MW01659873

Biographical Review of Cass, Schuyler and Brown Counties, Illinois

BIOGRAPHICAL REVIEW

—OF—

Cass, Schuyler and Brown Counties, Illinois.

Containing Biographical Sketches of Pioneers and Leading Citizens.

"Biography is the only true history."--Emerson.

CHICAGO:
BIOGRAPHICAL REVIEW PUBLISHING CO.
1892.

B52

CONTENTS.

PRESIDENTS OF THE UNITED STATES.

George Washington 9
John Adams 14
Thomas Jefferson 20
James Madison 26
James Monroe 32
John Quincy Adams 38
Andrew Jackson 47
Martin Van Buren 52
William Henry Harrison 56
John Tyler 60
James K. Polk 64
Zachary Taylor 68
Millard Fillmore 72
Franklin Pierce 76
James Buchanan 80
Abraham Lincoln 84
Andrew Johnson 93
Ulysses S. Grant 96
R. B. Hayes 102
J. A. Garfield 109
Chester A. Arthur 113
Grover Cleveland 117
Benjamin Harrison 120

BIOGRAPHICAL SKETCHES.

A

Adams, Wm T 244
Agnew, Jas M 321
Alexander, W L 288
Allard, Cad 271
Allen, A R 366
Allen, D H 382
Allison, Jos 430
Allphin, G W 133
Allphin, Z 134
Anderson, E. M 610
Anderson, Frank 320
Anderson, Robert 580
Anderson, V 405
Angier, F L 258
Arenz, J A 236
Armstrong, Thomas 568
Aten, C. L 438
Aten, Robert 391
Avery, Philander 181
Ayers, M 144

B

Bacon, H M 458
Bader, Wm 291
Bagby, John C 150
Baker, N W 541
Baujan, John 496
Baujan, H J 508
Barneycastle, G W 580
Barry, L T 378
Barton, Thos 406
Baxter, H B 337
Beatty, J J 563
Becker, Conrad 588
Beckwith, E. W 203
Bell, Ira 589
Bennett John L 238
Berry, F E 139
Berry, O A 232
Bertholf, Edward 520
Black, Isaac 549
Black, J F 128
Black John H 296
Black, J. M 174
Black, R S 616
Black, W T 132
Blackburn, B M 369
Bleyer, J W 523
Blose, D A 474
Bokemeier, Chas 246
Bolle, E H 488
Bollman, W C 201
Boone, N H 471
Bordenkircher, Geo 143
Bowe, Mrs M F 606
Boyd, Mark 160
Boyd, Richard 540
Brackenridge, W H 357
Bradbury, J T 159
Brannan, Stephen 521
Briar, Joseph 272
Brockman, Wash 131
Brockschmidt, Christian 503
Broker, Wm A 287
Brooks, Martin 164
Brown Robt 280
Browning, J J 398
Brumback, W L 504
Buck, J. J 318
Buracker, Wm 153
Burnside, Wm. H 361
Bush, Richard 533
Byrns, G A 341

C

Cady, F E 507
Cady, Henry 209
Cady, M E 283
Calef, S L 146
Campbell, G S 220
Campbell, Geo W 515
Campbell, L C 313
Campbell, Pauline 464
Campbell, Wm 365
Carles, L M 166
Carls, J H 458
Carr, David 446
Carter, Thomas H 259
Chalfant, T J 497
Clark, Abner A 323
Clark Elias 522
Clark, F A 439
Clark, J H 529
Clark, J K 187
Clark, J T 316
Clark, L W 188
Clark, T. J 206
Clark, W A 316
Cleek, M M 403
Clifford, Michael 176
Coil, A S 488
Coleman, Wm H 270
Colt, D P 389
Coningham, Grove 289
Conover, Geo 367
Cook, S W 541
Cosner, Jos L 350
Cox, Wm M 164
Cramer, Englebert 576
Crampton, S C 391
Craske, Henry 151
Crawford, Jas 170
Crum, G W 219
Crum, H. J 443
Crum, Jas 436
Crum, Thos J 312
Cunningham, A 343
Cunningham, James 416
Cuningham, T E 513
Curry, F M 161

D

Daniel, J W 413
Darnell Jesse 597
Davis, F E 360
Davis, J A 307
Davis, J H 415
Davis, W B 180
Davis, Wm J 199
De Counter, Samuel 311
Demaree, W L 381
Deppe, J H 396
De Witt, Jas 262
De Witt, Jas L 497
Dick, Levi 216
Dirreen, John 345
Dodds, David 371
Dodge, J S 290
Dorsett, C 420
Dorsett, W D 157
Downing, F E 584
Druse, W H 577
Duchardt, Christian 357
Dunlap, C M 491
Dunn, Chas N 136
Dunn, R H 865
Dupes, Christian 239
Dyson, Edwin 333

E

Edgar, A C 137
Edmonston, Enoch 195
Edwards, J M 507
Eifert, Geo H 260
Elliott, John 333
Ellis, S E 304
Emmerson, Wm T 588
Erwin, Geo. W 599
Erwin Lewis D 461
Evans, Hiram 437

F

Fields, G I 249
Fischer, Henry Jr 545
Flinn, J. C 387
Foote, John 618
Foster, H T 179
Frank, Ed S 449
Frankenfield, Theo 473
Freesen Wm 594
Frey, John Geo 485
Frisby, Geo W 525
Fulks R B 512
Funk, H C 612

G

Gapen, Thos . 587
Garm, Henry . . 442
Garner, I. R. . 581
Garner, W S 423
Gaut, W. P . 493
Gerrish, Cynthia 466
Gerrish, Jacob D . 466
Gibson, Ira N.... . 480
Gifford, Jos 233
Glandon, John 454
Glaze, W. W.... . . . 245
Glover, W S . . . 561
Goodell, J H . 385
Green, Nancy 198
Greenwell, Wm M 170
Greer, Geo . . 302
Greer, J L. 578
Greer, M W . 130
Greve, Henry . . . 417
Griffith, R H . 478
Griffith, W H . 558
Grimwood W. M . . 516
Grover, Jas . . . 519
Grover, H P . . 530

H

Hackman, E F . . . 211
Hackman, Wm . 235
Hageman, A L . . 567
Hagener, Ed 495
Hagener, John H 320
Hager, Lyman. . 432
Hale, Wm 505
Hall, E G . . 445
Hambaugh, J M . 601
Hammer, F. A . . 242
Hansmeyer, H . 127
Harbison, Martha J . . . 352
Harbison, Moses . 470
Harding, Peyton . . 548
Harris, Maro . . . 557
Harshey, Amos 450
Hash, Zachariah . . 490
Hayes, J W. 579
Heaton, Henry W. . . 401
Heaton, John . . . 379
Hedgcock, A J . . 193
Hedgcock, Joshua 344
Herron, David . . . 143
Herzberger, Conrad 399
Hierman H A . . 537
Higgins, Jackson 279
Hiles, Jas 219
Hill, A... . 575
Hill, Chas 451
Hill, Israel . . 359
Hills, John T 517
Hindman, Samuel . . 552
Hines, H . . . 433
Hinman, Mrs M . . . 536
Hines, H . 433
Hoffman, Geo H. 551
Hoffman, J C 511
Hood, S J 271
Horrom, Cyrus . . . 181
Horton, Job D 321
Howell, Jacob . . . 524
Howell, Thos S . 383
Hueschen, John . . . 421
Huff, G P 479
Huge, F W 512
Hunt, Jos 197
Huppers, Wm . . 136
Huss, C. J . 611
Huss, John. F. . . 301

I

Irwin, C N . 441

J

Jackson, Ezra . . . 205
Jackson, Mary . 590
Jaques, Hiram 256
Jockisch, Ernest . . 620
Jockisch, Wm 346
Johnson, C F 294
Johnston, D W C . 600
Jokisch, C T . 145
Jokisch, C G. . 141
Jokisch, Philip . . 377
Jones, C E. 210
Jones, Thos . 353
Juett, Chas H. 535

K

Kallasch, Adolph 402
Keil, H C . . 241
Keith, P R . 486
Kendrick, John G . 612
Kennedy, Charles 426
Kerley, King 410
Kerr, John 196
Kircher, John. . . . 607
Kirkham, Geo H . 527
Kloker, L F 298
Knight, Thos . 252
Korsmeyer, F. W 153
Korsmeyer, H H . 400
Korte, Henry C 273
Krohe, August . 562
Krohe, Henry W . 282
Krohe, Fred . . . 259
Krohe, Henry C . . . 310
Krohe, Lewis E 395
Krueger, C S . . . 467
Kruse, F H D . 465
Kuhl, George . . 277
Kuhlmann, Chris . . 381

L

Lambert, Wm J . 534
Lancaster, Reuben 352
Lane, C M . . 484
Lang, F C . 340
Larash, W I 308
Launer, T C . . . 595
Lawler, J. Thomas.... 480
Lawrence, Frank 429
Leach E D 317
Lee, W H.. 392
Leek, H. 477
Leeper, A A 330
Leib, E . . 571
Lewis, Azariah . . 222
Linn, D C 570
Listmann, John 374
Little, Robt 574
Logsdon, Aaron 476
Logsdon, Andrew. 526
Logsdon, Joseph . 531
Logsdon, Perry. . . 203
Lovekamp, H H 554
Lowry, A K . . 175
Lucas, G W . . . 407
Lucas, Newton. 155
Lucas, Wm 384
Lutterell, Mrs S B . . 348
Lyons, Daniel . 593

M

Main, Z E . . 318
Manlove, Wm B . 248
Marshall, A L . . . 399
Martin Rachel D 414
Matthew, James D . 332
Mayreis, Conrad . . 314
McCabe, Dr A A . 560
McCabe, John . . . 159
McCaskill, W H . 583
McClintock, J W . 539
McCormick, A B . . 425
McCoy, G W 344
McCreery, W T . 494
McDannold, J J . . 194
McDannold, T I 246
McFarland, R N . 324
McKee, Wm . 334
McMaster, R. B . . 230
McPhail, Angus . . . 536
Mead, A J . . . 200
Mead, R H... . . 212
Meats, Isaac . . 459
Merscher, J. W... . . 356
Merz, John. . . . 483
Meserve, N P . 563
Meservey, Joseph. 297
Meyer, Fred . 551
Meyer, F W 204
Meyer, Henry . . . 535
Meyer, H. C 329
Meyer, H W . . . 274
Milby, E T... 554
Miller, Aaron 280
Miller, Samuel . . . 592
Mills, R W 253
Milner, R 390
Misenhimer, Isaac . 515
Mohlmann, W G 234
Moore, Alex . . . 481
Moore J B . . 278
Moore, S A. . . 566
Morrell, Wm 434
Morris, J. W 473
Muhlert, Francis 585
Mumford, Wm N 404
Munroe, Thomas . . . 125
Murphy, J P 502

N

Neeley, James. 484
Neeley, J. E 544
Newbold, H Y 575
Newman, Robt 453
Nicholson, J S 244
Nieman, C. E 472
Niestradt, H C 553
Noble A L 342
Nokes, S. D. 261
Norbury, C J 237

O

Oetgen, Wm 142
Oetgen, H W 455
Orr, D W 588
Orwig, J W 572
Osborn, R J 370
Owens, D. W 394

P

Parke, Jos 544
Parke, Overton 349
Parrott, Thos P 227
Parsons, Norman 223
Patteson, Jonathan 138
Patterson, Jas M 359
Pence, Joseph 322
Perry, I 241
Perry, Jas 509
Perry, Wm 557
Persinger, L G 326
Petefish, S H 372
Pevehouse, I N 428
Phelps, Chas H 581
Philippi, P. P 358
Pilger, C 368
Pilger, Wm 306
Plaster Jeptha 498
Price, F C. 240
Price, Mrs Wm 140
Price, Wm T 305
Prince, F. R 424
Pruett, J S 167

R

Ranney, S. T 174
Ravenscroft, Mary F 411
Read, Jas. M. 468
Redman, B F 200
Redfield, T M. 361
Reeve, S. A 202
Reid Duncan, 294
Reno, W C 563
Rice, Chauncey 163
Rich, Robert 435
Richardson, Geo E 574
Rickard, P W 189
Rigg, J N 287
Rigg, Peter 309
Rink, Anton 295
Ritchea, George 319
Ritchey, Chas D 546
Ritchey, F T 601
Ritchey, Jacob 335
Ritter, Henry D 250
Robinson, J F 281
Robison, Jas N 172
Rogge, H H 404
Rohn, Casper 228
Rohn, J Henry 231
Rohn, Wm 483
Rottger, F W 179
Rowland, B L 564
Rowland, T. J. 510
Runkle, Darius 452
Ryan, Thos 249

S

Sandidge, John 299
Sands, R E 604
Saunders, Mrs C 555
Savage, Henry S 355
Scanland, S W 261
Schaad, Andrew 275
Schaar, Theodore 460
Schaeffer, C A 336
Schewe, Wm 569
Schisler, Lewis. 515
Schmitt, Geo J 485
Schmoldt, H M. 182
Schroder, Samuel M 292
Schroeder, H J 274
Schultz, H C 315
Schultz, John 468
Schuman, Adam 154
Scoggan, W D 172
Scott, E J 167
Scott, Leonidas 139
Scott, T W 188
Scott, T W 196
Seaman, J W 221
Seasly, Adam P 226
Seckman, Nancy P 264
Seeley, E H O 184
Serrot, Leonard 448
Settles, Gilderoy 444
Sewall, Wm 456
Shafer, Mrs E 169
Shank, John. 147
Shupe, W. K 331
Sielschott, A. H 177
Six, A D 214
Skiles, H A 518
Skiles, Oswell 375
Slack, N G 565
Smith, A. M 362
Smith, D G. 431
Smith, J. J. 495
Smith, T L 469
Snyder, Geo E 500
Snyder, J F 604
Snyder, J H 397
Snyder, J W 135
Spencer, J M 207
Spring, Ebenezer
Stark, Henry 429
Stephens, Daniel 229
Stevenson, Wm 373
Stock, Casper 422
Stout, A L 532
Stout, F M 350
Stover, D Marion 165
Stribling, I M. 418
Stutsman, J S 325
Sutherland, H R 567
Sutton, Nathan 327

T

Talkemeyer, Wm 459
Taylor, Duncan 192
Taylor, H W 217
Taylor, Robt 427
Teel, Jas A 185
Thomas, Peter 447
Thomas, Wm 571
Thompson, A M 301
Thompson, J D 218
Thron, David 525
Tinney, C M 368
Treadway, E N 269
Treadway, W. T 213
Trone, Geo W 149
Tureman, J H 614
Tyson, Wm T 266

U

Unland, John 284
Unland, Dr W G 591
Utter, G D 257

V

Van Deventer, J F 191
Van Deventer, L J 419
Van Deventer, T R 285
Ventres Henry 347
Vette, Henry 475

W

Wagner, George 388
Wagner, Gregory, Jr 364
Walker, C T 300
Walker, D N 265
Walker, John H 538
Walker, J S. 617
Ward Wm W. 393
Warden, F A 156
Watkins, Jas M 224
Watts, Thos W 463
Way, Wm A 309
Webb, Allen 542
Webb, John 586
Webb, J W 487
Weigard, Wm. 503
Wellfare, F E 162
Wells, R. 149
Wetzel, John B 311
Whetstone, Marcus 462
Wier, Geo H 598
Wight, Jesse 308
Williams, G W. 247
Williams, P S 420
Williams, R. E 501
Williams, T R 207
Wilson, B R. 618
Wilson, D D. 276
Wilson, Geo W & F M 619
Wilson, Jas M 613

Wilson, Thos........ 293
Wilson, Wm. B........ 613
Winhold, F........ 596
Witte, Henry F........ 251
Wood, Wm........ 489
Wright, S. G........ 492
Wyatt, W. M........ 408

Y

Young, Mrs. Almira........ 543
Young, J. A........ 231

Z

Zahn Henry........ 550
Zimmer, Lewis, Sr........ 573
Zimmer, Lewis, Jr........ 597
Zimmerman, Geo. W........ 440
Zimmerman, Jacob........ 389

Go: Washington

GEORGE WASHINGTON.

GEORGE WASHINGTON, the "Father of his Country" and its first President, 1789-'97, was born February 22, 1732, in Washington Parish, Westmoreland County, Virginia. His father, Augustine Washington, first married Jane Butler, who bore him four children, and March 6, 1730, he married Mary Ball. Of six children by his second marriage, George was the eldest, the others being Betty, Samuel, John, Augustine, Charles and Mildred, of whom the youngest died in infancy. Little is known of the early years of Washington, beyond the fact that the house in which he was born was burned during his early childhood, and that his father thereupon moved to another farm, inherited from his paternal ancestors, situated in Stafford County, on the north bank of the Rappahannock, where he acted as agent of the Principio Iron Works in the immediate vicinity, and died there in 1743.

From earliest childhood George developed a noble character. He had a vigorous constitution, a fine form, and great bodily strength. His education was somewhat defective, being confined to the elementary branches taught him by his mother and at a neighboring school. He developed, however, a fondness for mathematics, and enjoyed in that branch the instructions of a private teacher. On leaving school he resided for some time at Mount Vernon with his half brother, Lawrence, who acted as his guardian, and who had married a daughter of his neighbor at Belvoir on the Potomac, the wealthy William Fairfax, for some time president of the executive council of the colony. Both Fairfax and his son-in-law, Lawrence Washington, had served with distinction in 1740 as officers of an American battalion at the siege of Carthagena, and were friends and correspondents of Admiral Vernon, for whom the latter's residence on the Potomac has been named. George's inclinations were for a similar career, and a midshipman's warrant was procured for him, probably through the influence of the Admiral; but through the opposition of his mother the project was abandoned. The family connection with the Fairfaxes, however, opened another career for the young man, who, at the age of sixteen, was appointed surveyor to the immense estates of the eccentric Lord Fairfax, who was then on a visit at Belvoir, and who shortly afterward established his baronial residence at Greenway Court, in the Shenandoah Valley.

Three years were passed by young Washington in a rough frontier life, gaining experience which afterward proved very essential to him.

In 1751, when the Virginia militia were put under training with a view to active service against France, Washington, though only nineteen years of age, was appointed Adjutant with the rank of Major In September of that year the failing health of Lawrence Washington rendered it necessary for him to seek a warmer climate, and George accompanied him in a voyage to Barbadoes. They returned early in 1752, and Lawrence shortly afterward died, leaving his large property to an infant daughter In his will George was named one of the executors and as eventual heir to Mount Vernon, and by the death of the infant niece soon succeeded to that estate

On the arrival of Robert Dinwiddie as Lieutenant-Governor of Virginia in 1752 the militia was reorganized, and the province divided into four districts. Washington was commissioned by Dinwiddie Adjutant-General of the Northern District in 1753, and in November of that year a most important as well as hazardous mission was assigned him. This was to proceed to the Canadian posts recently established on French Creek, near Lake Erie, to demand in the name of the King of England the withdrawal of the French from a territory claimed by Virginia This enterprise had been declined by more than one officer, since it involved a journey through an extensive and almost unexplored wilderness in the occupancy of savage Indian tribes, either hostile to the English, or of doubtful attachment. Major Washington, however, accepted the commission with alacrity, and, accompanied by Captain Gist, he reached Fort Le Bœuf on French Creek, delivered his dispatches and received reply, which, of course, was a polite refusal to surrender the posts. This reply was of such a character as to induce the Assembly of Virginia to authorize the executive to raise a regiment of 300 men for the purpose of maintaining the asserted rights of the British crown over the territory claimed As Washington declined to be a candidate for that post, the command of this regiment was given to Colonel Joshua Fry, and Major Washington, at his own request, was commissioned Lieutenant-Colonel. On the march to Ohio, news was received that a party previously sent to build a fort at the confluence of the Monongahela with the Ohio had been driven back by a considerable French force, which had completed the work there begun, and named it Fort Duquesne, in honor of the Marquis Duquesne, then Governor of Canada. This was the beginning of the great "French and Indian war," which continued seven years. On the death of Colonel Fry, Washington succeeded to the command of the regiment, and so well did he fulfill his trust that the Virginia Assembly commissioned him as Commander-in-Chief of all the forces raised in the colony

A cessation of all Indian hostility on the frontier having followed the expulsion of the French from the Ohio, the object of Washington was accomplished and he resigned his commission as Commander-in-Chief of the Virginia forces. He then proceeded to Williamsburg to take his seat in the General Assembly, of which he had been elected a member.

January 17, 1759, Washington married Mrs Martha (Dandridge) Custis, a young and beautiful widow of great wealth, and devoted himself for the ensuing fifteen years to the quiet pursuits of agriculture, interrupted only by his annual attendance in winter upon the Colonial Legislature at Williamsburg, until summoned by his country to enter upon that other arena in which his fame was to become world wide.

It is unnecessary here to trace the details of the struggle upon the question of local self-government, which, after ten years, culminated by act of Parliament of the port of Boston. It was at the instance of Virginia that a congress of all the colonies was called to meet at Philadelphia September 5, 1774, to secure their common liberties—if possible by peaceful means. To this Congress Colonel Washington was sent as a delegate On dissolving in October, it recommended the colonies to send deputies to another Congress the following spring In the meantime several of the colonies felt impelled to raise local forces to repel insults and aggressions on the part of British troops, so that on the assembling of the next Congress, May 10, 1775, the war preparations of the mother country were unmistakable. The battles of Concord and Lexington had been fought Among the earliest acts, therefore, of the Congress was the selection of a commander-in-chief of the colonial forces This office was unanimously conferred upon Washington, still a member of the Congress. He accepted it on June 19, but on the express condition he should receive no salary.

He immediately repaired to the vicinity of Boston, against which point the British ministry had concentrated their forces. As early as April General Gage had 3,000 troops in and around this proscribed city. During the fall and winter the British policy clearly indicated a purpose to divide public sentiment and to build up a British party in the colonies. Those who sided with the ministry were stigmatized by the patriots as "Tories," while the patriots took to themselves the name of "Whigs"

As early as 1776 the leading men had come to the conclusion that there was no hope except in separation and independence In May of that year Washington wrote from the head of the army in New York: "A reconciliation with Great Britain is impossible. . . . . When I took command of the army, I abhorred the idea of independence, but I am now fully satisfied that nothing else will save us."

It is not the object of this sketch to trace the military acts of the patriot hero, to whose hands the fortunes and liberties of the United States were confided during the seven years' bloody struggle that ensued until the treaty of 1783, in which England acknowledged the independence of each of the thirteen States, and negotiated with them, jointly, as separate sovereignties. The merits of Washington as a military chieftain have been considerably discussed, especially by writers in his own country During the war he was most bitterly assailed for incompetency, and great efforts were made to displace him, but he never for a moment lost the confidence of either the Congress or the people. December 4, 1783, the great commander took leave of his officers in most affectionate and patriotic terms, and went to Annapolis, Maryland, where the Congress of the States was in session, and to that body, when peace and order prevailed everywhere, resigned his commission and retired to Mount Vernon.

It was in 1788 that Washington was called to the chief magistracy of the nation. He received every electoral vote cast in all the colleges of the States voting for the office of President. The 4th of March, 1789, was the time appointed for the Government of the United States to begin its operations, but several weeks elapsed before quorums of both the newly constituted houses of the Congress were assembled The city of New York was the place where the Congress then met. April 16 Washington left his home to enter upon the discharge of his new duties He set out with a purpose of traveling privately, and without attracting any public attention; but this was impossible. Everywhere on his way he was met with thronging crowds, eager to see the man whom they regarded as the chief defender of their liberties, and everywhere he was hailed with those public manifestations of joy, regard and love which spring spontaneously from the hearts of an affectionate and grateful people. His reception in New York was marked by a grandeur and an enthusiasm never before witnessed in that metropolis The inauguration took place April 30, in the presence of an immense multitude which had assembled to witness the new and imposing ceremony. The oath of office was administered by Robert R Livingston, Chancellor of the State When this sacred pledge was given, he retired with the other officials into the Senate chamber, where he delivered his inaugural address to both houses of the newly constituted Congress in joint assembly

In the manifold details of his civil administration, Washington proved himself equal to the requirements of his position. The greater portion of the first session of the first Congress was occupied in passing the necessary statutes for putting the new organization into complete operation. In the discussions brought up in the course of this legislation the nature and character of the new system came under general review. On no one of them did any decided antagonism of opinion arise. All held it to be a limited government, clothed only with specific powers conferred by delegation from the States There was no change in the name of the legislative department, it still remained "the Congress of the United States of America" There was no change in the original flag of the country, and none in the seal, which still remains with the Grecian escutcheon borne by the eagle, with other emblems, under the great and expressive motto, "*E Pluribus Unum.*"

The first division of parties arose upon the manner of construing the powers delegated, and they were first styled "strict constructionists" and "latitudinarian constructionists" The former were for confining the action of the Government strictly within its specific and limited sphere, while the others were for enlarging its powers by inference and implication. Hamilton and Jefferson, both members of the first cabinet were regarded as the chief leaders, respectively, of these rising antagonistic parties which have existed, under different names from that day to this. Washington was regarded as holding a neutral position between them, though, by mature deliberation, he vetoed the first apportionment bill, in 1790, passed by the party headed by Hamilton, which was based upon a principle constructively leading to centralization or consolidation. This was the first exercise of the veto power under the present Constitution It created considerable excitement at the time. Another bill was soon passed in pursuance of Mr. Jefferson's views, which has been adhered to in principle in every apportionment act passed since

At the second session of the new Congress, Washington announced the gratifying fact of "the accession of North Carolina" to the Constitution of 1787, and June 1 of the same year he announced by special message the like "accession of the State of Rhode Island," with his congratulations on the happy event which "united under the general Government" all the States which were originally confederated

In 1792, at the second Presidential election, Washington was desirous to retire, but he yielded to the general wish of the country, and was again chosen President by the unanimous vote of every electoral college At the third election, 1796, he was again most urgently entreated to consent to remain in the executive chair. This he positively refused. In September, before the election, he gave to his countrymen his memorable Farewell Address, which in language, sentiment and patriotism was a fit and crowning glory of his illustrious life. After March 4, 1797, he again retired to Mount Vernon for peace, quiet and repose.

His administration for the two terms had been successful beyond the expectation and hopes of even the most sanguine of his friends. The finances of the country were no longer in an embarrassed condition, the public credit was fully restored, life was given to every department of industry, the workings of the new system in allowing Congress to raise revenue from duties on imports proved to be not only harmonious in its federal action, but astonishing in its results upon the commerce and trade of all the States. The exports from the Union increased from $19,000,000 to over $56,000,000 per annum, while the imports increased in about the same proportion. Three new members had been added to the Union. The progress of the States in their new career under their new organization thus far was exceedingly encouraging, not only to the friends of liberty within their own limits, but to their sympathizing allies in all climes and countries.

Of the call again made on this illustrious chief to quit his repose at Mount Vernon and take command of all the United States forces, with the rank of Lieutenant-General, when war was threatened with France in 1798, nothing need here be stated, except to note the fact as an unmistakable testimonial of the high regard in which he was still held by his countrymen, of all shades of political opinion. He patriotically accepted this trust, but a treaty of peace put a stop to all action under it. He again retired to Mount Vernon, where, after a short and severe illness, he died December 14, 1799, in the sixty-eighth year of his age. The whole country was filled with gloom by this sad intelligence. Men of all parties in politics and creeds in religion, in every State in the Union, united with Congress in "paying honor to the man, first in war, first in peace, and first in the hearts of his countrymen."

His remains were deposited in a family vault on the banks of the Potomac at Mount Vernon, where they still lie entombed.

JOHN ADAMS.

JOHN ADAMS, the second President of the United States, 1797 to 1801, was born in the present town of Quincy, then a portion of Braintree, Massachusetts, October 30, 1735. His father was a farmer of moderate means, a worthy and industrious man. He was a deacon in the church, and was very desirous of giving his son a collegiate education, hoping that he would become a minister of the gospel. But, as up to this time, the age of fourteen, he had been only a play-boy in the fields and forests, he had no taste for books, he chose farming. On being set to work, however, by his father out in the field, the very first day converted the boy into a lover of books.

Accordingly, at the age of sixteen he entered Harvard College, and graduated in 1755, at the age of twenty, highly esteemed for integrity, energy and ability. Thus, having no capital but his education, he started out into the stormy world at a time of great political excitement, as France and England were then engaged in their great seven-years struggle for the mastery over the New World. The fire of patriotism seized young Adams, and for a time he studied over the question whether he should take to the law, to politics or the army. He wrote a remarkable letter to a friend, making prophecies concerning the future greatness of this country which have since been more than fulfilled. For two years he taught school and studied law, wasting no odd moments, and at the early age of twenty-two years he opened a law office in his native town. His inherited powers of mind and untiring devotion to his profession caused him to rise rapidly in public esteem.

In October, 1764, Mr. Adams married Miss Abigail Smith, daughter of a clergyman at Weymouth and a lady of rare personal and intellectual endowments, who afterward contributed much to her husband's celebrity.

Soon the oppression of the British in America reached its climax. The Boston merchants employed an attorney by the name of James Otis to argue the legality of oppressive tax law before the Superior Court. Adams heard the argument, and afterward wrote to a friend concerning the ability displayed, as follows: "Otis was a flame of fire. With a promptitude of classical allusion, a depth of research, a rapid summary of historical events and dates, a profusion of legal authorities and a

John Adams

LIBRARY
OF THE
UNIVERSITY OF ILLINOIS

prophetic glance into futurity, he hurried away all before him. *American independence was then and there born.* Every man of an immensely crowded audience appeared to me to go away, as I did, ready to take up arms."

Soon Mr. Adams wrote an essay to be read before the literary club of his town, upon the state of affairs, which was so able as to attract public attention. It was published in American journals, republished in England, and was pronounced by the friends of the colonists there as "one of the very best productions ever seen from North America"

The memorable Stamp Act was now issued, and Adams entered with all the ardor of his soul into political life in order to resist it. He drew up a series of resolutions remonstrating against the act, which were adopted at a public meeting of the citizens of Braintree, and which were subsequently adopted, word for word, by more than forty towns in the State Popular commotion prevented the landing of the Stamp Act papers, and the English authorities then closed the courts The town of Boston therefore appointed Jeremy Gridley, James Otis and John Adams to argue a petition before the Governor and council for the re-opening of the courts, and while the two first mentioned attorneys based their argument upon the distress caused to the people by the measure, Adams boldly claimed that the Stamp Act was a violation both of the English Constitution and the charter of the Provinces. It is said that this was the first direct denial of the unlimited right of Parliament over the colonies Soon after this the Stamp Act was repealed

Directly Mr. Adams was employed to defend Ansell Nickerson, who had killed an Englishman in the act of impressing him (Nickerson) into the King's service, and his client was acquitted, the court thus establishing the principle that the infamous royal prerogative of impressment could have no existence in the colonial code But in 1770 Messrs Adams and Josiah Quincy defended a party of British soldiers who had been arrested for murder when they had been only obeying Governmental orders, and when reproached for thus apparently deserting the cause of popular liberty, Mr. Adams replied that he would a thousandfold rather live under the domination of the worst of England's kings than under that of a lawless mob Next, after serving a term as a member of the Colonial Legislature from Boston, Mr. Adams, finding his health affected by too great labor, retired to his native home at Braintree.

The year 1774 soon arrived, with its famous Boston "Tea Party," the first open act of rebellion. Adams was sent to the Congress at Philadelphia, and when the Attorney-General announced that Great Britain had "determined on her system, and that her power to execute it was irresistible," Adams replied: "I know that Great Britain has determined on her system, and that very determination determines me on mine You know that I have been constant in my opposition to her measures. The die is now cast. I have passed the Rubicon Sink or swim, live or die, with my country, is my unalterable determination" The rumor beginning to prevail at Philadelphia that the Congress had independence in view, Adams foresaw that it was too soon to declare it openly. He advised every one to remain quiet in that respect, and as soon as it became apparent that he himself was for independence, he was advised to hide himself, which he did.

The next year the great Revolutionary war opened in earnest, and Mrs. Adams, residing near Boston, kept her husband advised by letter of all the events transpiring in her vicinity. The battle of Bunker Hill came on. Congress had to do something immediately. The first thing was to choose a commander-in-chief for the—we can't say "army"—the fighting men of the colonies. The New England delegation was almost unanimous in favor of appointing General Ward, then at the head of the Massachusetts forces, but Mr. Adams urged the appointment of George Washington, then almost unknown outside of his own State. He was appointed without opposition. Mr. Adams offered the resolution, which was adopted, annulling all the royal authority in the colonies. Having thus prepared the way, a few weeks later, viz., June 7, 1776, Richard Henry Lee, of Virginia, who a few months before had declared that the British Government would abandon its oppressive measures, now offered the memorable resolution, seconded by Adams, "that these United States are, and of right ought to be, free and independent." Jefferson, Adams, Franklin, Sherman and Livingston were then appointed a committee to draught a declaration of independence. Mr. Jefferson desired Mr. Adams to draw up the bold document, but the latter persuaded Mr. Jefferson to perform that responsible task. The Declaration drawn up, Mr. Adams became its foremost defender on the floor of Congress. It was signed by all the fifty-five members present, and the next day Mr. Adams wrote to his wife how great a deed was done, and how proud he was of it. Mr. Adams continued to be the leading man of Congress, and the leading advocate of American independence. Above all other Americans, he was considered by every one the principal shining mark for British vengeance. Thus circumstanced, he was appointed to the most dangerous task of crossing the ocean in winter, exposed to capture by the British, who knew of his mission, which was to visit Paris and solicit the co-operation of the French. Besides, to take himself away from the country of which he was the most prominent defender, at that critical time, was an act of the greatest self-sacrifice. Sure enough, while crossing the sea, he had two very narrow escapes from capture; and the transit was otherwise a stormy and eventful one. During the summer of 1779 he returned home, but was immediately dispatched back to France, to be in readiness there to negotiate terms of peace and commerce with Great Britain as soon as the latter power was ready for such business. But as Dr. Franklin was more popular than he at the court of France, Mr. Adams repaired to Holland, where he was far more successful as a diplomatist.

The treaty of peace between the United States and England was finally signed at Paris, January 21, 1783; and the re-action from so great excitement as Mr. Adams had so long been experiencing threw him into a dangerous fever. Before he fully recovered he was in London, whence he was dispatched again to Amsterdam to negotiate another loan. Compliance with this order undermined his physical constitution for life.

In 1785 Mr. Adams was appointed envoy to the court of St. James, to meet face to face the very king who had regarded him as an arch traitor! Accordingly he repaired thither, where he did actually meet and converse with George III.! After a residence there for about three years, he obtained permission to return to America. While in London he wrote and published an able work, in three volumes, entitled: "A Defense of the American Constitution."

The Articles of Confederation proving inefficient, as Adams had prophesied, a carefully draughted Constitution was adopted in 1789, when George Washington was elected President of the new nation, and Adams Vice-President. Congress met for a time in New York, but was removed to Philadelphia for ten years, until suitable buildings should be erected at the new capital in the District of Columbia. Mr. Adams then moved his family to Philadelphia. Toward the close of his term of office the French Revolution culminated, when Adams and Washington rather sympathized with England, and Jefferson with France. The Presidential election of 1796 resulted in giving Mr. Adams the first place by a small majority, and Mr. Jefferson the second place.

Mr. Adams's administration was conscientious, patriotic and able. The period was a turbulent one, and even an archangel could not have reconciled the hostile parties Partisanism with reference to England and France was bitter, and for four years Mr. Adams struggled through almost a constant tempest of assaults. In fact, he was not truly a popular man, and his chagrin at not receiving a re-election was so great that he did not even remain at Philadelphia to witness the inauguration of Mr. Jefferson, his successor. The friendly intimacy between these two men was interrupted for about thirteen years of their life Adams finally made the first advances toward a restoration of their mutual friendship, which were gratefully accepted by Jefferson.

Mr. Adams was glad of his opportunity to retire to private life, where he could rest his mind and enjoy the comforts of home By a thousand bitter experiences he found the path of public duty a thorny one. For twenty-six years his service of the public was as arduous, self-sacrificing and devoted as ever fell to the lot of man. In one important sense he was as much the "Father of his Country" as was Washington in another sense. During these long years of anxiety and toil, in which he was laying broad and deep, the foundations of the greatest nation the sun ever shone upon, he received from his impoverished country a meager support. The only privilege he carried with him into his retirement was that of franking his letters.

Although taking no active part in public affairs, both himself and his son, John Quincy, nobly supported the policy of Mr. Jefferson in resisting the encroachments of England, who persisted in searching American ships on the high seas and dragging from them any sailors that might be designated by any pert lieutenant as British subjects. Even for this noble support Mr. Adams was maligned by thousands of bitter enemies! On this occasion, for the first time since his retirement, he broke silence and drew up a very able paper, exposing the atrocity of the British pretensions.

Mr. Adams outlived nearly all his family. Though his physical frame began to give way many years before his death, his mental powers retained their strength and vigor to the last. In his ninetieth year he was gladdened by the popular elevation of his son to the Presidential office, the highest in the gift of the people. A few months more passed away and the 4th of July, 1826 arrived The people, unaware of the near approach of the end of two great lives—that of Adams and Jefferson—were making unusual preparations for a national holiday. Mr. Adams lay upon his couch, listening to the ringing of bells, the waftures of martial music and the roar of cannon, with silent emotion Only four days before, he had given for a public toast, "Independence forever." About two o'clock in the afternoon he said, "And Jefferson still survives." But he was mistaken by an hour or so; and in a few minutes he had breathed his last.

THOMAS JEFFERSON.

THOMAS JEFFERSON, the third President of the United States, 1801–'9, was born April 2, 1743, the eldest child of his parents, Peter and Jane (Randolph) Jefferson, near Charlottesville, Albemarle County, Virginia, upon the slopes of the Blue Ridge. When he was fourteen years of age, his father died, leaving a widow and eight children. She was a beautiful and accomplished lady, a good letter-writer, with a fund of humor, and an admirable housekeeper. His parents belonged to the Church of England, and are said to be of Welch origin. But little is known of them, however.

Thomas was naturally of a serious turn of mind, apt to learn, and a favorite at school, his choice studies being mathematics and the classics. At the age of seventeen he entered William and Mary College, in an advanced class, and lived in rather an expensive style, consequently being much caressed by gay society. That he was not ruined, is proof of his stamina of character. But during his second year he discarded society, his horses and even his favorite violin, and devoted thenceforward fifteen hours a day to hard study, becoming extraordinarily proficient in Latin and Greek authors.

On leaving college, before he was twenty-one, he commenced the study of law, and pursued it diligently until he was well qualified for practice, upon which he entered in 1767. By this time he was also versed in French, Spanish, Italian and Anglo-Saxon, and in the criticism of the fine arts. Being very polite and polished in his manners, he won the friendship of all whom he met. Though able with his pen, he was not fluent in public speech.

In 1769 he was chosen a member of the Virginia Legislature, and was the largest slave-holding member of that body. He introduced a bill empowering slave-holders to manumit their slaves, but it was rejected by an overwhelming vote.

In 1770 Mr. Jefferson met with a great loss; his house at Shadwell was burned, and his valuable library of 2,000 volumes was consumed. But he was wealthy enough to replace the most of it, as from his 5,000 acres tilled by slaves and his practice at the bar his income amounted to about $5,000 a year.

In 1772 he married Mrs. Martha Skelton, a beautiful, wealthy and accomplished

Th: Jefferson

LIBRARY
OF THE
UNIVERSITY OF ILLINOIS

young widow, who owned 40,000 acres of land and 130 slaves, yet he labored assiduously for the abolition of slavery. For his new home he selected a majestic rise of land upon his large estate at Shadwell, called Monticello, whereon he erected a mansion of modest yet elegant architecture. Here he lived in luxury, indulging his taste in magnificent, high-blooded horses.

At this period the British Government gradually became more insolent and oppressive toward the American colonies, and Mr. Jefferson was ever one of the most foremost to resist its encroachments From time to time he drew up resolutions of remonstrance, which were finally adopted, thus proving his ability as a statesman and as a leader. By the year 1774 he became quite busy, both with voice and pen, in defending the right of the colonies to defend themselves His pamphlet entitled: "A Summary View of the Rights of British America," attracted much attention in England. The following year he, in company with George Washington, served as an executive committee in measures to defend by arms the State of Virginia As a Member of the Congress, he was not a speechmaker, yet in conversation and upon committees he was so frank and decisive that he always made a favorable impression But as late as the autumn of 1775 he remained in hopes of reconciliation with the parent country.

At length, however, the hour arrived for draughting the "Declaration of Independence," and this responsible task was devolved upon Jefferson. Franklin, and Adams suggested a few verbal corrections before it was submitted to Congress, which was June 28, 1776, only six days before it was adopted During the three days of the fiery ordeal of criticism through which it passed in Congress, Mr. Jefferson opened not his lips. John Adams was the main champion of the Declaration on the floor of Congress. The signing of this document was one of the most solemn and momentous occasions ever attended to by man. Prayer and silence reigned throughout the hall, and each signer realized that if American independence was not finally sustained by arms he was doomed to the scaffold.

After the colonies became independent States, Jefferson resigned for a time his seat in Congress in order to aid in organizing the government of Virginia, of which State he was chosen Governor in 1779, when he was thirty-six years of age. At this time the British had possession of Georgia and were invading South Carolina, and at one time a British officer, Tarleton, sent a secret expedition to Monticello to capture the Governor. Five minutes after Mr. Jefferson escaped with his family, his mansion was in possession of the enemy! The British troops also destroyed his valuable plantation on the James River. "Had they carried off the slaves," said Jefferson, with characteristic magnanimity, "to give them freedom, they would have done right."

The year 1781 was a gloomy one for the Virginia Governor. While confined to his secluded home in the forest by a sick and dying wife, a party arose against him throughout the State, severely criticising his course as Governor. Being very sensitive to reproach, this touched him to the quick, and the heap of troubles then surrounding him nearly crushed him. He resolved, in despair, to retire from public life for the rest of his days. For weeks Mr. Jefferson sat lovingly, but with a crushed heart, at the bedside of his sick wife, during which time unfeeling letters were sent to him, accusing him of weakness and unfaithfulness to duty. All this, after he had lost so much property and at the same time done so much for his country! After her death he actually fainted away, and remained so long insensible that it was feared he never would recover! Several weeks passed before he could fully recover his equilibrium He was never married a second time.

In the spring of 1782 the people of England compelled their king to make to the Americans overtures of peace, and in November following, Mr. Jefferson was reappointed by Congress, unanimously and without a single adverse remark, minister plenipotentiary to negotiate a treaty.

In March, 1784, Mr. Jefferson was appointed on a committee to draught a plan for the government of the Northwestern Territory His slavery-prohibition clause in that plan was stricken out by the pro-slavery majority of the committee, but amid all the controversies and wrangles of politicians, he made it a rule never to contradict anybody or engage in any discussion as a debater.

In company with Mr. Adams and Dr. Franklin, Mr. Jefferson was appointed in May, 1784, to act as minister plenipotentiary in the negotiation of treaties of commerce with foreign nations Accordingly, he went to Paris and satisfactorily accomplished his mission. The suavity and high bearing of his manner made all the French his friends, and even Mrs. Adams at one time wrote to her sister that he was "the chosen of the earth." But all the honors that he received, both at home and abroad, seemed to make no change in the simplicity of his republican tastes On his return to America, he found two parties respecting the foreign commercial policy, Mr. Adams sympathizing with that in favor of England and himself favoring France.

On the inauguration of General Washington as President, Mr. Jefferson was chosen by him for the office of Secretary of State. At this time the rising storm of the French Revolution became visible, and Washington watched it with great anxiety. His cabinet was divided in their views of constitutional government as well as regarding the issues in France. General Hamilton, Secretary of the Treasury, was the leader of the so-called Federal party, while Mr. Jefferson was the leader of the Republican party. At the same time there was a strong monarchical party in this country, with which Mr Adams sympathized. Some important financial measures, which were proposed by Hamilton and finally adopted by the cabinet and approved by Washington, were opposed by Mr. Jefferson; and his enemies then began to reproach him with holding office under an administration whose views he opposed. The President poured oil on the troubled waters. On his re-election to the Presidency he desired Mr. Jefferson to remain in the cabinet, but the latter sent in his resignation at two different times, probably because he was dissatisfied with some of the measures of the Government. His final one was not received until January 1, 1794, when General Washington parted from him with great regret

Jefferson then retired to his quiet home at Monticello, to enjoy a good rest, not even reading the newspapers lest the political gossip should disquiet him. On the President's again calling him back to the office of Secretary of State, he replied that no circumstances would ever again tempt him to engage in anything public! But, while all Europe was ablaze with war, and France in the throes of a bloody revolution and the principal theater of the conflict, a new Presidential election in this country came on. John Adams was the Federal candidate and Mr. Jefferson became the Republican candidate. The result of the election was the promotion of the latter to the Vice-Presidency, while the former was chosen President .. In this contest Mr. Jefferson really did not desire to have either office, he was "so weary" of party strife. He loved the retirement of home more than any other place on the earth.

But for four long years his Vice-Presidency passed joylessly away, while the partisan strife between Federalist and Republican was ever growing hotter. The former party split and the result of the fourth general election was the elevation of Mr. Jefferson to the Presidency! with Aaron Burr as Vice-President These men being at the head of a growing party, their election was hailed everywhere with joy. On the other hand, many of the Federalists turned pale, as they believed what a portion of the pulpit and the press had been preaching—that Jefferson was a "scoffing atheist," a "Jacobin," the "incarnation of all evil," "breathing threatening and slaughter!"

Mr Jefferson's inaugural address contained nothing but the noblest sentiments, expressed in fine language, and his personal behavior afterward exhibited the extreme of American, democratic simplicity. His disgust of European court etiquette grew upon him with age. He believed that General Washington was somewhat distrustful of the ultimate success of a popular Government, and that, imbued with a little admiration of the forms of a monarchical Government, he had instituted levees, birthdays, pompous meetings with Congress, etc Jefferson was always polite, even to slaves everywhere he met them, and carried in his countenance the indications of an accommodating disposition.

The political principles of the Jeffersonian party now swept the country, and Mr. Jefferson himself swayed an influence which was never exceeded even by Washington Under his administration, in 1803, the Louisiana purchase was made, for $15,000,000, the "Louisiana Territory" purchased comprising all the land west of the Mississippi to the Pacific Ocean.

The year 1804 witnessed another severe loss in his family. His highly accomplished and most beloved daughter Maria sickened and died, causing as great grief in the stricken parent as it was possible for him to survive with any degree of sanity.

The same year he was re-elected to the Presidency, with George Clinton as Vice-President. During his second term our relations with England became more complicated, and on June 22, 1807, near Hampton Roads, the United States frigate Chesapeake was fired upon by the British man-of-war Leopard, and was made to surrender. Three men were killed and ten wounded. Jefferson demanded reparation England grew insolent It became evident that war was determined upon by the latter power. More than 1,200 Americans were forced into the British service upon the high seas Before any satisfactory solution was reached, Mr. Jefferson's Presidential term closed Amid all these public excitements he thought constantly of the welfare of his family, and longed for the time when he could return home to remain There, at Monticello, his subsequent life was very similar to that of Washington at Mt. Vernon. His hospitality toward his numerous friends, indulgence of his slaves, and misfortunes to his property, etc., finally involved him in debt. For years his home resembled a fashionable watering-place. During the summer, thirty-seven house servants were required! It was presided over by his daughter, Mrs. Randolph.

Mr Jefferson did much for the establishment of the University at Charlottesville, making it unsectarian, in keeping with the spirit of American institutions, but poverty and the feebleness of old age prevented him from doing what he would He even went so far as to petition the Legislature for permission to dispose of some of his possessions by lottery, in order to raise the necessary funds for home expenses. It was granted; but before the plan was carried out, Mr. Jefferson died, July 4, 1826, at 12 50 P. M.

JAMES MADISON.

JAMES MADISON, the fourth President of the United States, 1809-'17, was born at Port Conway, Prince George County, Virginia, March 16, 1751. His father, Colonel James Madison, was a wealthy planter, residing upon a very fine estate called "Montpelier," only twenty-five miles from the home of Thomas Jefferson at Monticello. The closest personal and political attachment existed between these illustrious men from their early youth until death.

James was the eldest of a family of seven children, four sons and three daughters, all of whom attained maturity. His early education was conducted mostly at home, under a private tutor. Being naturally intellectual in his tastes, he consecrated himself with unusual vigor to study. At a very early age he made considerable proficiency in the Greek, Latin, French and Spanish languages. In 1769 he entered Princeton College, New Jersey, of which the illustrious Dr. Weatherspoon was then President. He graduated in 1771, with a character of the utmost purity, and a mind highly disciplined and stored with all the learning which embellished and gave efficiency to his subsequent career. After graduating he pursued a course of reading for several months, under the guidance of President Weatherspoon, and in 1772 returned to Virginia, where he continued in incessant study for two years, nominally directed to the law, but really including extended researches in theology, philosophy and general literature.

The Church of England was the established church in Virginia, invested with all the prerogatives and immunities which it enjoyed in the fatherland, and other denominations labored under serious disabilities, the enforcement of which was rightly or wrongly characterized by them as persecution. Madison took a prominent stand in behalf of the removal of all disabilities, repeatedly appeared in the court of his own county to defend the Baptist nonconformists, and was elected from Orange County to the Virginia Convention in the spring of 1766, when he signalized the beginning of his public career by procuring the passage of an amendment to the Declaration of Rights as prepared by George Mason, substituting for "toleration" a more emphatic assertion of religious liberty.

James Madison

LIBRARY
OF THE
UNIVERSITY OF ILLINOIS

In 1776 he was elected a member of the Virginia Convention to frame the Constitution of the State. Like Jefferson, he took but little part in the public debates. His main strength lay in his conversational influence and in his pen. In November, 1777, he was chosen a member of the Council of State, and in March, 1780, took his seat in the Continental Congress, where he first gained prominence through his energetic opposition to the issue of paper money by the States. He continued in Congress three years, one of its most active and influential members.

In 1784 Mr. Madison was elected a member of the Virginia Legislature. He rendered important service by promoting and participating in that revision of the statutes which effectually abolished the remnants of the feudal system subsistent up to that time in the form of entails, primogeniture, and State support given the Anglican Church; and his "Memorial and Remonstrance" against a general assessment for the support of religion is one of the ablest papers which emanated from his pen. It settled the question of the entire separation of church and State in Virginia.

Mr. Jefferson says of him, in allusion to the study and experience through which he had already passed:

"Trained in these successive schools, he acquired a habit of self-possession which placed at ready command the rich resources of his luminous and discriminating mind and of his extensive information, and rendered him the first of every assembly of which he afterward became a member. Never wandering from his subject into vain declamation, but pursuing it closely in language pure, classical and copious, soothing always the feelings of his adversaries by civilities and softness of expression, he rose to the eminent station which he held in the great National Convention of 1787; and in that of Virginia, which followed, he sustained the new Constitution in all its parts, bearing off the palm against the logic of George Mason and the fervid declamation of Patrick Henry. With these consummate powers were united a pure and spotless virtue which no calumny has ever attempted to sully. Of the power and polish of his pen, and of the wisdom of his administration in the highest office of the nation, I need say nothing. They have spoken, and will forever speak, for themselves."

In January, 1786, Mr. Madison took the initiative in proposing a meeting of State Commissioners to devise measures for more satisfactory commercial relations between the States. A meeting was held at Annapolis to discuss this subject, and but five States were represented. The convention issued another call, drawn up by Mr. Madison, urging all the States to send their delegates to Philadelphia, in May, 1787, to draught a Constitution for the United States. The delegates met at the time appointed, every State except Rhode Island being represented. George Washington was chosen president of the convention, and the present Constitution of the United States was then and there formed. There was no mind and no pen more active in framing this immortal document than the mind and pen of James Madison. He was, perhaps, its ablest advocate in the pages of the *Federalist.*

Mr. Madison was a member of the first four Congresses, 1789–'97, in which he maintained a moderate opposition to Hamilton's financial policy. He declined the mission to France and the Secretaryship of State, and, gradually identifying himself with the Republican party, became from 1792 its avowed leader. In 1796 he was its choice for the Presidency as successor to Washington. Mr. Jefferson wrote: "There is not another person in the United States with whom, being placed at the helm of our affairs, my mind would be so completely at rest for the fortune of our political bark." But Mr. Madison declined to be a candidate. His term in Congress had expired, and he returned from New York to his beautiful retreat at Montpelier.

In 1794 Mr. Madison married a young widow of remarkable powers of fascination —Mrs. Todd. Her maiden name was Dorothy Paine. She was born in 1767, in Virginia, of Quaker parents, and had been educated in the strictest rules of that sect. When but eighteen years of age she married a young lawyer and moved to Philadelphia, where she was introduced to brilliant scenes of fashionable life. She speedily laid aside the dress and address of the Quakeress, and became one of the most fascinating ladies of the republican court. In New York, after the death of her husband, she was the belle of the season and was surrounded with admirers. Mr. Madison won the prize. She proved an invaluable helpmate. In Washington she was the life of society. If there was any diffident, timid young girl just making her appearance, she found in Mrs. Madison an encouraging friend.

During the stormy administration of John Adams Madison remained in private life, but was the author of the celebrated "Resolutions of 1798," adopted by the Virginia Legislature, in condemnation of the Alien and Sedition laws, as well as of the "report" in which he defended those resolutions, which is, by many, considered his ablest State paper.

The storm passed away; the Alien and Sedition laws were repealed, John Adams lost his re-election, and in 1801 Thomas Jefferson was chosen President. The great reaction in public sentiment which seated Jefferson in the presidential chair was largely owing to the writings of Madison, who was consequently well entitled to the post of Secretary of State. With great ability he discharged the duties of this responsible office during the eight years of Mr. Jefferson's administration.

As Mr. Jefferson was a widower, and neither of his daughters could be often with him, Mrs. Madison usually presided over the festivities of the White House; and as her husband succeeded Mr. Jefferson, holding his office for two terms, this remarkable woman was the mistress of the presidential mansion for sixteen years.

Mr. Madison being entirely engrossed by the cares of his office, all the duties of social life devolved upon his accomplished wife. Never were such responsibilities more ably discharged. The most bitter foes of her husband and of the administration were received with the frankly proffered hand and the cordial smile of welcome; and the influence of this gentle woman in allaying the bitterness of party rancor became a great and salutary power in the nation.

As the term of Mr. Jefferson's Presidency drew near its close, party strife was roused to the utmost to elect his successor. It was a death-grapple between the two great parties, the Federal and Republican. Mr. Madison was chosen President by an electoral vote of 122 to 53, and was inaugurated March 4, 1809, at a critical period, when the relations of the United States with Great Britain were becoming embittered, and his first term was passed in diplomatic quarrels, aggravated by the act of non-intercourse of May, 1810, and finally resulting in a declaration of war.

On the 18th of June, 1812, President Madison gave his approval to an act of Congress declaring war against Great Britain. Notwithstanding the bitter hostility of the Federal party to the war, the country in general approved; and in the autumn Madison was re-elected to the Presidency by 128 electoral votes to 89 in favor of George Clinton.

March 4, 1817, Madison yielded the Presidency to his Secretary of State and intimate friend, James Monroe, and retired to his ancestral estate at Montpelier, where he passed the evening of his days surrounded by attached friends and enjoying the merited respect of the whole nation. He took pleasure in promoting agriculture, as president of the county society, and in watching the development of the University of Virginia, of which he was long rector and visitor. In extreme old age he sat in 1829 as a member of the convention called to reform the Virginia Constitution, where his appearance was hailed with the most genuine interest and satisfaction, though he was too infirm to participate in the active work of revision. Small in stature, slender and delicate in form, with a countenance full of intelligence, and expressive alike of mildness and dignity, he attracted the attention of all who attended the convention, and was treated with the utmost deference. He seldom addressed the assembly, though he always appeared self-possessed, and watched with unflagging interest the progress of every measure. Though the convention sat sixteen weeks, he spoke only twice; but when he did speak, the whole house paused to listen. His voice was feeble though his enunciation was very distinct. One of the reporters, Mr. Stansbury, relates the following anecdote of Mr. Madison's last speech:

"The next day, as there was a great call for it, and the report had not been returned for publication, I sent my son with a respectful note, requesting the manuscript. My son was a lad of sixteen, whom I had taken with me to act as amanuensis. On delivering my note, he was received with the utmost politeness, and requested to come up into Mr. Madison's room and wait while his eye ran over the paper, as company had prevented his attending to it. He did so, and Mr. Madison sat down to correct the report. The lad stood near him so that his eye fell on the paper. Coming to a certain sentence in the speech, Mr. Madison erased a word and substituted another; but hesitated, and not feeling satisfied with the second word, drew his pen through it also. My son was young, ignorant of the world, and unconscious of the solecism of which he was about to be guilty, when, in all simplicity, he suggested a word. Probably no other person then living would have taken such a liberty. But the sage, instead of regarding such an intrusion with a frown, raised his eyes to the boy's face with a pleased surprise, and said, 'Thank you, sir; it is the very word,' and immediately inserted it. I saw him the next day, and he mentioned the circumstance, with a compliment on the young critic."

Mr. Madison died at Montpelier, June 28, 1836, at the advanced age of eighty-five. While not possessing the highest order of talent, and deficient in oratorical powers, he was pre-eminently a statesman, of a well-balanced mind. His attainments were solid, his knowledge copious, his judgment generally sound, his powers of analysis and logical statement rarely surpassed, his language and literary style correct and polished, his conversation witty, his temperament sanguine and trustful, his integrity unquestioned, his manners simple, courteous and winning. By these rare qualities he conciliated the esteem not only of friends, but of political opponents, in a greater degree than any American statesman in the present century.

Mrs. Madison survived her husband thirteen years, and died July 12, 1849, in the eighty-second year of her age. She was one of the most remarkable women our country has produced. Even now she is admiringly remembered in Washington as "Dolly Madison," and it is fitting that her memory should descend to posterity in company with that of the companion of her life.

JAMES MONROE.

JAMES MONROE, the fifth President of the United States, 1817–'25, was born in Westmoreland County, Virginia, April 28, 1758. He was a son of Spence Monroe, and a descendant of a Scottish cavalier family. Like all his predecessors thus far in the Presidential chair, he enjoyed all the advantages of education which the country could then afford. He was early sent to a fine classical school, and at the age of sixteen entered William and Mary College.. In 1776, when he had been in college but two years, the Declaration of Independence was adopted, and our feeble militia, without arms, amunition or clothing, were struggling against the trained armies of England. James Monroe left college, hastened to General Washington's headquarters at New York and enrolled himself as a cadet in the army.

At Trenton Lieutenant Monroe so distinguished himself, receiving a wound in his shoulder, that he was promoted to a Captaincy. Upon recovering from his wound, he was invited to act as aide to Lord Sterling, and in that capacity he took an active part in the battles of Brandywine, Germantown and Monmouth. At Germantown he stood by the side of Lafayette when the French Marquis received his wound. General Washington, who had formed a high idea of young Monroe's ability, sent him to Virginia to raise a new regiment, of which he was to be Colonel; but so exhausted was Virginia at that time that the effort proved unsuccessful. He, however, received his commission.

Finding no opportunity to enter the army as a commissioned officer, he returned to his original plan of studying law, and entered the office of Thomas Jefferson, who was then Governor of Virginia. He developed a very noble character, frank, manly and sincere. Mr. Jefferson said of him:

"James Monroe is so perfectly honest that if his soul were turned inside out there would not be found a spot on it."

In 1782 he was elected to the Assembly of Virginia, and was also appointed a member of the Executive Council. The next year he was chosen delegate to the Continental Congress for a term of three years. He was present at Annapolis when Washington surrendered his commission of Commander-in-chief.

With Washington, Jefferson and Madison he felt deeply the inefficiency of the old Articles of Confederation, and urged the formation of a new Constitution, which should invest the Central Government with something like national power. Influenced by these views, he introduced a resolution

James Monroe

LIBRARY
OF THE
UNIVERSITY OF ILLINOIS

that Congress should be empowered to regulate trade, and to lay an impost duty of five per cent. The resolution was referred to a committee of which he was chairman. The report and the discussion which rose upon it led to the convention of five States at Annapolis, and the consequent general convention at Philadelphia, which, in 1787, drafted the Constitution of the United States.

At this time there was a controversy between New York and Massachusetts in reference to their boundaries. The high esteem in which Colonel Monroe was held is indicated by the fact that he was appointed one of the judges to decide the controversy. While in New York attending Congress, he married Miss Kortright, a young lady distinguished alike for her beauty and accomplishments. For nearly fifty years this happy union remained unbroken. In London and in Paris, as in her own country, Mrs. Monroe won admiration and affection by the loveliness of her person, the brilliancy of her intellect, and the amiability of her character.

Returning to Virginia, Colonel Monroe commenced the practice of law at Fredericksburg. He was very soon elected to a seat in the State Legislature, and the next year he was chosen a member of the Virginia convention which was assembled to decide upon the acceptance or rejection of the Constitution which had been drawn up at Philadelphia, and was now submitted to the several States. Deeply as he felt the imperfections of the old Confederacy, he was opposed to the new Constitution, thinking, with many others of the Republican party, that it gave too much power to the Central Government, and not enough to the individual States.

In 1789 he became a member of the United States Senate, which office he held acceptably to his constituents, and with honor to himself for four years.

Having opposed the Constitution as not leaving enough power with the States, he, of course, became more and more identified with the Republican party. Thus he found himself in cordial co-operation with Jefferson and Madison. The great Republican party became the dominant power which ruled the land.

George Washington was then President. England had espoused the cause of the Bourbons against the principles of the French Revolution. President Washington issued a proclamation of neutrality between these contending powers. France had helped us in the struggle for our liberties. All the despotisms of Europe were now combined to prevent the French from escaping from tyranny a thousandfold worse than that which we had endured. Colonel Monroe, more magnanimous than prudent, was anxious that we should help our old allies in their extremity. He violently opposed the President's proclamation as ungrateful and wanting in magnanimity.

Washington, who could appreciate such a character, developed his calm, serene, almost divine greatness by appointing that very James Monroe, who was denouncing the policy of the Government, as the Minister of that Government to the republic of France. He was directed by Washington to express to the French people our warmest sympathy, communicating to them corresponding resolves approved by the President, and adopted by both houses of Congress.

Mr. Monroe was welcomed by the National Convention in France with the most enthusiastic demonstrations of respect and affection. He was publicly introduced to that body, and received the embrace of the President, Merlin de Douay, after having been addressed in a speech glowing with congratulations, and with expressions of desire that harmony might ever exist be tween the two nations The flags of the two republics were intertwined in the hall of the convention. Mr. Monroe presented the American colors, and received those of France in return. The course which he pursued in Paris was so annoying to England and to the friends of England in this country that, near the close of Washington's administration, Mr. Monroe, was recalled

After his return Colonel Monroe wrote a book of 400 pages, entitled "A View of the Conduct of the Executive in Foreign Affairs." In this work he very ably advocated his side of the question, but, with the magnanimity of the man, he recorded a warm tribute to the patriotism, ability and spotless integrity of John Jay, between whom and himself there was intense antagonism; and in subsequent years he expressed in warmest terms his perfect veneration for the character of George Washington

Shortly after his return to this country Colonel Monroe was elected Governor of Virginia, and held that office for three years, the period limited by the Constitution. In 1802 he was an Envoy to France, and to Spain in 1805, and was Minister to England in 1803 In 1806 he returned to his quiet home in Virginia, and with his wife and children and an ample competence from his paternal estate, enjoyed a few years of domestic repose.

In 1809 Mr. Jefferson's second term of office expired, and many of the Republican party were anxious to nominate James Monroe as his successor. The majority were in favor of Mr. Madison. Mr. Monroe withdrew his name and was soon after chosen a second time Governor of Virginia. He soon resigned that office to accept the position of Secretary of State, offered him by President Madison. The correspondence which he then carried on with the British Government demonstrated that there was no hope of any peaceful adjustment of our difficulties with the cabinet of St James. War was consequently declared in June, 1812 Immediately after the sack of Washington the Secretary of War resigned, and Mr Monroe, at the earnest request of Mr. Madison, assumed the additional duties of the War Department, without resigning his position as Secretary of State. It has been confidently stated, that, had Mr. Monroe's energies been in the War Department a few months earlier, the disaster at Washington would not have occurred.

The duties now devolving upon Mr. Monroe were extremely arduous. Ten thousand men, picked from the veteran armies of England, were sent with a powerful fleet to New Orleans to acquire possession of the mouths of the Mississippi Our finances were in the most deplorable condition. The treasury was exhausted and our credit gone And yet it was necessary to make the most rigorous preparations to meet the foe. In this crisis James Monroe, the Secretary of War, with virtue unsurpassed in Greek or Roman story, stepped forward and pledged his own individual credit as subsidiary to that of the nation, and thus succeeded in placing the city of New Orleans in such a posture of defense, that it was enabled successfully to repel the invader

Mr. Monroe was truly the armor-bearer of President Madison, and the most efficient business man in his cabinet His energy in the double capacity of Secretary, both of State and War, pervaded all the departments of the country He proposed to increase the army to 100,000 men, a measure which he deemed absolutely necessary to save us from ignominious defeat, but which, at the same time, he knew would render his name so unpopular as to preclude the possibility of his being a successful candidate for the Presidency.

The happy result of the conference at Ghent in securing peace rendered the increase of the army unnecessary; but it is not too much to say that James Monroe placed in the hands of Andrew Jackson the weapon with which to beat off the foe at New Orleans Upon the return of peace Mr. Monroe resigned the department of war, devoting himself entirely to the duties of Secretary of State. These he continued to discharge until the close of President Madison's administration, with zeal which was never abated, and with an ardor of self-devotion which made him almost forgetful of the claims of fortune, health or life

Mr. Madison's second term expired in March, 1817, and Mr. Monroe succeeded to the Presidency. He was a candidate of the Republican party, now taking the name of the Democratic Republican In 1821 he was re-elected, with scarcely any opposition. Out of 232 electoral votes, he received 231. The slavery question, which subsequently assumed such formidable dimensions, now began to make its appearance. The State of Missouri, which had been carved out of that immense territory which we had purchased of France, applied for admission to the Union, with a slavery Constitution. There were not a few who foresaw the evils impending. After the debate of a week it was decided that Missouri could not be admitted into the Union with slavery. This important question was at length settled by a compromise proposed by Henry Clay

The famous "Monroe Doctrine," of which so much has been said, originated in this way: In 1823 it was rumored that the Holy Alliance was about to interfere to prevent the establishment of Republican liberty in the European colonies of South America. President Monroe wrote to his old friend Thomas Jefferson for advice in the emergency. In his reply under date of October 24, Mr. Jefferson writes upon the supposition that our attempt to resist this European movement might lead to war:

"Its object is to introduce and establish the American system of keeping out of our land all foreign powers; of never permitting those of Europe to intermeddle with the affairs of our nation It is to maintain our own principle, not to depart from it."

December 2, 1823, President Monroe sent a message to Congress, declaring it to be the policy of this Government not to entangle ourselves with the broils of Europe, and not to allow Europe to interfere with the affairs of nations on the American continent, and the doctrine was announced, that any attempt on the part of the European powers "to extend their system to any portion of this hemisphere would be regarded by the United States as dangerous to our peace and safety."

March 4, 1825, Mr. Monroe surrendered the presidential chair to his Secretary of State, John Quincy Adams, and retired, with the universal respect of the nation, to his private residence at Oak Hill, Loudoun County, Virginia. His time had been so entirely consecrated to his country, that he had neglected his pecuniary interests, and was deeply involved in debt The welfare of his country had ever been uppermost in his mind.

For many years Mrs. Monroe was in such feeble health that she rarely appeared in public. In 1830 Mr. Monroe took up his residence with his son-in-law in New York, where he died on the 4th of July, 1831. The citizens of New York conducted his obsequies with pageants more imposing than had ever been witnessed there before. Our country will ever cherish his memory with pride, gratefully enrolling his name in the list of its benefactors, pronouncing him the worthy successor of the illustrious men who had preceded him in the presidential chair.

John Quincy Adams.

JOHN QUINCY ADAMS, the sixth President of the United States, 1825-'9, was born in the rural home of his honored father, John Adams, in Quincy, Massachusetts, July 11, 1767. His mother, a woman of exalted worth, watched over his childhood during the almost constant absence of his father. He commenced his education at the village school, giving at an early period indications of superior mental endowments.

When eleven years of age he sailed with his father for Europe, where the latter was associated with Franklin and Lee as Minister Plenipotentiary. The intelligence of John Quincy attracted the attention of these men and received from them flattering marks of attention. Mr. Adams had scarcely returned to this country in 1779 ere he was again sent abroad, and John Quincy again accompanied him. On this voyage he commenced a diary, which practice he continued, with but few interruptions, until his death. He journeyed with his father from Ferrol, in Spain, to Paris. Here he applied himself for six months to study; then accompanied his father to Holland, where he entered, first a school in Amsterdam, and then the University of Leyden. In 1781, when only fourteen years of age, he was selected by Mr. Dana, our Minister to the Russian court, as his private secretary. In this school of incessant labor he spent fourteen months, and then returned alone to Holland through Sweden, Denmark, Hamburg and Bremen. Again he resumed his studies under a private tutor, at The Hague.

In the spring of 1782 he accompanied his father to Paris, forming acquaintance with the most distinguished men on the Continent. After a short visit to England, he returned to Paris and studied until May, 1785, when he returned to America, leaving his father an embassador at the court of St. James. In 1786 he entered the junior class in Harvard University, and graduated with the second honor of his class. The oration he delivered on this occasion, the "Importance of Public Faith to the Well-being of a Community," was published—an event very rare in this or any other land.

Upon leaving college at the age of twenty he studied law three years with the Hon. Theophilus Parsons in Newburyport. In 1790 he opened a law office in Boston. The profession was crowded with able men, and the fees were small. The first year he had

J. Q. Adams

LIBRARY
OF THE
UNIVERSITY OF ILLINOIS

no clients, but not a moment was lost The second year passed away, still no clients, and still he was dependent upon his parents for support Anxiously he awaited the third year. The reward now came. Clients began to enter his office, and before the end of the year he was so crowded with business that all solicitude respecting a support was at an end

When Great Britain commenced war against France, in 1793, Mr Adams wrote some articles, urging entire neutrality on the part of the United States. The view was not a popular one. Many felt that as France had helped us, we were bound to help France. But President Washington coincided with Mr Adams, and issued his proclamation of neutrality. His writings at this time in the Boston journals gave him so high a reputation, that in June, 1794, he was appointed by Washington resident Minister at the Netherlands. In July, 1797, he left The Hague to go to Portugal as Minister Plenipotentiary. Washington at this time wrote to his father, John Adams:

"Without intending to compliment the father or the mother, or to censure any others, I give it as my decided opinion, that Mr. Adams is the most valuable character we have abroad, and there remains no doubt in my mind that he will prove the ablest of our diplomatic corps."

On his way to Portugal, upon his arrival in London, he met with dispatches directing him to the court of Berlin, but requesting him to remain in London until he should receive instructions. While waiting he was married to Miss Louisa Catherine Johnson, to whom he had been previously engaged. Miss Johnson was a daughter of Mr. Joshua Johnson, American Consul in London, and was a lady endowed with that beauty and those accomplishments which fitted her to move in the elevated sphere for which she was destined.

In July, 1799, having fulfilled all the purposes of his mission, Mr. Adams returned In 1802 he was chosen to the Senate of Massachusetts from Boston, and then was elected Senator of the United States for six years from March 4, 1804. His reputation, his ability and his experience, placed him immediately among the most prominent and influential members of that body. He sustained the Government in its measures of resistance to the encroachments of England, destroying our commerce and insulting our flag. There was no man in America more familiar with the arrogance of the British court upon these points, and no one more resolved to present a firm resistance. This course, so truly patriotic, and which scarcely a voice will now be found to condemn, alienated him from the Federal party dominant in Boston, and subjected him to censure.

In 1805 Mr. Adams was chosen professor of rhetoric in Harvard College. His lectures at this place were subsequently published. In 1809 he was sent as Minister to Russia. He was one of the commissioners that negotiated the treaty of peace with Great Britain, signed December 24, 1814, and he was appointed Minister to the court of St. James in 1815. In 1817 he became Secretary of State in Mr. Monroe's cabinet in which position he remained eight years. Few will now contradict the assertion that the duties of that office were never more ably discharged. Probably the most important measure which Mr. Adams conducted was the purchase of Florida from Spain for $5,000,000.

The campaign of 1824 was an exciting one. Four candidates were in the field Of the 260 electoral votes that were cast, Andrew Jackson received ninety-nine; John Quincy Adams, eighty-four, William H. Crawford, forty-one, and Henry Clay, thirty-seven As there was no choice by the people, the question went to the House of Representatives. Mr. Clay gave the vote of Kentucky to Mr. Adams, and he was elected.

The friends of all disappointed candidates now combined in a venomous assault upon Mr. Adams. There is nothing more disgraceful in the past history of our country than the abuse which was poured in one uninterrupted stream upon this high-minded, upright, patriotic man. There was never an administration more pure in principles, more conscientiously devoted to the best interests of the country, than that of John Quincy Adams; and never, perhaps, was there an administration more unscrupulously assailed. Mr. Adams took his seat in the presidential chair resolved not to know any partisanship, but only to consult for the interests of the whole Republic,

He refused to dismiss any man from office for his political views. If he was a faithful officer that was enough. Bitter must have been his disappointment to find that the Nation could not appreciate such conduct.

Mr. Adams, in his public manners, was cold and repulsive; though with his personal friends he was at times very genial. This chilling address very seriously detracted from his popularity. No one can read an impartial record of his administration without admitting that a more noble example of uncompromising dignity can scarcely be found. It was stated publicly that Mr. Adams' administration was to be put down, "though it be as pure as the angels which stand at the right hand of the throne of God." Many of the active participants in these scenes lived to regret the course they pursued. Some years after, Warren R. Davis, of South Caroliha, turning to Mr. Adams, then a member of the House of Representatives, said:

"Well do I remember the enthusiastic zeal with which we reproached the administration of that gentleman, and the ardor and vehemence with which we labored to bring in another. For the share I had in these transactions, and it was not a small one, *I hope God will forgive me, for I shall never forgive myself.*"

March 4, 1829, Mr. Adams retired from the Presidency and was succeeded by Andrew Jackson, the latter receiving 168 out of 261 electoral votes. John C. Calhoun was elected Vice-President. The slavery question now began to assume pretentious magnitude. Mr. Adams returned to Quincy, and pursued his studies with unabated zeal. But he was not long permitted to remain in retirement. In November, 1830, he was elected to Congress. In this he recognized the principle that it is honorable for the General of yesterday to act as Corporal to-day, if by so doing he can render service to his country. Deep as are our obligations to John Quincy Adams for his services as embassador, as Secretary of State and as President; in his capacity as legislator in the House of Representatives, he conferred benefits upon our land which eclipsed all the rest, and which can never be over-estimated.

For seventeen years, until his death, he occupied the post of Representative, towering above all his peers, ever ready to do brave battle for freedom, and winning the title of "the old man eloquent." Upon taking his seat in the House he announced that he should hold himself bound to no party. He was usually the first in his place in the morning, and the last to leave his seat in the evening. Not a measure could escape his scrutiny. The battle which he fought, almost singly, against the pro-slavery party in the Government, was sublime in its moral daring and heroism. For persisting in presenting petitions for the abolition of slavery, he was threatened with indictment by the Grand Jury, with expulsion from the House, with assassination; but no threats could intimidate him, and his final triumph was complete.

On one occasion Mr. Adams presented a petition, signed by several women, against the annexation of Texas for the purpose of cutting it up into slave States Mr. Howard, of Maryland, said that these women discredited not only themselves, but their section of the country, by turning from their domestic duties to the conflicts of political life

"Are women," exclaimed Mr. Adams, "to have no opinions or actions on subjects relating to the general welfare? Where did the gentleman get his principle? Did he find it in sacred history,—in the language of Miriam, the prophetess, in one of the noblest and sublime songs of triumph that ever met the human eye or ear? Did the gentleman never hear of Deborah, to whom the children of Israel came up for judgment? Has he forgotten the deed of Jael, who slew the dreaded enemy of her country? Has he forgotten Esther, who, by her *petition* saved her people and her country?

"To go from sacred history to profane, does the gentleman there find it 'discreditable' for women to take an interest in political affairs? Has he forgotten the Spartan mother, who said to her son when going out to battle, 'My son, come back to me *with* thy shield, or *upon* thy shield?' Does he remember Cloelia and her hundred companions, who swam across the river under a shower of darts, escaping from Porsena? Has he forgotten Cornelia, the mother of the Gracchi? Does he not remember Portia, the wife of Brutus and the daughter of Cato?

"To come to later periods, what says the history of our Anglo-Saxon ancestors? To say nothing of Boadicea, the British heroine in the time of the Cæsars, what name is more illustrious than that of Elizabeth? Or, if he will go to the continent, will he not find the names of Maria Theresa of Hungary, of the two Catherines of Prussia, and of Isabella of Castile, the patroness of Columbus? Did she bring 'discredit' on her sex by mingling in politics?"

In this glowing strain Mr Adams silenced and overwhelmed his antagonists.

In January, 1842, Mr Adams presented a petition from forty-five citizens of Haverhill, Massachusetts, praying for a peaceable dissolution of the Union. The pro-slavery party in Congress, who were then plotting the destruction of the Government, were aroused to a pretense of commotion such as even our stormy hall of legislation has rarely witnessed. They met in caucus, and, finding that they probably would not be able to expel Mr. Adams from the House drew up a series of resolutions, which, if adopted, would inflict upon him disgrace, equivalent to expulsion Mr Adams had presented the petition, which was most respectfully worded, and had moved that it be referred to a committee instructed to report an answer, showing the reason why the prayer ought not to be granted.

It was the 25th of January The whole body of the pro-slavery party came crowding together in the House, prepared to crush Mr. Adams forever. One of the number, Thomas F. Marshall, of Kentucky, was appointed to read the resolutions, which accused Mr. Adams of high treason, of having insulted the Government, and of meriting expulsion; but for which deserved punishment, the House, in its great mercy, would substitute its severest censure With the assumption of a very solemn and magisterial air, there being breathless silence in the audience, Mr. Marshall hurled the carefully prepared anathemas at his victim. Mr. Adams stood alone, the whole pro-slavery party against him.

As soon as the resolutions were read, every eye being fixed upon him, that bold old man, whose scattered locks were whitened by seventy-five years, casting a withering glance in the direction of his assailants, in a clear, shrill tone, tremulous with suppressed emotion, said

"In reply to this audacious, atrocious charge of high treason, I call for the reading of the first paragraph of the Declaration of Independence Read it! Read it! and see what that says of the rights of a people to reform, to change, and to dissolve their Government.'

The attitude, the manner, the tone, the words; the venerable old man, with flashing eye and flushed cheek, and whose very form seemed to expand under the inspiration of the occasion—all presented a scene overflowing in its sublimity There was breathless silence as that paragraph was read, in defense of whose principles our fathers had pledged their lives, their fortunes and their sacred honor. It was a proud hour to Mr. Adams as they were all compelled to listen to the words.

"That, to secure these rights, governments are instituted among men, deriving their just powers from the consent of the governed, and that whenever any form of government becomes destructive of those ends, it is the right of the people to alter or abolish it, and to institute new government, laying its foundations on such principles and organizing its powers in such form as shall seem most likely to effect their safety and happiness."

That one sentence routed and baffled the foe. The heroic old man looked around upon the audience, and thundered out, "Read that again!" It was again read. Then in a few fiery, logical words he stated his defense in terms which even prejudiced minds could not resist His discomfited assailants made several attempts to rally. After a conflict of eleven days they gave up vanquished and their resolution was ignominiously laid upon the table

In January, 1846, when seventy-eight years of age, he took part in the great debate on the Oregon question, displaying intellectual vigor, and an extent and accuracy of acquaintance with the subject that excited great admiration

On the 21st of February, 1848, he rose on the floor of Congress with a paper in his hand to address the Speaker Suddenly he fell, stricken by paralysis, and was caught in the arms of those around him. For a time he was senseless and was conveyed to a sofa in the rotunda. With reviving consciousness he opened his eyes, looked calmly around and said, "*This is the end of earth.*" Then after a moment's pause, he added, "*I am content*" These were his last words, and he soon breathed his last, in the apartment beneath the dome of the capitol—the theater of his labors and his triumphs. In the language of hymnology, he "died at his post," he "ceased at once to work and live."

LIBRARY
OF THE
UNIVERSITY OF ILLINOIS

Andrew Jackson

ANDREW JACKSON.

ANDREW JACKSON, the seventh President of the United States, 1829-'37, was born at the Waxhaw Settlement, Union County, North Carolina, March 16, 1767. His parents were Scotch-Irish, natives of Carrickfergus, who came to America in 1765, and settled on Twelve-Mile Creek, a tributary of the Catawba. His father, who was a poor farm laborer, died shortly before Andrew's birth, when his mother removed to Waxhaw, where some relatives resided.

Few particulars of the childhood of Jackson have been preserved. His education was of the most limited kind, and he showed no fondness for books. He grew up to be a tall, lank boy, with coarse hair and freckled cheeks, with bare feet dangling from trousers too short for him, very fond of athletic sports, running, boxing and wrestling. He was generous to the younger and weaker boys, but very irascible and overbearing with his equals and superiors. He was profane—a vice in which he surpassed all other men. The character of his mother he revered; and it was not until after her death that his predominant vices gained full strength.

In 1780, at the age of thirteen, Andrew, or Andy, as he was called, with his brother Robert, volunteered to serve in the Revolutionary forces under General Sumter, and was a witness of the latter's defeat at Hanging Rock. In the following year the brothers were made prisoners, and confined in Camden, experiencing brutal treatment from their captors, and being spectators of General Green's defeat at Hobkirk Hill. Through their mother's exertions the boys were exchanged while suffering from smallpox. In two days Robert was dead, and Andy apparently dying. The strength of his constitution triumphed, and he regained health and vigor.

As he was getting better, his mother heard the cry of anguish from the prisoners whom the British held in Charleston, among whom were the sons of her sisters. She hastened to their relief, was attacked by fever, died and was buried where her grave could never be found. Thus Andrew Jackson, when fourteen years of age, was left alone in the world, without father, mother, sister or brother, and without one dollar which he could call his own. He soon entered a saddler's shop, and labored diligently for six months But gradually, as health returned, he became more and more a wild, reckless, lawless boy He gambled, drank and was regarded as about the worst character that could be found

He now turned schoolmaster He could teach the alphabet, perhaps the multiplication table, and as he was a very bold boy, it is possible he might have ventured to teach a little writing But he soon began to think of a profession and decided to study law. With a very slender purse, and on the back of a very fine horse, he set out for Salisbury, North Carolina, where he entered the law office of Mr. McCay. Here he remained two years, professedly studying law. He is still remembered in traditions of Salisbury, which say

"Andrew Jackson was the most roaring, rollicking, horse-racing, card-playing, mischievous fellow that ever lived in Salisbury. He did not trouble the law-books much"

Andrew was now, at the age of twenty, a tall young man, being over six feet in height He was slender, remarkably graceful and dignified in his manners, an exquisite horseman, and developed, amidst his loathesome profanity and multiform vices, a vein of rare magnanimity. His temper was fiery in the extreme; but it was said of him that no man knew better than Andrew Jackson when to get angry and when not.

In 1786 he was admitted to the bar, and two years later removed to Nashville, in what was then the western district of North Carolina, with the appointment of solicitor, or public prosecutor. It was an office of little honor, small emolument and great peril. Few men could be found to accept it.

And now Andrew Jackson commenced vigorously to practice law. It was an important part of his business to collect debts. It required nerve During the first seven years of his residence in those wilds he traversed the almost pathless forest between Nashville and Jonesborough, a distance of 200 miles, twenty two times Hostile Indians were constantly on the watch, and a man was liable at any moment to be shot down in his own field Andrew Jackson was just the man for this service—a wild, daring, rough backwoodsman. Daily he made hair-breadth escapes. He seemed to bear a charmed life. Boldly, alone or with few companions, he traversed the forests, encountering all perils and triumphing over all

In 1790 Tennessee became a Territory, and Jackson was appointed, by President Washington, United States Attorney for the new district In 1791 he married Mrs. Rachel Robards (daughter of Colonel John Donelson), whom he supposed to have been divorced in that year by an act of the Legislature of Virginia. Two years after this Mr. and Mrs Jackson learned, to their great surprise, that Mr. Robards had just obtained a divorce in one of the courts of Kentucky, and that the act of the Virginia Legislature was not final, but conditional To remedy the irregularity as much as possible, a new license was obtained and the marriage ceremony was again performed.

It proved to be a marriage of rare felicity Probably there never was a more affectionate union. However rough Mr. Jackson might have been abroad, he was always gentle and tender at home, and through all the vicissitudes of their lives, he treated Mrs. Jackson with the most chivalric attention.

Under the circumstances it was not unnatural that the facts in the case of this marriage were so misrepresented by opponents in the political campaigns a quarter or a century later as to become the basis of serious charges against Jackson's morality which, however, have been satisfactorily attested by abundant evidence.

Jackson was untiring in his duties as

United States Attorney, which demanded frequent journeys through the wilderness and exposed him to Indian hostilities. He acquired considerable property in land, and obtained such influence as to be chosen a member of the convention which framed the Constitution for the new State of Tennessee, in 1796, and in that year was elected its first Representative in Congress. Albert Gallatin thus describes the first appearance of the Hon Andrew Jackson in the House:

"A tall, lank, uncouth-looking personage, with locks of hair hanging over his face and a cue down his back, tied with an eel skin, his dress singular, his manners and deportment those of a rough backwoodsman"

Jackson was an earnest advocate of the Democratic party. Jefferson was his idol. He admired Bonaparte, loved France and hated England. As Mr. Jackson took his seat, General Washington, whose second term of office was just expiring, delivered his last speech to Congress A committee drew up a complimentary address in reply. Andrew Jackson did not approve the address and was one of twelve who voted against it.

Tennessee had fitted out an expedition against the Indians, contrary to the policy of the Government A resolution was introduced that the National Government should pay the expenses. Jackson advocated it and it was carried. This rendered him very popular in Tennessee A vacancy chanced soon after to occur in the Senate, and Andrew Jackson was chosen United States Senator by the State of Tennessee John Adams was then President and Thomas Jefferson, Vice-President

In 1798 Mr. Jackson returned to Tennessee, and resigned his seat in the Senate. Soon after he was chosen Judge of the Supreme Court of that State, with a salary of $600 This office he held six years It is said that his decisions, though sometimes ungrammatical, were generally right. He did not enjoy his seat upon the bench, and renounced the dignity in 1804 About this time he was chosen Major-General of militia, and lost the title of judge in that of General.

When he retired from the Senate Chamber, he decided to try his fortune through trade. He purchased a stock of goods in Philadelphia and sent them to Nashville, where he opened a store He lived about thirteen miles from Nashville, on a tract of land of several thousand acres, mostly uncultivated. He used a small block-house for a store, from a narrow window of which he sold goods to the Indians As he had an assistant his office as judge did not materially interfere with his business.

As to slavery, born in the midst of it, the idea never seemed to enter his mind that it could be wrong. He eventually became an extensive slave owner, but he was one of the most humane and gentle of masters

In 1804 Mr. Jackson withdrew from politics and settled on a plantation which he called the Hermitage, near Nashville He set up a cotton-gin, formed a partnership and traded in New Orleans, making the voyage on flatboats. Through his hot temper he became involved in several quarrels and "affairs of honor," during this period, in one of which he was severely wounded, but had the misfortune to kill his opponent, Charles Dickinson For a time this affair greatly injured General Jackson's popularity. The verdict then was, and continues to be, that General Jackson was outrageously wrong If he subsequently felt any remorse he never revealed it to anyone.

In 1805 Aaron Burr had visited Nashville and been a guest of Jackson, with whom he corresponded on the subject of a war with Spain, which was anticipated and desired by them, as well as by the people of the Southwest generally.

Burr repeated his visit in September, 1806, when he engaged in the celebrated combinations which led to his trial for treason. He was warmly received by Jackson, at whose instance a public ball was given in his honor at Nashville, and contracted with the latter for boats and provisions. Early in 1807, when Burr had been proclaimed a traitor by President Jefferson, volunteer forces for the Federal service were organized at Nashville under Jackson's command; but his energy and activity did not shield him from suspicions of connivance in the supposed treason. He was summoned to Richmond as a witness in Burr's trial, but was not called to the stand, probably because he was out-spoken in his partisanship.

On the outbreak of the war with Great Britain in 1812, Jackson tendered his services, and in January, 1813, embarked for New Orleans at the head of the Tennessee contingent. In March he received an order to disband his forces; but in September he again took the field, in the Creek war, and in conjunction with his former partner, Colonel Coffee, inflicted upon the Indians the memorable defeat at Talladega, Emuckfaw and Tallapoosa.

In May, 1814, Jackson, who had now acquired a national reputation, was appointed a Major-General of the United States army, and commenced a campaign against the British in Florida. He conducted the defense at Mobile, September 15, seized upon Pensacola, November 6, and immediately transported the bulk of his troops to New Orleans, then threatened by a powerful naval force. Martial law was declared in Louisiana, the State militia was called to arms, engagements with the British were fought December 23 and 28, and after re-enforcements had been received on both sides the famous victory of January 8, 1815, crowned Jackson's fame as a soldier, and made him the typical American hero of the first half of the nineteenth century.

In 1817-'18 Jackson conducted the war against the Seminoles of Florida, during which he seized upon Pensacola and executed by courtmartial two British subjects, Arbuthnot and Ambrister—acts which might easily have involved the United States in war both with Spain and Great Britain. Fortunately the peril was averted by the cession of Florida to the United States; and Jackson, who had escaped a trial for the irregularity of his conduct only through a division of opinion in Monroe's cabinet, was appointed in 1821 Governor of the new Territory. Soon after he declined the appointment of minister to Mexico.

In 1823 Jackson was elected to the United States Senate, and nominated by the Tennessee Legislature for the Presidency. This candidacy, though a matter of surprise, and even merryment, speedily became popular, and in 1824, when the stormy electoral canvas resulted in the choice of John Quincy Adams by the House of Representatives, General Jackson received the largest popular vote among the four candidates.

In 1828 Jackson was triumphantly elected President over Adams after a campaign of unparalleled bitterness. He was inaugurated March 4, 1829, and at once removed from office all the incumbents belonging to the opposite party—a procedure new to American politics, but which naturally became a precedent.

His first term was characterized by quarrels between the Vice-President, Calhoun, and the Secretary of State, Van Buren, attended by a cabinet crisis originating in scandals connected with the name of Mrs. General Eaton, wife of the Secretary of War; by the beginning of his war upon the United States Bank, and by his vigorous action against the partisans of Calhoun, who, in South Carolina, threatened to nullify the acts of Congress, establishing a protective tariff.

In the Presidential campaign of 1832

Jackson received 219 out of 288 electoral votes, his competitor being Mr. Clay, while Mr Wirt, on an Anti-Masonic platform, received the vote of Vermont alone. In 1833 President Jackson removed the Government deposits from the United States bank, thereby incurring a vote of censure from the Senate, which was, however, expunged four years later. During this second term of office the Cherokees, Choctaws and Creeks were removed, not without difficulty, from Georgia, Alabama and Mississippi, to the Indian Territory; the National debt was extinguished; Arkansas and Michigan were admitted as States to the Union; the Seminole war was renewed; the anti-slavery agitation first acquired importance; the Mormon delusion, which had organized in 1829, attained considerable proportions in Ohio and Missouri, and the country experienced its greatest pecuniary panic

Railroads with locomotive propulsion were introduced into America during Jackson's first term, and had become an important element of national life before the close of his second term. For many reasons, therefore, the administration of President Jackson formed an era in American history, political, social and industrial. He succeeded in effecting the election of his friend Van Buren as his successor, retired from the Presidency March 4, 1837, and led a tranquil life at the Hermitage until his death, which occurred June 8, 1845

During his closing years he was a professed Christian and a member of the Presbyterian church No American of this century has been the subject of such opposite judgments. He was loved and hated with equal vehemence during his life, but at the present distance of time from his career, while opinions still vary as to the merits of his public acts, few of his countrymen will question that he was a warm-hearted, brave, patriotic, honest and sincere man If his distinguishing qualities were not such as constitute statesmanship, in the highest sense, he at least never pretended to other merits than such as were written to his credit on the page of American history—not attempting to disguise the demerits which were equally legible. The majority of his countrymen accepted and honored him, in spite of all that calumny as well as truth could allege against him His faults may therefore be truly said to have been those of his time; his magnificent virtues may also, with the same justice, be considered as typical of a state of society which has nearly passed away.

MARTIN VAN BUREN.

MARTIN VAN BUREN, the eighth President of the United States, 1837-'41, was born at Kinderhook, New York, December 5, 1782. His ancestors were of Dutch origin, and were among the earliest emigrants from Holland to the banks of the Hudson. His father was a tavern-keeper, as well as a farmer, and a very decided Democrat.

Martin commenced the study of law at the age of fourteen, and took an active part in politics before he had reached the age of twenty. In 1803 he commenced the practice of law in his native village. In 1809 he removed to Hudson, the shire town of his county, where he spent seven years, gaining strength by contending in the courts with some of the ablest men who have adorned the bar of his State. The heroic example of John Quincy Adams in retaining in office every faithful man, without regard to his political preferences, had been thoroughly repudiated by General Jackson. The unfortunate principle was now fully established, that "to the victor belong the spoils." Still, this principle, to which Mr. Van Buren gave his adherence, was not devoid of inconveniences. When, subsequently, he attained power which placed vast patronage in his hands, he was heard to say: "I prefer an office that has no patronage. When I give a man an office I offend his disappointed competitors and their friends. Nor am I certain of gaining a friend in the man I appoint, for, in all probability, he expected something better."

In 1812 Mr. Van Buren was elected to the State Senate. In 1815 he was appointed Attorney-General, and in 1816 to the Senate a second time. In 1818 there was a great split in the Democratic party in New York, and Mr. Van Buren took the lead in organizing that portion of the party called the Albany Regency, which is said to have swayed the destinies of the State for a quarter of a century.

In 1821 he was chosen a member of the convention for revising the State Constitution, in which he advocated an extension of the franchise, but opposed universal suffrage, and also favored the proposal that colored persons, in order to vote, should have freehold property to the amount of $250. In this year he was also elected to the United States Senate, and at the conclusion of his term, in 1827, was re-elected, but resigned the following year, having been chosen Governor of the State. In March, 1829, he was appointed Secretary of

M Van Buren

LIBRARY
OF THE
UNIVERSITY OF ILLINOIS

State by President Jackson, but resigned in April, 1831, and during the recess of Congress was appointed minister to England, whither he proceeded in September, but the Senate, when convened in December, refused to ratify the appointment.

In May, 1832, Mr. Van Buren was nominated as the Democratic candidate for Vice-President, and elected in the following November. May 26, 1836, he received the nomination to succeed General Jackson as President, and received 170 electoral votes, out of 283.

Scarcely had he taken his seat in the Presidential chair when a financial panic swept over the land. Many attributed this to the war which General Jackson had waged on the banks, and to his endeavor to secure an almost exclusive specie currency Nearly every bank in the country was compelled to suspend specie payment, and ruin pervaded all our great cities. Not less than 254 houses failed in New York in one week. All public works were brought to a stand, and there was a general state of dismay President Van Buren urged the adoption of the independent treasury system, which was twice passed in the Senate and defeated in the House, but finally became a law near the close of his administration.

Another important measure was the passage of a pre-emption law, giving actual settlers the preference in the purchase of public lands. The question of slavery, also, now began to assume great prominence in national politics, and after an elaborate anti-slavery speech by Mr Slade, of Vermont, in the House of Representatives, the Southern members withdrew for a separate consultation, at which Mr. Rhett, of South Carolina, proposed to declare it expedient that the Union should be dissolved, but the matter was tided over by the passage of a resolution that no petitions or papers relating to slavery should be in any way considered or acted upon.

In the Presidential election of 1840 Mr. Van Buren was nominated, without opposition, as the Democratic candidate, William H. Harrison being the candidate of the Whig party. The Democrats carried only seven States, and out of 294 electoral votes only sixty were for Mr Van Buren, the remaining 234 being for his opponent. The Whig popular majority, however, was not large, the elections in many of the States being very close.

March 4, 1841, Mr Van Buren retired from the Presidency. From his fine estate at Lindenwald he still exerted a powerful influence upon the politics of the country. In 1844 he was again proposed as the Democratic candidate for the Presidency, and a majority of the delegates of the nominating convention were in his favor; but, owing to his opposition to the proposed annexation of Texas, he could not secure the requisite two-thirds vote. His name was at length withdrawn by his friends, and Mr Polk received the nomination, and was elected

In 1848 Mr Cass was the regular Democratic candidate. A schism, however, sprang up in the party, upon the question of the permission of slavery in the newly-acquired territory, and a portion of the party, taking the name of "Free-Soilers," nominated Mr. Van Buren. They drew away sufficient votes to secure the election of General Taylor, the Whig candidate. After this Mr. Van Buren retired to his estate at Kinderhook, where the remainder of his life was passed, with the exception of a European tour in 1853. He died at Kinderhook, July 24, 1862, at the age of eighty years.

Martin Van Buren was a great and good man, and no one will question his right to a high position among those who have been the successors of Washington in the faithful occupancy of the Presidential chair.

WILLIAM HENRY HARRISON.

WILLIAM HENRY HARRISON, the ninth President of the United States, 1841, was born February 9, 1773, in Charles County, Virginia, at Berkeley, the residence of his father, Governor Benjamin Harrison. He studied at Hampden, Sidney College, with a view of entering the medical profession. After graduation he went to Philadelphia to study medicine under the instruction of Dr. Rush.

George Washington was then President of the United States. The Indians were committing fearful ravages on our Northwestern frontier. Young Harrison, either lured by the love of adventure, or moved by the sufferings of families exposed to the most horrible outrages, abandoned his medical studies and entered the army, having obtained a commission of ensign from President Washington. The first duty assigned him was to take a train of pack-horses bound to Fort Hamilton, on the Miami River, about forty miles from Fort Washington. He was soon promoted to the rank of Lieutenant, and joined the army which Washington had placed under the command of General Wayne to prosecute more vigorously the war with the Indians. Lieutenant Harrison received great commendation from his commanding officer, and was promoted to the rank of Captain, and placed in command at Fort Washington, now Cincinnati, Ohio.

About this time he married a daughter of John Cleves Symmes, one of the frontiersmen who had established a thriving settlement on the bank of the Maumee.

In 1797 Captain Harrison resigned his commission in the army and was appointed Secretary of the Northwest Territory, and *ex-officio* Lieutenant-Governor, General St. Clair being then Governor of the Territory. At that time the law in reference to the disposal of the public lands was such that no one could purchase in tracts less than 4,000 acres. Captain Harrison, in the face of violent opposition, succeeded in obtaining so much of a modification of this unjust law that the land was sold in alternate tracts of 640 and 320 acres. The Northwest Territory was then entitled to one delegate in Congress, and Captain Harrison was chosen to fill that office. In 1800 he was appointed Governor

W. H. Harrison

LIBRARY
OF THE
UNIVERSITY OF ILLINOIS

of Indiana Territory and soon after of Upper Louisiana. He was also Superintendent of Indian Affairs, and so well did he fulfill these duties that he was four times appointed to this office. During his administration he effected thirteen treaties with the Indians, by which the United States acquired 60,000,000 acres of land In 1804 he obtained a cession from the Indians of all the land between the Illinois River and the Mississippi

In 1812 he was made Major-General of Kentucky militia and Brigadier-General in the army, with the command of the Northwest frontier. In 1813 he was made Major-General, and as such won much renown by the defense of Fort Meigs, and the battle of the Thames, October 5, 1813. In 1814 he left the army and was employed in Indian affairs by the Government.

In 1816 General Harrison was chosen a member of the National House of Representatives to represent the district of Ohio In the contest which preceded his election he was accused of corruption in respect to the commissariat of the army Immediately upon taking his seat, he called for an investigation of the charge A committee was appointed, and his vindication was triumphant. A high compliment was paid to his patriotism, disinterestedness and devotion to the public service. For these services a gold medal was presented to him with the thanks of Congress.

In 1819 he was elected to the Senate of Ohio, and in 1824, as one of the Presidential electors of that State, he gave his vote to Henry Clay. In the same year he was elected to the Senate of the United States In 1828 he was appointed by President Adams minister plenipotentiary to Colombia, but was recalled by General Jackson immediately after the inauguration of the latter.

Upon his return to the United States, General Harrison retired to his farm at North Bend, Hamilton County, Ohio, sixteen miles below Cincinnati, where for twelve years he was clerk of the County Court. He once owned a distillery, but perceiving the sad effects of whisky upon the surrounding population, he promptly abandoned his business at great pecuniary sacrifice

In 1836 General Harrison was brought forward as a candidate for the Presidency Van Buren was the administration candidate; the opposite party could not unite, and four candidates were brought forward. General Harrison received seventy-three electoral votes without any general concert among his friends The Democratic party triumphed and Mr. Van Buren was chosen President. In 1839 General Harrison was again nominated for the Presidency by the Whigs, at Harrisburg, Pennsylvania, Mr. Van Buren being the Democratic candidate. General Harrison received 234 electoral votes against sixty for his opponent. This election is memorable chiefly for the then extraordinary means employed during the canvass for popular votes Mass meetings and processions were introduced, and the watchwords "log cabin" and "hard cider" were effectually used by the Whigs, and aroused a popular enthusiasm.

A vast concourse of people attended his inauguration. His address on that occasion was in accordance with his antecedents, and gave great satisfaction A short time after he took his seat, he was seized by a pleurisy-fever, and after a few days of violent sickness, died April 4, just one short month after his inauguration. His death was universally regarded as one of the greatest of National calamities Never, since the death of Washington, were there, throughout one land, such demonstrations of sorrow. Not one single spot can be found to sully his fame, and through all ages Americans will pronounce with love and reverence the name of William Henry Harrison

JOHN TYLER.

JOHN TYLER, the tenth President of the United States, was born in Charles City County, Virginia, March 29, 1790. His father, Judge John Tyler, possessed large landed estates in Virginia, and was one of the most distinguished men of his day, filling the offices of Speaker of the House of Delegates, Judge of the Supreme Court and Governor of the State.

At the early age of twelve young John entered William and Mary College, and graduated with honor when but seventeen years old. He then closely applied himself to the study of law, and at nineteen years of age commenced the practice of his profession. When only twenty-one he was elected to a seat in the State Legislature. He acted with the Democratic party and advocated the measures of Jefferson and Madison. For five years he was elected to the Legislature, receiving nearly the unanimous vote of his county.

When but twenty-six years of age he was elected a member of Congress. He advocated a strict construction of the Constitution and the most careful vigilance over State rights. He was soon compelled to resign his seat in Congress, owing to ill health, but afterward took his seat in the State Legislature, where he exerted a powerful influence in promoting public works of great utility.

In 1825 Mr. Tyler was chosen Governor of his State—a high honor, for Virginia had many able men as competitors for the prize. His administration was signally a successful one. He urged forward internal improvements and strove to remove sectional jealousies. His popularity secured his re-election. In 1827 he was elected United States Senator, and upon taking his seat joined the ranks of the opposition. He opposed the tariff, voted against the bank as unconstitutional, opposed all restrictions upon slavery, resisted all projects of internal improvements by the General Government, avowed his sympathy with Mr. Calhoun's views of nullification, and declared that General Jackson, by his opposition to the nullifiers, had abandoned the principles of the Democratic party. Such was Mr. Tyler's record in Congress.

This hostility to Jackson caused Mr. Tyler's retirement from the Senate, after his election to a second term. He soon after removed to Williamsburg for the better education of his children, and again took his seat in the Legislature.

John Tyler

LIBRARY
OF THE
UNIVERSITY OF ILLINOIS

In 1839 he was sent to the National Convention at Harrisburg to nominate a President General Harrison received a majority of votes, much to the disappointment of the South, who had wished for Henry Clay. In order to conciliate the Southern Whigs, John Tyler was nominated for Vice-President. Harrison and Tyler were inaugurated March 4, 1841. In one short month from that time President Harrison died, and Mr. Tyler, to his own surprise as well as that of the nation, found himself an occupant of the Presidential chair. His position was an exceedingly difficult one, as he was opposed to the main principles of the party which had brought him into power General Harrison had selected a Whig cabinet Should he retain them, and thus surround himself with councilors whose views were antagonistic to his own? or should he turn against the party that had elected him, and select a cabinet in harmony with himself? This was his fearful dilemma.

President Tyler deserves more charity than he has received. He issued an address to the people, which gave general satisfaction. He retained the cabinet General Harrison had selected. His veto of a bill chartering a new national bank led to an open quarrel with the party which elected him, and to a resignation of the entire cabinet, except Daniel Webster, Secretary of State.

President Tyler attempted to conciliate He appointed a new cabinet, leaving out all strong party men, but the Whig members of Congress were not satisfied, and they published a manifesto September 13, breaking off all political relations. The Democrats had a majority in the House, the Whigs in the Senate. Mr Webster soon found it necessary to resign, being forced out by the pressure of his Whig friends.

April 12, 1844, President Tyler concluded, through Mr. Calhoun, a treaty for the annexation of Texas, which was rejected by the Senate, but he effected his object in the closing days of his administration by the passage of the joint resolution of March 1 1845.

He was nominated for the Presidency by an informal Democratic Convention, held at Baltimore in May, 1844, but soon withdrew from the canvass, perceiving that he had not gained the confidence of the Democrats at large

Mr. Tyler's administration was particularly unfortunate. No one was satisfied. Whigs and Democrats alike assailed him. Situated as he was, it is more than can be expected of human nature that he should, in all cases, have acted in the wisest manner, but it will probably be the verdict of all candid men, in a careful review of his career, that John Tyler was placed in a position of such difficulty that he could not pursue any course which would not expose him to severe censure and denunciation

In 1813 Mr. Tyler married Letitia Christian, who bore him three sons and three daughters, and died in Washington in 1842. June 26, 1844, he contracted a second marriage with Miss Julia Gardner, of New York He lived in almost complete retirement from politics until February, 1861, when he was a member of the abortive "peace convention," held at Washington, and was chosen its President. Soon after he renounced his allegiance to the United States and was elected to the Confederate Congress He died at Richmond, January 17, 1862, after a short illness.

Unfortunately for his memory the name of John Tyler must forever be associated with all the misery of that terrible Rebellion, whose cause he openly espoused. It is with sorrow that history records that a President of the United States died while defending the flag of rebellion, which was arrayed against the national banner in deadly warfare

JAMES K. POLK.

JAMES KNOX POLK, the eleventh President of the United States, 1845-'49, was born in Mecklenburg County, North Carolina, November 2, 1795. He was the eldest son of a family of six sons and four daughters, and was a grand-nephew of Colonel Thomas Polk, celebrated in connection with the Mecklenburg Declaration of Independence.

In 1806 his father, Samuel Polk, emigrated with his family two or three hundred miles west to the valley of the Duck River. He was a surveyor as well as farmer, and gradually increased in wealth until he became one of the leading men of the region.

In the common schools James rapidly became proficient in all the common branches of an English education. In 1813 he was sent to Murfreesboro Academy, and in the autumn of 1815 entered the sophomore class in the University of North Carolina, at Chapel Hill, graduating in 1818. After a short season of recreation he went to Nashville and entered the law office of Felix Grundy. As soon as he had his finished legal studies and been admitted to the bar, he returned to Columbia, the shire town of Maury County, and opened an office.

James K. Polk ever adhered to the political faith of his father, which was that of a Jeffersonian Republican. In 1823 he was elected to the Legislature of Tennessee. As a "strict constructionist," he did not think that the Constitution empowered the General Government to carry on a system of internal improvements in the States, but deemed it important that it should have that power, and wished the Constitution amended that it might be conferred. Subsequently, however, he became alarmed lest the General Government become so strong as to undertake to interfere with slavery. He therefore gave all his influence to strengthen the State governments, and to check the growth of the central power.

In January, 1824, Mr. Polk married Miss Mary Childress, of Rutherford County, Tennessee. Had some one then whispered to him that he was destined to become President of the United States, and that he must select for his companion one who would adorn that distinguished station, he could not have made a more fitting choice. She was truly a lady of rare beauty and culture.

In the fall of 1825 Mr. Polk was chosen a member of Congress, and was continu-

James K. Polk

LIBRARY
OF THE
UNIVERSITY OF ILLINOIS

usly re-elected until 1839 He then withdrew, only that he might accept the gubernatorial chair of his native State. He was a warm friend of General Jackson, who had been defeated in the electoral contest by John Quincy Adams. This latter gentleman had just taken his seat in the Presidential chair when Mr. Polk took his seat in the House of Representatives. He immediately united himself with the opponents of Mr. Adams, and was soon regarded as the leader of the Jackson party in the House.

The four years of Mr Adams' administration passed away, and General Jackson took the Presidential chair. Mr. Polk had now become a man of great influence in Congress, and was chairman of its most important committee—that of Ways and Means. Eloquently he sustained General Jackson in all his measures—in his hostility to internal improvements, to the banks, and to the tariff. Eight years of General Jackson's administration passed away, and the powers he had wielded passed into the hands of Martin Van Buren, and still Mr. Polk remained in the House, the advocate of that type of Democracy which those distinguished men upheld.

During five sessions of Congress Mr. Polk was speaker of the House. He performed his arduous duties to general satisfaction, and a unanimous vote of thanks to him was passed by the House as he withdrew, March 4, 1839. He was elected Governor by a large majority, and took the oath of office at Nashville, October 14, 1839. He was a candidate for re-election in 1841, but was defeated. In the meantime a wonderful revolution had swept over the country W. H Harrison, the Whig candidate, had been called to the Presidential chair, and in Tennessee the Whig ticket had been carried by over 12,000 majority. Under these circumstances Mr. Polk's success was hopeless. Still he canvassed the State with his Whig competitor, Mr Jones, traveling in the most friendly manner together, often in the same carriage, and at one time sleeping in the same bed Mr. Jones was elected by 3,000 majority.

And now the question of the annexation of Texas to our country agitated the whole land. When this question became national Mr Polk, as the avowed champion of annexation, became the Presidential candidate of the pro-slavery wing of the Democratic party, and George M Dallas their candidate for the Vice-Presidency They were elected by a large majority, and were inaugurated March 4, 1845

President Polk formed an able cabinet, consisting of James Buchanan, Robert J Walker, William L Marcy, George Bancroft, Cave Johnson and John Y. Mason The Oregon boundary question was settled, the Department of the Interior was created, the low tariff of 1846 was carried, the financial system of the Government was reorganized, the Mexican war was conducted, which resulted in the acquisition of California and New Mexico, and had far-reaching consequences upon the later fortunes of the republic. Peace was made. We had wrested from Mexico territory equal to four times the empire of France, and five times that of Spain In the prosecution of this war we expended 20,000 lives and more than $100,000,000 Of this money $15,000,000 were paid to Mexico

Declining to seek a renomination, Mr. Polk retired from the Presidency March 4, 1849, when he was succeeded by General Zachary Taylor. He retired to Nashville, and died there June 19, 1849, in the fifty-fourth year of his age. His funeral was attended the following day, in Nashville, with every demonstration of respect. He left no children Without being possessed of extraordinary talent, Mr. Polk was a capable administrator of public affairs, and irreproachable in private life.

ZACHARY TAYLOR.

ZACHARY TAYLOR, the twelfth President of the United States, 1849-'50, was born in Orange County, Virginia, September 24, 1784. His father, Richard Taylor, was Colonel of a Virginia regiment in the Revolutionary war, and removed to Kentucky in 1785; purchased a large plantation near Louisville and became an influential citizen; was a member of the convention that framed the Constitution of Kentucky; served in both branches of the Legislature; was Collector of the port of Louisville under President Washington; as a Presidential elector, voted for Jefferson, Madison, Monroe and Clay; died January 19, 1829.

Zachary remained on his father's plantation until 1808, in which year (May 3) he was appointed First Lieutenant in the Seventh Infantry, to fill a vacancy occasioned by the death of his elder brother, Hancock. Up to this point he had received but a limited education.

Joining his regiment at New Orleans, he was attacked with yellow fever, with nearly fatal termination. In November, 1810, he was promoted to Captain, and in the summer of 1812 he was in command of Fort Harrison, on the left bank of the Wabash River, near the present site of Terre Haute, his successful defense of which with but a handful of men against a large force of Indians which had attacked him was one of the first marked military achievements of the war. He was then brevetted Major, and in 1814 promoted to the full rank.

During the remainder of the war Taylor was actively employed on the Western frontier. In the peace organization of 1815 he was retained as Captain, but soon after resigned and settled near Louisville. In May, 1816, however, he re-entered the army as Major of the Third Infantry; became Lieutenant-Colonel of the Eighth Infantry in 1819, and in 1832 attained the Colonelcy of the First Infantry, of which he had been Lieutenant-Colonel since 1821. On different occasions he had been called to Washington as member of a military board for organizing the militia of the Union, and to aid the Government with his knowledge in the organization of the Indian Bureau, having for many years discharged the duties of Indian agent over large tracts of Western

Zachary Taylor

LIBRARY
OF THE
UNIVERSITY OF ILLINOIS

country. He served through the Black Hawk war in 1832, and in 1837 was ordered to take command in Florida, then the scene of war with the Indians.

In 1846 he was transferred to the command of the Army of the Southwest, from which he was relieved the same year at his own request Subsequently he was stationed on the Arkansas frontier at Forts Gibbon, Smith and Jesup, which latter work had been built under his direction in 1822.

May 28, 1845, he received a dispatch from the Secretary of War informing him of the receipt of information by the President "that Texas would shortly accede to the terms of annexation," in which event he was instructed to defend and protect her from "foreign invasion and Indian incursions" He proceeded, upon the annexation of Texas, with about 1,500 men to Corpus Christi, where his force was increased to some 4,000

Taylor was brevetted Major-General May 28, and a month later, June 29, 1846, his full commission to that grade was issued. After needed rest and reinforcement, he advanced in September on Monterey, which city capitulated after three-days stubborn resistance. Here he took up his winter quarters The plan for the invasion of Mexico, by way of Vera Cruz, with General Scott in command, was now determined upon by the Govenrment, and at the moment Taylor was about to resume active operations, he received orders to send the larger part of his force to reinforce the army of General Scott at Vera Cruz. Though subsequently reinforced by raw recruits, yet after providing a garrison for Monterey and Saltillo he had but about 5,300 effective troops, of which but 500 or 600 were regulars. In this weakened condition, however, he was destined to achieve his greatest victory. Confidently relying upon his strength at Vera Cruz to resist the enemy for a long against Taylor to overwhelm him, and then to return to oppose the advance of Scott's more formidable invasion The battle of Buena Vista was fought February 22 and 23, 1847. Taylor received the thanks of Congress and a gold medal, and "Old Rough and Ready," the sobriquet given him in the army, became a household word. He remained in quiet possession of the Rio Grande Valley until November, when he returned to the United States.

In the Whig convention which met at Philadelphia, June 7, 1848, Taylor was nominated on the fourth ballot as candidate of the Whig party for President, over Henry Clay, General Scott and Daniel Webster In November Taylor received a majority of electoral votes, and a popular vote of 1,360,752, against 1,219,962 for Cass and Butler, and 291,342 for Van Buren and Adams General Taylor was inaugurated March 4, 1849.

The free and slave States being then equal in number, the struggle for supremacy on the part of the leaders in Congress was violent and bitter In the summer of 1849 California adopted in convention a Constitution prohibiting slavery within its borders Taylor advocated the immediate admission of California with her Constitution, and the postponement of the question as to the other Territories until they could hold conventions and decide for themselves whether slavery should exist within their borders. This policy ultimately prevailed through the celebrated "Compromise Measures" of Henry Clay, but not during the life of the brave soldier and patriot statesman July 5 he was taken suddenly ill with a bilious fever, which proved fatal, his death occurring July 9, 1850. One of his daughters married Colonel W. W. S. Bliss, his Adjutant-General and Chief of Staff in Florida and Mexico, and Private Secretary during his Presidency Another daughter was

MILLARD FILLMORE.

MILLARD FILLMORE, the thirteenth President of the United States, 1850-'3, was born in Summer Hill, Cayuga County, New York, January 7, 1800. He was of New England ancestry, and his educational advantages were limited. He early learned the clothiers' trade, but spent all his leisure time in study. At nineteen years of age he was induced by Judge Walter Wood to abandon his trade and commence the study of law. Upon learning that the young man was entirely destitute of means, he took him into his own office and loaned him such money as he needed. That he might not be heavily burdened with debt, young Fillmore taught school during the winter months, and in various other ways helped himself along.

At the age of twenty-three he was admitted to the Court of Common Pleas, and commenced the practice of his profession in the village of Aurora, situated on the eastern bank of the Cayuga Lake. In 1825 he married Miss Abigail Powers, daughter of Rev. Lemuel Powers, a lady of great moral worth. In 1825 he took his seat in the House of Assembly of his native State, as Representative from Erie County, whither he had recently moved.

Though he had never taken a very active part in politics his vote and his sympathies were with the Whig party. The State was then Democratic, but his courtesy, ability and integrity won the respect of his associates. In 1832 he was elected to a seat in the United States Congress. At the close of his term he returned to his law practice, and in two years more he was again elected to Congress.

He now began to have a national reputation. His labors were very arduous. To draft resolutions in the committee room, and then to defend them against the most skillful opponents on the floor of the House requires readiness of mind, mental resources and skill in debate such as few possess. Weary with these exhausting labors, and pressed by the claims of his private affairs, Mr. Fillmore wrote a letter to his constituents and declined to be a candidate for re-election. Notwithstanding this communi-

Millard Fillmore

LIBRARY
OF THE
UNIVERSITY OF ILLINOIS

cation his friends met in convention and renominated him by acclamation. Though gratified by this proof of their appreciation of his labors he adhered to his resolve and returned to his home.

In 1847 Mr Fillmore was elected to the important office of comptroller of the State In entering upon the very responsible duties which this situation demanded, it was necessary for him to abandon his profession, and he removed to the city of Albany. In this year, also, the Whigs were looking around to find suitable candidates for the President and Vice-President at the approaching election, and the names of Zachary Taylor and Millard Fillmore became the rallying cry of the Whigs On the 4th of March, 1849, General Taylor was inaugurated President and Millard Fillmore Vice-President of the United States

The great question of slavery had assumed enormous proportions, and permeated every subject that was brought before Congress It was evident that the strength of our institutions was to be severely tried July 9, 1850, President Taylor died, and, by the Constitution, Vice-President Fillmore became President of the United States. The agitated condition of the country brought questions of great delicacy before him. He was bound by his oath of office to execute the laws of the United States. One of these laws was understood to be, that if a slave, escaping from bondage, should reach a free State, the United States was bound to do its utmost to capture him and return him to his master Most Christian men loathed this law President Fillmore felt bound by his oath rigidly to see it enforced. Slavery was organizing armies to invade Cuba as it had invaded Texas, and annex it to the United States President Fillmore gave all the influence of his exalted station against the atrocious enterprise.

Mr Fillmore had serious difficulties to contend with, since the opposition had a majority in both Houses He did everything in his power to conciliate the South, but the pro-slavery party in that section felt the inadequcncy of all measures of transient conciliation. The population of the free States was so rapidly increasing over that of the slave States, that it was inevitable that the power of the Government should soon pass into the hands of the free States. The famous compromise measures were adopted under Mr. Fillmore's administration, and the Japan expedition was sent out

March 4, 1853, having served one term, President Fillmore retired from office He then took a long tour through the South, where he met with quite an enthusiastic reception In a speech at Vicksburg, alluding to the rapid growth of the country, he said

"Canada is knocking for admission, and Mexico would be glad to come in, and without saying whether it would be right or wrong, we stand with open arms to receive them; for it is the manifest destiny of this Government to embrace the whole North American Continent."

In 1855 Mr. Fillmore went to Europe where he was received with those marked attentions which his position and character merited. Returning to this country in 1856 he was nominated for the Presidency by the "Know-Nothing" party Mr. Buchanan, the Democratic candidate was the successful competitor Mr Fillmore ever afterward lived in retirement During the conflict of civil war he was mostly silent. It was generally supposed, however, that his sympathy was with the Southern Confederacy. He kept aloof from the conflict without any words of cheer to the one party or the other For this reason he was forgotten by both He died of paralysis, in Buffalo, New York, March 8, 1874

FRANKLIN PIERCE.

FRANKLIN PIERCE, the fourteenth President of the United States, was born in Hillsborough, New Hampshire, November 23, 1804. His father, Governor Benjamin Pierce, was a Revolutionary soldier, a man of rigid integrity; was for several years in the State Legislature, a member of the Governor's council and a General of the militia.

Franklin was the sixth of eight children. As a boy he listened eagerly to the arguments of his father, enforced by strong and ready utterance and earnest gesture. It was in the days of intense political excitement, when, all over the New England States, Federalists and Democrats were arrayed so fiercely against each other.

In 1820 he entered Bowdoin College, at Brunswick, Maine, and graduated in 1824, and commenced the study of law in the office of Judge Woodbury, a very distinguished lawyer, and in 1827 was admitted to the bar. He practiced with great success in Hillsborough and Concord. He served in the State Legislature four years, the last two of which he was chosen Speaker of the House by a very large vote.

In 1833 he was elected a member of Congress. In 1837 he was elected to the United States Senate, just as Mr. Van Buren commenced his administration.

In 1834 he married Miss Jane Means Appleton, a lady admirably fitted to adorn every station with which her husband was honored. Three sons born to them all found an early grave.

Upon his accession to office, President Polk appointed Mr. Pierce Attorney-General of the United States, but the offer was declined in consequence of numerous professional engagements at home and the precarious state of Mrs. Pierce's health. About the same time he also declined the nomination for Governor by the Democratic party.

The war with Mexico called Mr. Pierce into the army. Receiving the appointment of Brigadier-General, he embarked with a portion of his troops at Newport, Rhode Island, May 27, 1847. He served during this war, and distinguished himself by his bravery, skill and excellent judgment. When he reached his home in his native State he was enthusiastically received by

Franklin Pierce

LIBRARY
OF THE
UNIVERSITY OF ILLINOIS

the advocates of the war, and coldly by its opponents. He resumed the practice of his profession, frequently taking an active part in political questions, and giving his support to the pro-slavery wing of the Democratic party

June 12, 1852, the Democratic convention met in Baltimore to nominate a candidate for the Presidency. For four days they continued in session, and in thirty-five ballotings no one had received the requisite two-thirds vote Not a vote had been thrown thus far for General Pierce Then the Virginia delegation brought forward his name. There were fourteen more ballotings, during which General Pierce gained strength, until, at the forty-ninth ballot, he received 282 votes, and all other candidates eleven. General Winfield Scott was the Whig candidate. General Pierce was elected with great unanimity. Only four States—Vermont, Massachusetts, Kentucky and Tennessee—cast their electoral votes against him. March 4, 1853, he was inaugurated President of the United States, and William R. King, Vice-President.

President Pierce's cabinet consisted of William S. Marcy, James Guthrie, Jefferson Davis, James C Dobbin, Robert McClelland, James Campbell and Caleb Cushing

At the demand of slavery the Missouri Compromise was repealed, and all the Territories of the Union were thrown open to slavery The Territory of Kansas, west of Missouri, was settled by emigrants mainly from the North. According to law, they were about to meet and decide whether slavery or freedom should be the law of that realm. Slavery in Missouri and other Southern States rallied her armed legions, marched them into Kansas, took possession of the polls, drove away the citizens, deposited their own votes by handfuls, went through the farce of counting them, and then declared that, by an overwhelming majority, slavery was established in Kansas These facts nobody denied, and yet President Pierce's administration felt bound to respect the decision obtained by such votes. The citizens of Kansas, the majority of whom were free-State men, met in convention and adopted the following resolve

"*Resolved*, That the body of men who, for the past two months, have been passing laws for the people of our Territory, moved, counseled and dictated to by the demagogues of other States, are to us a foreign body, representing only the lawless invaders who elected them, and not the people of this Territory, that we repudiate their action as the monstrous consummation of an act of violence, usurpation and fraud unparalleled in the history of the Union."

The free-State people of Kansas also sent a petition to the General Government, imploring its protection In reply the President issued a proclamation, declaring that Legislature thus created must be recognized as the legitimate Legislature of Kansas, and that its laws were binding upon the people, and that, if necessary, the whole force of the Governmental arm would be put forth to inforce those laws

James Buchanan succeeded him in the Presidency, and, March 4, 1857, President Pierce retired to his home in Concord, New Hampshire. When the Rebellion burst forth Mr. Pierce remained steadfast to the principles he had always cherished, and gave his sympathies to the pro-slavery party, with which he had ever been allied. He declined to do anything, either by voice or pen, to strengthen the hands of the National Government He resided in Concord until his death, which occurred in October, 1869 He was one of the most genial and social of men, generous to a fault, and contributed liberally of his moderate means for the alleviation of suffering and want. He was an honored communicant of the Episcopal church.

JAMES BUCHANAN.

JAMES BUCHANAN, the fifteenth President of the United States, 1857-'61, was born in Franklin County, Pennsylvania, April 23, 1791. The place where his father's cabin stood was called Stony Batter, and it was situated in a wild, romantic spot, in a gorge of mountains, with towering summits rising all around. He was of Irish ancestry, his father having emigrated in 1783, with very little property, save his own strong arms.

James remained in his secluded home for eight years enjoying very few social or intellectual advantages. His parents were industrious, frugal, prosperous and intelligent. In 1799 his father removed to Mercersburg, where James was placed in school and commenced a course in English, Greek and Latin. His progress was rapid and in 1801 he entered Dickinson College at Carlisle. Here he took his stand among the first scholars in the institution, and was able to master the most abstruse subjects with facility. In 1809 he graduated with the highest honors in his class.

He was then eighteen years of age, tall, graceful and in vigorous health, fond of athletic sports, an unerring shot and enlivened with an exuberant flow of animal spirits. He immediately commenced the study of law in the city of Lancaster, and was admitted to the bar in 1812. He rose very rapidly in his profession and at once took undisputed stand with the ablest lawyers of the State. When but twenty-six years of age, unaided by counsel, he successfully defended before the State Senate one of the Judges of the State, who was tried upon articles of impeachment At the age of thirty it was generally admitted that he stood at the head of the bar, and there was no lawyer in the State who had a more extensive or lucrative practice.

In 1812, just after Mr. Buchanan had entered upon the practice of the law, our second war with England occurred. With all his powers he sustained the Government, eloquently urging the rigorous prosecution of the war; and even enlisting as a private soldier to assist in repelling the British, who had sacked Washington and were threatening Baltimore. He was at that time a Federalist, but when the Constitution was adopted by both parties, Jefferson truly said, "We are all Federalists: we are all Republicans."

The opposition of the Federalists to the war with England, and the alien and sedi-

James Buchanan

LIBRARY
OF THE
UNIVERSITY OF ILLINOIS

tion laws of John Adams, brought the party into dispute, and the name of Federalist became a reproach Mr Buchanan almost immediately upon entering Congress began to incline more and more to the Republicans In the stormy Presidential election of 1824, in which Jackson, Clay, Crawford and John Quincy Adams were candidates, Mr Buchanan espoused the cause of General Jackson and unrelentingly opposed the administration of Mr Adams.

Upon his elevation to the Presidency, General Jackson appointed Mr. Buchanan, minister to Russia. Upon his return in 1833 he was elected to a seat in the United States Senate He there met as his associates, Webster, Clay, Wright and Calhoun He advocated the measures proposed by President Jackson of making reprisals against France, and defended the course of the President in his unprecedented and wholesale removals from office of those who were not the supporters of his administration Upon this question he was brought into direct collision with Henry Clay. In the discussion of the question respecting the admission of Michigan and Arkansas into the Union, Mr Buchanan defined his position by saying:

"The older I grow, the more I am inclined to be what is called a State-rights man"

M de Tocqueville, in his renowned work upon "Democracy in America," foresaw the trouble which was inevitable from the doctrine of State sovereignty as held by Calhoun and Buchanan. He was convinced that the National Government was losing that strength which was essential to its own existence, and that the States were assuming powers which threatened the perpetuity of the Union. Mr Buchanan received the book in the Senate and declared the fears of De Tocqueville to be groundless, and yet he lived to sit in the Presidential chair and see State after State, in accordance with his own views of State rights, breaking from the Union, thus crumbling our Republic into ruins, while the unhappy old man folded his arms in despair, declaring that the National Constitution invested him with no power to arrest the destruction

Upon Mr. Polk's accession to the Presidency, Mr. Buchanan became Secretary of State, and as such took his share of the responsibility in the conduct of the Mexican war At the close of Mr Polk's administration, Mr. Buchanan retired to private life, but his intelligence, and his great ability as a statesman, enabled him to exert a powerful influence in National affairs

Mr. Pierce, upon his election to the Presidency, honored Mr Buchanan with the mission to England In the year 1856 the National Democratic convention nominated Mr. Buchanan for the Presidency. The political conflict was one of the most severe in which our country has ever engaged On the 4th of March, 1857, Mr Buchanan was inaugurated President His cabinet were Lewis Cass, Howell Cobb, J. B. Floyd, Isaac Toucey, Jacob Thompson, A. V. Brown and J S. Black.

The disruption of the Democratic party, in consequence of the manner in which the issue of the nationality of slavery was pressed by the Southern wing, occurred at the National convention, held at Charleston in April, 1860, for the nomination of Mr. Buchanan's successor, when the majority of Southern delegates withdrew upon the passage of a resolution declaring that the constitutional status of slavery should be determined by the Supreme Court.

In the next Presidential canvass Abraham Lincoln was nominated by the opponents of Mr. Buchanan's administration Mr Buchanan remained in Washington long enough to see his successor installed and then retired to his home in Wheatland. He died June 1, 1868, aged seventy seven years.

ABRAHAM LINCOLN.

ABRAHAM LINCOLN, the sixteenth President of the United States, 1861-'5, was born February 12, 1809, in Larue (then Hardin) County, Kentucky, in a cabin on Nolan Creek, three miles west of Hudgensville. His parents were Thomas and Nancy (Hanks) Lincoln. Of his ancestry and early years the little that is known may best be given in his own language: "My parents were both born in Virginia, of undistinguished families—second families, perhaps I should say. My mother, who died in my tenth year, was of a family of the name of Hanks, some of whom now remain in Adams, and others in Macon County, Illinois. My paternal grandfather, Abraham Lincoln, emigrated from Rockbridge County, Virginia, to Kentucky in 1781 or 1782, where, a year or two later, he was killed by Indians—not in battle, but by stealth, when he was laboring to open a farm in the forest. His ancestors, who were Quakers, went to Virginia from Berks County, Pennsylvania. An effort to identify them with the New England family of the same name ended in nothing more definite than a similarity of Christian names in both families, such as Enoch, Levi, Mordecai, Solomon, Abraham and the like. My father, at the death of his father, was but six years of age, and he grew up, literally, without education. He removed from Kentucky to what is now Spencer County, Indiana, in my eighth year. We reached our new home about the time the State came into the Union. It was a wild region, with bears and other wild animals still in the woods. There I grew to manhood.

"There were some schools, so called, but no qualification was ever required of a teacher beyond 'readin', writin', and cipherin' to the rule of three.' If a straggler, supposed to understand Latin, happened to sojourn in the neighborhood, he was looked upon as a wizard. There was absolutely nothing to excite ambition for education. Of course, when I came of age I did not know much. Still, somehow, I could read, write and cipher to the rule of three, and that was all. I have not been to school since. The little advance I now have upon this store of education I have picked up from time to time under the pressure of necessity. I was raised to farm-work, which

Your friend as ever
A. Lincoln

LIBRARY
OF THE
UNIVERSITY OF ILLINOIS

I continued till I was twenty-two At twenty-one I came to Illinois and passed the first year in Macon County. Then I got to New Salem, at that time in Sangamon, now in Menard County, where I remained a year as a sort of clerk in a store.

"Then came the Black Hawk war, and I was elected a Captain of volunteers—a success which gave me more pleasure than any I have had since I went the campaign, was elated; ran for the Legislature the same year (1832) and was beaten, the only time I have ever been beaten by the people. The next and three succeeding biennial elections I was elected to the Legislature, and was never a candidate afterward.

"During this legislative period I had studied law, and removed to Springfield to practice it In 1846 I was elected to the Lower House of Congress; was not a candidate for re-election. From 1849 to 1854, inclusive, I practiced the law more assiduously than ever before Always a Whig in politics, and generally on the Whig electoral tickets, making active canvasses, I was losing interest in politics, when the repeal of the Missouri Compromise roused me again. What I have done since is pretty well known"

The early residence of Lincoln in Indiana was sixteen miles north of the Ohio River, on Little Pigeon Creek, one and a half miles east of Gentryville, within the present township of Carter. Here his mother died October 5, 1818, and the next year his father married Mrs Sally (Bush) Johnston, of Elizabethtown, Kentucky. She was an affectionate foster-parent, to whom Abraham was indebted for his first encouragement to study. He became an eager reader, and the few books owned in the vicinity were many times perused. He worked frequently for the neighbors as a farm laborer; was for some time clerk in a store at Gentryville; and became famous throughout that region for his athletic powers, his fondness for argument, his inexhaustible fund of humerous anecdote, as well as for mock oratory and the composition of rude satirical verses. In 1828 he made a trading voyage to New Orleans as "bow-hand" on a flatboat; removed to Illinois in 1830; helped his father build a log house and clear a farm on the north fork of Sangamon River, ten miles west of Decatur, and was for some time employed in splitting rails for the fences—a fact which was prominently brought forward for a political purpose thirty years later.

In the spring of 1851 he, with two of his relatives, was hired to build a flatboat on the Sangamon River and navigate it to New Orleans The boat "stuck" on a mill-dam, and was got off with great labor through an ingenious mechanical device which some years later led to Lincoln's taking out a patent for "an improved method for lifting vessels over shoals" This voyage was memorable for another reason—the sight of slaves chained, maltreated and flogged at New Orleans was the origin of his deep convictions upon the slavery question

Returning from this voyage he became a resident for several years at New Salem, a recently settled village on the Sangamon, where he was successively a clerk, grocer, surveyor and postmaster, and acted as pilot to the first steamboat that ascended the Sangamon. Here he studied law, interested himself in local politics after his return from the Black Hawk war, and became known as an effective "stump speaker." The subject of his first political speech was the improvement of the channel of the Sangamon, and the chief ground on which he announced himself (1832) a candidate for the Legislature was his advocacy of this popular measure, on which subject his practical experience made him the highest authority

Elected to the Legislature in 1834 as a

"Henry Clay Whig," he rapidly acquired that command of language and that homely but forcible rhetoric which, added to his intimate knowledge of the people from which he sprang, made him more than a match in debate for his few well-educated opponents.

Admitted to the bar in 1837 he soon established himself at Springfield, where the State capital was located in 1839, largely through his influence; became a successful pleader in the State, Circuit and District Courts; married in 1842 a lady belonging to a prominent family in Lexington, Kentucky, took an active part in the Presidential campaigns of 1840 and 1844 as candidate for elector on the Harrison and Clay tickets, and in 1846 was elected to the United States House of Representatives over the celebrated Peter Cartwright During his single term in Congress he did not attain any prominence.

He voted for the reception of anti-slavery petitions for the abolition of the slave trade in the District of Columbia and for the Wilmot proviso, but was chiefly remembered for the stand he took against the Mexican war. For several years thereafter he took comparatively little interest in politics, but gained a leading position at the Springfield bar. Two or three non-political lectures and an eulogy on Henry Clay (1852) added nothing to his reputation.

In 1854 the repeal of the Missouri Compromise by the Kansas-Nebraska act aroused Lincoln from his indifference, and in attacking that measure he had the immense advantage of knowing perfectly well the motives and the record of its author, Stephen A Douglas, of Illinois, then popularly designated as the "Little Giant" The latter came to Springfield in October, 1854, on the occasion of the State Fair, to vindicate his policy in the Senate, and the "Anti-Nebraska" Whigs, remembering that Lincoln had often measured his strength with Douglas in the Illinois Legislature and before the Springfield Courts, engaged him to improvise a reply This speech, in the opinion of those who heard it, was one of the greatest efforts of Lincoln's life; certainly the most effective in his whole career. It took the audience by storm, and from that moment it was felt that Douglas had met his match Lincoln was accordingly selected as the Anti-Nebraska candidate for the United States Senate in place of General Shields, whose term expired March 4, 1855, and led to several ballots, but Trumbull was ultimately chosen

The second conflict on the soil of Kansas, which Lincoln had predicted, soon began. The result was the disruption of the Whig and the formation of the Republican party. At the Bloomington State Convention in 1856, where the new party first assumed form in Illinois, Lincoln made an impressive address, in which for the first time he took distinctive ground against slavery in itself.

At the National Republican Convention at Philadelphia, June 17, after the nomination of Fremont, Lincoln was put forward by the Illinois delegation for the Vice-Presidency, and received on the first ballot 110 votes against 259 for William L Dayton. He took a prominent part in the canvass, being on the electoral ticket.

In 1858 Lincoln was unanimously nominated by the Republican State Convention as its candidate for the United States Senate in place of Douglas, and in his speech of acceptance used the celebrated illustration of a "house divided against itself" on the slavery question, which was, perhaps, the cause of his defeat. The great debate carried on at all the principal towns of Illinois between Lincoln and Douglas as rival Senatorial candidates resulted at the time in the election of the latter, but being widely circulated as a campaign document, it fixed the attention of the country upon the former, as the clearest and most convincing exponent of Republican doctrine.

Early in 1859 he began to be named in Illinois as a suitable Republican candidate for the Presidential campaign of the ensuing year, and a political address delivered at the Cooper Institute, New York, February 27, 1860, followed by similar speeches at New Haven, Hartford and elsewhere in New England, first made him known to the Eastern States in the light by which he had long been regarded at home. By the Republican State Convention, which met at Decatur, Illinois, May 9 and 10, Lincoln was unanimously endorsed for the Presidency It was on this occasion that two rails, said to have been split by his hands thirty years before, were brought into the convention, and the incident contributed much to his popularity. The National Republican Convention at Chicago, after spirited efforts made in favor of Seward, Chase and Bates, nominated Lincoln for the Presidency, with Hannibal Hamlin for Vice-President, at the same time adopting a vigorous anti-slavery platform

The Democratic party having been disorganized and presenting two candidates, Douglas and Breckenridge, and the remnant of the "American" party having put forward John Bell, of Tennessee, the Republican victory was an easy one, Lincoln being elected November 6 by a large plurality, comprehending nearly all the Northern States, but none of the Southern The secession of South Carolina and the Gulf States was the immediate result, followed a few months later by that of the border slave States and the outbreak of the great civil war

The life of Abraham Lincoln became thenceforth merged in the history of his country. None of the details of the vast conflict which filled the remainder of Lincoln's life can here be given Narrowly escaping assassination by avoiding Baltimore on his way to the capital, he reached Washington February 23, and was inaugurated President of the United States March 4, 1861.

In his inaugural address he said· "I hold, that in contemplation of universal law and the Constitution the Union of these States is perpetual. Perpetuity is implied if not expressed in the fundamental laws of all national governments It is safe to assert that no government proper ever had a provision in its organic law for its own termination I therefore consider that in view of the Constitution and the laws, the Union is unbroken, and to the extent of my ability I shall take care, as the Constitution enjoins upon me, that the laws of the United States be extended in all the States In doing this there need be no bloodshed or violence, and there shall be none unless it be forced upon the national authority The power conferred to me will be used to hold, occupy and possess the property and places belonging to the Government, and to collect the duties and imports, but beyond what may be necessary for these objects there will be no invasion, no using of force against or among the people anywhere. In your hands, my dissatisfied fellow-countrymen, is the momentous issue of civil war. The Government will not assail you. You can have no conflict without being yourselves the aggressors You have no oath registered in heaven to destroy the Government, while I shall have the most solemn one to preserve, protect and defend it"

He called to his cabinet his principal rivals for the Presidential nomination — Seward, Chase, Cameron and Bates, secured the co-operation of the Union Democrats, headed by Douglas, called out 75 000 militia from the several States upon the first tidings of the bombardment of Fort Sumter, April 15, proclaimed a blockade of the Southern posts April 19, called an extra session of Congress for July 4, from which he asked and obtained 400,000 men and $400,000,000 for the war; placed McClellan at the head of the Federal army on General Scott's resignation, October 31; appointed Edwin M. Stanton Secretary of War, January 14, 1862, and September 22, 1862, issued a proclamation declaring the freedom of all slaves in the States and parts of States then in rebellion from and after January 1, 1863. This was the crowning act of Lincoln's career—the act by which he will be chiefly known through all future time—and it decided the war.

October 16, 1863, President Lincoln called for 300,000 volunteers to replace those whose term of enlistment had expired; made a celebrated and touching, though brief, address at the dedication of the Gettysburg military cemetery, November 19, 1863; commissioned Ulysses S. Grant Lieutenant-General and Commander-in-Chief of the armies of the United States, March 9, 1864; was re-elected President in November of the same year, by a large majority over General McClellan, with Andrew Johnson, of Tennessee, as Vice-President; delivered a very remarkable address at his second inauguration, March 4, 1865; visited the army before Richmond the same month; entered the capital of the Confederacy the day after its fall, and upon the surrender of General Robert E. Lee's army, April 9, was actively engaged in devising generous plans for the reconstruction of the Union, when, on the evening of Good Friday, April 14, he was shot in his box at Ford's Theatre, Washington, by John Wilkes Booth, a fanatical actor, and expired early on the following morning, April 15. Almost simultaneously a murderous attack was made upon William H. Seward, Secretary of State.

At noon on the 15th of April Andrew Johnson assumed the Presidency, and active measures were taken which resulted in the death of Booth and the execution of his principal accomplices.

The funeral of President Lincoln was conducted with unexampled solemnity and magnificence. Impressive services were held in Washington, after which the sad procession proceeded over the same route he had traveled four years before, from Springfield to Washington. In Philadelphia his body lay in state in Independence Hall, in which he had declared before his first inauguration "that I would sooner be assassinated than to give up the principles of the Declaration of Independence." He was buried at Oak Ridge Cemetery, near Springfield, Illinois, on May 4, where a monument emblematic of the emancipation of the slaves and the restoration of the Union mark his resting place.

The leaders and citizens of the expiring Confederacy expressed genuine indignation at the murder of a generous political adversary. Foreign nations took part in mourning the death of a statesman who had proved himself a true representative of American nationality. The freedmen of the South almost worshiped the memory of their deliverer; and the general sentiment of the great Nation he had saved awarded him a place in its affections, second only to that held by Washington.

The characteristics of Abraham Lincoln have been familiarly known throughout the civilized world. His tall, gaunt, ungainly figure, homely countenance, and his shrewd mother-wit, shown in his celebrated conversations overflowing in humorous and pointed anecdote, combined with an accurate, intuitive appreciation of the questions of the time, are recognized as forming the best type of a period of American history now rapidly passing away.

LIBRARY
OF THE
UNIVERSITY OF ILLINOIS

Andrew Johnson

ANDREW JOHNSON.

ANDREW JOHNSON, the seventeenth President of the United States, 1865-'9, was born at Raleigh, North Carolina, December 29, 1808. His father died when he was four years old, and in his eleventh year he was apprenticed to a tailor. He never attended school, and did not learn to read until late in his apprenticeship, when he suddenly acquired a passion for obtaining knowledge, and devoted all his spare time to reading.

After working two years as a journeyman tailor at Lauren's Court-House, South Carolina, he removed, in 1826, to Greenville, Tennessee, where he worked at his trade and married. Under his wife's instructions he made rapid progress in his education, and manifested such an intelligent interest in local politics as to be elected as "workingmen's candidate" alderman, in 1828, and mayor in 1830, being twice re-elected to each office.

During this period he cultivated his talents as a public speaker by taking part in a debating society, consisting largely of students of Greenville College. In 1835, and again in 1839, he was chosen to the lower house of the Legislature, as a Democrat. In 1841 he was elected State Senator, and in 1843, Representative in Congress, being re-elected four successive periods, until 1853, when he was chosen Governor of Tennessee. In Congress he supported the administrations of Tyler and Polk in their chief measures, especially the annexation of Texas, the adjustment of the Oregon boundary, the Mexican war, and the tariff of 1846.

In 1855 Mr. Johnson was re elected Governor, and in 1857 entered the United States Senate, where he was conspicuous as an advocate of retrenchment and of the Homestead bill, and as an opponent of the Pacific Railroad. He was supported by the Tennessee delegation to the Democratic convention in 1860 for the Presidential nomination, and lent his influence to the Breckenridge wing of that party.

When the election of Lincoln had brought about the first attempt at secession in December, 1860, Johnson took in the Senate a firm attitude for the Union, and in May, 1861, on returning to Tennessee, he was in imminent peril of suffering from popular violence for his loyalty to the "old flag" He was the leader of the Loyalists' convention of East Tennessee, and during the following winter was very active in organizing relief for the destitute loyal refugees from that region, his own family being among those compelled to leave

By his course in this crisis Johnson came prominently before the Northern public, and when in March, 1862, he was appointed by President Lincoln military Governor of Tennessee, with the rank of Brigadier-General, he increased in popularity by the vigorous and successful manner in which he labored to restore order, protect Union men and punish marauders On the approach of the Presidential campaign of 1864, the termination of the war being plainly foreseen, and several Southern States being partially reconstructed, it was felt that the Vice-Presidency should be given to a Southern man of conspicuous loyalty, and Governor Johnson was elected on the same platform and ticket as President Lincoln, and on the assassination of the latter succeeded to the Presidency, April 15, 1865 In a public speech two days later he said "The American people must be taught, if they do not already feel, that treason is a crime and must be punished, that the Government will not always bear with its enemies, that it is strong, not only to protect, but to punish In our peaceful history treason has been almost unknown The people must understand that it is the blackest of crimes, and will be punished" He then added the ominous sentence: "In regard to my future course, I make no promises, no pledges." President Johnson retained the cabinet of Lincoln, and exhibited considerable severity toward traitors in his earlier acts and speeches, but he soon inaugurated a policy of reconstruction, proclaiming a general amnesty to the late Confederates, and successively establishing provisional Governments in the Southern States. These States accordingly claimed representation in Congress in the following December, and the momentous question of what should be the policy of the victorious Union toward its late armed opponents was forced upon that body.

Two considerations impelled the Republican majority to reject the policy of President Johnson: First, an apprehension that the chief magistrate intended to undo the results of the war in regard to slavery; and, second, the sullen attitude of the South, which seemed to be plotting to regain the policy which arms had lost. The credentials of the Southern members elect were laid on the table, a civil rights bill and a bill extending the sphere of the Freedmen's Bureau were passed over the executive veto, and the two highest branches of the Government were soon in open antagonism The action of Congress was characterized by the President as a "new rebellion" In July the cabinet was reconstructed, Messrs. Randall, Stanbury and Browning taking the places of Messrs Denison, Speed and Harlan, and an unsuccessful attempt was made by means of a general convention in Philadelphia to form a new party on the basis of the administration policy

In an excursion to Chicago for the purpose of laying a corner-stone of the monument to Stephen A. Douglas, President Johnson, accompanied by several members of the cabinet, passed through Philadelphia, New York and Albany, in each of which cities, and in other places along the route, he made speeches justifying and explaining his own policy, and violently denouncing the action of Congress

August 12, 1867, President Johnson removed the Secretary of War, replacing him by General Grant. Secretary Stanton retired under protest, based upon the tenure-of-office act which had been passed the preceding March The President then issued a proclamation declaring the insurrection at an end, and that "peace, order, tranquility and civil authority existed in and throughout the United States." Another proclamation enjoined obedience to the Constitution and the laws, and an amnesty was published September 7, relieving nearly all the participants in the late Rebellion from the disabilities thereby incurred, on condition of taking the oath to support the Constitution and the laws

In December Congress refused to confirm the removal of Secretary Stanton, who thereupon resumed the exercise of his office, but February 21, 1868, President Johnson again attempted to remove him, appointing General Lorenzo Thomas in his place Stanton refused to vacate his post, and was sustained by the Senate.

February 24 the House of Representatives voted to impeach the President for "high crime and misdemeanors," and March 5 presented eleven articles of impeachment on the ground of his resistance to the execution of the acts of Congress, alleging, in addition to the offense lately committed, his public expressions of contempt for Congress, in "certain intemperate, inflammatory and scandalous harangues" pronounced in August and September, 1866, and thereafter declaring that the Thirty-ninth Congress of the United States was not a competent legislative body, and denying its power to propose Constitutional amendments. March 23 the impeachment trial began, the President appearing by counsel, and resulted in acquittal, the vote lacking one of the two-thirds vote required for conviction

The remainder of President Johnson's term of office was passed without any such conflicts as might have been anticipated He failed to obtain a nomination for re-election by the Democratic party, though receiving sixty-five votes on the first ballot July 4 and December 25 new proclamations of pardon to the participants in the late Rebellion were issued, but were of little effect. On the accession of General Grant to the Presidency, March 4, 1869, Johnson returned to Greenville, Tennessee. Unsuccessful in 1870 and 1872 as a candidate respectively for United States Senator and Representative, he was finally elected to the Senate in 1875, and took his seat in the extra session of March, in which his speeches were comparatively temperate He died July 31, 1875, and was buried at Greenville.

President Johnson's administration was a peculiarly unfortunate one That he should so soon become involved in bitter feud with the Republican majority in Congress was certainly a surprising and deplorable incident, yet, in reviewing the circumstances after a lapse of so many years, it is easy to find ample room for a charitable judgment of both the parties in the heated controversy, since it cannot be doubted that any President, even Lincoln himself, had he lived, must have sacrificed a large portion of his popularity in carrying out any possible scheme of reconstruction.

ULYSSES S. GRANT.

ULYSSES SIMPSON GRANT, the eighteenth President of the United States, 1869-'77, was born April 27, 1822, at Point Pleasant, Clermont County, Ohio. His father was of Scotch descent, and a dealer in leather. At the age of seventeen he entered the Military Academy at West Point, and four years later graduated twenty-first in a class of thirty-nine, receiving the commission of Brevet Second Lieutenant. He was assigned to the Fourth Infantry and remained in the army eleven years. He was engaged in every battle of the Mexican war except that of Buena Vista, and received two brevets for gallantry.

In 1848 Mr. Grant married Julia, daughter of Frederick Dent, a prominent merchant of St. Louis, and in 1854, having reached the grade of Captain, he resigned his commission in the army. For several years he followed farming near St. Louis, but unsuccessfully; and in 1860 he entered the leather trade with his father at Galena, Illinois.

When the civil war broke out in 1861, Grant was thirty-nine years of age, but entirely unknown to public men and without any personal acquaintance with great affairs. President Lincoln's first call for troops was made on the 15th of April, and on the 19th Grant was drilling a company of volunteers at Galena. He also offered his services to the Adjutant-General of the army, but received no reply. The Governor of Illinois, however, employed him in the organization of volunteer troops, and at the end of five weeks he was appointed Colonel of the Twenty-first Infantry. He took command of his regiment in June, and reported first to General Pope in Missouri. His superior knowledge of military life rather surprised his superior officers, who had never before even heard of him, and they were thus led to place him on the road to rapid advancement. August 7 he was commissioned a Brigadier-General of volunteers, the appointment having been made without his knowledge. He had been unanimously recommended by the Congressmen from Illinois, not one of whom had been his personal acquaintance. For a few weeks he was occupied in watching the movements of partisan forces in Missouri.

September 1 he was placed in command of the District of Southeast Missouri, with headquarters at Cairo, and on the 6th, without orders, he seized Paducah, at the mouth of the Tennessee River, and commanding the navigation both of that stream and of

U. S. Grant

LIBRARY
OF THE
UNIVERSITY OF ILLINOIS

the Ohio This stroke secured Kentucky to the Union, for the State Legislature, which had until then affected to be neutral, at once declared in favor of the Government. In November following, according to orders, he made a demonstration about eighteen miles below Cairo, preventing the crossing of hostile troops into Missouri; but in order to accomplish this purpose he had to do some fighting, and that, too, with only 3,000 raw recruits, against 7,000 Confederates Grant carried off two pieces of artillery and 200 prisoners

After repeated applications to General Halleck, his immediate superior, he was allowed, in February, 1862, to move up the Tennessee River against Fort Henry, in conjunction with a naval force. The gunboats silenced the fort, and Grant immediately made preparations to attack Fort Donelson, about twelve miles distant, on the Cumberland River. Without waiting for orders he moved his troops there, and with 15,000 men began the siege. The fort, garrisoned with 21,000 men, was a strong one, but after hard fighting on three successive days Grant forced an "Unconditional Surrender" (an alliteration upon the initials of his name) The prize he captured consisted of sixty-five cannon, 17,600 small arms and 14,623 soldiers. About 4,000 of the garrison had escaped in the night, and 2,500 were killed or wounded. Grant's entire loss was less than 2,000. This was the first important success won by the national troops during the war, and its strategic results were marked, as the entire States of Kentucky and Tennessee at once fell into the National hands Our hero was made a Major-General of Volunteers and placed in command of the District of West Tennessee

In March, 1862, he was ordered to move up the Tennessee River toward Corinth, where the Confederates were concentrating a large army, but he was directed not to attack His forces, now numbering 38,000, were accordingly encamped near Shiloh, or Pittsburg Landing, to await the arrival of General Buell with 40,000 more; but April 6 the Confederates came out from Corinth 50,000 strong and attacked Grant violently, hoping to overwhelm him before Buell could arrive; 5,000 of his troops were beyond supporting distance, so that he was largely outnumbered and forced back to the river, where, however, he held out until dark, when the head of Buell's column came upon the field. The next day the Confederates were driven back to Corinth, nineteen miles. The loss was heavy on both sides; Grant, being senior in rank to Buell, commanded on both days Two days afterward Halleck arrived at the front and assumed command of the army, Grant remaining at the head of the right wing and the reserve. On May 30 Corinth was evacuated by the Confederates In July Halleck was made General-in Chief, and Grant succeeded him in command of the Department of the Tennessee September 19 the battle of Iuka was fought, where, owing to Rosecrans's fault, only an incomplete victory was obtained

Next, Grant, with 30,000 men, moved down into Mississippi and threatened Vicksburg, while Sherman, with 40,000 men, was sent by way of the river to attack that place in front, but, owing to Colonel Murphy's surrendering Holly Springs to the Confederates, Grant was so weakened that he had to retire to Corinth, and then Sherman failed to sustain his intended attack

In January, 1863, General Grant took command in person of all the troops in the Mississippi Valley, and spent several months in fruitless attempts to compel the surrender or evacuation of Vicksburg; but July 4, following, the place surrendered, with 31,600 men and 172 cannon, and the Mississippi River thus fell permanently into the hands of the Government Grant was made a

Major-General in the regular army, and in October following he was placed in command of the Division of the Mississippi. The same month he went to Chattanooga and saved the Army of the Cumberland from starvation, and drove Bragg from that part of the country. This victory overthrew the last important hostile force west of the Alleghanies and opened the way for the National armies into Georgia and Sherman's march to the sea.

The remarkable series of successes which Grant had now achieved pointed him out as the appropriate leader of the National armies, and accordingly, in February, 1864, the rank of Lieutenant-General was created for him by Congress, and on March 17 he assumed command of the armies of the United States. Planning the grand final campaign, he sent Sherman into Georgia, Sigel into the valley of Virginia, and Butler to capture Richmond, while he fought his own way from the Rapidan to the James. The costly but victorious battles of the Wilderness, Spottsylvania, North Anna and Cold Harbor were fought, more for the purpose of annihilating Lee than to capture any particular point. In June, 1864, the siege of Richmond was begun. Sherman, meanwhile, was marching and fighting daily in Georgia and steadily advancing toward Atlanta, but Sigel had been defeated in the valley of Virginia, and was superseded by Hunter Lee sent Early to threaten the National capital; whereupon Grant gathered up a force which he placed under Sheridan, and that commander rapidly drove Early, in a succession of battles, through the valley of Virginia and destroyed his army as an organized force The siege of Richmond went on, and Grant made numerous attacks, but was only partially successful. The people of the North grew impatient, and even the Government advised him to abandon the attempt to take Richmond or crush the Confederacy in that way, but he never wavered. He resolved to "fight it out on that line, if it took all summer."

By September Sherman had made his way to Atlanta, and Grant then sent him on his famous "march to the sea," a route which the chief had designed six months before. He made Sherman's success possible, not only by holding Lee in front of Richmond, but also by sending reinforcements to Thomas, who then drew off and defeated the only army which could have confronted Sherman Thus the latter was left unopposed, and, with Thomas and Sheridan, was used in the furtherance of Grant's plans Each executed his part in the great design and contributed his share to the result at which Grant was aiming. Sherman finally reached Savannah, Schofield beat the enemy at Franklin, Thomas at Nashville, and Sheridan wherever he met him; and all this while General Grant was holding Lee, with the principal Confederate army, near Richmond, as it were chained and helpless Then Schofield was brought from the West, and Fort Fisher and Wilmington were captured on the sea-coast, so as to afford him a foothold, from here he was sent into the interior of North Carolina, and Sherman was ordered to move northward to join him. When all this was effected, and Sheridan could find no one else to fight in the Shenandoah Valley, Grant brought the cavalry leader to the front of Richmond, and, making a last effort, drove Lee from his entrenchments and captured Richmond

At the beginning of the final campaign Lee had collected 73,000 fighting men in the lines at Richmond, besides the local militia and the gunboat crews, amounting to 5,000 more Including Sheridan's force Grant had 110,000 men in the works before Petersburg and Richmond. Petersburg fell on the 2d of April, and Richmond on the 3d, and Lee fled in the direction of Lynchburg. Grant pursued with remorseless energy, only stopping to strike fresh blows, and Lee at last found himself not only outfought but also out-marched and out-generaled. Being completely surrounded, he surrendered on the 9th of April, 1865, at Appomattox Court-House, in the open field, with 27,000 men, all that remained of his army. This act virtually ended the war. Thus, in ten days Grant had captured Petersburg and Richmond, fought, by his subordinates, the battles of Five Forks and Sailor's Creek, besides numerous smaller ones, captured 20,000 men in actual battle, and received the surrender of 27,000 more at Appomattox, absolutely annihilating an army of 70,000 soldiers

General Grant returned at once to Washington to superintend the disbandment of the armies, but this pleasurable work was scarcely begun when President Lincoln was assassinated. It had doubtless been intended to inflict the same fate upon Grant, but he, fortunately, on account of leaving Washington early in the evening, declined an invitation to accompany the President to the theater where the murder was committed This event made Andrew Johnson President, but left Grant by far the most conspicuous figure in the public life of the country. He became the object of an enthusiasm greater than had ever been known in America. Every possible honor was heaped upon him, the grade of General was created for him by Congress, houses were presented to him by citizens; towns were illuminated on his entrance into them; and, to cap the climax, when he made his tour around the world, "all nations did him honor" as they had never before honored a foreigner

The General, as Commander-in-Chief, was placed in an embarrassing position by the opposition of President Johnson to the measures of Congress, but he directly manifested his characteristic loyalty by obeying Congress rather than the disaffected President, although for a short time he had served in his cabinet as Secretary of War.

Of course, everybody thought of General Grant as the next President of the United States, and he was accordingly elected as such in 1868 "by a large majority," and four years later re-elected by a much larger majority — the most overwhelming ever given by the people of this country His first administration was distinguished by a cessation of the strifes which, sprang from the war, by a large reduction of the National debt, and by a settlement of the difficulties with England which had grown out of the depredations committed by privateers fitted out in England during the war This last settlement was made by the famous "Geneva arbitration," which saved to this Government $15,000,000, but, more than all, prevented a war with England. "Let us have peace," was Grant's motto. And this is the most appropriate place to remark that above all Presidents whom this Government has ever had, General Grant was the most non-partisan He regarded the Executive office as purely and exclusively *executive* of the laws of Congress, irrespective of "politics." But every great man has jealous, bitter enemies, a fact Grant was well aware of.

After the close of his Presidency, our General made his famous tour around the world, already referred to, and soon afterward, in company with Ferdinand Ward, of New York City, he engaged in banking and stock brokerage, which business was made disastrous to Grant, as well as to himself, by his rascality. By this time an incurable cancer of the tongue developed itself in the person of the afflicted ex-President, which ended his unrequited life July 23, 1885. Thus passed away from earth's turmoils the man, the General, who was as truly the "father of this regenerated country" as was Washington the father of the infant nation.

RUTHERFORD B. HAYES.

RUTHERFORD BIRCHARD HAYES, the nineteenth President of the United States, 1877–'81, was born in Delaware, Ohio, October 4, 1822. His ancestry can be traced as far back as 1280, when Hayes and Rutherford were two Scottish chieftains fighting side by side with Baliol, William Wallace and Robert Bruce. Both families belonged to the nobility, owned extensive estates and had a large following. The Hayes family had, for a coat-of-arms, a shield, barred and surmounted by a flying eagle. There was a circle of stars about the eagle and above the shield, while on a scroll underneath the shield was inscribed the motto, "Recte." Misfortune overtaking the family, George Hayes left Scotland in 1680, and settled in Windsor, Connecticut. He was an industrious worker in wood and iron, having a mechanical genius and a cultivated mind. His son George was born in Windsor and remained there during his life.

Daniel Hayes, son of the latter, married Sarah Lee, and lived in Simsbury, Connecticut. Ezekiel, son of Daniel, was born in 1724, and was a manufacturer of scythes at Bradford, Connecticut. Rutherford Hayes, son of Ezekiel and grandfather of President Hayes, was born in New Haven, in August, 1756. He was a famous blacksmith and tavern-keeper. He immigrated to Vermont at an unknown date, settling in Brattleboro where he established a hotel. Here his son Rutherford, father of President Hayes, was born. In September, 1813, he married Sophia Birchard, of Wilmington, Vermont, whose ancestry on the male side is traced back to 1635, to John Birchard, one of the principal founders of Norwich. Both of her grandfathers were soldiers in the Revolutionary war.

The father of President Hayes was of a mechanical turn, and could mend a plow, knit a stocking, or do almost anything that he might undertake. He was prosperous in business, a member of the church and active in all the benevolent enterprises of the town. After the close of the war of 1812 he immigrated to Ohio, and purchased a farm near the present town of Delaware. His family then consisted of his wife and two children, and an orphan girl whom he had adopted.

It was in 1817 that the family arrived at Delaware. Instead of settling upon his

Sincerely
R. B. Hayes

LIBRARY
OF THE
UNIVERSITY OF ILLINOIS

farm, Mr. Hayes concluded to enter into business in the village. He purchased an interest in a distillery, a business then as respectable as it was profitable His capital and recognized ability assured him the highest social position in the community He died July 22, 1822, less than three months before the birth of the son that was destined to fill the office of President of the United States.

Mrs Hayes at this period was very weak, and the subject of this sketch was so feeble at birth that he was not expected to live beyond a month or two at most As the months went by he grew weaker and weaker so that the neighbors were in the habit of inquiring from time to time "if Mrs. Hayes's baby died last night." On one occasion a neighbor, who was on friendly terms with the family, after alluding to the boy's big head and the mother's assiduous care of him, said to her, in a bantering way, "That's right! Stick to him You have got him along so far, and I shouldn't wonder if he would really come to something yet" "You need not laugh," said Mrs Hayes, "you wait and see You can't tell but I shall make him President of the United States yet"

The boy lived, in spite of the universal predictions of his speedy death, and when, in 1825, his elder brother was drowned, he became, if possible, still dearer to his mother He was seven years old before he was placed in school His education, however, was not neglected His sports were almost wholly within doors, his playmates being his sister and her associates. These circumstances tended, no doubt, to foster that gentleness of disposition and that delicate consideration for the feelings of others which are marked traits of his character. At school he was ardently devoted to his studies, obedient to the teacher, and careful to avoid the quarrels in which many of his schoolmates were involved. He was always waiting at the school-house door when it opened in the morning, and never late in returning to his seat at recess. His sister Fannie was his constant companion, and their affection for each other excited the admiration of their friends

In 1838 young Hayes entered Kenyon College and graduated in 1842 He then began the study of law in the office of Thomas Sparrow at Columbus. His health was now well established, his figure robust, his mind vigorous and alert. In a short time he determined to enter the law school at Cambridge, Massachusetts, where for two years he pursued his studies with great diligence.

In 1845 he was admitted to the bar at Marietta, Ohio, and shortly afterward went into practice as an attorney-at-law with Ralph P. Buckland, of Fremont. Here he remained three years, acquiring but limited practice, and apparently unambitious of distinction in his profession His bachelor uncle, Sardis Birchard, who had always manifested great interest in his nephew and rendered him assistance in boyhood, was now a wealthy banker, and it was understood that the young man would be his heir. It is possible that this expectation may have made Mr. Hayes more indifferent to the attainment of wealth than he would otherwise have been, but he was led into no extravagance or vices on this account

In 1849 he removed to Cincinnati where his ambition found new stimulus Two events occurring at this period had a powerful influence upon his subsequent life. One of them was his marriage to Miss Lucy Ware Webb, daughter of Dr. James Webb, of Cincinnati, the other was his introduction to the Cincinnati Literary Club, a body embracing such men as Chief Justice Salmon P. Chase, General John Pope and Governor Edward F Noyes The marriage was a fortunate one as everybody knows Not one of all the wives of our Presidents was more universally admired, reverenced and beloved than is Mrs. Hayes, and no one has done more than she to reflect honor upon American womanhood.

In 1856 Mr. Hayes was nominated to the office of Judge of the Court of Common Pleas, but declined to accept the nomination Two years later he was chosen to the office of City Solicitor.

In 1861, when the Rebellion broke out, he was eager to take up arms in the defense of his country. His military life was bright and illustrious. June 7, 1861, he was appointed Major of the Twenty-third Ohio Infantry In July the regiment was sent to Virginia October 15, 1861, he was made Lieutenant-Colonel of his regiment, and in August, 1862, was promoted Colonel of the Seventy-ninth Ohio Regiment, but refused to leave his old comrades. He was wounded at the battle of South Mountain, and suffered severely, being unable to enter upon active duty for several weeks. November 30, 1862, he rejoined his regiment as its Colonel, having been promoted October 15.

December 25, 1862, he was placed in command of the Kanawha division, and for meritorious service in several battles was promoted Brigadier-General. He was also brevetted Major-General for distinguished services in 1864. He was wounded four times, and five horses were shot from under him.

Mr. Hayes was first a Whig in politics, and was among the first to unite with the Free-Soil and Republican parties In 1864 he was elected to Congress from the Second Ohio District, which had always been Democratic, receiving a majority of 3,098. In 1866 he was renominated for Congress and was a second time elected. In 1867 he was elected Governor over Allen G Thurman, the Democratic candidate, and re-elected in 1869 In 1874 Sardis Birchard died, leaving his large estate to General Hayes

In 1876 he was nominated for the Presidency. His letter of acceptance excited the admiration of the whole country. He resigned the office of Governor and retired to his home in Fremont to await the result of the canvass. After a hard, long contest he was inaugurated March 5, 1877 His Presidency was characterized by compromises with all parties, in order to please as many as possible The close of his Presidential term in 1881 was the close of his public life, and since then he has remained at his home in Fremont, Ohio, in Jeffersonian retirement from public notice, in striking contrast with most others of the world's notables.

LIBRARY
OF THE
UNIVERSITY OF ILLINOIS

J. A. Garfield

JAMES A. GARFIELD.

JAMES A. GARFIELD, twentieth President of the United States, 1881, was born November 19, 1831, in the wild woods of Cuyahoga County, Ohio. His parents were Abram and Eliza (Ballou) Garfield, who were of New England ancestry. The senior Garfield was an industrious farmer, as the rapid improvements which appeared on his place attested. The residence was the familiar pioneer log cabin, and the household comprised the parents and their children—Mehetable, Thomas, Mary and James A. In May, 1833, the father died, and the care of the household consequently devolved upon young Thomas, to whom James was greatly indebted for the educational and other advantages he enjoyed. He now lives in Michigan, and the two sisters live in Solon, Ohio, near their birthplace.

As the subject of our sketch grew up, he, too, was industrious, both in mental and physical labor. He worked upon the farm, or at carpentering, or chopped wood, or at any other odd job that would aid in support of the family, and in the meantime made the most of his books. Ever afterward he was never ashamed of his humble origin, nor forgot the friends of his youth. The poorest laborer was sure of his sympathy, and he always exhibited the character of a modest gentleman.

Until he was about sixteen years of age, James's highest ambition was to be a lake captain. To this his mother was strongly opposed, but she finally consented to his going to Cleveland to carry out his long-cherished design, with the understanding, however, that he should try to obtain some other kind of employment. He walked all the way to Cleveland, and this was his first visit to the city. After making many applications for work, including labor on board a lake vessel, but all in vain, he finally engaged as a driver for his cousin, Amos Letcher, on the Ohio & Pennsylvania Canal. In a short time, however, he quit this and returned home. He then attended the seminary at Chester for about three years, and next he entered Hiram Institute, a school started in 1850 by the Disciples of Christ, of which church he was a member. In order to pay his way he assumed the duties of janitor, and at times taught school. He soon completed the curriculum there, and then entered Williams College, at which he graduated in 1856, taking one of the highest honors of his class.

Afterward he returned to Hiram as President. In his youthful and therefore zealous piety, he exercised his talents occasionally as a preacher of the Gospel. He was a man of strong moral and religious convictions, and as soon as he began to look into politics, he saw innumerable points that could be improved He also studied law, and was admitted to the bar in 1859. November 11, 1858, Mr Garfield married Miss Lucretia Rudolph, who ever afterward proved a worthy consort in all the stages of her husband's career. They had seven children, five of whom are still living.

It was in 1859 that Garfield made his first political speeches, in Hiram and the neighboring villages, and three years later he began to speak at county mass-meetings, being received everywhere with popular favor He was elected to the State Senate this year, taking his seat in January, 1860.

On the breaking out of the war of the Rebellion in 1861, Mr Garfield resolved to fight as he had talked, and accordingly he enlisted to defend the old flag, receiving his commission as Lieutenant-Colonel of the Forty-second Regiment of the Ohio Volunteer Infantry, August 14, that year. He was immediately thrown into active service, and before he had ever seen a gun fired in action he was placed in command of four regiments of infantry and eight companies of cavalry, charged with the work of driving the Confederates, headed by Humphrey Marshall, from his native State, Kentucky This task was speedily accomplished, although against great odds On account of his success, President Lincoln commissioned him Brigadier-General, January 11, 1862, and, as he had been the youngest man in the Ohio Senate two years before, so now he was the youngest General in the army. He was with General Buell's army at Shiloh, also in its operations around Corinth and its march through Alabama. Next, he was detailed as a member of the general court-martial for the trial of General Fitz-John Porter, and then ordered to report to General Rosecrans, when he was assigned to the position of Chief of Staff. His military history closed with his brilliant services at Chickamauga, where he won the stars of Major-General

In the fall of 1862, without any effort on his part, he was elected as a Representative to Congress, from that section of Ohio which had been represented for sixty years mainly by two men—Elisha Whittlesey and Joshua R. Giddings. Again, he was the youngest member of that body, and continued there by successive re-elections, as Representative or Senator, until he was elected President in 1880. During his life in Congress he compiled and published by his speeches, there and elsewhere, more information on the issues of the day, especially on one side, than any other member

June 8, 1880, at the National Republican Convention held in Chicago, General Garfield was nominated for the Presidency, in preference to the old war-horses, Blaine and Grant, and although many of the Republican party felt sore over the failure of their respective heroes to obtain the nomination, General Garfield was elected by a fair popular majority. He was duly inaugurated, but on July 2 following, before he had fairly got started in his administration, he was fatally shot by a half-demented assassin. After very painful and protracted suffering, he died September 19, 1881, lamented by all the American people. Never before in the history of this country had anything occurred which so nearly froze the blood of the Nation, for the moment, as the awful act of Guiteau, the murderer. He was duly tried, convicted and put to death on the gallows.

The lamented Garfield was succeeded by the Vice-President, General Arthur, who seemed to endeavor to carry out the policy inaugurated by his predecessor

LIBRARY
OF THE
UNIVERSITY OF ILLINOIS

C. A. Arthur

CHESTER A. ARTHUR.

CHESTER ALLEN ARTHUR, the twenty-first Chief Executive of this growing republic, 1881-'5, was born in Franklin County, Vermont, October 5, 1830, the eldest of a family of two sons and five daughters. His father, Rev. Dr. William Arthur, a Baptist clergyman, immigrated to this country from County Antrim, Ireland, in his eighteenth year, and died in 1875, in Newtonville, near Albany, New York, after serving many years as a successful minister. Chester A. was educated at that old, conservative institution, Union College, at Schenectady, New York, where he excelled in all his studies. He graduated there, with honor, and then struck out in life for himself by teaching school for about two years in his native State.

At the expiration of that time young Arthur, with $500 in his purse, went to the city of New York and entered the law office of ex-Judge E. D. Culver as a student. In due time he was admitted to the bar, when he formed a partnership with his intimate friend and old room-mate, Henry D. Gardiner, with the intention of practicing law at some point in the West; but after spending about three months in the Western States, in search of an eligible place, they returned to New York City, leased a room, exhibited a sign of their business and almost immediately enjoyed a paying patronage.

At this stage of his career Mr. Arthur's business prospects were so encouraging that he concluded to take a wife, and accordingly he married the daughter of Lieutenant Herndon, of the United States Navy, who had been lost at sea. To the widow of the latter Congress voted a gold medal, in recognition of the Lieutenant's bravery during the occasion in which he lost his life. Mrs. Artnur died shortly before her husband's nomination to the Vice-Presidency, leaving two children.

Mr. Arthur obtained considerable celebrity as an attorney in the famous Lemmon suit, which was brought to recover possession of eight slaves, who had been declared free by the Superior Court of New York City. The noted Charles O'Conor, who was nominated by the "Straight Democrats" in 1872 for the United States Presidency, was retained by Jonathan G. Lemmon, of Virginia, to recover the negroes, but he lost the suit. In this case, however, Mr. Arthur was assisted by William M Evarts, now United States Senator Soon afterward, in 1856, a respectable colored woman was ejected from a street car in New York City. Mr. Arthur sued the car company in her behalf and recovered $500 damages Immediately afterward all the car companies in the city issued orders to their employes to admit colored persons upon their cars

Mr Arthur's political doctrines, as well as his practice as a lawyer, raised him to prominence in the party of freedom, and accordingly he was sent as a delegate to the first National Republican Convention Soon afterward he was appointed Judge Advocate for the Second Brigade of the State of New York, and then Engineer-in-Chief on Governor Morgan's staff In 1861, the first year of the war, he was made Inspector-General, and next, Quartermaster-General, in both which offices he rendered great service to the Government After the close of Governor Morgan's term he resumed the practice of law, forming first a partnership with Mr Ransom, and subsequently adding Mr. Phelps to the firm Each of these gentlemen were able lawyers

November 21, 1872, General Arthur was appointed Collector of the Port of New York by President Grant, and he held the office until July 20, 1878.

The next event of prominence in General Arthur's career was his nomination to the Vice-Presidency of the United States, under the influence of Roscoe Conkling, at the National Republican Convention held at Chicago in June, 1880, when James A Garfield was placed at the head of the ticket Both the convention and the campaign that followed were noisy and exciting The friends of Grant, constituting nearly half the convention, were exceedingly persistent, and were sorely disappointed over their defeat. At the head of the Democratic ticket was placed a very strong and popular man, yet Garfield and Arthur were elected by a respectable plurality of the popular vote The 4th of March following, these gentlemen were accordingly inaugurated; but within four months the assassin's bullet made a fatal wound in the person of General Garfield, whose life terminated September 19, 1881, when General Arthur, *ex officio*, was obliged to take the chief reins of government. Some misgivings were entertained by many in this event, as Mr. Arthur was thought to represent especially the Grant and Conkling wing of the Republican party, but President Arthur had both the ability and the good sense to allay all fears, and he gave the restless, critical American people as good an administration as they had ever been blessed with Neither selfishness nor low partisanism ever characterized any feature of his public service He ever maintained a high sense of every individual right as well as of the Nation's honor. Indeed, he stood so high that his successor, President Cleveland, though of opposing politics, expressed a wish in his inaugural address that he could only satisfy the people with as good an administration

But the day of civil service reform had come in so far, and the corresponding reaction against "third-termism" had encroached so far even upon "second-term" service, that the Republican party saw fit in 1884 to nominate another man for President Only by this means was General Arthur's tenure of office closed at Washington. On his retirement from the Presidency, March, 1885, he engaged in the practice of law at New York City, where he died November 18, 1886.

LIBRARY
OF THE
UNIVERSITY OF ILLINOIS

GROVER CLEVELAND.

GROVER CLEVELAND, the twenty-second President of the United States, 1885—, was born in Caldwell, Essex County, New Jersey, March 18, 1837. The house in which he was born, a small two-story wooden building, is still standing. It was the parsonage of the Presbyterian church, of which his father, Richard Cleveland, at the time was pastor. The family is of New England origin, and for two centuries has contributed to the professions and to business, men who have reflected honor on the name. Aaron Cleveland, Grover Cleveland's great-great-grandfather, was born in Massachusetts, but subsequently moved to Philadelphia, where he became an intimate friend of Benjamin Franklin, at whose house he died. He left a large family of children, who in time married and settled in different parts of New England. A grandson was one of the small American force that fought the British at Bunker Hill. He served with gallantry throughout the Revolution and was honorably discharged at its close as a Lieutenant in the Continental army. Another grandson, William Cleveland (a son of a second Aaron Cleveland, who was distinguished as a writer and member of the Connecticut Legislature) was Grover Cleveland's grandfather. William Cleveland became a silversmith in Norwich, Connecticut. He acquired by industry some property and sent his son, Richard Cleveland, the father of Grover Cleveland, to Yale College, where he graduated in 1824. During a year spent in teaching at Baltimore, Maryland, after graduation, he met and fell in love with a Miss Annie Neale, daughter of a wealthy Baltimore book publisher, of Irish birth. He was earning his own way in the world at the time and was unable to marry; but in three years he completed a course of preparation for the ministry, secured a church in Windham, Connecticut, and married Annie Neale. Subsequently he moved to Portsmouth, Virginia, where he preached for nearly two years, when he was summoned to Caldwell, New Jersey, where was born Grover Cleveland.

When he was three years old the family moved to Fayetteville, Onondaga County, New York. Here Grover Cleveland lived until he was fourteen years old, the rugged, healthful life of a country boy. His frank, generous manner made him a favorite among his companions, and their respect was won by the good qualities in the germ which his manhood developed. He attended the district school of the village and was for a short time at the academy His father, however, believed that boys should be taught to labor at an early age, and before he had completed the course of study at the academy he began to work in the village store at $50 for the first year, and the promise of $100 for the second year. His work was well done and the promised increase of pay was granted the second year.

Meanwhile his father and family had moved to Clinton, the seat of Hamilton College, where his father acted as agent to the Presbyterian Board of Home Missions, preaching in the churches of the vicinity. Hither Grover came at his father's request shortly after the beginning of his second year at the Fayetteville store, and resumed his studies at the Clinton Academy. After three years spent in this town, the Rev Richard Cleveland was called to the village church of Holland Patent He had preached here only a month when he was suddenly stricken down and died without an hour's warning The death of the father left the family in straitened circumstances, as Richard Cleveland had spent all his salary of $1,000 per year, which was not required for the necessary expenses of living, upon the education of his children, of whom there were nine, Grover being the fifth. Grover was hoping to enter Hamilton College, but the death of his father made it necessary for him to earn his own livelihood For the first year (1853-'4) he acted as assistant teacher and bookkeeper in the Institution for the Blind in New York City, of which the late Augustus Schell was for many years the patron In the winter of 1854 he returned to Holland Patent, where the generous people of that place, Fayetteville and Clinton, had purchased a home for his mother, and in the following spring, borrowing $25, he set out for the West to earn his living

Reaching Buffalo he paid a hasty visit to an uncle, Lewis F Allen, a well-known stock farmer, living at Black Rock, a few miles distant He communicated his plans to Mr Allen, who discouraged the idea of the West, and finally induced the enthusiastic boy of seventeen to remain with him and help him prepare a catalogue of blooded short-horn cattle, known as "Allen's American Herd Book," a publication familiar to all breeders of cattle. In August, 1855, he entered the law office of Rogers, Bowen & Rogers, at Buffalo, and after serving a few months without pay, was paid $4 a week—an amount barely sufficient to meet the necessary expenses of his board in the family of a fellow-student in Buffalo, with whom he took lodgings Life at this time with Grover Cleveland was a stern battle with the world He took his breakfast by candle-light with the drovers, and went at once to the office where the whole day was spent in work and study. Usually he returned again at night to resume reading which had been interrupted by the duties of the day. Gradually his employers came to recognize the ability, trustworthiness and capacity for hard work in their young employe, and by the time he was admitted to the bar (1859) he stood high in their confidence. A year later he was made confidential and managing clerk, and in the course of three years more his salary had been raised to $1,000 In 1863 he was appointed assistant district attorney of Erie County by the district attorney, the Hon. C. C. Torrance.

Since his first vote had been cast in 1858 he had been a staunch Democrat, and until he was chosen Governor he always made it his duty, rain or shine, to stand at the polls and give out ballots to Democratic voters. During the first year of his term as assistant district attorney, the Democrats desired especially to carry the Board of Supervisors. The old Second Ward in which he lived was Republican ordinarily by 250 majority, but at the urgent request of the party Grover Cleveland consented to be the Democratic candidate for Supervisor, and came within thirteen votes of an election. The three years spent in the district attorney's office were devoted to assiduous labor and the extension of his professional attainments. He then formed a law partnership with the late Isaac V. Vanderpoel, ex-State Treasurer, under the firm name of Vanderpoel & Cleveland Here the bulk of the work devolved on Cleveland's shoulders, and he soon won a good standing at the bar of Erie County. In 1869 Mr. Cleveland formed a partnership with ex-Senator A P. Laning and ex-Assistant United States District Attorney Oscar Folsom, under the firm name of Laning, Cleveland & Folsom. During these years he began to earn a moderate professional income, but the larger portion of it was sent to his mother and sisters at Holland Patent to whose support he had contributed ever since 1860 He served as sheriff of Erie County, 1870–'4, and then resumed the practice of law, associating himself with the Hon Lyman K. Bass and Wilson S. Bissell. The firm was strong and popular, and soon commanded a large and lucrative practice. Ill health forced the retirement of Mr. Bass in 1879, and the firm became Cleveland & Bissell. In 1881 Mr. George J. Sicard was added to the firm.

In the autumn election of 1881 he was elected mayor of Buffalo by a majority of over 3,500—the largest majority ever given a candidate for mayor—and the Democratic city ticket was successful, although the Republicans carried Buffalo by over 1,000 majority for their State ticket. Grover Cleveland's administration as mayor fully justified the confidence reposed in him by the people of Buffalo, evidenced by the great vote he received

The Democratic State Convention met at Syracuse, September 22, 1882, and nominated Grover Cleveland for Governor on the third ballot and Cleveland was elected by 192,000 majority. In the fall of 1884 he was elected President of the United States by about 1,000 popular majority, in New York State, and he was accordingly inaugurated the 4th of March following.

BENJAMIN HARRISON.

BENJAMIN HARRISON, the twenty-third President of the United States, 1889, was born at North Bend, Hamilton County, Ohio, in the house of his grandfather, William Henry Harrison (who was the ninth President of this country), August 20th, 1833. He is a descendant of one of the historical families of this country, as also of England. The head of the family was a Major-General Harrison who was devoted to the canse of Oliver Cromwell. It became the duty of this Harrison to participate in the trial of Charles I. and afterward to sign the death warrant of the king, which subsequently cost him his life. His enemies succeeding to power, he was condemned and executed October 13th, 1660. His descendants came to America, and the first mention made in history of the Harrison family as representative in public affairs, is that of Benjamin Harrison, great-grandfather of our present President, who was a member of the Continental Congress, 1774-5-6, and one of the original signers of the Declaration of Independence, and three times Governor of Virginia. His son, William Henry Harrison, made a brilliant military record, was Governor of the Northwest Territory, and the ninth President of the United States.

The subject of this sketch at an early age became a student at Farmers College, where he remained two years, at the end of which time he entered Miami University, at Oxford, Ohio. Upon graduation from said seat of learning he entered, as a student, the office of Stover & Gwyne, a notable law firm at Cincinnati, Ohio, where he applied himself closely to the study of his chosen profession, and here laid the foundation for the honorable and famous career before him. He spent two years with the firm in Cincinnati, at the expiration of which time he received the only inheritance of his life, which was a lot left him by an aunt, which he sold for $800. This sum he deemed sufficient to justify him in marrying the lady of his choice, and to whom he was then engaged, a daughter of Dr. Scott, then Principal of a female school at Oxford, Ohio.

After marriage he located at Indianapolis, Indiana, where he began the practice of law. Meeting with slight encouragement he made but little the first year, but applied himself

Benj. Harrison

LIBRARY
OF THE
UNIVERSITY OF ILLINOIS

closely to his business, and by perseverance, honorable dealing and an upright life, succeeded in building up an extensive practice and took a leading position in the legal profession.

In 1860 he was nominated for the position of Supreme Court Reporter for the State of Indiana, and then began his experience as a stump speaker. He canvassed the State thoroughly and was elected

In 1862 his patriotism caused him to abandon a civil office and to offer his country his services in a military capacity He organized the Seventieth Indiana Infantry and was chosen its Colonel Although his regiment was composed of raw material, and he practically void of military schooling, he at once mastered military tactics and drilled his men, so that when he with his regiment was assigned to Gen. Sherman's command it was known as one of the best drilled organizations of the army. He was especially distinguished for bravery at the battles of Resacca and Peach Tree Creek For his bravery and efficiency at the last named battle he was made a Brigadier-General, General Hooker speaking of him in the most complimentary terms.

While General Harrison was actively engaged in the field the Supreme Court declared the office of Supreme Court Reporter vacant, and another person was elected to fill the position. From the time of leaving Indiana with his regiment for the front, until the fall of 1864, General Harrison had taken no leave of absence. But having been nominated that year for the same office that he vacated in order to serve his country where he could do the greatest good, he got a thirty-day leave of absence, and during that time canvassed the State and was elected for another term as Supreme Court Reporter. He then started to rejoin his command, then with General Sherman in the South, but was stricken down with fever and after a very trying siege, made his way to the front, and participated in the closing scenes and incidents of the war.

In 1868 General Harrison declined a reelection as Reporter, and applied himself to the practice of his profession. He was a candidate for Governor of Indiana on the Republican ticket in 1876. Although defeated, the brilliant campaign brought him to public notice and gave him a National reputation as an able and formidable debater and he was much sought in the Eastern States as a public speaker. He took an active part in the Presidential campaign of 1880, and was elected to the United States Senate, where he served six years, and was known as one of the strongest debaters, as well as one of the ablest men and best lawyers. When his term expired in the Senate he resumed his law practice at Indianapolis, becoming the head of one of the strongest law firms in the State of Indiana

Sometime prior to the opening of the Presidential campaign of 1888, the two great political parties (Republican and Democratic) drew the line of political battle on the question of tariff, which became the leading issue and the rallying watchword during the memorable campaign The Republicans appealed to the people for their voice as to a tariff to protect home industries, while the Democrats wanted a tariff for revenue only. The Republican convention assembled in Chicago in June and selected Mr. Harrison as their standard bearer on a platform of principles, among other important clauses being that of protection, which he cordially indorsed in accepting the nomination. November 6, 1888, after a heated canvass, General Harrison was elected, defeating Grover Cleveland, who was again the nominee of the Democratic party. He was inaugurated and assumed the duties of his office March 4, 1889.

LIBRARY
OF THE
UNIVERSITY OF ILLINOIS

Thomas Munroe

THOMAS MUNROE, M. D., Rushville, Illinois.—There is, in the career of the earnest professional or business man, toiling on through the busy, work-a-day years of a long and arduous life, but little to attract the attention of an idle reader in search of a sensational chapter. But for the mind fully awake to the real meaning of human existence there are immortal lessons in the life of the man who, without other means than a strong arm, a true heart and determined will, conquers adversity, overcomes obstacles, and closes the evening of a long life with an honorable competence and good name. Such a man is the subject of this biography, Doctor Thomas Munroe.

Doctor Munroe was a son of John and Ann (Wells) Munroe, and was born at Annapolis, Maryland, January 4, 1807. His father and mother were both natives of Maryland; the former was born August 6, 1763, and the latter January 20, 1771. They were married May 14, 1789. The boyhood of Thomas Munroe did not differ much from that of other boys born of and reared by Christian parents, who held progressive and correct ideas of the higher duties and privileges of American citizenship. He entered school at an early age, and, being an apt scholar, made rapid headway in his studies and graduated from St. John's College with honors, having taken the full classical course.

After finishing at St. John's College, he decided to adopt the profession of medicine as his life-work. He began reading under the direction of Dr. Dennis Claude, and later entered the University of Maryland in Baltimore, from which he graduated with the degree of M. D. in 1829. All through his life, Dr. Munroe took a just pride in having upon his diploma the famous names of Drs. Roger B. Taney and Reverdy Johnson,—the first as Provost, the second a member of the executive committee of the University of Maryland.

After graduating, Dr. Munroe began the practice of his profession in Baltimore, but after twelve months concluded it was better for him to go West. In accordance with this wise conclusion, he closed up his business in Baltimore, and in 1834 removed to Illinois and settled in Jacksonville, where he remained until 1843, when he came to Rushville, and was actively engaged in professional labor until the breaking out of the civil war, when he offered his services to his country, and was commissioned Surgeon of the One Hundred and Nineteenth Illinois Volunteer Infantry. He participated in all the marches of the regiment, and was in all its campaigns and battles for two years; at the end of that period he was obliged to resign his commission on account of ill health. He returned to his home and resumed his practice, which he continued, with great activity and success, until a short time previous to his death, which occurred April 23, 1891.

Dr. Munroe was married October 5, 1841, to Annis Hinman, who was born at Utica. New York, December 10, 1815; her father, Benjamin Hinman, was a native of Southbury, Connecticut; he was a son of Deacon David Hinman, who was a son of Benjamin Hinman, who was a son of Benjamin Hinman, Sr., who was a son of Sergeant Edward Hinman, the first settler of that name in this country. (See genealogy published by R. R. Hinman, New York.) Mrs. Munroe's father was a soldier in the war of the Revolution. and had the title of Major; he was one of the early settlers of Little Falls, New York, and purchased a large tract of land there; he afterward removed to Utica, New York, and died in Pennsylvania in 1821, while making a business trip to the State. He married Anna Keyser, who was born at Fort Keyser, New York, a daughter of John Keyser, of Montgomery county, New York Her father was taken captive by the Indians during the Revolutionary war and was carried to Canada, where he was held for three years, his death occurred at Fort Keyser; his wife survived until August 9, 1863, she was living in Illinois at that time, her sons being among the pioneers of Brown county, they emigrated to the State in 1836, and were of a party that laid out the town of La Grange.

Children are indeed blessed who have educated and Christian parents to guide and direct those early impulses which have so much to do with the ultimate direction of ambition and mentality; and no family of children were ever more favored in this than the children of this good father and mother. The breadth of Dr Munroe's mind, his great wisdom in giving his children splendid educations and permitting them to select their own vocations, is manifest in the marked degree of success which has attended their efforts. The eldest son, Thomas, is one of the progressive and successful men of Muskegon, Michigan, being the head of the well-known firm of Thomas Munroe & Co, and the general superintendent of the Thayer Lumber Company, both of Muskegon In this double capacity he has acquired more than an ordinary fortune, and, with his marked success as a financier, he has won a greater meed of victory—that of the love and respect of all who know him.

The second son, James E. Munroe, resides in Chicago, and is engaged in the practice of law. He is a lawyer of good ability, fair attainments and great industry As the result of twenty years of labor at the bar he has acquiesced a large practice and a handsome competence.

The daughter, Mary A, of Rushville, is deeply interested in all that pertains to the betterment and advancement of mankind. She resides at the family home, the companion and comfort of her aged and gentle mother. Her brothers, Hinman and Charles G., are also residents of Rushville, the former being married and residing in a happy home, a close neighbor of his mother. Charles G is a member of the family at the old homestead, and is engaged with his brother Hinman in the lumber business, in which they are eminently successful. The youngest son is a resident of Muskegon, Michigan, where he holds a position of trust under his brother. Dr Munroe was related to such men as Jonathan Pickney, Nathan Hammond and William Munroe, all of whom occupy honored places in the early history of the United States from their participation in the notable events incident to those times. The fine engraved portrait of Dr. Munroe, which faces this sketch, was executed specially for this history An examination of the portrait will reveal better than word-painting the character of the man herein recorded.

In the death of Dr. Munroe, the city of Rushville lost one of the men whose great mentality, indefatigable energy and true Christian manhood did so much to make the city what it is. The following appeared in the *Schuyler Citizen* a short time after Dr. Munroe's death, and was written by his eminent co-laborer, Dr. J N. Speed:

"No man in the community performed more faithfully the duties of a citizen and a Christian, or led a more exemplary life than he did; and this could be as truly said of him during his army as well as his civil life. He was a life-long member of the Methodist

Episcopal Church, and always held one or more official positions; and, what is a little remarkable, he held the position of Recording Steward and Secretary in the Rushville Methodist Episcopal Church continuously for thirty-eight years, and then resigned by reason only of the infirmities of age. I doubt if in the memory of any person a like office has been filled for so long a time continuously by the same person, and certainly no more faithfully. He was very regular in his attendance on the means of grace. Even after the first admonition of his approaching affliction his seat at church, day and night, at prayer-meeting and class-meeting, was very seldom occupied by any other than himself. As a citizen he always took an active interest in the affairs of the public, and his influence was always on the side of the public welfare As a physician Dr. Munroe was ever studious and attentive, and his habit of study continued even after his active practice ceased, and in all his intercourse with his brother physicians he was the embodiment of professional rectitude, and in this respect he had no superiors and but few equals He was looked upon by all who knew him as a perfect gentleman He was always kind to the poor, and the resources of his skill and watchfulness were as faithfully extended to the pallet of the lowly as to the silken couch of the affluent, thus manifesting in his life the saying of the venerable Beerhaave, that 'the poor were his best patrons because God was their paymaster'"

HENRY HANSMEYER was born in Lippe-Detmold, Prussia, Germany, in 1833 He came of pure German ancestry and of hardy stock. His father, Fred Hansmeyer, married Wilhelmina Hoy of the same province. In 1849 they took passage for America and landed in New Orleans after a seven-weeks voyage Thence the family came up the Mississippi, to St Louis, where the mother and one child died of the cholera after being there one week The father and four children came on to Chicago, where Henry was attacked by the cholera and confined to the house for two weeks, later he joined his father and the other children at Watertown, and it was near there that the father died about one year later, being then in middle life.

Henry Hansmeyer is the second of the four sons yet living He came to this country in 1849 and lived on a farm in Jefferson county, Wisconsin, until 1851, working for $10 a month He came to Beardstown in 1851 and still worked by the month, for a time for $10, he saved his money, became a stock dealer and trader and did various things until he accumulated enough to purchase land In 1865 he found himself on safe ground for business, which he carried on successfully and extensively He was an active farmer and stock-raiser until 1880. In that year he retired from business and moved into Beardstown He owns a fine farm of 306 acres, 250 acres of which is under the plow and the rest is pasture, good land and all supplied with first class farm buildings He purchased this farm in 1865 and also owns some good residence property in Beardstown, the opera house building at Mount Olive, Illinois, and other residence property there.

He was married in Beardstown, in 1857, to Miss Catharina Schmidt She was born in Hesse-Darmstadt She was the daughter of the Rev. George and Kate Schmidt, who came to the United States in 1856, settling in Beardstown, where they died Mr Schmidt was for many years pastor of the Lutheran. He was a fine minister and an anti-slavery advocate, a Republican in politics and a leader in his community. Mrs. Hansmeyer is a great worker in the Lutheran Church and a very fine woman. They have four children: Augusta, wife of Henry Oetgen, a farmer in Schuyler county; Minna, wife of Henry Stock; Katie, wife of John Duvall, First State Bank of Beardstown; William, a miller by trade. Mr. Hansmeyer is a public-spirited citizen, a Republican in politics and a member of the Fourth Street Lutheran Church, of which he has been a Trustee for sixteen years.

JOSEPH FRANKLIN BLACK was born in Murray county, Tennessee, February 23, 1828. His father, William Black, was born near Milledgeville, Georgia, January 3, 1796, son of Thomas Gillespie Black, who was born in Markingham county, North Carolina, in January, 1772, whose father, William Black, a native of Maryland, removed to North Carolina. William Black was captain of a company of militia at the time the Revolutionary war broke out, and was one of the first who refused to take the oath of allegiance to the British government. He died soon after the war began. The maiden name of his wife was Beard, They were members of the Presbyterian church.

Thomas G. Black was reared and educated in his native State. He taught school several years. Removing from North Carolina to Georgia, he settled near Milledgeville, where he bought a tract of land and on it passed the residne of his life, dying in 1823. He was married February 26, 1795, to Polly Callahan, who was born April 7, 1773, daughter of William and Elizabeth (Shepard) Callahan, her father being of Irish and her mother of German descent. Mrs. Black went to Tennessee after the death of her husband, and from there to Illinois in 1825. Her death occurred in Morgan county, this State, in 1853. Grandfather and grandmother Black were members of the Presbyterian Church. They reared ten of their eleven children, viz.: William, Susanna, John, Cynthia, James, Thomas, Polly, Jefferson, Eleanor and Elizabeth. Rebecca died in infancy.

Willliam Black, father of the subject of our sketch, grew up and received his education in his native State, and went with the family to Tennessee directly after the death of his father. He was a natural mechanic and with his brother John established a a furniture factory in Maury county, remaining in business there till 1834. That year, with his wife and six children, he came to Illinois, their removal being made via the Cumberland, Ohio, Mississippi and Illinois rivers. He located four miles north of Winchester, in Scott county, where he bought eighty acres of prairie and eighty acres of timber land, paying $2.50 per acre for a part of it. He at once built a small frame house, containing two rooms, and commenced improving his land. In 1846 he sold this farm for $8 per acre. He then came to Cass county and bought 200 acres of land, located six miles southeast of Virginia, for which he paid $6 an acre. There was a double log house on this place, which the family occupied one year, at the end of which time they moved into the substantial brick house which Mr. Black erected, and which still stands. He also built a work shop. He, however, gave the most of his attention to farming. He lived there till after the death of his wife, when he went to Virginia and spent his last days at the home of his son, John, where he died October 3, 1884 December 4, 1823, he married Miss Mary S. Vaughn, who was born in Tennessee, November 1, 1803, daughter of Dixon and Susan Vaughn. She died on the home farm, January 29, 1881. Of the ten children born to them they reared eight, namely: Thomas G., Joseph F, William L., Richmond V., Green V., James B., Mary J. and John. Both he and his wife were reared in the Presbyterian Church, and after coming to Illinois they united with the Christian Church, of which they remained consistent members till the time of their death

Joseph Franklin Black, the subject of our sketch, was six years old when he moved to Illinois with his parents, and remembers distinctly many of the incidents connected with their removal and frontier life. At that time Central Illinois was sparsely settled and it was long before the advent of railroads here. Naples was the principal market for the surrounding country Mr. Black relates that at one time his father went to St Louis to mill. Instead of being gone one week, as he had expected, he was gone three weeks, and in the mean time the supply of meal gave out at home. By pounding corn in a mortar, the children made meal enough to last till their father's return. In 1836 three cooking stoves were brought to Jacksonville, one of which Mr. Black's father bought, paying $75 for it. Such a curiosity was this stove that the neighbors for miles around came to see it.

Joseph F. received his education in the primitive schools of Illinois. He inherited from his father a talent for mechanical work and early began to assist him in the shop At the age of twenty he began life on his own responsibility, commencing at once as a contractor and builder, and before he was twenty-one he bought 102 acres of land near the village of Philadelphia, for which he paid $3 50 an acre. He continued contracting and building for a time. Then for three years he was engaged in farming After that he moved to Philadelphia and devoted his time to the invention of farm machinery To him belongs the distinction of having invented and patented the first self-binder ever made. He took three different patents on it, and in partnership with his brother William got two patents on a gang plow. The value of such a man to a community cannot be estimated. Indeed, the worth of his inventive genius extends beyond his own community and State, being felt all over the world.

In 1867 he resumed farming and continued that occupation till 1876 That year he moved to Virginia and established himself as a contractor and builder. Many of the best store buildings and residences in this city are monuments to his skill. Nor have his labors been confined to Virginia He has done work in Springfield, Jacksonville, Beardstown, and various other places For some years past Mr Black has devoted his time to architecture, which he studied in his younger days, preparing plans and specifications and superintending the construction of buildings. He made the plans for the county jail and superintended its construction, also the two additions to the courthouse.

Mr Black was married May 17, 1849 to Mary F. Wilmott, a native of Illinois and a daughter of Charles R Wilmott They had five children, as follows: Charles W., born September 23, 1850, was married November 24, 1870, to Elsie Buckley, and has five children: Mabel, Roy, Mary, Stella and Clyde; Mary, born May 28, 1855, married Armstead Mains, and has seven children · Maude, Elma, William, Reatta, Toura, Lonese and Leslie;

Eva, born August 29, 1860, was married January 26, 1882, to William G. Payne; Robert, born September 22, 1864, was married October 18, 1889, to Maggie Gray and has two children, Edna and an infant; and Frank born March 23, 1868, married a Miss Elliott, and has one child, Edward. Mrs. Black died January 26, 1879, and in May, 1883, Mr. Black wedded Mary (Thompson) Skiles.

Mr. Black is a member of the Christian Church, as also was his first wife. His present companion has her membership with the Methodist Episcopal Church. Politically, he was formerly a Whig, but since the organization of the Republican party he has affiliated with it.

MARTIN W. GREER, a life-long resident of Rushville township, was born August 5, 1843, a son of James Greer, a native of County Tyrone, Ireland, born in the month of May, 1812. Martin Greer, the paternal grandfather of our subject, was also a native of Ireland, but of Scotch ancestry; he was a farmer by occupation, and spent his entire life in his own country; he married Lucy Crosier, who after the death of her husband came to America with her children; she died at the residence of her son James in 1870, at the age of eighty-three years. She was the mother of five children, all of whom came to this country: George, James, Jane, Richard and Robert. James Greer was a youth of eighteen years when he crossed the sea to America; he resided in the State of New York until 1836, and then came to Illinois, locating in Schuyler county. After is marriage he bought a farm on which he passed the rest of his life; he died in 1875. He was married in 1842, to Martha Wilson, a native of Nelson county, Kentucky, born October 15, 1818. Martha Wilson was the daughter of Elijah M. Wilson, who was born in Prince William county, Virginia, a son of Henry Wilson, also a Virginian by birth; Henry Wilson married Sarah Melton, who was a native of Virginia; they removed to Kentucky and were among the pioneers of the Blue-grass State. Elijah M. Wilson married Jane Hawley, a native of Virginia and a daughter of Absalom and Martha (Field) Hawley. He removed with his wife to Illinois, and entered a tract of Government land four miles south of Rushville; at the end of five years he sold this place for $600, and removed to Littleton township, where he purchased a farm on which he lived until his death. To them were born nine children: Martin W., Elijah M., William J., George S., Samuel E., Lucy J., Mary E., Maria E. and Vietta. Lucy married James Neill; Mary is the wife of Felix Jackson; Maria E. married Charles E. Lawler. The parents were both devoted church members, the father having joined the Methodist Episcopal Church in his youth; the mother first united with the Baptist Church, but after her marriage was a member of the Methodist Episcopal Church.

Martin W. Greer passed his youth on his father's farm, assisting in the labors of seed-time and harvest, and attending the district school a portion of each year. At the age of twenty-one years he began to teach school, and was engaged in this profession for a period of six terms. Aside from this experience he has been interested exclusively in agricultural pursuits, in which he has been more than ordinarily successful. He introduced the first Berkshire hogs into the county, and has a fine herd of short-horn cattle; his horses are of excellent pedigree, and he takes great pride in elevating the standard of all classes of live stock. At the time of his marriage Mr. Greer settled on the farm he now owns on section 34, Rushville township; he has good, substantial farm buildings, an orchard, and very attractive grounds surrounding his residence; in fact, the farm is one of the most desirable in the county.

He was married in April, 1867, to Susan H. Kruse, who was born in Rushville township, a daughter of Francis H. and Elizabeth Kruse, whose history appears on another page of this volume. Mr. and Mrs. Greer are the parents of five children living: Fred A., Luther M., Henry E., Millie M. and Owen J. The father is a member of the Methodist Episcopal Church, but the mother belongs to the Christian denomination. Politically, Mr. Greer has always, until the past two years, been a Democrat, and has been School Treasurer of Rushville township for a period of sixteen years; he has always been loyal to home interests and home industries, and is one of the most highly respected men in the county. For the past two years Mr. Greer has advocated the principles of the People's party and was nominated for Congress on that ticket for the Eleventh district by the convention held at Bushnell, June 11, 1892.

WASHINGTON BROCKMAN is one of the leading business men of Mount Sterling, where he was born September 13, 1844. His father, James, was born in Kentucky, and was there reared and educated. He turned his attention to the study of medicine when young. He graduated from Lexington Medical College, and in 1836 or 1837 he came to Illinois, locating in Mount Sterling, where he began his practice. It was at this time that he had a very narrow escape from being drowned by being caught in the high water at Meredosia. His practice extended into Pike and Morgan counties, where he had to go on horseback. He continued practicing until 18—, when he was elected Circuit Clerk, which position he held until his death. His wife's name was Sophia Price, of Scott county, Kentucky, the daughter of one of the pioneers of Brown county. Dr. Brockman was a Democrat; served as school commissioner of Brown county; was a member of the Second State Constitutional Convention; was one of the charter members of Hardin Lodge, No. 44, A. F. and A. M., and was buried with Masonic honors.

Washington was an infant when his mother died, and but eight years when his father died. His step-mother was left in limited circumstances with four children to care for, and consequently at thirteen years of age he went to live with an uncle. He remained with him about a year, and then went to live with another uncle, who owned a flour mill. For several years he worked in the mill, in a blacksmith shop and on a farm, and was also in a drug store in Mount Sterling. In September, 1861, he enlisted in Company K, Tenth Illinois Cavalry, and went to Missouri. His company was one of the four detached from the regiment and sent to join General Curtis after the Pea Ridge fight. They marched to Helena, Arkansas, and then participated in the capture of Vicksburg, after which he was granted a furlough of twenty days, which was extended to twenty days more, and then his health being poor he was assigned to duty in the drug department. He remained there by order of the physicians until the spring of 1864, when he was ordered to take charge of a company of the Veteran Reserve Corps. He was honorably discharged in December, 1864, as his term had expired, and he returned home and soon secured a position in the post office for thirty days, and then was clerk in the enrolling department of the Provost Marshal's office, remaining there until after the war, when the office was discontinued. He went to Macomb, Illinois, to secure a job, but not being successful he returned and bought a book and stationery store. In less than a year he sold out, and was employed at various kinds of work for a few months, and then purchased one-half interest in another book and stationery store; later he bought the interest of his partner and conducted the busines alone. He carries a full line of books, stationery, wall paper, sporting goods and other goods of like nature. In 1886 he opened a buggy repository and farm implement business and conducted it successfully for six years, but in 1892, owing to poor health, he was obliged to sell that branch of the business.

He was married, in 1865, to Estella J. Leeped, of Mount Sterling, daughter of Johnson and Catherine (Dawson) Leeped. Mr. and Mrs. Brockman have four living children: George Leon, Clarence Eugene, Ernest Edgar and Percy Washington. Mr. Brockman organized the Isaac McNeil Post, of which he is a member, No. 289, G. A. R. He is also a member of Unity Lodge, No. 310, I. O. O. F. He is a charter member of the Mount Sterling Lodge, No. — A. O. U. W.; and of the Crescent Lodge, I. O. M. A.; also a Fellow-craft member of Hardin Lodge, No. 44, A. F. and A. M. He and his wife are greatly respected by their host of friends. He is one of the directors of the Mount Sterling Building and Loan Association, and is vice-president of the Mount Sterling Electric Light and Power company, which he helped to organize.

Politically he is a strong Republican, having cast his first ballot in 1864 for "honest Old Abe" Lincoln, and from this party he has never departed, believing that the principles of said party are just and true.

WILLIAM T. BLACK, a prominent farmer of Woodstock township, was born in Dubois county, Indiana, March 18, 1821. When he was four years old his parents removed to Schuyler county, and here he has since resided. He remained under the parental roof until he had attained his majority, and then he started out in life on his own account; he first rented a farm in Woodstock township, which he cultivated one year, and then removed to Rushville township.

He was united in marriage, October 30, 1842, to Matilda Matheny, a native of Morgan county, Ohio, born March 29, 1823. Her parents, Andrew and Sarah (Harris) Matheny, were natives of New England and Virginia respectively; they emigrated to Illinois in 1835, purchased a farm in Schuyler county, and there spent the balance of their days. Both the paternal and maternal ancestors were patriots and fought in the war of the Revolution. Mrs. Black is one of a family of four children. After his marriage, Mr. Black rented land for a few years longer, and in 1849 bought 120 acres, on which he built a small frame house; this was his home until 1867, when he sold the place and purchased 280 acres in Woodstock township. In 1869 he erected a dwelling, which has since been enlarged and remodeled; he has made all the improvements on the farm, and has developed it into one of the most desirable in the township. He carried on a general farming business, and is considered one of the leading agriculturists of the county.

Mr. and Mrs. Black are the parents of six children: Austin married Nancy King, and they have one son; Athelinda is the wife of Richard Kettenring, and the mother of two sons; Harriet A. died at the age of forty-two years; William H. married Rachel Boiles, and they have seven children, five sons and two daughters; Richard married Jane Stevens, and they have two sons and a daughter; Franklin P. married Sarah Kennedy, and they have two sons.

Politically, Mr. Black affiliates with the Democratic party; he has filled the office of Assessor for three years, and in 1877 he was elected Justice of the Peace, and is the present incumbent. He is a member of the Farmers' Alliance. In his religious faith he is a Baptist. He has endured all the vicissitudes of life on the frontier, and has accumulated his property entirely by his own exertions. He has always employed the most correct business methods, and has the respect of the entire community.

GEORGE W. ALLPHIN, section 15, Huntsville township, was born in Kentucky, September 13, 1830. He is the son of Reuben and Susan (Brumbeck) Allphin. He was five years old when the family came to Illinois. He was reared on the farm and helped improve the new land. He attended such schools as those early days afforded, when they had log houses, with slabs for seats, and holes on the south side for windows. In the spring of 1850 he crossed the plains to California, and followed mining for four years, and was successful, returning by way of New Orleans. On his return he purchased eighty acres, on which he now resides. The land was unimproved and covered with timber. He now owns 115 acres of land, and has the same well improved. He has also a fine quality of stock. He is a Republican in politics, although he was a Democrat for thirty years. He has been Justice of the Peace and held many minor offices. He has been a successful man, having made his money since 1854, when he came to Illinois, settling in Huntsville.

He married, December 10, 1854, Miss Atlanta Wilson, daughter of Jamison Wilson. She was born in Huntsville township, in February, 1835. Mr. and Mrs. Allphin have had six children, three living: Anna, wife of James Burmood; Calvin and Sherman. They were members of the Cumberland Presbyterian Church for many years, and when that society failed they united with the Methodist Episcopal Church. Mr. Allphin is a member of Huntsville Lodge, No. 365, A. F. & A. M., and of Cyclone Lodge, I. O. O. F. He and his wife are highly respected citizens of Huntsville.

Jamison Wilson, the oldest living settler in Huntsville township, was born in what is now Grant county, Kentucky, November 29, 1829. His parents, John R. and Rachel (Junip) Wilson, were early settlers in this part of the State. He resided in Kentucky until 1836, and then came to Illinois, locating in Cass county, but finally settled in Adams county. They had eight children, of whom the subject was the oldest. The second child was Polly; the others were Nancy, Jane, Sarah, Lucy, Dora and Robert. Jamison Wilson was reared a farmer, and in 1834 he came to Illinois and settled in Huntsville township. He entered and purchased land, where he resided until quite recently. He became the owner of 207 acres of land. He continued to reside on a farm until 1886, since which he has resided with his daughter, Mrs. Allphin. In politics he was a Republican, and a Justice of the Peace for a time. He has been a church member all his life, having been connected with different denominations, as convenient.

He was married in 1832, to Miss Ellen Thornhill. She was born in Kentucky in 1810, being a daughter of John and Jane Thornhill. She died July 23, 1881. They had seven children: Ulysses resides in Linn county, Kansas; Atlanta, now Mrs. G. W. Allphin; Melvina married Solomon Rawson, of Jacksonville, Iowa, and died in 1862; Mary married John Rawson, and resides in Grant county, Kansas; Lucurgus resides in Frederick, Illinois; Palenicus resides on the old homestead; and Xenophon resides in Huntsville township, Illinois.

ZEBULON ALLPHIN resides on section twenty-two, Huntsville Township, and is not only a prosperous farmer, but a specimen of 1835, born in Boone county, Kentucky, in July, 1832. His father Reuben Allphin, was a native of Kentucky in 1801, and was the son of Zebulon Allphin, born in Virginia, but emigrated to Kentucky, where he died at the age of ninety-six years. He had nine children, of whom two are still living: William, Dollie, Jackson, Luke, Shelton, Ransom, Rebecca, Nancy and Reuben. All came to Schuyler county except Dollie and Ransom, who removed to Kentucky. Father of subject was a small boy when the family removed to Kentucky and was reared a farmer and overseer on his father's plantation. He married Susan Brumbeck. She was born in Virginia in 1800. In 1835 they came to Illinois and settled at Camden. Some time after they settled on section ten, Huntsville township, where he purchased a claim. In 1840 he removed to Rushville and remained five years, when he enlisted in the Mexican war. In 1848 he came to McDonough county. In 1850 he returned to Schuyler county, and after the Civil war went to St. Joseph, Missouri, where he pursued farming until 1870. He then returned to Schuyler county and passed his remaining years with his children. His wife died in 1852. They had eight children: William, Zarilda Thornhill, Sarah Hills, Henry, James, George W., Zebulon, and Susan Brumbeck. The parents were members of the Cumberland Presbyterian Church. The father is buried in Rushville and the mother in Huntsville. Mr. Allphin was a Democrat, and held local offices. He was reasonably successful as a farmer, notwithstanding he was an uneducated man.

Zebulon was but three years old when he came to Schuyler county and lived with the family until he was married. He was educated at the district schools.

He was married in 1852, to Mary L. Calvin, daughter of Samuel and Phoebe Calvin, and a native of Ohio. After marriage Mr. Allphin settled where he now resides and soon purchased 160 acres of unimproved land. He has since resided on the same, and now owns over 240 acres of land. He is a general farmer, dealing in live stock. Mr. and Mrs. Allphin have eight children: William C. resides in Carthage, Missouri; James Henry resides in Huntsville township; Addie, wife of Frank Seward, resides in Huntsville township; Cornelia, wife of Harvey Hoover of Clark county, Missouri; George M., at home;

Leonidas, of Huntsville; and Jessie, at home.

Mr. Allphin is a Democrat in politics. He has been Supervisor several times and has held minor offices. His wife died February 25, 1890. She was a member of the Methodist Episcopal Church. Mr. Allphin is a member of Huntsville Lodge, No. 465, A. F. & A. M. He has made all his property himself.

JOHN W. SNYDER, a well known and highly respected citizen of section 20, Buena Vista township, became a resident of Schuyler county in 1834. He is a native of Virginia, having been born in Frederick county of that State, June 4, 1823. His father, Jacob Snyder, was a farmer. He married Margaret Hughes, and in 1834 emigrated to Illinois, locating in Buena Vista township, where he at first rented land, but later purchased a tract, adding to it from time to time until he owned about 500 acres. This he improved by erecting a good substantial residence and commodious barns for his grain and stock, and in time brought the land to a high state of cultivation. He died September 28, 1865, aged sixty-seven years. His wife, the mother of our subject, had died on November 7, 1849, at the early age of fifty-one years. She was a woman of intelligence and warm impulses, a faithful wife and fond mother, and left many friends to mourn her loss. They had four children: John W., James, now residing near Hamilton, Illinois; Joseph, a resident of Littleton township, Illinois; and George Edward, residing in Buena Vista township, same State. The parents were consistent members of the Methodist Protestant Church, and contributed to its support. Politically the father was a Democrat, but was never an office seeker, or politician in the modern sense of the term.

The subject of our sketch, John W. Snyder, was but a mere boy when his parents came to Illinois, since which time he has continued a resident of Schuyler county. He was reared to log-cabin life on a farm, and received his education in a log schoolhouse. He lived at home until he attained to the age of manhood. He married, June 18, 1848, Miss Cynthia Blackley, a daughter of William and Jane Blackley. She was born in Tennessee, November, 1825. After his marriage our subject resided on the farm on which he still lives. He commenced with 260 acres of land, with no improvements, and now owns 190 acres, well improved with good house and barns for grain and stock and other modern improvements, while his land is well cultivated, being devoted to mixed farming.

Mr. and Mrs. Snyder have had nine children, six of whom are living. Sarah Jane was born June 21, 1849, and married Harvey Cole. She died in Buena Vista township May 3, 1878, leaving three children. Margaret E. was born December 12, 1850, and resides at home. Martha E. was born April 3, 1853, and died June 18, 1856. Mary E. was born April 3, 1853, and married George Warrington, and resides in Buena Vista township. Lydia F. was born November 18, 1859, and resides at home. Louisa A. was born December 27, 1862, and married Ross Pittman, and now resides in Rushville, of Schuylor county, Illinois. Cynthia B. was born October 9, 1864, and died December 15, 1864. Hannah L. was born May 24, 1867, and resides at home. Mazie C. was born September 25, 1868, and lives with her parents at home.

Mr. Snyder affiliates with the Democratic party, and has been honored by his constituents by an election to the office of Justice of the Peace, in which capacity he served his county ably and well. Like his parents before him, he is a Protestant Methodist, to the support of which church he contributes.

Commencing life with little means, he has, by industry and economy, accumulated a competence, and by reason of his honest dealings and cordial manner he has won the friendship and good will of the community.

WILLIAM HUPPERS, an old and successful business man of Beardstown, was born in the Rhine province, October 1, 1839. His parents lived and died in their native province. His father, Gearheard Huppers, was a mechanic and small farmer, and had been quite active in local matters of his native town. He died at the age of eighty-six. His mother, who died at the age of eighty-one, before her marriage bore the name of Elizabeth Waltham. They were members of the German Reformed Church.

Mr. Huppers was well reared, and when thirteen years of age, after attending public school, was apprenticed to the tailor's trade. After completing his time he started out as a journeyman workman, going to Belgium, where he spent six months, and then proceeded to Paris, where he remained for two years, and then came to the United States, stopping first in New York and then Columbus, Ohio, and later coming to Beardstown. Here he has made all his money, having, when he landed in Columbus, less than one dollar in his pocket. He now does a large and lucrative business as merchant tailor and gentlemen's furnisher, at the corner of Main and State streets. He arrived in Beardstown and established a similar business with Mr. Miller, who continued with him until 1881; since then Mr. Huppers has carried the business on very successfully alone. He has been a leader in many local enterprises. He is interested in the Beardstown Electric Light and Power Company, is a director of the First State Bank, and is a member of the Board of Education. His fellow-citizens have always known where to find him in public matters.

He was married in Arenzville, to Minnie Henkel, of Hesse Darmstadt. She came with her mother to this country when she was twelve years of age. Mrs. Henkel, a much respected member of the church, died in Beardstown, aged fifty-three years. Mr. and Mrs. Huppers are the parents of two children: Lula A., who was educated in Beardstown, but completed her course in the university at Evanston, Illinois, and is now a skilled teacher in vocal and instrumental music; Harry C., twelve years of age, is at home. Mr. and Mrs. Huppers are leading people in this city, Mrs. Huppers being a member of the First Lutheran Church. Mr. Huppers is a member of the order of F. & A. M., a member of Cass Lodge, No. 23, of Clark Chapter No. 29, and is Treasurer in both. He is a sound Republican in politics.

CHARLES N. DUNN, a successful farmer and stock-raiser of Beardstown, was born here, and has always lived on this farm. His father was John Dunn, of Cornwall, England, born in 1822. He grew up in his native country as a farmer boy and with his brother Luke came to the United States in the '40s, on a sailing vessel from Liverpool and landed in New York and came from there to Beardstown. Soon afterward he came out to his present location where he purchased 160 acres of wild land, which is now owned by his son. On this place John Dunn began life as a young single man and here made farming a success. He was married to Caroline Treadway, who was born in Maryland, but had come to Cass county when young, as her parents were old settlers. They soon accumulated 320 acres of fine land in what is known as the Sangamon bottoms and here John Dunn died in 1877, aged fifty-five years. His wife survived him until 1885, when she died, aged seventy-two years. She was a noble, good woman and the best of neighbors. Mr. Dunn was an honest man and both he and his wife were highly esteemed members of the Methodist Episcopal Church.

Charles Dunn is the youngest of a family of eight children, four of whom are yet living, Mary Paschal, now living in Morgan county; Sarah Kuhlman, living near Virginia, this county; William, a farmer in Butler county, Kansas; and Charles, who has never been married. He is a sound Republican of good habits and sound principles. He has been a very successful farmer and stock-raiser and now owns a fine farm of 160 acres, well improved and with a fine set of farm buildings. The place has been his own for fifteen years, and is where he was born and resides.

AMAZIAH C. EDGAR was born at Virginia, Cass county, Illinois, May 12, 1845. His father, George Edgar, was a native of Franklin county, Kentucky, and was there reared and married; he emigrated to Illinois at an early day, and was one of the honored pioneers of Schuyler county. After a few years he removed to Cass county, Illinois, and located at Virginia, engaging in farming near that place. In 1849, when the gold fever swept this country, he joined the train of emigrants journeying to the Pacific coast. He remained in the Golden State sixteen years, and then returned to Illinois, and resumed agricultural pursuits in Cass county; his death occurred soon after his return. He was united in marriage to Elizabeth Nall, a native of Kentucky and a daughter of Gabriel and Fanny (Tuttl) Nall. To them were born four children: Martha, Robert, Amaziah C., the subject of this biography, and Henrietta.

Mr. Edgar received his education at Virginia, and in early life was thrown upon his own responsibility; he also assisted in the support of the family, and by industry and economy managed to save his earnings until he could get a start in the world. He resided at Virginia until after his marriage, and then removed to Macon county, Illinois, and purchased a farm near Niantic; here he was engaged in agricultural pursuits until 1882, when he sold this land and came to Rushville, where he lives a retired life.

He has been twice married: In 1868 he was united to Julia (Carr) Cook, a native of Cass county, Illinois, and a daughter of David Carr; her first husband was John Cook, and her death occurred in 1875. Mr. Edgar's second marriage was in 1878, to Eliza E. Ford, a native of Arkansas and a daughter of Elias E. Ford; her father was a Kentuckian by birth and one of the pioneers of Macon county, Illinois; he removed thence to Arkansas in search of health, but soon returned and now lives a retired life at Niantic; he married Sarah McDonald, a native of Ohio. Mrs. Edgar died at Las Vegas, New Mexico, April 23, 1892, on the thirty-fourth anniversary of her birth; she had gone there in quest of health, but the hand of death was laid upon her, and she was called from this life to the reality of the future. She was the mother of two children: Effie May and Ballinger. Mr Edgar had one child by his first marriage, named Nevada. Politically he has always been a Democrat, and a stanch supporter of the principles of the party He represented Niantic on the County Board of Supervisors for six years, and as a member of the County Central Committee He was president of the Macon County Fair Association four years He is a member of Rushville Lodge, No 9, A F and A M In all the walks of life his action has been characterized by that integrity and honor which insures the respect and confidence of the entire community

JONATHAN PATTESON was born in State of Virginia, June 1, 1797 His father was Charles Patteson, also a native of Virginia, who removed from that State to Green county, Kentucky about the year 1800, and was thus one of the pioneers of that locality He bought a tract of timber land, and erected thereon a log cabin, in which were domiciled the family. They were in a wilderness and were compelled to live off the products of their little place and the game that was found in abundance in the woods Mr Patteson was an owner of slaves, and they cultivated flax and cotton, and used to card, spin and weave all the cloth for the entire family They were compelled to be self-supporting, and knew little of the outside world because railroads were unheard of, newspapers rarely seen, and even steamboats had but just been heard of He continued to reside in Green county until his death His wife, the mother of our subject, was Regina DeGraphenreidt, a native of North Carolina, who died when our subject was but four years of age

Our subject, Jonathan Patteson, is the only survivor of a family of six children. He was reared on the farm in Kentucky and was there married At quite an early age he went to live with a merchant in Columbia, Adair county, and there he remained, clerking in a store, until he was married He then went to that part of Adair county now included in Russell county, and took charge of a paper mill. Soon after his location there, Russell county was organized, and the first court was held in his house He lived there until 1837, at which time he came to Illinois While in Kentucky he lived on a small stream, six miles from the Cumberland river. This little stream was known as Greasy creek. He built a flat boat, and himself and family, accompanied by Thomas J Garrett, floated down to the Cumberland river and there took a steamer and continued on down to the Ohio, thence down to the Missssissippi, thence up the Mississippi and Illinois rivers, stopping at Erie (now Frederick), Schuyler county This country was then an utter wilderness, filled with wild animals and with a few scattering pioneers, almost as wild as the animals He bought a tract of 160 acres, two miles east of town, covered with heavy timber, upon which two log cabins had been erected and a few acres cleared by the former owner He paid $2,000 for the entire tract, which was then considered a very high price Here he lived and labored until 1871, when he came to Rushville and has since lived there retired from active business. He is the oldest man now living in Schuyler county. Generally his health has been good, but of late years he has suffered with rheumatism, though his mind and memory are yet well preserved During his long life he has witnessed the introduction of railroads and steamboats, telegraph lines, and when he came to Illinois, as he passed through Louisville, he traded for two stoves, the first ever brought to Schuyler county. They were rough, primitive affairs, which would now sell for about three dollars, but for which he paid the sum of seventy dollars. In 1822 he was married to Miss Matilda Caldwell, a native of Columbia, Kentucky, and a daughter of William and Eliza (Pyles) Caldwell. To himself and wife have been born seven children: Eliza M., Charles R., William C., Harriet J., Laura, Matilda and Louisa Caroline. Of these children all are living except the daughter, Laura, who died in 1872.

LEONIDAS SCOTT, one of the prominent citizens of Rushville, Schuyler county, Illinois, is a native of this county, born September 7, 1855 (for family history, see sketch of Mrs. T. W. Scott). He was united in marriage March 25, 1874, to Melinda B. Demaree, a native of Mercer county, Kentucky, born August 9, 1855. Her parents, Holdman and Martha J. Demaree, were also natives of Mercer county, Kentucky. They emigrated to Schuyler county in 1857, and bought land on which they lived until death; they had born to them eight children, six of whom are living. Mrs. Scott's grandparents were Virginians by birth, and were among the pioneers of Kentucky.

Mr. and Mrs. Scott have two children: Laura B. was born March 18, 1876, and Catherine, born August 16, 1888. Mr. Scott passed an uneventful youth, being reared to the occupation of a farmer; after his marriage he remained on the home farm until 1887, when he purchased his present residence in Rushville. He rents his farm, which consists of 200 acres, and devotes his time to the breeding of fine horses. Netty Thorn is a very fine animal belonging to his stables, and he has sent out some of the most promising horses that are on the turf to-day.

Our worthy subject is a member of the Knights of Pythias, and takes an active interest in the order. His wife belongs to the Christian Church. They are giving their children a good education, and are thus providing them with a legacy of which no man can defraud them.

FREDERICK E. BERRY, one of the managers of the National Union store at Rushville, was born in Schuyler county, Illinois, December 23, 1841, a son of Daniel and Mary A. (Crow) Berry, natives of Washington county, Pennsylvania. Samuel Berry, the paternal grandfather, was also a resident of Washington county, Pennsylvania. Daniel Berry was reared to the occupation of a farmer; he emigrated to Schuyler county, Illinois, in an early day, and settled in Rushville township, where he purchased eighty acres of land, partially improved; here he lived until his death in 1871; his widow still resides on the home farm. They had a family of nine children, all of whom grew to mature years: William C. died in Rushville, leaving a family; Daniel died in California; George G. died at Tombstone, Arizona; Sarah is the wife of Morris Hobart; Elizabeth married C. L. Easley; Mary A. is the wife of W. R. Milby; Frederick E. is the subject of this sketch; Martha M. is the wife of A. V. Quinn; John S. died in New York city; Frederick E. was brought up amid rural scenes, and attended the common schools.

When the great Civil war arose between the

North and South, he was not slow to espouse the cause of the Union, and May 10, 1861, he enlisted in the service of the State Government; and May 24, 1861, enlisted for three years in Company G, Sixteenth Illinois Volunteer Infantry, and spent the summer and fall of 1861 in Missouri; in January, 1862, he went to Cairo and afterward joined Pope's army in the siege of New Madrid; he participated in the capture of Island No. 10, the siege of Corinth, and was afterward stationed at Big Spring, Mississippi; next at Tuscumbia, Alabama, and took part in the retreat of Negley's and Palmer's brigades; next they were at Decatur and Nashville, Tennessee, remaining at the latter place during the two months of the siege; he was at Stone river, at Nashville, and during the siege of Chattanooga was at Kelly's Ferry. January 1, 1864, he was transferred to the Sixtieth Illinois Volunteer Infantry, and took part in the battles of Tunnel Hill and Buzzard Roost Gap; he was transferred March 1st to the Sixteenth Regiment, which he joined in the beginning of the war, and served until May 2d, when he began the Atlanta campaign; he went as far as Burnt Hickory, and there was ordered back, and June 13th, at Chattanooga, was discharged. He returned to his home, and resumed the more peaceful pursuit of agriculture.

Mr. Berry was married January 3, 1867, to Miss Maggie Milby, a daughter of Benjamin and Mary Milby, a native of Delaware, born January 30, 1845. He then took charge of his father's farm, which he managed until the fall of 1891. In October of that year the branch store of the National Union Company was organized; he was made manager at Rushville; this company does a general mercantile business, carries a well selected stock, and is worthy of the generous patronage received. Mr. Berry owns the old homestead left by his father, which consists of 178 acres.

Mr. and Mrs. Berry have had born to them a family of five children: Katie is the wife of Miles Van Horn; Anna, Elizabeth, Grace and Fred E. In politics Mr. Berry is independent, although he formerly affiliated with the Republican party. He has been Tax Collector and served as a member of the School Board. He belongs to the Grand Army of the Republic, and has been Commander of Colonel Harney Post, No. 131; he is also a member of the A. O. U. W., and is Secretary of the County Alliance. He has also been interested in public movements, and has been a loyal supporter of home industries. He is a man of superior business qualifications, and through strictly honorable methods he has accumulated considerable property.

MRS. WILLIAM PRICE, a resident of Rushville, Illinois, has the honor of being one of the earliest settlers of Schuyler county, Illinois, her parents removing there in 1826. She was born in Crawford county, Indiana, October 8, 1816, a daughter of Wiliam and Cassie (Frakes) McKee, whose history appears on another page of this volume. She recalls many incidents of life on the frontier, and has not forgotten the privations and hardships endured by those who were courageous enough to undertake to subdue the wild land and convert it into fertile farms. She was married at the age of sixteen years, to William Price, a native of Tennessee, born October 8, 1809, a son of Samuel and Beersheba (Atchily) Price; his father removed from Tennessee to Illinois, and was a pioneer of Schuyler county; he afterward removed to Arkansas, and lived there until after the death of his wife, when he returned to Illinois; he spent his last years at the home of Mrs. Price in Rushville. William Price was reared in his native State, and there learned the trade of a blacksmith; he remained in Tennessee until 1830, when he emigrated to Schuyler county, Illinois, where he resided until his death. At the time of his marriage he settled on the land now occupied by Mrs. Mary Price, which was the gift of her father; he followed his trade, and at the same time superintended the cultivation of his farm; he made many excellent improvements, erecting good buildings, and bringing the land to a high state of productiveness. His death occurred March 21, 1887.

Mrs. Price has four children living; John married Margaret Owen; George married Emma Meador; Agnes is the wife of Oscar B. Hite; James F. married Nannie Bodenheimer.

In his political views Mr. Price adhered to the principles of the Republican party. He was a man of great integrity of character, and enjoyed the respect of all who knew him.

CHARLES GOTTHELF JOKISCH, an old settler and farmer of Cass county, now deceased, was born in Saxony, Germany, February 27, 1819. He was one of nine children. His grandfather, believing that opportunities for young men were better in the United States than in Germany, urged his two sons and their families to emigrate to this country. This they did early in the thirties, and began in Cass county on Government land, and here the father of Gotthelf died in what is now Bluff Springs precinct, at about the age of fifty. He had accumulated

a fine property and left an estate valued at twenty-five thousand dollars. His aged father also died here. (For fuller history of family see biography of William Jockisch.)

Charles Gotthelf grew up an industrious boy, and was ever afterward identified with the best interests of the county, but unfortunately died before he was very old. In spite of his early death he left an estate that was very valuable. His death occurred in March, 1874, in the fifty-fourth year of his age. By industry and economy he first was able to buy a small farm, and from time to time increased it until he owned a property of 350 acres, most of it in a high state of cultivation. He was a quiet, good man, gave his entire time to his business, never engaged in politics, except to vote the Republican ticket.

He was married here to Elinore Carls, of Hanover, Germany, November 1, 1846. Her mother had died in Germany, and she came to this country with her father and other members of the family in 1843, and has since lived in the borders of Cass county. (For family history, see biography of Louis M. Carls.) Mrs. Jokisch is the youngest of the family now living. She has two brothers, George and Henry, both of this county. She is a well preserved lady and very intelligent. She and her husband were life-long members of the Methodist Episcopal Church.

She is the mother of ten children: Theophilus, Otto, George and Matilda (Loomis) are deceased; those living are: Maurice W., a farmer living in Virginia; Mary E., a noble character, living at home; Philip J., a very successful farmer of this township; Amelia Hackman, a native of this county; Edward F., a successful farmer in Virginia; Harry J., now running the homestead, is a well educated farmer. He attended the high school of Virginia, and also the Wesleyan University at Mt. Pleasant, Iowa, and the Illinois State Normal School. He taught recently in the schools of Beardstown. He is industrious and knows how to put his education to good use. He clings to the same political faith as did his father, and bids fair to do that parent honor.

WILLIAM OETGEN, one of the old settlers and successful farmers living in Cass county, was born in Hanover, Germany, May 31, 1817. He came of pure German ancestry. His father, G. Henry, was a native of the same place in Germany, born in 1787 and died December 26, 1820. He was a blacksmith, as were all his brothers and his father before. They were all members of the Lutheran Church. The name of his mother was Helen L. Veslage, a native of Hanover, who survived her first husband, and in 1823 married Dr. J. C. A. Seeger, who came to the United States in 1831, and in 1832 was joined by his wife and our subject. The family settled in Philadelphia, Pennsylvania, in September, 1832, where Mr. Oetgen learned the shoemaker's trade. Mr. Oetgen made a quick passage of twenty-eight days and landed in New York City. In 1834 his parents came to Beardstown, and were joined a year later by our subject. They both died here, but left no children: hence Mr. Oetgen is the only one of his family now living that came from Germany. Mr. Oetgen landed in this county July 25, 1835. He began here a poor boy and worked for years for $8 a month; later he received as much as $12.50 a month, and in 1843 farmed one year as a renter, and in 1844 purchased his first land not far from Beardstown city. This consisted of 290 acres, which he improved, and in 1859 he purchased 126 acres on section 20, township 18, range 11, where he now lives. He later added 120 acres, and then seventy acres more, and again eighty acres, all of which is valuable and some of which is worth more than $100 an acre. He has been one of the leading men of the county, and has had all the experiences of a pioneer. Being a smart and intelligent man he has a fine memory, and can tell in a very interesting manner of the condition of things in the past history of the county. He has been a good citizen.

He was married, in Cass county, to Catherine Middlebusher, born in Hanover, near Osnabruck, December 23, 1826, and came to the United States in 1835, and to Cass county with her parents, Adam and Petro N. (Ketwick) Middlebusher, who died here of cholera two weeks after landing in Beardstown. They were members of the Lutheran Church, and while only in this country a short time they came in a day when their names should be associated with the other pioneers. Mrs. Oetgen was yet very young when her parents died, and was partly reared by the mother and step-father of Mr. Oetgen. She is yet living. She was married, April 7, 1843, to Mr. Oetgen, and has proved herself a good, true wife. They are the parents of eight children, of whom Mary and Hannah died young. John recently died in Beardstown, leaving a wife and two bright children. He had been educated at Poughkeepsie, New York, and was book-keeper for Henry Keil. At the time of his death he was a promising young man and a worthy member of the family. The living are: Helen Fricke, of Lafayette county, Missouri; Henry William, who married Augusta Hansmier, a farmer in Schuyler county; and George C., who married Henrietta Reichert, and also on the old homestead; Martha, wife of Louis Leonhard, working Mr. Oetgen farm in this township; and Edward L., on the home farm. The latter was appointed in 1890 as a census enumerator in this county. The children are all smart and self-sustaining, and are all active Republicans.

DAVID HERRON, a prominent farmer of Bainbridge township, was born in county Down, Ireland, in June, 1829, a son of Robert Herron, who was born in the same county; the paternal grandfather, Robert Herron, was a native of Ireland, of Scotch ancestry. The father of our subject learned the trade of linen weaver at a time when this work was done on hand looms, and followed this occupation through life. He married Mary Cleland, a daughter of Thomas and Jane (Bell) Cleland, natives of Ireland, of Scotch lineage. After the death of her husband, Mrs. Herron emigrated to America, in 1850, and spent the last years of her life in Schuyler county, Illinois. She was the mother of eight children: Sarah, Robert, Thomas, Jane, David, John, William and Hugh. David Herron passed his youth in his native country, and there received his education. In 1850 he determined to try his fortunes in the New World, and accordingly, the 27th day of March, sailed from Belfast on the vessel Annie, and landed at the port of New York after a voyage of forty-nine days. He went directly to Ohio, via the Hudson river and Erie canal to Buffalo, and thence by lake to Cleveland; from that city he went by team to Mahoning county. He began to learn the tanner's trade, but on account of ill health abandoned the plan; he then went to work in the iron furnaces and continued there for two years, after which he engaged in farming; he was employed by the month until 1858, when he came to Schuyler county, Illinois, and purchased 160 acres of land; about eighty acres of this tract were cleared, and a log cabin had been built, which was their first Illinois home. Mr. Herron has added to his first purchase of land until he now owns 240 acres, more than half of which is under a high state of cultivation; he has erected a good set of frame buildings, and has developed the place into one of the most desirable in the township.

He was united in marriage, in 1857, to Mary Hull, who was born in Mahoning county, Ohio, a daughter of Logan and Annie (Ross) Hull, of the same county; Mrs. Herron's paternal grandfather, Benjamin Ross, was a native of New Jersey, and one of the earliest settlers of Mahoning county; he was a man of much energy and enterprise, and erected the first mill operated by water power in Mahoning county. Mr. and Mrs. Herron are the parents of six children: Jane, Thomas, Blanche, Lula, Mary A. and Robert L., who died in 1865. They are consistent members of the Methodist Episcopal Church. Politically Mr. Herron affiliates with the Democratic party.

GEORGE BORDENKIRCHER, Chairman of the County Board of Supervisors, was born on a farm in Ohio, May 1, 1842. His father was named Wendal, and was born in Germany; and his father, David, was born in Germany, and there married and came to America about 1833 and settled in Coshocton county, Ohio. He bought a large tract of land there, and lived there until his death. Wendal was eighteen years old when he came to America, and he resided with his parents until his marriage, when his father gave him land in Coschocton county, and he lived there until 1851, when he moved to Indiana and lived there until 1856, and then came to Illinois and settled in Mount Sterling township, and bought a tract of unimproved land with a set of log buildings Their first home was a log hut. He quickly improved his land, erected frame buildings and lived there until 1878, when he removed into the city of Mount Sterling, and now lives retired. His wife's name was Mary Stons, born in Germany, and came an orphan girl to America. When she died in Mount Sterling she left four children.

George attended school both in Ohio and Indiana. He remained on the farm with his father until his enlistment, August 8, 1862, in Company D, One Hundred and Nineteenth Illinois Volunteers, and remained with the regiment until the close of the war, being in all the various marches, campaigns and battles of his regiment. He worked his father's farm in 1867, then bought eighty acres of land in section 14, Mount Sterling township, which is included in his present farm. He has in all 180 acres of land.

He was married, April 10, 1866, to Florentine Meyer, born in Alsace, Germany, April 29, 1846. Her father came to America in 1851 and settled in Ohio, and his wife and seven children followed him two years later. He followed his trade of tailor for four years in Cincinnati, and then moved to Mount Sterling and continued the business. Mr. and Mrs. B. have six children living: Emily, Edward, Anna, Albert, Celestine and Freddie. Our subject with his family is a member of the St. Joseph Catholic Church. He is a Democrat in politics, and is now serving his third term as Supervisor and second term as chairman of the board, and is president of the Brown County Agricultural Society. He is also a member of the Western Catholic Union, and his wife is a member of the Sacred Heart Society.

MORTIMER AYERS, M. D., a leading member of the medical fraternity in Schuyler county, Illinois, has been a resident of Rushville since October 1, 1873. He was born at Springfield, Illinois, June 25, 1848, a son of Grover and Jane (Stockdale) Ayers. The father was a native of New York state, born near Penn Yan, May 21, 1818, and emigrated to Wapakoneta, Ohio, with his family at an early day. There he was married, and in 1844 he emigrated to Illinois, and settled at Springfield; here he embarked in a general mercantile trade, which he carried on until 1862, when he retired from active life; he removed to Vermont, Fulton county, in 1876, and there passed the remainder of his days; his death occurred in 1880; his wife survives him, and is a resident of Vermont, Illinois. He was very prosperous in business and accumulated a competency. In his religious faith he was a Baptist. The family consisted of five children: Bryon W., died in Springfield, Illinois; Ada is the wife of George W. Whitney; Sylvanus resides in La Fayette, Indiana; the fourth born is the subject of this sketch; Grover died at Springfield, at the age of twenty years.

Dr. Ayers passed his boyhood days at Springfield, and attended the public schools until he was fifteen years of age. He then entered the United States Navy as midshipman, and served in this capacity for three years; the greater portion of this time was spent at Annapolis, Maryland, although he made several cruises. In 1866 he returned to Springfield, and began the study of medicine, soon afterward going to St. Louis, where he continued the pursuit of the science under the direction of Prof. T. G. Comstock. He entered the Homeopathic Medical College of Missouri at St. Louis, and was graduated in the spring of 1868. He then located at Pana, Illinois, where he engaged in practice. He had not yet attained his majority, being only twenty years of age, and he soon decided to enter the navy; when he reached New York, however, he went on board a merchant vessel as surgeon, sailed to South America, and was absent three years. Returning to the United States at the end of that period, he located at Rushville, Illinois. He has taken several special courses in medicine, the last of which was at the Royal Ophthalmic Hospital, London, England; he has been a close and careful student of all topics pertaining to the science and practice of medicine, and has made his mark as a skillful physician. He is the only member of the Homoepathic school in Rushville.

Dr. Ayers was united in marriage, July 15, 1874, to Miss Dora Hill, a daughter of Major William Hill, and a native of Littleton township, Schuyler county. Two children have been born to them, Ethel and Olive. In his religious faith the Doctor is a Presbyterian. He is a member of the Masonic order, belonging to the blue lodge, chapter and commandery; he has held the office of Commander of Rushville Commandery, No. 56, K. T.

Major William Hill was born in Lancashire, England, June 27, 1825. At the age of twenty-one years he emigrated to America, and became one of the pioneers of Schuyler county in 1846. He was a cabinetmaker by trade, and followed this vocation for ten years. He married Rachel Knowles, a daughter of Joseph Knowles, who came to the United States with his family aboard the same vessel with the Major. After abandoning his trade he was interested in a flouring mill, but when the Civil war broke out he was one of the first to respond to the call for troops; he raised a company, which was mustered into the service as part of the Engineer's Regiment of the West; he was elected Captain, served through the entire conflict, and was mustered out with the rank of Lieutenant Colonel by brevet; he had arisen in regular order to the rank of Major. After the war he became a member of the firm of J. & J. Knowles & Co., and was connected with this firm until his death, which occurred March 25, 1877. His wife died April 12, 1877. They had a family of five children, four of whom lived to mature years: Maria, wife of C. M. Cowan, of York, Nebraska; Mary A. is Deputy County Clerk of York county, Nebraska; Dora is the wife of Dr. M. Ayers; Laura was the wife of the late Luther Jackson, of Rushville.

Major Hill was a staunch Republican, and took a prominent part in local affairs. He was a man of plain and unpretentious manner, true to his convictions, and worthy of the esteem in which he was held.

CARL TRAUGOTT JOKISCH, a good farmer and stock-raiser of sections twenty-eight and twenty nine, township eighteen, range eleven west, was born in Germany near Bautzen, January 4, 1822. He is the fifth of his father's children and the oldest one now living. He was thirteen years of age when his parents left Germany for the United States in the fall of 1834, coming on a sailing vessel and landing in New

Orleans, January 1, 1835. They came up the Mississippi and Illinois rivers to Beardstown, landing February 2, 1835, and have as a family since been identified with the history of the county. The mother died in the latter part of January, 1835, at St. Louis, while the family were on the way. She was only forty two years of age. She was always a member of the German Lutheran Church, as was her husband who survived her.

Traugott has always been a farmer in the county to which he came so many years ago. He was raised by an uncle, C. G. Jokisch, now deceased, the father having died in 1851. The father had obtained new lands in this county and here spent the remaining years of his life. (See William Jokisch, this book.)

The farm of our subject has a beautiful location near Bluff Springs, in the Illinois river valley, where he owns a fine and well improved farm of 235 acres, with substantial farm buildings.

He was married, in this county to Mary Ellen Carls, born in Hanover in 1834. She came with her parents to the United States and Cass county in 1845 and has since lived here, being a true helpmate to a good husband. She is an honest, good woman. She was the daughter of John Frederick and Elizabeth Carls, natives of Hanover, who came with their family to this country, but misfortune overtook them. Early after landing the father was killed by an accident while building a house for his family in Beardstown. A piece of timber fell on him and caused his death. He was then in the prime of life, being then about thirty-eight. He was a very skillful cabinet-maker, a good citizen and devoted Christian for many years. His wife survived him for four years and then died, in Beardstown, in 1849, of the cholera, which was epidemic at that time. She was a Christian woman.

Mrs. Jokisch has one sister and two brothers. The sister, a widow, is Mrs. Elizabeth Kuhl, living in Pekin, Illinois; Henry is a farmer in Montana; and John F. is a farmer in Cass county, Illinois. They are both married.

Mr. and Mrs. Jokisch and family are members of the Methodist Church, and are very good, moral, upright people. Mr. Jokisch is a Republican in politics. Mr. and Mrs. Jokisch are the parents of twelve children, four of whom are deceased: John W. died an infant; Edward, married, left a wife and one child; Philipena died at the age of thirty-six, leaving two children; Ida died in Montana when twenty years of age. The living ones are: Louis, a teacher for more than twenty years in Central Illinois, and is single; Emme, wife of Charles Wilson, farmer and fruit-grower of Virginia; Elizabeth, wife of Adam Hegeman, farmer in this county; Albert W., living near the homestead, farming; George F., living in the east end of the county on a farm; Richard, at home, helping on the farm; Cora and Tillie are also at home.

S. L. CALEF, one of the old, representative families of Cass county, lives on a fine farm on section nine, township eighteen, range eleven, where he owns 320 acres, all well improved except a few acres, and all lying in the familiar and famous Sangamon bottom. On this fine land he has erected two sets of fine buildings. He came to the county in the fall of 1844, when he was a man of small means, but in a year's time he was able to purchase his first land of eighty acres and began to farm on his own account. Soon after this he bought another eighty, and some years later invested in 160 acres more, making 320 acres in all. He has as fine land as there is in the county, and it is all paid for. He has a comfortable bank account in addition, and is considered one of the well-to-do men of the county. He gave up active farming some fifteen years ago, and since that time has been taking life easy, having rented his farm to William Coleman (see biography). Mr. Calef came to this county and State from New Hampshire, where he was born, near Plainfield, Sullivan county, June 25, 1820. He came of New England parents, born in New Hampshire, of English ancestry. His father, Nathaniel Calef, was a native of Salisbury, New Hampshire, son of Benjamin Calef, who was born in New Hampshire, and lived and died in Salisbury, New Hampshire, being a farmer all his life. He was an old man when he died, and had always been a prominent member of society. He married a New Hampshire lady who li ed and died there when quite old. Nathaniel Calef was married twice. He was married for the first time to Miss Elizabeth Hall, who died on the farm where they had settled after marriage. She left several children, of whom John Hall Calef is still living. He is on the old Calef farm in New Hampshire, and is an old man, aged eighty-six. His second wife, mother of subject, was Sarah Pettengill, she having been first married and borne a family to a Mr. Little, who died, and she married Nathaniel Calef, to whom she proved a good and faithful wife. She bore him our subject and a daughter, Lucinda, who became Mrs. Harrington, and died in New Hampshire, as did her mother, both old people. Nathaniel Calef, the oldest half-brother of the subject of this sketch, was a soldier in the war of 1812.

Our subject was married in Cass county to Lucy A. Main. She was born, reared and educated in Geauga county, Ohio, in 1829, and came to Illinois when young, settling on a farm in Cass county with her parents, Lodrick and Ann Eliza (Beard) Main. They were early settlers and improved their farm, and died when old people. They were natives of Connecticut and went to Ohio when young, marrying in Genaga county, from which they came to Cass county, Illinois.

Mr. and Mrs. Calef have no children, but have raised and helped several young people. They are very well known people and have made a host of friends for themselves during their lives in this county. Mrs. Calef is a Methodist, and her husband is a Republican in politics.

JOHN SHANK, a successful farmer, horticulturist and florist, and a prominent citizen of Mount Sterling, Illinois, was born in Franklin, Johnson county, Indiana, July 11, 1843. His paternal grandparents were John and Catherine (Dosing) Shank, the former a native of Pennsylvania and of German descent, while the latter was of French ancestry. The former was an early settler of Ohio, when that State was the frontier of civilization, his last days having been passed at his home in Preble county, near Eaton, that State. His son, William Shank, the father of the subject of this sketch, was born in Montgomery county, Virginia, in May, 1821, and was twelve years of age at the time of his father's death. After this event his mother removed with her family to Indiana, and located in Johnson county, near Morgansville. Here William Shank grew to manhood, and, in 1842, married Julia E. Mc-

Cord, a native of Tennessee Her parents were John and Mary (Brown) McCord, both of Scotch-Irish descent, who emigrated in an early day from Virginia to Tennessee, whence, about the year 1836, they removed to Indiana They resided in that State nearly twenty years, when finally, in 1855, they removed to Illinois Here the father purchased land in Moultrie county, near the village of Bethany, on which he and his wife settled, and where his death occurred in 1865, lamented by all who knew him William Shank and his young wife preceded her parents to Illinois by eleven years, having removed thence in 1844, two years after their marriage They settled in Pea Ridge township, Brown county, where William bought a tract of land, a portion of which was heavily timbered. Here they resided for many years, the wife, mother of the subject of this sketch, dying in 1889, universally beloved and mourned

John Shank, whose name heads this biography, was thus about a year old when his parents removed to the Prairie State, which was then new and sparsely settled. Here, in the freedom of a wild expanse, he grew to manhood,—physically strong and athletic, and mentally acute and active,—receiving the educational advantages afforded by his surroundings and circumstances.

On the breaking out of the great Civil war, with all the enthusiasm of youth and patriotism, he rallied to the defense of his country's flag, enlisting in Company B, Fiftieth Volunteer Infantry, on August 20, 1861, and serving until the close of the war The most important engagements in which he participated were the siege of Corinth, Shiloh, Corinth and Resaca In January, 1864, he re-enlisted or veteranized, and was given a furlough of thirty days. After the battle of Resaca, at Rome, Georgia, he was placed on detached duty in the Commissary Department of General Sherman's army, where he continued until cessation of hostilities He was honorably discharged with his regiment at Springfield, Illinois, on July 14, 1865.

He then, like thousands of others, resumed his former peaceful occupations, engaging, during the first year of his return, in farming. Later, he embarked in mercantile pursuits at Clayton, Illinois, remaining there for about three years, when he sold his business and acted as traveling salesman for about eight years, making Clayton his home. During the latter period, he bought a part of his father's land in Pea Ridge township, and, discontinuing traveling, he engaged in general farming, making a specialty of horticulture. In 1874 he engaged in the nursery business and raising of small fruits, in which he continued successfully for some time Finally, in 1884, he removed to Mount Sterling, the county seat, his present home, where he continued the nursery and fruit business, to which he later added that of floriculture. His natural adaptability and careful attention to business have resulted in well-merited success, while his liberal methods and uniform courtesy have secured for him a constantly increasing patronage, until he now realizes a comfortable income from these various industries

Mr. Shank was married in 1867, to Miss Sue Mead, an estimable lady and a native of Morgan county, Ohio. She was a daughter of Zaccheus and Margaret (Logue) Mead, the former a native of New York, where he was reared and married. He and his wife were prominent and esteemed pioneers of Morgan county, Ohio, where they resided many years, the father finally expiring there, regretted by his family and many friends The mother still survives, and makes her home with her daughter, Mrs. Shank.

Mr. and Mrs. Shank have four children: Jesse E., Samuel M., Nora A. and Joe H.

Politically, Mr. Shank affiliates with the Republican party. Religiously, he is a member of the Presbyterian Church, while his wife belongs to the Methodist Episcopal denomination. Both are esteemed residents of Mount Sterling, to the social and financial status of which they have given material aid by their energy, public spirit and sterling worth.

GEORGE W. TRONE, one of the most practical and progressive farmers of Schuyler county, has resided here since he was a youth of fifteen years. He was born in Carroll county, Maryland, April 4, 1849, a son of Adam Trone, a native of York county, Pennsylvania. The father was a miller by trade, and followed that vocation in Pennsylvania and Maryland; he settled in Carroll county before his marriage, and resided there until 1858, when he removed to Illinois and settled at Astoria, Fulton county; there he operated a mill until 1863, when he invested in land in Rushville township; the remainder of his life was devoted to agriculture. He was united in marriage to Rebecca Erb, a native of Carroll county, and a daughter of John Erb. The paternal ancestors of our subject were of German extraction, while those on the mother's side were of Irish origin. Mrs. Trone still resides on the farm in Rushville township. George W. received his education in the common schools of his native county, and at Astoria and in Rushville township. When but a boy he began to assist his father in the mill, but he preferred farming, and did not follow the trade any length of time. After the family removed to Rushville township he was occupied on the farm until he attained his majority.

In 1871 he bought a tract of land in Bainbridge township, one-half of which he sold afterward. In 1880 he purchased the farm he now occupies; it consists of 150 acres of land in Rushville township, and the most of it is in a high state of cultivation. In 1883 he sold fifty-three acres. Mr. Trone devotes his entire time to farming and stock-raising; he breeds high-class registered stock, and frequently exhibits at the county and State fairs, and as frequently carries off the prizes.

He was married in 1874 to Sarah R. Boise, a native of Rushville township and a daughter of Matthew Boise; they have three children: Libbie E., George Carl and Earl R. The mother is a worthy member of the Methodist Episcopal Church. Politically, Mr. Trone affiliates with the Democratic party.

RENSSELAER WELLS was born in Lorain county, Ohio, February 22, 1823. He was the son of Charles and Elizabeth (Durand) Wells. The latter was a native of Connecticut, came to Illinois when subject was eleven years old, and settled in Littleton township, this county, and died at Rushville, aged sixty-five years. His wife was born in the same county as her son, and she died on the old farm, aged thirty-five.

Subject remained at home until his marriage, when he bought his present farm and put up a log cabin, where they lived for several years, until he built the frame house in which they lived until 1871. He then built their present fine residence, which cost $3,500. He has now about 500 acres of land, where he carries on mixed farming, and he has made this farm one of the finest in the county.

He was married in 1844, to Rebecca Rose, born in Morgan county, Illinois, daughter of Randolph and Rebecca (Bazier) Rose, the latter of Kentucky. Mrs. Rose died in this county. Mr. and Mrs. Rose were among the earliest settlers, and Mrs. Wells was one of eight children, five yet living. Mr. Wells is one of seven children, two yet living.

Mr. and Mrs. Wells have had seven children: George, married and has three children, Randolph, married and has two children; William, at home; David, married and has two children; Charles, married and has one child; Mary A., single and at home. They have all been well educated. Mr. and Mrs. Wells are members of the Christian Church, and Mr. Wells is a Democrat, voting first in 1844. He takes no active part in politics.

He traces his grandfather Durand back to his residence in France, of which country he was a native, first settling in Ohio, where he died when a very old man.

Mr. and Mrs. Wells are very good people, and are highly respected by all who have the pleasure of knowing them.

HON. JOHN C. BAGBY, attorney at law, was born in Glasgow, Barren county, Kentucky, January 24, 1819. His father was Rev. Sylvanus M. Bagby, a native of Louisa county, Virginia, born September 29, 1787. His grandfather was Richard Bagby, a native of the same county, and his great grandfather was John Bagby, a native of Scotland, who went from there to Wales, where he married and lived a number of years, and then came to America in colonial times, accompanied by his family, and settled in Virginia. He settled in Louisa county, where he became a prominent planter and slave owner. Richard Bagby, the son of John Bagby, and grandfather of our subject, was also a planter and passed his entire life in Louisa county. His wife was Miss Sarah Kimbrough, a native of the Old Dominion and of Welsh descent. The father of our subject, Sylvanus M. Bagby, was left an orphan at an early age and was cared for by an uncle, John Bagby, of Rocbkridge county, Virginia. He learned the carpenter trade, and in 1808 removed to Kentucky, and was one of the early settlers of Glasgow. While there, in June, 1813, he married Miss Frances S. Courts, a native of Caroline county, Virginia, born May 17, 1793, her father, John Courts, being a native of England, and an early emigrant to Virginia. His wife was Frances Winn, a native of Culpeper, Virginia.

Sylvanus M. Bagby was converted in early youth and joined the Baptist Church. He became a preacher of that demonination, but did not give up his trade as a carpenter, which he followed during the week, preaching on Sundays. He remained a member of the Baptist Chnrch until 1828, when he accepted the religious doctrines of Alexander Campbell, whom he assisted in organizing a Christian Church in Barren county, and was from that time forward a minister of that denomination. He resided in Glasgow until 1842, when, with his wife and eight daughters, he journeyed overland to Illinois, stopping at Rushville, where he engaged in the mercantile business. Later he purchased a farm, a portion of which is now inclnded in the city, upon which is located the railroad depot. He died in 1848, having lived a useful, pious and honorable life. His wife passed away in 1858. She reared ten children as follows: Albert K., who still resides in Glasgow; Martha A. Hall; Frances H. Montgomery; Clara Ramsey; Sarah C.; Elizabeth Lusk; Mary M. Doyle; Emily C., Zorelda VanHosen, and our subject, John C.

In the school of Barren county our subject, John C. Bagby, was educated, supplementing the same by an attendance at Bacon College, which at that time was located in Georgetown, but later was removed to Harrodsburg. He continued at this college until his graduation as a civil engineer, in 1840, when he returned to Glasgow, and taught school five years, devoting his spare moments to the study of law with Judge Christopher Tompkins of that town. He was admitted to the bar in 1846 and in April of that year came to Rushville and began the practice. In 1847 he formed a partnership with William A. Minshall, which partnership continued until 1848, when Mr. Minshall was elected Circuit Judge. Mr. Bagby, with the exception of the time spent in Congress, continued the practice of law until he was elected Circuit Judge in 1885. He cast his first presidential vote for William Henry Harrison, and was a prominent Whig and Free Soiler until 1856, when he was one of seven to organize the Republican party in this county. He continued a Republican until 1872, when he branched off and voted for Horace Greeley, since which event he has affiliated with the Democratic party. He has filled various offices of trust, and in 1874 was elected a member of Congress. He served as Circuit Judge six years, entering upon his duties in 1885. He has been a member of Rushville Lodge, No. 9, A. F. & A. M., for forty-six years, and was Master of the lodge eleven terms. He was one of the organizers of Stapleton Chapter, No. 9, R. A. M., and has been a member of the order of the Sons of Temperance. On October 1, 1850, he married Miss Mary A. Scripps, a native of Cape Girardean county, Missouri, and daughter of George H. and Mary (Hyler) Scripps. They have been blessed with nine children: Mary Frances; John S.; Virginia Ellen, who died at the age of eleven years; Albert; Morris; George Henry, who died aged twenty-seven years; William Ray, who died in infancy; Catherine B.; Arthur F. and Edwin H.

HENRY CRASKE, a member of the State Board of Equalization, a resident of Rushville, and one of its most prominent citizens, was born in Bury St. Edmunds, Suffolk county, England, September 26, 1845. His father, James Craske, was born in the same place, January 4, 1798, and his grandfather was also a native of England, where he passed his entire life. James Craske was the only one of his children to come to America. He was reared and educated in his native land and lived there until 1862, when he came to this country and located at Little Falls, New York, where he still lives, at the unusual age of ninety-four years. His wife's maiden name was Eliza Clark, a native of Barton Mills, England, and died in Bury St. Edmunds, of the same country, in 1849. Her children were named Marianne, Sarah, James, Caroline, Elizabeth and Henry, all of whom were reared to maturity.

The original of this sketch and the youngest of the family was educated in the public schools of Bury St. Edmunds, and when fifteen years of age joined his older brother and sisters in America. He located in York State, where he continued to reside. On September 5, 1862, he enlisted in Company A, One Hundred and Fifty-second New York Volunteer Infantry, and served with distinction until the close of the war He was in the Second Army Corps, of the second division, and at different times was connected with the First, Second and Third Brigades. At the battle of the Wilderness, May 6, 1863, he was wounded in the head by a minie ball while charging the enemy's lines, a portion of his skull being torn away On the following day he fell into the hands of the enemy and lay on the field without medical attendance for fourteen days The provisions of the rebels ran short and they sent word to the Federal commander that he might supply his wounded with food and medicine. Consequently a forage train was sent upon the field when Mr. Craske managed to crawl aboard and in that way escape to the Union lines He remained in the hospital until the last of June, when he joined his regiment and remained with it in all its campaigns, marches and battles until he was honorably discharged, July 14, 1865.

Upon the termination of his military career he returned to York State and on December 23, 1865, was united in marriage to Miss Ellen Maria Jones, a native of Little Falls and a daughter of Elijah and Jane Jones, born respectively in England and New York. On the 23d of April, 1866, he came West, and located in Springfield, Illinois, and there followed his trade, that of a dyer, until March 28, 1868, when he removed to Rushville and resumed his trade, continuing until 1870, when he went to Decatur and lived a year and a half and then returned to Rushville and engaged in the grocery business and in buying and shipping produce to St. Louis, Chicago, New York and Boston, continuing the same for a number of years Mr. and Mrs. Craske have seven interesting children: Geneva A, Caroline Elizabeth, Mamie, Frances C, Harry Barton, Lillian M. and John A Logan Fraternally Mr Craske is a member of Rushville Lodge, No 9, A F & A M ; Rushville Chapter, No 184, R A M ; and Rushville Commandery No 56, K. T. He is also a member of the A. O U W and of Security Lodge, No. 31, I. O. M. A.; and also of Colonel Harney Post, No 131, G. A R

Mr Craske has taken considerable interest in politics and in that difficult and doubtful field has distinguished himself He was elected a member of the State Board of Equalization in 1888, and in 1885 was the originator of the scheme in the Thirty-fourth District which elected a Republican Representative to the State Legislature, thus breaking the dead lock which had tied up the General Assembly for months and ended in the election of John A Logan for United States Senator. The following letter explains itself, and shows how the part taken by Mr. Craske contributed to Republican success:

LELAND HOTEL, Springfield, Ill.
May 20, 1885

HENRY CRASKE,

My Dear Sir: The election is over and the victory is ours To the Thirty fourth Representative District we are indebted for the vote that gave us the majority in the Legislature, and to you, my dear sir, there is much due for the organization and success. You were the first man who suggested to me the possibility of carrying the district I wrote you then, saying the plan was a good one Of course, great credit is due to all our friends who aided in carrying out the programme from whom I would not wish to detract anything; but to you I give the credit as the originator of the plan which was a success, and to you I now return my grateful acknowledgments. Your friend,

JOHN A. LOGAN.

It should be said by way of explanation, that in the Thirty-fourth General Assembly the two houses were a tie on joint ballot and in consequence there was a dead lock in the Senatorial contest which continued under great excitement for months. On the 12th of April, a Democratic member of the Thirty-fourth Senatorial District died, and a special election was called for May 6th to fill his seat. In that district the Democrats had a majority of 2,000, and therefore felt certain of electing their nominee. Mr. Craske wrote a letter suggesting a still hunt and the plans to be pursued to secure success. His plan was submitted to General Logan and by him to the Republican caucus, and were adopted and acted upon. The result fully met their anticipations, the Republican nominee was elected, the Democrats were out-generaled and astonished, and even the people in distant States were filled with surprise. The movement was so adroit that General Logan pronounced it the most daring piece of political strategy, so successfully executed, since the days of Alexander the Great.

WILLIAM BURACKER was born on a farm in township 17, range 9, Cass county, Illinois, September 14, 1846.

His parents, Philip A., and Jane (Holzman) Buracker, were born, reared and married in Page county, Virginia, and in 1844 came to Illinois, making the journey with a team. They located on the farm on which their son William was born, and there resided six years. They then moved to a farm in range 10, of the same township, where they passed the rest of their lives. The father died May 28, 1891, at the age of sixty-eight years. The mother passed away in 1873. They reared three children, William, Alfred and George. Alfred is deceased.

William Buracker was reared and educated, and has passed his life thus far, in his native county. He was brought up on the farm, and has since been engaged in agricultural pursuits. When he attained his majority he commenced farming for himself on his father's land, and in 1870 his father gave him the farm he has since occupied, which is located in section 27, township 17, range 10. In connection with his agricultural pursuits he is also engaged in stock raising.

In 1868 Mr. Buracker was united in marriage with Helen C. Heslep, a native of Cass county, and a daughter of Thomas and Catherine Heslep. Mr. and Mrs. Buracker have two children, Philip T. and Katie.

Politically, Mr. Buracker has always affiliated with the Democratic party, and is a most efficient member of the same. He was elected a member of the Board of County Commissioners in 1885, and was re-elected in 1888. In this capacity he has always worked for the good of the entire county, ever taking a bold stand in favor of the right.

FRED W. KORSMEYER, one of the most successful men of this locality, lives on section 30, township 17, range 12. He is a German, being born in Hanover, January 15, 1838. His parents were J. H. and Mary (Lovecamp) Korsmeyer, who were born in the same place, and descended from the best German blood. When our subject was thirteen years of age they came to the

United States in the fall of 1851. They took the usual passage of their fellow countrymen, from Bremer to New Orleans, and from there up the Mississippi and Illinois rivers to Beardstown They located very near the present home of our subject, and here they lived and died, the father about sixty, and the mother seventy They had always been members of the German Lutheran Church and are remembered as good, honest German settlers of that early day Our subject and a brother, Herman, are the only living members of the family.

Mr. Korsmeyer began farming on his own account about the time of his majority His first was a purchase of 140 acres, and he increased it from time to time until he now owns 600 acres, the most of which is under the plow He has made many improvements on the farm he has owned for the past thirty years He has very fine land, lying in the bottoms of the Illinois river, and adjoining the Meredosia lake

Mr Korsmeyer was married in Cass county, to Miss Minnie Miller, who came from her birthplace, in Hanover, Germany, when young Her parents settled in Beardstown, where her father died some years ago, at the home of his daughter, as did also his wife They had lived to good old age and had been valued members of the Lutheran Church. Mrs. Korsmeyer is the youngest of three children. Her two brothers are Fred, a Morgan county farmer, and Henry, who lives in Springfield Mr. and Mrs Korsmeyer have seven living children· Henry and Herman assist in running the farm, Emma, William C., Christian, and Theodore and Charles, the twins, live at home The children are all naturally bright, and the parents intend to educate them thoroughly. The family is Lutheran in religion, and Mr Korsmeyer is very prominent in the politics of his township, being a Democrat, and has held almost all of the local offices He is now a candidate for County Commissioner, and so popular is he that this means a certain election They are among the most prominent people in the township

ADAM SCHUMAN, one of the enterprising and successful young farmers of section 13, range 12, owning a farm of 120 acres which he has occupied since the death of his father, John A Schuman, in October, 1886, has been the proprietor of the farm where he was born, reared and educated The date of his birth is February 13, 1851 Since he came into possession of the farm, he has greatly improved it and made it very successful, having it well stocked and employing good farm hands Although only a young man, he is ambitious and is bound to succeed.

Adam is the only son of John Adam and Katie (Loab) Schuman, both natives of Germany, of good ancestry They were born, reared and educated in Germany, and while yet young came in the early forties to America, sailing from Hesse Darmstadt, arriving after several weeks' voyage in New Orleans, coming from there to St. Louis, Missouri Here he stopped for a short time and unfortunately was taken sick and was taken to the hospital. As soon as he was able to leave he came to Beardstown, with the help of an old friend, Valentine Thron After his arrival in Beardstown, he worked for six months for Mr. Thron to repay him for his kindness; later John A Schuman was engaged as a butcher for a time, but later purchased land on section 13, township 17, range 12, at which place he spent the remainder of his life as a farmer, dying at the age of sixty-six. He was a good and worthy citizen, straightforward and upright in all his dealings with his fellow men. He was a prominent member and a good worker in the German Methodist Church, to which he was a generous supporter, being always ready to help everything that tended toward the advancement of good principles. The Sunday-school received much of his attention. He was a sound Democrat in politics. His wife died some years before in 1865, when she was forty years of age. She was a good, Christian woman, a faithful wife and devoted mother, a kind neighbor and a worthy member of the Emanuel Methodist Episcopal Church, near Arenzville.

Adam was the only son in the family, but there were four daughters, Lizzie, wife of George Hauffman, farmer of this township; Mary, wife of Joseph Pierce, of Bluff Springs precinct; Lydia, wife of William Schute, also of Bluff Springs; and Amelia, wife of Charles Johnson, a farmer of Beardstown.

Mr. Schuman was married, at Arenzville, to Miss Lizzie Thron, a native of this county, being born, reared and educated here. She is the daughter of Valentine and Margaret (Bier) Thron, natives of Hesse Darmstadt, Germany. They were young, single people when they came to the United States, settling in Illinois, where they were married, in the city of Beardstown, where Mr. Thron engaged in wagon-making, and was thus engaged for some years, when he purchased land in the early fifties in township 17, range 12, and there lived for some years. Later he removed to Arenzville, and there his wife died, in January, 1884. She was then quite an old woman and a worthy member of the Lutheran Church, to which she had belonged all her life. She was a good, kind wife and mother, and was highly respected by all her neighbors. Mr. Thron now makes his home with his daughter, Mrs. Schuman, and passed his eighty-second birthday in June, 1892. He has been a good, hard-working man all his life and a consistent member of the Lutheran Church. He is a Democrat in politics.

Mr. and Mrs. Thron were the parents of nine children, six yet living and all are married, being successful in life. Mr. and Mrs. Schuman are active workers in the Emanuel Lutheran Church, and Mr. Schuman takes especial interest in the Sunday-school. He is a good and worthy man.

Mr. Schuman and his wife are the parents of six children: John W., Mary L., Fred G., Liddy E., Elmer and Myrtle.

NEWTON LUCAS, a resident of Pea Ridge township, was born in what is now Cooperstown township, December 11, 1838. His father, D. R. Lucas, was one of the pioneers of Brown county, born in Butler county, Ohio, March 21, 1810. His father, John Lucas, was born September 7, 1760, in Virginia, and was a soldier in the Revolutionary war. He was taken prisoner by the Indians and by them taken to Kentucky and Ohio. He was pleased with the country, and after the close of the war located in Kentucky, but failed to secure a good title to his land and lost it, and then went to that part of Ohio now included in Butler county, secured a large tract of land in the Miami bottom, improved a farm, residing there until his death June 15, 1836. His wife's name was Jemima Robbins, who was born November 19, 1768, who died on the home farm, November 22, 1831, aged sixty-three years. She was the mother of twelve children. Daniel Robbins Lucas was raised in his native county, but when a young man went to Indiana and commenced the study of medicine

In January, 1836, he came to Mt. Sterling. Illinois, and commenced to practice his profession. He also engaged in teaching and in the mercantile and lumber business About 1843 he purchased land in Lee township, and resided there the greater part of the time until his death, which occurred January 26, 1884 His wife's name was Sarah Ann Keith, to whom he was married in 1836; she was born in Hardin county, Kentucky, December 14, 1817, and died March 22, 1890. She was the mother of twelve children, their names are. William, Newton, Martha, Ann (now dead), Mary E, George W. Henry C (now dead), John H, Ethan A, Helen A. (now dead), Daniel W, Benjamin F., James E. Three dead and nine living, seven of whom live in the county. one, B F, lives in Colorado I. E. lives in Missouri. Newton received his earlier education in the pioneer schools which were held in the log houses with furniture of the most primitive kind, where the teacher boarded around among the scholars; as soon as he was large enough to manage a yoke of oxen he worked upon the farm He caught the Pike's Peak fever in the spring of 1860, went across the plains in an ox wagon to the Rocky Mountains, returned in July of same year He met with an accident December 25, 1860, while cutting a tree for firewood; in trying to get out of the way of some falling limbs, the tree struck and crushed his hip, making a cripple of him for life. He was appointed route agent on mail route from Clayton, Illinois, to Keokuk, Iowa, in 1864, but after some two months' service resigned; taught school during the winter of 1862–'63 at what is now Fargo, in this county, taught at Ashland, Adams county, during the winter of 1869–'70; remained with his parents until he was married in 1865, then farmed and operated a saw mill until the spring of 1871, when he moved to Scotland county, Missouri, and operated a saw mill for three years; then moved to Memphis, Missouri, and went into the hay business with his brother for two years; moved back to Brown county, Illinois, engaged in farming and running a sawmill, operated a sawmill on Sangamon river bottom during the winter of 1880–'81, moved to Mt Sterling in the spring of 1882, and operated a steam thresher, lived there until December, 1883, then bought the farm he now lives upon; owns 220 acres; farm is well improved and has good buildings; the house he built himself

In politics he is a Republican; cast his first ballot for Abraham Lincoln for president, and Richard Yates for governor; has always been a Republican; and was a delegate to the Republican State Convention, May 4, 1892.

August 29, 1865, he married Barbara Frank, who was born in Davison county, North Carolina, February 21, 1842, daughter of William and Sarah (Winkler) Frank. Mr. and Mrs. Lucas have three children. Minnie S, William D, Ruth R. Minnie is the wife of Henry L Lee and has two children; they live in Maxwell City, New Mexico

---

B. A. WARDEN, senior member of the firm of Warden & Son, proprietors of the Rushville *Republican*, was born in Clermont county, Ohio, January 2, 1839. His father, Moses Warden, was a native of Pennsylvania, and in his youth was converted to the Christian religion and became a preacher of the gospel; he learned the trade of a saddler, and followed this vocation in addition to his ministerial labors. When quite a young man he went to Ohio, and there was married to Margaret Anderson, a native of Brown county, Ohio Mr. Warden lived in Bethel, Clermont county, and there worked at his trade and preached in the Methodist Episcopal Church; later he purchased a farm near Bethel, and engaged in agriculture; there he passed the last days of his life. His only brother, Richard Warden, settled in the same county, and there spent the remainder of his life The mother of our subject died in 1851. There was a family of seven children Anderson, William, Martha L, Salathiel L, Margaret L., Sarah E., and Francis A.

Francis A was a lad of twelve years when his father died, and one year later the mother passed away; he was then cared for by his older brothers and sisters, and was reared and educated in his native county At the age of seventeen years he began clerking in a drug store at Felicity, Ohio, and was thus employed for two years; at the end of this period he became a partner in the business, which was continued until 1876 In that year he came to Shelby county, Illinois, and engaged in mercantile trade, which he conducted eight years. Ray Warden, son of Francis A, having learned the art of printing, engaged in the business at Stewardson and Cowden, Shelby county, conducting a paper at each place for a year; at the end of twelve months he went to Augusta, Hancock county, and published the Augusta *Eagle* for eight years; during all this time his father was a partner in the business, and in January, 1891, they (F. A Warden and son, S. R. Warden,) came to Schuyler county, and established the Rushville *Republican*. This is a well edited sheet, newsy, and a loyal supporter of Republican principles.

Mr Warden was married in 1863, to Olive B. Leffingwell, a native of Williamsburg, Ohio, and daughter of Sidney and Melissa Leffingwell Five children have been born to them: S. Ray, F. Ella, Louise, Mary E, and Jessie.

During the late civil war, Mr. Warden supported the Government of the Union; he cast his first vote for Abraham Lincoln, and has since affiliated with the Republican party; he and his wife are worthy members of the Methodist Episcopal Church He belongs to Rushville Lodge, No 9, A F. and A. M, to the Knights of Honor Lodge, No 990, and to Augusta Camp, M. W A

WILLIAM D DORSETT was born in Randolph county, North Carolina, December 28, 1828 His father was Azariah Dorsett, a native of the same State, who was a cooper by trade, but he also followed farming for a livelihood. In 1835 he came in a six-horse wagon with his family, consisting of a wife and twelve of his fourteen children, to Illinois, camping out over night on their entire trip to Schuyler county. They settled in what is now Huntsville township, and a little later bought a tract of land upon which a few acres had been broken and a log cabin erected. The cabin was a very rough, primitive concern, with a roof of boards rived by hand, and a chimney of sods After a little while this was replaced by a more pretentious and comfortable structure. Here he resided until his death in 1840. His widow died the following morning, and both were buried in the same grave. The mother was formerly Mary Beckerdite, of North Carolina, who reared to maturity fourteen children.

Our subject, William D Dorsett, was six years old when he was brought to Illinois by his parents, and he well remembers the wild animals that could be seen almost daily in the woods and on the prairie. At that time it was easy to find an abundance of wild honey, as an experienced bee-hunter could tell the location of a bee tree by watching the flight of the insect. Gristmills were very scarce, and often could not be reached at all. In this extremity the early settlers were compelled to grate their corn and wheat by hand, and Mr Dorsett recollects having eaten many a meal of this homely food At first the people of this vicinity had to go to mill fifty miles below Quincy, and were absent several days. He was quite young when his parents died, and was taken to live with an older brother. He bought forty acres of land in Birmingham township, at $10 an acre, paying for it by installments. When he began housekeeping, after his marriage, he had neither table nor chairs to commence with, and instead thereof had three bee-hives, one of which was used as a table and the other two for stools Some kind person presented them with a dry-goods box, which was made to serve as a cupboard, and a bedstead was presented to them by Mrs Dorsett's father This was considered a great luxury But this little home, though humble and rude, was made comfortable and bright by Mrs Dorsett, who took great pride in making it cozy and comfortable. Mr Dorsett went to work with a will, was very industrious and his wife very economical, and together they have come to prosperous circumstances and a happy home He secured early employment as a rail-splitter, like Abraham Lincoln, and it was not his fault that he did not reach the presidency instead of Mr. Lincoln. The first money he thus earned was used to buy his first table After a period of seven years he was the owner of sixty acres, free from incumbrance, which he then traded for 100 acres in Huntsville township, and at the close of his career as a farmer in Illinois he was the owner of 400 acres of rich Huntsville soil and a section of land in Texas. In 1883 he rented his farm and came to Rushville, and has since lived a retired life.

On the 15th of November, 1849, he was married to Elizabeth Ann Pendleton, who was born in Hardin county, Kentucky, July 11, 1832. Her father was Edwin Pendleton, a native Virginian, and her grandfather was James Pendleton, also of that State Her father was reared in his native State, and went to Kentucky when a young man, and was there united in marriage. He learned the shoemaker's trade, which he followed for a few years, and in 1830 came to Illinois He came the entire distance on horseback, accompanied by his wife and eldest child. Upon his arrival here his entire possessions consisted of two horses and 50 cents in money One of the horses died soon after crossing the Ohio river He located in Huntsville township, entered land from the Government, upon which he built a log house and commenced to improve his farm Mrs Dorsett's mother was a thorough pioneer woman and knew how to make cloth from flax and cotton Her daughter, Mrs. Dorsett, learned the art, and after her marriage made all the clothing for her family. Mr and Mrs Dorsett have had six children: Martha L., Hattie E., Joshua E., Ellis Benson, Hardin Wallace and Alvin De W. The parents are members of the First Methodist Episcopal Church of Rushville.

Both Mr and Mrs. Dorsett in their youth attended the pioneer schools of this county, where they learned "readin', ritin' and rithmetic,"—the three R's, as they were termed. The schoolhouse, of course, was a log building, and a very rough one at that. The seats were made of slats, and wooden pins served for legs. Holes were bored in the wall, pins inserted, and a board laid thereon served as a desk upon which the older scholars, with quill pens, learned to write. The windows consisted of a section taken out of the side of the house and the aperture covered with greased paper, which served to admit the light.

JOHN T. BRADBURY was born in Harrison county, West Virginia, March 4, 1840. His father is James Lee Bradbury, born in Virginia in 1816. He was reared on the farm and when he was twenty-three he went to Kentucky and engaged in teaching for some forty years. He came to Illinois in the fall of 1847, bringing his wife and two children. They came across the country in a lumber wagon and a horse team. It took them about thirty days to make the trip. Mr. Bradbury soon secured a school in Brown county. They soon moved into Mt. Sterling, where they lived until 1858. Mrs. Bradbury died in 1857, in the prime of her life, thirty-six, leaving five children to mourn her loss, namely: John T.; Nancy, deceased; James R., carpenter; Margaret Mallory; William, a farmer on the bluffs of the Illinois river.

John was brought up to be industrious and was well educated. At sixteen he began to study under Dr. Witty at Mt. Sterling. In summer he took charge of the farm, but in the winter studied under the instruction of the able Dr. Witty. In 1859 he went to the Missouri Medical College at St. Louis, and graduated in 1861. He opened his first office in Ripley, but very soon closed it and went to Hiawatha, Kansas, in the spring of 1861. Here he remained, practicing until 1863, when he returned home and enlisted in the One Hundred and Nineteenth Illinois Infantry, Company D. He was in the service three years, but most of the time as hospital surgeon. He was mustered out at Mobile, Alabama. In the spring of 1865 he returned to Missouri, at Parke, in Sharon county, and opened an office, where he practiced for about a year, when he returned to Versailles, in Brown county. Here he opened an office and drug store. In 1872 he sold out and came to Cooperstown, where he has resided since. He has had a large practice these many years and has felt the need of rest at times. He has been Postmaster during the Harrison administration.

He was married in 1861, in Mt. Sterling, to Viola Hatcher, daughter of E. and Maria N. (Brisbin) Hatcher, the former from North Carolina, the latter from Lancaster county, Pennsylvania. She was born in Madison, Indiana. The family came to Illinois in 1856.

Mr. and Mrs Bradbury have had seven children, only three of whom are now living: Samuel E. married to Ellen Logsden, two children; James Mitchel married Kate Hurlett; George Anderson, a youth of fifteen. They have all been educated. Dr. Bradbury is an Odd Fellow and a stanch Republican. He and his wife are very estimable people and are highly respected by all.

JOHN McCABE, well-known in business circles in Schuyler county, Illinois, was born in Coshocton county, Ohio, September 11, 1828. His father, John McCabe, Sr., was a native of Pennsylvania, but was taken to Ohio when quite young by his parents; there he learned the blacksmith's trade, which he followed until 1844. In that year he emigrated to Indiana and settled in Marion county, here he resumed his occupation, remaining for three years. In 1847 he came to Illinois, and settled in the town of Woodland, he afterward entered a tract of land on which he erected a log house; he followed his trade until 1862, when he enlisted in the war He died in 1863, while in the service His wife died in Rushville, Illinois. They reared a family of eight children Our subject resided with his parents until he had attained his majority, when he started out in life for himself; he had worked in a brick-yard three or four seasons, and at the age of twenty-two years he embarked in this business on his own account His first yard was at Littleton, where he conducted a business for two years; thence he removed to Macomb, where he continued until 1862 In June of that year he enlisted in Company A, Eighty-fourth Illinois Volunteer Infantry, and served until the close of the war The most important battles in which he participated were Stone River and Chickamauga; in the latter he was wounded, and so disabled from active duty in the field, when he had sufficiently recovered he was made hospital steward, and served the remainder of the war in that capacity. He was mustered out in August, 1865, after which he returned to Macomb There he remained until the spring of 1866, when he came to Rushville and engaged in the manufacture of brick In 1879 he added machinery for the manufacture of tile, and his products find a ready sale at the yard.

Mr. McCabe was married in 1851, to Mary Clark, a native of Indiana and a daughter of Henry and Margaret Clark Four children have been born to them. James is engaged in business with his father, Arthur is a resident of Versailles, where he is engaged in the practice of medicine, Howard C lives in Rushville, Cora married Allen Walker, and also resides in Rushville; two children died in infancy. The parents are consistent members of the Methodist Episcopal Church, the father joined in May, 1842, and the mother ten years later For thirty years Mr McCabe has been Steward of his church. He is a zealous advocate of temperance, and an ardent supporter of the Prohibition party He is a member of the Tile Manufacturers' Association, and has been treasurer of this body for a number of years He belongs to Colonel Horney Post, No 156, G A R, and is actively interested in its welfare. He is a man of energy and entertains progressive views upon questions of public interest, supporting those movements which tend to aid and elevate the masses

MARK BOYD, a pioneer farmer of Rushville township, now retired from active labor, was born in county Armagh, Ireland, February 6, 1823, a son of William Boyd, a native of the same county. The paternal ancestors were natives of Scotland William Boyd was reared to the life of a farmer, and when he had arrived at man's estate he emigrated to America; this was previous to the war of 1812, and he remained three years; at the end of that period he returned to Ireland, was married, and resided there until 1838. In that year he sailed with his wife and three children for the port of New York, the voyage consuming three weeks He engaged in teaming in New York city, and resided there until 1868, when he bought a farm of 120 acres, on which he lived until his death, February 10,

1868 He married Maria Boyd, who died in Rushville, in 1868; she was the mother of three children Esther J, Mark and Samuel Mark Boyd was a child of five years when he crossed the deep blue sea with his parents. He received his education in New York, the school which he attended being located on Seventeenth street, near Eighth avenue

In 1841 he began to learn the trade of a baker, and followed this calling until 1860, when he went to Orange county, New York; he was employed on a farm until 1867, when he came to Schuyler county, Illinois His first investment here was in a farm of eighty acres, and to this he has made additions until he now owns nearly 200 acres, in Oakland and Rushville townships There he made his home until 1892; in February of this year he removed to Rushville, where he is living in the quiet enjoyment of the reward his years of industry and toil have won.

Mr Boyd was married in New York city, September 11, 1845, to Sarah Fourgeson, the daughter of Daniel Fourgeson Her paternal grandfather, John Fourgeson, was a native of Scotland, and removed to county Derry after his marriage, where he purchased a farm and passed the remainder of his life He married Ann Kennedy, also a native of Scotland Daniel Fourgeson, their son, spent his entire life on the farm where he was born; he married Mary Fulton, a descendant of Scotch ancestors, but a native of county Derry, Ireland, Mrs. Boyd and her sister Elizabeth, wife of Duncan Taylor, were the only members of their family who came to America Mrs. Boyd sailed from Liverpool in 1850, and after twenty-one days on the water reached the port of New York Our subject and wife are the parents of three children. Maria J., Elizabeth and Sarah Maria married James Bill and is the mother of three children; Robert W., Henry and Charles, Elizabeth is the wife of George Manlove, and has a family of three children,—Bessie, Annie and Mark; Sarah married Elijah Wilson, and has a family of six children, Nellie, Annie, Maud, Henry, Walter and Jennie

Mr and Mrs. Boyd were reared in the Presbyterian Church, and have always adhered to that faith. They are people of much force and stability of character, and have reared a family who are an honor to them and a credit to the community in which they live

FRANCIS M. CURRY, a highly respected citizen of Mount Sterling, was born in Scott county, Kentucky, April 9, 1825, a son of John R Curry, who was born October 19, 1803. The paternal grandfather, Alexander Curry, the honored founder of Mount Sterling, Illinois, was born October 14, 1770, in the State of Maryland, the son of Archibald Curry, a native of Scotland, who emigrated to America in colonial times and settled in Maryland, where he passed the remainder of his life Alexander Curry was a pioneer of Scott county, Kentucky; he purchased a tract of land on the Lexington pike, on which he lived until 1830, when he came to Illinois, he was accompanied by his wife and children, and made a settlement in Brown county, which was then a part of Schuyler county. As soon as the land came into market he entered 2,000 acres, including the present site of Mount Sterling, he erected a double log house on the lot now occupied by the Christian Church, which was used at the same time as a dwelling, a justice's room and a meeting-house. He did not keep a hotel but entertained travelers free of charge He was the first Justice of the Peace and the first Postmaster of Mount Sterling In 1833 he laid out the town, and June 21 of that year occurred the first sale of lots. His son, Robert, had the first store in the place, the goods being brought by teams from St. Louis. He continued a resident of the place until his death in 1842 The maiden name of his wife was Elizabeth Nutter, a native of Delaware, born August 20, 1776. They reared a family of nine children: Daniel, Robert N., John R, Olivia, Sarah, Nancy, Leah, Mary and Harriet.

John R Curry was reared and married in Kentucky, and came from the Blue Grass State with his parents. He located on land his father gave him near Mount Sterling, and engaged in farming He died November 17, 1882. He married Belle Brockman, a native of Scott county, Kentucky, born May 15, 1804; she died December 17, 1875. They reared a family of five children. Francis M, James R, Elizabeth, Alexander A. and Mary B Francis M was a child of five years when he came to Illinois with his parents He received his education in the pioneer schools which were taught in the primitive log structures, often without a floor, and furnished with puncheon seats and puncheon desks; the building was erected without nails, and light was admitted by an opening in the wall, which was made by taking out a part of the log, in cold weather this hole was covered by a piece of greased paper At the age of fourteen years Mr Curry began clerking, receiving $12.50 a month the first year, and boarding himself After a few years he engaged in business on his own account, which he conducted successfully a number of years.

He was married September 21, 1853, to Mary Clements, a native of Bourbon county, Kentucky, born March 26, 1829 Her father, William H Clement, was born in Kentucky, and died in that State in 1834; he married Maria Givens, a daughter of John and Ruth Givens. Mr. and Mrs Curry are the parents of five children. Lizzie B, Ida M., Mattie G., Frank C and Charles A; the oldest son, William, died at the age of three and a half years The father and mother are members of the Presbyterian Church Politically our subject has been identified with the Democratic party, but he is a Prohibitionist both in principle and practice He is a man of many excellent traits and has the respect and confidence of the entire community.

FREDERICK E. WELLFARE, foreman of the copper shops of the Quincy Railroad at Beardstown for the past nine years, was born in Candage, Erie county, New York, June 23, 1858. He was but one year old when his parents moved to Illinois He is the son of John Wellfare, who was born in England, of English parentage, and was yet a small child when his parents brought him to the United States and settled in New York. Here he grew up in the town of Candage and acquired a complete knowledge of the coppersmith's trade, also tin, sheet-iron and pipe fitting, and, having become skilled in these departments of mechanical work, he came in 1859 with his family to Illinois. Here he was connected for about two years with a prominent manufacturer of copper pipe, sheet copper and brass goods, and his skill secured him the foremanship of the shops Finally he was offered a partnership, but refused it and went to Aurora to take charge of the copper shops of the main line or Chicago division of the Quincy Railroad

He was afterward connected with this large corporation for about thirty years, but owing to failing health he had to withdraw and entered into the hardware business, in 1883, in Aurora; but, not receiving the proper relief for his malady (catarrh of the head), he went to Kansas, and after two years, not being able to stand the heated winds, he went in 1886 to Los Angeles, California, and there opened and has since carried on a first-class restaurant. He is now about sixty years of age. He was married in Youngstown, New York, to Harriet Myers. She was born and reared in the Empire State, and was of German parentage. She is yet living and is about three years her husband's junior. They are members of the Presbyterian Church, and Mr. Wellfare is a sound Republican in politics.

Our subject is the eldest of three sons and three daughters yet living. He began when about twelve years of age with his father in the Quincy shops. Here he has remained with the exception of about three years. One year he was with his father in his hardware store at Aurora, and later was one year with the Chicago, Milwaukee & St. Paul Railroad, with headquarters at Dubuque, Iowa, and the last year with the Kansas City, St. Joseph & Council Bluffs Railroad, with headquarters at St. Joseph, Missouri. Since then he has been in the employ of the Quincy Railroad, for the last eleven years at Beardstown. He is a practical and thorough workman in his department. He also does the tin and sheet-iron work for the St. Louis division, and the steam-pipe fitting for it also.

He was married in Aurora, to Miss Almira Warner, of New York, born in 1862. She was brought to Cook county in 1867, and reared near the city of Chicago. She is the daughter of John P. and Julia (Havens) Warner, both now living near Aurora. Mr. Warner is a stock-breeder, and he and family live on a farm one mile southeast of Aurora.

Mr. and Mrs. Wellfare are good, hard-working young people. Mr. Wellfare is a member of the Ark Lodge, No. 116, I. O. O. F., of Beardstown. He is a sound Republican. Mr. and Mrs. Wellfare are the parents of two bright little children,—Lydia, aged seven, and Dare, aged four.

CHAUNCEY RICE, a well known and reliable druggist, and dealer in all kinds of goods generally carried by those in this business, was born in St. Lawrence county, New York, February 21, 1830. He was yet young when his parents moved to Ohio in 1842, and to Illinois in 1846. They were natives of New York. His father was born in Herkimer county, and came of New England stock, his parents being natives of Connecticut, and the family came of Welsh ancestry. Andrus Rice, father of our subject, married a Miss Mary Parks, of Vermont.

Chauncey is the eldest of the four surviving children. Mr. Rice has been in the drug business, and in the building he now occupies ever since 1859. He was in the same business in Rushville, Illinois, from 1850 to 1856, and hence is one of the oldest druggists in the State. He has seen the State struggle through many changes in the last fifty years. Nearly all the railroads have been built since then. He has taken an active part in the building up of the city himself, and has lent a helping hand to all enterprises, and has attended closely to business, and has made money. He was a director and stockholder in the old Cass County Bank, and a stockholder in the first State bank since it started. He is also a member and stockholder of the Beardstown Building and Loan Association.

He was first married in Hancock county, Illinois, to Miss Emily J. Denney, of Bond county, Illinois, but reared and married in Hancock county. She died in Nebraska, when in the prime of life, leaving three children: James, a commercial traveler in Iowa; Mary J., wife of Henry J. Nead; Chauncey A., now with a theatrical troupe in the West. Mr. Rice was married for the second time, to Elizabeth J. Knight, of Beardstown, but born in England. She died here April 4, 1892, aged about fifty years. Mr. Rice and wife have always been identified as members of the Methodist Episcopal Church. He is a member of the order of I. O. O. F., and Knights of Honor.

MARTIN BROOKS, editor of the Mount Sterling *Examiner*, was born in Jacksonville, in 1836. His father, Samuel S., came from Connecticut, of Scotch ancestry.

Martin commenced very young to learn the trade of printer, and was employed in different places until 1863, when he came to Mount Sterling, and with his brother Samuel bought the office and good will of the Mount Sterling *Union*, a weekly paper, and changed the name to the Mount Sterling *Record*. He was elected Circuit Clerk in 1864, and served eight years, and then bought an interest in the Mount Sterling *Message*, and two years later sold out, and was clerking in the courthouse for a time. In 1879 he bought the furniture and lease of the Lambert House, and kept hotel two years, and then resumed clerking in the courthouse. In 1883, he was elected Police Magistrate, and served two terms. In the meantime, with George S. Campbell he bought the Mount Sterling *Examiner*, and has been its editor ever since.

He was married in 1867, to Sophia S. Price, of Brown county, who died in 1869. In 1872 he was married to Nannie Kendrick.

He has two daughters by his second marriage: Mabel Claire and Bernice A. He belongs to Hardin Lodge, No. 44, A. F. & A. M., is a Democrat, and he and his wife belong to the Christian Church.

WILLIAM M. COX, M. D., one of the leading members of the medical profession in Brown county, Illinois, was born five miles from Jacksonville, Morgan county, Illinois. His father, Charles Cox, was a native of Virginia, and removed from that State to Kentucky, where he married; he afterward removed to Indiana, and thence to Morgan county, Illinois, where he was one of the early settlers; he located there previous to the "winter of the deep snow" (1830–'31), and experienced all the hardships and privations of that year. His brother, Hon. Jerry Cox, settled there at the same time. He entered a tract of Government land, on which he erected a log cabin. For several years after his settlement there wild game was plentiful, and the merchandise was brought from St. Louis by teams. The first railroad in the State was the one from Jacksonville to Naples, and the cars were first drawn by horses. Mr. Cox improved his farm, built good frame buildings, and resided there several years. He removed to Adams county and bought a farm, on which he made his home one year; at the end of that time he sold and moved to Hancock county, where he purchased a large tract of land opposite Keokuk; there he was extensively engaged in general farming, raising and feeding large numbers of live-stock, and carrying on a profitable business. He married Rachel N Craig, who was born in Kentucky and died at her home in Hancock county; his death also occurred at the home farm They had a family of seven children, six of whom grew to mature years William M., their son, received his education in the public schools, and at the age of nineteen years turned his attention to the study of medicine, his first work was done under the direction of Dr. McGougin, of Keokuk, and he afterward entered the medical department of the Iowa State University, from which he was graduated in 1860, ten years later he received a diploma from the College of Physicians, New York, and in 1878 he was graduated from the College of Physicians and Surgeons, Keokuk, Iowa. He began the practice of his profession at Bloomfield, Iowa, in 1860, and upon the breaking out of the Civil war he entered the United States service as First Surgeon of the Third Iowa Cavalry; after three months he was stricken with typhoid fever and was compelled to resign his position In 1862 he settled in Liberty, Adams county, and remained there until 1877, when he came to Mount Sterling, where he has since been in active practice He has been an indefatigable worker, a close student, and has kept fully abreast of the times upon all subjects pertaining to the great science.

The fire of May, 1892, destroyed his library, which was one of the most extensive and valuable to be found in Illinois outside the city of Chicago.

Dr. Cox was united in marriage to Effie M Morris, who was born in Payson, Adams county, Illinois, a daughter of Israel and Emily H. Morris Of this union one child has been born, Eleanor M. The mother and daughter are members of the Presbyterian Church Politically, the Doctor affiliates with the Democratic party He is a member of Hardin Lodge, No 44, A. F & A M ; of the Chapter, R. A. M , and of Delta Commandery, No 48, K T. He belongs to the Adams County and American Medical Societies, and is highly esteemed in professional, business and social circles for his many excellent traits, his ability as a physician, and his unswerving devotion to his country's interests

D. MARION STOVER is the present superintendent of schools in Schuyler county, Illinois He was born in Bainbridge township, this county, October 27, 1848, a son of Samuel Stover, a native of Page county, Virginia, born in November, 1813; he was a son of Samuel Stover, whose father was also named Samuel Stover The parental great grandfather, who lived in Shenandoah county, Virginia, married Barbara Lionbarger The paternal grandfather emigrated to Ohio in 1816, and was a pioneer of Licking county; he purchased a tract of land on which was a log house and other scant improvements; there were no market towns, and cattle and other live-stock had to be driven to Baltimore and other eastern markets; the wife carded and spun and wove the cloth with which her children were clothed, the maiden name of the paternal grandmother was Susanna Brumback, a native of Virginia, who died in Licking county, Ohio She reared a family of thirteen children; the father of our subject was a child of three years when his parents removed to Ohio; there he was reared, receiving his education in the subscription schools that were taught in the primitive log cabin. He remained with his parents until he attained his majority, and then started out in life for himself. He first rented land and carried on farming in this way for three years; at the end of that time he turned his attention to the carpenter's trade, which he followed until 1845, when he came to Illinois; he made the journey overland, accompanied by his wife and one child. He settled in what is now Bainbridge township, on land which he had purchased previous to coming here, the quarter section costing $150. Then there were no railroads, and grain had to be delivered at river towns. Mr. Stover went to work diligently to improve his farm, erecting substantial buildings, and placing the land under good cultivation; he lived on this place until 1888, when he rented it and removed to Rushville, where he has since lived a retired life. He was married to the mother of our subject in 1842; her maiden name was Maria Campbell, a native of Richland county, Ohio, and a daughter of Peter L. Campbell; he was born in 1799, and was but one year old when his parents removed to Ohio, and there he was reared and married to Agnes Jones; in 1844 he emigrated to Illinois, and settled in Schuyler county, where he became a prominent citizen; he and his wife are both deceased. Mrs. Stover has also passed from this life; seven of her children survive her: Milton L., Oscar A., D. Marion, Horace T., Rollin M., Robert C. and Zelm E.

D. Marion Stover spent his early days upon the farm, and attended the rural schools during the winter season. Although his opportunities were very limited he was diligent and used his time to the best advantage. At the age of twenty-one years he began teaching, and has since become well-known among the educators of the county. In 1886 he was elected to the office of county superintendent of schools, in which he has served continuously since that time. Familiar with all the needs of the child, he is very efficient in this capacity, and has brought the schools to a high grade of excellence. Politically he is a Democrat. He is a member of Rushville Lodge, No. 9, A. F. & A. M.

LOUIS W. CARLES, a well-to-do and successful farmer and stock-raiser, living on section 30, township 18, range 11, was born in this township in 1847, and was here reared and educated. He is the son of George H. Carles, born in Germany in 1818. He was of pure Germany ancestry. His wife's name was Elizabeth Crims, and she died at the age of sixty-one. She and her people were members of the Lutheran Church. The father and his children, in September, 1844, started for the United States, landed in New Orleans, and on the largest steamer then running on the Mississippi they came to Beardstown. They arrived January 10, 1845, having been three months on the way. Soon after landing Mr. Carles and one son purchased land in the county, and before long the family became large land owners. Here Mr. Carles, Sr., spent the last years of his life, and died when eighty-six years. He had always been identified with the Lutheran Church as had his parents before him. George H. Carles, Jr., has, since he came to this county been a resident near Bluff Spring station. He is yet smart and active, and runs the homestead, having many friends in the county, among the early settlers. He was married in

1842, in Hanover, to L. O. Nora Deydrick. She was born and reared in Germany. Mrs. George Carles is yet living, and is quite feeble. She is a Lutheran, as is her husband. Mr. Carles is a Democrat.

Louis is the only surviving member of quite a large family. Mr. Carles has been a resident of this county all his life. He has a fine farm of 160 acres, well supplied with good farm buildings. He still attends to overlooking everything himself. He is a well informed man of good judgment, and is a prominent citizen.

He was married, in this county, to Caroline Musch, daughter of John and Albidena (Leppe) Musch. Her father came from Germany, and now resides in Virginia, Cass county; and her mother was born on the vessel from which she was named on the passage from Germany to America. She died in this county when past middle age. Mr. Musch has married a third wife, who is still living.

Mr. and Mrs. Carles of this notice are energetic young people and faithful members of the Lutheran Church. They are the parents of eleven children, two of whom died young: George H., Jr.; Gustav A., Robert G., William M., Herman H., Louis W., Jr., Julius O., J. Albert and Paul B. The whole family is an honor to the county in which they live.

EUGENE J. SCOTT, one of the leading farmers and stockmen of Schuyler county, Illinois, was born at Georgetown, Scott county, Kentucky, June 3, 1845. He passed a quiet, uneventful youth, remaining under the parental roof until his marriage. He was first united to Miss Ida V. Watson, March 15, 1877. She was born in Collinsville, Illinois, February 7, 1847, and died in Schuyler county, Illinois, January 1, 1881; her father was a physician, who died when she was yet a child. By this marriage one child was born, Eugene W., the date of his birth being February 6, 1879, and the place Rushville township. Mr. Scott was married a second time, April 10, 1888, when he was united to Miss Nora L. Finch, who was born in Greenfield, Greene county, Illinois, July 6, 1855, a daughter of Thomas and Eliza Finch. Mr. and Mrs. Scott are the parents of one child, Thomas F., born May 28, 1889.

Mr. Scott lived on a farm four years after his marriage, and then rented the land and removed to Rushville; here he owns a pleasant residence, and is very comfortably situated. He makes a specialty of the breeding of fine horses and cattle, his favorite stock being Hambletonian horses and red-polled cattle; he has some of the finest animals in the State, in which he takes a just pride.

In politics he is allied with the Democratic party. He is a member of the school board, and in this capacity has done his utmost to further educational advancement. In all the walks of life his actions have been characterized by the highest integrity, and he is well worthy of the confidence reposed in him by his fellow-men.

JACOB S. PRUETT, who for many years has been prominently identified with the agricultural interests of Schuyler county, was born at St. Mary's, Hancock county, Illinois, December 3, 1834, a son of Constant Pruett. His father was a native of Roane county, Tennessee, and his grandfather was a farmer of that State, and spent his entire life within its borders. Constant Pruett was reared and married in Tennessee, and emigrated to Illinois in 1829, accompanied by his wife and one child; they journeyed on horse-back to Kentucky, and then secured a cart in which they completed the trip. They first settled in Cass county, but at the end of a year removed to Hancock county, where Mr. Pruett entered a tract of Government land; on this he built a log house in which Jacob S., the subject of this sketch, was born. In 1835 he sold the place and moved to McDonough county, entering eighty acres of land on what is now section 33, Bethel township; he built a log cabin on the east side of the tract, and a few years later erected one on the west side, in which he lived until his death in March, 1890, aged eighty-nine years. He married Susan Schoopman, of Roane county, Tennessee; her father, Jacob Schoopman, started to Illinois in an early day; he fell ill on the way and died before reaching his destination; his widow came to this county, and died in Bethel township. Jacob S. is one of a family of nine children: he was an infant when his parents moved to McDonough county; he attended the pioneer schools which were taught in the primitive log house, with the yet more primitive furnishing of puncheon seats and desks of the same pattern; the children were dressed in cloth of their mother's own weaving; there were no railroads, and wheat was hauled to market sixty miles distant, and sold at twenty-five cents a bushel. Our subject remained with his parents until he was twenty years of age. He then began life for himself. Having no capital he rented land in Bethel township for two years, and at the end of two years purchased forty acres of his father's original entry, and later he purchased the adjoining land across the county line on section 4, Brooklyn township.

In 1861, at the first call for troops, he enlisted in the Sixteenth Illinois Volunteer Infantry, and reported at Springfield; thence he went to Quincy, but the quota was filled before his arrival; therefore he returned to his home, and in February, 1862, he again enlisted, entering Company I, Sixty-second Illinois Volunteer Infantry, for a term of three years or during the war; the regiment was organized at Anna, Illinois, and mustered in at Cairo; thence he went to Paducah, Kentucky, and then to Columbus, and then to Kenton, Tennessee, where Companies I and K were detailed to guard a railroad trestle; while on duty here he was taken ill, and was honorably discharged; he returned home and resumed agricultural pursuits.

In March, 1864, he started with four companions overland to Montana; at the end of one hundred and five days he arrived at Idaho Gulch, and there was engaged in cutting hay for three months, at $50 per month; then he and his brother and Solomon Pestel, engaged in the live-stock trade. In the spring of 1866 he disposed of his interest, and began teaming between Virginia City and Salt Lake. In the fall of the same year he returned to his home, and again took up agricultural pursuits. He was very successful, made investments in land as his means increased, until he is now the owner of 360 acres; this is cultivated by his sons. He resided on the farm until 1882, when he removed to Rushville.

Mr. Pruett was first married March 4, 1855, to Jane Stoneking, who was born in Pennsylvania, August 29, 1833, a daughter of Joseph and Rebecca Stoneking, and died August 1, 1881. Mr. Pruett was married a second time, February 1, 1883, when he was united in marriage to Mrs. Mary J. (Mooney) Eales, a native of Henderson county, Kentucky, and a daughter of Henry L. and Octavia (Kelley) Mooney, and widow of George Eales. Mr. Pruett has five children born of his first marriage: Nicholas, Susan, Eliza A., Harriet and Mary; one child has been born of the second union, named Charles. Mrs. Pruett had by her first union six children: Effie E., Addie E., Edward Clarence, Zelma A., Cora V. and Kate. Politically our subject affiliates with the Democratic party, having cast his first presidential vote for Buchanan. He was elected Sheriff of the county in 1882, and served in this capacity four years. He was a zealous, capable officer and enjoyed the entire confidence of his constituency. Mrs. Pruett is a consistent member of the Christian Church.

MRS. EMELINE SHAFER, of Lee township, was born in Kingston, Luzerne county, Pennsylvania, December 9, 1808. Her father was Peter Shafer and her mother was Elizabeth Shoals, both of Pennsylvania. Grandfather Shoals and his wife both came from Germany and both were sold for their passage, as was the custom in those days, that their time for one year should be sold to pay their passage. Being sold to the same man in Philadelphia they became acquainted, and when they left this place they were married and walked the whole distance from Philadelphia to the Wyoming valley along the banks of the Susquehanna river. Here they soon became tenant farmers, and by industry and economy they became owners of a good farm there. Mrs. Shafer had grown up in the same neighborhood with her husband, and though marriage did not change her name, she was not related to him. Of course their means were very small, but their neighbors were in the same condition. After nine years they moved to Ohio by team. This was a pleasant trip of two weeks in 1834. They lived four years in Union county, four more in Madison county, and then traded their nice farm of 100 acres with good buildings and orchard for 160 acres of timber, two miles west of Mt. Sterling village, getting $200 in cash. They again took up the line of march, bringing with them their four children. They moved into an old log stable near their land, which they made tenable for a short time. Mr. Shafer was tired of his trade when he found that much of the fine timber had been cut, and upon making inquiry he found that the man who had taken much out of this timber had used it to fence eighty acres near what is now Fargo. They settled this by trading an eighty of Mr. Shafer's for the improved eighty that had been fenced with his timber. This was the place where Mrs. Shafer now lives, on which there was a comfortable, but rough house 16 x 16, with a fireplace and stick-and-mud chimney. They have lived here ever since. Here Mr. Shafer died in 1864, aged sixty nine years. They had buried three small children in Ohio and had eight living at his death, although all had gone from home but three. Charles Shafer and his brother Hiram D. were soldiers in the One Hundred and Seventeenth Illinois Volunteers Infantry from Brown county; Charles returned to die at his brother's at Mound Station at the age of twenty eight years. Hiram was in active service as a musician for over three years; Francis was in the ranks from February, 1864, to September of the same year. Of the eleven children born to Mrs. Shafer, seven are still living. Benjamin and Francis are at home conducting the farm for their venerable old mother. She has 170 acres in this farm. She has three motherless grandchildren with her, Maude, Cora and William. Perry Shafer, the eldest son, is a farmer in Kingman county, Kansas; Denison is a farmer in Smith county, Kansas; Wealthy Ann is the wife of Thomas Crabb, a farmer in Smith county, Kansas; Emeline, wife of Jordan Madison, a farmer in Leavenworth, Kansas; and Caroline, wife of James Wilson, a farmer in Kingman county, Kansas.

This grand old lady is now nearly eighty-four years of age and is still as vigorous as most women at fifty years. She thinks nothing of walking three or five miles and attends church regularly in the village. She has a lively recollection of much of her experience in pioneer life. She tells how they shelled the corn by driving the horses over it on the barn floor and drew it sixteen miles to the river market and then sold it for ten cents a bushel. She tells her children that a person can live entirely on corn meal, because she has tried it. All of her experiences, with many of her rough ones, are told with a zest which shows the stuff that this old heroine was made of, and it is refreshing to hear her speak of it as a rich romance in which she took part.

JAMES CRAWFORD, of township 17, range 10, Virginia, is a native of Ireland born in 1833. His parents were William and Margaret (Patterson) Crawford, both natives of Ireland who came to America after marriage, about 1843. They located near what is now Virginia, where they spent their lives. Both parents are interested in the Virginia cemetery. They had four children, two of whom are now living.

James grew to manhood on his father's farm. He has always worked hard and has accumulated property valued at thousands of dollars, all the result of his own industry and economy. He owns 540 acres of land surrounding the town of Virginia, for which he has refused $100 per acre. He gives his whole attention to stock-raising and feeding. He and his son are now feeding about 500 head of three to four year old steers. He is raising about 300 acres of corn this year (1892). The voters of the family are Democrats, and the family are among the representative citizens of Virginia. They have been raised in the Presbyterian faith. This is not a long-lived family, the members generally dying young.

He was married in Jacksonville, in 1868, to Miss Jane Elliott, of Virginia, born in 1841. They have five children: Fannie, Willie, James, Maggie and Floy; two died in infancy,—Henry C. and Thomas Elliott. Willie is now of age and is supporting himself by farming a portion of the homestead, feeding 125 head of cattle.

Mr. Crawford is an outspoken man, who speaks exactly what he thinks, and these qualities indicate the honesty of his nature, as he scorns to gain the favor of men by flattery. He has given his children a good education. He is a man of almost unlimited means, yet he spends his days in toil, feeling that his work is not yet accomplished, though he feels the weight of advancing years. He is a man of sterling honesty and the county is indebted to such men as he for much of its prosperity. He has resided for forty-five years on his farm.

WILLIAM M. GREENWELL, an intelligent and progressive citizen of Cooperstown, Brown county, Illinois, and a prosperous farmer, was born in Meade county, Kentucky, June 27, 1842.

His parents were George and Amanda (Rentfro) Greenwell, both natives of Kentucky, the former born in 1816, the latter in

1813 The father's grandparents came from Germany His paternal grandfather was a well-to-do-farmer in Kentucky, who died in middle life, leaving a widow and seven children, four sons and three daughters George, the father of the subject of this sketch, had charge of the homestead farm for many years, and was married there. In the spring of 1846, he and his family removed to Brown county, Illinois; his brother William had preceded him in 1840, and had erected a gristmill on Crooked creek. This was for many years the only water-power mill nearer than Quincy, and did a large custom business, and could have been sold at one time for $10,000 George and his family made their home with this brother for about six weeks, when, having sold their homestead in Kentucky, the father and brothers bought eighty acres near Mount Sterling, on which there were good improvements, paying for the farm $800 They added to their original purchase from time to time, until they had 280 acres, which continued to be their permanent home, and on which the father still resides. Here the father lost his first wife, mother of the subject of this notice, who died in 1882. aged seventy years They were the parents of ten children, five now living. They lost an infant son, and a daughter, Sarah J., at the age of twelve years Mary E, unmarried lives at home; William M, of this sketch, Horace D, a successful farmer of Cooperstown township; Henry H served six months in the army, in Kansas, where he was accidentally drowned, in 1862; Harriet A married John G. Dennis, and died in 1872, aged twenty-two years, leaving one daughter, who lives with her grandfather; Amy I., wife of N. B Cox, a prosperous farmer of Cooperstown township, Benjamin S. was a schoolteacher of high reputation, a self-educated man, and very enthusiastic in his work, whose early death was, no doubt, due to overwork, he went to California for his health, and taught while there, he came back home and died, at the age of twenty-eight; George F, the youngest, is at home, an invalid.

William M., whose name heads this sketch, was but a child when he accompanied his father to Brown county, Illinois, where his youth was spent At the age of nineteen years, he volunteered his services to the Union, and enlisted in October, 1861, in the Tenth Illinois Cavalry, for three years. He served four years and three months, and was with his regiment most of the time He entered the service as a private and came out as an Orderly.

Within two years after his return to civil life he was married, and after marriage settled on forty acres of land in Ripley township, which property he had bought while in the army, paying for it $1,350 Four years later, he sold this land for $2,150, and bought sixty-seven acres in Cooperstown township, on which he farmed for eight years. He then again sold out, disposing of his farm of 107 acres for $3,000, and buying his present place of 160 acres. Since then he has bought an additional eighty acres a mile and a half away, making, altogether, 240 acres which he now owns, all of which he is farming

He was married on December 26, 1866, to Mary Ann Bates, an estimable lady and a native of Brown county, Illinois, where she was born in 1845 Her parents are William H. and Mary A (Price) Bates, well-to-do and esteemed residents of Brown county They have had eight children, seven now living: a son died in infancy, James, aged twenty-five, married Julia Six, and has one son; Oscar, aged twenty-one is at home, as are also all the rest,—William, aged nineteen; Lilly Pearl, sixteen; Amanda, twelve; Lettie, eight; and Laura, aged six.

Although a Republican in politics, he has been once elected as census enumerator, and once as Assessor of a strongly Democratic township. In the discharge of his official duties, as in his private life, he has displayed superior ability and unimpeachable integrity. He is a member of the G. A. R., and belongs to Isaac McNeil Post at Ripley. He and his wife and two sons have been for a number of years earnest and useful members of the Christian Church, of which he is an Elder.

Aside from his highly respectable family relations, his father having been for many years a prominent resident of the State, he has gained for himself, by continued industry, upright dealing and uniform courtesy, both financial prosperity and the universal esteem of his fellow men.

WILLIAMS D. SCOGGAN was born in Lee township, Brown county, Illinois, December 28, 1843. His father was Isham Scoggan, born 1807, in Shelby county, Kentucky. He was the son of William Dotson Scoggan, who settled in Kentucky at a very early day, living to be a very old man, rearing seven children. Isham was the eldest son and on coming to this county he bought 320 acres of land and in 1839 brought his wife and two children. They made this journey by team. Some eight or ten years later his brothers and one sister came, and with them the aged father and mother. The mother of our subject was his father's second wife and was named Eliza Jane Arnold. Her parents were Kentucky farmers who lived and died there, leaving a family of nine children. The father of Mr. Scoggan died September 8, 1861, in his fifty-seventh year, leaving 700 acres of land and other property. The mother, in her seventy-eighth year, is still living, but is in feeble health.

William received a common school education and was reared to a farm life. He is now engaged in stock-farming, raising great numbers of cattle and horses. He has from 150 to 200 head of stock. His land is very fertile and he is able to rasise upon it corn, wheat, oats and hay and, as it is rolling and has natural drainage, he has not been obliged to do much tilling.

He was first married in Kansas, in 1875, but he lost his wife and one child within two years. He was at that time a farmer of Labette county, and remained there nine years. He owned 320 acres, which he sold and then returned to Illinois to the old homestead. His present wife was Susie Long, a native of Morgan county, Illinois, and daughter of Andrew and Lizzie (Buckton) Long. He was married September 30, 1891. Mrs. Scoggan is a Methodist, his mother a Missionary Baptist, his niece a Campbellite, and he himself represents the outside world, supporting them all. He is an ardent Republican.

JAMES N. ROBISON of Lee township, was born in Huntingdon county, Pennsylvania, November 22, 1823. His father, Henry Robison, was born in the same county, April 22, 1798, and his father was born in Scotland, but spent his last years in Huntingdon county, dying when his son Henry was six years old. Henry after his father's death was obliged to earn his own living and remained on a farm in the same county until 1824, and then with his wife and infant son emigrated to Ohio and lived near Cadiz for two years, then returned to Westmoreland county, Pennsylvania, there engaged in farming and dealing in stock He bought stock in Ohio and drove the across the mountains to Philadelphia. He made considerable money, which he expended on a stage line, but failed in that enterprise In 1837 he came to Illinois with his wife and four children by team to Pittsburg, then by way of the steamer, Rion, to Phillips Ferry, landing in Pike county In August of that year he rented some land and exercised his natural good judgment in stock and farming and in six years' time was able to purchase land He first bought eighty acres, which he soon sold and then bought 160 acres near Pittsfield, Pike county He occupied that farm a number of years, then sold it and moved to Adams county, lived there a few years, then bought three miles west of Perry, pike county, and there remained until his death in 1870. The maiden name of his wife was Margaret Taylor, who was born in Huntingdon county, Pennsylvania, daughter of Robert and Mary (McElroy) Taylor. She died at her home, August 1, 1867

James was in his fourteenth year when his parents came to Illinois. At that time this section of country was but little improved, and deer, wolves and wild-cats were plentiful. There was no railroads for years and the river towns were the only markets He resided with his father until twenty-one and then with a horse which his father gave him he started out for himself. He went to school during the winter and worked for his board. In the following spring he rented land and farmed for three years and then bought 160 acres in Lee township It was military land and he soon lost that on account of a faulty title, but he then bought another farm, of 120 acres. He has been a resident of Lee township since 1847, with the exception of one year in Adams county. He now has 700 acres in Lee township, 480 in Buckhorn township, 225 acres in Pike county and 370 in Johnson county, Kansas

He was married December 1. 1847, to Mary E. Caughenon. She was born in Huntingdon county, Pennsylvania, January 14, 1829. Her father, Henry, was born in Lancaster county, Pennsylvania, and his father, John, as far as known was born in Pennsylvania of German ancestry He came to Illinois in 1887, settled in Pike county, then moved to Pea Ridge in Brown county, bought a farm and lived there until his death The maiden name of his wife was Dorathea Lawrence of Lancaster county. She died in Pike county The father of Mrs. Robison was reared and married in Pennsylvania and resided there until 1836, and with his wife and four children came to Illinois. He lived in Pike county for two years and followed his trade of miller and then built a mill on McGrees creek and operated it for ten years. He then traded the mill for a farm, three miles west of Mt. Sterling, remained four years, then traded the farm for a stock of goods, engaged in the mercantile business in Clayton, Adams county, and remained there until his death in 1859. The first name of his wife was Agnes, daughter of William and Nancy (Tayler), likely natives of Ireland and Pennsylvania The grandfather was of Scotch ancestry. Mrs. Robison's mother died in Clayton in 1889.

Mr. and Mrs. Robison have eight living children: Henry, Mary, William, Robert, Enos M , Fred, Belle and Walter The first child, Margaret, the wife of Rev. J O Jennings, died in California. January 29, 1891.

Three others died in infancy. Mr. and Mrs. Robison are members of the Presbyterian Church, and he has served as Trustee of the church and his wife has taught in the Sunday-school. He has been a Republican since the formation of the party.

JAMES M. BLACK, dealer in hard coal and wood, was born in Indiana county, Pennsylvania, October 12, 1835. He was the son of John W. Black of the same county, who was one of thirteen children. All grew to maturity, and the sons were mechanics by trade. John W. Black was a blacksmith by trade. After he came West he was foreman of the Boyles Scales Company of St. Louis, Missouri, for some years, and, later came to Beardstown and established himself with Mr. T. A. Fisher, another old blacksmith. He was later with Messrs. Milner and Hill. He did business as a smith and a manufacturer of wagons and buggies. He went to Pike's Peak in the early sixties and was a miner there for some time. He secured his claim, but later came back to Vandalia and died there, about fifty years of age. He was married in his native county, to Marget A. Shankle, of early English ancestry. She was born in Indiana county, Pennsylvania, where her parents lived and died. She died when in St. Louis, after the birth of five children, when she was in the prime of life.

James M. Black came to this town, Beardstown, in 1851. From here he went to Iowa, and after residing there for six years came to Beardstown in 1861 and engaged in teaming until 1870, when he established his coal business.

He was married in Polk county, Iowa, June 11, 1857, to Miss Mary Shepherd. She was born in Kentucky and came with her parents, Benjamin and Minerva Shepherd of Kentucky, to Polk county, Iowa, and for some years following the marriage of their daughter. Mr. Shepherd died in Peoria county. Mrs. Shepherd still lives there, about ninety years of age. Mrs. Black died at her home in Beardstown, in 1878. She had three children, namely: Francis Ellen, born January 21, 1862, died May 6, 1864; Edward Franklin, born March 1, 1865, married Grace Putnam, and now lives in Virginia, where he is agent for the Quincy & Missouri Railroad; and Harry L., born October 6, 1870, who is still at home and assists his father. Mr. Black is a Republican and is chairman in one of the local district Republican central committees. He is a member of the Methodist Church. He is a working member of the A. O. U. W., and has managed their financial affairs for six years. He has been the representative to the Grand Lodge.

STEPHEN T. RANNEY, a well known member of commercial circles in Mount Sterling, was born in Elkhorn township, Brown county, Illinois, January 1, 1847, a son of Solomon Ranney. The paternal grandfather, Stephen Ranney, was a native of the State of New York, and his father emigrated from Wales in colonial times, and settled in New York State. Stephen Ranney was a lawyer by profession, and had a large and profitable practice. He was married to Olive Jaqnes, a native of New York State, who lived to the advanced age of ninety years. Solomon Ranney removed from New York to Ohio in an early day, and in 1842 came to Illinois; he spent a few years in Cass county, returned to Ohio, and again came to this State; he located the second time in Brown county, and as his means were limited he did not invest in land; he is now a resident of Pike county, Illinois His wife's maiden name was Melinda Reeves, a native of Virginia, who died in 1849.

After the death of his mother, Stephen T. Ranney was taken in charge by his paternal grandmother, and was reared by her in Elkhorn township In his youth he divided his time between the work on the farm and attending the common school

There were no events of great importance connected with his career until 1864. In November of that year he enlisted in Company G, Fiftieth Illinois Volunteer Infantry, and served until the close of the war He was honorably discharged at Louisville, Kentucky, July 13, 1865, after which he returned to his home He was variously employed for several years, but finally purchased land in Elkhorn township, which he cultivated until his removal in 1882, to Mount Sterling, where he has since made his home.

Mr Ranney was married in 1877, March 3, to Melinda C. Perry, who was born November 12, 1847, in Brown county, Illinois Of late years he has been one of the most prominent real-estate dealers in the place, having laid out an addition and built more residences in the past ten years than any one other individual; he erected the Ranney Block, one of the handsomest business structures in Mount Sterling, and has been one of the most enterprising and energetic supporters of the county's interests

Politically he is identified with the Democratic party He served as Justice of the Peace in Elkhorn township, has represented the Second Ward on the Board of Aldermen, and in 1882 was elected Sheriff of the county; four years later he was elected Treasurer of the county, and in 1890 he was made Justice of the Peace He has been a director of the Building and Loan Association since its organization, and in all the walks of life has shown himself a stanch, reliable man, worthy of the confidence reposed in him by the community in which he lives

HON ALEXANDER K LOWRY was born in Armstrong county, Pennsylvania, November 7, 1829, a son of Joseph Lowry, a native of Franklin county, Pennsylvania The paternal grandfather, Adam Lowry, was a native of Ireland, but was the descendant of Scotch ancestors; he emigrated to America, accompanied by his family about the year 1780, and settled near Chambersburg, Franklin county, Pennsylvania; he died at the age of ninety-five years in Armstrong county, Pennsylvania His son Joseph learned the blacksmith's trade, but engaged in agricultural pursuits in Armstrong county, where he had settled previous to his marriage; he bought a tract of timber land, cut out the trees to make a spot for the erection of his cabin, and also built a shop where he followed his trade in connection with his farming; he there spent the remainder of his days, his death occurring in 1853. He married Elizabeth Kerr, a native of Armstrong county, Pennsylvania, and a daughter of William Kerr, who was born in the north of Ireland, of Scotch ancestry, he settled in Pennsylvania after landing in America, and he and his wife there spent the remainder of their days

Alexander K Lowry was reared and educated in the county of his birth; he taught school one term in Indiana county, Pennsylvania, and in 1848 and 1849 was engaged in clerking in a country store From

1850 to 1853 he was bookkeeper for the owners of the furnaces in Bedford county, and from 1853 to 1855 he was clerking. Before the end of the latter year he emigrated to Iowa, going via the Ohio and Mississippi rivers to Keokuk, and thence by team to Poweshiek county, being one of the first settlers in Grinnell. At that time there was not a mile of railway in the State of Iowa; the central and western portions of the State were very sparsely settled, and the Missouri river bounded the frontier. Mr. Lowry began business by opening a hotel, and soon after was appointed Postmaster upon the establishment of an office at that point. He remained at Grinnell about a year and a half, and then went to Pennsylvania, the home of his youth. It was not long, however, before he emigrated to Dakota county, Nebraska, where he purchased a claim of Government land and on which he remained six months. Returning to Grinnell at the end of that time he embarked in mercantile trade, and also began the study of law. He was admitted to the bar in 1858, and soon after came to Macomb, Illinois, where he engaged in practice until 1861; in this year he removed to Mount Sterling, and devoted himself to legal work until 1864, when he made a trip to California, going via the Isthmus. Arriving in the Golden State he opened a hotel, which he kept for three years at Marysville, and then came back to Illinois, the return trip being made via the Nicaragua route.

Mr. Lowry has been twice married; in 1855 he was united to Sarah McCartney, a native of Indiana county, Pennsylvania, who died in 1870. Mr. Lowry's second marriage occurred in 1872, when he was united to Martha J. Means, who was born one mile from Mount Sterling, Brown county, Illinois; she died in February, 1888. Two children were born of the first marriage, Clara B. and Hattie; the latter is the wife of James L. Gray, and has one child, Mary Vivian.

In politics Mr. Lowry affiliated with the Democratic party until 1869, but since that time he has supported the principles of the Republican party. He was elected County Superintendent of Schools in 1861, was County Treasurer in 1863, and in 1886 was elected a member of the State Legislature. In these various offices he discharged his duties with marked ability, reflecting great credit upon himself as well as his constituency. At the present time he is a member of the School Board, filling the office of president.

REV. MICHAEL CLIFFORD has been pastor of St. Mary's Church, Mount Sterling, Illinois, for more than twenty years, and during this time has been a faithful servant to his Master, and has won the esteem and admiration of the people with whom he has labored. He was born in county Limerick, Ireland, and his ancestors for many generations were natives of the same county. He received his early education in the Latin school at Charleyville, county Cork, and later became a student at All Hallow's College, Dublin, from which institution he was graduated in 1862. In July of the same year he crossed the sea to America, and came directly from the seaboard to Illinois.

His first charge was at Bunker Hill, Macoupin county; thence he was sent to Sangamon county, and removed from this point to Morgan county, where he remained until 1872, when he came to Mount Sterling and took charge of St. Mary's congregation.

This is the first Roman Catholic Church of Mount Sterling, having been founded more than fifty years ago; the present structure is a handsome brick edifice, with a seating capacity of 500, and the membership numbers 185 families. The parochial school under the care of the church is in charge of the Dominican Sisters, and has an attendance of eighty-five. Since Father Clifford has been pastor of St. Mary's, improvements have been made to the extent of over $10,000; a residence for the priest and one for the Dominican Sisters are included in the work accomplished by him. He has been devoted to the interests of his people, and in him they find that wise counsel and loving admonition which has been a safe guide on the pathway of life.

A. H. SIELSCHOTT, Beardstown, Illinois.—The United States, the grandest government that shelters a people, possesses alone of all the governments of the world, the privilege which makes it possible for each individual to force his way through the ranks of the many and become one of the few. Emerson says "it is purpose that differences men," and the man who, by birth or its equivalent, enjoys the possibilities of a high and noble purpose, under such a government, and who through energy, tact, and strict integrity overcomes the obstacles that engulf smaller men, who levels the impossibilities of other men to his own convenience and makes them his opportunities, is that man of purpose, and is by the law of natural selection a leader. It is to such men that society and progression owes its highest attainments; and it is of one of those whose straightforward career has made his name worthy the pages of history, that this sketch is written.

A. H. Sielschott was born in the busy province of Hanover, Germany, in 1835. He is a son of Frederick and Amelia Sielschott, who were also natives of Hanover. His parents were of that sturdy conservative element that has enriched the great Empire of Germany and advanced it to the front rank in the world's history of great soldiers and statesmen, and placed it in close touch with the advance of civilization and the fellowship of men. They were farmers owning their land, and as is characteristic of that eminently worthy husbandry, were given entirely to the cultivation of their land, leaving travel to those who were less inspired with the habits of their forefathers. They were never outside the borders of their loved fatherland, but lived out their allotted time, happy, and contented, with the pleasures and prosperity their home life and patriotism afforded them. They each attained the good age of three score years and ten.

The boyhood of A. H. Sielschott was practically the same as that of other boys whose parents were devoted to labor and frugality. At the age customary in his native land, Mr. Sielschott entered the public schools and acquired a classical education in his native tongue. After leaving school and being of a decidedly progressive temperament and endowed with a full share of native pluck, he decided to leave his home and try for his fortune in the broader fields of America. In the early part of 1854 he left Bremen on the steamer Hansa, ticketed for New York. Arriving there he soon pushed boldly westward and reached Beardstown in the fall of that year. Here he decided to remain, and here with but a five-dollar gold piece in his pocket he began the life that has been so full of good for himself and also for the community. Mr. Sielschott did not waste any time looking for an easy job, but with determination and energy took hold of the first honest work that presented itself. He was familiar with farm work and naturally bent his energies in that direction He engaged to work on a farm, and went at it with a will. While working and while resting he kept his brain busy evolving plans for the future, and speculating honestly, and with a method well worked out, he advanced step by step in popularity and position until he had acquired not only a comfortable income but the higher victory, namely, the confidence and respect of all who knew him In 1876 he was elected by a large majority to the office of Sheriff, and so satisfactorily did he discharge the duties of his office that he was repeatedly re-elected until he had held the office for an unbroken period of ten years. After ten years in office Mr. Sielschott had reason to hope for a rest from public service, but he was almost immediately elected to the office of County Treasurer, and held that important office until 1890, a period of four years. In 1889 the First State Bank of Beardstown was organized and Mr. Sielschott was elected its president, an office which he has continued to hold ever since Under his wise direction the bank has prospered, and is to-day one of the richest banking organizations in the State Its principles are sound, and it enjoys a financial solidity far beyond any possible event or turn in values.

Mr. Sielschott's record in the government affairs in the city and county is a most unusual and remarkable one. In addition to the fourteen years in which he discharged the important duties of Sheriff and Treasurer of the county, he has served five terms as Mayor of the city of Beardstown. A single term in any office, no matter how important, seldom determines a man's fitness for high commendation. It is the repeated voice of the people in recalling a man to public office—in making him his own successor year after year—that establishes beyond question that man's ability and worthiness

Mr Sielschott has also served many times as delegate to County and Congressional conventions. He is a Democrat, believing the principles of that great party to be in closer touch with the needs of the people, and in greater harmony with the progress of the age than all the planks, principles and platforms of all other political parties combined. In a word he believes Democratic doctrine everlastingly right, and all opposition thereto everlastingly wrong. He has always supported these principles fully and faithfully, and has done more than one man's share to establish purity in office and the great truth that public office is a public trust

In business life Mr. Sielschott has been a promoter of many important enterprises, one of the most important of which was the construction of the fine bridge that spans the Illinois river at Beardstown. He is, also, identified with many other worthy and prosperous enterprises.

In March, 1862, Mr. Sielschott was married to Miss Ellen Piper, of Beardstown, a native of Hanover, Germany, who at the age of seven accompanied her parents to the United States and settled in Beardstown They were worthy and consistent members of the Lutheran Church. They died after having attained the good old age of four-score years.

Mr. and Mrs Sielschott have three children: A. F. Sielschott, of the firm of Spring & Sielschott, of Beardstown; Alice A. and Martha M. are still members of the family home. Both of the young ladies have received a splendid education, and both are prominent in social matters The family worship at the Congregational Church.

Socially Mr. Sielschott is a leading member of the Masonic fraternity. Personally he is kind, courteous and affable. In a word, he possesses just such a personality as the intelligent reader would expect to find in conjunction with such an admirable record.

HENRY TRUE FOSTER, the well-known first settler of Beardstown yet living, was born on February 3, 1815, in Lincoln county, Maine. He grew up and acquired a practical education at Warren and Newcastle, and when seventeen years of age went to Bangor, Maine, and spent three years in the clothing store of Thomas Furber, the first store of that kind in the city. When twenty years of age he came with his father to Illinois, where they had landed interests. After landing at Meredosia, on the Illinois river, he came to Beardstown, where Mr. Foster has since resided. He has engaged in a variety of occupations, having been a farmer, merchant, manufacturer, grain buyer, packer, and dealer in grain. He was an active business man and was very successful in his many business ventures. He is generous to a fault, and never paused to consider his personal gain or loss if an enterprise was started that was likely to prove a benefit to the city. It was through his personal efforts that the railroads were run to Beardstown. In 1861 he was appointed Postmaster of the place and held the office for seven years, and in 1868 was placed at the head of the municipality of Beardstown. He infused new life into the place by promoting the welfare of the city. He introduced new enterprises, and it is doubtful if there is another citizen of the city who has devoted so much time and energy to the development of that place as Mr. Foster. He has been a prominent Republican in politics since the organization of the party. He has been an active worker in that party in local matters. President Lincoln and he were personal friends, and he was a member of the State Central Committee during the second campaign of Mr. Lincoln. He is a member of the Congregational Church of which he is a Deacon and of which he was for years a Trustee. Mr. Foster was one of those who voted for William H. Harrison in 1836 and 1840.

Mr. Foster was married in Beardstown, 1839, to Mary De Haven, of Philadelphia, Pennsylvania. She was born, reared and educated in that city and came west when a young woman. She died at her home January 11, 1888, at the age of seventy-seven. She ever proved herself a true and noble wife and mother, and her death was deeply felt by those she left behind her. She left two sons: Edwin C., who married Isabel Dale and who now resides in Waterloo, Iowa; and Robert Harry, who married Emma Logan and they live in Minneapolis, Minnesota. They are both prosperous young men.

FREDERICK W. ROTTGER, one of the most successful and enterprising business men of Mount Sterling, was born near Mendon, Prussia, August 8, 1844. His father, William Rottger, was born in the same country, and there was reared and married. In 1845 he determined to try his fortunes in the New World, and left his family behind until he should seek out a home for them in the strange, new land. He located in Morgan county, Illinois, where he died about a year later. His wife was left in very humble circumstances, with four little children. In 1850 she brought her family to

America, sailing from Bremen and landing in New Orleans; thence they came via the Mississippi and Illinois rivers to Naples, and completed the journey to Jacksonville by rail. Frederick W. was bound out to E. S. Hendrickson, a farmer then residing in Morgan county, with whom he remained until he had attained his majority. His early life was spent on the farm, but he managed to learn the art of telegraphy, and came to Mount Sterling to accept a position with the Wabash Railway Company as station agent. For more than a quarter of a century he has had charge of the company's business at this point, and by his years of faithful service has gained the entire confidence of the officials of the corporation. After he had been in Mount Sterling a short time he began contracting for railroad ties, and has carried on this business continuously since that time. In 1874 he purchased an interest in the lumber business of C. M. Dunlap, and in 1882 bought the entire concern, since which time he has conducted the trade alone. In 1878 he added the grain business to his own interests, and has done a large amount of buying and shipping. He also has immense agricultural interests, and owns 800 acres of fine farming land in Pea Ridge township.

Mr. Rottger was married October 18, 1865, to Eugenia Peters, a native of Steubenville, Ohio, and a daughter of Stebbens and Alicia (Tracy) Peters; of this union five children have been born: Eugenia, Nina, Myrtle, Frederick W. and Winnifred. Mrs. Rottger is a consistent member of the Presbyterian Church. Our worthy subject belongs to the Masonic order, being a member of Hardin Lodge, No. 44, A. F. & A. M., Delta Commandry, No. 48, K. T., and the Quincy Consistory. Politically he is identified with the Democratic party, and has represented the people of his township in many of the local offices; he was the first Mayor of Mount Sterling, and has been a member of the County Board of Supervisors. He is also the choice of his party to represent Brown county in the State Legislature. He is a man of unquestioned integrity, true to his friends, and strong in the purposes he considers just and right.

WILLIAM B. DAVIS, proprietor of the *Democrat Message*, was born in La Fayette county, Missouri, July 10, 1865. His father, Henry K. Davis, was born in Wheeling, West Virginia, and his father, Samuel H. Davis, was a printer, and at one time published a paper in Wheeling, and later in Peoria, Ill. He spent his last days there. His son was also a printer, and followed his trade many years. He issued the first daily paper ever published in Peoria, and the first ever published in Champaign county, and during the war published the Lexington *Union* at Lexington, Missouri. It was a strong Union paper, and there his life was fraught with much danger. Later he established the Daily *Advertiser* at Kansas City, and it is now known as the Kansas City *Times*. Among the other places where he published papers were Paris, Texas, and Warrensburg, Missouri.

In December, 1874, he came to Mount Sterling and bought the Mount Sterling *Democrat* and continued its publication until his death, April 6, 1886. His wife's name was Mary Davis, of Cumberland, Maryland, a daughter of John Davis. She now resides at Mount Sterling, where she has reared six children.

William was ten years old when he came to Mount Sterling, and at the age of eighteen he began to learn the trade of printing in the office of the *Democrat.* In 1886 he bought the office and good will of the *Message* and consolidated it with the *Democrat* under the name of the *Democrat Message.* His mother still retains a half interest in the paper.

He married, in 1888, Laura G. Givens, of Mount Sterling, Illinois, daughter of John and Maria Putman Givens. They have one child, Catherine Maria. Mrs. Davis belongs to the Methodist Episcopal Church, Mr Davis is a Democrat in politics, and belongs to the Cincinnatis, No. 287, K. P.

CYRUS HORROM dates his birth in Dearborn county, Indiana, September 4, 1820. His father, Benjamin Horrom, was born in New York state, and when a young man moved to Ohio. A few years later he continued his way westward, and took up his abode in Dearborn county, Indiana, where he lived till December, 1828. At that time he started with his wife and nine children for Illinois, making the removal with ox teams, and landing in Cass county the following March. Here he entered a tract of Government land in township 18, range 10, and erected a log house. The maiden name of his wife was Sarah Austin, she being a native of the same locality in which her husband was born. They reared nine children, and on the home farm the parents died.

Cyrus Horrom was eight years of age at the time the family moved to Illinois. At the time Central Illinois was sparsely settled, and in the northern part of the State the only inhabitants were Indians. Game of all kinds was plenty throughout the State, and the people dressed in homespun. Little of the land in Cass county had been entered, most of it belonging to the Government. The means of transportation being limited, farm produce necessarily brought a low price. Corn was ten cents per bushel, good steers sold at half a cent per pound, and pork brought seventy-five cents per hundred pounds.

Mr. Horrom lived with his parents till he reached his majority. He then went to Marshall county and worked on a farm three months. Returning to Cass county, he rented land of his father, and in 1845 settled on the farm he now owns and occupies. This farm is located on section 17, contains 145 acres, and is well improved with good buildings, etc.

Mr. Horrom was married in 1845, to Mary J. Briar, a native of Pennsylvania, and a daughter of James and Mary (Davis) Briar. Joseph Briar, a sketch of whom appears elsewhere in this volume, is a brother of hers. Mr. and Mrs. Horrom have seven children living, viz: John H., Matilda J., Mary E., William H., Martha Ellen, Preston W., and Cora Alice. Charles, Addie, Millard and George A. are deceased.

PHILANDER AVERY, one of the large land owners of Schuyler county, resides on section 26, Camden township. He first came to the county in 1832, being a native of Franklin county, Ohio, born June 13, 1823. His parents, David and Margaret (Adams) Avery, were natives of Pennsylvania and Ohio. The grandfather of the subject was born in Ireland, but came to the United States when a boy and for some time was a sailor. He then farmed and followed the carpenter trade. Some time after his children were settled he emigrated to Illinois, settled in Schuyler county, where he died at the age of eighty-five. His wife also died in Schuyler county. They had ten children: Stephen, Chancey, Pelatin, Nancy, Maria, Daniel, William, Polly, Betsy and Sarah. The father of the subject was born in New York State, July 1, 1797, and when a boy removed with the family to Ohio, where he worked at the trade of carpenter. He was married in 1821, in Ohio, to Margaret Adams, who was born in Franklin county, Ohio. In 1832 he came to Colwell, Illinois, and resided for eight years in Rushville, then settled in Woodford county, where he entered some land. He next spent three years in Missouri and on his return went to Camden township, where he owned eighty acres. He died in 1851, aged fifty-five years. His wife died two months later, aged fifty-four. They had nine children, Matilda, deceased; Rebecca, deceased; Nancy, deceased; Sarah Carter, deceased; Elizabeth J., deceased; Charles resides at Industry, Illinois, and Zavin, deceased.

Philander is the second of the family. He came with the family to Illinois and has remained a farmer ever since. After his marriage he removed to Knoxville, where he resided until 1851 and then returned to Schuyler county and purchased eighty acres of land in Camden township and has since been a resident of the place. He now owns 700 acres of land and deals largely in live stock. He has always been a good, hard-working man, and is known well and favorably all over the county. He is a Democrat in politics and has always been an outspoken man. He is uneducated in schools, but has been educated in the great school of experience.

He was married in 1842 to Mrs. Meeks, *nee* Bryant. She was born in Stokes county, North Carolina, and married there, coming to Illinois with her husband, Mr. Meeks. She had three children by him: Miria, Columbus and Helen. She bore her second husband two children: Mary Ann, who was drowned in a stream near home when fifteen, and James, who resides in Camden township. Mrs. Avery died, November 16, 1891.

Mr. Avery is a member of Camden Lodge, No. 648, A. F. & A. M. He is worth a good deal of property, which he has made himself.

James Avery was born in Knox county, Illinois, July 30, 1844. He has always lived with his father, although he owns 120 acres of land himself. He is a Democrat and has been Highway Commissioner and member of the School Board. He is a member of Camden Lodge, No. 648, A. F. & A. M. He has worked as a carpenter.

He was married in 1868, to Martha Dixon, daughter of Lawone and Hannah Dixon. She was born in Brown county, in 1848. They have one son, La Fayette, born July 3, 1870.

HENRY M. SCHMOLDT, Beardstown, Illinois.—It is the constitutional privilege of every American to aspire to the highest honors within the gift of the people; and when such aspiration is supplemented by progressive and well balanced mentality, backed with integrity, tact and energy, it follows as a law of natural selection that such a man is a leader among his fellow men. It matters not whether his father be a prince of fortune, or an humble mechanic; the law of selection, made natural by the inspired principles of our constitution, remains the same; for under the beneficent and noble doctrine of a true republican government, monarchial succession is relegated to the repellent past, and all men are born equal—equal in the right of law and privilege, the only aristocrat being the man possessing a wealth of brains Such a man may have an academic sheepskin learnedly inscribed as an early voucher to his mentality and title to distinction. When such is happily the case the man simply rises the more rapidly, simply obtains an earlier hold upon the confidence and respect of his fellow men. The history such a man makes becomes his own property, so to speak, and not alone an embellishment of the future. His progress has outstripped time, and he lives to read, in accredited form and in the suffrage of approval of his fellow men, the story of his life How eminently fitting to a good life is such an honor, and how few men enjoy it! It is one of those few, a man who, though still in the morning of his life, has made a record worthy the pages of history that this sketch is written.

Henry M. Schmoldt was born in Cass county, Illinois, September 19, 1858 He is the eldest son of Robert G and Johanna (Blohn) Schmoldt, both natives of Hanover, Germany. Robert G. Schmoldt was the eighth son of Herman Schmoldt, a wealthy land owner in Hanover. The father of Henry M. Schmolt spent a portion of his early life upon the ocean In 1852 he was married, by the American consul at Hamburg, to Miss Johanna Blohn, of Hanover, after which he emigrated to the United States, locating in New York city. In July of the following year he removed to Beardstown, where with his good wife he enjoys the fruits of a well-earned competence and good name.

In 1890, at the retirement of his father from business, Henry M Schmoldt, in company with his brothers, Adolph E. and Robert W., assumed full control of the extensive business built up by their father, a business which with the advent of younger blood at the helm has made additional strides in the favor of the public The boyhood of Henry M Schmoldt was full of active usefulness and hard work. At the usual age he entered the public school at Beardstown, and to this, the education there obtained, was added a commercial course of study in a business college in St. Louis, Missouri, after which he took a course at Asbury (now Depauw) University, Greencastle, Indiana.

In 1876, he returned to Beardstown and associated himself with his father in the manufacture of cooperage supplies, and has continued in the business ever since, the firm now being Schmoldt Bros. & Company This firm also deals extensively in lumber and house-furnishing supplies.

Mr Schmoldt, of whom this sketch is written, is one of the younger war horses in the Republican party, and has widened his strength and wisdom in office by having been repeatedly elected to the office of Mayor of Beardstown, besides having served as Alderman for several years He is a hard worker, scrupulous and exact in his dealings with men, and a staunch advocate of the principles of the great party, in whom and through whom he sees the great truths which his party believes have made America what it is. He is, however, more of a statesman than a politician; for politicians are not generally given to great scruples in matters of conscience in politics, and Mr. Schmoldt is, but it is the honest, straightforward man that wins a lasting meed of victory in politics as well as in social and business life; and such is the record of Mr. Schmoldt. In the local counsels of the Republican party he is an able and welcome adviser.

On May 12, 1880, Mr. Schmoldt was married to Miss Lena Earhardt, of Beardstown, daughter of the late Dr. Fred Earhardt, an old and leading physician of Cass county. They have one child, a daughter, whom they have named Jennie.

Socially, Mr. Schmoldt is a prominent member of the Masonic fraternity, and also of the Odd Fellows. Personally he is kind, courteous and affable.

E. H. OWEN SEELEY is on of the oldest settlers of Schuyler county and resides in Rushville. He was born at Thetford, Orange county, Vermont, December 15, 1811. His father, Luke Seeley, was born in the same town October 15, 1792. The grandfather, Sheldon Seeley, was a native of New England and it is supposed was born in Vermont, at least he was one of the pioneers of Thetford where he followed agricultural pursuits. At a very early day he went to Ohio, prospecting, but was taken sick while there and died near Sandusky. His wife was Deborah Bowker, a native of New England, who died at Thetford at the age of about ninety years.

Luke Seeley was reared and married in his native State. Upon reaching manhood he engaged in mercantile pursuits, which he continued in Vermont until 1818, when he removed to Franklin county, New York, and there lived on a farm for about one year. He then moved to Malone, New York, and engaged in merchandising, conducting at the same time a cabinet shop and employing a foreman to carry it on. In 1828 he came to Illinois to look at his piece of land in the military tract, but then went back to New York in September, 1830, and returned to Illinois with his family. He started on the 12th of September, and journeyed with a two-horse team to Buffalo, thence by lake to Cleveland, thence by team to Columbus, Ohio, where he remained until the 27th of October, and then with a company of fourteen families made the overerland journey by team to Schuyler county, and after forty days on the road arrived at Rushville. He located on land just north of Rushville, but one year later moved to the village and started the first nursery in Schuyler county, which he conducted successfully until his death October 15, 1856. His wife, and the mother of our subject, was formerly Miss Electa Owen, a native of Milton, Vermont, and the daughter of Elijah Owen. She died in Rushville, May 10, 1834. Both parents were substantial citizens, good neighbors, and enjoyed the high esteem of all who knew them.

Our subject, E. H. Owen Seeley, was educated at Malone Academy. One of the friends of the family, Dr. Waterhouse, had lost his only son and he expressed his desire to have our subject go to Burlington, Vermont, and study medicine, and to this the father assented. It was considered necessary that he should have a Latin education and accordingly he secured a Latin grammar, Cicero's Orations, Ainsworth's Latin and English Dictionary, the Iliad of Homer and the Bucolics of Virgil in two volumes; but at this juncture, on the eve of his departure, and after his father had procured him a suit of sheep's-gray clothing, his mother objected to his going, and instead thereof he entered a shop to learn the cabinet trade, but he still had his books that he had purchased, and in 1830, when he came West, he traded his books for a rifle, as it was evident that he would have much more use for that instrument of death in the wilds of Illinois than for his classic, Latin works. Soon after his arrival here, he bought the lot on the corner east of the court house, and in 1831 began undertaking The first person he buried was the fourth body consigned to the cemetery at this place When the cholera swept the town in 1834, taking off thirty persons or more, himself and one other person conducted all the burials For many years he was the only furniture dealer and undertaker in the city. He continued an active business until 1878, but since then has been mainly retired

On the 26th of September, 1839, he married Catherine A. Haskell, a native of Troy, New York, whose father was Joseph Haskell of New Hampshire Joseph Haskell was left an orphan at an early age, and upon arriving at adult years, went to York State, where he followed blacksmithing. In 1831, accompanied by his wife and family, he came by team to Wheeling, West Virginia, and then by the Ohio, Mississippi and Illinois rivers to Beardstown. He did not settle on the land he had previously bought in Schuyler county, but established himself in Rushville, then a little hamlet He bought the land now occupied by the court house and erected thereon a frame dwelling, in which the mother of Mrs Seeley taught the first school in the village. Mr. Haskell followed the trade of a mason and resided here until his death, October 2, 1864 The maiden name of his wife was Clarissa Pier She was born in Poultney, Vermont, March 5, 1792, and died August 10, 1879 in Rushville.

Mr Seeley has always been a Democrat, and in 1847 and 1848 was Assessor and Treasurer of this county He visited every house in the county and made his returns in ninety days From 1857 to 1861 he served as Postmaster To himself and wife were born six children Charles, Albert, Frank, Dora William L. and Ella. Dora died at the age of five years. Mrs. Seeley joined the Methodist Church at the age of ten years and has been a consistent member ever since She has in her possession the manuscript of a history of Rushville written by her mother several years ago.

JAMES A TEEL, a pioneer of Schuyler county, and one the most successful farmers and stock-raisers of the State of Illinois, was born in Washington county, Pennsylvania, July 19, 1830 His father, Henry P. Teel, was born in New Jersey; and it is thought that the grandfather, John Teel, also was a native of New Jersey The great-grandfather, Captain John Teel, commanded a company in the war of the Revolution; he spent his last years in Beaver county, Pennsylvania, and was buried with military honors; his widow came to Illinois and spent her last days here John Teel served five years in the regular army, and participated in the struggle of 1812; he emigrated from Pennsylvania and spent the last years of his life in Guernsey county, he married Huldah Haines, a native of the Keystone State; she also died in Guernsey county Henry P. Teel was a millwright by trade, and followed this vocation in Pennsylvania until 1833, when he came to Illinois, accompanied by his wife and two children; the trip was made via the Ohio, Mississippi and Illinois rivers to Erie, and thence by team to Rushville; here he lived two years, and then removed to the Territory of Iowa, locating at Fort Madison, where he lived one year; he then came back to Schuyler county, and resumed work at his trade. He saved his money, and in 1845 he purchased a tract of school land on section 16, Rushville township, in connection with his trade he superintended the cultivation of this land, and resided on the farm until his death, which occurred March 21, 1878. He married Martha Ann Mathews, who was born in New Castle, Delaware, November 11, 1811, her father, James Mathews was born on the sea when his parents were emigrating to America; Thomas Mathews, the great-grandfather of our subject, was born in Ireland, of Scotch ancestry, after emigrating to America he settled in Delaware, but later removed to Pennsylvania, locating in Washington county; he afterward came to Ohio, where he spent the remainder of his days, he married Margaret Steward, a native of Ireland. James Mathews, the maternal grandfather, was a paper-maker by trade, learning the business at New Castle, Delaware; after his marriage he removed to Washington county, Pennsylvania, and thence to Kansas, where he spent the last days of his life in Cherokee county; he was a thirty-third degree Mason, and his funeral was conducted by that body. Henry P. Teel and wife reared a family of seven children: James A the subject of this notice, Huldah A., John T, William, Alice, Henry and Cass. The parents are members of the Presbyterian Church; Mr. Teel affiliates with the Democratic party.

James A Teel was four years of age when his parents came to Schuyler county to reside, settlers were few, and wild game abounded. At Fort Madison also the Indians were numerous, Black Hawk and Keokuk being prominent chiefs, well remembered by Mr Teel. He attended the pioneer schools of Schuyler county, which were taught in log school houses, furnished in primitive style; the seats were made of slabs with wooden pins for legs, and the desks for the older scholars were constructed after the same pattern; the pens were made by the teacher from goose-quills. Cooking was done by a fire-place, and the children were clothed in home-spun of the mother's own weaving. James A resided with his parents until he was nineteen, and then, in 1849, he emigrated to California, joining the great throng that pressed to the gold fields of that State; he was one of a company of sixty who made the journey overland with ox teams, walking the entire distance. He arrived at Biddle's Bar out of funds; he soon found employment in the mines, and worked two days and a half at $9 per day; he then began mining on his own account, and remained there until 1851, when he returned to his home via the Nicaragua route and New York In 1853 he made another trip across the plains, spent a few months in the golden State, and returned by way of the Isthmus He engaged in farming in Rushville township, and soon turned his attention to the breeding of fine cattle. In 1856 he located on a farm which he still owns on section 2, Rushville township; this tract consists of 570 acres, and is improved with good substantial buildings; Mr Teel lived there until March, 1891, when he removed to the farm where he now resides, one mile north of the courthouse; he owns nearly 1,200 acres of land, all in Rushville and Buena Vista townships

He was married July 29, 1856, to Miss Elizabeth Smith, a native of Rushville township, born December 24, 1834, a daughter of Jonathan and Nancy (Skiles) Smith (see sketch of William Wood). Mr and Mrs Teel have four children living: Herschel V, Neosho May, Marshall E. and Walter H · the oldest child, Everett L., was born July 14, 1866; he was graduated from the law department of the State University, Madison, Wisconsin, in the class of 1890, and his death occurred in October, of the same year.

In early days Mr. Teel belonged to the Whig party, but for many years past has affiliated with the Democratic party. He has served as collector of Rushville township, and has been a member of the county Board of Supervisors. He is a stock-holder in the Schuyler County Agricultural Society, and has made an exhibit at the second fair held in the county, receiving two silver spoons as premiums; his herd of short-horns has been seen at many county fairs in Illinois since that time, and has been awarded sweep-stakes and other prizes on different occasions. Mr. Teel is a stock-holder in the Schuyler Hotel Company, and also in the Bank of Schuyler County. He is a man of superior business qualifications, and his judgment in all matters pertaining to agriculture is highly esteemed throughout the county and State.

JOHN K. CLARK, a well-to-do and prominent farmer, living on sections 31 and 32, Township 18, Range 11, Cass county, Illinois, where he owns a fine farm, well improved and well supplied with farm buildings, of about 400 acres, lying in the Sangamon valley, near Bluff Springs, was born in this county, in what is now Monroe precinct, in 1828. He is the oldest man in Cass county that was born here. The family later came to what is now Bluff Springs precinct in 1846, and here the parents afterward lived. Prior to coming to Bluff Springs they had lived for a time in Morgan county, Illinois, and also in Schuyler county, later in Henry county, Iowa, and there the father, Thomas, struck the first stake of what is now Mount Pleasant, Iowa. Some time after this his attention was called to a beautiful spring located about three miles east of Mount Pleasant, and during his four years' sojourn in Henry county, Iowa, when it was all new ground, unbroken, he remained there. Later he sold and returned to Illinois, and in 1840 located in Cass county, where he became a prominent citizen and spent his remaining days there, dying in the vicinity of Bluff Springs, in 1852. He was sixty-seven years of age at his death. He was a good, well-known citizen of this county. He was born in Kentucky, and was the son of Thomas Clark, Sr., who was born in London, England, and came to America when a young man, settling in Kentucky, in Barren county, and there lived for some years as a prominent pioneer. He was married, and while yet in middle life was attacked by the Indians and murdered, and his house burned down. The mother died a natural death in Kentucky when quite an old woman. Thomas Clark, Jr., had followed his brother, William M., to Illinois, the latter coming here in the early '20s and settling in Morgan county. He is now dead. Thomas Clark was married in Kentucky to a lady of that State, Julia Ann King, of Scotch-Irish stock. She labored with her husband in building a home in those early days in Illinois. She died some fourteen years after her husband, and was about seventy-six years old. She was a Methodist.

John is the eldest son of four yet living children. His sister, Mrs. Mary Loosley, is the eldest, being a widow and now lives with him. Another brother, Owen W., was a teacher for many years in the public schools and taught penmanship in twenty-seven States, and also in the Dominion of Canada. He is single, as is our subject. Another sister is Martha, wife of Judge D. N. Walker, of Virginia. Two brothers and three sisters, now dead. Rev. William Clark, the older, was a member of the Methodist Episcopal

Conference, and preached the gospel for forty years. Thomas was a well-to-do farmer and owned a fine farm near Bluff Springs, where his widow, two sons and a daughter, still reside. Cynthia, the oldest daughter, was a member of the Methodist Episcopal Church, and lived a consistent Christian life, and died at the age of seventy-two. Rebecca and Jane were also members of the Methodist Church. They died younger.

John Clark is one of the prominent men of the county and takes an active part in local matters. He is a Democrat, a live, good fellow who enjoys life as it comes. He started Bluff Springs, built the first house and store, old the first merchandise, and was Postmaster of the place. This was about 1872. His brother Owen was also Postmaster for some time, and both brothers were teachers.

THOMAS W. SCOTT, M. D., Rushville, Illinois, is a son of Thomas W. and Catherine (Fitzgerald) Scott, whose history is fully given in another biographical sketch in this work. He was born in Scott county, Kentucky, April 18, 1848, and was but a child when his parents came to Illinois. Here he grew to manhood; he attended the common schools, and also enjoyed the opportunities afforded in the academy at Monmouth, Illinois. He assisted his father in the farm work, and thus gained an intelligent comprehension of agriculture as a science.

In 1881 he began the study of medicine at Mount Vernon, Missouri, under the preceptorship of Dr. G. L. Knapp; he subsequently attended lectures at the Missouri Medical College, St. Louis, and was graduated with the degree of M. D. in March, 1884. He immediately located at Mt. Vernon, Missouri, and the following year removed to Rushville. He is a close student of his profession and the science of medicine, and is fully abreast of the times upon all subjects pertaining thereto. The July (1892) session of the Board of County Supervisors appointed him County Physician.

In addition to his professional duties the Doctor finds time for horticultural pursuits, and is very successful; he also raises poultry, breeding the best grades. He owns a farm east of Rushville, which is cultivated under his supervision.

Politically he is identified with the Democratic party, although he gives little attention to politics beyond exercising his right of suffrage. He is an honored member of the Knights of Pythias. He is a man of great energy and enterprise, and in all the walks of life has earned the success and merited the prosperity that has attended him.

LUKE W. CLARK, M. D., has been a close student of his profession for many years, and long ago won an enviable reputation as a skillful practitioner. He was born in Pike county, Ohio, September 6, 1841. His father, Ebenezer Clark, was a native of the State of New York, and was there reared and married, his wife's maiden name being Julia A. Wilcox, also of the Empire State. His early life was spent amid rural scenes, in closest touch with Nature, who is always a wise and gentle teacher. He attended the common schools, and in his youth began the study of botany and medicine; there was not a tree or plant in the State of Illinois with which he was not as familiar as with the members of his own household. He emigrated to Ohio, and there was engaged in agricultural pursuits; he was still devoted to the study of medicine, and after the family came to Illinois and located at Rushville, in 1845, he began the practice of his profession, which he continued to the time of his death. While for many years he enjoyed a wide and paying practice, he did not accumulate wealth; he was kind to the poor and did much for charity; in his death the poor lost one of their stanchest friends. In politics he was an ardent supporter of Republican principles; in his religious faith he was also possessed of the courage of his convictions, denying any future state; he did not approve of secret societies. His wife died in February, 1892; they had born to them nine children, all of whom lived to years of maturity: Marcus, a physician, died at Vermont, Illinois, in 1892; Franklin is a farmer in McDonough county; Victor is a farmer in Adair county, Missouri; Luke W. is the subject of this sketch; Albert R. is practicing medicine at Vermont, Illinois; Mary married Dr. B. F. Taylor, and died at Vermont, Illinois; Lucy is the wife of Jacob Trout, of Rushville; Cornelia is the wife of C. P. Neill; Emaline married William Barber.

Dr. Luke W. Clark received his literary education in the common schools of Rushville, and at the age of sixteen years began the study of medicine under the preceptorship of his father, with whose botanical remedies he became familiar. After finishing his medical education he came to Rushville and engaged in practice with his father. He is now one of the oldest physicians in Schuyler county, and has a large and lucrative practice.

Dr. Clark was married, in 1872, to Miss Frances Schenk, a daughter of John Schenk, and a native of Fulton county, Illinois.

Four sons have blessed this union: Wheeler, Myron, Earl and Homer.

The Doctor is a member of the State Medical Eclectic Society; in all his professional relations he has preserved that integrity and honor which graced the name of his father. He has been a close student of the science of medicine, and employs a set of remedies which have come to be known as "Clark's Family Medicines," and are now manufactured for the trade. In politics he affiliates with the Republican party.

PETER W. RICKARD, an intelligent and progressive farmer of Cass county, Illinois, residing in township 19, range 9, was born in Windham county, Connecticut, August 26, 1823.

His parents were Peter and Mary (Healy) Rickard, both natives of Massachusetts, the mother's birth having taken place in Dudley, of that State. The father died one month previous to the birth of the subject of this sketch. Grandfather Rickard was a brave and efficient soldier in the Revolutionary war, and died in the service. The Rickard family is of French ancestry and took a prominent part in early Colonial times. Our subject's mother was a daughter of Stephen and Rhoda (Marcy) Healy, also natives of Massachusetts, both of whom were related to old and respected families of that State. They died in the Bay State between the ages of seventy and eighty years. Both her father and grandfather were distinguished soldiers in the Revolutionary war, although the fame of her grandfather, Major Nathan Healy, rather outshone that of her father, the elder gentleman receiving a liberal pension from the Government for his able services in that memorable struggle The Healys were originally from England, and, as far as known, were successful farmers. On the maternal side, Mr. Rickard's mother was an own cousin of William L Marcy, at one time Governor of New York Their revered parents had eight children, of whom our present subject is the sole survivor; some of these were tradesmen and successful merchants. The mother died in Windham county, Connecticut, aged about sixty-nine years, universally lamented for her kindly ways and Christian character.

The subject of this sketch lived with his mother until he was eight years of age, when he went to live with a brother-in-law, with whom he remained until he was fourteen He, then, found employment by the day or month, and at the same time diligently prosecuted his studies in the free school, which he continued to attend until he attained the age of twenty-one.

He then started for the West, Illinois being the objective point, then on the extreme frontier. In these days of rapid transit, it is interesting to note, by way of contrast, the time consumed by the journey. He went by cars and boat to New York city, and thence, via the Erie canal and Cumberland stage route, to Philadelphia and Wheeling, which took four weeks' time. He thence proceeded by the rivers to Beardstown, Illinois being twenty days en route, arriving at the latter place in the fall of 1844. He taught a subscription school for several terms, after which he taught a free school, continuing thus for many years, teaching in the winter and farming during the summer. He first purchased 120 acres in his present township, on which he settled soon after marriage He afterward kept a general store for a year in Chandlerville, when, in 1857, he sold his first farm and bought 240 acres, on which he now resides He lived on the old farm while the present one was being prepared for occupancy Besides this valuable and extensive property, he owns a fine tract of forty acres, in this vicinity, all of which is devoted to mixed farming, in which he is very successful, being numbered among the most prosperous farmers of the county

Mr Rickard was first married June 22, 1846, to Miss Elizabeth Pease, an intelligent lady, and a native of Ohio. Her parents were Aborn Pease and wife, natives of Connecticut, prominent and early settlers of Illinois, who died at an advanced age. By this marriage, Mr. Rickard has one son, Henry A , who was born February 12, 1848; he married Julia Hardin, and has two children Mr. Rickard's union was destined to be of short duration, his wife dying on the old farm, in the twenty-seventh year of her age

November 5, 1854, Mr. Rickard was again married, his second wife being Miss Mary Harbison, an estimable lady, a native of this county and a sister of Moses Harbison, a prominent resident of this locality. (See sketch in this book.) By this marriage there was one child, now deceased This union was also suddenly dissolved by the hand of death, before whose power all must bow. This gentle and beloved lady expired October 6, 1856, leaving many friends to mourn her untimely taking away.

April 21, 1856, Mr. Rickard was married to Miss Mary C. Taylor, well and favorably known in this community, where she was born March 21, 1840 Her parents, Henry B and Mary P (Hawthorn) Taylor, are honored pioneers of Illinois. Mrs Rickard was a pupil of her husband when he taught school here in the early day. She is well informed and intellectual, being well adapted to be a companion to a person of her husband's superior ability and training.

By this marriage there have been nine children, five now living; all born on this farm. Those surviving are: Charles E., born July 28, 1860; John T., born June 29, 1862; Francis M., born October 8, 1867; Mary, born March 4, 1871; James A., born December 25, 1879.

Mr. Rickard was formerly an old-line Whig, and cast his first vote for William H. Harrison, at a time when there was no tickets, each person writing the name of the candidate of his choice. He has taken an active interest in the politics of his township, and has held the position of superintendent and other local offices, discharging his duties in his several capacities with ability and integrity.

Mr. and Mrs. Rickard and all the family are earnest and useful members of the Congregational Church, of which Mr. Rickard is a Deacon and Trustee. The entire family are prominent in temperance work and all matters tending to the material and moral advancement ot the community.

Although caring less for pedigree than our English cousins across the water, yet we tacitly admit that tendencies and early training have much to do with shaping a man's career through life. While Mr. Rickard has worked out his own prosperity and salvation, yet he has, no doubt, often drawn inspiration from the contemplation of the virtues of his illustrious ancestors, whose example he has insensibly been led to emulate.

JOSEPH FENTON VAN DEVENTER was born in Highland county, Ohio, June 25, 1826, a son of Jacob Van Deventer, who was born in Loudoun county, Virginia, a descendant of the colonial settlers who came from Holland in the early history of this country. The father of our subject was reared and married in Virginia, but removed to Ohio, where he was a pioneer of Highland county; there he bought a tract of timber-land, erected a log cabin, and made it his home until the fall of 1832, when he sold and came to Illinois; he was accompanied by his wife and children, and his brother and family. The trip was made overland, and after a journey covering three weeks he arrived in Schuyler county, which portion is now included in Brown county; he made a claim to a tract of Government land, bought a log cabin, and lived there until his death in 1833. He was twice married, the second wife being the mother of Joseph F. Her maiden name was Jane Rogers, and she was born near Paris, Kentucky, a daughter of Thomas Rogers; she kept the family together until her death in 1843. Joseph F. was a child of six years when his parents emigrated to the frontier; most of the land was owned at that time by the Government, the country was thinly settled, and the river towns were the only market-places. He attended the pioneer schools until he was old enough to assist on the farm; the mother had rented land which the sons cultivated. In 1850 Joseph and his brothers, Thomas and Henson, and a Mr. Adams and his son, crossed the plains to California; they started with ox teams March 27, and arrived at Weavertown, August 27. They engaged in mining thirty-five miles east of Sacramento until the following spring, and then went to Humboldt, and from that point across the mountains to Weaverton; there they resumed mining and continued the industry until June, 1852, when they started to Sacramento. They turned their attention to feeding cattle now, and followed the business until 1853, when they returned to Illinois, coming by the Isthmus to New York, and thence overland to their prairie home. Mr. Van Deventer and his brothers, Thomas, Barnett and Henson, combined their interests in farming and stock-raising, and bought land at different times, until they owned at one time 3,500 acres; Barnett and Henson are now deceased.

Our subject was married in 1868 to Lutitia Givens, who was born at Mt. Sterling, Brown county, Illinois, a daughter of John A. and Mary F. (Curry) Givens, pioneers of Brown county. Mr. and Mrs. Van Deventer have two children living, Homer G. and Lloyd T. They are both members of the Presbyterian church. He was formerly a supporter of the principles of the Whig party, but has been a Republican since the organization of that body. He is a man of honor and unquestioned integrity, and has the respect of his fellow-men.

DUNCAN TAYLOR, a well-known citizen of Rushville township, is a citizen of the Republic by adoption, his native land being Scotland; he was born in Perthshire, in March, 1819, a son of Collin and Mary (Watt) Taylor, natives of the same shire. The parents spent their lives in their own country; they reared a family of eight children, named as follows: Jane, Thomas and John, twins, James, Margaret, Duncan, the subject of this biographical sketch, Ann and Catherine. Duncan Taylor and his brother James were the only members of the family who emigrated to America; James entered the service in the Florida war, and was never heard of after leaving Boston. Our subject was reared and educated in Scotland, and resided in that country until he was eighteen years of age. He then went to London, England, and there followed the baker's trade until 1843. In that year he emigrated to the United States, embarking on board a sailing vessel at Liverpool, which landed in New York after a voyage of thirty days. He worked at his trade in New York city until 1848, and then started toward the setting sun. The city of Chicago at that time had a population of a few thousand people, but there was not a railroad entering the place, and stages ran to St. Louis and other important points. Mr. Taylor engaged in work at his trade in Chicago, and remained there a year, coming at the end of that time to Rushville.

At the breaking out of the civil war he abandoned his private interests, and in August, 1861, he enlisted in Company G, Twenty-eighth Illinois Volunteer Infantry, and was with his regiment in all the marches and campaigns; the most important battles in which he took part were Fort Henry, Fort Donelson, Shiloh, Jackson, Miss, and the sieges of Corinth and Vicksburg. He was honorably discharged August 26, 1864, the term of his enlistment having expired.

He returned to his home and resumed his former vocation, which he pursued a number of years; he was successful in his business operations, and at different times invested in and, until he now owns three farms in Woodstock township.

Mr. Taylor was married in 1843 to Elizabeth Fourgeson, a native of Ireland, and a daughter of Daniel and Mary (Fulton) Fourgeson. Four children were born of this union, two of whom are living, Robert and William, twins; Sarah and Mary are both deceased. Robert married Ann Beck, and has four children; William married Adele Vandavenor; Sarah was the wife of Richard Lawler, and Mary married Charles Reed; she left two children. Mr. and Mrs. Taylor are worthy and consistent members of the Presbyterian Church. In politics Mr. Taylor is an ardent supporter of Republican principles. He is a member of Colonel Harvey Post, No. 131, G. A. R. He is a man of superior business ability, is honorable in all his dealings, and worthy of the confidence his fellow-men repose in him.

ANDREW J. HEDGCOCK, a prosperous farmer and esteemed citizen of Schuyler county, Illinois, was born in Davidson county, North Carolina, November 25, 1831, and is a son of John and Temperance (Bodenhamer) Hedgcock. Three generations of the family were born in the old North State: the subject of this sketch, his father, John, and his grandfather, Elisha. The originator of the family in that State was Elisha's father, John, who removed to North Carolina from within sixteen miles of Baltimore, Maryland. This was about six years before the Revolutionary war. William, an older brother of John's, was a soldier in that war; and it is more than probable that John also fought with the Colonies for independence. Elisha, son of John, spent his whole life in North Carolina. He had four sons, all dead but one. His son, John, a farmer, removed to Illinois in 1834, with his wife and three children. The long trip was made overland with a one-horse wagon, and consumed about eight weeks. He at first settled near Rushville, but afterward removed to Birmingham township, where he bought seventy-nine acres of wild land. On this he built a log cabin, 16 x 18 feet, in which his family lived for sixteen or eighteen years. He then erected a nice frame house, where he resided until his death, at the age of seventy-five years. He was well and favorably known in his community, and was sincerely mourned by many friends. In politics, he was originally a Whig, but joined the Republican party on its organization. He was a devout church member, and interested in all good works. His worthy wife died on the same farm, aged fifty-five years.

Andrew is one of the eight children, seven of whom are yet living, nearly all in this county. He remained on the old farm until he was twenty-two years old working with his father at the cooper trade, and attending the subscription school. He married early in life, and rented a farm for two years, but at the end of that time he bought eighty acres that were but little improved, on which he built a log house. Here they lived for four years and then he replaced the old house by a neat frame one. He has 520 acres now, and it is divided into several as good farms as are in the county, all having fine farm houses and buildings upon them. Mr. Hedgcock has always been a strong Republican in politics, and voted for John C. Fremont. He and his wife are prominent members of the Congregational Church, he having joined in 1857.

He was married April 17, 1855, to Miss Martha P. Hall, of Iredell county, North Carolina. She is the daughter of Robert S. and Annie (King) Hall. Her parents were married in 1819 and came to Illinois in the spring of 1835, for the purpose of freeing their slaves, of whom they had some eleven or twelve by inheritance, which they succeeded in doing after several years of trouble and expense. They had ten children. Mr.

Hall was a good man, and always acted up to his convictions of right and wrong. He lived in Indiana for some time and then returned to Illinois, and died here at the age of seventy-two. The whole family were very prominent wherever they lived.

Mr. and Mrs. Hedgcock had eight children, seven of whom are still living: Robert S., born February 28, 1856, married Laura Balton, and they have three children; Mary J., born September 10, 1857, married Albert S. Glass, and they have one child; John F., born November 3, 1861, married Anna E. Wade, and they have four children. He is Township Treasurer, to which office he was elected in 1886. He is a farmer, and resides on his own farm. The fourth child, Bessie E., born June 14, 1864, married George Dorsett, and they have one child; Matilda A., born September 25, 1866, and Anna E., born May 16, 1875, are both at home. Lillie E., born November 8, 1870, married William E. Dorsett, September 10, 1891.

All but two of the children have been at Plymouth High school, of which three are graduates. Most of the family are active in church work, and the occupation of them all is farming and stock raising. This is a family of whom the county may well be proud.

HON. JOHN J. McDANNOLD, a prominent citizen of Brown county, is the subject of the following biography, and is cheerfully accorded a space in this history. He was born on the homestead in Pea Ridge township, Brown county, Illinois, August 29, 1851. His father, Thomas I. McDannold, was born near Mt. Sterling, Kentucky, a son of John McDannold, a native of Virginia. The great-great-grandfather of our subject, Alexander McDannold, was born near Aberdeen, Scotland, and emigrated to America in colonial days; he settled near Culpeper Court House, Virginia, and spent the remainder of his life in that State. John McDannold removed from Virginia to Kentucky and was an early settler of that State; he improved a farm on which he lived the remainder of his days. Thomas I. McDannold grew to manhood in his native State, and came to Illinois. After his marriage he purchased a tract of wild land in Pea Ridge township; there he built a small frame house, and began the task of reducing his land to cultivation. As his means increased he made other investments in land, and now owns 500 acres. He was united in marriage to Mary E. Means, a native of Kentucky and a daughter of Major John and Patsey (Parker) Means. They reared a family of four children: John J., Thomas R., George R. and Clara. John J. received his early education in the district schools, and this training was supplemented by a course at the Quincy high school, one term at Farwell's English and Classical school, and two years at Dr. Corbin's private school.

Supplying himself with the necessary books, he returned to the home farm, and began the study of law. In 1873 he entered the law department of the Iowa State University at Iowa City, and was graduated from that institution in 1874; December 25th of that year he opened an office in Mt. Sterling, and has since devoted himself to legal work.

He was united in marriage, in 1876, to Miss Cora Harris, who was born in Macomb, Illinois, a daughter of Dr. Ralph and Mary Harris. Two children were born to Judge and Mrs. McDannold, Malcolm and Helen.

Judge McDannold has filled various offices of trust and honor; he has served as a member of the School Board, has served in the City Council, has been Mayor of the city, Master in Chancery for seven years, and County Judge for six years; the last named position he resigned in 1892. He was made the nominee of the Democratic party for Congress at the convention held at Jerseyville, in May, 1892, being the first man in Brown county to receive this distinction. He is a member of Hardin Lodge, No. 44, A. F. & A. M., of the chapter, and of Delta Commandry, No. 48, K. T. In his profession he has been very successful, and has attained a prominent position among the members of the bar of Illinois.

ENOCH EDMONSTON, a member of the county Board of Supervisors, representing Bainbridge township, is one of the prominent citizens of Schuyler county, and is entitled to recognition in its annals. He was born in Carroll county, Missouri, March 2, 1856, a son of Enoch Edmonston, Sr.; the father was born in Buncombe county, North Carolina, July 20, 1801, a son of Baziel Edmonston, who removed from Maryland, his native State, to North Carolina, and thence to the Territory of Indiana, in 1808; he was a pioneer of Dubois county, and there spent the last years of his life. He was married to Hannah Rose, who was born in North Carolina and died in Indiana. Enoch Edmonston, their son, was reared in Indiana and was married there. In 1829 he emigrated to Illinois with his brother, spent the summer in Schuyler county, and in the autumn returned to Indiana. In 1834 he again came to the State, accompanied by his family; he made the trip overland with two teams, camping on the way, and located on a tract of land that was afterward found to be patent land; he then removed to section 31, where he resided a short time, soon making a claim to a tract of Government land on section 29; he erected a house on this place, made some improvements, and lived there until he purchased land on section 32. As he prospered he added to his landed estate, and at one time owned about 1,000 acres. In 1855 he rented his farms, and went to Carroll county, Missouri, where he purchased land and resided for two or three years; at the end of that time he returned to Schuyler county, where he was living at the time of his death, August 2, 1872. He was twice married; the first wife was Susan Allen, a native of Buncombe county, North Carolina, and a daughter of Daniel and Celia (Hyde) Allen; she died in 1854; the second marriage was to Sarah (Barbee) Newsom. Mr. Edmonston was prominently identified with the best interests of the county; for six years he was Sheriff of the county, and was Treasurer for two years, discharging his duties with marked ability and fidelity.

Enoch Edmonston, Jr., was two years old when his parents returned from Missouri to Illinois. He received his education in the common schools, and had the advantage of a term at a business college in Quincy. For a period of three years he was engaged in business at Quincy, and with the exception of that time he has given his attention exclusively to agricultural pursuits; he now occupies the old homestead. He was married in March, 1885, to Nancy Ater, a native of Cass county, Illinois, and a daughter of John J. and Mary Ater, natives of Morgan county, Illinois, and pioneers of Cass county. Mr. and Mrs. Edmonston are the parents of four children: Belle, Roy, Floss and Fay. Independent in thought and action, Mr. Edmonston has never been associated with any political party, but cast his first vote with the Labor party, and now gives his support to the organization known as the People's party. He is a member of Woodstock Grange, No. 443, P. of H.

JOHN KERR, Rushville.—America has drawn her population from every continent and all the islands of the sea. Ireland has contributed her quota, sending many of her sturdy sons, who have aided in the development and growth of the New World, and pushed their way to the frontier, that the path might be made for the onward march of civilization. John Kerr, proprietor of the Schuylerville coal mine and one of the prominent agriculturists of Schuyler county, Illinois, is a native of County Fermanagh, Ireland, born near Five-mile Town, July 15, 1840. His father was also a native of the Emerald Isle, but the grandfather was born in Scotland, although he spent his last days in County Fermanagh. The father was a weaver by trade, and operated a hand loom with great skill; later in life he became the proprietor of a shop, and employed several men; the last years of his life, however, were devoted to farming, the land being leased; he married Rebecca Wier, a native of Scotland, and to them were born eight children.

John Kerr and his brother Alexander emigrated to America in 1864, the latter settling at Newark, New Jersey; they were the only members of the family who came to this country. Our subject was reared and educated in his native land, and followed agricultural pursuits. He did not bring his family with him to the United States, as it was to them an untried land, and he wished to be able to return if the prospects were not fair. He was first located at Whitestone on the Hudson, his wife and children joining him there the following year. Later on he went to Newark, New Jersey, and was employed in the woolen mills until 1872. In that year he removed to Illinois, and purchased eighty acres of land, ten miles north of Rushville; here he lived a year, and then sold out, buying ten acres near Rushville. Two years later he had the good fortune to open a coal bank, and since that time he has been busily engaged in operating the same; he ships to northern Illinois and Wisconsin, and carries on a profitable trade. He has invested in lands at different times, and now owns one hundred and ninety and a half acres, lying three quarters of a mile from the courthouse.

Mr. Kerr was united in marriage in 1862, to Miss Eleanor Bell, a native of County Fermanagh, Ireland, and a daughter of Robert and Ann Bell. Eight children have been born to them: Joseph, Catherine, Robert, Annie, Fred, William, Burt and May.

Politically, Mr. Kerr adheres to the principles of the Republican party, and is a thoroughly loyal citizen of his adopted country.

THOMAS W. SCOTT, deceased, was born in Montgomery county, Maryland, December 2, 1808. His father, Amos Scott, was a native of the same county, born in 1777, of Scotch-Irish ancestors, who were among the early settlers of this country. He was reared to agricultural pursuits, and resided in Maryland until 1814, when he removed to Kentucky. The journey was made with teams to the Ohio river, and thence down that stream on flatboats. Mr. Scott located near Georgetown, Scott county, and was engaged in planting until 1832, when he came to Schuyler county, Illinois, and settled on land in Buena Vista township, which his son Thomas W. had purchased; there he and his wife spent the remainder of their days; her maiden name was Nancy West, and she was born in Montgomery county, Maryland; she was the mother of two sons and five daughters. Thomas W. was a child of six years when the family removed to Kentucky, and there in the Blue-Grass State he was reared and educated. In 1829 he came to Illinois, making the trip on horseback, and located at Rushville, which was but a hamlet; the surrounding country was thinly settled, and much of the land was yet owned by the Government. He embarked in the mercantile trade at Rushville, opening the first store of the kind in that place; he carried on a business there until 1835, and then returned to Scott county, Kentucky. He bought the Blue Springs farm, five miles west of Georgetown, and cultivated this land with slave labor; he lived there until 1851, when he sold out and returned to Rushville, Illinois. He was engaged in conducting a general loan and brokerage business until his death, which occurred January 22, 1885.

Mr. Scott was twice married; his first wife was Adeline Johnson; she was born in Scott county, Kentucky, and died there in 1834; the issue of this marriage was one son, R. J., now living at Brookfield, Missouri, a physician. The second marriage was December 20, 1840, when he was united to Catherine Fitzgerald. She was born one mile from Lexington, Kentucky, October 30, 1822, a daughter of Jesse Fitzgerald, a native of Colfax county, Virginia. The paternal grandfather, William Fitzgerald, was also a Virginian by birth, but removed to Kentucky, being one of the earliest white settlers there. On account of the hostility of the Indians, he with several others lived for some time in the fort at Boone Station. Later he purchased land in Fayette county, and resided there until his death. Jesse Fitzgerald was a young child when his parents moved to Kentucky. He was reared to the occupation of a farmer, and owned land one mile from Lexington which was cultivated by slaves. He married Lucretia Shellars, a native of Maryland and a daughter of William Shellars.

Mrs. Scott has nine children living: Josephine, Eugene J., Mary F., Thomas W., Catherine, Leonidas, Winfield, Mentor and Florida. The parents were both consistent members of the Christian Church. Mr. Scott cast his first vote for General Jackson, and was all his life an ardent supporter of the principles of Democracy. He was a man of much force and integrity of character, and his name is honored among the pioneers of Schuyler county.

JOSEPH HUNT, farmer, of section 2, township 17, range 10, post office Virginia, was born in Kentucky, September 19, 1824. His parents moved to Sullivan county, Indiana, when he was one year old. Here he grew to manhood, coming to Illinois when he was twenty-five and stopping two years in Sangamon county. From there he went to Cass county, thirty-eight years ago. His parents were John R. and Hannah (Davis) Hunt. Both were natives of Kentucky, and the grandfather was also a Kentuckian, who ived to be ninety years old. Both parents died in Sullivan county, Indiana. They had eleven children, of which large family Joseph was the eldest. Eight of the children are still living. John Wesley died in Nashville during the war, being a soldier; Dora was killed accidently with a scythe, and George died in mature years, leaving a family. Levi, James, Sarah A., Mary, Elizabeth, Martha and Macia all live in Sullivan county, Indiana.

Joseph enlisted in August, 1862, in Company D, One Hundred and Fourteenth Illinois Infantry, and was assignod to duty with the army of the Cumberland. He participated in the siege of Vicksburg under General Grant. From there he went to the battle of Jackson, returned to Memphis, and was in that fight; next engaged in the fight at Champion Hills, and from there went to the Black River, where he built a bridge under fire from the enemy. He was under General Thomas at this time. He guarded a pontoon bridge for about six months, and while there heard of the surrender of Lee and Johnson. He was discharged in August, 1865, having served three years. Joseph was home but once during his service, and that was on a sick furlough. He had the erysipelas while in service and it injured his eyes so much that he was nearly blind, and a furlough was necessary. He has never recovered from the effect of it. He receives a small pension, on account of heart disease.

He was married on the farm where he now lives, to Durinda B. Freeman, February 12, 1854. They have had two children: James Henry, the eldest, is married and resides in Leadville, Colorado. He has been keeping hotel until recently. He is now employed at the Government Fish Hatchery. He has one child, Bernice. Ida married John T. Drinkwater, and lives near by. They have two sons, Ralph and Joe. Mr. Drinkwater is a breeder of road and draft horses.

Mr. Hunt is a staunch Republican, although the rest of the family were Democrats. He and his wife are members of the Cumberland Presbyterian Church and are worthy people and are highly respected by their hosts of friends. Mr. Hunt does not belong to any social orders.

MRS. NANCY GREEN was born in Ohio, November 30, 1824, and lived there until two or three years of age, and then came to Kentucky with her parents. They were James and Lovey (Tolle) Tolle, both born in Virginia, who had gone to Ohio in an early day. In 1836 they concluded to move West and sold every thing except some household goods, and with a two-horse wagon came overland and first settled in Schuyler county for two months. They then came to Brown county and entered eighty acres of land and bought 160 more of that partly improved, and hewed out a log hut in which they lived until about 1850. They then sold out again and went to Grundy county, Missouri, where Mr. Tolle bought an improved farm of 160 acres and there lived until his death, but he had sold the farm before this. He was living at the home of his daughter Sarah when he died, aged about seventy-four years. The mother of our subject died at the same place, aged about sixty-five years. There were ten children, four of whom are yet living. The father was a wheelwright and chair-maker. The grandparents on the mother's side were Reuben and —— Tolle, and the paternal grandparents were William and Diana Tolle.

The marriage of our subject took place January 28, 1843, to Mr. Hiram Green, who was born in Culpeper county, Virginia, December 25, 1817. He was the son of

John and Sarah (Newby) Green, who lived in Virginia all their lives and died about middle age. The husband of our subject came to Illinois about 1838, with some of his relatives, and worked by the month for some time, but was a cooper at the time of his marriage. He bought a farm of 160 acres in the county of Brown from a man who had improved it; but Mr. Green built a log house and there they lived for about six years, and then he bought another eighty acres and built a better house. There the family lived until 1873, when he sold it and bought his present farm of 240 acres on which are all improvements. He died August 2, 1877. He was a Democrat in his politics but did not bother much about them.

Our subject and her husband started with nothing and at the time of his death had acquired as fine a farm as there is in the county. They were faithful members of the Union Baptist Church for years, and he was an active member, assisting in the building of it and was lamented by all at the time of his death.

Mrs. Greene, the estimable lady whose sketch we are presenting, is well known in the township where she and her husband have shown to the world a life of married felicity. She has been the beloved mother of fourteen children and is not only esteemed above all others by her immediate family but by the neighborhood. We close this short notice with the names of her family. Mary Jane is at home; Sarah is married and has two children; Lovey M. is married and died leaving four children; Ann G. is married and has seven childre; Juliet is married and has five children; William F. is married and has six children; Celinda E. is married and has five children; Angeline is married and has four children; George W. is married and has three children; Purlina is married and has two children; Olive; Almira is married but has no family.

Mrs. Greene looks after the farm herself and rents to her son George, who carries on a very successful mixed farming.

WILLIAM J. DAVIS, of Lee township, was born in Adams county, Illinois, in 1845. His father, Washington, was born in Virginia about 1822, and his father, Edward, was a Virginia farmer who emigrated to Illinois in 1837, where he died at an advanced age, in Adams county. They came by land the most of the way. The mother of William J. was Nancy Chipman of North Carolina, a daughter of David Chipman, who came to Illinois in 1835. She survived her husband.

William Davis had a good common-school education, was reared to farm life, and this has been his vocation except a little agency as a salesman in fruit trees. He remained at home until twenty-six years of age, when he married Maggie, daughter of George and Hannah (Ferguson) Colgate. She was born in Pike county, of which her parents were early settlers. Her mother died about 1877. Her father is living, at the age of seventy-five.

Mr. and Mrs. Davis settled on a small farm near Clayton in 1874. Three years later they sold there and moved to their present home in Brown county, buying sixty acres for $2,-250. He rents part, and farms about 120 acres a year. They have been greatly blessed, and have not lost any of their ten children. They are, Charles E., Adelbert, Walter, Harriet, Jackson, Julia, George, Belle, Mary and Nellie. This family is all comely, bright and dutiful; and are being carefully educated.

Mr. Davis is a Missionary Baptist, he is also a Democrat, but is not strongly partizan. While he has been very busy raising stock and engaged in general farming he has had time to become a successful bee-keeper in the last six years. He is School Director and a very active member in his church. His family is highly thought of in the community as is he himself.

BENJAMIN F. REBMAN, a farmer and dairyman, was born in Schuyler county, Illinois, at Pleasant View, January 12, 1848. He was the seventh child in a family of nine born to John and Margaret (Huffman) Rebman, the former of whom was born at Strasburg, Germany, and the latter near the same place. They emigrated to America in 1830 and were married in New York city in 1832. They lived in New York State about four years, when they removed to St. Louis, and after remaining there two years removed to Beardstown, Illinois, where they lived four years more. At the end of that time they moved to Schuyler county and here they both died, Mrs. Rebman in 1877 and her husband four years later. Mr. Rebman was a mechanic by trade.

Benjamin Rebman, after the slight schooling he was able to obtain in the country schools, at the age of eighteen, engaged in farming, working by the month for farmers until he had accumulated enough to begin business for himself. He has been engaged in the dairy business for some years and has supplied the city of Beardstown with vast quantities of milk. This taken in connection with his extensive farming yield him a nice income. He was engaged in the manufacture of brick, but sold out recently.

He was married in this county January 1, 1879, to Mrs. Louisa Curry, daughter of Anthony Messeren, one of the pioneers of Schuyler county. He was a very successful farmer, being a representative of an agricultural family for generations back. He went from Germany, his birthplace, to the West Indies, when he was six years of age. The uncle who was taking him to America died on the voyage and the child was adopted by a West Indian planter. Here he grew to manhood, and came to Illinois in 1832 and entered a large tract of land in Schuyler county, where he lived until the time of his death in 1859. His wife survived him for twenty-two years. They had five children, two of whom died in infancy.

Mr. and Mrs. Rebman have had three children: Anthony, deceased; Gale and Herman Blane. His religious views are those of a free-thinker; is Republican in politics.

ANDREW J. MEAD is located at Huntsville and is the oldest physician in Schuyler county, as he has been located at this place since March, 1840. He was born in Henry county, Kentucky, April 4, 1815, being a son of William and Mary (Scott) Mead.

He grew to manhood in his native State, passing his boyhood on the farm. At the age of thirteen he commenced to clerk in a store and continued there four years. He then lived with Dr. Gosle, with whom he studied medicine until he was twenty-one and then practiced with him one year. He then went to Indiana, whence he came to Illinois and located at Huntsville. He had been on a visit to Missouri, and on his return stopped in Huntsville, where he met some old Kentucky friends who induced him to locate in this place. He has had a large practice and is well and favorably known.

He married in December, 1843, Mary J. Briscoe, born near Perryville, Kentucky, June 2, 1825, daughter of George H. and Eliza K. (Ewing) Briscoe. She died December 4, 1891. They had four children: Alice, died, aged six years; Richard Homer, see sketch; William B., a physician in Kansas, graduate of Rush Medical College; and Clara, wife of Charles Everson, of Huntsville. Both sons studied medicine with their father and both graduated before they were twenty-one years of age. The Doctor is a Democrat in politics and has always been an active worker in the party. He never accepted any office, as his profession occupied all his time. He is a man who is liberal in his religious views. No one is more highly respected and admired than this same pioneer doctor of Huntsville.

WILLIAM C. BOLLMAN, Postmaster at Browning, is a native of Pike county, Illinois, born March 13, 1839. His parents were John and Rebecca (Hedgen) Bollman. Both were natives of Ohio and came to Illinois in 1837, locating in Pike county, where the father died in 1850, and the mother died in Quincy, of the cholera, when it was raging there. There were seven children by this marriage, and two by the former one. The brothers and sisters of William were: Michael, deceased; our subject was the next child; Samuel, still living in Pike county, married; John, deceased; Orville, deceased; Sarah Massey of Fulton county, Illinois; Mary O., married; Aaron Finton resides near Pittsfield, Illinois. The other two are dead.

William grew to manhood in Pike county, and married there Miss Amanda Preston, of Ohio. Her parents were John and Hannah Preston. The father died when Mrs. Bollman was a child, but the mother died in Browning with her daughter, Mrs. Bollman.

Mr. Bollman farmed for many years in Pike county, and then removed to Browning, Schuyler county, where he lived until 1861, when he enlisted in Company H, Third Illinois Cavalry, as a private, and became Quarter Master Sergeant of his regiment. He served four years and two months, and participated in the battles of Pea Ridge; was with Sherman when he made the attack on Haines' Bluff, at Vicksburg; was at the capture of Arkansas Post, and from thence to Hollow Springs, Mississippi; did scouting duty in Mississippi, and afterward had a serious engagement at Gravelly Springs, Tennessee, and he was also engaged in many other skirmishes and battles of less importance. After the surrender of the rebel armies, the regiment was sent across the plains to award the Indians, and remained there until October, 1865. They were mustered out at Minneapolis, October 10, 1865. Mr. Bollman returned to Browning, and engaged in farming, and remained in that business until 1887, when he engaged in mercantile business. He was appointed Postmaster in 1890, and still holds that position.

Mr. and Mrs. Bollman have had nine children, but only one of that number is living, Frank, now twenty-three years of age, is married and resides in Beardstown, Illinois. The Bollman family are of German and Irish origin. Mr. Bollman is a Republican, though he entered the army as a Democrat, but changed his views while in the service, and has faithfully voted with the Republican party ever since. He is a member of the G. A. R., also of the I. O. O. F. Browning Lodge, No. 309. He is a P. G., and has represented his lodge for two years at the Grand Lodge of the State. Mr. and Mrs. Bollman are members of the Methodist Episcopal Church.

Mr. Bollman was not the only member of his family who served in the late war; a brother, Samuel, served three years in the Ninety-ninth Illinois Infantry. Both escaped injury, except to general health.

SIMON A. REEVE, who has long been closely connected with the agricultural interests of Schuyler county, is a native of the State of Illinois, born at Springfield, December 28, 1828. His father, John Reeve, was a native of New York, and the paternal grandfather was born in the same State; the latter is supposed to have visited Illinois at an early day, as he purchased land in Fulton county. John Reeve was still a youth when he accompanied his parents to Kentucky, and there he was married to Betsey Ross, a Kentuckian by birth; from the Brue Grass State he removed to Indiana, and thence to Illinois, being one of the pioneers of Springfield; he resided there some years before it became the capital city of the commonwealth. In 1829 he came to Schuyler county, and settled in Bainbridge township on land his father had given him; the tract was heavily timbered, and there were no improvements. Mr. Reeve erected a log house, and began the task of placing the land under cultivation. He resided there until after the death of his wife, which occurred in 1843, when he returned to Indiana; in a few years he came back to Illinois and located in Peoria county, where he spent the last days of his life. His death occurred in his seventy-fifth year. Simon A. Reeve was but an infant when his parents removed to Schuyler county; here he was reared amid the privations and hardships incident to life on the frontier; the country was thinly settled, Indians still roamed the prairie, and wild game was abundant. The mother spun and the sister wove all the cloth with which the children were dressed. Our subject attended the pioneer schools taught in the primitive log house, and in early youth began to earn his own living; for some time he received as compensation only his board and clothing; later he had $8 or $9 per month, which he considered excellent wages. He afterward learned the cooper's trade, which he followed a number of years, and at this vocation earned the money with which he bought the first land he owned. An incident worthy of note as illustrating the value of neighbors as compared with that of land, is furnished in the act of the father of the subject of this sketch: When he settled on 160 acres of land in Schuyler county, his neighbors were few and far between, and in order to secure a near neighbor, Mr. Reeve sold fifty of his 160 acres to a gentleman for $25, upon the condition that he would reside upon it. Mr. Reeve has been very successful as a farmer, and has accumulated considerable amount of property; to his oldest son he has given 107 acres, to another 91 acres, and now occupies a farm of 120 acres, which is well improved.

Mr. Reeve was married, in 1854, to Miss Jane Orr, a native of county Tyrone, Ireland, and a daughter of Joseph and Mary (Burnside) Orr. Two sons have been born of this union, William H. and Pulaski; the former married Harriet E. Ackley, who was born in Adams county, Illinois, a daughter of Latham and Pauline (Spangler) Ackley; their three children died in infancy: Pulaski married Mary I. Ward, and they have one child living, named Bertha. Mr. and Mrs. Reeve are consistent members of the Methodist Episcopal Church. In his political opinions Mr. Reeve adheres to the principles of the Democratic party.

E. WALKER BECKWITH was one of the early settlers of Bainbridge township, Schuyler county, Illinois, and is entitled to recognition as a member of that worthy band of men and women who penetrated the wilderness of the frontier, and made the way for the onward march of progress. He was born at Stephentown, Rensselaer county, New York, August 17, 1798, and is a son of Elisha Beckwith, a native of New England, and grandson of Elisha Beckwith, Senior; the latter was a sailor and followed the sea for many years, visiting the principal ports of the world; he spent his last years in Chenango county, New York. The father of our subject was reared to agricultural pursuits; from Stephentown he removed to Chenango county, New York, where he was one of the early settlers; he bought a tract of timber land there, and erected a log house; he cleared a farm, made many valuable improvementss, and spent his last years in that home. He married Mary Walker, a daughter of James Walker; she survived him many years, coming to Illinois after his death; she died in Hancock county.

E. Walker Beckwith grew to manhood among the primitive surroundings of Chenango county, New York; there were no railroads, and Albany was the principal market town; the mother spun and wove the cloth with which her children were clothed. Here he remained until he was about twenty-six years of age, and then pushed his way to Ohio; after a year spent in that State he went to Indiana, and while a resident of the Hoosier State was engaged in various occupations; he once made a trip on a flat-boat, loaded with produce, to New Orleans. He lived in Indiana seven years, and then came to Illinois, locating in Schuyler county; as before stated, he was one of the early settlers in Bainbridge township, and with the exception of four years spent in Hancock county, Illinois, this has been his home for the past forty years.

He married Mary Waugh, a native of Kentucky and a daughter of Thomas and Sally Waugh. She died in 1886. Of this union five children were born: James, Charles, Norman, Stephen and Emily J. Stephen resides on the home farm, and has the management of the same; he married Elizabeth Kline, May 8, 1884, and they are the parents of three children: Olie T., Fidelia and Minnie E.

Mr. Beckwith is a consistent member of the Baptist Church, as was also his wife. He is a man of honor and integrity, and has the respect of the entire community.

HON. PERRY LOGSDON, a citizen of Schuyler county, is a man whose name is honored where it is known. He was born in Madison county, Kentucky, July 8, 1842, a son of Joseph and Lucy (Parker) Logsdon (see sketch of Joseph Logsdon). Until the age of eighteen years he passed an uneventful life amid the scenes of his childhood, but this quiet was then rudely disturbed by the breaking out of the Civil war between the North and South. In 1861 he enlisted in Company H, Fiftieth Illinois Volunteer Infantry, and served his country faithfully until the cessation of hostilities,

July 13, 1865, being the date of his discharge. He participated in every engagement of his company, and when the war was ended he returned to his home, with the rank of First Lieutenant.

Mr. Logsdon was married September 5, 1867, to Miss Lizzie Byers, who was born in Schuyler county, Illinois, March 12, 1850, a daughter of William and Eleanor (Stutsman) Byers (see sketch of John S. Stutsman). Mr. Byers was born in the Blue-grass State, and removed to this county in 1847, where he spent his last days; the date of his birth is May 22, 1826, and his death occurred February 24, 1862; his wife was born August 23, 1828, in the State of Indiana. The paternal grandparents of Mrs. Logsdon were John and Elizabeth Byers; he died in 1827, and she survived until 1857. After his marriage, Mr. Logsdon settled on land which is a portion of his present farm; the dwelling was a log house which was raised the day General William Henry Harrison was inaugurated President of the United States; there he lived six years, and then removed to his present home. He first bought 106 acres of choice land, to which he added 120 acres later on; to this he added two eighty-acre tracts, and is now the owner of one of the most desirable farms in the county; a portion of this land is rented, and the rest is devoted to general farming.

To Mr. and Mrs. Logsdon have been born seven children, four of whom are deceased: Luella was born on the home farm, August 5, 1869; Julia was born July 31, 1873; Charles P. was born January 6, 1880. Mr. Logsdon has for many years been identified with the political movements of his county; he has been Assessor, was Supervisor two years, and has been School Director; in 1884 he was elected a member of the State Legislature, and in 1888 was re-elected by a large majority. He is a Republican, but carried a Democratic district. While a member of the Legislature he was on several committees of importance, among which were these on Penal and Reformatory Institutions, Canals and Rivers, Insurance, Drainage, and Farm Drainage. He discharged his duties with marked ability, and such was the dignity and courtesy of his bearing as to command the respect of his allies as well as opponents. Throughout all his career, Mr. Logsdon has borne himself with a deep sense of honor which has insured a name above reproach, a credit to his ancestry and a legacy of great worth to his posterity. In the terrible conflict of this nation he was a brave, courageous soldier; in the private walks of life he has been as much the hero. He is a prominent member of the G.A. R. at Rushville, and takes an active interest in this organization.

F. WILLIAM MEYER, a prosperous farmer and stock-raiser of section 17, range 11, was born in Westphalia, Prussia, Germany, in 1838. In 1849, he came to America with his parents (see biography of Fred Meyer) and has been living in this country ever since. Here he grew to manhood, obtaining a little knowledge of English and English books. While he is not a well educated man he has good judgment and is very intelligent He is the eldest of his father's family, of whom all are married and live in the United States. Mr. Meyer owns a well improved farm of 160 acres, all under the plow with first-class farm buildings, all erected by himself. Beside this fine farm he owns seventy acres of good grass land and eighty acres of timber land. These lands are all earned by his own hard work. He follows general farming and stock-raising and breeds cattle from a first-class stock.

He was married the first time to Caroline Telkemeyer, born in Cass county, in 1845, where she was reared and educated. She came of German parents who came to the United States and settled in Cass county where they lived and died, the mother when young and the father, William, when about sixty-five. They were earnest members of the German Lutheran Church. Mrs. Meyer died at her home in this county in 1879, on Easter Sunday of that year. She was thirty-three years of age, a true, good wife and mother, and a devout member of the Lutheran Church. She was the mother of three children: Mary at home with her father; Minnie and Emma, also at home. They are intelligent young women. Mr. Meyer was married the second time in Schuyler county, to Lizzie Gise, of Hesse Darmstadt, born in 1849. She came to the United States when a young woman with her father, John, the mother having died in Germany. They settled in Cass county. Later, Mr. Gise went to Oregon and died there when an old man. He and his family were Lutherans. Mr. and Mrs. Meyer have one child, Lucy. They are members of the Lutheran Church, and are true, good people. Mr. Meyer is a Republican in politics.

EZRA JACKSON is a Hoosier by birth, born in Scott county, February 26, 1823. His father, Samuel Jackson, was a native of North Carolina, and his grandfather, Solomon Jackson, was probably a native of the same State. The grandfather was a powerful man and lived to the great age of ninety-eight years. He enlisted three different times in the Colonial army during the Revolutionary war, the first two enlistments being as substitute. He served during nearly the entire war, and was very young when he first enlisted. He was a shoemaker by occupation, but also taught school, and remained in North Carolina until the formation of the Territory of Indiana, when he came there, too, and settled in what is now Scott county. He was thus one of the earliest settlers and pioneers of Indiana. He bought land and lived there until his death. For many years he drew a pension from the Government for his services and patriotism during the Revolutionary war. He visited Schuyler county several times, but finally died in Jefferson county, Indiana.

Samuel Jackson, the father of our subject, was quite a young man when he went to Indiana. He married and lived there until 1829, and then, accompanied by his wife and five children, all drawn by two yoke of oxen, hitched to an old-fashioned wagon, came to Illinois in search of a home. There was scarcely an inhabitant on the broad prairie then, and not a laid-out road in Schuyler county. He located in what is now Bainbridge township, moving into a vacant log cabin, which the family occupied for two years, buying in the meantime a tract of land upon which was a rude log cabin and five or six acres of cleared land, the remainder of the farm being heavy timber. There was little value then in standing timber, no matter how large and fine, and accordingly the great trees were cut down, rolled together, and destroyed by the torch. This was necessary in order to clear the land for cultivation. Upon this farm he resided until his death in 1839. He was an industrious, exemplary citizen, and an honor to the great and historic name of Jackson. The maiden name of his wife, the mother of our subject, was Esther Close, who was born within two miles of Albany, New York. Her father was a native of England, who came to America at the age of thirteen. He married a Connecticut lady, and came to Scott county, Indiana, in a very early day, being one of its pioneers.

Our subject, Ezra Jackson, is one of seven children born to his parents, viz.: Zadok, Ezra, Calvin, Elizabeth, Jesse, Solomon and Mary J. When Ezra was five years of age, he was brought to Schuyler county, where he grew to manhood. He was reared on the farm, and remained there until the age of twenty years, when he commenced to learn the trade of a cooper, after following which a few years, he conducted a hotel for one year in Frederick. In 1865 he bought property at the corner of Liberty and Lafayette streets, Rushville, where he kept hotel for twenty years. He then removed the building standing there and erected the brick store building now occupying the site of the hotel. For some time he has been retired from active business. He was married, in 1846, to Emily Brunk, who was born in Morgan county, Illinois, June 8, 1829, the daughter of Jesse and Eliza (Day) Brunk, natives of Kentucky, and pioneers of Morgan county. Mr. and Mrs. Jackson's living children are; Owen, Felix, Mary Ellen, Effigene, Martha and Frederick. Mr. Jackson is a Democrat in politics.

THOMAS J. CLARK was born in Huntsville township, Schuyler county, September 16, 1853. His father, Harrison, was born in Logan county, Kentucky, February 15, 1811, and he was the son of Abner Clark.. The father of our subject was reared and married in his native township and resided there until 1833, when he emigrated to Illinois. He was accompanied by his wife and child, and his brother-in-law, Mr. Wilgus, and family. They owned a wagon together, and each one had his own horse, and in this way made an overland journey to Illinois and located in Schuyler county. When he landed here his entire wealth consisted in his interest in the wagon, his horse and $150. He lived at Mount Sterling one year, then entered a tract of Government land in what is now Huntsville township, Schuyler county. He wanted a quarter section of land, but that would have cost more money than he had, consequently he entered eighty acres, and as soon as he obtained the money he entered the remainder of the quarter. As every other settler, he first built a log cabin on the place and commenced to improve his farm. For several years there were no railroads, and he hauled his wheat to Quincy, forty miles away. He commenced very soon to deal in stock, and was very successful both as a stock-dealer and farmer. He continued to purchase land until he had about 500 acres. Here he continued until his death in 1883. His wife was named Lydia Coffman, of Hardin county, Kentucky, born August 3, 1815. Her parents came from Germany, and were early settlers of Kentucky. She died in 1860.

Thomas was educated in Schuyler county, and two years at Lincoln University. In 1875 he went to Sedgwick county, Kansas, purchased a farm twelves from Wichita and there engaged in farming for two years, when he went into Wichita and engaged in the grain business. He remained there two years and then went to McPherson, where he engaged in the same business, there built an elevator and shipped the first car load of grain ever shipped from that station. After two years he returned to Illinois and purchased the farm where he now resides in Pea Ridge township. It contains 240 acres, and is one of the finest in the county.

He was married in 1874, to Virginia, daughter of John S. Anderson. She was born in Huntsville township. Mr. and Mrs. Clark have seven children: Helen, Arthur R., Chester L., John H., Paul, Mary A. and Stanley.

Mr. Clark joined the Cumberland Presbyterian Church when sixteen years of age, and is an Elder in the church and has officiated both as Superintendent and teacher in the Sunday-school. Politically he is a stanch Republican, and is a member of the County Central Committee. In 1890 he was special agent of the Government to make note of the recorded indebtedness of the Twelfth Congressional District. He has served several terms as Secretary of the Mount Sterling Mutual Insurance Company, which office he now holds. Mr. Clark is well read, keeps posted on all general questions, is also a forcible writer, and is one of the prominent men of the township.

THOMAS R. WILLIAMS, Superintendent of the Cass County Poor Farm, was born in Bertie county, North Carolina, June 1, 1850. He is the son of Williamson A. and Margaret (Thomas) Williams, natives of Bertie county, North Carolina. The family is an old one in the State. The parents lived on a farm until after the birth of six children, and in the fall of 1856 removed to Illinois by wagon, and settled in this favored section, not far from Bluff Springs. They rented for two years, and then purchased the farm where they lived, when the mother died in May, 1884, three-score-and-ten. She was a member of the Methodist Episcopal Church. Her husband remained on the farm for two years longer, and then went to Beardstown, and one year later came to Bluff Springs, and here spent his last years, dying in October, 1888. He was a good citizen, a member of the Methodist Episcopal Church, a stanch Democrat, and a very worthy man.

Our subject and his brother are the only members of the family now living. Mr. Williams has lived in this county since he was six years of age, and has been a practical farmer since he was twenty-two years of age. He took charge of the Poor Farm in 1887, after his brother had managed it for eight years. It is located at Bluff Springs, and consists of more than 100 acres of fine land. It is well managed by Mr. Williams.

The average poor in attendance all the time is about twelve, and there is but one feeble-minded person among them.

Our subject was married in this county to Sophia Reichert, born in Beardstown, in 1857, reared and educated in Cass county, and a daughter of Conrad and Sophia Reichert, of Germany. The mother died in the prime of life, in Cass county. Mr. Reichert was married the second time to Mrs. Withroe, and they live in Beardstown, now quite old.

Mr. and Mrs. Williams have three children: Charles F., John F. and Howard, all at home. The family belongs to the Methodist Episcopal Church, and Mr. Williams is a Democrat. The county has the right man in the right place.

JOSEPH M. SPENCER, an intelligent and progressive citizen of Ashland, Illinois, and an honored veteran of the late war, was born in Gibson county, Indiana, October 24, 1842.

His parents were Joseph and Elizabeth (Hayhurst) Spencer, both of whom were natives of Morgantown, Virginia, the father of Welsh and the mother of German ancestry. They were married in Miami county, Ohio, removing thence to Indiana, from where they came to Morgan county, Illinois, in 1849. The parents and younger children later removed to Kansas, where the father died in 1870, leaving his family and many friends to mourn his loss. He was a man of superior intelligence and generous impulses, and was very popular among his associates, who keenly felt his loss. His devoted wife, whose greatest interest was the welfare of her husband and family, returned to Illinois after her husband's death, finally expiring in Morgan county, Illinois, in 1879, deeply lamented by all who knew her and who appreciated her many excellent qualities of mind and heart

This worthy couple were the parents of seven children, four of whom are now living: Job H, the eldest, died in Arkansas, in April, 1890, leaving two children, his wife having previously died; John D served three years in the Forty second Indiana Infantry, is now married and is a prosperous farmer of Gibson county, Indiana; William S. resides in Buena Vista, Colorado: he is a widower and has a family; Rebecca, wife of William A Baldwin, lives in Loami, Sangamon county, Illinois; Amos and Simeon died in youth.

The subject of this sketch accompanied his parents to Illinois when he was seven years of age, and his boyhood and early manhood was spent in this State, in the quiet pursuits of farm and home life. These peaceful, happy days were disturbed by the Civil war, and young Joseph enlisted at Springfield, on September 15, 1861, in Company K, Thirty-third Illinois Infantry He was in the Department of Missouri, and was taken prisoner by the notorious Jeff Thompson, at the battle of Blackwell Station, in October, 1861, and was paroled on the same day Jeff said " they could either take the oath of allegiance, receive a parole, or be shot;" that he had "no use for prisoners." It was at this battle that Mr. Spencer saved the life of General Lippincott, a service which the General appreciated until the day of his death, and the heroic act afterward brought many courtesies to the subject of this sketch. He was offered a commission as Second Lieutenant, but declined it as a reward for doing his duty We pause to exclaim, In what other country could such an incident have occurred? Truly, America rears kings, not ordinary men!

Mr. Spencer was seven months under parole, when he returned to the right of his command, at Village Creek, Arkansas, and took part in the fight at Cotton Plant, which occurred the following day Here, he captured Colonel Harris' horse, sword and two revolvers. This was the Colonel who commanded the Texas Legion in that engagement. Mr. Spencer was next engaged in battle at Port Gibson, May 1, 1863; he had been in several unimportant battles during the interim, but this was the next general engagement He was at Champion Hills and Black River Bridge; after which came the siege of Vicksburg, where he dug in the ditches and was under fire for forty-seven days. Here, he received a sunstroke, and was sent to St. Louis on a hospital boat. It was then that he realized fully the saying that misfortunes never come singly, for, while *en route*, he fell down a hatchway, striking on his head and causing deafness in his left ear, from which he has never recovered.

He rejoined his regiment at New Orleans, in February, 1864, they being on their way home on veteran furlough. Mr. Spencer re-enlisted as a musician, and accompanied the boys home. Afterward, he returned to New Orleans, where he did garrison duty until the Mobile campaign, when the regiment was badly decimated by a railroad wreck, which killed and wounded many men. Mr. Spencer was assigned to the Sixteenth Army Corps, under General A. J. Smith, and participated in the fight at Spanish Fort. He then went to Montgomery, Alabama, and thence to Selma, of the same State, whence he and the command moved forward to Meridian, Mississippi. From there they went to Vicksburg, and, later, to Yazoo, where Mr. Spencer was mustered out of service, November 24, 1865, after a continuous service of more than four years.

His duty done, his thoughts naturally turned to procuring a means of livelihood. It was then that he turned his attention to learning the business of painting and decorating, which he has followed most of the time ever since, In 1866, he went to Kansas, where he remained until 1874, at which time he removed to Iowa. While in Missouri, in the winter of 1862, he met with a very painful accident, in which he lost one finger and had another severely injured, which, although not incapacitating him from work, has, at times, seriously interfered with his dexterity. In 1880, he finally returned to Ashland, Illinois, to which place he is attached by all the associations of his childhood. Here he and his family have since resided, in a substantial and comfortable home surrounded by neat and attractive grounds, the whole place breathing the air of thrift and content. Besides this, Mr. Spencer is also the owner of other valuable property.

He was married, August 7, 1870, to Miss Mary E. Gard, an estimable lady, who is a native of Morgan county, Illinois, of which place her parents, Ephraim and Paulina Gard, were worthy pioneers. Her eldest brother, John S., died in the United States service, while waiting for his discharge, after the close of the war. Mrs. Spencer was the second of six children, only three of whom now survive: William, Mary and Lydia.

Mr. and Mrs. Spencer have three daughters, Ella, Anna and Lulu, all of whom are at home, the second being a teacher in the public schools. They are all highly intellectual and have been liberally educated. Mrs. Spencer and the two older daughters rae useful members of the Christian Church.

Mr. Spencer is a straight Republican in politics, and takes an active interest in all public affairs.

He is a prominent member of John L. Douglas Post, No. 592, in which he served for two terms as Quartermaster, and one term as Officer of the Day. He is an Ancient Odd Fellow, to which order he has belonged for a number of years.

Any one who has read thus far in the life of this noble, upright man, will not be at a loss to make deductions in keeping with his exemplary character. Unaided, he has attained to prominence and acquired a comfortable income for himself and family, while his numerous generous qualities appeal successfully to the hearts of his countrymen.

HENRY CADY, of Huntsville, came to this county in 1840. His grandfather, Reuben Cady, has been written up in the biography of M. E. Cady. His father was Horace Cady, and he married also a

Miss Cady, but no relation. Mr. Horace Cady was a farmer, and emigrated to New York State, settling near Rochester. Here they stayed until 1840, when they came to Illinois, settled in Camden, and the father purchased 120 acres of land. He later resided for four years near Farmington, Fulton county, then returned to Schuyler county and passed the remaining years of his life on the farm on which he first settled. He died January, 1851. His wife died November, 1870. They had ten children, namely: Hezekiah, died in Sacramento, California; Daneford, now in Camden township; Elizabeth, now Mrs. I. G. Cady, of Camden township; Lucia married Perry Anderson, and is now dead; Henry; Reuben died in Camden township; Orin died at Memphis, Tennessee, while in the army; Philinda married Cyrus Anderson, of Huntsville township; Emeline, now Mrs. Richard Mead, of Rushville. This large family have commanded the respect and esteem of every one wherever any of them have gone.

Henry Cady was born in Otsego county, New York, December 3, 1828. He came with the family to Illinois, and learned the blacksmith's trade in 1849. He started a shop in 1854 and continued it for six years. He then settled where he now resides and purchased land, but still continued his trade until 1870, when he discontinued the blacksmith shop and devoted himself to farming. He now owns 320 acres of land, on which he has made many valuable improvements. He follows stock-raising and has produced some very fine cattle. He has been Supervisor one term, and Road Commissioner still another term.

He was married in 1855, to Emeline Plunkett, of Camden township. They have had eight children: Adelia, now Mrs. Edwin Elliott; Amelia, died in childhood; Amanda, now Mrs. Greeley Clark; Frank, died at eighteen; Everett is at home; Mary is also at home, and the youngest child is Stowell R. Mr. Cady is a Democrat in politics, and the family are members of the Christian Church. Mr. Cady is a man who has made his property himself, and has been a man of good habits all his life.

C. E. JONES, prominently connected for the last twelve years, as division road master between Bushnell, Illinois, and St. Louis, Missouri, of the St. Louis division of the Quincy Railroad, with headquarters at Beardstown, was born on a farm near Baldwinsville, New York, February 11, 1847. He was there reared and educated, becoming early acquainted with hard work. At the age of sixteen, he enlisted in the Scott's Nine Hundred Cavalry, but before he reached the front he was overtaken by his father, and compelled to return home. In 1863, he enlisted in Nine Hundred of New York State Militia, and served until July, 1864, when he enlisted in Company A, One Hundred and Eighty-fifth New York Regiment Volunteer Infantry, Colonel Jennings and Captain O. K. Howard, commanding, and this regiment was assigned to First Division of the Fifth Army Corps. He fought as a brave soldier at Hatcher's Run, Petersburg, Weldon and Quaker roads and Five Forks; was in the pursuit of Lee, and was at Lee's surrender at Appomattox, where his company lost their First Lieutenant, the last man killed of the Army of the Potomac, and, later, he participated in the grand review at Washington, District of Columbia. He had many narrow escapes from capture and wounds, especially while serving as a scout for General Chamberlain, and for the period of nine months his was one of the fighting regiments of the war. He was one of the first to obtain a piece of the famous apple tree at Appomattox Court House, where Lee held his last consultation with his staff and decided to surrender. He is honestly proud of his military record, and was honorably discharged June 11, 1865.

His connection with the Chicago, Burlington & Quincy Railroad system began in 1867, and after a period of two years' service with the bridge department, with headquarters at Galesburg, he helped in the construction of the large railroad bridges over the Mississippi river at Burlington, Quincy and Hannibal, Missouri. He was also engaged between Hannibal and Moberly, Missouri. Later he was assistant track layer for the new road. then known as the Hannibal and Naples, now part of the Wabash system. All these years he has proven himself a good man, and his promotion has been won by his own efforts. He helped build what is known as the Louisiana branch of the Q. system, and after the completion of that road he became section foreman, and later extra gang foreman, which is on line of regular promotion, and after nine years was promoted to assistant road master of the St. Louis division, with headquarters at Beardstown. Two years later he became roadmaster from Bushnell to St. Louis. He now has control of 136 miles of track, with two yards, thus putting him over a large number of men. Since May, 1880, he has been the Q. road-master, and has achieved a just prominence by his indomitable energy and devotion to the interests of the company. He is a good citizen, and a leader in all local and public matters.

For several years he has been a working member of McLane Post, No. 97, G. A. R., of Beardstown, of which he is now Past Commander. He is also a member of the Beardstown Lodge, K. of P., No. 207, and was a charter member and the first Chancelor Commander, serving for three terms, and is now Deputy Grand Master of the district, and has taken an active part in all its work, and he is a member of the orders of Woodmen and Workmen. He is also active in local politics, is Chairman of the Republican County Central Committee, and has been a member of the Board of Education. He belongs to the Roadmasters' Association of America, is an ex-Vice President of it, and is a member of the Executive Board.

He was married in Quincy, Illinois, to Almira E. Stedman, of Pike county, formerly of Wilkes Barre, Pennsylvania. She was only twelve years old when her parents came to Illinois, and she grew up in Pike county. Their living children are: Bertha, Anna, Althea, Ray and Almira Edrie.

EDWARD F. HACKMAN, a farmer of section 26, township 17, range 12, was born at his father's home, in this county, November 28, 1857. He is the second son and fifth child. His parents were John Frederick and Inglehert (Meyer) Hackman, natives of Hanover, Germany, coming of pure German ancestry. They came to America in 1835, with their respective families. They grew up, were married in Cass county, and soon afterward settled on a farm in Indian Creek precinct, and later, they came to Arenzville precinct, where they purchased their present home. They bought from time to time, and made improvements, and now have a beautiful home. (For further particulars, with regard to ancestry, see biography of William Hackman.)

Edward was reared on his father's farm and remained there until he was twenty-five years old. He has since tilled his own farm. He has resided on the farm he now owns for eleven years, and last year, 1890, he bought it. It is a fine farm, and he has made many improvements upon it. It contains 240 acres.

He was married here to Amelia Jokish, an accomplished young lady, born and reared in the county. Since her marriage, she has been a devoted wife and mother. (For family history, see biography of C. G. Jokisch.) Mr. and Mrs. Hackman are the parents of five children: Elmer, Orville E., Cora M., Morton H., and Earl R. All are bright, smart children. Mr. and Mrs. Hackman are members of the Emanuel Methodist Episcopal Church, of which Mr. Hackman has been Steward for five years. He is a Republican in politics, and is very prominent in politics.

Mr. John Frederick and wife have lived honored lives in the county, and their sons and daughters are a credit to them. The father and sons are all strong Republicans, and the former is seventy-five years of age, but he is in poor health, and for the past ten years has been retired from active business. He was one of the first members of the Emanuel Methodist Episcopal Church of this place. His wife is also a member of the same, and is seventy-two years of age. They have eight children living: Wilhelmenia, widow of Henry Winkle, residing in Beardstown, mother of three bright daughters; Herman; Sophia, wife of M. L. Korse, a hardware dealer of Beatrice, Nebraska; Matilda is at home keeping house for her parents; Edward; Sarah, wife of Philip Jokisch; Henry, of the firm of Korse & Hackman, hardware dealers at Beatrice, Nebraska.

Herman Hackman is a prominent young farmer and stock-raiser, yet single, of section 30, township 17, range 11. He manages his father's old homestead of 319 acres, and has run it on his own account for the past ten years. He was born on this farm, May 6, 1850, and was reared and received his first education in the county; later he attended a commercial school in St. Louis. He has always followed the vocation of farming, and is a hard-working young man. He, like his father and brothers, is a staunch Republican in politics, and a Methodist in religion.

DR. RICHARD HOMER MEAD is a native of Schuyler county, born in Huntsville, January 16, 1847, being a son of Andrew J. and Mary (Briscoe) Mead. He was educated in Huntsville. When he was sixteen years old he enlisted in Company K, Eighth Iowa Cavalry, at Camp Roberts, Davenport, Iowa. From there they went to Nashville, Tennessee, and were on duty in the mountains during the winter of 1863–'64. In the spring they were on the left wing of General McCook's cavalry, with Sherman's army on his advance on Atlanta, participating in the engagements of that campaign, besides other engagements. There was fighting every day for 100 days. They then returned north, and were the first forces to oppose Hood's crossing the Tennessee river. They retreated before Hood's advance to Duck river, where they prevented his advance until the battle of Franklin, in which they participated, also in the battle of Nashville, when they pursued Hood's army to the Tennessee river. In the spring of 1865 they were in Wilson's cavalry, and fought two engagements in the mountains in Alabama after the war was over, not having received notice of the signing of the terms of the surrender. They next were sent in pursuit of Jeff. Davis, to Macon, Georgia, where he was captured. Mr. Mead was then mustered out, August 28, 1865. He was taken prisoner on McCook's raid in the rear of Atlanta, but escaped in a few hours. One half of his company died at Andersonville prison. After the war he returned to Illinois and resumed the study of medicine, which he had commenced in the office of his father. In November, 1865, he entered the medical college at Keokuk, Iowa, graduating with the class of 1867. He then located at Huntsville, and practiced with his father until 1872, when he went to Texas and spent five years with the I. & G. N. Railroad Company. In 1878 and 1879 he attended the St. Louis Medical College, and then resumed practice at Huntsville, and continued until 1884. Dr. Mead had thus received a good medical education, but his literary education was limited to the schools of Huntsville; however, he applied to the Civil Service Commissioner for examination, and passed in the class of Burlington, Iowa, receiving an appointment as Pension Clerk at Washington, District of Columbia, August 18, 1884, being the fifteenth man from Illinois who passed the examination. March 2, 1885, he became a permanent member of class 1, and in October of the same year he was promoted to class 2. April 24, 1886, he was detailed to the field as special examiner, and worked in Maine, New Hampshire and New York. December 28, 1886, he resigned his position, but being an honorably discharged soldier he can re-enter the service at any date, without an examination. He returned to Huntsville, where he resumed his practice, and where he has remained ever since. He usually spends the winter months in the Southern States. Dr. Mead has had a large practice, and has always attended to his patients regardless of weather, bad roads or illness.

He was married October 3, 1889, to Mary, daughter of James N. and Martha (Parrish) Ward, and they have one child,—Clara Briscoe.

Dr. Mead has voted the Democratic ticket for years, but now supports the People's party. He is a member of the Huntsville Lodge, No. 465, A. F. & A. M.; Augusta Chapter, No. 78, R. A. M., and Almoner Commandery, No. 32, K. T., also of Cyclone Lodge, No. 635, I. O. O. F., of which he is one of the organizers. He attended the National Columbian Medical Association at Washington, District of Columbia, in 1884–'85–'86. He is very active in G. A. R. matters, is a member of George A. Brown Post, No. 417, of the Department of Illinois, and always attends the annual National Encampment.

WILLIAM T. TREADWAY came to Cass county (then Morgan) with his parents in 1829. He was the son of Edward and Elizabeth (Anderson) Treadway, natives of Maryland, raised near Baltimore. They moved from there after marriage, to Hamilton county, Ohio, and from there to this county. The family is English-Scotch. They had eight children, of whom the subject was the fourth; only three are living, and he is the oldest. They are Edward, Owens and Elizabeth. The parents died here and are interred in the Monroe cemetery.

William was born in Hamilton county, Ohio, August 22, 1819, hence was ten years old when he became a resident of Cass county. Sixty-three years of his life have been spent in this county, forty-one of them on his present farm. He was educated in the subscription schools, grew to manhood a farmer, and followed that occupation all his life. He is now enjoying the fruit of his early industry, and is living a retired life. During his residence in this county Mr. Treadway has witnessed a wonderful transformation from a wilderness to a populous and prosperous community. His farm in this precinct was partly improved when he bought it, and this was his first real estate in the county, though he spent about twenty-one years here before this purchase. He is a Democrat in politics, and has held the various county and precinct offices. He owns 290 acres of tillable land, has a good house and fair improvements. His farming is divided between grain and stock-raising. The Treadway family has always been noted as a robust race, always enjoying long lives, and have been represented in America for six generations.

He was married in this county, in 1850, to Mary McHenry, who has borne him nine children, all living: Jacob, Margaret, Mary, Nancy, James, John, Louisa, Joseph and Jefferson. Two daughters and one son are unmarried. The others are all married and are farmers, except Joseph, who is in the agricultural business at Virginia City. Mrs. Treadway died in 1879, and her husband is still unmarried.

ALEXANDER D. SIX, M. D., one of the successful surgeons and physicians of Versailles, was born in Morgan county, now Scott, in 1828. His father, David Six, was born in Tennessee, in 1799, and his father, John Six, was a native of the Shenandoah valley, Virginia, and his grandfather, the great-great-grandfather of the Doctor, was banished from Germany on account of his tendency toward mutiny, and settled in this country, where he founded the family of Six on American soil. The offence for which he was exiled from his native land was a small one, it being the infringement of the game laws with regard to hunting rabbits. His grandson, John, took a very active part in the Revolutionary war, and though a youth was one of the prison guards at Yorktown. His wife was Mary Duvall, of Pennsylvania, and they were married in the State where he was following his trade of carpenter and joiner. After marriage they removed to Tennessee, where their seven sons were born. This gentleman was a typical frontiersman and hunter, and was a pioneer of Tennessee, Kentucky and Illinois. The father of our subject, David, and his brother, John, were the pioneers of that family to Illinois, coming in the spring of 1823, landing near Springfield in June, making the journey with pack horses and bringing their families with them, David having two children, while his brother had but one. In a year or two they came to the western part of Morgan county, and their parents and brothers followed to Illinois a couple of years afterward, making the journey with covered wagons. The entire party was very poor, having nothing but their outfits and their willing hands, ready to engage in whatever offered itself. John Six had a family as follows: Abraham Six, died in Scott county, aged sixty-seven, leaving three sons and two daughters; Daniel, died in the same county, about the same age, leaving eight or nine children to mourn his death; John, the next, and his family are all buried, he dying in 1857, aged sixty-seven; Jacob, moved to Arkansas and died at an advanced age, leaving a large family; David, father of subject; Isaac, farmer of Scott county, where he died about the same age as his other brothers; William died at the same age; Mary, wife of

James Taylor, of Scott county, a farmer, and they had a medium family; Elizabeth, wife of William Parker, died in Arkansas, leaving a large family; Catherine is still living with her daughter, in Missouri, aged ninety years, and is in fair health of mind and body; she had five children, Nancy, wife of Simon Taylor, died when about seventy, leaving twelve or thirteen children These children were all farmers, or the wives of farmers, and they all crossed the plains to Illinois. The father and mother of the subject lived on a farm of 140 acres, near Mount Sterling, where the father died, aged fifty-nine years, leaving eleven living children and one deceased daughter of five years. The name of the children were: Nancy, wife of a Mr Green, of California, has a large family; Martha, died in Missouri, aged forty-eight, leaving the nine children she had born to her husband, George Scott, Daniel, a farmer of Mount Sterling, has a family of two daughters and the same number of sons, Abraham, a farmer two miles east of Mount Sterling, has seven children; Alexander D, subject, Mary, died, aged forty-eight, in California, near Los Angeles, being the wife of Irving Carter, by whom she had six children; Isabella died when five years old, William died near Mount Sterling on the homestead, aged fifty-four, leaving a wife and two daughters, Elizabeth, now Mrs. William Bowen, of Knox county, Missouri, has six daughters; Cynthia, widow of W A Sieles, lives on her farm in Missouri with her seven children; Oliver P. and James K. are both bachelors on the home farm This family is among the earliest of the settlers, and the Six prairie in Mount Sterling is named after them.

The Doctor was reared to farm life and received his primary education in the log schoolhouses, with the puncheon floors and slab seats, without backs The school that he attended, principally, was held in Mount Sterling He left the subscription school at eighteen and went for a year to the Mount Sterling Academy when he was twenty-two. tion school of the neighborhood held in the log After this he taught school for four years, reading medicine all this time. He finished his medical course in Rush Medical College, Chicago, graduating in the class of 1859, beginning his practice at Mount Pleasant. He went to Colorado in 1860 and two years later made an exploring trip through Idaho and Montana. He spent two years in Colorado and four years in Montana, and was one of the nineteen who discovered the gold mines in the last named State, at Big Hole, not long before the discovery of the Bannock mines. He was interested in these and other mines during the four years he spent in this State, but returned home, across the plains, by stage, a journey of 2,200 miles, an easier journey than the trip out, which was made with ox teams.

The Doctor bought his present farm of 400 acres about 1873, of J P. Hambaugh for $9,000, with no buildings but the old log-cabin He built his farm house in 1875 and his barns in 1880 and 1889, one being 36 by 40 and the other 36 by 48. His farm is a grain and stock one, he raising wheat, corn and hay, feeding his stock at home At times he has as many as forty-two head of horses, which he raises from colts He has built a warehouse on his own land, at Perry Spring Station, where they ship a great deal of grain and stock.

This gentleman was married, in Lee township, to Elizabeth Osborn, still living They have three living children, but have buried one daughter, Jessie, aged nine years She was a lovely child and her untimely death cast a gloom over the entire household. The living children are: Charles, aged twenty-four; Fred H., twenty-two; and Mattie, the pet of the household, aged eight. The sons are both regular farmers, and are now conducting the stock farm. Both have received a good business education, and are still single, residing at home. The little daughter is a sweet child and fills, to some extent, the aching void left by her departed sister.

The Doctor still practices, but only pursued his profession exclusively for about two years. He was of a great deal of use in the mines, where his professional skill was often called into play, at one time being blown up from a premature discharge of a blast of powder; the Doctor was injured, and it was some time before he recovered, having narrowly escaped death. This gentleman is a member of no secret society or creed, and believes in Democracy, but is hardly within party lines. He and his family are highly respected.

LEVI DICK, one of the most prominent citizens of this section, was born in Simpson county, Kentucky, February 17, 1815, son of Peter and Christina (Shutt) Dick. Peter Dick was born in one of the Carolinas, and reared to farm life. He came to Illinois in the fall of 1829, bringing his wife and eight children all the way from Simpson county, Kentucky, where he had settled at a very early day. The journey lasted about twenty-two days, and they settled in Sangamon county, where they raised one crop, and then, in the winter of 1831, removed to near the present home of our subject, buying 160 acres of partly improved land, nine or ten acres being broken, and a small log house erected on the land. In this cabin they lived for two years, until Peter rebuilt it, and in the remodeled house this esteemed gentleman ended his days, aged seventy years. His wife was born in the same county as himself, and died on the old farm, aged sixty-eight. These two had eight children, five yet living. Peter Dick was a son of John and ——— Dick, also natives of one of the Carolinas, who died in Kentucky, when very old. Subject's mother was a daughter of Henry and Polly Shutt, natives of Germany, who came to Illinois at an early day, dying here when very old. The entire family, on both sides, pursued farming to a great extent. Peter Dick and wife were very poor when they came to Illinois, and so were unable to provide for their children, who were forced to take care of themselves.

Our subject was no exception to this rule, and everything he has was earned by himself. He remained on the farm, working with his father until his marriage. His education was received at the district and subscription schools. After his marriage, Mr. Dick settled in a log cabin, about 18 x 20, in which he lived until 1852, when he moved into his present fine house. The fine home and farm now owned by Mr. Dick presents a great contrast to the wild prairie found by his father and mother when they came to this region in search of fortunes. Wild deer and game of many kinds abounded. Mr. Dick is inclined to think, however, that pioneer life had its pleasures as well as trials, as he says that the people were much more sociable in those days than now.

Mr. Dick was married the first time to Emmatiah Leeper, in 1839. This lady was born in Kentucky, and was a daughter of Robert and Mary Leeper. Mrs Dick died on the farm where he now lives, aged about thirty-five years; by this wife he had nine children, three now living, namely: Amos, married to Matilda Armstrong, two children; Robert L. married Amanda Sutton, three children; Martha A. married Alonzo Sutton, five children. Mr. Dick was married a second time, to Mary Morgan, born in Kentucky, died on the old home farm, aged fifty-three. She bore him two children, Eliza C. and George L., the latter now in Oregon. The former married N. B. Orr, of Delaware county, Iowa, born in 1856, son of Thomas and Caroline Orr, and they have three children.

Mr. Dick's fine farm of 300 acres is managed by his son-in-law, Mr. Orr, who carries on a mixed farming, and waving fields of grain now occupy the prairie where, half a century ago, deer were found in flocks of seventy-five.

Mr. Dick, like his father before him, is a stanch Democrat, and cast his first vote for Martin Van Buren. Mr. Dick and his father helped build the first church and schoolhouse in the section, and has taken a deep interest in church and school matters ever since. He and his family are all church attendants and worthy, good people.

HENRY W. TAYLOR, a prominent farmer of Brooklyn township, and an honored pioneer of the county, was born in Trumbull county, Ohio, in February, 1824, a son of Alexander and Betsey (Scott) Taylor, natives of Pennsylvania; the father died at the age of fifty-five years, and the mother died at the advanced age of eighty years, at Burlington, Iowa. The paternal grandfather, Matthew Taylor, was born in the north of Ireland, of English parents. He emigrated to the United States in 1772, and settled in Pennsylvania; he died in Huntingdon county, at the age of ninety-seven years. His wife, whose maiden name was McIlheny, was born in Ireland, of Scotch-Irish ancestors; she lived to be ninety-five years old. Alexander Taylor came to Ohio in 1810, and cleared a farm out of the heart of the forest. His wife, Betsey Scott, was a daughter of Nehemiah and Mary (Wick) Scott; her father was a native of Long Island, and was a descendant of Scotch ancestry, and the mother of Washington county, Pennsylvania; both died in Trumbull county, Ohio. The Taylor family have been prominent in the affairs of both church and State, possessing great intelligence and culture.

Henry W. Taylor received superior educational advantages, and at the age of nineteen years began teaching school; he followed this profession two years, and then took a course of law in a private school. After his graduation he engaged in practice, but in a short time the California gold fever swept this country, and he determined to go to the Pacific coast. He made the journey overland with four yoke of oxen, and was on the way from the 1st of April until October 22. He remained four years, and was engaged in mining during that time.

He was married June 8, 1853, to Miss Cornelia Manlove, a native of Rushville, Schuyler county, Illinois, and a daughter of Jonathan D. and Sophronia (Chadsey) Manlove. Mrs. Taylor's father was born in North Carolina, came to Illinois in an early day, and was married in Schuyler county in 1826. (This was the third marriage in the county.) Mr. and Mrs. Taylor have three children living: Marian H. married T. D. Lewis, and has three children; Ida M. is at home; Fannette married Dr. J. E. Camp, and is the mother of three children.

After his marriage Mr. Taylor lived in Rushville township, and was engaged in operating a lumber-yard and building a plank road until 1857, when he sold his entire possessions and removed to Brooklyn township. He developed a farm of 900 acres out of prairie and timber land, made many valuable improvements, and has one of the best places in the county. He and his wife are members of the Presbyterian Church, of which he is an Elder. Politically he affiliates with the Republican party; his first vote was cast for Zachary Taylor, but at the formation of the Republican party he gave his allegisance to that organization, and cast his suffrage for J. C. Fremont. He was Justice of the Peace for sixteen years, was Supervisor for two terms, and has served on the school board. In connection with his large agricultural interests, Mr. Taylor has carried on a mercantile business since before the war, purchasing his first stock in February, 1861. He makes a specialty of raising fine, blooded stock, and has done much to elevate the standard in this section. He is a self-made man, and a citizen in whom Schuyler county takes just pride.

JAMES D. THOMPSON, one of the successful farmers of Woodstock township, is entitled to the space that has been accorded him in this history of Schuyler county, and following is a brief outline of his career. He is a native of Crawford county, Pennsylvania, born March 30, 1823, a son of William and Mary (Peterson) Thompson. The paternal grandfather, William Thompson, Sr., was born in Ireland, and when a boy crossed the seas to try his fortunes in the New World. He was a carpenter by trade, and followed his vocation all his life; he and his wife attained the good old age of three-score and ten years. William Thompson, Jr., was a native of the Keystone State, and resided there until 1837, when he came to Illinois; he was a millwright by trade, and worked at that occupation several years. Two years after coming to this State he purchased land in Brown county, on which he settled the 14th day of May. In the fall of the same year his death occurred, at the age of fifty-four years and seven months; he left a wife and six children. The family then rented land for a period of eight years, and at the end of that time located on the tract purchased by the father. The mother died in Brown county, at the age of eighty-six years. Her parents, James and Elizabeth (Abbott) Peterson, were of English and German descent, and died in Pennsylvania, at the ages of ninety-one and ninety years respectively. James D. Thompson is one of a family of ten children, five of whom are living. He remained under his parents' roof until he was married; this event occurred April 3, 1856, when he was united to Miss Margaret E. Grosclande, a native of France, born April 27, 1830. Her parents, James F. and Catharine E. (Jonte) Grosclande, emigrated to the United States in 1833, and located in Woodstock township, Schuyler county, Illinois; he died here September 30, 1878, at the age of seventy-four years, and she September 15, 1878, at seventy-two years; they reared a family of eleven children. Mrs. Thompson's paternal grandparents died in 1878, the grandfather September 30, and the grandmother September 16. Peter J. Jonte, the maternal grandfather, was born in February, 1776, and died October 2, 1846; his wife, Susan Landon, was born March 25, 1774, and died June 7, 1842.

Mr. and Mrs. Thompson are the parents of six children: Mary E. is married, and the mother of three children; William J. is married, and has six children; Jefferson E. is married, and has three children; Emily L. is married, and the mother of a family of three; Charles W. is married; and Lorena M. is at home.

Mr. Thompson has been prominently connected with the agricultural interests of the county, and owns about 300 acres of choice land; he has been School Director for twenty-three years, and has held other local offices, always discharging his duties with a fidelity that won the entire confidence of his constituency. Politically he affiliates with the Democratic party.

DR. GEORGE W. CRUM, farmer and physician, town 17, range 11, section 35, post office Arenzville, was born on the homestead adjoining. (See sketch of James Crum.) Dr. Crum began his education in the district schools. From there he went to the Illinois College at Jacksonville for one year, and then attended two years at the State Normal School at Normal, Illinois. He then attended three years the Illinois Wesleyan College, receiving the degrees of B. A. and M. A. from that popular institution. From there he went to Adrian, Michigan, to complete his scientific course. He received the degree of B. S. at Adrian, and completed a full classical course at the Wesleyan College. He studied medicine under private tutors during his vacations, and then attended the St. Louis Medical College, receiving the degree of M. D. in 1874. His close application to study had undermined his health, and he felt obliged to retire to the farm to recuperate. On completing his professional course he entered upon the duties imposed by the office of hospital physician, but this was terminated by failing health. He intends to resume practice during the coming year.

He was married August 21, 1878, to Mollie E., daughter of Dr. David Malone, now deceased. Mrs. Crum was born in Posey county, Indiana. They have two children, Cora and Olga, eleven and thirteen years old.

The Doctor is not an aggressive politician. He owns a farm of 160 acres of well-improved land, adjoining that of his father. Mrs. Crum is a lady of fine literary attainments, a graduate of the Athenæum College at Jacksonville, Illinois. Her only brother is a physician there. Her sisters, Alice, Emma and Rosa, all married into representative and prominent families. Alice was the wife of William Morrison, and died in Iowa; Emma became the wife of Robert McCurdy, of Princeton, Indiana; and Rosa married Elijah Needham, of Virginia, Illinois. She is not now living. Mrs. Crum is a member of the Christian Church, and her husband is a member of the I. O. O. F. and the A. O. U. W. They are very worthy people.

JAMES HILES, general farmer and stock raiser of Beardstown, was born in Salem county, New Jersey, January 4, 1822 His father, John, was a native of the same place, was there engaged as a truck-raiser, and afterward ran a large farm in Mannington township, and still later was engaged in farming and truck-raising near Bridgeport. He died at the age of ninety-six, after leading a quiet, peaceable life. His wife's name was Sarah Chrispen, also born in Salem county She came of an old Quaker family Her own mother and a sister were speakers among Friends for many years She and her husband, however, adhered very closely to the Methodist Episcopal Church, of which they were working members. She died at the age of ninety.

James grew up in New Jersey, and was married March 7, 1844, and about this time commenced farming in Marion county, and followed it for about nine years; then he was a butcher in Woodtown two years He came here in 1856, first he engaged as a butcher and farmer at Brighton, Illinois, for two years, and then went to Greenfield While at those towns he furnished the meat for the workmen on what is now the Quincy railroad, while it was building He followed that business there for three years He was a poor man when he reached here, but has since acquired a good property It is now thirty-one years since he came to Cass county, engaging first in farming He has been very successful, because of a progressive nature, and because he understood the nature of the soil. He soon began the growing of sweet potatoes and watermelons, and this has occupied most of his time for twenty five years He raises from 2,000 to 2,500 bushels annually, and a large number of melons. He is very well known, and is respected as a hard worker and a good citizen. His place consists of fifty-nine acres, where he has lived but a few years.

He was married in Woodtown, New Jersey, to Sarah Kidd, who was born and reared in Salem county, born in 1818. Her parents, Joseph and Jane Kidd, lived and died on the old farm in Salem county, New Jersey, members of the Presbyterian Church. Mr and Mrs Hiles have had ten children, among whom were two sets of twins, who died when young The three living children are. Elizabeth, wife of Thomas Reeves, farmer and gardener, near Beardstown; James, a farmer in Cass county, and Charles, a farmer and trucker, near Beardstown. Mr and Mrs. Hiles are good people: both have been active members of the Methodist Episcopal Church for more than fifty years. Mr Hiles has never been a chewer or smoker of tobacco, has never been intoxicated, nor has he ever used a profane word. He has been a life-long Democrat.

GEORGE S CAMPBELL was born in Missouri township, Brown county, Illinois, April 12, 1857 His father, William O F. Campbell, was born in Logan county, Kentucky, in 1815, and his father, Owen Campbell, was a native of Orange county, North Carolina, while his father, John Campbell, came from Ireland to America in Colonial times, and served in the Revolutionary war. The grandfather of our subject went to Kentucky with his parents when quite young He was married to Mary, the daughter of William Clark, a native of North Carolina, and a soldier in the Revolutionary war. Owen Campbell resided in Logan county until his death, during the war of 1812 He greatly opposed England and was killed during a dispute relating to the great measures which were then attracting the attention of everyone. He left a farm of sixty-two acres The father of our subject resided in Kentucky until 1835, when he emigrated to Illinois, and settled on that part of Schuyler county now included in Brown county He had a tract of land in what is now Missouri township, but at that time they were included in Schuyler county Here he resided until his death in 1891. His wife, whose maiden name was Caroline Stubblefield, was born in Kentucky, in 1819, and died in 1870. He was a firm member of the Cumberland Presbyterian Church, but after coming to Illinois he united with the Christian Church, and served as an Elder seven years; and also preached. He was a great bible student, and a Democrat in politics. He also served as Justice of the Peace for seven years.

George S. Campbell was educated at the Mt. Sterling schools. He lived with his father until 1872. At that time he began to learn the printer's trade in the office of the *Gazette* of Mt. Sterling, and this has been his business ever since. He has worked at his trade in different places, and in 1878 purchased the *Examiner*, a weekly paper devoted to the interests of the people in general, and the Democratic party in particular.

He was married, in 1886, to Miss Alta M. Larkin, born in Brown county, daughter of John and Mary Larkin. They have had two children, Earl and Elsie. Mr. Campbell is a Democrat in politics, and is a member of Jephtha Lodge, No. 100, I. O. O. F., and also the Encampment of the I. O. O. F., the I. O. M. A. and Modern Woodmen.

JOHN W. SEAMAN, an old representative citizen and successful stock raiser, was born in Jefferson county, Virginia, six miles north of Harper's Ferry, September 21, 1820. His father, Joseph, was also a native of Jefferson county, and was engaged there for years as a boatman on the Shenandoah and Potomac rivers, and kept a public inn for some time. His parents, who lived and died there, were American born, but of German ancestry, the father being in the Revolutionary war. Joseph J. was a soldier in a Virginia regiment, was in many engagements, and for some time was stationed at Baltimore, Maryland. His wife was Nancy Deaver, who was born and reared in Jefferson county, and came of similar ancestry as her husband. After the birth of their children, of whom our subject is the youngest, Joseph Seaman and wife, in the spring of 1832, came West, taking a boat at Wheeling, and came down the Ohio, and up the Mississippi and Illinois rivers, and landed at Beardstown when it was a hamlet of a few houses. There the family lived for some years, Mr. Seaman following the trade of carpenter. He later went to Frederick, Schuyler county, and there died when sixty years of age. His wife died the next day, at about the same age. They had many acquaintances among the pioneers of Cass county.

John is the only surviving member of the family that came from Virginia to Illinois. He came here in 1832, found it new and unbroken, and has lived to note the many changes that have taken place during the past thirty years. He reached here about the time the Indians left the county, and hence has been closely connected with all pioneer history. He has seen the county settled, all the roads laid out and built, all the school houses built, all the railroads and all the other improvements made that have made this the garden spot of Cass county. His farm of about 500 acres, highly improved and well stocked, is located in section 16, township 18, range 11 west. He can boast of the character of his soil, except 100 acres on a sand ridge, and sixty-five acres in the bluffs. He purchased the place in 1852, and its present substantial condition is due to his perseverance and industry.

He was married in this county, to Mary E. Thompson, born in New York, in 1828. She came to this county with her parents, George B. and Hannah Thompson, late in the '30s. Both lived and died in the county, Mr. Thompson being a farmer, and at one time a merchant in Beardstown. Mr. and Mrs. Thompson were quite well known as pioneer settlers of this county, the former dying in Beardstown, about seventy years of age, and the latter in 1850. Mrs. Seaman was one of five children. A brother, Seth Thompson, now at the soldier's home at Quincy, Illinois, and Mrs. Seaman, are the only remaining members of the family.

Mr. and Mrs. Seaman are members of no church, but are good, moral people, and are beloved by all who knew them. He is not an office seeker, but is a decided Democrat in politics.

They are the parents of eleven children, four of whom are dead: Frank, Harriet, Charles and an infant. Those living are: John, a farmer on the old homestead, married Ida Kruse; George, a machinist living in Cass county, married Susie Reiket; Fred, at home helping on the farm; Hannah Heaton, living in Washington, on a farm; Cora, wife of James Heaton, also lives in Washington; Anna S. Pearn, near Virginia, Illinois; and Bertha S. Hale, of Springfield, Illinois.

The entire family are excellent people, and excellent representatives of Cass county.

AZARIAH LEWIS, a prosperous and influential farmer of Cass county, Illinois, residing in township 18, range 9 west, was born in Washington county, Kentucky, March 15, 1813, and is a son of William and Elizabeth (Burns) Lewis. The Lewis branch of the family is of Welsh ancestry, while that of Burns descended from German ancestry. The father of our subject participated in the war of 1812, for which he also received a pension and a soldier's warrant, which were contined to his widow. He was born in Virginia, and accompanied his parents to Kentucky at an early day. He continued to reside in the latter State until 1828, and then, with his wife and seven children, started for Illinois, at that time the extreme frontier. They made the journey with a two-wheeled cart, which was drawn by a pair of small oxen, preceded by horses. They were four weeks on the journey, and most of the family came on foot. They were among the very earliest settlers of Illinois, the country being then wild and abounding with game. On their arrival in Morgan (now Cass) county, they had only fifty cents between them; and all who were able went out to work by the day and month—worked on farms, split rails, and did whatever they found to do. The honest, hard-working father was finally enabled to enter forty acres of Government land, in Mason county, where he built a small cabin, in which he resided until his death in 1844, at the age of fifty-five years. His devoted wife survived him many years, dying at the age of seventy-eight years, on the original forty acres which she had assisted in reclaiming from a wilderness. By her careful management she had accumulated a nice little property. She was the mother of eleven children, of whom, as far as known, five now survive.

The subject of this sketch attended a subscription school for a short time in his youth, but owing to his father's limited means and the scarcity of schools he had but few educational opportunities. He continued to reside at home until his marriage, working on farms in his vicinity by the day and month. After his marriage, he settled on a farm in the eastern part of Cass county, which he rented and worked on shares by the month, where he continued for four or five years. He then bought forty acres of fertile farming land, on which he built a log cabin, 16 x 16 feet, into which he and his family moved. Here he continued to live and industriously improved his farm, for two years At the end of this time, he sold out and again rented land, on which he lived for about five years He then bought forty more acres of partly improved land, which he continued to work for seven or eight years, when he again sold out and bought 110 acres in the immediate vicinity. On this latter place, he continued to live until 1856, at which time he purchased his present farm Here he now has 120 acres, which he has carefully cultivated to mixed farming, besides which he has made a specialty of stock-raising, having now some very fine specimens of cattle. By unremitting industry, able management and careful economy, he has prospered, and is now virtually retired from active business, and is enjoying in comfort the fruits of his early toil

Mr. Lewis first was married in February, 1832, to Miss Sarah Graham, an intelligent lady, who was an orphan, and a native of Green county, Kentucky By this marriage, there were seven children, five of whom are yet living: the elder, Elizabeth, is married and has seven children and ten grandchildren, Nancy Jane W is married and has eleven children and sixteen grandchildren; Mary A. married, has four children and two grandchildren, Caroline, married, has five children and one grandchild; Kilbourn, married, has eight children The devoted wife and mother died in 1863, aged forty-six years, leaving her family and many friends to mourn her loss

October 4. 1864, Mr Lewis was again married, his second wife being Mary E. Clark, an estimable lady, who was born in Marietta, Ohio, August 28, 1823 Her parents were John S. and Mary E. (Pearse) Clark, both natives of Ohio. Grandfather Pearse was a brave soldier in the Revolutionary war, and drew a pension for his services in that struggle. Her father was born in Cincinnati, and was an old sailor and river boatman In 1826 he brought a boat load of salt to Illinois, landing at Beardstown Thence he proceeded to Morgan county, where he settled on a farm, on which he continued to live until three years previous to his death He then sold out and bought property in town, where he resided, retired from business pursuits, until his death, at the age of seventy-three years. He was a very energetic man and was popular among his associates, being widely known throughout this State His wife died at the same place as her husband, aged sixty-five years She was an intelligent woman of kindly impulses, and much beloved by those who knew her They were the parents of fourteen children, of whom, as far as known, three or four now survive By the second marriage Mr. A Lewis has one son, Charles, born July 4, 1868, who is now married and has one child

Whatever success has blessed Mr Lewis' efforts is entirely due to his own persistence and intelligence, and he richly deserves the prosperity which he now enjoys.

NORMAN PARSONS, now retired and living quietly at his home at the corner of Fifth and Washington streets, is one of the old settlers, having come here in 1854 He was born in Hartford, Connecticut, November 6, 1811, and was a child only a few years old when his parents, Moses and Elsiby (Pease) Parsons, with a colony of twenty families, during the war of 1812, came overland with teams to Geauga county, Ohio. They arrived in June, 1814, and made a settlement in the heavy timber of that new, unbroken country, surrounded by Indians and plenty of game. He there lived until the country was well improved, when he died some years ago at the advanced age of eighty-seven years. His wife had died some five years before. They were Methodists, and the father and seven sons were all Republicans.

Norman Parsons served with his State militia, went through all the promotions from First Lieutenant to Colonel of his regiment. He was one of the organizers of the G. A. R. at Beardstown.

After his arrival in Beardstown he became a member of the firm of Fischer & Parsons, wagon manufacturers, who did business for two years. A company was then established known as Putnam & Parsons, doing a general tombstone business. This continued for two years, and at this time Mr. Parsons bought a stock of goods at Falls City, Nebraska, where he lived for one year, and then returned to this county, where he secured and began to improve 175 acres of land near Beardstown. Here he continued until 1861, when he enlisted in the Third Illinois Cavalry and was soon after made Sergeant of Company C. He served three years in the army of the West. At Germantown, Tennessee, he veteranized and was made First Sergeant of Company F. of Third Illinois Cavalry, re-organized, and served until the fall of Richmond. He returned to St. Louis, Missouri, with his regiment in 1865, and later was sent to Fort Snelling, Minnesota, to protect the whites against the Indians. He was honorably discharged at St. Paul, Minnesota, June 20, 1865. He was in all the great battles of his division of the army, and had many narrow escapes, and at one time was surrounded by General Forrest's men and made his escape only by his military tactics. He was a man of daring and bravery. He returned to Beardstown in 1865, made a trip to Nebraska on horseback, and spent some time there looking after his real-estate interests.

He was appointed Postmaster of this place by President Grant in his first term, and held it for eighteen years consecutively, and had in the meantime served as Justice of the Peace. He was one of the organizers of the Republican party in Geauga county, Ohio, and was vice-president of the first anti-slavery society organized in that section.

He was first married in Ohio, to Amanda F. King, who died in 1852, aged thirty-four. She left two sons: Melbourne, living in Beardstown, and William; both of these gentlemen made very fine records indeed in the war of the rebellion. Mr. Parsons was married a second time to Mrs. Catherine Saunders. She has three children by a former marriage, namely: John, a mercantile bookkeeper; George, who was a member of Battery B, Second Illinois Light Artillery, in the late war; and Elva J., a lady of superior talent, and a teacher in the high school, and is now the wife of Mr. Saunders.

SQUIRE JAMES M. WATKINS, a popular Justice of the Peace and one of the most prosperous farmers of Cass county, Illinois, residing in township 18, range 9, was born in Richmond precinct, same county, February 5, 1839.

His parents were Elijah and Lydia A. (Montgomery) Watkins, both natives of Kentucky, the former born in Green county, in 1797, and the latter a native of Hart county. His father's parents were Samuel and Mary (McClure) Watkins, the former a native of Wales and the latter of Maryland. Samuel Watkins came to America when a very young man and settled in Maryland, where he was married, and whence he removed to Kentucky. He was a prominent pioneer of the latter State, in which he made his home for many years, and where he died at the age of eighty-five years His wife also died in that State, aged sixty-five or seventy years. They were the parents of twelve children, eleven of whom survive Two of these, Lewie and Hank, were brave and efficient soldiers in the war of 1812. The mother of this subject was a daughter of Simpson and Salle (Gum) Montgomery. She was one of five children, two of whom were half brothers Her father was of Scottish descent, his parents never coming to America, and her people were mostly farmers. Her father was a boatman, and lost his life by being struck on the head with a gun.

The father of the subject of this notice resided at home until he attained the age of nineteen He then worked for a while by the day and month in Kentucky until he had accumulated some means, and when, about the year 1833-'34, he emigrated with his wife to Illinois, at that time the frontier of civilization. They came overland with one wagon, drawn by oxen, and brought some stock. They first located in Wayne county, but shortly afterward removed to Menard county, where he continued to live until 1838, when he sold out and came to Cass county. Here he first rented land for five or six years, then bought eighty acres, a few of which were broken, and the place having an old log house on it This house served as their home for about a year, when it was replaced by a better one. The father was an exceedingly energetic man, and his success in this new country was a foregone conclusion. He added, from time to time, to his original purchase, until he possessed 300 acres of choice farming land, 160 of which was received from the Government. His death occurred on the old homestead in 1884, to the great sorrow of many friends, who esteemed him for his ability, industry and uprightness of character. He and his worthy wife were earnest and useful members of the Primitive Baptist Church, and he helped to build the first church in his locality. He displayed his usual activity in church and all good work, and acted as a Deacon for many years

The subject of this sketch was reared to farm work and attended subscription school during the winters, working on his father's farm in the summer. Owing to his busy life, his education was limited, and he is essentially a self-educated and self-made man. Extensive reading, supplemented by excellent judgment and an active mind, have combined to render himself successful in life and a leader among men. He lived at home until after his marriage, and the following year moved to his father-in law's farm, on which he remained until the next year. He then bought twenty-five acres, a few of which were broken, and built on it a box house, 16 x 18 feet. He and his family lived in this house for twelve or fourteen years, when he erected his present substantial and comfortable home. He has lived on the same place ever since, which now contains 120 acres, devoted to mixed farming, and is one of the finest farms in the county.

He was married June 14, 1859, to Miss Nancy Jane Lewis, an estimable lady and a daughter of Azariah and Sarah Lewis, a sketch of whom appears in this work She was born April 4, 1842 They have eleven children, as follows: Sarah E, born March 10, 1860, married H. Speulda, and they have seven children; they live in South Dakota; Charles L., born October 16, 1861, married Susan McNeil, a native of this county; they have three children; Simpson Lee, born November 13, 1863, married Ida Taylor, and lives in Chandlerville; William B, born December 28, 1867, married Belle Miller, and they have two children, he lives in this neighborhood; Laura, born December 15, 1865, married James Cooper, and they have three children; John R, born March 29, 1870, married Dora Lucas, and they have one child, Azariah, born August 20, 1872. Stella M, born December 19, 1874, Miamia B, born June 16, 1877; Josephine, born August 28, 1880; Casper, born June 25, 1884. All of Mr Watkins' children have had educational advantages

Mr Watkins is an old Andrew Johnson Democrat, and cast his first vote for Stephen A. Douglas With the exception of his vote cast for General Weaver for President, he has voted a straight Democratic ticket ever since. Acknowledging his ability, his constituents have sought the advantage of his judgment and experience by electing him to various local offices. He went from the school room to the position of school director, in which capacity he has served ever since He has held the responsible position of Justice of the Peace for twenty years, discharging his duties with justice and impartiality.

His wife is a faithful member of the Primitive Baptist Church, and, both by her in-influence and means, contributes to its support.

Mr Watkins' life is a brilliant example of what may be accomplished by intelligent and persistent effort, which not only insure material prosperity but also crown their votaries with honor and happiness

ADAM P SEASLY, a progressive and enterprising young farmer of Oakland township, was born in Carroll county, Maryland, in 1860. His father, Adam Seasly, now a resident of Adams county, Pennsylvania, is a native of Germany, but emigrated to America when a young man, he was reared to the life of a farmer, and also mastered the blacksmith's trade in his own country. After arriving in this country he went directly to Pennsylvania, and there was married to Elizabeth Cook, a daughter of Benjamin Cook; she died in early womanhood in Pennsylvania, leaving two sons and a daughter· Mary, Adam P· and George; Mary died in infancy, and George lived only a few years. At the age of three years Adam P was taken by Henry Riffle, and under his care was reared to manhood

In the spring of 1869 Mr. Riffle came from Pennsylvania to Illinois, and located at Vermont, Fulton county, he was a plasterer by trade, and followed that calling in connection with farming. Mr. Riffle had no children of his own, but adopted a son and daughter, for whom he carefully provided. Adam P. Seasly, the son, was given a good education, and was taught the printer's trade

Mr Seasly was married in 1881, to Miss Rebecca E. Kost, of Fulton county, Illinois, a daughter of John and Catherine Kost, natives of Pennsylvania. Mr. Kost is a carpenter and farmer, and in 1850 he emigrated to Illinois and settled in Fulton county. He is now one of the wealthiest resident land owners in this section, but is retired from active business pursuits. Mr. Seasly engaged in agricultural pursuits in Fulton county, which he continued until 1885, when he removed to his present farm of eighty acres; he rents an additional eighty acres, and is carrying on a successful business. To him and his wife have been born three children: Ross H., Edgar and Ruth.

Politically our subject affiliates with the Democratic party; he has served as School Trustee, and has always been a liberal supporter of home industries and enterprises.

THOMAS P. PARROTT, an intelligent and public-spirited citizen of Buena Vista township, is a pioneer of 1831, since which time his interests have been identified with those of his favorite county. He is a native of Kentucky, having been born in Glasgow, that State, on September 3, 1825.

His father, Josiah Parrott, was a native of Maryland, having been born in Talbot county, that State, on July 20, 1800. He had no school advantages, but acquired an excellent business education in Glasgow, Kentucky, to which place he early removed. He was possessed of unusual financial ability, and had a remarkable aptitude for mercantile pursuits. In time he became the owner of three stores, one at Glasgow, one at Thompsonville, and another at Gainesboro, Tennessee. He was married in Kentucky, to Nancy G. Bransford, a native of Rockingham, Virginia, in which place she was born on July 27, 1807. She was a daughter of Thomas Bransford, a prominent citizen of that place.

In 1830 Mr. Parrott came to Rushville, Illinois, which was then a new and sparsely settled country, and opened a store at that place. He had at that time $60,000 and a large stock of goods. After starting his store, he returned to Kentucky, and in the spring of the following year, 1831, he removed his family to Rushville, where he continued in business for more than forty years, being the oldest merchant of that place. He also started several other stores at the same time, in different towns, one at Beardstown, and another at Princeton, while he had still another at Pulaski. All were general stores and all carried large stocks of goods. He possessed very great energy and excellent financial ability, and was eminently successful in business. He invested largely in land, and became the owner of thousands of acres of the richest land of Schuyler county. He voted with the Whig party, and later with the Republican, but never desired to hold office. He was a member of the Masonic fraternity, being one of the charter members of the lodge in Rushville. He was a prominent member of the Methodist Episcopal Church, of which he was a liberal supporter. He helped to build the first Methodist church in Rushville, and contributed toward the erection of the present handsome edifice.

Mr. Parrott's first wife died on July 26, 1835, leaving four children to the care of her husband, and many friends to mourn her loss. She was a woman of intelligence and many charms of character, a faithful wife and fond mother, and was much lamented by all who knew her. The children were: Thomas P., subject of our sketch; James H., now a real-estate man of Omaha, Nebraska; John B., who died in Buena Vista, unmarried; and Susan, who died unmarried.

Mr. Parrott was subsequently married again, his second wife being Catharine Scripps, a native of Missouri. They had twelve children: George, deceased; Maria, who married

Colonel William McAlister, and died in Rushville; Lydia, married; Sarah, who married Albert Clark, and died in Kearney, Nebraska; Josiah, a traveling salesman; Catharine, deceased; Charley, a resident of Lincoln, Nebraska, and was for many years a banker in Omaha; Walter, a wholesale dealer in hats, caps and notions, in Chicago; Frank, deceased; Marcus, a resident of Omaha; Ellen, deceased; and Lewis, a real-estate man of Omaha, Nebraska.

The father died at his home, surrounded by his family and friends, on May 29, 1881, aged eighty-one years, much lamented as a faithful friend and fond husband and father.

The subject of our sketch was but a mere boy when the family came to Rushville in 1831. He attended school in Rushville, and when young began to assist in the duties about his father's store, and when grown, became a partner. The confinement of indoor work, however, did not agree with his health, and consequently, during the war he located on a farm in Buena Vista township. He is now the owner of 320 acres of highly cultivated land. Besides his farming interests, he is largely engaged in stock-raising, being a breeder of shorthorn and red-polled cattle, and of Morgan and Clyde horses, and has some of the finest specimens of the various breeds to be found in the country.

On January 25, 1848, he was married to Sarah Wright, a daughter of E. M. and Sarah Wright. She was born in Syracuse, New York. Their happy married life was doomed to be of short duration, for, after little more than a year, on November 12, 1849, his wife died, leaving to his care one child, Sarah G., now the wife of Insco Marine, and resides at Beatrice, Nebraska.

On October 10, 1860, our subject was married again, his second wife being Emma Window, born in Macomb, Illinois, a daughter of Rev. William H. Window. Her father was a Methodist Episcopal minister, widely and favorably known in Illinois. They had eight children, two sons and six daughters: Susan, wife of E. H. Lugg, of Warsaw, Illinois; William; Grace; Harry; Catharine; Ida; Blanche and Margaret. The faithful wife and devoted mother died on July 22, 1890, much mourned by her family and friends. April 13, 1892, Harry married Miss Carrie McCormick, of Buena Vista.

Our subject affiliates with the Republicans in politics, and though averse to office has, at the earnest solicitation of his numerous friends, served in some local positions of trust, to the entire satisfaction of his constituents. He is, like his father before him, a liberal supporter of the Methodist Episcopal Church, which denomination has found in him an earnest and sympathetic friend.

Of high integrity and morality, of rare ability and warm impulses, he enjoys the confidence of his fellow citizens, and the esteem of his family and a host of friends.

CASPER ROHN, a general farmer in sections 32 and 33, range 12, township 18, Beardstown precinct, has a well improved tract which has been his farm for twenty-one years. He was born on a part of the farm which he now owns, September 23, 1842. His parents were Henry and Elizabeth (Longore) Rohn. They both came to America and were married after landing in St. Louis, and later came to Beardstown (for further history, seehistory of J. Henry Rohn, this book). They were very early settlers, having come to the county three years after the Indians had left the State.

Mr. Casper Rohn has been a hard-working man, has been moderately successful, and has made his way in the world by his own efforts.

He was married first to Mary Jockissh, of Cass county, Illinois, and resided in this county until her death in 1876, at the age of twenty-five years. She was a good, kind wife and mother, and left her husband four children: Lizzie Eveland, living in Fulton county, Illinois; Clara, at present in Jacksonville, Illinois; Philip is at home on the farm, and George, who lives at Boody, Illinois. Mr. Rohn was married a second time in this county, to Delia Dunn, born in Morgan county, daughter of an old settler. Her father now lives in Missouri, but her mother died there some years ago. Mr. and Mrs. Rohn are the parents of six children: Lulu, Walter, Frank, Charles, Samuel and Ruth. They are associated with the people of the Methodist Episcopal Church, and Mr. Rohn is an ardent Republican. Mr. Rohn is an honest, peaceable, home loving German citizen, and he and his worthy wife are greatly esteemed by their hosts of friends.

DANIEL STEPHENS has been closely identified with the history of Schuyler county, Illinois, since 1836, and it is fitting that his name should appear in this volume. He was born in Davidson county, North Carolina, April 4, 1819, a son of Alexander Stephens, who died in 1825; the mother of our subject, whose maiden name was Mary Dealy, was a native of New Jersey; she was married a second time in Illinois, spending the last of her life in Bainbridge township. Daniel Stephens, in early life, became inured to the hard labor of a farm; he made the most of his opportunities to secure an education, but as there were no free schools and his father was in limited circumstances, the advantages offered him were very few. He lived in North Carolina until 1836, when he emigrated to the West, and settled in Illinois; the entire journey was made overland with teams, and the country reached was little better than a wilderness. Mr. Stephens settled in that portion of Schuyler county which is now included in Brown county, but he had no means to invest in land, and so was obliged to work for wages; he received $12 a month, and from this small sum saved enough to make a beginning. In 1841 he settled on a tract of patent land that is now a part of his farm, and three years later he bought eighty acres, for which he paid $170; this place was covered with timber and brush, and in the heart of the forest he erected a cabin that afforded protection and shelter; he courageously undertook the task of placing the land under cultivation, and as he prospered he invested in other lands, until he now owns 572 acres, lying in Bainbridge and Woodstock townships.

Mr. Stephens was married January 26, 1840, to Rebecca Kimbel, a native of Simpson county, Kentucky, and a daughter of Samuel and Elizabeth Kimbel. Of this union were born seven children: George W., William M., David, Samuel, John R., Samantha Jane and Olive.

George W. Stephens has been three times married, his present wife being Ann Irvin; they have seven children: William M. has been married twice, Martha J. Eason being the second wife; he has eight children; David married Martha Landreth, and has a family of seven children; Samuel married Cornelia Persinger, and has four children; John married Mary J. Macombs, and has one child; Samantha J. is the wife of Richard Black, and has three children; Olive married L. F. Nooner, and is the mother of four children. Mr. Stephens has thirty-five grandchildren and three great-grandchildren.

ROBERT B. McMASTER was born in Highland county, Ohio, February 3, 1827, a son of David McMaster, who was born in county Down, Ireland. The paternal grandfather, John McMaster, was a native of Ireland, of Scotch ancestry. He emigrated to America in 1807, and settled in Rockbridge county, Virginia, where he lived until 1818. He removed to Ohio in that year, and located in Highland county. He bought a tract of heavily timbered land, built a log cabin in the midst of the forest, and resided there until his death. He married Jennie McKee, of County Down, Ireland; she died on the farm in Highland county, the mother of four children: James, David, Arthur and Robert. David McMaster, the father of our subject, was a lad of twelve years when his parents crossed the sea to America. He was married in Virginia, and lived there until 1816, when he removed to Kentucky; at the end of one year he went to Highland county, Ohio, where he was among the pioneers; he bought a tract of timber land, erected the characteristic log cabin with a mud-and-stick chimney, and began the task of clearing a farm. Cincinnati was the nearest market-town, sixty miles distant, wild game was abundant, and the mother carded, spun and wove the cloth with which her children were dressed. In 1836 Mr. McMaster sold this farm and came to Illinois, accompanied by his wife and six children; they made the journey in a four-horse wagon, camping on the way. He first located in Fulton county, and in 1838 came to Schuyler county, and rented until he bought land in Rushville township, where he resided until his death in 1866. His wife's maiden name was Elizabeth Wardlaw, a native of Rockbridge county, Virginia, and a daughter of William and Mary Wardlaw, natives of Scotland. They reared a family of six children: Mary C., William W., John M., Robert B., Jane C. and Sarah A.

A lad of nine years, Robert B. McMaster came to Illinois, and well remembers many incidents of the journey and the trials and privations to which they were subject on the frontier. He attended the pioneer schools, and received a training which fitted him for the ordinary duties of life. He remained with his parents until 1850, and in March of that year started for the Golden State. He took the overland route, and accomplished that perilous journey without accident or disaster. He arrived in California in July, and at once engaged in mining; he continued this industry until 1852, when he returned to Illinois. He bought land included in the tract he now owns on section twenty-two, Rushville township, and has been one of the most progressive and prosperous farmers of the county. He was actively engaged in agricultural pursuits until 1884, when he purchased property in and adjoining Rushville, and erected a handsome residence which he now occupies.

Mr. McMaster was married in 1853, to Rachel Quinn, and they had a family of three children: Curtis died at the age of twenty-eight years; Jennie died in infancy; Mary married Marshall Finch, and has two sons, Robert and Wade T. Mrs. McMaster was born in Hardin county, Kentucky, November 14, 1836, a daughter of Thomas Quinn, a native of Virginia. He married Nancy Kennedy, a native of Hardin county, Kentucky, and a daughter of Peter and Rachel (Colvon) Kennedy. In 1837 they moved to Illinois with their family of eight children, and settled in Schuyler county; the father died in 1844, but the mother survived until 1886, in her eighty-fifth year.

J. HENRY ROHN, farmer and stock-raiser, living on the old homestead in township 18, range 12, of the precinct of Beardstown, was born at the same place, September 20, 1837. He is the eldest member of the family. The father, Henry, was a native of Hesse-Darmstadt. Henry Rohn, Sr., had grown up, but was yet single, when he came to the United States with his brother John, and after a long, tedious passage, they landed in New Orleans, and from there proceeded to St. Louis. Here he stopped and married the girl who had come with him from the same province. Her name was Elizabeth Longore, and they soon came to Cass county and entered, in the year 1837, Government land. They added to it from time to time until he owned 1,300 acres, made by him and his thrifty wife. He was $105 in debt when he landed in Beardstown, having to borrow money to come there. He continued on this same land, improving it until his death in 1891. He was then nearly eighty-six years of age. He was a well-known pioneer, a successful farmer, a good neighbor and husband, and an active member of the Methodist Episcopal Church. His wife is yet living, aged eighty-one years, smart and active, making her home with her son William, and is still an active member of the Methodist Episcopal Church.

J. Henry has lived on the farm he now owns all his lifetime. It consists of 820 acres, and of this 500 acres are under the plow, with good farm buildings. He has owned the old homestead for fifteen years.

He was married in this county to Malinda Wagle, born in Brown county, in 1840. Her father was Jephtha Wagle, of Madison county, Kentucky, who was married there and came to Brown county as an early settler, and later moved on a farm near Arenzville, and there lived and died. His wife is yet surviving, at the age of eighty years, making her home in this county. Her maiden name was Phœbe Todd, and she was a relative of Mrs. Abraham Lincoln. Mr. and Mrs. Rohn are the parents of four children: Albert and Louis H. are both at home helping on the farm, and Carrie and Nettie are twins, and both are bright and intelligent children. The whole family are Methodists, and are good types of German citizens. Mr. Rohn is a stanch Republican.

JOHN A. YOUNG, one of the most prominent and prosperous agriculturists of Schuyler county, resides on section 21, Buena Vista township. The following space will be devoted to a brief biography of which he is the subject. He was born in Schuyler county, on the farm which he now occupies, June 14, 1832, a son of John Young, a native of Ireland; the paternal grandparents were John and Margaret Young. John Young emigrated to America when a young man, and stopped for a time in Philadelphia; thence he continued his journey to the West, and after locating in Rushville he sent for his parents; they left their native land, crossed the sea, and made a home in the new world; they now reside in Buena Vista township, at a good old age. There were born to them three sons and two daughters: John, William K., Alexander, Margaret and Elizabeth. The father of John A. Young was married at Rushville to a daughter of Hugh McCreary, a native of Ireland, who came to America aboard the same ship as her husband, and it was on this voyage that they met. He died in early life, the date being February 8, 1835; he was a farmer, and had entered land in Buena Vista township; the wife died June 14, 1883; they had two children: James M. died in infancy; John A. is the only surviving member of the family. During his boyhood days he lived with his mother and relatives; from early childhood he was self-sustaining, working for his board; he attended school until sixteen years of age, and then settled with his mother on the homestead that had been entered by the father. In 1852 he went to California, making the journey overland, and remained on the Pacific coast six years; he was engaged in mercantile and agricultural pursuits, and was reasonably successful. He returned via the Isthmus and New York city; he made a visit to relatives in Philadelphia, and then came to his old home. Here he resumed agricultural pursuits, making many improvements in the way of erecting buildings; his mother resided with him until her death.

The homestead originally consisted of 130 acres, twenty acres of which Mr. Young sold to raise the money to go to California. He now owns 580 acres in one body, well stocked, and in a high state of cultivation. He gives especial attention to the breeding of live-stock, and has a fine herd of short-horns, and some horses of excellent pedigree.

Mr. Young was united in marriage October 13, 1869, to Miss Mary L. Clark, a daughter of Rev. John Clark; she was born in Schuyler county, Illinois, April 1, 1847, and died May 15, 1878; she was the mother of four children: Carl C., born August 9, 1870, is in the employ of the Illinois Steel Company; Anna F., born August 3, 1872, is a student at De Pauw University, Greencastle, Indiana; Sarah E., born August 23, 1874, and James H., December 10, 1876. Mr. Young was married a second time, November 24, 1881, to Miss Elizabeth De Witt, a daughter of James and Ellen (Little) DeWitt; she was born at Littleton, Schuyler county, May 22, 1855; five children were born of this union: one died in infancy; Mary was born September 19, 1882; John D., April 5, 1884; Dwight M., September 28, 1885; Ellen L., April 16, 1888. Mrs. Young is a consistent member of the Methodist Episcopal Church.

In addition to the business interests already mentioned, Mr. Young has investments in real estate in Duluth and other points; he is also a stockholder in the Bank of Rushville, and is one of the directors of the same. Politically he is identified with the Republican party; he has been Supervisor of his township, but his private affairs have so taken his time that public office has not been sought. He is a man of broad intelligence, and the strictly honorable methods he has employed in his business career has won him the entire confidence and respect of the community.

O. A. BERRY, foreman of the blacksmith shops of the Rock Island and St. Louis division of the Chicago, Burlington & Quincy railroad, located at Beardstown, was born in Medina, Ohio, February 12, 1852. He came when five years of age to Aurora, Illinois, with his parents. He grew up there and received a common school education and learned his trade. His father, Thomas E Berry, had come from England to Medina, Ohio, there learned the carpenter's trade and was married to Anna Pierce, who was also of English birth. In 1857, Thomas Berry, wife and four children, settled in Aurora, where he still lives, aged seventy-three years, and is still hearty enough to work at his trade. His wife died in 1887. They were both members of the Congregational Church.

Mr Berry came here from Aurora and was for one year foreman of the Chicago division of the Chicago, Burlington & Quincy railroad He has been twenty-six years with this company and has never lost a month's time, nor been suspended. He won his promotion by attending strictly to business.

He was married in Aurora, to Ella Irwin, who was born, reared and educated in the same place She was the daughter of Jerry Irwin, a prominent and successful tailor of Aurora, who died in 1881 His wife still lives in Aurora. They were both Roman Catholics. Mr. and Mrs Berry have one child, Maude. He is a member of the Masonic order. He is a sound Republican, but not an office-seeker.

JOSEPH GIFFORD, a well-to-do and highly esteemed farmer of Versailles township, Brown county, Illinois, where he has lived for twenty years, was born in Cambria county, Pennsylvania, in December, 1833

His parents, Joseph and Sarah (Davis) Gifford, were both natives of the Keystone State, where his father was born in 1802 His paternal grandfather, also named Joseph, was of English parentage, and is thought to have been born in England He was a prosperous farmer in Huntingdon county, Pennsylvania, and left, at his death, a good estate to his family, consisting of five sons and four daughters, all of whom became heads of families, some attaining a great age. One son was more than ninety years of age when last heard from, and, if still living, as is quite probable, he is nearly a hundred. The father of the subject of this sketch moved from Pennsylvania directly to Brown county, Illinois, in 1856, and rented land near the village of Cooperstown, where he resided for thirteen years, until his death in 1869, at the age of sixty-seven years. He left a widow and five children, four sons and one daughter: David, a successful farmer in Iowa; Joseph, of this sketch, John and Isaac, both prosperous farmers of Nebraska; and Jemima, who married Manuel Whited, and died in Nebraska, aged forty-two years, leaving five children.

The subject of this sketch was reared to hard labor, and had but few educational advantages Before he was eleven years old, he worked in the Sligo Pig Iron Works, in Clarion county, Pennsylvania. When eighteen years of age, he commenced life for himself, and what little education he possesses has been gleaned by the dusty, toilsome wayside of life Fortunately his parents dowered him with an unclouded intelligence and a robust constitution, and inculcated in him a love of truth and integrity, and trained him to habits of industry and economy

He was married in his twenty-first year, to Lucinda Hovis, of Venango county, Pennsylvania, August 3, 1854, and continued to live in the Keystone State until the fall of 1868, when they removed to Brown county, Illinois. They made the journey overland with a team, bringing six children with them. They were four weeks en route, and, the weather being propitious, their journey was a continual pleasure trip and picnic. They camped in their tent and covered wagon at night, and cooked their meals by the way. Arriving in Brown county, Illinois, they located on forty acres of their present farm for which they paid $650. There were no buildings on the place at the time, and only fifteen acres of it were cleared. They had brought but little means with them, and went in debt $450, since when they have purchased forty more acres, are out of debt, and have most of the farm well improved.

Prior to coming to Illinois, in September, 1862, Mr. Gifford went as a volunteer in Company E, Sixteenth Pennsylvania Cavalry, from Franklin, Pennsylvania. He was on duty all of the time from his enlistment until his discharge at Lynchburg, Virginia, June 17, 1865, except when he was sick in the hospital with typhoid pneumonia, from June 4 to August 16, 1863. He was in some forty-six engagements, some of which were hotly contested. Among these was the battle of Hatcher's Run, which he thinks was worse than that of the "Bull Pen." His last year of service was spent under the command of General Phil. Sheridan.

Mr. and Mrs. Gifford have had ten children, nine of whom survive: Sarah, married George Green, and died, aged twenty-five years, leaving two sons; Ernest, a prosperous farmer of Elkhorn township, married Alice Lewis, and has two children; Maggie married Morgan Grady, a successful farmer of Pike county, Illinois; Laura married Frank Sellers, a well-to-do farmer of Iowa, and has one daughter; Ida married George B. Alexander, and has two children; Julia married John Orr, a progressive farmer of Cooperstown township; Hattie married William Tolle, an estimable laboring man of Versailles township, and has one son; Mattie and Mollie, twin sisters, are intelligent and active young ladies, who relieve their mother of much of the household work; Joseph W., the youngest, a youth of sixteen, is at home, and does much of the hard labor on the farm. Mr. Gifford, who has toiled hard for many years, is taking a needed rest whenever he can do so.

In politics Mr. Gifford is Democratic, and has been honored by his constituents several times with public office. Besides minor positions of trust, he has served two terms as Justice of the Peace, and was re-elected for the third term, but declined to qualify, thinking he had done his share of such service.

Religiously he and his worthy wife are earnest and useful members of the Methodist Episcopal Church, to which they have belonged many years.

Mr. Gifford's history would serve as an example for many poor, young men, starting in life. A careful analysis of his prosperity would be found to consist in intelligent and persistent effort, supplemented by uprightness of dealing, careful economy and uniform courtesy in all the various walks of life.

WILLIAM G. MOHLMANN, proprietor of the furniture and undertaking establishment at the corner of Main and Jefferson streets, was born in the city of Beardstown, July 10, 1866. His father, William, was born in Prussia and was the son of Henry, who was also a Prussian. He grew up there and learned the trade of cabinet maker. He married a Prussian lady of good family, and after most of their children were born, and when their son William was thirteen years old, in 1849, came to the United States. He finally settled in Beardstown and established a business, which was managed by Henry Mohlmann until his death in 1881, at the age of seventy-eight years. It was afterward carried on by William Mohlmann until his death in 1891. He was a good business man, a public-spirited citizen and one that did much for the city. His wife, as well as mother, is still living, the latter being about eighty years of age. The mother of William G. was named Lydia Lohmann, a Prussian. She was yet young when she came with her parents to the United States, and her mother is still living, smart, bright and active. The whole family were identified with the Lutheran Church.

William G. Mohlmann is the second of seven children. He grew up and obtained a practical education, and learned his business by growing up in it. He afterward took a course in the College of Embalming in Chicago. The business was established by the grandfather, Henry, in 1858. Until 1876 most of the goods were manufactured by the firm. At that time William F. became sole proprietor, and in 1891 William G. became half owner, and after the death of his father the sole proprietor. The convenient building now in use was recently built by the present owner. It was completed in July, 1891. Mr. Mohlmann occupies a double store, basement and first and second floors, 50 x 80 feet, all stocked with goods.

He was married in Virginia, February 18, 1892, to Miss Rose Leggett of North Carolina. Mr. and Mrs. Mohlmann are young society people of Beardstown. Mr. Mohlmann is a member of the blue lodge and chapter, A. F. & A. M. of Beardstown and Rushville, and Commandery No. 56, and Senior Deacon in blue lodge and Royal Arch Captain in chapter. He is no office-seeker, but is a Democrat in politics. He is yet a young man, but full of business and is bound to succeed.

WILLIAM HACKMAN, a practical German farmer and stock raiser of section 30, township 17, range 11, is the owner of a good farm where he lives. He was born in Hanover, near the city of Osnabrück, in 1820, September 13th. He was the third son born to John E. and Maria (Struve) Hackman, natives of Hanover, who came of pure German blood. After his marriage he settled down in his native land as a farmer, on a small scale, and here all the children were born, but later in life Mr. Hackman sold out all his interests in his native land and set sail from Bremen for the United States, with his wife and family. After a voyage of seven weeks and two days, they landed at Castle Garden, coming on at once to Illinois via Albany, New York, Buffalo, across Lake Erie, landing at Cleveland, across the canal, down the Ohio to Cairo, up the Mississippi river to St. Louis, and thence up the Illinois river to Beardstown, in June, 1835. The father purchased 120 acres in township 12, range 11, but before they were settled he sickened and died. He had procured the deed, so his family had the farm. He was only fifty-eight years of age and had been in the country but a few months. The widow mother moved on the farm with her children, and they began their life as farmers in a new country. Some years later she went to live with her only daughter, Mary Bushman, of Beardstown, where she died when seventy-two years of age. She lived to see her children all well married and settled in life. Mrs Hackman joined the Methodist Church in this county and died in that faith. Her husband was a Lutheran.

William and a brother Fred are the only surviving children, the latter also being a farmer at Arenzville. William grew to manhood in this county He is now the owner of two fine farms of 320 acres in all, both having a complete set of farm buildings on them, built by Mr Hackman. The land is in a fine condition and yields good crops

He was married in this county to Elizabeth Meyer, born in Germany, in 1828 She was a small child when brought to America by her parents. They made their first settlement on the farm now owned by Mr Hackman It was on this farm that Mr and Mrs Meyer both lived, and died when they were thirty years old. They were Lutherans in religion. Mrs Hackman is one of seven children, of whom she and a sister, Mrs Fred Hackman, of this county, and a brother, Henry, a retired farmer of Oregon, are the only surviving members. The next year, July, 1835, after they came to America, Mr and Mrs Meyer died, and Mrs Hackman was reared by a Mrs Freeman Skinner. She has been a true, good wife to a devoted husband for the past forty-five years

Mr and Mrs. Hackman are the parents of six children: one, Matilda, died when young, one, William E, died when twenty-two; and Louisa, after her marriage to George Keoneke, to whom she bore five children The living children are, Louis; Lucinda, wife of Theo. Heierman, a farmer in Morgan county, Illinois; and they have one child

Mr and Mrs. Hackman are regarded as being among the good, kind and hospitable old settlers of the county. They are upright, Christian people, being members of the Emanuel Methodist Episcopal Church, two miles from Arenzville Mr Hackman and son are sound Democrats in politics.

Mr Louis Hackman is now the manager of his father's old homestead, and he is conducting it in a way that reflects great credit on him. He is a hard-working man, and thoroughly understands his business, as the fine condition of his fields testify He was married to Amelia Kors of this county, and they are the parents of three as bright little ones as any one need care to see. Mr. Louis Hackman has been County Commissioner for the past nine years.

The whole family are just the kind of people that make Cass county so prosperous, and if there were more like this worthy German and his son, the prosperity of the State would be greatly increased.

JUDGE JOHN A ARENZ, now retired from active life and living at his pleasant home on the corner of Sixth and State Streets, was born on the river Rhine, near Cologne, in 1810, October 28. He is the only member of the family that came to this country now living, His parents lived near Cologne, Germany, and the father, Francis, died there when past ninety years of age; he was a prominent and successful man and was an officer in the army of his country, and received a pension for some years before his death. His wife lived to be an old lady over seventy-five years old

Mr Arenz came to this country in 1835, on a sailing vessel from Bremen. He landed in Baltimore city and another brother followed Mr. Arenz to this country, and he died in this State some twelve years ago, leaving a family Mr Arenz had been carefully educated in civil engineering and other branches; was one of the corps of men that measured the State of Prussia He was the principal of a public school, and was given a license to practice as an attorney at law. He was admitted to the bar about the time he was elected County Judge Mr Arenz had followed his brother Francis to this country, he having come some time before, being the first member of the family that left the old world for the new. Our subject came to this county in 1835, and the State was still unsettled in great part His brother's was the only frame house for miles around and wild game of every kind abounded. There were no railroads and but few wagon roads The people were kind and good hearted Mr. Arenz had come to the State from Baltimore, crossing the mountains to Wheeling, West Virginia, coming down the Ohio river to St Louis on a boat, It took fourteen days to make the trip, the boat often sticking on sand bars. After landing in St Louis he came to Cass county, and after some time he and his brother Francis laid out the town of Arenzville in the southern part of Cass county There they established a saw mill, gristmill and general store, and ran it for some time successfully. Later Francis died and Mr. Arenz came to Beardstown and has since made it his home. Francis died in Jacksonville, in 1856, in the prime of life, and was considered one of the foremost men of the State. He was one of the State Board of Agriculture and was a Director of the same. He also organized the local board of Cass county, which has continued ever since The State Board passed commendable resolutions on the death of Mr Francis Arenz, for his earnest, hard work.

Mr. John Arenz became prominent as soon as he came to the county and was soon elected Justice of the Peace, and has held other local offices. He was elected to the office of Probate Judge, being the second elected in the county He held the office for many years. He was elected first Mayor of Beardstown, in 1850, and has filled the office twice, subsequently He has been city Alderman and Treasurer, and served for many years He has been an admirer of the principles of his party, Republican. He was a Whig until the dissolution of that party and he then ardently espoused the cause of the new party from the time of its organization. He has always been regarded as a representative man

He was married, in Beardstown, to Mary Miller, of Kentucky, and she died at her home in this city in 1886, aged seventy years. She was the daughter of Captain William Miller, of Kentucky, a soldier in the Black Hawk war, having served as Captain of a company from Jacksonville, Illionis, where he was a pioneer, but later he came to Beardstown, where he died at an advanced age He was a prominent man Judge Arenz and wife had three children, Francis W died when young; Maria L., wife of Philip Kuhl, a merchant of this city, who have two children, and Anna, wife of Omer S. Spring, of Peoria, Illinois, a wholesale grocer and confectioner; they have one daughter, Mary L.

CHARLES J. NORBURY, one of the old and best known men of Cass county, was born in Philadelphia, May 22, 1812 His father, Joseph B, was a native of Northumberland, Pennsylvania, grew up and obtained his education in Philadelphia, became an attorney, and was so engaged until his death at sixty years of age He was a well known citizen of that city. His mother, Rebecca Frick, was born in Northumberland county, coming of German parents, and died a consistent member of the Dutch Reformed Church

Mr Norbury, after obtaining his early education, became a clerk in a wholesale house in Philadelphia In the spring of 1836 he came to Beardstown via Pittsburg, the Ohio, Mississippi and Illinois rivers. He has since been a resident of this place. He first began as a clerk for William Bassett, who was a dealer in flour and dry goods and agent for the steamboats on the rivers. After this Mr Norbury was associated with several gentlemen, and later entered into business relations with George Plahn, which continued until 1884, when Mr Norbury retired from active business In these years he had become one of the best known men of the county, respected for his honesty and as one who was a friend in need He never accumulated a large fortune, but possesses a modest competence.

He was married in Beardstown, in 1839, to Elizabeth Spence of Tennessee, born October 16, 1822 She was the daughter of Rev. Thomas Spence, a prominent Methodist minister of Tennessee, who came to Illinois in the early thirties, having been a pioneer minister in the early history of the State Mr and Mrs Norbury are working members of the Congregational Church. He is not an office seeker, but has always been a Whig and a Republican, voting first for William H. Harrison and last for his grandson Having always lived a temperate life, notwithstanding his age, he has a clear eye and sound faculties. He and his wife are the parents of thirteen children, nine of whom are living Those living are: Rebecca, widow of D. H Flickwin and living in Beardstown; Jennie, now wife of Judge S P Dale, Cañon City, Colorado, William remains at home; Paralee, the wife of O. K Ruechler, lives in Jacksonville, Illinois; Arthur also lives at Jacksonville; Elizabeth resides in Denver; Anna, wife of William D Epler, resides in Beardstown; Frank is a physician in charge of the male annex of the insane asylum at Jacksonville; Mamie is the wife of G B. Hegardt, assistant United States Engineer at Fort Stephens, Oregon He built the Government jetties at the mouth of the Columbia river.

JOHN L. BENNETT, born in McDonough county, Illinois, December 13, 1832, is the son of Isaac Bennett, born in North Carolina, May 22, 1808. He married in White county, Tennessee, Mary Lynch, April 8, 1834 She was the daughter of Charles and Mary Lynch The latter was born August 7, 1814. Her parents, who were farmers, reared eight children, the father dying in Tennessee, at the age of forty-five, her mother in Hancock county, Illinois, aged eighty-four years. Grandfather Bennett died in Kentucky in 1831, and his wife in Hancock county at the age of eighty years She came to Illinois in 1834, her son, Isaac, coming with her They first settled in McDonough county, coming from Tennessee in ox carts, taking about eight weeks to the trip They were in humble circumstances, and lived in McDonough county for two years, and then went from there to Hancock county, where they took up a claim of 160 acres of wild land with no improvements. They built a rude log cabin, in which they lived and reared most of the children. He made a good farm of this, for which he paid and took a deed in 1838. They had eleven children: John L., the second, is a farmer and stock grower of Hiar township, McDonough county; Mary Jane was the wife of Philo McPeigh, who died and left two children; Norelan is a large farmer of Hancock county, and has three children; Barbary Ann was the wife of George Bradly, and died, leaving four children; Rufus, a farmer of Hancock county, Illinois; Lorinda, killed by a kick from a horse at the age of eleven; Zilpha died at fourteen; Jeremiah, a wealthy ranchman and stock-grower of Texas; Lucinda, wife of William Duncan, died leaving five children; Phœbe is married and resides in St. Louis, and has two children.

John L. Bennett had very limited opportunities for obtaining an education: could barely read when a young man. He had to begin hard work when but a child, plowing corn when only eleven years old. He has worked very hard all his life until very recently. He was and is still a very rugged and strong man, and could endure anything and everything, even the ague which shook him while a lad.

He was married at twenty-one and soon left home. His wife was Elizabeth Carder, born in Indiana, where she was reared, daughter of Cooper B. Carder, of South Carolina, who came to Illinois in 1839. Her mother was a Miss Dudney, of Tennessee. Mr. and Mrs. Carder came to Illinois in 1839, where the latter died in 1853, leaving Elizabeth to care for the home. Mrs. Bennett's father, nearly eighty years of age, is living with her on the farm, of 180 acres.

Mr. and Mrs. Bennett have had a hard struggle to get this farm. They worked rented lands for some years and then bought their first land in 1864, fifty-five acres of timber for $700, paying one-half down. This was in Hancock county, and they sold this and bought where they now are. They have owned as much as 230 acres since. Mr. Bennett has done general farming all these years, and for the past few years has owned stock horses. He stands three fine stallions, two of them full blood, imported Clydesdale. He keeps from fifteen to twenty head of horses, some cattle and many hogs. Turns off as high as forty horses.

They have had twelve children, have buried two daughters and three sons; four died in infancy and early childhood. Eliza Ann, the first born, married Samuel Reeves, and died at thirty years of age. Those living are: Mary M., wife of William Neff, farmer in Hancock county, with two children; Charles Edward married Allie Buck, a farmer; John M. married Nancy White, resides with his parents and is running the home farm; Henry is single and has a tonsorial establishment in Chicago; Edgar is married to a Miss Swanson and resides in Chicago; Otto, in Hancock county; Homer, still a child, is at home. Mr. Bennett is a straight Democrat. He and his wife are highly respected by all who know them.

CHRISTIAN DUPES, of the firm of Dupes & Blohm, dealers in general merchandise and farm implements, was born in Monroe precinct, Cass county, where he has always lived. He was reared and educated in his native county as a farmer. He is the son of David Dupes, a native of Pennsylvania, who came to Illinois when a young man early in the forties. He was married, in 1844, in Schuyler county, to Katie Neathamer, a native of Pennsylvania, who was reared in her native State. She came when young to Schuyler county, Illinois, and was married to Mr. Dupes at the early age of fourteen. After their marriage Mr. Dupes began their married life on a farm, but in 1845 he moved to Cass county, and they settled in Monroe precinct, where he afterward owned 300 acres in this county and 160 in Ottawa county, Kansas. He continued to live in Monroe precinct until his death, on section 26, township 18, range 11, in 1888. He was then seventy-three years of age, and had been a successful farmer, a good citizen and a stanch Democrat. His wife still survives him, living at the old homestead, at the age of sixty-two years. She is the mother of six sons and three daughters still living, and two sons deceased.

Christian is the eldest child, and has never married. He was engaged as a farmer for many years, and was very successful, owning some very valuable property in the village of Bluff Springs. His present business was established in October, 1888, under the present firm name, but recently Mr. Dupes sold the store to A. W. Blohm, but retains the realty. After the first year they increased their capital and capacity to double its original size, and are now doing a large and lucrative business.

He is independent in politics, and is an ambitious young man, still in the prime of life, being only a little over forty years of age. He is a good citizen and a reliable business man. He is the Assistant Postmaster of the place, L. A. Jones being the Postmaster.

FLAVIUS C. PRICE, one of the oldest of the native born settlers of Mount Sterling, was born December 12, 1838. His father, William D. Price, was born in Kentucky, near Leesburg, July 17, 1817. Grandfather of subject, William D. Price, was born in Virginia, and removed from there to Kentucky, being one of the pioneers of that state. He spent his last years at Lexington. He served in the war of 1812, and was taken prisoner by the British.

Father of subject was reared in Kentucky, and came from there to Illinois about 1833, and located in that part of Schuyler county now included in Brown county. He entered a tract of Government land on section 2, built a log house, and at once commenced to improve a farm. He was a resident there till his death, which occurred in 1848. The maiden name of mother of our subject was Eliza A. Taylor. She was born in Fayette county, Kentucky, October 17, 1817, daughter of John and Elizabeth Taylor. Her parents came from Kentucky to Morgan county in 1832, and thence to Brown county in 1834. Mother of subject died February 1, 1871.

Subject was reared and educated in his native township. When his parents settled here, and for years afterward, the country was but little improved, and deer, turkeys, wolves and other game abounded. He attended the pioneer schools. These were taught in a log house, the seats made of slabs, one side hewn smooth, and wooden pins for legs. There were no desks, but holes bored in the wall, pins inserted, and a plank laid on them served as a desk for the larger pupils.

He continued to reside with his mother on the farm till 1862, when, August 8, he enlisted in Company D, One Hundred and Nineteenth Illinois Volunteer Infantry. The regiment was organized at Quincy, in October, and was one of the most active regiments in the army. He was with the regiment in all its various marches, campaigns and battles. The most important battles were the siege and capture of Fort de Russey, Pleasant Hill, Yellow Bayou, Nashville, Tennessee, and Forts Spanish and Blakely. He was discharged with the regiment and returned home, and resumed farming till 1882, on the lot where he now resides in section 1, Mount Sterling.

He was married May 10, 1861, to Narcissa Wilson. She was born in Brown county, Illinois, daughter of James L. Wilson. She died August 9, 1886. He was again married on October 23, 1887, to Miss Nancy Sullivan; she was born in Scotland county, Missouri. He has one child living by first marriage, Julia E., and by second marriage, one daughter, Calista. Julia E. married Wm. Jones, of Scott county, and has one daughter, Ethel.

Our subject is a Republican in politics. He and his wife are both members of the Christian Church, as also was his first wife.

HENRY C. KEIL, a large and very successful dealer in all kinds of hardware, stoves and tinware, was born in Hesse-Darmstadt, Germany, November 7, 1848. He grew up, attained his education and learned his trade of tinner in his native country. His father, Johanas Keil, is yet living in Germany at his old home, and is seventy years of age. He has been all his life a farmer. He had married a Miss Elizabeth Moell, a native of his own province. She died at the age of sixty years. She and her husband had belonged all their lives to the German Lutheran Church.

Henry Keil is the eldest of four children. After coming to this country and locating in Beardstown in 1867, he went back by way of Hamburg, Germany, in 1873; he returned to Beardstown in the spring of 1874, and has since lived here. He followed the tinner's trade for some time. He began business for himself in 1876, and has from that time on been increasing his stock and his trade. He carries a full line of first-class goods in a fine brick store of his own building, which he erected on Main street in 1890. He is a live man, full of business, and one who works for the best interest of his city and county. He has been a stockholder in the First National bank since it was started, first as a private bank in 1877, and later a national bank in 1887.

He was married in Beardstown, to Sophia Weis. She was born at Hamilton Station, Cass county, and was there raised and educated. She is the daughter of John and Catherine Weis, who both died on their old farm in Cass county. They were pioneers in Cass county, having come about 1840. Mr. and Mrs. Keil are members of the Lutheran Church, as were their parents. They have three smart children: Alma, Arthur and Edwin, all still at home.

Mr. Keil is a Republican in politics, has been Alderman of the city for several terms, and is a fine man in every way.

ICHABOD PERRY, one of the early settlers of this county, residing in Mount Sterling, was born in Claiborne county, Tennessee, July 18, 1815. His father, Edmond Perry, was a native of North Carolina and served in the war of 1812, receiving a land warrant for 160 acres; but it is not known that this was ever located. His father came from the same State, and removed from there to Claiborne, Tennessee, where he purchased land and carried on farming until 1831, when he came to Illinois

He spent his last years in Brown county. The maiden name of his wife was Rebecca Yarberry, also a native of North Carolina. She died in Brown county, also. Their son, Edmond, was a natural mechanic, but never learned a trade, and as he was very fond of hunting, he put in a good deal of time in that way. He resided in Tennessee until 1831, when, with his parents and others and wife and ten children, he emigrated to Illinois, and after four weeks overland travel landed in Morgan county. He rented a log cabin, three quarters of a mile from Jacksonville, and there spent the winter, and in the spring of 1832 came to that part of Schuyler that has been included in Brown county. He settled on a tract of vacant land in what is now Cooperstown township, and at once built a log cabin in the usual manner of the settlers, with rough hewn logs and puncheon floor. He lived in that place for about a year when he found out that he had built his house on the wrong land. He then moved to the adjoining quarter and put up a log cabin there, and later purchased this land, paying therefor $200, mostly in property. It was military land. This included the southwest quarter of section thirty, and he turned his attention to the improvement of the land, and resided in this locality until his death. The maiden name of his wife was Rachel Bridges, daughter of William and Sarah Bridges, who moved from Tennessee to Missouri in 1831, and spent the rest of their days there.

Ichabod was sixteen years old when he came to Illinois with his parents. The country was sparsely settled and but little improvement has been made anywhere. For some years the people lived on the produce of their farms and on the wild game that abounded in the forests. His mother used to card, spin and weave, and dressed her children in homespun made by her own hands. The father, being a skilled hunter, used to kill a great many deer. He dressed the skins, and in the winter the boys used to wear pants made of that material. Ichabod received his early education in the public schools of Tennessee. These were taught on the subscription plan, each family paying according to the number of children sent. He made the best of his opportunities, and in later years has improved his mind by extensive reading. He remained with his parents until he was twenty one and then began life for himself. In 1836 he went to the Territory of Iowa. At the time of his marriage he located on wild land in section 24, of Mount Sterling township, which he occupied for fifty-three years. He bought other tracts of land at various times, and at one time was the owner of 800 acres. He has assisted each of his children to homes, and now lives with his daughter, Mrs. Ward.

In 1838, he married Martha Bell, born in Kentucky, January 1, 1818, daughter of Robert and Jennie Bell. She died January 7, 1892. He has four children living: Oliver H., married to Martha McMillian; Lewis C., married first to Columbia Sharon, and for his present wife, Julia Dennis; Ethan Allen, married Delia Sharon; and Mary, married to William Ward. Mr. Perry is an ardent supporter of Republican principles. In 1846, etc., when he was a Democrat, he was Justice of the Peace two terms.

FRANKLIN A. HAMMER, of the firm of Beatty & Hammer, dealers in all kinds of hardware and farmers' implements, was born on the banks of the Shenandoah river, in Buckingham county, Virginia, April 10, 1829 He is the son of John Hammer, who, with two other brothers, had come from Germany prior to the Revolution The family was started in this country by the grandfather of Mr Franklin Hammer, who settled in Virginia, and lived and died there at an advanced old age His son grew to manhood in Virginia, and participated in the war of 1812 After that war was over he moved to the Shenandoah valley and farmed in Rockingham county for some years, when he went to Morgan county, Illinois, and started his life in that State as a general mechanic and blacksmith and wagon-maker In 1843, he removed to Beardstown and opened up a livery stable and hotel, which he ran until 1848, when he sold out and bought a farm six miles from Beardstown, and lived on it for some years, farming and improving it to a great extent. At the end of that time he again moved to Beardstown, and died at the age of eighty, in 1868. He was a good man and citizen and well known pioneer He was a Methodist in religion, and a Democrat in politics. He married in his native county, Miss Elizabeth Marica, of Virginia. She died on the farm in Cass county, at the age of forty-six. She was a member of the Lutheran Church He was married a second time, to Cynthia Dalton She died on the farm in Cass county, without issue, when quite old.

Franklin is the only surviving member of his father's three children. He came to the State of Illinois in 1835, when but a small boy, with his parents, settling in Arcadia, Morgan county, Illinois, and later, in 1843, the family came to Beardstown, and his father settled on a farm in Cass county Our subject returned to Beardstown and was connected for many years in the livery business, buying and selling horses and preparing them for fancy roadsters He was a true admirer of the noble, intelligent animal, and his judgment in regard to the worth of a horse was very good. In the old days he could drive four-in-hand as well as a western stage driver. He still retains his fondness for them, and has all his old power of judging them. In 1874, he sold out his livery and horse business, except as a breeder of the Hambletonian horses, that he continued until 1877, when he became president of the old Cass County Bank. He continued in this capacity until 1883, when he resigned in order to enter into a partnership with Mr. Beatty, he buying the stock of Mr. Rearick. He had been a stockholder in the Cass county bank ever since its organization in 1866 It had been previously an insurance business. The present firm of Beatty & Hammer is noted for the full line of reliable goods they carry They are located on Main street. Mr. Hammer has always taken an active part in all the affairs of the town. He has made judicial investments in various ways, and has made considerable money.

Mr. Hammer was married in Cass county, to Miss Margaret A Lee, of the same county of Cass. Her parents, Caleb and Matilda (Higgins) Lee, were natives of Maryland, and after marriage came, in 1828, to Cass county, Illinois, and settled there. He was a farmer, and spent the remainder of his life on the farm that he purchased upon coming to the county

Mrs Hammer is the youngest of four children, and all were born in Cass county. She and her husband are the parents of two children living· John, in business with his father; and Nellie, wife of Charles Ireland, a conductor on the Ohio & Mississippi railroad Mr Hammer is a Democrat in polities, and he and his wife are members of the Congregational Church. He has been the Treasurer and Assessor of the county one term.

WILLIAM T. ADAMS was born in Logan county, Kentucky, March 7, 1831. His father, Benjamin Adams, was born in Maryland, and his father was also from Maryland. He was also a farmer, who left Maryland for Kentucky about 1815, settled in Logan county and resided on his farm until his death. His wife's name was Sarah Bell, and she also died in Logan county. Benjamin Adams was about ten years old when his parents moved to Kentucky, and there he was reared, married and lived until 1830, when he came to Illinois and settled in what is now Brown county. He was accompanied by his wife and three children. He made the entire journey by team, making it in three weeks. He rented land a mile north of Mount Sterling for one year, and then bought timber land in sections 2 and 3 of the same township. He at once built a log cabin, making a comfortable home, although he had to hew the logs and build it himself. He lived upon the same farm until his death in 1873. His wife's name was Perneta Clark, born in Logan county, Kentucky, whose father, Abner, came from North Carolina, an early settler of Logan county, where he lived until 1835. He then sold out and came to Illinois, and bought in what is now Missouri township, improved his farm and resided there until his death. His wife's name was Nancy Gorham, of Kentucky. The mother of our subject is still living at the old home, aged eighty-six. He was two years old when he came with his parents to Illinois. Of course, in those days the people were obliged to live on game, fish and the product of their land. He, as many other pioneer boys, went to school in a log hut with seats of slabs. Holes in the side of the building served for windows. He resided with his father until his marriage, when he settled on the farm where he now resides.

He married, September 21, 1854, Ann Eliza Buvinger, of Martinsburg, Virginia, born November 15, 1853. Her father was born in Maryland, and her grandfather in Germany. The latter located in Baltimore when he came to America, and continued there until his death. The father of Mrs. Adams was a hatter. He went when a young man to Virginia, and there married Margaret McCormick, and in 1834 moved to Champaign county, Ohio, and in 1852 came to Illinois. He purchased a home in Mount Sterling, and here resided until his death. Mr. and Mrs. Adams have four living children: Charles B., who married Sarah Briggs; Sarah, married to William Briggs; Thomas, married to Julia Harris; and William E.

J. S. NICHOLSON, editor of the Beardstown *Illinoian*, was born in Oldham, Lancashire, England, in 1832. The family left Liverpool on the anniversary of the Queen's marriage, and, like so many emigrants, had a slow passage to New Orleans, thence up the Mississippi river, settling at last, after a journey of eleven weeks with teams, at Jacksonville. In 1850 the family settled on improved lands near Beardstown. They farmed this land. Part of the family moved to Rome, Peoria county, where the father died, aged seventy-three years, four months and twenty-eight days. He had been a good, quiet citizen. The war of the Rebellion changed his politics and he became a decided

Republican in his old age. His wife, formerly Miss Mary Needham, died February 9, 1881. She had been a good, kind wife and mother, and both she and her husband were consistent members of the Methodist Church, having been so connected for thirty-five years.

The subject of our sketch commenced life here as an office boy at the office of a paper of which he later became the proprietor and editor. The history of journalism in Beardstown began as early as 1834, when F. Arenz, the brother of Judge Arenz, became the editor of the Beardstown *Chronicle and Illinoian*, a kind of land advertiser. The next paper was started by Judge Emmons in 1845, and this was later owned by C. D. Dickinson, and he was followed by J. M. Sherman. Soon after it became the property of B. C. Drake, who ran it under the name of the *Central Illinoian.* When the war broke out the office was closed and the editor enlisted. The paper was re-organized by R. S. Mitchell, the property becoming owned by a stock company. Following the election of 1863 it became the property of L. W. Reavis, who continued to be the owner until 1866. The next year the paper was the property of A. J. Miller and was edited by Judge Emmons, and in 1877 Mr. Nicholson became the manager and proprietor. He was his own editor, and except for a short interval in 1883, has continued to run it successfully as a semi-weekly, under the name of the *Illinoian.* He is a thorough and practical newspaper man and the columns display his ability. His paper is run in the interests of the Republican party, and he has taken hold of all matters that tend toward reform. He has always been a great admirer of Abraham Lincoln and relates Mr. Lincoln's early experiences here with an especial pride and enthusiasm.

He was married in this city, in 1860, to Miss J. D. C. Harris, who came from England with her parents when a young woman. She died here in 1873, leaving four children, of whom but one is still living, Charles B., a member of the firm of Merry & Nicholson of St. Louis, Missouri. Mr. Nicholson was married for the second time, in this city, to Miss E. J. Buck. She was born, reared and educated in Cass county, and she has been a good wife and mother, and is an intelligent lady. Her one child is a son named Edgar E., a bright lad of twelve years. Mr. and Mrs. Nicholson are members of the Methodist Episcopal Church. He is a Republican in every sense. He has frequently been a delegate to the State and District Conventions and once a member of the State Central Committee.

WILLIAM W. GLAZE was born February 18, 1825, in Scioto county, Ohio. His father, Jacob Glaze, was born in the same county, but his father was a native of Virginia, although he died in Scioto. Mr. Glaze, Sr., was a farmer all his life, and died in the county where his entire life was spent, in 1844. His wife was a member of the Reardin family, a native of the same county as her husband, and she lived until 1891. She left three children living.

William Glaze moved to Brown county in 1856, by team, with his family. Here he has remained ever since on the land he bought when he came to the county. He built a house when he brought his family, as the old one-story house that was on the place when he bought it burned down. Times were hard after his arrival in Illinois. The banks of the State were in bad repute and money was scarce. Mr. Glaze had a great deal of difficulty in paying his taxes the first year. He served as Supervisor two terms.

He married Miss Elizabeth M. Coleman, a native of Scioto county. They have six children; May J., Maggie F., Carrie F., Julia H., Thomas H. and A. J. Mr. Glaze has been a member of the I. O. O. F. for twenty-six years and has filled all the important offices in the order. He once represented the order at the Grand Lodge. Two of his children live at home.

CHARLES BOCKEMEIER, general farmer and stock-raiser, was born in Prussia, not far from the river Rhine, August 16, 1835. His father, Charles, lived and died in Prussia, a blacksmith by trade. His wife came to the United States six months after his death, joining her sons in Cass county, dying at the age of eighty-two. She and her husband were life-long members of the Lutheran Church. Charles was a young single man when in 1854 he set out for the United States. He took the usual route via New Orleans, Mississippi, Ohio and Illinois rivers, to Beardstown, and joined his brother Casper, who had come here two years before. He has been in the county for more than thirty years, and what he now owns he has made by his own efforts. He has owned his present place for fourteen years. It consists of 160 acres, some well improved, and some very fine pasture land. He is at present Commissioner of road district No. 3, of Cass county.

He was first married to Miss Barbara Gemming, of Germany, who came to the United States when a young woman. At her death she left three children: Mrs. Anna Flammo, of Pekin, Illinois; Mrs. Lena Herety, wife of a railroad employé, and Mrs. Emma Nortrup, of Scott county, Illinois. He was married a second time, near Beardstown, to Mrs. Loise Wubker; her maiden name was Loise Schewe. She was born in Prussia, came here when a young woman, was first married in Cass county, to Henry Wubker, and by that marriage had seven children. Mr. and Mrs. Bockemeier have two sons, Charles and William. They attend the Lutheran Church, and are highly respected members of it. Mr. Bockemeier is a sound Democrat and an excellent man.

THOMAS I. McDANNOLD, an extensive farmer of Pea Ridge township, was born in Bath county, Kentucky, July 5, 1826. His father, John, was born in Montgomery county, Kentucky, in 1797, and his father, Reuben, was born in Culpeper county, Virginia, in 1750; and his father, Alexander, was born near Aberdeen, Scotland, coming to America in colonial times, and settled in Culpeper county, Virginia, where he spent the rest of his days. Reuben emigrated to Kentucky at an early day, secured a large tract of land, which he improved with slave labor, and resided there until 1834, then sold out and emigrated to Pike county, Missouri, settled near Clarksville, bought a farm and resided there until his death in 1854. John learned the trade of tanner and conducted the business in Owensville, Kentucky, and in connection with it engaged in the mercantile business. He resided there until his death in 1834. He was a Whig in politics, and served several years as Sheriff of the county. In 1834 the mother of our subject emigrated to Illinois, making the journey in a two horse wagon. She located at Springfield, where two brothers lived. Her father gave her some land, a part of which is now included in the land in Springfield and the rest at Buffalo Heart Grove. She married a second time, and lived near Springfield for a season, and then moved to Jacksonville and spent her last days there.

Thomas was in his eighth year when they came to Illinois, and remembers many of the incidents of the journey. At that time Vandalia was the capital of the State, and Springfield was only a village of 2,000 inhabitants. There was no railroad in Illinois, and St. Louis and Beardstown were the nearest markets for supplies. He went to school at Springfield, and resided there until 1844, and then went to his grandfather's in Pike county, Missouri. He remained with his grandfather one year, and in 1845 came to Mount Sterling, and in the next year, in company with his brother-in-law, General Singleton, purchased a tract of land in Missouri township, which he occupied two years, and in 1848 purchased the place where he now resides. He is well known as a practical and successful farmer, and has purchased land at different times, and now owns some 400 acres. His improvements rank with the best in the county.

He was married in March, 1849, to Mary Elizabeth Means, born in Lewis county, Kentucky, January 1, 1828. Her father, Major John Means, was born in the same county, and his father, John Means, born in Pennsylvania, went from there to Kentucky with his family and was one of the pioneers of Lewis county. The removal was made with pack-horses. He secured a tract of land on which he engaged in farming, and on which he remained until his death. His wife's name was Elizabeth Elton, born near Philadelphia, and she died in Lewis county, at the age of ninety-six. The father of Mrs. McDannold learned the trade of a blacksmith, which he followed in Lewis county until 1835, and then with his wife and three children came to Illinois. He settled in that part of Schuyler county now included in Mount Sterling, and bought a tract of land one mile east of the city, and remained there until his death in 1863. The name of his wife was Martha Parker, born in Culpeper, Virginia, and died in Mount Sterling in 1884. Mr. and Mrs. McDannold have four living children: John J., Thomas R., George R. and Clara L. They are members of the Presbyterian Church. Mr. McDannold was formerly a Whig, but has been a stanch Republican ever since the formation of the party. For seventeen years he has been director on the County Agricultural Board, and for six years has been its vice-president.

GEORGE W. WILLIAMS was born in Lancaster county, Pennsylvania, March 17, 1826. He was the son of Thomas and Margaret (Young) Williams. The former was a native of New York, and died in St. Louis, Missouri, when George was about four years old. Mrs. Williams was born in Pennsylvania, and died in Brown county, at the home of her son, aged seventy-eight.

George W. Williams was bound out to the trade of saddler at the age of eight, and remained there until he was seventeen, working for his board and clothes. At the expiration of his apprenticeship, he hired out at ten dollars a month, and worked for six months before he went to St. Louis, and worked under instructions for two years, and then traveled for two years. In 1849 he started a shop in St. Charles, Missouri, and continued there until the next year, when he started for Mt. Sterling. He remained there only one summer, and then opened a shop in Versailles.

In 1852 he sold out and crossed the plains to California with a team of oxen. He engaged in mining at Michigan Bar, and followed it for several months, when the city was burned. He then went to the mines, but that fall opened a shop in Red Bluff, and managed it until 1858. He then returned by way of New Orleans to Versailles, and again opened a shop. In a year or two he went on a farm, which he had bought previously, of 240 acres, partly improved. He built a log cabin 16 by 18 feet and lived there until 1863, when he built a two-story frame house and various farm buildings. Mr. Williams retired from farm work in the spring of 1891, and bought a nice house with twelve acres surrounding it in Mt. Sterling, just out of the city limits. He has been Assessor and School Director. He is a strong Democrat, though he cast his first vote for Taylor.

Mr. Williams was married in Versailles, Illinois, October 11, 1858, to Miss Juliet Ross, of Kentucky. She was the daughter of Richard Ross. Mr. Ross is still living, but his wife is dead. Mr. and Mrs. Williams have four children yet living, three being dead. Those still living are: Frank, married and having a bag works at the old home; Lydia, married; Charley and Edith are at home.

Both Mr. and Mrs. Williams are very estimable people, and are very influential among their large circle of friends.

WILLIAM B. MANLOVE was born in Schuyler county, December 28, 1830, near the town of Rushville. He is the son of Jonathan and Charity (Bodenhamer) Manlove. The former was a farmer of North Carolina, and came to this county in the fall of 1830, traveling over land all the way, and settled near Rushville, where he stayed the first winter. The next spring he went south and settled near Sugar Grove; and in 1834, he sold and moved to Birminghan township, and bought a farm where our subject still lives, of eighty acres. He put up a log house, in which the family lived. During the building of this house the father died, at the age of twenty-eight, leaving a wife and three children, of whom William was the eldest. The mother wove cloth for a living, and kept the old farm, and later married a second time, dying at the home of her son, William. William Manlove, Sr., was of English descent. The family were all farmers as well as can be ascertained. They left North Carolina on account of slavery.

William stayed at home until he was nineteen years old, assisting his mother and attending school in winter. After he became nineteen, he engaged to work for a neighbor at 50 cents a day, but worked for him only two months, and then went to his first free school, the other being a subscription school. He worked out by the month for a year, and then returned home, and buying out the heirs settled there. He had one yoke of oxen at that time.

He was married in 1853, to Miss Abigail Swisegood, who was born in North Carolina, and came with her parents to Illinois in 1846, being the daughter of John and Elizabeth Swisegood. She was one of six children, five yet living.

At his marriage he had only a small farm, but by dint of hard labor he has increased it to 900 acres of as fine land as there is in the county. He commenced work, plowing corn at 25 cents a day, taking his pay in bread and meat, which he carried to his mother who hired him out. He never went into debt for anything, but by great economy and much self-denial he succeeded in buying some land, and afterward stock. He feeds two or three cars of cattle and hogs, and has always been a man devoted to his home.

He voted the first time for Fillmore and the Republican ticket ever since, as his father was an old-line Whig. The whole family are considered good, honest people, and highly respected by everybody, making no pretensions. He built his present home in 1865, and was visited by the soldiers returning from the war. All of his land is in this township, and 600 acres of it is highly cultivated. He had six children, five living, namely: Eli, the eldest, is deceased; Laura A., John J., Isabell V., Tad J. and Emberry J. A grandson, William, a son of his oldest son, lives with them.

GEORGE I. FIELDS was born in Wythe county, Virginia, May 16, 1837. His father, John D. Fields, was born in Rappahannock county, Virginia. His grandfather was a native of Scotland and came to this country at an early date and settled near Richmond, Virginia. Here he died at the advanced age of 100 years. Mr. John D. Fields was a brick mason and a farmer. He attended to his trade and had his sons work the farm. He lived on his farm until his death in October, 1868, when he was ninety-six years old. He was a Sergeant in the war of 1812, and made a fine record in the naval service, especially at Norfolk, Virginia. He was honorably discharged. He received his land warrant for 160 acres, which he sold. His wife's name was Nancy E. Williams, a native of Culpeper county, Virginia. She died in Wythe county, Virginia, after a happy married life of sixty years. Mr. and Mrs. John D. Fields had seven children, three of whom are still living.

Mr. George I. Fields is the youngest of the family. He left his home in 1867 and settled in Versailles, Brown county, Illinois. Until that time he had been a farmer, but from then until 1884 he was engaged in milling. Since then he has engaged in newspaper work as editor and publisher of the Versailles *Enterprise*.

He was married to Ellen P. McWane April 16, 1865. She was born in Nelson county, Virginia, and is still spared to her family. They have had nine children, six of whom are still living, namely: Maggie V. Nancy E., Emma J., Addie D., Lonie and Stella May.

Mr. Fields has been elected Tax Collector for the township seven times. He is a Republican in politics and is the Chaplain of the blue lodge, A. F. & A. M. He connected himself with the Methodist Episcopal Church in 1870, and has been a Class-leader and exhorter most of the time. Mr. and Mrs. Fields are worthy members of society and are greatly esteemed by their host of warm friends.

THOMAS RYAN, Supervisor of Buena Vista township, resides on section 20, Schuyler county, Illinois. He was born October 20, 1845, and raised in this county. His parents were Charles and Margaret (Strong) Ryan. His father was born in Ohio, but removed with his parents to Frederick, Illinois, where he married, and settled in Buena Vista township in 1833. He was a brickmaker, and burnt the first brick ever made in Rushville. He also worked at the shoemaker's trade. He finally located on land in section 21, where he improved this farm of 120 acres, besides which he owned 320 acres more. He erected good substantial buildings on this place and otherwise improved and cultivated the land. Here he resided until the time of his death, which occurred January 9, 1891. His wife, mother of our subject, died December 16, 1879. They had eight children, five sons and three daughters: John, deceased; George, now residing in Texas (Grapevine); Catharine, wife of Thomas Armstrong; Louisa, wife of Alexander Young; Charles, deceased; Thomas, the subject of our sketch; William; and Margaret E., wife of Thomas Stoughel.

The subject of our sketch was reared on the home farm, and received his education at the country schools of that district, residing at home until he was twenty-three years of age. In 1868, he was married to Ellen Shields, daughter of Joshua and Julia (Futler) Shields. She was born in Ohio, June 16, 1847. Her parents were natives of Pennsylvania and New York, who came to Illinois in 1857, locating in Rushville. Mr. Shields served in the late civil war, being a member of the One Hundred and Nineteenth Regiment, and died while in the army. His wife, mother of Mrs. Ryan, is still living, in Canton, Illinois.

Mr. and Mrs. Ryan have had twelve children, eight of whom are living, the latter being Martin, Josie, Homer, Minnie, Herman, Clarence, Lula and Lena, the last two being twins.

Mr. Ryan is one of the most successful farmers of the county, owning 160 acres of highly improved and cultivated land, devoted to mixed husbandry. He has a comfortable home and large barns for his grain and stock, besides other modern improvements.

Politically, he affiliates with the Democratic party, and has been honored by his constituents by being elected to the office of Supervisor of his township.

He is a respected member of the community on account of his many admirable traits of character, and has the good will of a large circle of acquaintances.

HENRY D. RITTER was born August 6, 1819, son of Michael and Barbara E. (Schafer) Ritter. The former was born in 1795, being of German ancestry. By occupation he was a stone mason, and in 1812 he went to the German and French war and served as a soldier for nineteen or twenty years, and was an officer at the time of his death, at the age of fifty-one years. He was the son of Reinhart Ritter, who were natives of the same place. They were farmers. Subject's mother was born in Germany in 1796, and died when about sixty-five. Her parents lived to be very old people.

Henry was one of seven children, two of whom are living, and he is the eldest. He remained at home until he was twenty-five years old and worked as a clerk. He sailed in the Mentor for America from Bremen, Prussia, and arrived in New York after a voyage of six weeks. Here he remained for eighteen months, engaged in painting and the manufacture of parasols and umbrellas. From there he went to Virginia and followed the business of painting houses for three years, when he married and came to Ohio, settling in Fayette county, where he bought a house and four acres of land, and there lived until 1854, when he sold and came to Illinois in the fall, settling where he now lives. Here he bought 120 acres of land, which he improved, and in the same winter he added eighty acres to the farm. There was a log house on the land in which they lived until 1861, when he built his present house. He later bought 120 acres, and then eighty acres more, making in all 400 acres. He rents almost all of his land, and has practically retired from active business. Mr. Ritter has always been a Democrat, and has filled nearly every office in the county. He was School Trustee and Assessor for twenty years, Justice of the Peace for twelve years, Constable and Coroner four years, Sheriff two years, Commissioner two years, Supervisor eight years, and was chairman of the Board of Supervisors for a time, and he is considered one of the most prominent men in the county.

He was married April 24, 1848, by Rev. William N. Scott, near Petersburg, Hardy county, Virginia, to Miss Lucinda E. Hall, born in Virginia on the south side of Blue Ridge mountains, April 13, 1823. She was a daughter of James and Judy (Taylor) Hall. James Hall was a native of Virginia, and followed farming. When Mrs. Ritter was three years old the family moved to Rockingham county, Virginia, where they lived several years and then moved to Hardy county, and bought a farm, on which he erected a log house, where he lived a year or two, and then built a new and better hewn-log house in another neighborhood, about a mile from the first one. Here he spent the remainder of his life, dying at the advanced age of one hundred and two years, on his birthday. He was the father of eighteen children, seven boys by his first wife and eleven children by the second one, Judy Taylor. Seven of the latter are still living. One of the sons, Henry, by the latter marriage, was starved to death in one of the prisons of Richmond, Virginia, during the war of the Rebellion. Mrs. Judy Hall was a native of Virginia, and a daughter of George Taylor. She died in Hardy county, aged seventy years. Mrs. Ritter and her brother went to school in the old subscription schools where the parents paid according to the number of children sent; and Mr. Hall had so many children he could not afford to send more than two or three at a time. Mrs. Ritter remembers her first teacher, a Mr. Nick Hawk, who managed to keep school the entire year in a log house with benches of slabs, without backs. Their slates and pencils were pieces of soapstone and slate that they could find in the neighborhood of the school.

Mr. and Mrs. Ritter have had eleven children, nine yet living: Mary E., married Calvin Hill; Judy V. married Henry C. Hill, seven children, six yet living; Justina C. married Calvin S. Hill, eight living children; Calvin Z. married Viola Weatherby; George W. married Sylvina Weatherby, one child; Douglas J., at home with his father at work on the farm; Elisa Jane, married William H. McDaniel, five children; James H. S. married Mattie Shelton, four children; Franklin W. living at home; Martha O. and Martha Ann died when small.

Mr. Ritter is a member of A. F. & A. M. Lodge, No. 108, at Versailles, and the Meredosia Chapter and Council, No. 56, and also of I. O. O. F., Irene Lodge, No. 72, of Versailles, and Encampment of I. O. O. F.

He follows general mixed farming and is a well educated man, being educated in Germany.

HENRY F. WITTE, a practical farmer and stock-raiser, lives on a good farm in section 3, township 18, range 11, where he owns 120 acres of fine prairie land and forty acres of timber. He bought this land in 1862 and has since been successful as a farmer. He was born in Harford, Menden, Westphalia, Prussia, Germany, on August 9, 1824. He is the son of Fred and Minnie (Isserman) Witte, natives of Prussia, Germany, where they married and began life as farmers. There, too, all the family was born, and in 1855 the parents, with three children, set out for this country, taking passage on a sailing vessel, the Berker, from Bremen, leaving September 8, 1856, and landed in New Orleans after a voyage of nine weeks and two days. From there they came up to Beardstown on a steamer, landing here November 24, 1855. Here the parents lived and died, the father when about seventy years old and the mother when ten years younger. They were members all their lives of the Lutheran Church.

Henry had two brothers and a sister that finally came to this country, Henry being the only one now living. He was a single man when he made the voyage and worked for two years in the Park House and brick yards in Beardstown.

In 1856 he was married in Beardstown to Minnie Vette, born near the birthplace of her husband. Her mother had died in Germany, and her father, Fred Vette, followed his daughter to the United States and spent his last years, dying in Cass county when nearly eighty years old. He and his wife were life-long members of the Lutheran Church. Mrs. Witte had come to the United States when a young woman, in 1855, on the same vessel that brought her future husband. They were married about eighteen months after landing. They have lived and labored to build up a good home. They have reared a large and intelligent family of eight children, two deceased, Carrie and Edward, aged eight years and one month, respectively. Those living are: William H., a farmer in Arenzville, married Sophia Roegge of this county; Bertha, wife of Ed. Krohe, in Hickory precinct; Anna, wife of Frank Lebknecher, farmer in this county; Mariah, wife of Albert Krohe of Hickory precinct; Lizzie, wife of William Roegge, a farmer near Arenzville; and Minnie, who is still at home and cares for her parents. She is an intelligent and accomplished young lady and is greatly beloved by her parents. The entire family are members of the German Lutheran Church, and Mr. Witte is a stanch Republican.

When Mr. Witte was a young man he traveled extensively in Germany, and was in the regular German army from 1845 to 1847, but was not in the Revolution of 1848. He and his family are highly respected by all who know them.

THOMAS KNIGHT was born in Cornwall county, near Land's End, England, August 14, 1836. His father, Thomas Knight, was also born in Cornwall, of Cornish parents, and followed the trade of cooper until he came to this country in 1846. He first settled in Meredosia and then came into Cass county, where the family has since made their home. The father had brought a little money with him and was able to buy forty acres of land. He became a farmer, which business was entirely new to him. He was very industrious and had good judgment and all the family became well off. The father died there, after having increased his property to 264 acres. His wife survived him some years, and died when past four-score years. She was remarkable for being a very beautiful old lady and a very consistent member of the Methodist Episcopal Church.

LIBRARY
OF THE
UNIVERSITY OF ILLINOIS

R. W. Mills

Mr. Knight is one of a family of six, of which all are still living. He is one of the wealthy and influential men of Beardstown, and is now living at the corner of Eleventh and Washington streets, where he recently purchased a fine home, and has lived here ever since he retired from active life on his farm He has been a successful farmer and stock-raiser in Hickory precinct. He was a progressive farmer and kept up with the times His possessions amount to 520 acres, most of it under the plow and suppled with the finest improvements. As he was only ten years of age when he reached Cass County, he is one of the oldest settlers of the county

Mr. Knight was married in Beardstown, to Emma Dunn of Cornwall, England, where she was reared She came to Illinois with her brothers when yet a young girl and settled in Cass county, where she and her brother John still reside. Mr and Mrs Knight have six children. Robert, who married Delia Thiveaght, daughter of a farmer of Monroe, Illinois; Minnie married Fayette Post, a railroad conductor on the Ohio & Mississippi, living in Beardstown; Myrtle married L W. Berry, train dispatcher on the Chicago, Burlington & Quincy railroad; Albert and Eddie are at home, as is also the youngest, Clarence Lloyd. Mrs. Knight and some of the children are members of the Methodist Episcopal Church. Mr Knight, since he became of age, has become a Democrat, and his party elected him to the office of County Commissioner He is a strong local worker for his party.

RICHARD WATSON MILLS, one of the leading attorneys of Cass county, Illinois, was born in Jacksonville, Morgan county, this State, August 3, 1844.

His father, Chesley Mills, was born near Lebanon, Tennessee son of James Mills, a native of the eastern shores of Maryland, James Mills was born during Revolutionary times, a son of John Mills, who lost his life in the Revolutionary war, and in Maryland he was reared. When a young man he went to Tennessee, married the daughter of Isaac Lindsey, located a few miles from the Hermitage, and resided there until 1808. That year he removed to the Territory of Missouri and located three miles from Hannibal, being one of the earliest settlers there. He improved a large farm and resided on it till the time of his death Isaac Lindsey, his father-in-law, was a resident of Eastern Maryland at the breaking out of the Revolutionary war. He was loyal to the crown, but preferred not to fight on either side; so he sought the furtherest bounds of civilization, taking up his abode in the wilderness eight miles from the Hermitage. At that time the Indians were numerous and often there was trouble with them For a long time the settlers all lived in block houses He improved a farm in the locality which is still known as Lindsey's Bluff, and resided there till his death

Chesley Mills learned the trade of plasterer and bricklayer, which he followed till his death, in 1844 He married Harriet Cadwell, a native of Edwardsville, Madison county, Illinois, born on January 10, 1814, daughter of Dr George Cadwell. Dr. Cadwell was born and reared in Vermont, and in 1799 went to Kentucky with his father-in-law, Matthew Lyon. He objected strenuously to the institution of slavery, and in 1804 came to the Territory of Illinois, becoming one of the original settlers of Madison county He resided there till 1820, when he went to Morgan county with his wife and children, making the journey with flatboats via the Mississippi and Illinois rivers to Naples. He located near Lynnville, being the first physician to settle in Morgan county, and continued practice there till the time of his death. The maiden name of his wife, grandmother of the subject of our sketch, was Parmelia Lyon. She was born in Vermont. Her father, Matthew Lyon, was born in Ireland, of Scotch ancestry, and when a young man came to America and located in Vermont, where he married the daughter of Governor Chittenden, the first governor of Vermont. He took part in the Revolutionary war and attained the rank of General. After the war, he represented Vermont two terms in Congress He was the first victim under the Sedition Act, the charge being that of speaking disrespectfully of John Adams, the President of the United States. He was sentenced to six months' imprisonment and fined $1,000; served his time in jail and paid his fine In 1799, he emigrated to Kentucky and located in Lyon county, which is named in honor of him He founded the town of Eddyville, the county seat of Lyon county, and became a prominent and wealthy man He was a slave owner and trader. While residing there he was sent as a representative to Congress. He removed from Kentucky to the Territory of Arkansas, was among the pioneers of Helena, and soon after his arrival there was sent as delegate to Congress. He died in Arkansas about 1825.

The mother of our subject now resides in Jacksonville. She reared five children. Thomas, spent his last years in Dakota; Emily, married Thomas W. Jones, of Ritchie, Will county, Illinois; Martha, married Henry Demarest; George, resides in San Francisco, California, and is a member of the Judson Manufacturing Company of Oakland.

Richard W. Mills received his early education in the district schools. He was in his seventeenth year when the war broke out, and he enlisted in Company B, Tenth Illinois Volunteer Infantry, and went with the company to Cairo. He was there rejected on account of his age, and returned home He had been at home, however, only a few days when he again enlisted, this time in Company F, Nineteenth Illinois Volunteer Infantry, and was accepted. He went South with his regiment and remained with it till after his term of service had expired. He participated in the battles of Stone River and Mission Ridge, and was in the reserve at Chickamauga. After his return home he received an academic education at Jacksonville, after which he taught school four years During that time he commenced the study of law with Judge Cyrus Epler, and in May, 1870, was admitted to the bar He practiced with Judge Epler till 1871, and January 6 of that year he came to Virginia, where he has since been engaged in a successful law practice

February 4, 1873, he married Matilda A Tate, a native of Cass county, Illinois, and a daughter of Dr. Harvey Tate She died March 26, 1884. His second marriage was consummated November 29, 1889, with Nellie W. Epler, a native of Cass county, her parents being William and Jennie Epler.

Mr. Mills is a member of Virginia Lodge, No 544, A F. & A M , Clark Chapter, No 29, R. A. M.; Hospitaller Commandery, No 31, K T Politically, he has always affiliated with and been an ardent and efficient worker in the Republican party. He has served as Master in Chancery

Mrs Mills' father, William Epler, a resident of the city of Virginia, was born in what is now Princeton precinct, Cass county, Illinois, April 15, 1835 His father, John Ep ler, was born in that part of Lancaster now included in Dauphin county, Pennsylvania, April 15, 1795. His father, the great-grandfather of Mrs. Mills, Abram Epler, was born in the same locality. His father, great-great-grandfather of Mrs. Mills, John Epler, was born in Germany, and was reared there to young manhood, and in 1734, with his brother Peter, came to America They located near Reading, Berks county, Pennsylvania They were Lutherans and established a church of that denomination there. Peter's descendants removed to Northumberland county; John's removed to that part of Lancaster now included in Dauphin county in 1768. He purchased a tract of land there, which he occupied till his death in 1782 A natural bowlder marks his resting place, upon which is inscribed a shield, his name and the date of his death The farm which he owned is now in possession of his great-great-grandson He reared three sons and one daughter

Abram Epler was reared and married in Pennsylvania, and resided there till 1798 Then, with his wife and three children, he removed to Kentucky, making the journey across the mountains with teams, down the Ohio river on flatboats to the Falls of the Ohio, landing at the site of the present city of Louisville. He remained there two years; then crossed the river into Northwest Territory, and located in what is now included in Clark county, Indiana. There he erected a log cabin in the wilderness. In 1807 he built a stone house there, which is still standing, it being the oldest stone house, in a good state of preservation, in the State of Indiana. He resided there until 1832, when he came to Illinois He died in Cass county in 1837. The maiden name of his wife was Anna Oldweiler. She was born in Lancaster county, Pennsylvania, October 26, 1768, and died at the home of her son George, May 3, 1847 There were eleven children born to them, all of whom reached adult years: Elizabeth Norris, John, Nancy Austin, Abram, Catherine, Blizard, Jacob, David, Sarah Weir, Isaac, George, Mary Short.

John Epler, grandfather of Mrs Mills, was but three years old when his parents moved to Kentucky, and five years old when they moved to the Northwest Territory There he was reared and married He resided in Clark county till 1831, when with his wife and six children, he came to Illinois; made the journey with teams, and after three weeks' travel landed in Cass county. He bought a tract of land on which he engaged in farming and was very successful in his operations. From time to time he purchased other lands until he became the owner of 1,200 acres in Cass and Morgan counties. He spent the last years of his life in Virginia and died May 25, 1876. The maiden name of his wife was Sarah Beggs She was born in what is now Clark county, Indiana, April 28, 1800 Her father, Charles Beggs, was born in Rockingham county, Virginia, October 30, 1775, and his father, Thomas Beggs, was born in the same county He took part in the Revolutionary war and died in the service Charles Beggs was reared and married in Virginia, and resided there till 1798, when he moved to Kentucky In 1799 he removed to the Northwest Territory and settled in that part now included in Clark county, Indiana He served in the war of 1812, and fought with Harrison at the battle of Tippecanoe; was an old Whig, and personal friend of General Harrison; served in both the Indiana Territorial and State Legislatures; resided in Clark county till 1829 In 1829 he came to Illinois and was one of the pioneers of Morgan county. He bought a tract of land and resided on it till his death, October 21, 1869. The maiden name of his wife was Martha Trumbo. She was born in Rockingham county, Virginia, March 16, 1778, and died May 12, 1811. Four of her children grew to maturity: Elizabeth, Sarah, Mary and George. The grandmother of Mrs. Mills died January 11, 1882. Twelve of her children were reared: Charles, Abram, Cyrus, Mary A. Barrett, Sarah Fairbank, Elizabeth Hall, John M., William, David, Myron L., Ellen Prince, and Albert G.

William Epler, father of Mrs. Mills, was reared in his native county, and received his early education in the pioneer schools here, and subsequently attended Illinois College, Jacksonville. He has been prominently identified with the business interests of Virginia many years. The maiden name of Mrs. Epler, wife of William Epler, was Jane Abigail Woodman. She was born at Paw Paw, Michigan, March 6, 1838. From a genealogical record of the Woodman family, compiled by Jabez H. Woodman, we learn that there were two brothers, Edward and Archalaus Woodman, natives of Christian Malford, a parish in Wiltshire, England, came to America in 1635, and settled in Newbury, Massachusetts. There descendants are numerous and are scattered in various parts of the United States. It seems from this that Mrs. Mills is a descendant of Edward. The second in line was his son Edward, the third in line his son Archalaus, the next in line Archalaus' son Joseph, born May 4, 1714. He married Bridget Willey in 1762. He died in Wheelock, Vermont, November, 1807. His son John, great grandfather of Mrs. Mills, married Sarah Foy. He died at Lyndon, Vermont, December 6, 1853, aged ninety years. His son, David Woodman, gra[illegible] Mrs. Mills, [illegible] New Eng[illegible], July 27, 1793. He [illegible] from New England to New York State, thence to Michigan, and from there to Oketo, Kansas, where his death occurred August 28, 1892, aged ninety-nine years and one month. His wife, grandmother of Mrs. Mills, was Abigail Gray. The mother of Mrs. Mills died in the State of Nebraska, October 2, 1863, in the twenty-sixth year of her age. Mr. Epler, father of Mrs. Mills, now has a piece copied from an English history, that was published in 1615, that gave an account of the trial and burning at the stake at Lewis, in Sussex, England, of Richard Woodman, June 22, 1557, on account of his religious convictions. He was tried before the Bishops of Chichester and Winchester. He was very tenacious of his opinions, as are said to be some of the Woodmans of the present day. The parents of Mrs. Mills were married at the home of the bride's brother-in-law, Colonel John B. Culver, at Duluth, Minnesota, April 12, 1859. At that time Duluth was an Indian trading post, and they were the first white settlers ever married there. Mr. Epler was there in the employ of the United States Government as a civil engineer.

HIRAM JAQUES was born in Schoharie county, New York, August 17, 1814. He was the son of Jesse and Maria (Boice) Jaques. They both died in New York. They had twelve children, but only one or two are living. Hiram remained at home with his parents until their death, when he worked by the month until the spring of 1837, when he came to Illinois by the Ohio, Mississippi and Illinois rivers, with one of his brothers and two neighbors. They first [illegible] by day, month or [illegible] two years, and then took an interest in a saw and grist mill, and later bought it all and 200 acres of land.

Mr. Jaques was married in 1838 or 1839, to Nancy Reeves of Kentucky, where her father and mother were early settlers. They had very few neighbors, but there was an abundance of wild game. Mr. Jaques has lived on the farm he first purchased ever since his marriage, except two or three years. He first built a log house in which they lived until the present one was built.

They have had nine children, four of whom are yet living: Louisa, wife of Dr. Scanland (see sketch); Alma, married, and has one child; he served four years during the late war, was wounded three times, and now resides at Colorado Springs; Nephi Jaques served in the Tenth Illinois Cavalry two years and has since died, leaving two children; Rachel, who married Mr. Scanland, and has three children living; George, married, and has two children ;Walace W., married.

Mr. Jaques has always been an Andrew Jackson Democrat, and now votes the People's ticket, as he is now a member of that party, although he voted for Andrew Jackson. He has been engaged in general farming all his life, and he and his wife are greatly respected by all who know them.

GEORGE D. UTTER, a prosperous farmer and stock-raiser of Frederick, Schuyler county, Illinois, was born in that place on November 13, 1846, the youngest child of John and Charlotte (Brines) Utter. Both of his parents were natives of Allegany county, New York, where the father was born November 11, 1810, and the mother April 11, 1807. In 1815, when five years of age, his father came to Palmyra, Illinois, where his youth and early manhood were spent. He was there married to Charlotte Brines, December 5, 1834, and in 1839 removed with his wife and family to Schuyler county, same State, settling on the Rushville road, near Pleasant View. There he and his worthy wife spent their remaining days, rearing six children, two boys and four girls, of whom two boys and one girl now survive. October 15, 1887, the family were called upon to mourn the loss of the devoted wife and mother, who had unselfishly watched over their interests for so many years. On February 14, of the following year, the honest, hard-working father also departed this life, as if unable to endure separation from his beloved companion. Both of these worthy people enjoyed the esteem of their entire community.

George, whose name heads this biography, was the baby of the family, and now weighs 240 pounds, which shows what Illinois can produce under favorable circumstances. He was trained to farm life and educated in the public schools of his native county, and now resides within one mile of his birthplace. By industry, economy and careful management, he has accumulated a competence for himself and family. He owns an excellent farm of 240 acres, which was originally purchased by his father, and is numbered among the successful farmers of Schuyler county.

March 14, 1867, he was married in Schuyler county, to Miss Priscilla J. Ward, who was born in Bainbridge, that county, April 10, 1848. Her parents, Apollos and Jane (Bramble) Ward, were among the first settlers of Schuyler county. Her father was a native of Hamilton county, Ohio, where he was born July 29, 1805. Her mother was born February 23, 1815, and their marriage occurred June 23, 1835. Her mother still survives, and is universally respected.

Mr. and Mrs. Utter have seven children: Arthur Frank, born January 9, 1868, married Clara Bradman February 27, 1889, and lives on a farm near by; Albert Marion, born October 29, 1870; Alice May, born September 4, 1873; Pulaski, born November 30, 1876; Amy Florence, born January 10, 1880; Mary Viola, born October 21, 1883; and Cora Minnie, born October 30, 1889. All of these are under the parental roof, and form a typical happy family.

Politically, Mr. Utter affiliates with the Democratic party. Religiously, he and his wife are prominent members of the Methodist Episcopal Church South.

Mr. Utter's prosperity is due to his persistent efforts and honorable dealings in all the walks of life. He is one of the representative men of his county, and deservedly enjoys the esteem of his fellow men.

FRANKLIN L. ANGIER, chief clerk of the Locomotive and Car Department of the St. Louis Division of the Chicago, Burlington and Quincy Railroad, was born in Vermont at Waterbury, where he was reared until twelve years of age. He was the son of Aaron Angier of New Hampshire. His father was American of French ancestry. Aaron was a Baptist clergyman and married in Vermont, Miss Eliza Luther. She came of good family of Scotch descent. After marrying, Rev. Mr. Angier continued his work in the church of his faith until 1850, when he moved to New York State, and after four years moved to Illinois in 1854. He died a few months after his arrival in this State, in Bureau county, while yet in active work, being then only forty-seven. He was a hard-working, logical preacher, fluent talker and a worthy citizen. His wife survived him until 1863, and then died at the age of fifty-four. They had ten children.

When Franklin Angier was twelve they removed to Elbridge, New York, and here he was educated until he was sixteen, when the family removed to Illinois, where he has since resided. Except three years in the army, he has been engaged in clerical work. He enlisted from Geneva, Illinois, in September, 1861, in Company B, Fifty-second Illinois Volunteer Infantry, Captain E. A. Bowen and Colonel Wilson in command. The latter named official did not retain his command very long, but was succeeded by Colonel T. W. Sweeny. The regiment was in the Fifteenth Army Corps of the Army of the Tennessee. They fought their first battles at Fort Donelson, Shiloh and siege of Corinth and battle of Corinth under General Rosecrans, and in October, 1863, Mr. Angier was discharged, and in May, 1864, re-enlisted and joined Company G, One Hundred and Thirty-ninth Illinois Volunteer Infantry, remaining until expiration of service, October 28, 1864. They were garrisoned at Cairo, Illinois. He served in the capacity of First Lieutenant all the time he was in the One Hundred and Thirty-ninth Regiment.

After coming to this State Mr. Angier lived in Bureau county for a short time, and was married there to Adaline Smith, born in Rochester, New York, in 1838, but was reared in Illinois, where her parents had moved when she was young. Her father, Alonzo Smith, was a farmer and died in Bureau county in 1865, when in middle life. His wife is still living and resides with her daughter Mrs. Angier. She is eighty-four. She has been a worthy member of the Baptist Church for years.

Mr. and Mrs. Angier are members of the Baptist Church. Mr. Angier is a Republican in politics, and a Master Mason, being a member of Cass Lodge, No. 23, and Clarke Chapter, No. 29, of Beardstown. He has been Master and is now Secretary of the lodge. Is a member of McLane Post, No. 97, Grand Army of the Republic.

They have seven children: Mary, wife of C. E. Sperry, a painter of Aurora, Illinois; Frank is a clerk under his father and married Maude Foster; Florence is at home; Carl and Earl (twins), and Charles and Dana are all four at home. They all have received the advantage of a good education and are refined, intelligent young people.

FRED KROHE was born in Cass county, September 30, 1849, and was reared in Beardstown, which has been his home. He is the son of Fred Krohe, Sr., who was born in Saxony, Germany, May 8, 1809, and who died November, 1880, in Beardstown. He was a young man when with his parents he came to the United States. He married in Cincinnati, Sophia Hoverkluf, who was born in Hanover, Germany, in 1816, and died March 20, 1888. She had come with her parents to the United States to Cass county, both dying there. She had a family of six children, of whom three are living.

Mr. Krohe is a man who has devoted his time to his business and the amassing of a fortune. He has now retired and is living in Beardstown, and is living on the corner of Washington and Third streets. He has made a fortune and owns some very valuable property, and is owner of the opera-house block and some fine property in the county. He has lived in this county all his life, except three years in Omaha, Nebraska, where he has some property interests.

He was married in Beardstown, to Elizabeth Stock of Cass county, a native of the same county. She was born February, 1846. She cwas reared and educated in this county and is the daughter of Henry and Elizabeth Stock, natives of Prussia. Mr. and Mrs. Stock, were wealthy and well-known members of the county, and were members of the Lutheran Church.

Mrs. Krohe died at St. Louis, May 9, 1892; she was a good and worthy woman, who had always lived in Cass county and was associated with its history. Since her death Mr. Krohe has lived in his home at Beardstown.

THOMAS H. CARTER was born in Little York, York county, Pennsylvania, October 11, 1823. His father, Bushnell Carter, a native of Connecticut, came when a young man to Pennsylvania, where he married Julia L. Barber, an estimable lady. He was an educated man, a successful lawyer, and died in early manhood. After the death of his mother our subject was taken by his father to an uncle in Connecticut, and there he grew to manhood. When twenty years of age he became a school teacher, and so continued until 1847, when he went to Canfield, Ohio, where he began the study of law under Judge Newton. He was admitted to the bar in 1852, after graduating from Ballston, New York. About this time, with a young wife, he made his way to Beardstown, and engaged in partnership in a general law business with a cousin, Carter Van Vleck, who had come here some years before. In later years he was connected in a legal way with Henry Philips, of Virginia, Illinois, but after some years he had sole charge of the business himself. He became well-known through the State as one of the legal lights of the day, and has figured in it prominently. He has amassed a good farm property in Missouri, which is still in the family. He was not a politician, but he had been City Attorney of Beardstown, and from 1858 to 1861 he was Postmaster of the place. He was held in high esteem for his upright character and good qualities. He was a Democrat, a Master Mason, a good moral man and a great lover of home.

He was married to Miss Maria L. Peck, in Warren, Litchfield county, Connecticut, where he was reared. She was born in the same place December 13, 1825, and was a daughter of Phineas and Phoebe (Taylor) Peck, both of Litchfield. Mr. Peck was a farmer and purchased the old Peck homestead, which is yet in the family. His death occurred July 11, 1870, at the age of seventy-seven. He was a strong, active man, and both he and his wife were members of the Congregational Church, as are also their children. Mr. and Mrs. Carter had one son, Augustine P., now chief clerk of Superintendent Johnson of the Montana Central Railroad of Helena, Montana. He married Miss Frances B. Henderson, of Monmouth, a daughter of Colonel Henderson, a prominent man of Warren county. Mr. and Mrs. Augustine Carter and wife have one bright daughter, Marcia P., named for her grandmother.

Mr. Carter died while in Peoria, Illinois, for treatment, on March 19, 1886, leaving to his many friends a memory most pleasing to cherish.

GEORGE HENRY EIFERT settled in Schuyler county, January 13, 1857. He was born in Hesse-Darmstadt, Germany, February 11, 1823. He had five brothers and two sisters; the former all came to the United States, where the brother, John, died in Schuyler county; George also died there, while Ludwig died in this county; Valentine went away during the civil war, and was never heard from again.

George was the youngest, but his father died when only forty-one years old, so he had to work very hard, as there were nine small children left. He came to the United States and first stopped in Maryland with a Dunkard preacher two years, when the minister sent him to Ohio. He went to Preble county, Ohio, and in 1854 he sent to Germany for Margaret Roth. She came to America from Hesse-Darmstadt in 1826, June 21, all by herself. When she arrived in Ohio she and Mr. Eifert were married. In 1855 they came to Illinois and rented land in Schuyler county, which was but little improved. Here he passed his remaining years. Before his death he became the owner of 417 acres of land and put up fine buildings on the land, and he also raised stock. His death occurred November 17, 1884. His wife is still living on the homestead. They had four children: George, Charles W. and two who died in infancy. Mr. Eifert was a Democrat in politics, a Methodist in religion, and was an earnest, good man, dying happy and satisfied.

When he was married he borrowed $50, and that was all he had. When he came to Illinois he was worse off yet, as he then had only $20. He purchased a stove and wash-tub, and they began housekeeping without a chair, table, knife or fork, and slept on the floor a whole month before they could afford to buy a bedstead, but they worked hard and prospered.

George Eifert is the elder son of George and Margaret Eifert. He was born in Preble county, Ohio, August 6, 1856. The family came to Illinois, and he has since resided here, where he has followed farming.

He was married, November 17, 1878, to Sarah Hale, daughter of William and Margaret Hale (see sketch). She was born in Schuyler county, Illinois, in 1858. They have two children: Carl and Warren. Mr. Eifert has part of the old homestead, where he follows stock-raising. He is a Democrat in politics and a member of the Methodist Church South. He and his wife are highly respected citizens of their section, and are admired by every one who knows them.

CAPTAIN SYLVESTER D. NOKES was born in Franklin county, New York, February 11, 1835. His father was John Nokes, born March 20, 1809, and his grandfather was Jacob Nokes, of New England. He was a farmer who died at an advanced age in Brown county, Illinois, and his wife's name was Mary —, who bore him seven children. She died in Brown county about ten years after her husband, aged eighty years. John Nokes came West from New York in 1842, and settled in Brown county on 160 acres of new land, it being part of his present farm. He brought his wife and six children with him in a covered wagon. He rented for several years and then built a hewed-log house. Much of his land was prairie of the most productive kind. He resided on this farm about twenty years.

The Captain was a volunteer in the One Hundred and Nineteenth Illinois Infantry, Company E, enlisting August 9, 1862. He went as Second Lieutenant, and was mustered out as Captain, to which post he was promoted in 1864, in the place of Captain Munford, resigned. He was absent from his command on account of a gunshot wound in the thigh received on the Red river. He was all through that campaign, was in the two days' fight before Nashville, Tennessee, and in the charge on Fort Blakely. He has sixty acres of orchard land, apples, peaches and grapes. He keeps ten to twelve horses, fifteen to twenty head of cattle and fattens about fifty hogs per year. His orchards return him the best interest on his money. He built their fine brick farm house in 1881. The schooling of the Captain is limited, but he is well informed and a great reader.

He was married about the age of twenty, to Anna J. Dodd, who was nearly sixteen. She was the daughter of William and Julia Ann Richardson Dodd. Her father was of Green county, Illinois, and her mother of Bradenburg, Kentucky.

The living children of Captain and Mrs. Nokes are: Mrs. Carrie Bradney, living in Missouri; Mrs. Mary V. Wright, at home; Oscar E., living at the Mounds; Birdie May, a young lady at home; Irwin Grant; and Jessie.

The Captain has been a Republican, but now is an Alliance man. He is justly proud of his war record.

DR. SIDNEY W. SCANLAND was born in Carroll county, Kentucky, October 13, 1834. He was the son of Thomas B. and Agnes W. (Searcy) Scanland, who were also born in Kentucky. Thomas followed the trade of cooper when a young man, and was married at the age of twenty-six, in Kentucky. In 1840 he came to Illinois. He settled first in Elkhorn township, and lived there two years on his first farm.

He built a frame house, but in 1842 he bought in section 16 120 acres, and still later bought more land, until he had acquired nearly 400 acres. He improved his farm, built several houses and barns, and died October 14, 1885, aged seventy-seven years, respected by all who knew him. He was the son of William Scanland, a native of Kentucky. William had come to Illinois in 1846, and settled in Pike county, where he and his wife lived and died very old people. They spent their last days in Pittsfield, Illinois. Our subject's mother was born in Carroll county, Kentucky, May 3, 1812, and died in Versailles, January 20, 1888, at the home of her daughter, Mrs. Susan McCoy. Her parents died when very old people in Kentucky.

Sidney was one of six children: four are yet living. One brother, George, was taken prisoner in the late war, and died five months later at Macon, Georgia. Our subject is the only professional man in the family now living, but some of his father's brothers were prominent physicians. He remained at home until eighteen years of age, attending school, and after that taught school for some time, and during this time was obliged to board around among the neighbors, as they did in those times. During the years of his teaching he was educating himself, and when about twenty-six years of age, began to study medicine. After marriage, in 1860, he settled on the old farm where he had always lived, and in December, 1863, he enlisted in Company K, Tenth Illinois Cavalry, and remained in the service until January, 1866.

Before this time he had attended lectures at Rush Medical College. After the war he settled in Chambersburg, Pike county, and practiced for seven years. He then came to this county, taught school one winter, then bought a little farm in 1875, and has practiced medicine ever since. He has 100 acres of the old homestead and takes life very easy. He has taken an active part in everything that has taken place in the county, and has contributed time and money to advance the interests of the People's party. He is a prominent member of the G. A. R. in Isaac McNeil Post, also a lecturer in the Farmers' Alliance, and President of an Anti-horse-thief Association.

He was married to Louisa L. Jaques of this county (see sketch of Hiram and Nancy Jaques). They have four children: Sidney H., George A. and Birdie C. are in California; and Florence Z. is the wife of Oscar McCoy still living at home.

Dr. Sidney W. Scanland has always been a representative man of Elkhorn township; has twice been elected Justice of the Peace, and is at present acting as Notary Public.

REV. JAMES DE WITT was born at Hope, Warren county, New Jersey, November 5, 1817, a son of James and Anna (Coates) De Witt; the father was born in Sussex county, New Jersey, and about the year 1842 emigrated to Michigan; he located on a farm in Oakland county, and there passed the remainder of his days; he died at the age of eighty-six years; the mother was also a native of New Jersey, and died in Michigan, at the age of seventy years. They reared a family of eight children, seven of whom are living: one son was a merchant, another a tanner, and a third was a millwright, but they are now engaged in agricultural pursuits. James De Witt, Jr., remained at home with his parents until he was thirteen years of age, and then began clerking for an older brother; at the end of two years he secured a position as clerk in a general store, and three years later he went to Pennsylvania, where he was employed as a clerk by his brother. In the spring of 1838, he left the Keystone State, and came by rail, canal and river, to St Louis, the journey was continued by water to Warsaw, where he disembarked, and from that point he walked to Schuyler county. The first summer of his residence here he clerked for Dr Benjamin V. Teel, and then returned to New Jersey, where he spent the summer of 1839, and in the fall of 1839 he came again to this county and secured a position with the firm of Wilson & Greer, which he held until 1842

Mr. De Witt was united in marriage, January 25, 1842, to Miss Ellen Little, a native of Columbia, Lancaster county, Pennsylvania; she died in this county at the age of sixty-one years; seven children were born of this union, six of whom are living· James L is married and has three children, John M. is married and has three children; George W ; Elizabeth is married and the mother of four children; Cyrus L is married; William A. is the youngest Mrs De Witt was a daughter of James and Rebecca Little, natives of Ireland, who emigrated to the United States in 1801, and died in Schuyler county, Illinois, the father, at the age of seventy, and the mother at eighty-four years of age Mr. De Witt was married a second time, October 3, 1883, to Mrs. Catharine H. (Pittinger) Waddell She was born in Hancock county, West Virginia, April 30, 1837, a daughter of Nicholas and Elizabeth (Matthewson) Pittinger, natives of Ohio and Pennsylvania respectively; the father died at the age of seventy-two years, and the mother at eighty-five; they removed to Illinois in 1838, and settled in Fulton county, where they resided two years, thence they came to Schuyler county, and here passed the last days of their life, the Matthewson family is of Irish descent Mrs. De Witt's first marriage was to William Waddell, and of this union was born one child, Clementine Mr Waddell died in Fulton county, Illinois, at the age of thirty-three years

After his first marriage, Mr. De Witt settled in Rushville, and clerked for his father-in-law until 1844, when he engaged in business for himself, his partner being Mr. Greer; he conducted the business with different partners until 1850, when he sold out and removed to Littleton township, where he and his brother-in-law conducted a general store for four years; the firm was then changed, Mr. De Witt retaining his interest for another period of four years; the old firm then resumed business, and in 1862 he sold out. He now resides on the farm which was given his wife by her father, and devotes much of his time to agriculture; he has added to the original tract, and built the residence they now occupy.

Mr. De Witt received his elementary education in the district school, but it was through his own efforts that his advanced studies were carried on; he was under theological instruction only one year, but during that time made great attainment. For more than fifty years he has been a local minister in the Methodist Episcopal Church, and during that half century he has accomplished much work for the Master He has performed the marriage ceremony 130 times, and has as often been called to administer the last sad rites of burial. In the affairs of the State, as well as of the church, he has taken a prominent part; he has been Postmaster, Collector, and Deputy Marshal, to take the census of one-half of the county, in 1870; and in 1874-'75, he was a member of the State Legislature from Schuyler county, representing the people with great credit to himself and to their best and highest interests. Politically, he adheres to the principles of the Republican party. In all the walks of life he has borne himself with that dignity and rectitude worthy of his calling, and has made a record that will bear the scrutiny of ages.

NANCY P. SECKMAN was born in Harrison county, Kentucky, August 18, 1814. Her father, James Taylor, and her mother, Katie Bishop, were both born in Maryland, near Snow Hill. They went to Kentucky, when young, were married there, and were well-to-do farmers. They moved to Illinois in the fall of 1832, when this daughter was nineteen years old. They brought ten children with them in a prairie schooner, being twenty-one days on the route. They hired a man to bring them with his five-horse team, and they brought three horses and saddles of their own. They had a most delightful time, a continual picnic of twenty-one days, from the time they left the old Kentucky home until they arrived at grandfather Taylor's in Morgan county. They bought 160 acres in what is now Scott county, and this they made their permanent home. They had two more children in Illinois, making twelve in all, and all but two grew to adult age, Mrs. Seckman being the eldest. The mother died at the age of sixty-five, on the farm in Scott county; the father lived many years after, but finally passed away at the ripe old age of eighty-five years, leaving a fine estate to the ten remaining children.

Mrs. Seckman had very little schooling in the every-day school, as they were then termed. She was married in her twenty-second year to Jonathan W. Seckman, born near Chillicothe, Ohio, in 1810. His father was William Seckman, and his mother, Susan Wright, both from farmer families of Ohio. They came to Illinois after this son came. Jonathan came here a poor young man, and began working for the low wages of those times. He drove teams and broke prairie, and worked and earned and saved, until in his thirtieth year he had two horses, six oxen, and several head of horned cattle, and some hogs. He was married to our subject, March 31, 1844, and began domestic life on an island in Menard county, on lands his father owned. They purchased forty acres in 1842, in Cooperstown township, near the present home of Mrs. Seckman. He traded a good house and his last horse for it. He worked out by the day and paid for the use of a six-horse team, with which he tilled the land for the first crop. Their life on the island for the three years they were there, was a living death from fever and ague, and when they left for Brown county they were reduced in means, having but $40. They bought a log house on an adjoining claim, which they moved on their small farm. The timber was large and dense on this land, and he built his old house on and over several large stumps. They moved into this abode, January 1, 1842, and in about two years he bought eighty acres adjoining. In 1865, they built the present commodious frame house in which Mrs. Seckman now resides. Here he died, August 8, 1885, aged seventy-five, leaving his widow with seven living children. They had buried one daughter when an infant, and one son, John William, aged twenty-eight. He left a wife and son. Mr. Seckman owned at his death 720 acres of land, and several lots in Mount Sterling. These lands are well-stocked and well-improved. He was well and favorably known in this section. His life of toil was not only successful financially, but he left a good record to his devoted wife. His father had been a preacher among the United Brethren, and he also left a large estate to a large and honorable posterity.

The names of Mrs. Seckman's living children are: James R., a farmer of Nebraska, has five children; Kittie J., wife of William Shultz, of Nebraska, has twelve children; Charles H., farmer on part of the old homestead, has six children; George D., also a farmer on the homestead, ten children; Jonathan, farmer in Brown county, eight children; Joseph L., also on the homestead, seven children; Archie, also on the homestead, in the house with his mother, four children.

Mrs. Seckman says that she is a monument of God's mercy and love. She has had great health and strength during life, has worked hard in the house and field, has helped make fence, stack grain, and has done everything in the house from rocking the cradle to spinning and weaving. She is now as strong and vigorous as ever, and her mind is as strong as ever, and in every respect she is a remarkable old lady.

DARIUS N. WALKER, ex-Judge of Cass county, Illinois, and a resident of Virginia, is a native of the Old Dominion, born in Fauquier county, February 16, 1834. Of his life and ancestry we record the following facts:

Solomon Walker, junior and senior, father and grandfather of the Judge, were also Virginians by birth, and the former was a native of Fauquier county. The latter suffered privations and hardships in the various campaigns of the Revolutionary war, being in the service seven years, and never fully recovered his health afterward. He spent his last years in Culpeper county, Virginia. The maiden name of Grandmother Walker was Frances Taylor. Her father was a native of England, and when but a small boy was kidnaped by sailors, brought to America and bound out until twenty-one years of age. He spent his last years in the State of Virginia. Solomon Walker, Jr., learned the trade of tanner, and followed his trade in connection with farming in Fauquier county, remaining a resident of that place until 1855. Then he sold his interests there and came to Illinois, locating in Virginia precinct, Cass county, on a farm he purchased a mile and a half east of the present courthouse site. He engaged in agriculture and remained a resident there till after the death of his wife. He spent his last years at the home of his son, Judge Walker, where he died, in 1889, in the eighty-sixth year of his age. His wife, Emma Wilkins, was born in Prince William county, Virginia, daughter of Thomas Wilkins. She died on the home farm in 1879. Nine of her children reached adult years.

Judge Walker was reared and educated in his native State, and when a mere boy he commenced to assist his father in the tanyard and on the farm. He is a natural mechanic, and while a resident of Virginia worked a portion of the time at the millwright trade. He came to Cass county with his parents in 1855, and lived at home until he was twenty-three years old; was then employed at farming and carpenter work. April 15, 1862, he started with others for Oregon. They went by rail to St. Joseph, at that time the terminus of the railroad, and thence by boat to

Sonora, Missouri. There they equipped themselves with ox-teams and provisions, and on the 12th of May started on their journey across the plains, arriving at the present site of Baker City, Oregon, August 23. He remained at Auburn, near Baker City, till February, when he went to Placerville, Idaho Territory, and engaged in mining, remaining there until the fall of 1864. Then he went to San Francisco, and from there went to New York, via Panama; thence to Cass county, Illinois. Soon afterward he bought a farm in Virginia precinct, which he sold the following fall, came to Virginia and engaged in work at the carpenter's trade. In the fall of 1868 he purchased a tin and stove store, and carried on that business until 1873, when he was elected Police Magistrate of Virginia, and devoted his attention to the duties of that office. In 1880 he visited the Rocky mountains. He went as far as Western on the railroad and thence by stage to Leadville, Colorado. Five months later he returned to Virginia and has since resided there.

Judge Walker was married in the fall of 1861, to Elizabeth Adams, who was born in Morgan county, Illinois, daughter of William and Mildred (Bryant) Adams. She died in 1873. In January, 1876, he married Martha E. Clark, a native of Schuyler county, Illinois, her parents being Thomas and Annie Clark. He has two children living by his first marriage: Emma E. and John L.

Politically, the Judge has always affiliated with the Democratic party. He served as Police Magistrate from 1873 to 1882; has also served as Alderman and Mayor. In 1882 he was elected County Judge, was re-elected in 1886, and served two full terms. He is a member of Saxon Lodge, No. 68, I. O. O. F., and Washington Lodge of Mutual Aid. Mrs. Walker is a member of the Presbyterian Church, while the Judge is a Baptist.

WILLIAM T. TYSON, a widely and favorably known citizen of Bainbridge township, Schuyler county, Illinois, an honored veteran of the late war, and one of the most prosperous farmers of the State, is a worthy representative of a prominent family of distinguished patriots, who sealed their devotion to their country long before she became a distinct nation, and who, by their united and continued efforts, have contributed in no small measure to her steady advancement to her present glorious position among the countries of the world.

Zephaniah Tyson, the distinguished grandfather of the subject of this sketch, was born in Virginia in 1771, and was thus by birth placed on the arena of the most stirring events of that age. It is not surprising, therefore, that he should have developed that surprising precocity which the time itself tended to foster. Born of patriots, breathing the air of patriotism, and drinking in those noble sentiments which have filled the hearts of heroes since the world began, he early put by the pastimes of youth, assuming with ease and pleasure the responsibilities and cares of a man and a soldier. At the age of nineteen years he enlisted in the Indian war, and served under that able and celebrated patriot, General Wayne. Again, in the war of 1812, he was still found fighting under the starry flag; and later took part in the battle of Tippecanoe, under General Harrison. Amidst all these warlike engagements, he found time to cultivate the friendship of the little god of love, who directed his shafts from behind the bright glances of Miss Margaret De Long, an amiable and intelligent Virginian, and a descendant of an old and esteemed family of that State. In 1830, he removed to Illinois, which was then a new and sparsely settled country, where he settled on a farm on the southeast quarter of section 3, township 1 north, range 1 west of the fourth principal meridian, where he continued to live until his death in 1849, at the age of seventy-eight years, universally and sincerely lamented.

George Tyson, an able son of a great father, was born in 1807, on the Muskingum river, in Ohio. In those times, the young apparently matured much earlier than in our present indolent age, for we find this youth leaving home and starting in pursuit of his fortune long before he was fully grown. He went to Cincinnati, where he found work, and where he soon afterward purchased a flat-boat, with which he commenced trading and trafficking with the natives on the Ohio river. In 1829, he married Miss Lucinda Bellamy, a native of Culpeper county, Virginia. Soon afterward he sold his flat-boat, and with the proceeds purchased a team, with which the young couple made the trip overland from a point on the Ohio river to Schuyler county, Illinois, where they settled on a farm in the southeast quarter of section 11, township 1 north, range 1 west. Fortune smiled on their industrious efforts, and in time Mr. Tyson accumulated considerable property, having 480 acres of choice agricultural land, besides owning a steam saw and grist mill. In 1866, he went West and has never been heard from since. The faithful wife and devoted mother survived her husband's probable death ten years, expiring September 10, 1876, in her sixty-seventh year, leaving a bereaved family and many friends to mourn her loss.

William T. Tyson, the subject of this notice, was born April 2, 1841, in a log house, situated forty rods from his present large and comfortable residence. His early life was spent on the home farm, and he attended the country schools of his vicinity, where he received a good common-school education, sufficient to enable him to teach several schools in his township. At the age of sixteen, he accompanied his parents to Moniteau county, Missouri, where his father bought a farm of 160 acres on the Pacific railroad, and ran a woodyard in connection with his farm, there being an abundance of excellent timber on the land. In the fall of 1858, young William accompanied his parents to Henry county, Missouri, where his father bought 300 acres of excellent prairie land, on the west half of the southeast quarter of the southwest quarter of section 21, in township 43, of range 28. Here the family continued to reside until the breaking out of the Civil war, when the mother and younger children returned to the old homestead in Illinois. It was then that young William displayed that patriotism for which his family was famous, by raising the first flag ever hoisted in the county after the nomination of Abraham Lincoln. He raised a pole fifty feet high, to which was attached a flag fourteen by twenty-one feet, with a rail resting on the top of the pole. He was several times ordered to take it down, but as often refused to do so.

This sentiment of love for his country culminated in his enlistment in the United States service as a private in Company D, Cass County Regiment of Cavalry, Missouri Home Guards, on June 27, 1861, to serve three years, or during the war, and was discharged at Harrisonville, Missouri, February 28, 1862, by reason of General Order No. 25, paragraph three, Headquarters Department of Missouri, December 14, 1861. He participated in several engagements, the most important of which were Parkersville and Harrisonville, Missouri, July 18 and 19, 1861 He was selected for Second Lieutenant of the company, and lacked but a few votes of being elected He was one of the soldiers who helped to guard the first wagon train of provisions to Lyon's army, after the battle of Wilson's creek, Missouri. Soon after his discharge, he started for Illinois, and was obliged to cross the entire State of Missouri from west to east at a very dangerous time of the war

On August 12, 1862, Mr. Tyson re-enlisted in the army as a private in Company D, 115th Regiment, Illinois Volunteers, for three years or during the war During his service he did his full share of marching, fighting, scouting, picketing, digging and suffering, as well as participating in the foraging and picnicking, of which Uncle Sam's boys are generally believed to have had a large amount During this term of service he took part in a number of prominent engagements. He was in the battle of Franklin and Harpeth river, April 10, 1863 He was in Rosecrans' campaign from Murfreesboro to Tullahoma, Tennessee, from June 23 to 30, 1863. He participated in the battle of Chickamauga, September 18, 19 and 20, 1863; and was in the Dalton raid, under General Palmer, from February 21 to 27, 1864 He was also in the charge on Tunnel Hill, Georgia, May 7, 1864, and took part in the battle of Resaca, May 15 and 16, 1864.

He was one of that brave little band of forty-two men who formed Company D, under Captain Hymer's command, who held their own against such fearful odds at Buzzard's Roost gap, Georgia. They were stationed at the block house at that point, in July, 1864, where on August 15, they were attacked by Wheeler's cavalry, but Company D opened such a fire of shot on the attacking party that the cavalry were obliged to retire. Again, on October 13, Hood's army of 40,000 came to the block house and opened fire on the inmates with musketry and artillery, 133 cannon balls being fired at the fort This little band of Spartans, however, held the attacking party in check for ten hours, when they were finally forced to surrender. In this engagement, five were killed, six wounded and thirty-seven taken prisoners The prisoners, among whom was the subject of this sketch, were marched to Cahaba, Alabama, where they were confined for ten days in Castle Morgan, which was named in honor of the daring Confederate raider, John Morgan. Owing to the crowded condition of the prison, they were sent to Millen, Georgia, where they were when General Sherman sent General Kilpatrick's Cavalry, on November 22, to rescue them if possible The preceding evening, however, they were loaded on the cars and sent to Savannah, and thence on down the coast to Thomasville, Georgia, and from there across the country to Andersonville In this famous, or rather infamous, prison, Mr. Tyson was confined for three months: at the end of that time he was sent to Vicksburg, where he was paroled, exchanged, and loaded on the Henry Ames, one of those magnificent floating palaces for which the lower Mississippi was famous in *ante-bellum* days He was in this way transferred to St. Louis, and there paid off, and given a thirty days' furlough to go home. At the expiration of this time he returned to Springfield, Illinois, where he received his final pay and discharge, on June 14, 1865 As typical of the appreciation in which Mr. Tyson was held by his commanders, may be mentioned the remark of Captain Hymer, who said to him. "I know you were one of my best soldiers, and were always in the line of duty" Mr Tyson was on detached service in the Signal Corps, at Wartrace, Tennessee; and while stationed at Tullahoma, that State, was headquarter clerk for General Jesse H Moore While in Kentucky, Mr Tyson was a guest of the great Kentucky statesman, Cassius M Clay, at that time absent in Russia, but whose absence was amply compensated for by the cordiality and hospitality of Mrs Clay, her daughter and daughter-in-law, with whom he had the pleasure of dining

By the spring of 1867, Mr. Tyson had saved up $500, with which he purchased 160 acres of land in section 11, township 1 north, range 1 west. This event foreshadowed another, which transpired in the fall of the same year, and which was but the fulfilling of the saw, to provide a cage before getting the bird He was married November 10, 1867, to Miss Sarah J. Scott, an estimable lady, and a resident of Schuyler county, Illinois. Their happy married life, however, was destined to be of short duration, for on February 22, 1878, the faithful wife and mother expired at home, in the midst of her family and friends. She was widely known and greatly beloved on account of her practical Christian virtues and kind heart. They had four children. Jesse C, Laura, Leora and Stella, the latter of whom died in infancy; there are now two grandchildren.

In 1880, Mr. Tyson was appointed Census Enumerator for Bainbridge township, to which position he was reappointed on May 20, 1890 He is in very comfortable circumstances, and owns as fine a farm as there is in the country, which is provided with good improvements and is moderately and well stocked.

In politics he has always been a Republican, and is opposed to oppression in any form.

A duty done is always a source of pleasure and pride to the one performing it. This is essentially true at all times and at all places, but how much more so must it be when the performance involves danger and perhaps death; when, as in the late war, the champions of justice and freedom were baptized with fire and with blood It is then that duty assumes her heaven-born spirit, and pours into the heart the balm of unspeakable joy and that peace which passeth understanding

EDWARD N TREADWAY, a farmer of Beardstown, was born in Hamilton county, Ohio, February 23, 1825. His father was Edward Treadway, a native of Maryland, of English stock. He grew up as a farmer in Maryland, and married Elizabeth Anderson, who was reared and educated in Hartford county, Maryland She came of Scotch ancestry. He and his wife moved to Hamilton county in 1816, and later came to Illinois, into Cass county, and settled in what is known as the Monroe precinct. This was in 1829 The wife died about two years after the family settled in this county, being then only in middle life. Her husband spent his last days with his children, and died in 1859, being then about seventy-five years of age He and his wife were recognized as very early pioneers of the county

Mr. Treadway has lived in this precinct since he was ten years of age, and has become known as one of the old settlers He is a farmer on the same land which he went upon when he became of age. It is in sections 29 and 30, and consists of 160 acres, and is known as the Sangamon bottoms. It is all improved He also owns 120 acres of timber land which is very valuable.

He was married in this county, to Sarah Phelps, of North Carolina, the daughter of William and Margaret (Measles) Phelps, who were born, reared and married in North Carolina. They came North with their family and settled in the precinct of Beardstown. Mr. Phelps is yet living, a hale, hearty old gentleman, but Mrs. Phelps died some years ago.

Mr. and Mrs. Treadway attend the Methodist Episcopal Church in this city, and are worthy, good citizens with a host of friends. They are the parents of five living children: Martha Predshaw, now living on a farm in this county; William, at home assisting his father; Hans, living in McDonough county; Anna and Bertha at home. Mr. Treadway is a consistent Democrat.

WILLIAM H. COLEMAN, general farmer and stock-raiser, running the large cattle farm of 320 acres, and also owner of nearly 600 acres in the precinct of Philadelphia, all in Cass county, has lived in the county for thirty-two years, has always been engaged as a farmer and has always been quite successful. He began here as a poor man, and worked for $10 a month for the first four years, and after that began to farm on the Calef farm, which he has since run as a renter, and out of his savings he has purchased the large farm of 600 acres which he also runs on his own account, in connection with his rented farm, making nearly 1,000 acres that are under his control. He has been a hard-working man and has made all he has since he came to this county in 1860.

He was born in Westphalia at Menden, in Prussia, Germany, in 1840. He was reared in his native country, and after he came to this county he attended the public schools through the kindness of his benefactor, S. L. Calef, whose place he has worked on since 1860. He reveres this kind gentleman and his wife as he would his parents, and his long residence on their farm show what their opinion is of his honesty and faithfulness.

Mr. Coleman is the son of Gotlieb Coleman (spelled in the German Kuhlmann), and the latter came to the United States in 1870. He made his home with his son, William, until his death in 1886. He was then eighty-two years of age. He was a good old man and an active member of the Lutheran Church. He had married a German lady who lived and died in her native country, being only thirty-two years of age. Her maiden name was Mary Markman. She left six children at her death, of which William and a brother Henry, now a married farmer in Virginia precinct, this county, are all that are now living. William and his brother Henry came to the United States when young and single, coming in the spring of 1860 from Bremen, Germany, to New Orleans in a sailing vessel, Mary Margaret, with 636 passengers on board. After a thirty-nine days' voyage, they landed in New Orleans and came up the Mississippi river on a steamer to St. Louis, and from there to Beardstown, where they have both since lived, and have become good and successful farmers and reliable German citizens.

William was married in this county to Nancy McLin, born in Morgan county, where she was reared and educated. She has lost her parents, the mother dying in Morgan county, at the age of forty, the father in Cass county, aged sixty years, having always been a farmer by occupation.

Mr. and Mrs. Coleman are the parents of five children, yet living; four are deceased; those living are: Ellen M., wife of Perry Davis, a farmer of Virginia; Charles E., at home helping on the farm; Edgar, John and Arthur, all at home on the farm.

Mrs. Coleman is a member of the Methodist Episcopal Church, and Mr. Coleman is a sound Republican. He has been very active in local politics, and once run for County Commissioner, running ahead of his ticket several hundred votes. He and his wife are good, hard-working people and are justly entitled to the success they have attained.

SIDNEY J. HOOD, of the firm of Allard & Hood, publishers and editors of *The Evening Star* and *The Star of the West* of Beardstown, was born in Spring Green, Sauk county, Wisconsin, October 10, 1864. He was reared and educated at that place and acquired a knowledge of the carpenter and mason trades, but later went into the newspaper business. His father, Captain Thomas R. Hood, came from Pennsylvania to Wisconsin when a small child with his parents, Moses and Sarah Hood, natives of Pennsylvania, but who died in Wisconsin. Thomas R. Hood grew up as a farmer and carpenter, and when the war broke out he enlisted in the Sixth Wisconsin Regiment Light Artillery as a volunteer and served three and one half years, and was honorably discharged as Captain of his company. He had led his men through the battles of Corinth, Shiloh and other active engagements, and was much beloved by the members of his company. He had married Eliza A. Seiders, daughter o Joseph and Elizabeth (Keifer) Seiders. They had come West at a very early day, settling in Sauk county on Government land, and the same on which Joseph Seiders and wife lived and where Mr. Seiders died, a very old man, in the spring of 1888. His wife, who is yet living, at the age of eighty, is yet very active and interested in her surroundings. She and her husband were members of the United Brethren Church.

Our subject is the second of three children, and since his thirteenth year he has supported himself. At the age of seventeen years he began work at his native home at Spring Green on a paper known as the *Weekly Home News*. He has always regarded these early days in Spring Green as the palmy days of his life as well as of his newspaper work. In 1889 he came to Arenzville, Cass county, Illinois, and started the *Arenzville Argus*, and at the same time the *Chapin Boomerang*, and ran the papers for about sixteen months, when he sold out and came to Beardstown, where he has since lived. For some time, also, he was a worker on the *Laramie* (Wyoming) *Sentinel*, Bill Nye's old "first love." The first issue of the *Daily Star* took place March 7, 1892; present firm was started February 24, 1892. Both the daily and weekly papers are very prosperous. Mr. Hood is a very energetic man, and being a practical printer understands thoroughly the management of a newspaper.

Mr. Hood is still unmarried. He is an ardent Republican.

CAD ALLARD, the present Postmaster of Beardstown, and editor and proprietor of the *Star of the West*, was born in Virginia, Illinois, August 31, 1854. His father was Dr. L. S. Allard, one of the pioneer physicians and druggists of Cass county, and was one of the most forcible political writers of Central Illinois. He started and conducted for many years the *Cass County Courier* and was an active worker in politics. He served his country in the war of the Rebellion, entering it as a Captain and coming out a Colonel; also in the Mexican war as a Lieutenant. He is a Republican and is now a resident of Hot Springs, Arkansas. His mother was a Miss Sarah F. Payne, of Lexington, Kentucky, and is yet living. The complete history of Beardstown could not be given without a brief mention of the paper known as the *Weekly Star of the West*, a strong Republican paper, and the *Evening Star*, which is neutral. The energetic editor and proprietor, whose name heads this article, is entitled to the credit of making a success of a daily in so small a city and a weekly paper which is read by an intelligent public throughout a wide territory. The daily *Star* is but one year old, but has already won the confidence of the people. The *Weekly Star* has had an existence since 1888, and is now one of the leading Republican sheets of the West. It has just moved into elegant new quarters on Main street, with editorial and counting room on the ground floor. The editor handles every subject ably and without fear or favor; he is a practical newspaper man, a strong and forcible writer; and his life from the time he was fourteen has been spent in newspaper work. He began work in his father's office in Virginia, Illinois, from whom in 1872 he leased it. Young Allard ran this paper for some time and then took a partner named Mat. Summers, changing the name of the paper to the *Virginia Gazette*. His health failing he went to Arkansas and took charge of the Fort Smith *New Era*, then the property of the United States Marshal of Western Arkansas and the Indian Territory, which was the oldest and first Republican paper of the State. Two years after he went to Hot Springs, where for six years he ran a paper called the *Daily News*. There he lost his wife and soon after closed out his interests and went to Kansas thence he returned to Cass county, where he has made some grand strides forward, not only as a newpsaper man but as a local politician. His mode of handling the tariff question has attracted attention, and at the late State Convention, at which he was a delegate, he was one of the committee selected to draft the platform, which was accepted without a change or objection. He is the present treasurer of the Illinois Republican Press Association, and is a leading member of the K. of P., Beardstown Lodge, No. 207. It is worthy of remark that he is a newspaper man who neither drinks, smokes nor chews.

He was first married to Libbie Peak, who died at Hot Springs, Arkansas. He was married a second time May 20, 1890, to Miss Annie Jockisch, a well known young lady of Beardstown, who was reared and educated in this city, and is especially skilled in music. Her father is William Jockisch, a retired farmer and one of the directors of the Fourth National Bank. Beardstown society would not be complete without them.

JOSEPH BRIAR, one of the old settlers of Hickory precinct, Cass county, Illinois, was born in Pittsburgh, Pennsylvania, February 3, 1823, son of James Briar, a native of Ireland. His grandparents were born in Ireland, of Scotch ancestry, and spent their entire lives in their native land. James Briar was reared and married in Ireland and came to America about 1815. He first lived in New York city and afterward in Philadelphia, Baltimore and Pittsburg. He was a contractor on Government works, and while in New York city was engaged in building lighthouses in New York harbor. Subsequently he was one of the contractors on the building of the State prison at Alleghany. In the fall of 1836 he came to Illinois. He spent the winter at Beardstown, during which time he looked around for a location suitable for a home, and in the spring entered a tract of Government land in the Sangamon river bottoms. As there were no improvements on his land, he rented an improved farm east of Virginia, and a part of the family settled on that farm while the rest took up their abode on the land he had entered, and at once began its improvement. He resided on this place until his death, February 22, 1844. The maiden name of his wife was Mary Davis. She was born in Ireland, and died on the home farm. They reared nine children.

Joseph Briar was thirteen years old when he came to Illinois with his parents. There were no railroads in this State at that time, and their removal was made via the Ohio, Mississippi and Illinois rivers, landing at Beardstown November 19. Beardstown was then a small place, but was the market and depot for supplies for many miles around. Central Illinois was sparsely settled and much of the land still owned by the Government, while in the northern part the surveys were yet incomplete. Deer, wild turkeys, prairie chickens, and other game abounded. He resided with his parents till attaining his majority, when he settled on the farm he now owns and occupies. This place is located on section 4, township 18, range 10, and includes 122½ acres of the best of Sangamon river bottom land. He has erected a nice set of frame buildings and enjoys all the comforts of a pleasant home.

In 1847 Mr. Briar married Mary A. Harris, a native of England, who came with her parents to Cass county when she was a girl. She died in 1853, and the following year he married Eliza Smith, a native of New York State. There are two children living by the first marriage: Martha J. and Emily D. Of the seven children born by his present wife, four are living: Joseph, Harry, Frank and Annie. Lillie, Bertie and Effie are deceased.

Mr. and Mrs. Briar are members of the Cumberland Presbyterian Church.

HENRY C. KORTE, general farmer of section 4, township 17, range 11, was born in Kurhessen, Germany, January 2, 1840. He grew up at home, and in 1855 came to this country with his parents and three children. They set sail from Bremen, Hanover, on a sailing vessel, landing after an eight weeks' voyage on the vessel Oldenburg in Baltimore, and from there by railroad to Springfield, Illinois, and from there by wagon to Beardstown, Cass county. The father, Conrad, started a blacksmith shop, that being the trade he learned in Germany and carried it on for twenty years, dying at the age of seventy-six. He was a good worthy citizen and a member of the Lutheran Church. He was a Democrat in politics. His wife survived him about ten years and died at the age of seventy-two. She was also a Lutheran. Her maiden name was Christina Meyer. Henry, a sister, Mrs. Sophia Krohe, and a half sister, Mrs. Catherine Fischer, are the surviving members of the family.

Mr. Henry Korte began here as a poor man and worked as a farm laborer, beginning for himself in 1863, having been in the county since 1856. He purchased his first land in 1889. He has a fine farm in the section where he lives.

He was married in this county to Wilhelmina Krohe, born, reared and educated in Cass county, near the farm where she now lives. She is the daughter of August and Christine (Jokisch) Krohe, natives of Germany who had come to America when young and single, and were married in Cass county, where they made their home, the mother dying in 1889, aged over seventy. Mr. Krohe is still living in this county and is eighty years old. He and his family were always Lutherans and Mr. Krohe continues in the faith of his youth.

Mrs. Korte is one of seven children, being the third, and has been a good and faithful wife and mother. She has borne her husband four children: Albert H., married Mary Hessler of this county, and they live on Mr. Henry Korte's farm; Arthur G., single and a farmer on his own account, living at home; Edward, at home assisting his father; and Amelia, at home.

Mr. and Mrs. Korte, with their family, are Lutherans, and Mr. Korte and his sons are all Democrats. They are worthy good people.

HENRY W. MEYER, a successful farmer and stock raiser of section 7, township 18, range 11, was born near Arenzville, this county, in 1853, December 26. He is the younger of the children, Fred and Catherine Meyer, the latter now deceased and the former yet living (see biography). Henry is the only one of the family who was born in the county. He was reared and educated in his native county. He has a farm of 133 acres, all well stocked. He has farmed it on his own account for thirteen years. He has spent his entire life in this county, as a farmer on his father's homestead. He also has sixty acres in another part of the county, of which part is under the plow.

He was married in this county, near where he now lives, to Minnie Kloker, of Cass county, born March 6, 1858. She was reared and educated in her native county, where she spent the remainder of her short life, dying at her home at the age of thirty-four, June 28, 1891. She was a good wife and mother, and her loss was deeply felt not only by her sorrowing family, but by all who knew her. She had been a member of the Lutheran Church since early girlhood. She was the mother of four children: Irvin E., Fred W., Lewis W., Rudolph J.; and they are all deceased excepting the youngest. Besides, the parents have adopted a girl, named Nora M. Mr. Meyer has reason to be proud of his children and his record here in the county, where he has always been a good, true citizen, a faithful member of the Lutheran Church and a staunch Republican.

HENRY J. SCHROEDER, one of the old and well known contractors and builders of Beardstown, was born in the kingdom of Hanover, Germany, in 1833. His father, Fred Schroeder, had always been a farmer, and he died when about 74 years of age, at Beardstown, and his wife died some time later, aged seventy-eight. The family came to the United States in 1844, and came straight to Beardstown upon landing in New Orleans. They came by the usual route up the Mississippi river to St. Louis, and from there up the Illinois river to their destination. Henry was a boy of eleven when he came to this city, and has since made it his home. He grew up, learning the trade of carpenter, and worked as journeyman for a time, and later was with his father-in-law, Henry Mohlman, in his substantial planing mill for some years. It was the first business of the kind in the city, and the firm was successful in doing work for a large territory and for all the lumber yards of the city. The railroads that came into the city interfered with the business, and Mr. Schroeder sold out his interest and launched into the flour-mill business; but a change in the making of flour came about, and to change from buhr to roller process required large outlays: so Mr. Schroeder traded his mill off for a farm and went back to his trade as a carpenter and a contractor. He has since followed his trade, and has built many of the houses and public buildings of Beardstown. Among some of the buildings that he has constructed are the Park house, leading hotel of the city, opera house and many others that all bear testimony to the skill of the contractor and builder. He has dealt extensively in real estate, and has an interest in the Mohlman and Schroeder block, one of the best in the city. He also owns one of the argest and best two-and-one-half-story brick houses in the city. He has been a leading worker in local matters and a truly good citizen. For many years he has been a Democrat in politics, and his party once made him Alderman of the city. He has retired, to a certain extent, from active business and now enjoys the fruit of his labors. His sons succeed him: so there is no necessity for him to exert himself in regard to his business interests.

Mr. Schroeder was the first child that his parents had. He was followed by four sisters, but no brothers. The family were Lutherans, as are most of the German families, and were noted for their thrift and honesty. He has only one sister living, Jeanie Walch, of Leavenworth, Kansas.

He was married in Beardstown, to Miss Anna Mohlman, born in one of the Rhine provinces, Germany, in 1841, a daughter of Henry Mohlman, and when young she came to this country with her parents, and has since resided here. She is an intelligent woman, a good, kind wife, mother and neighbor. Mr. and Mrs. Schroeder have seven children, namely: Edward, a contractor of Beardstown, married to Mrs. Annie Balsemier; Dilla, wife of Charles Heinzes, of Beardstown; Henry G., a trimmer by trade, with Mr. Henry Keil, a hardware merchant of this city, and married to Miss Mene Wipker; George, at home, a carpenter; Rhoda, Walter and Edith: the last three named are all at home. Mr. Schroeder has a married daughter, Sarah, wife of Charles Kreke, a furniture dealer of this city. She is a child by a former marriage to Miss Dora Christiana, now deceased.

Mr. and Mrs. Schroeder are members of the Fourth Street Lutheran Church, and are liberal supporters of the same, of which Mr. Schroeder used to be a Trustee.

ANDREW SCHAAD, who for many years has been identified with the agricultural interests of Cass county, Illinois, and who is a resident of Hickory precinct, was born in Hesse-Darmstadt, January 4, 1836.

John Schaad, his father, was a son of John Schaad, and both passed their lives and died in Germany, the former in 1852. Grandfather Schaad was all his life engaged in agricultural pursuits. His son, John, became a civil engineer, and was engaged in surveying for canals, railroads and turnpikes. His wife, *nee* Katherine Hamel, was born in the same locality as her husband, she being the daughter of Christian Hamel. She came to America in 1853, the year following Mr. Schaad's death, and spent her last years in Cass county, Illinois. She reared four children: Thomas, Charles, Andrew and Mary. Thomas and Charles both married and reared families, and spent their last years in Cass county. Mary is the wife of Henry Walter, and lives in Arenzville.

The subject of our sketch attended school in Hesse-Darmstadt until 1853, when he accompanied other members of the family to America. They set sail from Havre de Grace September 15, 1853, on the sailing vessel Farera, and landed at New Orleans after a voyage of forty-five days. There was cholera on board the vessel, which rendered the voyage an unpleasant one. From New Orleans they came north by river to Beardstown. Andrew and his brothers rented land and farmed together, being successful in their operations. Subsequently Andrew and Charles bought a tract of land on sections 6 and 7, township 18, range 10, and farmed together a few years. The former has been a resident of what is now Hickory precinct since 1858, and is now the owner of 320 acres of land, 177 acres of which are the finest tillable land, located on sections 6, 7, and 8, township 18, range 10. He has erected a nice set of frame buildings, and is comfortably situated to enjoy life.

In 1866 Mr. Schaad married Miss Miza Taylor, a native of Scotland, and a daughter of Neill Taylor. He and his wife are the parents of three children Robert, Kate and Maud.

Politically Mr. Schaad is a stanch Republican. He is a member of the County Central Committee, Highway Committee in District No. 2, and has served as a member of his District School Board for thirteen years. Both he and his wife are members of the Cumberland Presbyterian Church.

DAVID D. WILSON, a popular and successful business man of Virginia, Cass county, Illinois, dates his birth in Oldham, Lancashire, England, November 23, 1841. His father, James Wilson, was born in the same shire, his parents having passed their lives in England. James Wilson and his brother, Thomas, and three sisters, were the only members of the family who came to America. Thomas settled in Cass county in 1841, and has since made his home here.

James Wilson was reared and married in Oldham, and was there employed in a cotton factory till 1842, in the spring of which year he sailed for America, embarking at Liverpool and landing at New Orleans. He came up the Mississippi and Illinois rivers into Illinois, and located in Cass county. He subsequently moved to Jacksonville, and five years later to Springfield, his death occurring at the latter place in 1850. His wife was, before her marriage, Miss Amelia Taylor, and she, too, was a native of Lancashire. Her death occurred in Cass county a few months after their arrival in this county.

After the death of his father, David D. was taken in charge by a family in Sangamon county, and with them he lived until he was fourteen. From that time he cared for himself. He found employment with his brother-in-law till 1860, and at that time commenced to learn the trade of carpenter. His employer soon emigrated to Iowa, and in 1861 young Wilson turned his attention to the trade of printer, at which he worked in the office of the Jacksonville *Journal*.

In 1862 he enlisted in the One Hundred and First Illinois Regiment Volunteer Infantry, and was in the State service one month. When the regiment was mustered in, he was rejected on account of a crippled hand. In 1864 he enlisted in Company B, One Hundred and Thirty-third Regiment Illinois Volunteer Infantry, this time being accepted. He served till the term of his enlistment expired, when he was honorably discharged. He then went to Nashville, Tennessee, expecting to work at his trade, but was taken sick and soon afterward returned to Illinois. After his recovery he farmed in Morgan county one year. Then he worked at his trade in Jacksonville for a time. In 1875 he came to Virginia, being employed in the office of the *Gazette* from March till July of that year. Next we find him engaged in the grocery business, which he still continues, and in which he has been eminently successful. He began with a small stock of goods, his natural business ability secured him a good trade, and he is now ranked with the successful business men of the town.

Mr. Wilson is a man of family. He was married, in 1866, to Martha Taylor, a native of Morgan county, Illinois, and their union has been blessed by the birth of four children: Mamie, Ella G., Herbert S. and Mabel.

He and his wife are members of the Christian Church. Politically he is a Republican, favoring prohibition.

GEORGE KUHL was born in Hesse-Darmstadt, Germany, in 1807. His parents, Christian and Elizabeth (Ganz) Kuhl, were very old when they died, the father at the age of eighty-three, the mother at the age of eighty-five and one-half years. They were members of the Lutheran Church. When George was yet a young man he embarked for America in the ship Baltimore in 1833. After a voyage of eight weeks he landed in Baltimore and went from there to Richmond, Virginia, and followed his trade of baker. He soon left that city, however, and came to Beardstown, Illinois. He was the first of his family to venture across the ocean, but was later joined by his parents and other brothers and sisters. He is the eldest of a large family that comes of good German stock. His youngest brother is a Lutheran clergyman of Carthage, Illinois, and he and George Kuhl are all that are left of the family.

When Mr. Kuhl came to Beardstown in 1835 he had but twenty-five cents in his pocket. The city was then very small, and the country was new. He began his business career in Beardstown as a baker. He soon gained a footing and found a sale for his wares, both in the little town and on the boats that were on the river. He made money and after twelve years established a large grocery store. Later he made it a general store, and added to it all the time until he became a large pork packer and grain dealer. Those were the times to make money, and during the war times he was one of the largest dealers on the Illinois river. He had two large grain houses that were destroyed by fire, and he lost some $4,000 in a paper mill. This made no difference to Mr. Kuhl's business enterprise. In spite of his losses he has made a large amount of money, and he now enjoys it in a beautiful home that he erected, that cost him some $15,000 when completed. It is furnished with every modern improvement. He has always had the best interests of the city at heart, and has done everything he could toward building it up. He has been a hard worker, and is the best kind of a citizen, and one that has a good deal of influence with all classes not only in the city but all over the county. He has been a leader in all tending to improve the city. He was one of the originators, and is one of the principal supporters of the German Church, and has contributed liberally to its support. His party (Republican) has rewarded his faithful services by making him Alderman of the city. He is a very temperate man and one that scorns anything mean or low. He has now retired from business, and is taking a merited rest, but he still takes a strong and deep interest in all that occurs in the city's history.

He was married for the first time to Christanna Belger, who was born in Saxony and came to this country when young in 1836. She died at Beardstown when about thirty years of age. She left four children, one of whom is dead. Mrs. Lizzie Rearick died after her marriage. The three living ones are: William P., who is in the grocery business, married Mary Shepherd; George S., a dry-goods merchant, married Julia Buck; Philip, a successful dry-goods merchant of Beardstown, married Mamie L. Arenz. Mr. Kuhl was married for the second time in this city to Mary E. Hemminghouse, *nee* Mashmeier. She was a German by birth and came to the United States with her parents in 1834. Landing in New York city they came by water route to Beardstown. Ten days after their arrival her father died, and her mother died some six months later. Mrs. Mary Kuhl was first married in her native country to the Rev. William Hemminghouse. He had charge of a German Lutheran mission; after some ten years he became a Methodist, and was a missionary through the West. He died when he was forty years old. He left six children, all dead but two daughters: Minnie, wife of George Schultheis; Henrietta, wife of Chris Kuhl. By their marriage Mr. and Mrs. Kuhl have four children: Louis, a clerk for Philip Kuhl in Beardstown, and married to Emma McVey, now deceased; Henry E., a clerk in Nashville, Illinois, married Allie Means; Mary, a teacher in the High School of Springfield, and she is an accomplished lady, and a graduate in English and German; Lydia, wife of Rev. M. D. Hornbeck, a minister of the Methodist Church.

JAMES B. MOORE, a soldier in the late war, was born in Newark, Delaware, November 26, 1819. His father, John, was born in the same place, October 9, 1791, and his grandfather, Archibald, was a native of Jamestown, Virginia. The great-grandfather of our subject was born in Ireland, of Scotch ancestry, and came to America and settled in Virginia, where he spent his last years. Archibald moved from Virginia to Newark, Delaware, bought land from Joseph Eagle, and there spent his last years as a farmer. The farm is still owned by his descendants. The name of his wife was probably McDonald, and as far as known, she spent her entire life in Newcastle county. John always followed agricultural pursuits, and the house where he was born was his home throughout his entire life. His wife was Mary Webb Temple of Chester county, Pennsylvania, whose father, Samuel, was born in the same locality, and whose grandfather, Caleb, was also a native of Pennsylvania. He was a Magistrate for several years under King James. He was an extensive land owner, owning the land, including Chad's Ford and Burningham in Chester county, where the battle of Brandywine was fought. He spent his last years in Chester county, was a Quaker. and reared his family in the same faith. The grandfather of our subject was an extensive farmer and stock-raiser and spent his last days in Chester county His wife was Elizabeth Clements The mother of James died near Newark, Delaware, October 1883, aged eighty-three.

James was reared and educated in Newark, attending school quite steadily until twenty years of age, when he engaged in farming for five years He then became a merchant for one year, but sold out and turned his attention to the study of law in the office of John M. Clayton, and in 1848 was admitted to the bar, and the same year came to Mt. Sterling He practiced here until his enlistment, July 15, 1861, in Company G, Third Illinois Cavalry, and served eight months. He was honorably discharged on account of disability incurred in the service. He then accepted the position of Provost Marshal of the Ninth Illinois District, and served in that capacity two and one-half years On account of failing eyesight, he resigned and returned home. Although not totally blind, he is so nearly so as to incapacitate him for the practice of his profession, and he lives retired in his pleasant home he has built in Mt. Sterling

He married Cordelia Merritt on September 8, 1851 She was born in Naples, Illinois. Her father, Joseph, was born in Sussex county, Delaware, July 16, 1803. When he was eight years old his parents went to Ohio The removal was made with two horses attached to a cart. They located in Pickaway county, where they lived until 1828, and then moved to Illinois, and were among the first settlers of Morgan county Later they bought land in Pea Ridge township, lived there until 1850, when they came to Mt. Sterling, where they continued to reside for the remainder of their days. Mr Merritt died in 1890 His wife died in Mt Sterling in 1875. She was Rebecca Drew and was born in Ohio

Mr. and Mrs Moore have had ten children: Joseph, James B , Kate, Will, Eugene, Annie, Sladie, Lottie, Jennie and George Mr Moore has been a member of the Republican party since its formation. Mr. and Mrs Moore are among the best people of Pea Ridge and are greatly respected by all who know them

JACKSON HIGGINS, of Brooklyn, Illinois, was born in Morgan county, Ohio, in 1832 His father, Daniel, was born in Green county, Pennsylvania, January 20, 1807, and his father, Joseph, was born near Harrisburg, Pennsylvania, and was engaged in farming He was born in 1777. and died in 1840, marrying Polly Henderson, and raising a family of twelve children He was drafted into the war of 1812, but sent a substitute. Daniel was married February 28, 1828, in Green county, Pennsylvania, to Sarah Brewer They moved from there to Morgan county, Ohio, about 1830. In the fall of 1838, they came to Illinois with a small horse and wagon, bringing four small children, being twenty-six days on the road. There were six families in the party The trip was a pleasant one, and the winter following was mild. They found the grass very tall, gone to seed, all kinds of game, and very recent marks of the buffalo remaining Agues and fevers were universal.

Mr. Higgins is the oldest resident in this part of Schuyler county. He took up eighty acres of school lands, and soon obtained a deed, which he has held until he came to live with his son. He was a tailor by profession, having learned his trade in Waynesburg, Pennsylvania, when a young man, having worked at it much of the time. In those early days the wives carded, spun and wove wool and flax, and Mr. Higgins in his trade, served the neighborhood well. His wife died, November, 1880, aged seventy-four years, leaving four living children, ten having been born. Mr. Higgins, in his eighty-sixth year, is bright and active.

Jackson has been a farmer all his life. He started on forty acres, and has from time to time added to it until his farm is now 227 acres, all fenced and more than one-half under the plow. There is some timber and large pasturage.

He was married in 1858, to Sarah, daughter of William and Polly, (Fowler) Burnett of England, but who have been residents here for many years. They have two sons, William Harrison, married, residing on the home farm, and John R., married, and also on the farm, They are all Democrats and Methodists. Mr. Higgins has been Justice of the Peace for four years and has served the county as Road Commissioner.

AARON MILLER was born in Fayette county, Pennsylvania, March 27, 1837. He was the son of Warwick and Mary (More) Miller of the same place. He was the son of William and Rebecca Miller, both of whom died at a good old age. Mr. William's mother was the daughter of Aaron and Mary (Hanney) More, who were natives of Pennsylvania, where they spent their lives and died at a good old age. Warwick was one of nine children, seven of whom are still living, and his wife is one of six children, one of whom alone survives.

Aaron Miller is one of seven children, all living. He remained at home until twenty-eight years of age, having spent his time in attending school, farming and wagoning. After his marriage Mr. Miller lived in Pennsylvania on his father's farm, but in 1869 he came to Illinois and bought eighty acres of land, later adding to it 360 acres. He has been a general mixed farmer and very successful.

He was married January 6, 1866, to Martha Robinson, born in 1836, daughter of William and Elizabeth (More) Robinson. The Robinson ancestors came from Ireland. Elizabeth More was born in Fayette county, Pennsylvania, and died there, aged fifty-seven years. She was a daughter of Colonel More, who was in the war of 1812. The Mores were of Scotch descent and first settled in Maryland, and all were honest mechanics or farmers. Mr. and Mrs. Miller have three children, Robert W. and Ruth, living at home, and Mary, a teacher of music, all graduates of the Plymouth school. Mr. and Mrs. Miller are members of the Congregational Church of Plymouth. Mr. Miller is a Republican and voted for Abraham Lincoln for his first term.

HON. ROBERT BROWN was born at Rushville, Schuyler county, Illinois, October 19, 1835, a son of John and Jane (Beckett) Brown; the father was a native of Fayette county, Kentucky, and emigrated to this State about 1831, settling at Rushville; he was a carpenter by occupation, and followed this calling until his death at the age of fifty-eight years; the mother was born in Bourbon county, Kentucky, and died in this county at the age of sixty-six years; they had born to them a family of ten children, five of whom are living Robert Brown remained at home until he was thirty-one years of age, when he was married At the age of twenty-four he was practically at the head of a large family, but he early developed remarkable business ability, and was quite equal to the cares that devolved upon him.

He was united to Miss Mary M. S. Hoffman, October 31, 1866 She was born in Woodstock township, Schuyler county, Illinois, September 7, 1845, a daughter of Samuel and Margaret C (Narding) Hoffman· Samuel Hoffman was a native of Berks county, Pennsylvania, and emigrated to Illinois in 1838, and here spent the remainder of his life; he was a soldier in the Mexican war, and died of a fever contracted in the service, at the age of twenty-eight years, he was a son of Joseph and Mary (Meyers) Hoffman, natives of Pennsylvania, Margaret C Narding was born in France, October 26, 1822, and emigrated with her parents to America in 1823, they first settled at Cincinnati, Ohio, and in 1839 came to Illinois and located in Woodstock township, Schuyler county Mr. and Mrs Brown have had born to them five children, four of whom are living Robert W, born October 26, 1868; Lilly J., born April 28, 1870; Herman H, born June 14, 1875; Edward C., born August 24, 1880

After his marriage Mr. Brown bought eighty acres of land, a portion of the farm he now owns; as his means increased he invested in land, and now has 400 acres in a body in Woodstock township In 1881 he replaced the old log house which had been a home for so many years with a modern structure, and he has made many valuable improvements upon the place; he does a general farming business, but makes a specialty of high grades of blooded stock.

Politically, Mr. Brown was identified with the Democratic party, but was elected to the State Senate by Democrats and Grangers by a majority of 1,476; he served four years, giving entire satisfaction to his constituency; he was a member of several important committees, and always showed a wise consideration of the subject in question. He was a member of the School Board for fiteen years, and has favored elevating the educational standards, and has filled the office of Supervisor He is a member of the Masonic fraternity, and belongs to the State Grange In addition to the business interests mentioned, Mr. Brown is a stockholder in the Bank of Rushville. He is a man of excellent business ability, his judgment carrying great weight. He has accumulated his property through his own unaided efforts, and he is in every way worthy of the esteem in which he is held.

JOHN F. ROBINSON, County Clerk of Cass county, is one of the prominent and influential men of the county. He is eminently a self-made man. Beginning life a poor boy, he has worked his way up to his present position of wealth and influence, being now classed with the leading citizens of his county A review of his life gives the following facts:

John F. Robinson was born in Crawford county, Ohio, May 31, 1851 His father, Andrew D. Robinson, was a native of the same State, and a son of James Robinson, one of the pioneers of Ohio. Andrew D was quite young when his father died, and he was reared by his mother He married in Ohio, and resided there till 1852. That year, leaving his wife with her parents, he started for California, making the journey with teams across the plains. At that time there were no white settlers between the Missouri river and California, except the Mormons. After his arrival in the Golden State, he engaged in packing provisions to the mines, and subsequently assisted in operating the first threshing-machine in that State. He remained there till 1856, when he returned East via the Isthmus route, and located in Linn county, Iowa, on a rented farm between Marion and Cedar Rapids. A year later he bought a partially improved farm in Spring Grove, two miles and a half west of Paris, where he lived till 1887. Leaving his son James in charge of the farm, he then removed to Center Point, where he now lives retired. The maiden name of his first wife, mother of John F., was Elizabeth E. Wachtel. She was born in Ohio, and her death occurred in Iowa, in 1865. The maiden name of his second wife was Eva L. Putney. He reared five children by his first wife, and of those born to his second wife three are living.

The subject of our sketch was an infant when his father went to California. In 1854, when he was three years old, he was taken by his mother and her parents to Iowa, making the journey with a horse and buggy. Iowa at that time was thinly settled, and there were no railroads in the State for two years afterward. Young Robinson attended the common schools, and advanced his education by attendance at the State University. In 1871 he came to Cass county, Illinois, to seek his fortune, landing here with no capital save a willing hand and a determination to succeed in life. He found employment on the farm, working by the month in summer, and during the winter of 1871-'72 he attended school in Chandlerville. The following ten years he taught school a part of each year. In 1874, he made his first purchase of real estate—a farm of 120 acres in Richmond precinct. Since then he has been an extensive and successful dealer in both farm and city property. He now owns four farms in Cass county, and a half interest in five other farms here. He is also interested in farm land in Clarke county, Iowa, and has city property in Kansas City, Missouri, and Eureka Springs, Arkansas.

In March, 1873, Mr. Robinson married Caroline (Houghton) Davis, who died April 19, 1874, leaving one child, Ada L. In August, 1879, he was united in marriage with Mary J. Witty, by whom he has two children, Lavina E. and Lee E.

Politically, he has always affiliated with the Democratic party. He cast his first vote for Horace Greeley. While teaching school he devoted a portion of his spare time to the study of law.

In 1882, Mr. Robinson was elected to the office of County Clerk of Cass county, for the legal term; was re-elected in 1886, and again in 1890.

Fraternally, Mr. Robinson is associated with Virginia lodge, No. 544, A. F. & A. M.; Clark Chapter, No. 9, R. A. M.; Hospitaller Commandery, No. 32, K. T.; Ashland Lodge, No. 341, I. O. O. F.; and Virginia Camp, M. W. A.

HENRY W. KROHE was born at Beardstown, Illinois, November 27, 1841, and died suddenly at his home in that city, of heart failure, December 19, 1889. He grew up here, and in 1862, when just about of age, he started for Calfornia, with an uncle and aunt. Going to New York, they took a steamer to Aspinwall, crossed the Isthmus of Panama, and was landed by a Pacific steamer at the city of San Francisco, where Mr. Krohe remained for some time. Later, he went to Portland, Oregon, Umatillia, Vancouver Island, etc., and thence up to British Columbia, and back again into California. He was amongst the Cherokee Indians, whose language he learned to speak well. He spent four years as a miner, and had a varied experience, making and losing money.

In 1866, he returned to Beardstown, and shortly afterward he went in partnership with his brother-in-law, George Schneider, into the saloon business, and together built the opera-house block, in 1873; but when it was nearly completed it was blown down by a terrible storm, July 4, 1873. It was rebuilt by them the same year. About eight years ago, Mr. Krohe sold his share of the opera-house block to his brother, Fred Krohe, who is still the proprietor of the same, with his brother-in-law, George Schneider, now of Omaha, Nebraska.

In 1869, he engaged in the manufacture of mineral and soda water, in which business he continued until the time of his death. He was well known as a hard-working business man. He built several nice dwelling houses, which became the property of his widow.

He was married at Jacksonville, Illinois, February 11, 1875, to Miss Bertha A. Eberwein, a native of Cass county, born December 2, 1846, daughter of J. C. H. and Maria Eberwein, who were born in Germany, and came to the United States when very young. Mrs. Eberwein died in 1847, leaving two little girls, Caroline and Bertha, both having good homes at the time they were married. Mr. Krohe and wife were reared in the faith of the Lutheran Church. He was a genial and pleasant man, a Democrat in politics, but not an office seeker. He leaves no children, but a widow, to mourn his early death; and Beardstown lost one of its best citizens when Mr. Krohe died.

MERIC E. CADY resides at Camden, and is numbered among the respected pioneers of Schuyler county. He was born in Tolland county, Connecticut, January 22, 1828, being a son of Isaac F. and Sarah (Chapman) Cady, natives of Connecticut. Isaac F. Cady in early life learned the trade of a carpenter, and, being a natural mechanic, also worked at the blacksmith trade. He could make anything in iron or other work in his line.

He first married Clarissa Hunt, who died, leaving seven children, five girls and two boys. He then married Sarah Chapman, and after two children had been born, he with his family came to Illinois, in 1835, via canal, Lake Erie and canal, to the Ohio river, where he purchased a boat, and came to Quincy, Illinois, and in the fall of 1835 he settled in Camden township, where he entered several hundred acres of land, and resided there till his death, which occurred in 1847, aged seventy-two years, six months and two days.

By his first marriage there were seven children, namely: Isaac G., H. H. Franklin, Angeline, Caroline, Emaline, Adaline and Mary Ann. By his second marriage, he had Francis E. and Meric E. The mother of our subject, by former marriage to I. A. Jones, had five children; Austin, Alonzo, Revilo, Charles W., and one died young. All the children were born in Connecticut, and the parents and fifteen children came to Illinois. The mother of our subject died aged eighty-one years.

Meric E. Cady was reared on the farm, and being a natural mechanic he worked somewhat in that line In 1850, he crossed the plains to California, where he worked in the mines for one year, and then went on a ranch In 1853, he came home via the Isthmus and New Orleans, and took 124 head of cattle and thirteen head of horses across the plains to California, and remained there till 1855, when he returned home via New York.

He was successful while in California, and on his return home he resumed farming, till 1882, becoming the owner of 268 acres, on which he made many improvements. When he removed to Camden village, he built a store, and with his son engaged in general mercantile business, and so continued ten years, since then he has lived a retired life He sold his farm in 1891, and purchased another of 130 acres, in Camden township

In March, 1856, he married Eliza A. Melvin She was born in Maine, in the town of Reidfield, 1835, daughter of John and Eunice Melvin, who settled in Schuyler county, in 1851 Our subject continued farming till 1882

Mr. and Mrs. Cady have three children living, and one dead Everett F. is a farmer in Camden township; Charles W died at the age of nineteen years, Eugenia and Addie In politics, Mr Cady is a Democrat, and has held local offices

Mr. and Mrs. Cady are members of the Christian Church. Mr Cady is a Royal Arch Mason, being the Master of the Camden Lodge, No 648, A F. & A M, a position he has held for several terms

JOHN UNLAND, of Beardstown, a practical farmer and stock-raiser, was born in Hanover, Germany, July 30, 1833. He was young when he came to this country with his father, Rev. Casper H Unland. The latter grew up a farmer, was well educated and became early in life interested in religion and while yet a young man began to exhort and preach experimental religion For this he was persecuted by the State church. He married Maria Calres in Hanover, and, after the birth of eight children, to better their condition they set out for the United States. They left on a sailing vessel October 20, 1844, and landed in New Orleans after a journey of eleven weeks They landed in Beardstown in the latter part of January, 1845, which was very remarkable, as the river is usually frozen at that time. They settled near Bluff Springs, on what is now known as the Tom Clark farm. After five years Mr. Unland sold, and purchased land five miles northwest of Arenzville, where he lived and died at the age of eighty-one years, his death occuring March 8, 1890. He was prominent in Cass county as a farmer and Methodist preacher, a good, noble man, a Republican, and the only one of his family who came to this country.

John is the second child of a family of thirteen, of whom nine are married and all have families He remained at home until he became of age and was married in this county to Elizabeth Christinaner, born in Germany She came with her parents when but three years old to Beardstown. Her father, Yost Christinaner, died at the age of eighty, and her mother died about the age of eighty, also. The name of the latter was Gustling. She and her husband were members of the Methodist Church and old settlers and good people of Cass county. Mrs. Unland was carefully reared by good parents She is the mother of seven living children: George married Nancy Henners and is a farmer in Morgan county; Lucinda, a widow with two children, lives with her father; Mary Higginson lives near Philadelphia, Cass county; and Nattie, Frank, Henry and William (the twins) live at home.

Mr. Unland has lived in this county since 1845 and has been one of its good citizens. He has lived on the farm, except three years, and he has put in all the improvements. He purchased it in June, 1860, and settled there in 1861. He has 200 acres in section 17, township 18, range 11, and his good farm buildings and fine improvements show that he thoroughly understands his business. He and his wife are both active members of the Methodist Church, of which Mr. Unland has been Class-leader since his twentieth year. He is a licensed exhorter. He is a sound Republican, but no office seeker.

THOMAS R. VAN DEVENTER, a prosperous farmer and stock-raiser and esteemed citizen of Brown county, Illinois, for the past fifty-five years a resident of section 15, Versailles township, was born in Fayette county, Ohio, in 1819.

His parents were Jacob and Jane (Rogers) Van Deventer, the former a native of old Virginia, and the latter of Paris, Kentucky. His father's parents were Jacob and Mary (Slater) Van Deventer, the former born in Holland in 1743, and the latter a native of Glasgow, Scotland. The young Hollander was a powder-maker by trade, and came to America in early manhood. He was married in New Jersey, on the Delaware river, and soon after went to Virginia, where he and his young wife located on a farm, which was situated on the south branch of the Potomac river. He engaged in farming, and having an excellent water-power in the river, also manufactured gun-powder. It was in the latter capacity that he rendered signal service to the patriots at the time of the Revolutionary war, providing them with powder with which to blaze their way into independence. He served for a short time in the regular army in that memorable conflict, and participated in the battles of Yorktown and Valley Forge. He was also a member of the Home Guards, although he did not take part in the engagement in which they distinguished themselves for bravery and efficiency. This worthy patriot and his wife were the parents of eight children, five sons and three daughters: William; Isaac; Jacob; Peter; Cornelius; Sarah, who married Jacob Judy; Mary, wife of George Timmons; and Peggy, wife of Daniel Timmons brother of George. The mother of this family died, aged eighty years, while the father expired four years later. They had met with many financial losses, and left only a small estate in worldly goods, although a rich heritage of honor and good deeds followed and influenced their children through life. Some of this family were of small stature, like the gentleman whose name heads this notice, but the majority of them, both men and woman, were large, erect and finely formed. Sarah was six feet tall, while Jacob, the father of the subject of this sketch, was a veritable giant, standing six feet six inches in his socks and weighing 240 pounds. Although possessing great strength and undaunted courage, he was most peaceable and kind. He was twice married. His first wife was Magdalene Buffenbarger, a member of a wealthy Ohio family. She died early, leaving two children—a son, Jethero, and a daughter, Elizabeth. The former now lives in Versailles, Illinois; and the latter resides in Indiana. Late in the fall of 1815 the father remarried, his second wife being the mother of the subject of this biography. A short time afterward, he and his brother, with their families, six persons in each household, came from Fayette county, Ohio, to Schuyler, now Brown county, Illinois. This journey of more than 400 miles was made in three weeks, with two large covered wagons and eight horses, four animals under saddle The father of our subject brought some means with him, realized from the sale of his farm in Ohio He first settled in Schuyler, now Brown county.

Eight years earlier Cornelius Van Deventer visited the Illinois bottoms, where he secured a claim. Five acres of this he fenced and planted to corn and pumpkins, and after completing their cultivation returned to his family On his return in the fall, great was his surprise to find his crop intact, not an ear of corn or a pumpkin being missing.

The stalwart and much beloved pioneer, Jacob Van Deventer, died in 1833, aged fifty-three years, leaving a bereaved family and many sorrowing friends His worthy wife survived him nine years, dying aged about forty-eight years They were the parents of six boys and two girls, to-wit: T. R, J. F, H. D, and B B., boys; girls, Caroline and Duan, one child, Pembrook Berbeck Van Deventer, died when small; the others were the subject of this notice, J F, H. D and B B. In 1838, she bought fifty-three acres of heavily timbered land, which had a small enclosure cleared, in the center of which was a hewed-log house, for which she paid $600 This forms part of the present large farm of the subject of this sketch He and his brothers formerly owned this farm of 800 acres in partnership, but J F. Van Deventer, of Mount Sterling, now owns another farm of 2,200 acres near by, which he is farming on a large scale. Their specialty is stock-raising, including horses, cattle and hogs. On the land cultivated by our subject and his other brother, there is now a substantial farm residence, which they erected in 1866, besides which there are large barns and an excellent granary, which they built in 1880, all of which are models of their kind. They breed and raise from fifty to sixty head of dehorned short horn cattle annually, and have fed each year, for some thirty-five years, about 250 head, which they ship to market, together with many which they buy to sell. They now own ninety head of horses, and breed and raise ten to twelve head a year, most of which are draft horses, but some are for the saddle. They send to market from 200 to 300 hogs a year, beside shipping of their own stock from eight to ten car loads annually Thus will be seen what a prominent part they take in the development of this country, which results in their own prosperity and provides work for numerous attendants

In politics, Mr. Van Deventer affiliates with the Republican party, the principles of which he has endorsed for many years

Notwithstanding his marvelous achievements in life, we have yet to chronicle the most wonderful feat of his existence, namely, his abstaining from matrimony. How he has escaped the wiles of the fair sex is truly phenomenal, unless we revert to his other superior accomplishments. However, we will not congratulate him yet, remembering he will not be free from danger until he has left this mundane sphere.

His early educational opportunities were limited, but he inherited a clear and strong intellect, as well as superior physical strength, and, by much reading and reflection, has over come these early disadvantages Besides being one of the most successful of men finacially, he enjoys, by reason of his integrity of character and uniform courtesy, the universal friendship of his fellow men.

WILLIAM A. BROKER was born in Lippe-Detmold, Germany, March 19, 1837. He was a boy of eleven years of age when his parents, Samuel and Sophia (Haupfer) Broker crossed the Atlantic in the spring of 1849, to New Orleans, and thence up the Mississippi river to St. Louis. This was during the year of the great cholera epidemic in that city, and within a few days the father and three of the children died, the mother and William having it severely, but recovering. When they were able to leave, the mother and her four small children moved to a farm near Watertown, Wisconsin. About one year later the mother died of cholera morbus, she being then fifty years of age. Mr. and Mrs. Broker had always been members of the German Reformed Church.

Mr. William Broker is the youngest of the children yet living. He is now pattern-maker for the St. Louis division of the Quincy railroad, which is located at Beardstown. He has been a resident of the same city since 1851. He was only fourteen years old when he arrived at Beardstown, and learned the trade of a practical carpenter mechanic under C. A. Bushman. After learning his trade he worked on his own account, and later became a carpenter for the old Rockford company. In 1869, when the railroad was bought up by the Quincy company, he became their pattern-maker in 1879. He has ever since been regarded as a good, reliable workman, and a true, straightforward man, and his long association with the railroad company is a recommendation of him as a citizen.

He was married in Beardstown to Miss Dorothea Kratz, who was born in Hesse-Darmstadt, Germany, in 1844, and was twelve years of age when her parents emigrated to this country. They have seven children: Frank, living at home, is a machinist; Sophia and Katie are at home, they having been well educated in the high school of the city; William is learning the machinist trade; Minnie, Amelia and Samuel are at home. Mr. and Mrs. Broker attend the Lutheran Church. Mr. Broker is a Republican, and a member of the A. O. U. W. He is highly respected by all.

JAMES N. RIGG, of the firm of Rigg & Smith, merchants of Camden, one of the well-known pioneers of Brown county, settled in 1869 at Camden. He was born in Anderson county, Kentucky, January 18, 1826, being a son of Richard and Margaret (Utterback) Rigg, natives of Virginia. Each removed with their respective families to Kentucky, where they were married. In 1831 they emigrated to Illinois and settled in what is now Brown county, but was then a part of Schuyler. Mr. Richard Rigg purchased land near Mount Sterling, and entered land, and then became the owner of 400 acres of land on which he made many improvements. His death occurred in 1879, aged eighty-four years. His wife died in 1877, aged eighty-four years. They were members of the Baptist Church, of which Mr. Rigg was a Deacon. He had already made money when he started farming in Illinois, and added to his fortune in this State. He and his wife had three sons and four daughters:

Elizabeth, married to John B. Annmos, deceased; Susan A., married to J. P. Singleton, of Mount Sterling; Eliza married James A. Parker, who died in Brown county; James N.; Peter, a farmer; and John J. died in Brown county. By a former marriage Richard had two children, William T. and Sarah.

James was only five years of age when the family came to Illinois. He was reared on the farm and resided there until he grew to manhood, attending school in the log schoolhouses of the section, where the teaching was as rude as the furniture. After his marriage James purchased a farm in Brown county, and continued on it until he came to Camden in 1869, when he sold his farm of 160 acres and with his father-in-law, Willis Watts, engaged in general merchandising in Camden, under the firm name of Watts & Rigg, and continued business for ten years. Mr. Rigg continued alone some years, until 1881, when the cyclone passed through the town; his store and dwelling-house were badly injured, and his family were badly hurt. He subsequently associated with his son-in-law in business, under the firm name of Rigg & Donnell. This firm continued two years. At the end of that time his present partner purchased an interest in the business, and the name was changed to Rigg & Smith.

He was married in 1849, to Emily I. Watts, daughter of Willis Watts. (For family history see history of Dr. B. P. Watts.) Mr. and Mrs. Rigg have five children: John J., of Keokuk, Iowa; Richard W. is a physician of Pulaski, Illinois; Francis M. is in the insurance business at Quincy, Illinois; Olie married John Donnell, a farmer of Iowa; and Gertrude, at home.

In politics he is a Democrat. He has been Supervisor of Camden township, until he declined to accept the office, and during this time was chairman of the Board of Supervisors of Schuyler county for four consecutive years. He has held many of the offices of the township. He has been Justice of the Peace for seven years, and been prominent in local politics, frequently having been a delegate of the county and district conventions. Mr. Rigg is a member of the Baptist Church, and his wife of the Christian Church. He has devoted his attention to merchandise, and is one of the oldest merchants in the county. He and his wife are respected throughout the county, where they are well known, and Mr. Rigg is regarded as a reliable, honest business man.

WILLIAM L. ALEXANDER, of section 30, Huntsville township, settled in the county in 1861. He was born in Russell county, Virginia, December 19, 1836. His parents were William and Mary (McReynolds) Alexander. The grandfather of our subject was John Alexander, born in the north of Ireland. He came to the United States, where he settled and pursued farming. He married and reared a large family. His son William was born in 1802 and was a farmer, marrying in Virginia. In 1840 he came to Illinois and settled in Adams county, North East township, where he became the owner of 400 acres of land on which he made good improvements. He died in 1887, his wife having died a few years previously. They were members of the Presbyterian Church and the father was a Democrat in politics. He was poor when he settled in Illinois, owning only a horse and wagon. They had thirteen children, all of whom attained their majority: Nancy, John, Mary, Rachel, Margaret, William L., Davis, Daniel, Mitchell, Martha, Samuel, Robert Wilson and Rebecca.

William L. was reared on the farm. In 1862 he enlisted in Company I, Eighty-fourth Illinois Infantry, and served until the close of the war. He was in the battles of Perryville, Kentucky, Stone river and Chickamauga, Tennessee, and the Atlanta Campaign. He returned with General Thomas and participated in the fight at Franklin and Nashville. He was mustered out at Camp Harker, Tennessee. He was a non-commissioned officer. At the battle of Kenesaw Mountain he received a gunshot wound in the head, for which he now receives a pension.

After the war he returned to Schuyler county, where he owned sixty acres of land, purchased in 1864. He has since pursued farming and now owns 541 acres of land and has two good sets of farm buildings. In addition to his farming he has raised stock and dealt in the same. Since 1889 he has rented all his land.

He was married in 1861 to Rachel J. Derry, daughter of Basil and Sarah Derry. She was born in Adams county, near Quincy. Mr. and Mrs. Alexander have four children: Martha A., wife of William H. Naylor, resides in Baxter Springs, Kansas; Edward died, aged nineteen; Emma, wife of Edward Straub of Galesburg, Illinois; Keely L. is at home. In politics Mr. Alexander is a Democrat and has been a member of the School Board. His wife is an earnest Christian lady, but not a member of any sect. Mr. Alexander has made his property and is a well-to-do man, richly deserving the respect in which he is held by all who know him.

GROVE CONINGHAM, deceased, was a native of New York city, born December 27, 1816. His father, Grove Coningham, Senior, was born in Londonderry, Ireland, about 1766. He emigrated to New York city at an early age and married Betsy Baldwin, of Putnam county, New York. They had nine children, of whom the subject of this sketch was the eighth. The father died in December, 1831, in New York city. His wife survived him thirty-eight years.

Our subject received his education in New York and at the age of sixteen came to Schuyler county, Illinois. In 1843 he returned to his native city and lived there for three years, then returned to Illinois and settled in Schuyler county in 1851. He made a trip to California in 1851 and remained for two years employed in the custom house. This was his business and had been from his youth, as he had been associated with his father in the same for years. In 1853 he returned to his old home in Frederick and settled there. There he resided until his death in 1891, February 21. Mr. Coningham was a business man for many years as a member of the firm of Farwell & Company, which lasted from 1855 to 1870. He was a stanch Republican in politics and an ardent supporter of the war and a friend of the soldiers. For two years after the dissolution of the firm of Farwell & Company he served as steamboat agent, and subsequently as Tax Collector, and held other positions of trust and responsibility. In 1866 he was appointed Postmaster at Frederick, which position he held for over twenty years. Mr. Coningham was a man of sterling worth and integrity. He was of a jovial disposition that made him friends wherever he was. He was noted for his firm adherence to the right whatever the cost might be. He was a worthy communicant of the Episcopal Church.

He was married in Frederick, Illinois, to Sarah H. Beal, in 1856. She is the daughter of Jesse O. and Sarah (Vail) Beal, born in

Coshocton county, Ohio, March 21, 1836. Her father came of German ancestry, and her mother traces her genealogy back to the Vails who came to Plymouth. Of a family of nine only three are now living Her brother Foster was a soldier in the Mexican war and is buried on Mexican soil. Samuel now resides in Frederick, a farmer; Julia resides in DeWitt, Iowa, and Mrs Coningham is the third living one of that once large family.

Mr. and Mrs. Coningham had seven children, namely Charlie, married, and lives in St Louis, a telegraph operator, Grove, unmarried, located at San Francisco, in the insurance business; Jesse is employed in the registry department of the St. Louis post-office, a position he has held for eight years; Betsy, now Mrs Moses, resides in Pueblo, Colorado; Grant, the yongest, named for the noted general, is married, employed in a saw mill and resides with his mother Mrs Coningham is a worthy member of the Christian Church, and has always been respected and liked by her large circle of friends.

JOHN S. DODGE, one of the most prominent farmers of Littleton township, Schuyler county, Illinois, was born in Bloomington, McLean county, this State, March 14, 1837. His parents, Solomon and Betsey (Springer) Dodge, were both natives of Ohio, his father being a carder and filler by trade His mother's ancestors were originally from Cork, Ireland. In 1833, his parents came by way of the Ohio and Mississippi rivers to Bloomington, Illinois, where our subject was born in his father's hotel, which was the first in that town, called the Caravansary. His father retired about twenty-five years before his death, he being ninety-one years of age and his wife seventy-two' when they died at the home of their son, the subject of our sketch His godfather, Israel Dodge, was from Scotland, and died in Marietta, Ohio, aged seventy-five years.

Our subject came to this county in 1846, and bought the farm on which he at present resides, which he has since much improved by the erection of a substantial residence and barns, and has the land well cultivated. He is one of ten children, five of whom are now living, two boys and three girls. He is the only farmer, all the others being merchants and mechanics.

Mr. Dodge remained at home until he was eighteen years of age, attending district school and helping his father. He then herded cattle for a couple of years, after which he worked around at different places until he was twenty-one years of age. He was, at the end of this time, married to Miss Emily Hoyt, on December 24, 1855, a native of Detroit, Michigan, where she was born November 2, 1836. Their happy married life was doomed to be of short duration, for three years later his wife died in Wahpeton, Minnesota, aged twenty-two years. She was an intelligent woman, with many charms of person and character, and was much regretted by all who knew her Her people were from New York State.

Mr. Dodge, after about eight years, married Miss Rachel Moore, on January 11, 1866, who was born in Buena Vista township, this county, June 15, 1838. Her parents, Thomas and Mary Moore, were pioneers of this county, and highly respected people. They are now both dead, her mother surviving her father by several years. She was one of twelve children, nine of whom are now living.

After his marriage Mr. Dodge rented a farm in this county, which he cultivated until the time of the war; when, on February 1, 1862, he enlisted in Company I, Sixty-second Illinois Infantry, under Captain Joseph McLean, and served for three years and four months in the army, and was on detached duty for two months. He was sick in 1864 and was in the regimental hospital. In 1865, on May 2, he was honorably discharged at Smithfield. Mr. Dodge and D. Wheat are the only ones left in Springfield township, who were members of that company.

After the war Mr. Dodge bought his present farm, which at that time was unimproved and had only a log house on it. It hardly resembles the same farm now, for he has erected a substantial residence, besides commodious barns for his grain and stock, besides other modern conveniences for the facilitating of agricultural pursuits. He has bought eighty more acres of land, making his present possessions 240 acres, all of which is under a good state of cultivation. Besides his farming interests, he is largely interested in stock-raising, making a specialty of cattle, in which he is very successful.

Our subject and wife have had eight children, six of whom still survive: Avey E., born in this county, was educated at Bushnell College, and studied music at Shenandoah, Iowa, and is now teaching music; Homer P. is at home; he was educated at Bushnell College; Fannie T. is at home, and was also educated at Bushnell College; Adda A.; Ruby J. and True; the last three are living a home with their parents.

Mr. Dodge is at present a Republican, although he went to war as a Douglas Democrat; after that international struggle he voted with the Republicans. His first vote was cast for John C. Fremont. His constituents have seen fit to honor him with public office, and he has served as Assessor and Commissioner of Highways, in which capacity he has rendered eminent satisfaction to all. He is a member of George Brown Post, of Brooklyn, also of No. 320, G. A. R., and affiliates with the A. F. & A. M., No. 766, of Littleton, of all which societies he is a prominent and esteemed member.

Of superior ability, high integrity and morality, he also adds the gentler virtues of sociability and amiability, thus commanding the respect and affection of all alike.

WILLIAM BADER, proprietor of the village of that name, was born in Preble county, Ohio, in 1826. His parents were Jeremiah and Sarah (Thompson) Bader. The father was a native of Germany, and the mother of Pennsylvania. They had eleven children, of whom eight are now living, namely: Mary, now Mrs. Hopkins, residing in Mason county; Sarah A., now Mrs. Gibbs, residing in Hancock county; Rosanna, now Mrs. Bleeker, of Pasadena, California; Margaretta, now Mrs. Doane; Jeremiah died when seventeen; John L., now residing in Kansas; Benjamin F., residing at Vermont, Illinois; Henry O., residing on a farm near Bader. The family moved from Ohio to Brooming township, Schuyler county, in 1846, and the parents both died on a farm near what is now known as Baders.

The early life of our subject was passed on the farm, and later he learned engineering and operated a saw and grist mill for many years. He then went into the lumber business in Ohio, where he conducted a mill before he removed to Illinois, he not coming until 1857. Here he continued his business in the lumber mill, and accumulated a large fortune. He and his wife have been enjoying some of their money by spending a year in California, on account of her failing health.

He was married November 9, 1856, in Randolph county, Indiana, to Miss Mercy A. Hunt, a daughter of Rev. William Hunt, of the Methodist Episcopal Church, a pioneer of Randolph county, Indiana, although he was a native of Kentucky.

Mr. and Mrs. Bader have no children of their own, but they have reared two as their own; the first one died, but the present one is still living, and is a young lady of seventeen. Mr. Bader is extensively engaged in the grain business, and owns 160 acres of land, a warehouse, several residences and two-thirds of a brick building in Baders. His wife is a member of the Christian Church and he is a member of the Masonic fraternity and of I. O. O. F. He is a Democrat in politics and has served three terms as a member of the Board of Supervisors of his county. He has been School Treasurer for fifteen or sixteen years, and has held various positions of trust and responsibility.

SAMUEL M. SCHRODER, a rising young business man of Oakland township, and one of the most progressive agriculturists of Schuyler county, was born in McDonough county, Illinois, in 1860, on the 27th day of April. His father, Nicholas Schroder, was a native of Germany, but emigrated to America with his mother when a lad of eleven years, in 1837; his father, John Schroder, died in the Fatherland about the year 1830, leaving a widow and three sons in very humble circumstances; the names of the sons are Christopher, Carson and Nicholas. They sailed from Bremen to New York, landing after a voyage of six weeks; they came direct to Pennsylvania, and from there to Schuyler county, and settled on a tract of Government land which the brave mother and stanch, energetic sons converted into a farm of great fertility and value. Nicholas went to California, taking the overland route; he mined for seven years, meeting with fair success, and then returned to Illinois, purchasing a farm of 160 acres in McDonough county. He was married in 1858 to Lucinda Phillips, a daughter of Samuel and Amy Philips, who were settlers in Illinois as early as 1840; they had a family of two daughters and a son: Amy Ann, wife of John W. Danners; Ada L., wife of Robert Robertson; and Samuel M., the son, is the subject of this notice. The parents came to Schuyler county in 1864, and purchased 220 acres of land in Oakland township, on which they lived until 1889, when they went to Vermont; here they bought a home in which they are now living in quiet enjoyment of the reward of their labors.

Samuel M. Schroder was reared to the life of a farmer, and received his education in the common schools. His opportunities were somewhat limited, but this lack has been more than overbalanced by wide reading and clear thinking upon all the topics of the day.

Mr. Schroder was united in marriage, in 1880, to Miss Sarah E. Smith, a native of Fulton county, Illinois, and a daughter of John and Rebecca (Barcus) Smith, natives of Pennsylvania and Illinois, respectively. Mr. and Mrs. Schroder have buried an infant daughter, and have three children living: Harry W. was born December 22, 1882; Cleveland B. was born March 3, 1884; and Maud, November 2, 1889.

Mr. Schroder first settled on eighty acres of land, and has since bought the eighty acres adjoining it; he also owned 280 acres in Schuyler and McDonough counties, which he recently sold at a handsome profit, after cultivating it four years. He does a general farming business, making a specialty of corn and wheat in the cereal line, and cattle, horses and hogs in live-stock. He has represented the people of his township in various local offices, and has always been a stanch supporter of home interests and home industries. He was elected vice-president of the J. Wershon Bank in June, 1892, and is a stockholder of this corporation. He is possessed of excellent business qualifications, and has met with marked success in all his undertakings. Always employing the most honorable methods, he has the highest regard and esteem of the entire community.

THOMAS WILSON, President of the Schuyler County Bank, and a leading financier and business man of Rushville, Illinois, was born near Five-Mile Town, in county Tyrone, Ireland, in March, 1812. Both his grandfather, Thomas, and father, Thomas, were natives of the same county. They were of well-known and esteemed Scotch ancestry, who were sturdy, rugged farmers, and passed their entire lives in their native land. His father was reared to manhood in his native county, where he married Jane Greer, also a native of the Emerald Isle. They resided in Ireland until 1843, when they commenced the long journey to America. Unfortunately the wife and mother died in England while en route, leaving six children and a bereaved husband. These children were: William, Thomas, Joseph, George, Jane and Robert, all of whom came to America, except George, and located in Illinois. The father settled first in Schuyler county, Illinois, where he remained four years, after which he removed to Hancock county, locating near Nauvoo, where he resided until death. He was an intelligent, pious, good man, and was greatly esteemed by all who knew him.

The subject of this sketch was reared and educated in Ireland, where he continued to live until 1832, when, at the age of twenty years, he emigrated to America, sailing from Derry in the sail vessel William Ewing. He landed in Philadelphia after a tempestuous voyage of seven weeks, a stranger in a strange land. He found employment in the City of Brotherly Love, at the weaving trade, and continued to operate a loom until the fall of the year of his arrival. He then removed to Lancaster county, that State, where he obtained employment on the farm of his uncle, James Little. He continued there until 1834, when he removed to Pittsburg, Pennsylvania, securing employment on a farm near that city. Three years later he went to Illinois, going via the Ohio, Mississippi and Illinois rivers, to Rushville, Schuyler county. At that early period the country was sparsely settled, and some of the land was still owned by the Government. Rude log houses dotted the country. At that time Rushville was an insignificant village, with nothing like its present pretentious appearance. Mr. Wilson immediately engaged in merchandising in a small way, buying his goods in St. Louis and transporting them by way of the river in summer and by wagon in winter. His business gradually increased until he became, in time, a prominent merchant of the town. Since 1872 he has been interested in banking, and upon the organization of the Schuyler County Bank he was elected its president, bringing to this position unusual financial ability and extended experience.

He was married September 18, 1834, in Pittsburg, Pennsylvania, to Miss Susan Clark, an estimable lady, a native of Lancaster county, that State, and a daughter of John and Eleanor (Greer) Clark. They have three children: Anne Jane, wife of James P. Clark; John; and Lorinda, wife of John T. Sweeney. Eleanor and Sarah Elisa are deceased. Eleanor died in December, 1860, after finishing her education at Monticello in 1857; and Sarah died in February, 1883, leaving three children; she was the wife of Hiram Graff.

Mr. and Mrs. Wilson are earnest and useful members of the Methodist Church, and are prohibitionists in principle. They are worthy people, and enjoy the esteem of the entire community.

DUNCAN REID was born in Forfarshire, Scotland, August 12, 1809, son of William and Grace (McKenzie) Reid. His parents were natives of Scotland, and passed their lives there. Reared and educated in his native land, Duncan Reid then learned the trade of tailor. On account of ill health, however, he sought out-door employment, turning his attention to the stone-mason's trade. He resided in Scotland till 1855.

October 10, 1839, he married Jane Wilkie, who was born in Fifeshire, Scotland, November 19, 1818, daughter of William and Euphemia (Gaul) Wilkie. Their union was blessed by the birth of six children: William, Jean, Susan, Margaret, Stuart and Duncan. Mrs. Reid and her two oldest children are members of the Cumberland Presbyterian Church, her son being a ruling Elder in the church. Miss Susan Reid is a teacher in the Kensington school, Chicago.

In 1855, accompanied by his wife and four children, he came to America, setting sail from Liverpool in May in the Aurora, and landing at New York after a voyage of five weeks. He came directly to Illinois and settled in Cass county. For six years he cultivated rented land, and during that time, by his energy and good management, not only supported his family but also laid by a snug little sum. He then purchased the property on which his family now reside, it being at that time a tract of wild land, covered with timber and brush. Here he built his cabin, which served as the family home until further prosperity enabled him to erect a comfortable frame residence. His death occurred here on the 14th of April, 1883. Mr. Reid was a self-made man, and one who was held in high esteem by all who knew him.

CHARLES F. JOHNSON, practical farmer and truck-raiser of Beardstown, was born in Salem county, New Jersey, April 7, 1863. He lived in his native State until thirteen, when his parents came to Cass county, settling in Beardstown. The father, Chalkley Johnson, followed his trade as a carpenter until February, 1884, when he and all their children, but one, Charles, went to Sedgwick county, Kansas, and settled on a farm, where the father and mother both live. The latter's maiden name was Luwesia Lippencott. Both were natives of Salem county, New Jersey, where they were reared, married and all their children were born. They had four, of whom our subject is the youngest, and of whom three are yet living,—Charles and two sisters, Mrs. Mary McKennel, of Sedgwick county, Kansas, and Mrs. Ella Crater, now living in Beardstown.

Mr. Johnson has a fine farm of 238 acres, most of it located in township 18, range 11. He has owned it for four years, having managed it on his own account for two years previously. Since he bought it he has made considerable improvement in the buildings. When he was twenty-one years of age he began to raise truck, making a specialty of sweet potatoes. He has been a hard worker and is very successful in everything he undertakes. He has made his large property by his own efforts.

He was married in this county, to Amelia Shuman, born in Hagener Station, Cass county, in 1866. She was reared and educated here, and is a good woman. She is the daughter of John Shuman, who was a native of Germany, coming to America when a young man and settling in Cass county, where he spent his last days as a farmer, dying in 1888, aged sixty-eight. He was a good man and a member of the German Methodist Episcopal Church. He was a Democrat in politics. His wife died in 1867, after the birth of five children, of whom Mrs. Johnson is the youngest. All the other children are now married. Mrs. Shuman was born in Germany, and her maiden name was Kate Loeb. She was a good wife and mother, and a member of the German Methodist Episcopal Church.

Mr. Johnson and wife have three children, —Viola, Gurtre and Nettie. They are members of the Methodist Episcopal Church, and Mr. Johnson is a Republican in politics. They are worthy, good people.

ANTON RINK, a successful brewer of Beardstown, was born on the river Rhine, August 9, 1833. He is the only member of his family now living in this country. His mother died in Germany when he was only two years of age. In 1850, and after his father's second marriage, he left the old country, and after a long and weary trip finally settled in Perry county, Missouri, where the father died four years later. His wife married a second time, and continued to live in Perry county until her death in 1890.

Mr. Rink came here from Missouri after he had spent ten years on a farm and had made some money to put into a business. He then was poor, but is now very wealthy, and has become so by his own efforts, and has been a real benefit to the town in which he lives. He arrived in 1864 and purchased a part in the brewery run under the name of A. Rink & Co. In 1867 he built a large brick brewery, with a capacity of 5,000 barrels per annum. The business has been successful, being represented on the road by himself and son in a commercial way. He is also a wholesale liquor dealer, running other places of business in the city. He is a stockholder, a promoter and original director of the First State Bank of Beardstown. He has been interested in all local matters affecting the good of the city ever since he came here, including the building of a wagon bridge across the Illinois river. He has been City Treasurer, and is a Democrat in politics. Mr. Rink, a sincere man, has not only been ambitious, but is also successful in earning a good reputation for ability, honesty, industry and executiveness.

He was married, in 1865, to Margaret Schultz, who was born in the same province and near her husband in Bavaria, Germany, and came, when twelve years of age to Menard county, Illinois. Her parents lived and died in Germany. They were members of the Catholic Church. Mr. and Mrs. Rink were the parents of eight children, five of whom are living: John and Amil assist their father in his business; Jessie is a teacher of music and has been well educated; Clara, now at home, was educated at Quincy, Illinois; and Arthur is in the deaf and dumb institute at Jacksonville, he being a deaf mute. Mr. and Mrs. Rink and family are members of the Catholic Church and take an interest in social matters.

JOHN H. BLACK, a prominent citizen of Woodstock township, is a representative of one of the earliest families of Schuyler county, and is entitled to a space in this history. He was born in Woodstock township, August 2, 1842. His father, James P. Black, was a native of Mecklenburgh county, North Carolina, a son of Richard S. Black (see sketch of Isaac Black). James P. Black removed to Indiana at the age of fourteen years, and resided there until 1826. Then, with his bride, he came to Illinois; the "wedding journey" was accomplished with a yoke of oxen, the bridegroom walking most of the distance. He located in Woodstock township, and there entered a tract of Government land which he began to improve. It was in this year that the county was organized; there were few white settlers. Indians were numerous, and the frontier was not far removed toward the setting sun. Mrs. Black's maiden name was Mary Padgett; she was born in Kentucky, a daughter of John and Eleanor Padgett, and died on the home farm in 1851. Our subject, John H. Black, received his education in the common schools of Woodstock township, and at the Western Seminary, Rushville. At the age of nineteen years he began teaching in Woodstock township, and was actively engaged in educational labors for more than twenty years.

In 1867 he removed to Richfield, Adams county, and there purchased a home in which he lived for a few years; his next change was to Quincy, where he bought city property, and thence he removed to Camp Point, where he lived five years; at the expiration of that period he returned to Quincy and made his home there until 1878, when he sold out and bought the farm he now occupies on section 12, Woodstock township.

Mr. Black was united in marriage in 1862, to Telitha Parke, a native of Brown county, Illinois, and a daughter of Oliver H. F. and Mary (Logsdon) Parke, natives of Kentucky, and pioneers of Brown county, Illinois. Of this union five children have been born: Mary, Nettie, John R., Lelia and J. Charles. The father and mother are members of the Church of God. Mr. Black has held various offices of trust, and has represented Woodstock township on the county Board of Supervisors for three terms. For twelve years he was Superintendent of Schools in Adams county, and did much to elevate the educational standard. He is a man of rare force and uprightness of character, and has the respect and confidence of the entire community.

MARQUIS L. CRUM, of township 17 north, range 10, section 32, was born about two and one half miles from his present location, January 16, 1851. His parents were James and Christina (Ream) Crum. The father was born in Indiana, in 1806. His mother came from Ohio, and married in this county, in 1833. The father came to the county in 1832, the mother with her parents, who settled in this neighborhood. The father was of German descent, and was the father of twelve children. His wife died May 1, 1878, and the father has since married again, and resides on the old homestead. Marquis was educated in the public schools, and then attended the State Normal school for two years, and the Illinois Wesleyan University four years, graduating in the scientific course in 1874, receiving the degree of B. S., and three years later the degree of M. S. was conferred upon him. Being in very poor health at this time, he resumed farming, and this has proven so beneficial, under the favorable circumstances surrounding him, that he has continued to follow it.

He was married, March 30, 1875, to Fannie Stubblefield, of Funk's Grove, McLean county, born there September 17, 1853. They became acquainted while attending the university, which she attended about three years. Her family are old settlers in that county. Mr. and Mrs. Crum have four children: Edith, the eldest, now sixteen, has been attending the Illinois College at Jacksonville, and expects to complete a course in one of the higher institutes of learning; Arthur E. and Oral C. are bright boys; and Rena F., now three years old, is the pet of the family. Mr. Crum owns a farm of 700 acres, principally devoted to stock. He breeds shorthorn cattle, and uses the Percheron-Norman horses, his father-in-law being an importer of this breed of horses in Bloomington. He also owns a stock farm of 240 acres near Kirksville, Missouri, and usually buys his stock in Missouri and ships here. They are members of the Methodist Episcopal Church, and Mr. Crum belongs to the A. O. U. W. He is a Democrat. He has been associated with the Farmers' Alliance, and was the State president of it for eighteen months. He declined a re-election. He was a delegate from Illinois to the national convention at Ocala, Florida, and Mr. Crum describes this trip as the finest he ever made. He has three nice tenement houses on his extensive farm where his employees reside. He hires four or five men by the year, usually married men, and furnishes them with house, fuel and garden.

JOSEPH MESERVEY, of Elkhorn township, was born here, June 22, 1841. He is the son of Joseph and Eliza Meservey. Joseph was the son of Nathaniel, both of Vermont. He spent his life there and died when nearly ninety years of age. Joseph followed the business of shipping horses for nine years, and then went into a distillery, and then sold out and came to this State at an early date.

He continued at home until his marriage, worked with his father, and attended the subscription school when able. When he married he had a little farm, and afterward he bought more land. He now owns 760 acres, which he earned himself. He carries $10,000 life insurance. He runs a large quarry by machinery. This is a new industry, and will employ fully thirty men, and the machinery will require an outlay of nearly $8,000. He is a Republican in politics, and voted first for Abraham Lincoln.

He was married, June 15, 1865, to Melvina Jane Wilson, born in Pike county, Illinois. (See sketch of George Wilson for history of Mrs. Meservey's family). Mr. and Mrs. Meservey have nine children: Clara M., Warren R., George O., Maggie B., Elwood, Lorena E., Herbert H., Herman H., and Amy A. Warren R. married Cora V. Moore, of Brown county, and has two children: Estel V. and Nina.

The family belong to the Methodist Episcopal Church, and the daughters are members of the Epworth League. They are a family that commands the respect and esteem of their host of friends.

LOUIS F. KLOKER, a practical and extensive farmer, occupying his fine farm in section 30, township 17, range 11, was born in Beardstown, May 20, 1836. Here he was reared and educated and has always been a resident. His father was Louis Kloker, Sr., a native of Hanover, Germany, belonging to an old German family. He had been a wagon maker, the only son of his father's family, and after growing up, about 1832, he came to the United States on a sailing vessel. After a voyage of thirteen weeks he landed in New Orleans, and came on to Beardstown, via the Mississippi river. He began work as a mechanic, and died about 1839. He was known as a hard-working young man of good habits, and was a member of the Lutheran Church. He left two sons, our subject and a brother Henry, who died when thirteen years of age. He married Mary Raube, also a native of Hanover, who had come to America in the same vessel with Mr. Kloker. They married soon after landing in Beardstown. She is the only member of her family in this country. After the death of her husband, Mrs. Kloker was married again to Fred Wedeking, who had come on the same vessel and at the same time as Mr. Kloker. After her second marriage they lived in Beardstown until 1844, when they settled on a farm southeast of Beardstown, and there Mrs. Wedeking died, December 25, 1857, aged forty-two. Mr. Wedeking died there also in 1887, aged seventy-six. He and his wife were good Lutherans, and very honest people.

After the death of his father, Louis was carefully reared by his mother and stepfather, and since their death he has been taking care of himself. Mr. Kloker formerly lived in township 17, range 12. He has made the most of his property by his own efforts, and now owns 280 acres, which is highly improved, and has upon it good farm buildings. He also owns forty acres in timber land.

He was married in this county to Mrs. Minnie Yost, *nee* Scheide. She was born in Prussia, in 1833, and came to Cass county, Illinois, with her mother. Her father died in Germany, in the prime of life. After they had come to this country they first settled in St. Louis, and there Miss Scheide was first married. She outlived all her husbands, and died at the home of her daughter, Mrs. Kloker, May 20, 1888. She was born February 8, 1794, and hence was ninety-four years of age: she was a strong, stout woman all her life. She and her people were Lutherans.

Mr. and Mrs. Kloker are working members of the St. Peter's Lutheran Church, near Arenzville, of which he has been Trustee for some years. For thirty years he has been active in school work in the township. In politics he is a Republican. They are parents of six children: Henry, farming on the home place; John A., a farmer in this county; Edward, also a farmer in this county; Lena, wife of William F. Duval, a farmer of this county; Herman and Fred are at home on the farm.

Mrs. Kloker had three children by a former marriage with Ernest F. Yost, formerly a successful farmer of this county, and a native of Germany. They are. Mary, wife of Ernest J. Boes, now of Beardstown; Louisa, wife of Henry H. Meyer, a family in this county; and Minnie, deceased, dying at the age of thirty-two, after her marriage with Henry W Meyer.

JOHN SANDIDGE, one of the most intelligent and prosperous farmers of Oakland township, Schuyler county, was born in the State of Kentucky in 1829 His father, Daniel Sandidge, was a native of Virginia, born in 1804; there he married Pamelia Tate, born in the same place in 1803. The paternal grandfather of our subject, John Sandidge was a Virginian by birth; he married a native of Virginia, and in an early day removed to Kentucky, settling in Lincoln county, he became a wealthy planter, owning a large number of slaves. They had a family of nine sons and four daughters Daniel, Clayton, Joshua, James, Larkin, John, Wyatt, Madison, Pullum, Emily, Patience, Amanda, and Leanta, all grew to adult age and had families excepting Emily, who died in early childhood. The father met with death by accident, his team running away and throwing him from the carriage. He was an octogenarian, and his wife died seven years later, nearly eighty years old. The eldest son, Daniel Sandidge, removed from Kentucky to Illinois in 1831, bringing his wife and five children, they first located at Canton, and removed thence to Industry township, McDonough county; here Mr. Sandidge took up 160 acres of Government land which he improved for two years, selling it at the end of that time; he moved to Eldorado township and bought a claim to 160 acres, on which he lived until 1840, he again sold, and purchased another tract of the same number of acres, and lived on this until 1850, when he sold and bought 160 acres in Oakland township, Schuyler county

His wife died in Eldorado township, at the age of forty-two years, leaving a family of ten children. He married a second time, the union being to Cynthia Phillips, who bore him a daughter and son He died in 1882, aged seventy-eight years; the wife died in June, 1891, at the age of eighty-four years The surviving members of this family are named as follows: Lucy J., John, Mrs. Jonah Lindsey, Harriet, wife of Elisha Goruch, Mrs Nathan Lindsey, Daniel, Charles, Larkin, Ellen, wife of Mike McCarty.

John Sandidge, our worthy subject, was reared to the life of a farmer, but in his twenty-first year left home and went to California; the trip across the plains proved a very enjoyable as well as novel one, and he spent ten years in the Golden State, engaged in mining and raising live-stock In 1860 he returned to Illinois via the Isthmus, remained one month, and then went back to California In 1871 he came home via the Union Pacific route, the object of this visit being to claim his bride

He was married November 19, 1871, to Miss Emma Stockton, and they returned to California by rail It proved a pleasant trip for her, and Mr Sandidge sold his interests there, and came back to Illinois in 1873. He has lived much of his time since 1873 in Vermont, Illinois, where he owns a pleasant home He bought a farm of 400 acres recently, and owns 200 acres in McDonough county. Mr and Mrs Sandidge have one son and a daughter· John F. is nineteen and Ida

Leah is fifteen; both are receiving excellent educational advantages. The son has a decided taste for agriculture, and intends making that his life occupation. Mr. Sandidge had the severe misfortune of losing his sight in 1882, the cause being brought about by his becoming overheated

Mrs Stockton, mother of Mrs. Sandidge, is now eighty-five years of age, but is bright and vigorous; she is a native of Fayette county, Pennsylvania, but came to Illinois in 1839; she was married to Daniel Stockton in 1842, he died in January, 1883, aged eighty-three years She well remembers the first steamer of the Ohio river, named the Adventure, and relates many interesting anecdotes of early days.

Mr Sandidge is a Prohibitionist, but in former days was a Democrat, casting his vote for Horace Greeley, whom he esteemed one of the greatest men and most gifted writers He carries on a general farming business, but makes a specialty of raising live-stock, giving his preference to short-horn cattle He plants from forty to seventy acres of corn, gathering as high as eighty bushels to the acre; he sows from thirty to seventy acres of wheat, but one of his practices is the rotation of crops, and he seeds to clover every third year. He is a man of good, sound judgment, and has made a marked success of every industry to which he has turned his attention

COLUMBUS T WALKER, of Virginia precinct, is a native of Fauquier county, Virginia, born May 12, 1838. His parents were Solomon and Emma (Wilkins) Walker Both were natives of Virginia, father born in 1804, and the mother four years later They removed to Cass county, Illinois, in 1855, and located on a farm near Virginia; here they both died, the mother in 1881, and the father in 1890. They had nine children William W., Darius N., Peter L., Columbus T., Mary F., Churchill A., David T, Jennie E and James T

Columbus T. was nineteen years old when he came to this county, and has resided here ever since. He attended the schools in this precinct after arriving in the county He first learned the tanner trade, and also learned to be a leather dresser, but did not follow the business after leaving Virginia. He has been a farmer all his life He has a farm of 100 acres, on which he has excellent improvements. He is a Republican in politics, although all his brothers are Democrats He has held all the township offices, and has been School Director for fifteen years, also Road Commissioner and Judge of Election, etc. He is a member of the Presbyterian Church, of which he is a Deacon, having held that office for twenty years He is a member of the I. O. O F, and has been since 1859, and now is a Past Grand of Saxon Lodge, No 68.

He was married in Cass county, February 8, 1866, to Emma J Angier, a native of Cass county, born October 10, 1846. Her parents were Addison G. and Annie E. (Wilson) Angier of Ohio. They were among the earliest settlers in Cass county: mother is still living in the county, but father died April 7, 1890.

Mrs. Walker died March 16, 1889, leaving seven children She was aged forty-two at her death The children are: Ella G, born December, 1865, married Edward Tink, and died in 1892, leaving two children; Edward A, born in December, 1868, married and resides in Kansas City; Hattie M., born May, 1871, married Charles Etchison, and resides in Virginia precinct; Louie F., born August,

1875; Charles H., born April, 1878; George R., born April, 1881, and Dollie, born March, 1884. He married for his second wife, Mrs. Leona Walker. She was a native of Cass county, and the daughter of George and Permelia (Freeman) Arenat. Mrs. Walker is a member of the Christian Church.

Mr. Walker is a man of representative type,—a distinction among his fellows attained by his honest, straightforward business methods and fine social qualities. His successes in life justly merit for him the approbation of business associates and competitors, and from the same source he receives warm sympathy for the late reverses which in a degree have temporarily checked his usual flourishing condition.

JOHN F. HUSS, general farmer and stock raiser in section 1, township 17, range 11, has entire charge of his father's homestead of more than 300 acres of fine land, under good improvement. The buildings are large and comfortable, and the place is well stocked. Mr. Huss has had the place under his personal control for nearly three years, and has shown himself to be a very successful farmer. He was born in this county, May 27, 1866. He was reared and has always lived on the farm where he was born. He received his education in the country schools. He is the fourth son of Christian Huss, who was born in Germany, of German parentage, and came to the United States alone. Mr. Huss, Sr., emigrated to this country in the '50s, settling in Beardstown. He purchased two other farms before he obtained his present homestead. The latter he conducted himself, until the spring of 1889. He is now about sixty years of age, hale and hearty, has made all of his large property since he has come to this country. He is a member of the Lutheran Church, and a stanch Democrat. (For further family history, see biography of C. J. Huss.)

Our subject is one of nine children, seven of whom are still living. Mr. Huss, of this notice, was married in this county to Miss Minnie Buck, born in this county, in 1868, daughter of Jasper J. Buck. (See biography of Mr. Buck for history.) She has no family, is a very smart, intelligent woman, and is one of the kind women of the community, and is so known everywhere. She and her husband are popular young people, and highly respected by all their neighbors. Mr. Huss takes quite an interest in local politics, and it may be predicted that he will be elected by the Democratic party to fill many of the offices of the county.

ALFRED M. THOMPSON, a farmer and stock raiser of township 17 north, range 11 west, section 36, Virginia post office, was born on the farm where he now lives, February 27, 1850. His parents were Oswell and Elizabeth (Henderson) Thompson. Both were born near Chillicothe, Ohio, the father in 1806, and the mother, September 22, 1813. They came to Illinois with their parents in the same year, 1827. The father's parents located on the farm which Alfred now owns, and the mother's people located near Arcadia, Illinois. They were married here, in 1829. They had eight children: Ada, wife of I. J. Swibling, a well-to-do farmer and stock raiser near Ashland, Illinois; Mrs. Mary J. Black, the eldest, resides in Virginia; she has been married twice, her first husband being Mace Skiles; W.

Howard resides in Jacksonville, Illinois, and runs a feed and sale stable; he also owns a fine tract of land near that of the subject, Sarah Ellen married Jacob Epler, who died soon after, and she married Mr Andrew App, her home is now at Seattle, Washington, where she married her second husband; she is now in Europe; Alfred; David; Albert and Abigail; the two latter deceased, the former in childhood, the latter in middle life, leaving a family. The youngest of the family is the first child mentioned, Ada

Alfred was reared and educated in his native county, and at the State Normal School, which he attended two years He returned home and resumed farming.

He was married in this county, September 10, 1872, to Meranda L Payne, daughter of W B. and Esther (Stevenson) Payne, natives of Kentucky, where Mrs Thompson was born June 25, 1854. They have had five children: Howard, born in 1876, died in 1883, from scarlet fever; David, born in 1878, at home, Nellie died at the age of three months; Edith, born in 1881, at home, Everett, born in North Dakota, and died in infancy

In the spring of 1883, Mr Thompson leased his farm and went to Bismarck, North Dakota, for the purpose of recuperating his health There he remained seven years, returning in a greatly improved condition He again took possession of the farm upon which he was born, and still operates it with hired assistance. He owns a fine farm of part timber and part prairie, upon which he has made many improvements He lives in the house in which he was born, which is in a good condition and is a building that does credit to the neighborhood.

Mr. Thompson is a Democrat in politics, and has been School Director and Road Commissioner Served one year as County Assessor of Burley county, North Dakota, resigning that office when he decided to return to Illinois, two years ago He and his wife are members of the Methodist Episcopal Church, in which he takes a deep interest, and also in the Sunday-school work, and he subscribes liberally to the support of same.

The Thompson family were among the first settlers in the county Few indeed can go back as they, in their residence here The family were of German origin, though long since established in America

Mr. Thompson owns 800 acres of land in Burley, North Dakota, which he rents, has 320 acres of wheat on it this year (1892), he furnishing the seed and receiving one-half of the threshed grain

GEORGE GREER was born near Five-mile town, county Tyrone, Ireland, August 1, 1814 His father was also a native of Ireland and was named Robert. The grandfather, George Greer, it is thought, was born on the same farm, and all were of Scotch ancestry. The grandfather was a farmer by occupation, and was also a prominent contractor of public works and improvements. He passed away in his native county. His wife, whose maiden name was Jane Martin, was born in county Fermanagh, and was also of Scotch stock Both were members of the Methodist Church The grandfather was an eccentric but able man, with independent views, and erected a stone church in his own yard.

The father of our subject was also a farmer and a successful contractor and spent his entire life on the farm where he was born His wife was Catherine Lendrum, who was born in the same locality, and was the daughter of

John and Elizabeth (Erskine) Lendrum, also of the same county and also of Scotch descent. The Erskines were very prominent people, not only in Ireland but in England also, where they were connected by ties of blood with nobility and royalty, and boasted a coat of arms, a motto, and an honored name. Both the parents of our subject were Methodists. The mother came to America at the age of forty-six years, and passed her last days at her home in Rushville. She reared a large family of thirteen children as follows: George, John, Elizabeth, Jane, Joseph, James, Robert, Eleanor, Erskine, Lendrum, Lucinda, Andrew and Alexander. All the members of this family were born in Ireland, and our subject was the first to cross the ocean, sailing from Derry on the 14th of April, 1832, in the vessel William Ewing, and landing in Philadelphia on the 7th of June.

When our subject reached Philadelphia he was a stranger and in limited circumstances. He soon found employment in that city, but the cholera broke out with great violence, whereupon he went to Lancaster county and engaged in farming, and there resided until the 13th of February, 1836, when he went by stage to Pittsburg, thence down the Ohio by the steamer Ben Bolt (her first trip), and up the Mississippi and Illinois rivers to Beardstown. Soon afterward he located at Rushville, and for some time was engaged in exploring the surrounding country. In the fall of 1836 he returned to Pennsylvania, and in July, 1837, again came to Rushville, where he has since resided. For many years he was a successful merchant and was associated in business with Thomas Wilson, but is now retired. He has been one of the most substantial and upright of Rushville's business men.

On the 6th of April, 1837, he was united in marriage to Miss Ann J. Clark, a native of Lancaster county, Pennsylvania. Her parents were John and Eleanor (Greer) Clark. Mr. and Mrs. Greer have two children living, Susanna and Almira D. The former is the wife of Henry Brown, and has three living children: Olie, Eleanor and Lynn; Almira is the wife of Edwin P. McClure, and has two children, George H. and Margaret M. Mr. and Mrs. Greer are Methodists, and he is a straight Republican.

JESSE WIGHT, farmer of township 17, range 10 west, Little Indian post office, was born in Delaware county, New York, February 13, 1828. His parents were Harvey and Judith (Jenkins) Wight—father born in New Jersey and the mother near Bunker Hill, Massachusetts. Both died the same week in New York State. Of a family of twelve, Jesse was the second youngest. The family has been scattered, some to Michigan, others to Pennsylvania and one to Illinois.

Jesse came to Beardstown on May 1, 1846, and hired out to work on a farm in this precinct, where he continued to work in that way for four or five years. He then rented land for several years, and about thirty years ago purchased his first real estate in Illinois. He was raised and educated in New York, and left there at twenty-two. Mr. Wight, by industry and economy, has accumulated a snug property, where he now lives in comparative ease. He owns a fine farm of 107 acres in a good state of cultivation, and raises grain and stock. Mr. Wight has never seen any of his father's relations, and hence knows but little of his family's genealogy.

He was married here in 1851, to Margaret Taylor, of Montgomery county, Ohio, who was born in 1826. Mr. and Mrs. Wight have eight children: Abigail, the eldest, married Taylor Berry, and lives in Morgan county; William is a farmer and lives in Nebraska, where also lives John I.; Amos Harvey lives on his father's farm; Lizzie J. Parker is now a widow and resides at home with her father; Mollie is still unmarried and lives at home. Mr. and Mrs. Wight are members of the Presbyterian Church, and Mr. Wight is a member of the Republican party. He has held various positions of trust in the precinct.

Amos Harvey, the youngest son of the above, now managing his father's farm, was born in this precinct, February 14, 1859. He grew to manhood on the farm and attended the public schools. He was a farmer one year in Dakota and was otherwise employed there for one year. He was also one season in Nebraska, herding cattle and running a threshing machine.

He was married, January 15, 1891, to Ollie Gilpin, born in Morgan county, Illinois, June 9, 1871. Her parents were James and Becky Gilpin. Her father was a soldier during the late war and is a pensioner. Mr. and Mrs. Wight have one child, Nettie May, born January 9, 1892. Mrs. Wight died at their home August 24, 1892. Mr. Wight is a member of the I. O. O. F., and in politics is a Republican.

SAMUEL E. ELLIS, a citizen of Littleton township, is so closely identified with the history of Schuyler county that this volume would not be complete were an outline of his career omitted from its pages. He was born in Oakland township, Schuyler county, Illinois, April 30, 1846, a son of James and Nancy (Harmon) Ellis.

James Ellis was a native of Mason county, Kentucky, a son of Elijah and Phœbe (Payton) Ellis, natives of Virginia; his parents emigrated to Kentucky at an early day and engaged in agricultural pursuits; later they came to Illinois, where they passed the remaider of their days; both lived to be eighty-four years of age. Their son, James, was reared to the occupation of a farmer, and in 1844 he came to Illinois and settled on the land where Samuel E. was born; he purchased a quarter section for $1,200, and undertook the task of placing it under cultivation; there were few improvements, and the dwelling was a small log-cabin; this furnished them shelter four years, when a frame building was erected, in which Mr. Ellis lived until he passed from this life at the age of seventy-seven years. Politically he supported the Republican party, and took an active part in local affairs; he was Assessor and Collector, and a member of the School Board for many years. He was one of the leading members of the Christian Church, and did the work of a pioneer in the cause of Christianity. He and Simon Doyle were Trustees of the society. Mr. Ellis was twice married: his first wife, Nancy Harmon, bore him seven children, of whom Samuel E. is the youngest; she was born in Bracken county, Kentucky, and died in Schuyler county, Illinois, at the age of thirty-four years. Her parents, Samuel and Elizabeth Harmon, were natives of Kentucky, and passed their lives in the Blue-grass State. The Harmon family is of German descent, and the Ellis family is of Scotch lineage.

Samuel E. Ellis had superior educational advantages in his youth, and made the most of his opportunities; he attended the district school, and was a student at Abingdon College, Knox county, Illinois, after which he entered the teacher's profession, which he followed for more than twenty years. He was united in marriage to one of his pupils, March 12, 1874; her maiden name was Julia E. Jones, a native of this county, and a daughter of James W. and Harriet E. Jones; her parents removed from Ohio to Illinois in 1854, and settled in Schuyler county at Pleasant View; the father died at the age of fifty-nine years, but the mother still survives; they had born to them a family of ten children, only three of whom are living. The father and a son, George W., were soldiers in the late war, and died of disease contracted while in the service.

Mr. Ellis enlisted in Company K, One Hundred and Thirty-seventh Illinois Volunteer Infantry, in 1864, and re-enlisted in February, 1865, in Company I, One Hundred and Fifty-fifth Illinois Volunteer Infantry. Although the period of his service was comparatively short he was in many important engagements, and at Memphis lost an ear; he receives a small pension, which is totally inadequate, in consideration of the injury received.

The family of Mr. and Mrs. Ellis consists of eight children: Jessie H., Lulu M., Laura G., Emma Z., Fannie L., Anna Belle, Ida M. and Carrie B.; Virgil died in infancy. The parents are members of the Christian Church, and since 1867 Mr. Ellis has been an Elder of the same; for twelve years he has been superintendent of the Sabbath-school. He and Simon Doyle were the principals and furnished most of the money to build the Christian Church in 1871–'72 He is a member of Colonel Horney Post, G. A. R., and has been an active worker in the organization for years; he belongs to Lodge No. 24, I. O. O. F. Politically he adheres to the principles of the Republican party, and cast his first vote for General Grant's first term. He was once elected Justice of the Peace, but did not serve.

In 1888 he purchased the farm on which he now lives with his family; the tract contains over 200 acres, and is one of the most desirable in the township. Of late years Mr. Ellis has abandoned the profession of teaching, having made an admirable record as an educator. He now devotes his time to agricultural pursuits, and is meeting with gratifying success.

WILLIAM T. PRICE, a progressive farmer of Virginia precinct, Cass county, Illinois, was born in Morgan county, same State, November 6, 1840.

His parents were Adam and Susan (Rosenberger) Price, both of German descent, and natives of Rockingham county, Virginia, where they lived to maturity and were married. In 1833 they removed to Morgan county, Illinois, where the father entered and improved a large tract of Government land. In 1852 they moved to Virginia precinct, Cass county, where they settled on a farm on which they passed the remainder of their lives. The greatly esteemed and lamented father passed away February 1, 1875, his worthy wife surviving him until September, 1881. They, with five infant children, are interred in Bethlehem cemetery, the ground of which was donated by them for a public burial place. They were both devout Christians, who rendered valuable service for many years to the Methodist Episcopal Church, in which the father filled, at different times, all the offices ever conferred on lay members. "Uncle Adam," as he was familiarly known, was a person of marked individuality and strong convictions, whose sterling integrity and earnest advocacy of all principles of justice won for him many friends where he was so well known. Of their twelve children, seven attained maturity, six now living (1892) John W., the eldest son, is a large landowner in Wilson county, Kansas He married Maria Ganse, an estimable lady, and both are prominent in church and social circles. William T., whose name heads this biography, is the next in order of birth, Anna Eliza married James V. Rawlings, a prosperous farmer of Virginia precinct; Adam C is a successful farmer of Douglas county, Illinois; Mary E. married Charles E Strickler, of Sibley, Iowa; Amanda J, unmarried, resides in Virginia, and Sarah E, the youngest, married Alfred Griffin, of Nokomis, Illinois, and died in 1885

The subject of this sketch spent his boyhood and early manhood on his father's farm and obtained a rudimentary education in the public schools. Amid these rural, peaceful scenes, he passed his time in the companionship of parents and friends until he attained his majority, when this happy state was rudely broken by the discordant notes of war. With youthful enthusiasm and patriotism, he enlisted in Company D, One Hundred and Fourteenth Illinois Volunteer Infantry for three years He participated, with his command in the siege of Vicksburg and in many of the numerous battles which occurred in and around that almost invulnerable stronghold. In the engagement at Guntown, Mississippi, his regiment suffered severely, many being killed or wounded, while the remainder, including the subject of this notice, were captured and incarcerated in the prison at Andersonville, where Mr Price was confined four months He was eventually transferred to Millen, Georgia, via Savannah, that State; and; a month later, was sent to Florence, South Carolina, arriving there November 28, and remaining there until February of the following year He was then sent, with other prisoners, to Richmond, Virginia, there paroled and sent North, and on arriving in St Louis was granted thirty days' furlough. When in prison, Mr. Price gladly exchanged a valuable watch for an old, ragged blanket, considering it one of the best trades of his life. He was in the prison at Andersonville when five comrades were hung for stealing from their mates, whom they murdered to conceal their theft A court, organized from among the prisoners, passed sentence on them and witnessed the execution It was also while he was in prison that the "Providence" spring burst forth, originating as it by magic and yielding to the famishing prisoners an abundant supply of cold water of clearest crystal

On the expiration of his furlough, he returned to Montgomery, Alabama, and three weeks later the war closed and he returned to his home, resuming the duties which had been interrupted three years before

On December 29, 1870, he was married to Augusta R, daughter of William and Elizabeth (Clutch) Marshall, pioneers of Cass county, James Marshall, her grandfather, having located in the county as early as 1825. Her father was of Scotch descent; while her mother was of Welsh ancestry, who emigrated to America in Colonial times, was in Waynesville, Ohio, and reared a Quakeress Her father entered and improved the land on which Mr. Price's house now stands, while the beautiful, towering, maple trees which adorn the place are attractive memorials of his taste and enterprise, being planted half a century ago by his hands. This was his home until death, when his widow and three children removed to Jacksonville, this State, where Mrs. Price was married. Her mother remained there until her death in 1874. In 1883, Mr. Price was called upon to mourn the death of his wife, which occurred on the old homestead.

tural pursuits.

ex perience, Mr. Price has followed agricul-

With the exception of his three years' war

Politically he affiliates with the Republican party. Religiously, he is an earnest member of the Methodist Episcopal church, and contributes liberally to the advancement of that and all other worthy objects.

JAMES A. DAVIS, farmer and stock-grower, post office, Virginia, Illinois, was born one and one-half miles south of Ashland, Cass county, Illinois, October 29, 1824. His parents, James and Elizabeth (Foster) Davis came to Cass county in 1822. The father settled on Indian creek, where he improved a little farm, which he afterward lost by another man "entering him out." He was born in Kentucky in 1796, coming here from Monroe county, and died, March 6, 1856, in this county. Mother was born in Cumberland county, Tennessee, in 1800, and is still living. She resides with her son George, who owns the old homestead in township 17, range 11. She was the mother of fourteen children, eight of whom are still living. Mr. and Mrs. Davis, Sr, moved from Ashland to the place where the mother now lives, when James, Jr., was four years old. Here he grew to manhood, was taught in the subscription schools of that day and was reared a farmer. At twenty years of age he learned the house carpenter trade which he followed until seven years ago. He worked five years in Beardstown, afterward returned to his home neighborhood, where he worked fifteen years inside five miles of his home, and was never out of a job.

He was married in Beardstown in 1849, to Martha A., daughter of Philip Schaeffer, a farmer who had come from Montgomery, Ohio, in 1832. Her birth was September 16, 1830. Mr. Davis has witnessed a wonderful development in Cass county during his sixty-eight years' residence here. His first memory of the country is as a vast wilderness, the settlers few and far between, with only occasionally a horse-power mill where the farmers had their grists ground by turns, often remaining all day to get one sack of corn ground. Mr. Davis has seen men reaping wheat on ground which is now covered with heavy timber, the early settlers preferring to clear up the timber land, some of which has since gone back to its primitive state. Mr. and Mrs. Davis have six children: Minerva, wife of Richard Way, residing in Cass county; Valentine, residing in Butler county, Nebraska, a farmer: Sarah Ellen, who wedded A. C. Robinson, living near Virginia, Illinois; James Philo, residing three miles south of Virginia; Cyrus Edward resides six miles east of the same place, and Charles L., a farmer living in Douglas county, Illinois. On July 21, 1884, Mr. Davis suffered the loss of his estimable wife, to whom he had been married thirty-eight years. A glowing tribute to her memory, as a lady of great worth, appears in a clipping in the local paper, in which appears the action of the I. O. O. F. lodge in the premises, of which she and her husband were valued members. She was a worthy member of the

Union Baptist Church. Mr. Davis was married to his second wife, Mrs. Elizabeth Smith, March 16, 1887. Her maiden name was Thompson, and she was born in Ohio in 1840, They are both members of the Union Baptist Church, in Virginia, and takes an active interest in Sunday-school and church work. He is a member of Saxon Lodge, No. 68, I. O. O. F., and of Advance Encampment, both located at Virginia. He has held various official positions in this town. He voted the Democrat ticket until the nomination of Tilden, when he voted the Greenback ticket for several years, but is now a Prohibitionist and has always advocated temperance and sobriety, and the legal control of the liquor traffic. He joined the Sons of Temperance in 1849, and has worked for the cause all his life. He uses neither tobacco nor liquor, and is one of the representative men of Cass county, and his family is one of the first established here.

WILLIAM I. LARASH, editor and proprietor of the Rushville *Citizen*, a weekly newspaper devoted to the interests of the people, is a native of Pennsylvania, born at Allentown, Lehigh county, October 2, 1851. His father, Isaac Larash, was also a native of the Keystone State, and his grandfather was descended from the French Huguenots; the latter was a planter by occupation, and passed his life in Pennsylvania; the father learned the tailor's trade, and carried on that business at Catasauqua, Pennsylvania; thence he removed to Illinois in 1852, and followed his trade in this State for several years. He finally purchased a farm in Spring Lake township, Tazewell county, and still resides there. He married Esther Ann Kildare, a native of Pennsylvania, who still survives. They are the parents of nine children: John, Elizabeth, Lucinda, William I., Mary, Charles, George, I., Addie M. and Walter. Our subject was the infant when the family began their life upon the frontier. He was reared and educated in Pekin, Tazewell county, and at the age of fourteen years went to learn the printer's trade; he served an apprenticeship of two years in the *Republican* office, never losing a half day's time. In 1869 he went to Omaha, and there found employment in a job and commercial printing office; this occupied him four or five months, and then he made a journey to the plains on a buffalo hunt. He was next located in Nebraska, where he followed his trade for a time; thence he went to St. Louis, and then home. He devoted some time to agriculture, and afterwards returned to his trade; he was on the Peoria *Review* until the paper changed hands. Then, with three other printers and two editors, one of whom was R. J. Burdette, he assisted in the founding of a paper which was named the Peoria *Evening Review*; an injunction was served upon them, and the name was changed to the Peoria *Injunction*. Mr. Larash was connected with with this paper a short time, and then was in different cities until 1875, when he came to Rushville, and took charge of the *Citizen* office. In 1879 he purchased the entire outfit with the good will of the paper, and has since managed its publication. He has a job-office in connection, and has won a wide patronage.

Mr. Larash was married March 21, 1878, to Emilia Ann Horney who was born in Littleton township, Schuyler county, Illinois, July 16, 1857, a daughter of Lenodias and Jane (Crawford) Horney. To them three children have been born: Lenodias H., Lizzie H. and

Winnie J. Politically, Mr. Larash affiliates with the Republican party, and was a delegate to the State Convention in 1880. He is a member of Rushville Lodge, No. 9, A. F. & A. M., Rushville Chapter, No. 184, R. A. M., and to Rushville Commandery, No. 56, K. T. He and his wife are earnest members of the Methodist Episcopal Church, joining that society in 1877, since which time he has been a Class-leader.

WILLIAM A. WAY, farmer and stock-grower, section 6, range 10, township 17, post office, Virginia, was born in Morgan county, Illinois, October 5, 1842 He was the son of Jesse and Melinda (Guin) Way, early settlers in Morgan county. The father came to the county in 1832, and has been a resident of either Morgan or Cass county ever since, and now resides in Virginia city. The mother died in Virginia in 1880, leaving six children: Elizabeth, the eldest, married T. H. Williams and died in Nebraska; Mary died when twelve years of age; Richard is a farmer, residing in Cass county, Virginia precinct; Stephen is the same, and John died at the age of twenty-six years.

William attended the public schools and then learned the carpenter trade, intermingled with farming. He enlisted August 11, 1862, in Company I, One Hundred and Fifteenth Illinois Volunteer Infantry, and was assigned to duty in the army of the Cumberland. A few days after the battle of Chickamauga, while on a scouting expidition, composed of details from the different regiments, he was taken prisoner with several others. He was sent to Richmond, via Atlanta, and was kept there about six weeks, quartered in the Smith building, near Libby prison. He was then taken to Danville, Virginia, kept there five months, and then to Andersonville, where he remained about eight months. From there he was sent to Charleston, and on from there to Florence. At this place he was paroled December 7, 1864, after fourteen months and thirteen days imprisonment. To say that he suffered a thousand deaths during this long confinement is no exaggeration. He was attacked with scurvy while in Andersonville and suffered greatly from that cause. Even to this day his limbs are scarred and measurably deformed. After this he was sent to Annapolis, Maryland, and then home, remaining there three months under treatment. He rejoined the regiment at Shield Mill, and remained there until the end of the war. He was discharged June 11, 1865, and returned to Virginia, Illinois.

He was married December 24, 1868, in Cass county, to Hattie Davis, daughter of Julia Ann and Edward Davis, old settlers of Cass county. Mr. and Mrs. Way have four children: Lenora married D. J. Parkison, a railroad employé; Walter, Linnie and John L. are all under the parental roof.

Mr. Way's grandfather was a soldier in the war of 1812. Mr. Way is independent in politics, voting for men rather than for parties. He is one of the men that a grateful country would delight to honor.

PETER RIGG, a prominent farmer of Missouri township, Brown county, is a native of Anderson county, Kentucky, having been born there, March 11, 1830. His grandfather, also Peter, came from England

and settled in Virginia when it was yet a colony of Great Britain, serving in the Revolutionary war. He resided on the banks of the Potomac river for many years, but finally removed, at an early period, to Bourbon county, Kentucky, and later resided twenty years in Anderson county, Kentucky. From there he removed to Shelby county, Kentucky, where he died. He reared an interesting family of six children, of whom Richard Watson, father of our subject, was the second. Richard was born in Virginia in 1789, and grew to manhood in that State, but was married in Anderson county, Kentucky, to Elizabeth George, a native of Kentucky. Her father came from the Carolinas. This marriage ceremony took place in the early part of 1812. Mrs. Rigg died, and in the fall of 1830 Mr. Rigg married Peggy Utterback. By his first marriage he had two children: William T., an honored citizen of Missouri township; and Sarah, who married Henry Ausmus, but died April 17, 1852. By the second marriage he had seven children: Elizabeth, wife of John B. Ausmus, of Texas; Susan, wife of Joshua P. Singleton, of Missouri township; Eliza J. married James M. Parker and died August 13, 1855; James N. (see sketch;) Margaret, wife of Abner Cogburn, of Hancock county; our subject; and John, who died November 24, 1852.

In the fall of 1831 Mr. Rigg moved from Kentucky to Illinois, first stopping in Morgan county. He then settled in Schuyler county, in that part which is now in Brown county, on section 20, Missouri township. Here he improved a farm, where he resided until his death, October 23, 1869.

Mr. Peter Rigg was reared on a farm until manhood and remained at home until his marriage in 1852, when he was united to Mary E. Clark, daughter of William A. Clark. She was born in Logan county, Kentucky, March 7, 1833.

Mr. Rigg continued to reside on the homestead, of which he became owner. He now has 190 acres of land and carries on mixed farming, to which he has given his entire attention.

Mr. and Mrs. Rigg have had nine children, three of whom grew up. They are: William C., born December 14, 1863, married February 4, 1890, to Nettie Miller, and they have one daughter, Myrtle, born in 1891; Melissa born August 22, 1871, married March 15, 1892, to Eldred Yowell, resides in Monroe county, Missouri; Richard W., born July 8, 1874.

Mr. Rigg is a stanch Democrat in politics and has served his township as School Treasurer and Commissioner of Highways.

He is an old regular Baptist in religion. He has been a hard-working man all his life and richly deserves all the prosperity that he now enjoys.

HENRY C. KROHE, a practical farmer living on a fine farm, a part of the old, Jokisch homestead, was born in Beardstown March 3, 1848. This farm was secured by Henry's grandfather and consists of sixty acres, all well improved with good farm buildings. Mr. Krohe also owns twenty acres more. He has lived on this farm for many years and also operates many other lands. He is the third son of seven children. He obtained his education in the public schools. His father, August Krohe, a native of Germany, was the son of Godfred and Rosena Krohe, and the family all left Germany in 1835 and after a trip of some months landed in New Orleans, and some weeks later in Beardstown.

They obtained land in the valley of Bluff Springs and here the grandparents died when past eighty. They were well known people and good Lutherans. August Krohe came here as a young man with his parents as above noted. He became of age here and a farmer, and is now living at home, having retired from active work. He was married here, to Christiana Jokisch, who came to this country on the same vessel as her husband. She was a worthy wife for more than fifty years and died in April, 1889.

Mr. Henry C. Krohe was married, near his present residence, to Christina Menge a native of Germany, born in 1852. She was only one year old when her parents came to Cass county in 1853. Here the father died fourteen years ago, but the mother is still living. They have always been Lutherans, as are Mr. and Mrs. Krohe of this notice. Mr. Krohe is a Democrat, but has never been an office holder. They have six children: Bertha C., Lydia S., Rosa A., Felix J. A., Paulina W. and Matilda L.

They are excellent people and are connected with some of the best famlies of Beardstown.

JOHN B. WETZEL, of section 5, Browning township, was born within three miles of his present home, July 7, 1843. His parents, Christopher and Sarah (Cook) Wetzel, came to Fulton county, Illinois, in 1836, settling on the farm where the father now lives. He was born in Carlisle, Pennsylvania, in 1813, and in the same year his mother was born in Augusta county, Virginia. The latter died in Fulton county, Illinois, March, 1889. The Wetzel and Cook families were both of German origin.

Mr. Wetzel received his education in the public schools of the district and grew to manhood on the farm and has always been a farmer. He owns 282 acres of land in sections 4 and 5, Browning township. This land is highly improved, his residence, erected in 1888, being a very handsome building of modern architecture. On his south farm he also has a good residence, comfortable surroundings, and he takes pride in his fine stock, and usually purchases from the stock yards in Chicago such cattle as he desires to feed; he also deals in hogs. He markets fruit by the car-load. The entire family are members of the United Brethren denomination and all are active in Sunday-school and church work. He has been a Class-leader and a Sunday-school superintendent for many years.

He was married in Astoria, in December, 1866, to Amanda E. Bryan of Virginia, whose parents, Thomas and Emeline (Lutz) Bryan, removed to Fulton county about 1853. Mr. and Mrs. Wetzel have three children, all living; Nettie F., Willard P. and Ina J., the first two living on the old Wetzel homestead. Ina J. is the wife of William Dean, a farmer, The two daughters have enjoyed the advantages of two years' attendance at the Rushville Normal School taking this after their public-school course, but do not care to teach. Mr. Wetzel is a Republican and has served as member of the County Central Committee. He is active and energetic in political work.

SAMUEL DE COUNTER, one of the largest land-owners in Woodstock township, was born in Brown county, Illinois, October 4, 1827, a son of Peter Frederick and Nancy (Scounts) De Counter. They were married in 1824, near Boon's Lick, Missouri. The father was a native of France, and emigrated to the United States in 1820; five years later he came to Brown county, and the following year brought his family here; he bought land which he converted into a fertile farm, residing upon it until his death at the age of eighty-four years; his wife also died in the county, at an advanced age; she was a Virginian by birth. Two children were born to them: a daughter, now deceased, and the subject of this sketch. Samuel remained at home until he was twelve years old, and then his father married Mary Manser, who died ten years later.

Samuel engaged in driving a peddling wagon until he was twenty-five, and then began his career as a farmer. He has been twice married; his first union was to Miss Catharine Miller, a native of Summit county, Ohio; she died in Brown county at the age of thirty-one years, leaving three children. Frederick is married and the father of five children; Morris L. is married and has seven children; Emma is married and the mother of seven children. Mr. De Counter was married a second time in 1860, to Mas Harriet Stubbs, who was born in Floyd county, May 17, 1826, and was the mother of two children. Her parents, William and Jane (Gailey) Clark, father a native of Kentucky and the mother of Pennsylvania, emigrated to Illinois in 1852, and died in this State at an advanced age; they have ten children, two of whom are now living. By his second marriage Mr. De Counter had one daughter, who died at the age of twenty-one years, leaving one boy, Clarence Southey.

Politically, he adheres to the principles of the Democratic party, but takes no active interest in the movements of that body. He has been one of the most energetic and enterprising of farmers, and has amassed a handsome estate. He has always pursued strictly honorable methods, and has an enviable reputation wherever his name is known.

THOMAS J. CRUM, of Virginia, Illinois, was born within one mile of his present residence, July 9, 1835. He is the eldest living son of James and Christina (Ream) Crum. (Parental history is given in the history of James Crum elsewhere in this book.)

Thomas was raised to manhood on a farm and attended the subscription schools of the neighborhood. He has always lived on the farm given him by his father upon attaining his majority. To this he has added until he now has 450 acres in this farm, besides 800 acres of land in Burleigh county, North Dakota. He has been a resident here for over fifty years and has witnessed wonderful changes in the country. He remembers very well when there was but very little improved land near him. He is a Democrat in politics.

He was married March, 1857, to Miss Sarah A. Henderson, daughter of William and Lucinda Henderson, who were among the early settlers in this, then Morgan county. She was the eldest of twelve children, seven of whom are now living. The mother died in Morgan county and the father in Henry county.

Mr. and Mrs. Crum have had eleven children, nine of whom are still living, namely; Charles, married, operating the Dakota farm; Theresa M., wife of Edward D. Sommers, resides at Colorado Springs, Colorado; Oscar M. is in the publishing business at Jacksonville, Illinois; William S., wholesale grocer in Joliet, Illinois; Ollie, now Mrs. Strong, resides at Winfield, Kansas, husband a farmer; Eben Ross, Mary L., Henry Obed, and Thomas Austin are still at home. A pair of twins died in infancy. The family are members of the Protestant Methodist church. Mr. Crum is an Ancient Odd Fellow, lodge having surrendered its charter during the late war. The Crum family is quite extensively represented in this county, where they are well and favorably known citizens who have by their industry accumulated a comfortable property. The aged father, now in his eighty-sixth year, is one of the solid landmarks of early pioneer days in Cass county.

LEWIS CASS CAMPBELL, a prominent and esteemed resident of Camden village, Illinois, was born on a farm in Camden township, February 23, 1851. His father, John Milton Campbell, was born in Harrison county, Kentucky, March 30, 1807, and was a son of James and Jane (Campbell) Campbell, natives of Scott county, Kentucky. Both of the grandfathers of John Milton Campbell bore the name of Campbell and were born in Scotland, but emigrated to America and died in the Colonies in the decade of 1700. John Milton's maternal grandmother was a Cellers. His maternal uncle, Lindsey Campbell, married a widow by the name of Graham. Her son, Furgerson Graham, died in Schuyler county, Illinois, at the residence of his son-in-law, Singleton Wright, deeply lamented for his many sterling qualities of character. William Campbell, an own cousin of John Milton Campbell, on his father's side, married a sister of Furgerson Graham. John Milton's father, James Campbell, was a skilled mechanic, who passed nearly all of his life in Kentucky, and died in Pendleton county, that State, aged eighty-six years. He was twice married, having by the first marriage five children, and one child by his second. John Milton was the oldest of the family, and his early life was spent on his father's farm. He received a fair education, and, under the instruction of his father, became a good mechanic. He afterward taught school and worked at his trade. He was married in Kentucky, to Ann Lake, and, in 1832, came to Illinois to look over the country. Being favorably impressed, he removed to the latter State in November, 1835. He entered and settled on land located on the southwest quarter of section eight, in Camden township, Schuyler county, where he improved a farm. His health failing in 1845 he passed a few years in the South, afterward returning to his farm. His first wife died in Kentucky, leaving one child, Thomas J. In 1850, Mr. Campbell was again married, his second wife being Miss Mary A. E. Aldrich, of Putnam county, Indiana, born June 8, 1826. She was a daughter of Samuel and Elizabeth (Strupp) Aldrich, natives of North Carolina, of English and German ancestry, respectively. She accompanied her sister to Illinois in 1847, and lived in Schuyler county. John Campbell died December 20, 1880, sincerely mourned by all who knew him. A Democratic in politics, he took an active part in all local affairs of importance. He frequently held office, being elected at various times to all positions in the gift of the county; he served one term as County Surveyor, and for many years as Deputy Surveyor. He was the clerk of his party, and, being a fine penman, the records of the county are remarkable for their neatness and legibility. He was a devout member of the Christian Adventist Church. His worthy wife survives him and resides in Camden. She also is an earnest and useful member of the church to which her husband belonged. This estimable couple were the parents of four children: Lewis, Stephen, James I. and Emma J.

Lewis was reared a farmer and educated in Camden township. After his marriage he resided on the farm of his father-in-law, but upon the death of his wife he returned to his mother's farm and managed it for some years, until 1885, when he married again and settled in Camden village and opened a hotel. He also engaged in farming and the carpenter trade, putting up some of the best buildings in the county, outside of Rushville. He afterward sold the hotel and devoted his attention to his trade. He has 240 acres of land and some valuable property in Camden village. Hard as Mr. Campbell has worked, it is nothing to the privations that his father had to endure. He was the pioneer school teacher of the county, and besides pursuing that occupation he made maple sugar and split rails to get the money with which to enter his land and purchase saddle-bags to carry his surveying tools in. What farmer of to-day has to endure such hardships?

He was married to Alice Callison in 1875, the daughter of John L. and Eliza (Smith) Callison. She was born in 1857, and died April, 1879. Mr. Campbell was again married in 1885, his second wife being Alice L. Irvin, a native of Littleton township and a daughter of Osburn and Martha Irvin. They have had one child, Paul Irvin, born July 26, 1891.

Mr. Campbell is independent in politics, being a supporter of the Farmers' Alliance, and has filled the office of Town Clerk. He is a member of Camden Lodge, No. 648, A. F. & A. M., of which he is Senior Warden. He is also correspondent for the *Rushville Times*, editing the Camden department. He was for many years an active member of the Patrons of Husbandry.

CONRAD MAYREIS, of Beardstown, was born in Hesse-Darmstadt in 1842. His parents lived and died in the same place. He was given a common German schooling and when fifteen years of age came to this country and came on at once to Beardstown, Illinois, having left a sister, Sophia, in New York city, who had been the first of the family to cross the ocean. Sophia has been employed by the same family for the last forty years. Their family is represented by two other sisters, Caroline and Mary and brother John. Mr. Mayreis came here in 1857, learned the trade of boot and shoe maker and followed it until 1861. He then enlisted in Company K, Fourteenth Illinois Volunteers, Captain Reynolds in command, the regiment being known as the Springfield regiment, Colonel Palmer (ex-Governor) in command. Mr. Mayreis served with his regiment as Corporal of his company for two years and three months, in the Army of the Tennessee, and fought in the battles of Fort Donelson, Pittsburg Landing, Corinth, siege of Pittsburg and other minor engagements. He escaped unhurt and received honorable discharge at Vicksburg, Tennessee, and on his return to Beardstown engaged in the boot and shoe business from 1864 to 1886 and in the meantime superintended work on a farm, which he has improved and owns in Cass county. He started his present business of dealer in wines and liquors, in 1885, at the corner of Main and Washington streets and has since connected with it a well kept cafe. He is also agent for the Anheuser-Busch Brewing Company of St. Louis at this place.

He was married in this city to Miss Anna Mooman, who was born at Bielefeld, Germany, in 1844 and came with her parents when she was two years of age to the United States. The family settled at Beardstown where Mr. and Mrs. Mooman both died, being consistent members of the Lutheran Church. Mr. Mayreis is the father of seven children: Frank, a partner in his father's business; Edward, who runs the restaurant; Conrad, at present running the farm; Minnie, wife of E. Rink; Henry, who is at an institute in St. Louis; Louis is at home in the public school; and Maria is also at home. Mr. Mayreis is a sound Republican in politics and has taken an active part in local matters, having an interest in the advancement of the city and county. Mr. and Mrs. Mayreis are leaders among their people and their children have all received a good education. They are all highly respected and admired by their large circle of friends.

JUDGE HERMANN C. SCHULTZ, a highly respected citizen of Schuyler county, Illinois, is an American by adoption, his birth-place being Prussia, Germany; the date, October 2, 1832. His father, Johannes Schultz, was a native of the same country, and was engaged in the sugar refining business: he married Elizabeth Felech, a native of Germany, who survived him many years; she emigrated to America in 1852, and spent the last days of her life in Texas; he died in 1846, and she passed away in 1858. Hermann Schultz was reared and educated in his native land, and at the age of fifteen years went to learn the baker's trade; having served an apprenticeship of three years, he worked as a journeyman in different cities for two years; at the end of that time he sailed from Hamburg for America, and after a voyage of two months, arrived in Galveston, Texas. He was employed with various occupations in that State until 1857, and in that year came to Schuyler county, Illinois. He rented land until 1862, and in August of that year he enlisted in the One Hundred and Eighth Illinois Volunteer Infantry, and served until the declaration of peace. He participated in the battles of Vicksburg and Arkansas Post, was at the siege and capture of Vicksburg, and also took part in the engagement at Spanish Fort. He was mustered in as a private, but was discharged as First Sergeant, in August, 1865. He then returned to his home and resumed his agricultural pursuits, which he continued until he was elected to the office of Judge of the Probate Court, of Schuyler county.

In 1854, Judge Schultz was united in marriage to Anna Heidenreich, a native of Saxe-Weimar, and a daughter of Adam Heidenreich; the father emigrated to the United States with his family, in 1851, and in 1857 he came to Schuyler county, Illinois, where he passed his last days. Judge and Mrs. Schultz are the parents of nine children: Hermann H., Charles S., Julius C., Callie, Laura, Emma, Ferdinand, Nellie and Peter. Charles S., Laura and Nellie are deceased. The Judge and his wife are members of the Methodist Episcopal Church, and he is also a member of Schuyler Lodge, No. 209, K. of P., and of Astoria Lodge, No. 100, A. F. & A. M. Politically, he affiliates with the Democratic party, and is an ardent supporter of its principles. He has served twenty years as Justice of the Peace, and ten years as a member of the County Board of Supervisors. He was elected to his present office in 1890, and has discharged the duties devolving upon him with a wisdom and justice that have dispelled all doubt as to his ability. He has been a liberal contributor to all movements tending to advance the county's interests, and is numbered among her most loyal citizens.

WILLIAM ANTHONY CLARK, the subject of this brief sketch, was born in Logan county, Kentucky, February 16, 1811. His ancestors were residents of North and South Carolina, his father having been born in Orange county, North Carolina, August, 1770, his early home being not far from Guilford Court House, and he could hear the cannon during the battle at that place. He often referred to that incident in later life. After the battle a division of the British army encamped near his mother's house, for several days. His mother was unprotected as her husband had died when Thomas, the father of subject, was five years old. Thomas was reared in North Carolina, and, braving the dangers of the wilderness, he crossed to Kentucky, settling in Logan county, about 1795. Here he married Mary Anthony, daughter of Philip Anthony, pioneer of Kentucky. Here Thomas Clark lived until the fall of 1839, when he came to Illinois, and settled in Missouri township, where he died in 1847.

W. A. Clark was one of a family of thirteen children, being the third. His boyhood was passed in Logan county, Kentucky, where he attended the schools of seventy years ago, which were only provided with benches of split logs, heated by a fire-place, and lighted by windows of greased paper. This gentleman was married, April, 1832, to Mehala Roberts, daughter of John Roberts. She was born in Maryland, but reared in Washington county, Virginia.

Mr. and Mrs. Clark resided in Logan county, Kentucky, until 1837, and three children were born to them there. They then came to Illinois, and rented land for one year, then entered eighty acres in Pea Ridge township, but five years later settled in Missouri township, on section 17, and with his two sons became the owner of 600 acres of fine land in the aforesaid section. Mr. Clark was a member of the Presbyterian Church, having joined it in 1833. He voted for Henry Clay, but afterward became a Democrat in politics. Mr. Clark was a poor man when he came to Illinois, but by his earnest endeavors and hard work he managed to accumulate a large fortune.

John Thomas Clark, the son of the above mentioned gentleman, is one of the prosperous farmers of Missouri township, residing on section 17. He was born in Pea Ridge township, June 12, 1844. The family removed to Missouri township about 1850, settling on section 17, where the father accumulated a large farm, dying December 16, 1890, while his wife died June 10, 1875. John is one of five children, namely: Mary E., wife of Peter Rigg; Sarah J., wife of J. M. Parker; Martha, wife of T. B. Ansmus, of Camp Point; William N.; and John, who is the youngest of the family. He was reared on the home farm until he attained his majority, when he became a partner with his father. They bought land and carried on farming, cultivating about 300 acres of land. John now owns 255 acres of land, on which he has a fine class of farm buildings. He carries on farming and deals in stock.

Mr. Clark was married, October 24, 1870, to Amanda Carter, daughter of John B. and Elizabeth (Bell) Carter, born in Brown county, January 3, 1851. John B. Carter, the father of Mrs. Clark, was born in Tennessee, and was a son of Joseph Carter. They came to Illinois in 1830, and first stopped in Brown county, but Joseph Carter later removed to McDonough county, where he died. His son John grew to manhood, and was married in Brown county, and had one child, but it died in infancy. He later married Elizabeth Bell, and settled in Lee township, Brown county. He then removed to Clayton, Adams county, where he enlisted, and was mustered into service in the Eighty-fourth Illinois Volunteer Infantry, Company I, serving three years. After the war he resided in Brown county, until 1869, when he removed to Crawford county, Kansas, where he died in 1872. His wife also died, in Kansas, in 1883. He and his wife had seven children, of whom Mrs. Clark was the eldest.

Mr. and Mrs. Clark have three children: Daisy, Arthur A. and Oliver B. Mr. Clark is a strong Democrat, and a member of the Masonic fraternity. He and his charming wife are among the most prominent people of their township, and enjoy the respect of all who knew them.

ELIAS D. LEACH, M. D., deceased, for many years one of the prominent citizens of Rushville and a leading member of the medical profession, was born near Youngstown, Ohio, March 26, 1823, a son of Benjamin and Hannah (Raynor) Leach, pioneers of Mahoning county, Ohio. His father died when he was two years old, so that as he advanced in years he was obliged to make all the opportunities that he enjoyed; when he had received a sufficient education he engaged in teaching, and soon turned his attention to the study of medicine; his leisure time was fully occupied in this pursuit, and he finally entered the office of Dr. Packard, of West Greenville, Pennsylvania. In 1844 he became a student in the Medical Department of the Western Reserve College at Cleveland, Ohio. He studied and taught alternately, securing the means with which to carry on his own education, and had the gratification of receiving a diploma in 1848.

Dr. Leach came directly to Illinois, and for a short time practiced in Virginia, Cass county; thence he removed to Frederick, Schuyler county, where he resided until 1853. In that year he came to Rushville, and embarked in mercantile trade, as a member of the firm of Little, Ray & Co.; this relationship continued until 1863, when the Doctor withdrew, and devoted his entire time to his private interests and professional duties until 1880; he then returned to commercial circles and continued in business until 1890, when he was obliged to retire on account of ill health; he died in September of that year.

He was three times married, his third wife, the mother of his children, being Harriet J. Paterson; she was born in Russell county, Kentucky, a daughter of Jonathan Paterson, whose history will be found on another page of this volume. Dr. Leach was united to her in marriage December 4, 1856, and to them three children were born, two of whom survive: Warren and Lawrence W. The former married Molly McCreary, and they have two children, Mark and Nina. Junius F., the oldest child, was born March 21, 1858, and died October 9, 1887. Dr. Leach was reared to the faith of the Christian Church, to which he always adhered. Politically he was identified with the Democratic party, and served his county in the capacity of Treasurer; he was a capable official and discharged his duties with a fidelity that won him the confidence of the people regardless of party ties. In all the walks of life he was true to the trusts resting with him, and in his death the county lost a citizen of great worth and high merit.

ZUAR E. MAIN was born on the farm he now owns, section 16, township 18, range 11 west, Cass county, March 30, 1849. He was reared and educated in this county, and has a fine and well improved farm of 167 acres, and forty acres in timber, and has a fine home in this county also. His grandfather was Joshua, who was born, lived and died in Willington township, Connecticut. He died at about the age of ninety, coming of English parents and was a prominent farmer in his township. His wife's name was Jernsha Lee, who lived and died in Connecticut. They were good religious people, and raised a large family. The father of our subject, Loderick L. Main, was born near Stafford Springs, Connecticut, in 1796, grew up to the carpenter's trade, and later was a seaman for a few years. After that he came to Ohio, settling near Burton, and there married Ann E. Beard, of New York State. In 1837 they came to Illinois, and settled on a farm now owned by our subject, Zuar Main, east of Beardstown. Here Mrs. Main died, in the prime of life, in 1838, leaving several children: Amos B., Lucy Ann, Curtis, Lewis and Myron. Mr. Main married a second time, in Cass county, Sarah Calef, born near Lebanon, New Hampshire, and came when a young woman with her sister to Cass, and was married in 1840 to Mr. Loderick Lee Main. Her death occurred October 25, 1873, at the age of sixty-six. Mr. Main, (Loderick Lee) died at the same place in 1883. He was one of the well known settlers of this county, and he and his wife were strong Methodists. Our subject is one of five children. Znar E. Main (fourth child), Ann E., Luther, Mary, Daniel L. (fifth child).

He was married in this county to Ellen McKean, born and reared in the county. Her parents were John and Nancy (Childress) McKean, natives of West Virginia. They were married at Charlestown, West Virginia, and started on a wedding tour to the West, early in the '30s, settling in Monroe precinct, Cass county. On this they lived and died, he at the age of sixty-two and she forty-seven. They were well-known good people. McKean was a native of Pennsylvania, and was reared in Ohio and married in West Virginia. He was the father of nine children, of whom six are yet living.

Mrs. Main is a smart, intelligent mother of three children; two are deceased,—Minta and Lucas A. Miss Minnie, a bright young lady and a good girl, is the only child living. Mr. and Mrs. Main attend the Methodist Episcopal Church, and Mr. Main is a sound Republican. He is a member of the order of Masons and of the A. O. U. W., and is a very good citizen.

JASPER J. BUCK, deceased, was one of the good farmers and citizens of Arenzville. He was the youngest of thirteen children. His father, Jasper Buck, was born in Bertie county, North Carolina, in 1792; removed to Cass county, Illinois, about 1825 or '30, where he died in 1846; his mother,

Sophia Buck, survived her husband ten years, dying in 1856. Of the twelve brothers and sisters of the subject of this sketch, four only survive at this writing (1892), viz.: Sarah, wife of Conrad Reining; John H.; Albert; and Betsy, wife of Richard Davis.

Jasper J., whose name heads this biography, was married to Miss Mary A. Morrison, February 27, 1862. They have four children: Josephine, born January 5, 1863, wife of William J. Kircher; John A., born September 4, 1864; Elizabeth M., born December 12, 1868, wife of John Huss; and Edward A., born October 8, 1872.

In 1864, Mr. Buck enlisted as a soldier, but as his two children were young, and his wife sickly, he withdrew and employed a substitute.

He was known as a good and true man, and was loved and respected by all. He was identified with no church organization, though he was a professed Christian. He was a member of the I. O. O. F. and in politics was a Democrat of the Jacksonian type.

After a long, painful illness, he died September 25, 1883, leaving a wife and four children to mourn his loss. Since his death Mrs. Buck has had the management of the farm of eighty acres, left her by her husband, She has raised her family of four children, two of whom are married and doing for themselves; two, John and Edward, are at home. She is a true Christian woman, and a useful member of the Presbyterian Church.

GEORGE RITCHEA, deceased, was one of the honored pioneers who braved all the dangers and privations of the frontier, and labored earnestly and indefatigably to to prepare the way for the march of progress and the advancing steps of civilization. He was a native of Montgomery county, Ohio, born near Dayton, February 19, 1814, a son of James Ritchea; his father was born in the north of Ireland, but emigrated to the United States, and was an early settler of Montgomery county; there he passed the remainder of his life. His son, George Ritchea, came to Illinois at an early day, and located in Schuyler county; the journey was made overland, as there were then no railroads; the products of the farm were shipped down the river, and all commerce was carried on in the most primitive style.

Mr. Ritchea engaged in the lumber business, rafting his stock for market down the river; later he embarked in the mercantile trade at Rushville, being one of the earliest merchants in the county. After his marriage he settled on a farm four miles from Rushville, and engaged in agriculture until his death, March 5, 1887. He was united to Lucinda Walker, a native of Hardinsburgh, Kentucky, and a daughter of Henry and Elizabeth Walker. To them were born five children, two of whom now survive: Francis P. and Anna Kate; Mary E. died January 10, 1888, aged forty-three years; George D. died in November, 1888, aged thirty-five years. Francis P. owns and occupies a farm joining the old homestead; Anna Kate, the surviving daughter, owns the homestead. She received a good education at Abingdon College, and also took a course at the Gem City Business College. At the age of sixteen years she began teaching, and has followed this profession in Illinois and Colorado, meeting with marked success and making an enviable reputation among educators of the West. Mr. and Mrs. Ritchea were worthy and consistent members of the Christian Church. Politically he affiliated with the Republican party, and was a staneh supporter of its principles. He was a man of excellent business ability, and although he began the struggle of life single-handed and alone, having no capital excepting that with which nature had provided him, he amassed a considerable amount of property. He employed the highest and most correct business methods, and had an enviable reputation as a man of integrity and honor.

JOHN H. HAGENER, of the firm of Hagener & Bros., was born January 7, 1850, in Beardstown, where he has lived all his life. His father, William Hagener, was born in the kingdom of Hanover, Germany, and in 1841 he crossed to St. Louis, and upon his arrival he married Eleanora Peters, who had come over on the same vessel from the same province that he had. Shortly after their marriage they went to Beardstown, and here resided until Mr. Hagener's death, which event occurred in the fifty-eighth year of his life. Mr. and Mrs. Hagener were leaders among their class, and Mr. Hagener was instrumental in the building of the Lutheran Church, and he and his wife were among the first members of it. Mr. Hagener purchased a piece of land in 1842, which has become very valuable since that time. He followed his trade of mechanic, and later began contracting and building, and in 1861 entered into the lumber business. He continued the latter business until the time of his death. He was a good and influential man, and his loss was felt by all who knew him. His wife is still living at the age of seventy-three, but is very feeble.

Mr. John Hagener is in a business that was established in 1875, and he and his brother do a large and thriving business in the lumber and house-furnishing supply trade, and also a large grain buying and selling business. They have a large mill and their elevator has a capacity of 50,000 bushels. They are doing a 300,000-bushel-grain business. They have warehouses at Concord, Arenzville, Browning and Hagener, and they keep local agents at the places mentioned. Their milling trade is well represented in the two leading brands of flour known as Best Patent and Four Leaf. Part of their goods are shipped to Europe. Both brothers are stockholders and directors in the First National Bank of Beardstown, and John Hagener is the vice-president, and has occupied that position ever since the bank was organized, in 1887. The bank is capitalized at $50,000 with a surplus of $20,000, and J. H. Harris is the president, and Thomas K. Condit occupies the position of cashier. Mr. John Hagener is a School Trustee and a Director in the Mutual Loan and Savings Association. He is a Republican in politics and is a hard-working, industrious citizen, ready to promote anything tending to the improvement and development of his town.

He married Miss Kate Pappmeier, of Beardstown. She was born and reared in Beardstown, and her father is in the store of Pappmeier & Sons. Mr. and Mrs. Hagener are leaders in their society, and are Lutherans in religious beliefs. They have five children, all of whom are living at home: Nora, Fred R., Emma, Lewis and Arthur.

FRANK ANDERSON, a widely and favorably known citizen of Schuyler county, is Superintendent of the poor farm of that county, in which capacity he has served since March 1, 1891. He was born in Schuyler county, in Huntsville township, on May 15, 1836, and has lived in that vicinity ever since. His parents were William and Prudence (Wallingsford) Anderson, both natives of Kentucky, who were married in their native State, coming to Illinois in 1835, and locating in Huntsville township, where they cleared and improved a farm of 640 acres. On his property he built a substantial and comfortable residence, besides barns for grain and stock, and added many other modern improvements, the land being under a good state of cultivation. He died in August, 1887, aged eighty-seven years. His wife still survives at the age of eighty-five years, supported and comforted by her kind and loving children.

The paternal grandparents of our subject, Andrew Anderson and wife, were natives of Kentucky, who removed to Schuyler county, Illinois, in an early day, locating near Rushville, where the grandmother died. The grandfather died in Camden township. They had eight children, six sons and two daughters: William, father of our subject; John, Jeremiah, Riley, Jackson and Perry, and two daughters.

The parents of our subject had ten children, of whom seven arrived at maturity. Cyrus died in Huntsville township, Illinois; Andrew, died in Huntsville township; Jane married Danforth Cady, and now resides in Camden township; Vincent resides in Huntsville township; our subject comes next in order; John died in Camden township; and Sarah, now Mrs. Samuel McCadann, of Camden township.

Our subject was reared on a farm in Huntsville township, and on January 1, 1858, was married to Harriet Kniss, daughter of Samuel and Polly Kniss, and a native of Indiana. After his marriage he resided with his wife on a part of the homestead, where he pursued his trade of blacksmithing, and also conducted a farm. He resided here until he took charge of the County Poor farm. He owns 171 acres of well improved land in Huntsville township, which is under a good state of cultivation. The poor farm contains 310 acres of land in section 26, of Buena Vista township, there now being thirty-one inmates of the home. This farm almost pays expenses, being well conducted under the able management of the subject of our sketch and his estimable wife.

Mr. and Mrs. Anderson have three children: Isabel, wife of Henry Powell, of Huntsville township; Millie and Fred.

Mr. Anderson affiliates with the Democratic party, though taking no active interest in politics aside from desiring the advancement and welfare of his native county and State. Socially he is a member of Camden Lodge, No. 648, A. F. & A. M.

Sober and intelligent, honest and industrious, kind and obliging, he has gained the good will of his fellow citizens and the affectionate regard of a host of friends.

JAMES M. AGNEW, a liberal-minded and progressive citizen of Littleton township, Schuyler county, Illinois, was born in Erie county, Pennsylvania, December 24, 1825. His parents were George and Esther (Sleight) Agnew, both natives of New York State and Genesee county. They went to Pennsylvania in an early day, where they followed farming until 1849, when they removed to Illinois, then a new country and very sparsely settled. They located in Rushville, where they resided until their death, his father living to be seventy-two years of age, and his mother sixty-eight. His grandparents lived in New York State, and lived to be very old people, his grandfather being Samuel Agnew

The subject of our sketch was one of nine children, of whom three are living. He lived at home until twenty-one years of age, when he removed with his parents to Illinois in 1849, working by the month until he was married He was married on June 12, 1851, to Miss May J. Bunnell, who was born in the same place as our subject Their happy married life was, however, of short duration, his wife dying in Rushville, aged twenty-five years.

He was married a second time on April 27, 1853, his second wife being Delilah Hodgson, a native of Indiana. They had five children, four of whom are now living, viz.: Millard F., single, Oral M , married, and has one child; James E., married to Miss Edgar; Ralph D , now in Kansas His second wife died, aged forty years, leaving to him the care of their children. She was much regretted by a large circle of friends, being a faithful wife and fond mother.

Mr. Agnew was married some years later to Mrs. Louisa Ham, who was born in Indiana They have one child, Jessie, now living at home.

After his first marriage Mr. Agnew rented land near Rushville, on which he lived for a couple of years. He then rented another piece, on which he remained for three years, when he again moved, remaining four years in the last place, when he removed to Littleton township, where he rented land for five years, at the end of which time he purchased a farm of 160 acres of wild land This he has improved by the erection of buildings, and has the land well cultivated. He has a comfortable home and other modern improvements. His land is devoted to mixed husbandry, in which he is very successful

Mr. Agnew has been a Republican ever since the organization of that party. His first presidential vote was cast for General W. H Harrison He and family are members of the Methodist Episcopal Church, to the support of which denomination he is a liberal contributor. Honest, intelligent, moral, liberal and progressive, Mr. Agnew enjoys the good will of the community, and the esteem of a large number of friends.

JOSEPH PENCE, of township 17, 7 north, range 10 west, section 18, was born in Rockingham county, Virginia, March 10, 1814 His parents were John and Mary (Smith) Pence, both being natives of Virginia They had three sons and five daughters, Mr. Pence, of this sketch, is the only survivor One brother died in Davis county, Iowa, and two sisters also died in the same place. The other three sisters died in Cass county, Illinois, and the remaining brother in Scott county, Illinois. The parents both died in Rockingham county, Virginia, the father in June, and the mother in September, 1834.

Mr Joseph Pence was married in Page county, Virginia, in 1837, to Sarah A Samuels, of the same county, born in 1812 After marriage the young couple went to Kentucky and remained until 1838, when they removed to Morgan county, Illinois. From there they went to Cass county, Illinois, where they have since resided Mr. Pence bought 205 acres of land, which he has greatly improved. Mrs Pence died in 1878, and her husband still mourns her loss. Mr. Pence has always been a Democrat and has held the various offices in his township, and was a member of the I. O. O. F.

Mrs. Pence bore her husband six children, namely: Joseph W., a farmer in Iowa, is a widower with nine children; Sarah Ellen, a widow who keeps house for her father. The other children are dead. The daughter married Thomas D. Chapman, who was born near Pittsburg, Pennsylvania, January 27, 1842, and was a soldier in Company I, One Hundred and Fifteenth Illinois Infantry, serving three years and three months. He returned home somewhat broken in health, and never entirely recovered, dying August 5, 1885. He left four children and a widow to mourn his loss. The children were: Louie, now Mrs. P. H. Caldwell; Charles F., Albert B. and Joseph H. are all at home with their grandfather, the first named being a member of the Sons of Veterans. Mrs. Chapman was born on the farm on which she now resides, and has always lived there. She is a member of the Providence Presbyterian Church. Her husband was a member of the Masonic order.

ABNER A. CLARK of section 31, Camden township, is one of the pioneers of 1835, born in Logan county, Kentucky, February 6, 1823. His father, Abner Clark, was born in North Carolina. He removed to Kentucky when a young man and became a farmer. He married Nancy Gorum, of Kentucky. In 1835 he came to Illinois and settled in what is now Missouri township, Brown county. He entered land and resided there until January, 1847, when his wife died, and in consequence he moved to Schuyler county and lived with a son until his death in August, 1849. He had entered considerable land, and at his death still owned 240 acres of land. He had been a Whig in politics and Presbyterian in religion for many years prior to his death. He had ten children: Calvin, born May 30, 1805, died March 14, 1880; Perneta, born December 10, 1806; William, born March 1, 1809, died March 7, 1855; Harrison, born February 15, 1811, died March 18, 1883; Inetta, born August 26, 1813. died June 1, 1838; Terlina, born October 26, 1815, died January 15, 1890; Delila, born October 26, 1815; Catherine, born June 19, 1818, died June 7, 1841; Francis A., born September 11, 1820; and Abner A., born February 6, 1823.

Abner was reared on the farm and attended such schools as the newly settled locality offered. After the death of his mother he resided with a brother until 1847, when he settled where he now resides, on 160 acres of land. He began housekeeping in a log cabin, which in time was supplanted by the present residence, which is a comfortable frame structure. He now owns 440 acres of land. His home contains 320 acres, he having added to the original 160. He has been a stock-raiser as well as a farmer, but now has all his land rented.

He was married, May 27, 1847, to Elizabeth J. Sims, daughter of David and Sarah E. Sims. She was born in Sangamon county, Illinois, February 6, 1832. Mr. and Mrs. Clark have had five children, namely: Francis M., born in 1849, died February 25, 1853; Luticia, born 1851, died March 8, 1853; Nancy P., born in 1852, married Daniel M. McCaskill of Brown county, two children, Carrie and Roy A.; Levi G., born 1857, married Lizzie R. Bond April 20, 1880, her death occurring November 13, 1882; was married to Amanda Cady, daughter of Henry Cady, resides in Schuyler county, three children: Asa A., Alta and Frank F.; Fred D., born 1868, resides at home.

Mr. Clark is a Republican in politics and a Baptist in religion, being Moderator of the society. He and his wife are respected by all who know them.

ROBERT NELSON McFARLAND, the oldest settler of Brown county, is now residing in Versailles. He was born in Harrison county, Kentucky, April 1, 1818. His father, William McFarland was born in the same county. There is little known of his grandfather except that he spent his last years in Harrison, Kentucky. His father was reared and married in Ohio, but resided in Kentucky until 1819, when his nearest neighbor was ten miles distant. He next moved to Green county, Ohio, and was one of the earliest settlers there. He lived there until 1822, when, with his wife and four children he made the journey to Illinois, cooking and camping by the way. He located in Sangamon and died there. At the time of their location there, this county was sparsely settled. The greater portion was owned by the Government. Springfield was but a hamlet, the capital of the State then being Vandalia.

His mother continued to live in Sangamon county until 1824. She accompanied her sister and her sister's husband, Cornelius Van Deventer, whom she afterward married, to what is now Brown county, where she resided until her death.

Mr. McFarland was six years old when he came to Brown county, and remembers well many of the incidents of its settlement. At that time their nearest neighbors, the Indians, were more numerous than the white people.

When Mr. Van Deventer came he laid claim to a tract of Government land, two and one half miles east of the present site of Versailles, and there built a log cabin in which was taught the first school in Brown county, Hannah Burbank being the teacher. For some years after they came here there were no mills convenient, and during one winter the family subsisted almost entirely on lye hominy. In time there was a mill, operated by horse-power, introduced into the county, and Mr. McFarland used to go, in common with others, and during the long ride would subsist on parched corn, wild game and wild honey. There were no railroads, no steamers on the Illinois river and no markets.

Of course our subject was reared to agricultural pursuits. His first farm was a tract of 100 acres, which he occupied until 1865, when he sold and purchased a farm of 210 acres, and at the present time he is living retired in the pleasant village of Versailles.

He was married December 31, 1839, to Margaret W. McFarland, who died in 1879, leaving four living children: Lucinda Van Deventer; Mary Whitehead; Robert N.. who married Ann Augusta Van Deventer; and Louis, who is still single.

JOHN D. HORTON, one of the progressive and enterprising farmers of Littleton township, was born in Schuyler county, Illinois, September 21, 1845, a son of Lewis and Priscilla (Christman) Horton. His father was a native of Luzerne county, Pennsylvania, and there grew to be mature years, he drove a stage until 1842, when he made a trip to Illinois, coming via the rivers to La Grange; he settled on the farm now occupied by our subject, purchasing the tract of 160 acres for $350, he erected a log house which was a comfortable home until 1866, when the present structure was built In 1852 he crossed the plains to California, returning in 1856 by way of New York city; he was accompanied by his son Fred, who afterward went to Texas, where he died. His life was devoted to the pursuit of agriculture; in politics he was a Democrat until 1856 when he cast his suffrage for Lincoln, but he was not actively interested in the movements of the party His wife died in Schuyler county at the age of eighty-six years; before his death she made a trip to California, visiting a daughter residing there. John D. Horton is one of a family of ten children, four of whom are living. He was first married September 2, 1869, to Miss Mary E Foster, of Schuyler county, who died July 8, 1870 He was again united in marriage February 17, 1875, to Miss Elizabeth Nichols. She is also a native of this county, born in Littleton township, July 13, 1856, a daughter of Reuben and Elizabeth (Agnew) Nichols. (See sketch of James (Agnew.)

Mr and Mrs Horton are the parents of four children, all of whom are living: Lewis R., born February 24, 1879; Warren, born March 22, 1881; Craig C, born May 14, 1884, and Jessie C, born January 17, 1890. Mr Horton received his education in the common school at Rushville and remained under the parental roof until his marriage; after this event he settled on the homestead, and has since that time been engaged in agriculture Politically he is identified with the Republican party; he has represented the people of his township in various local offices, discharging his duties with much ability and admirable fidelity. His wife has been for many years a member of the Methodist Episcopal Church. They are both people of great stability of character and enjoy the respect of all who know them Their ancestors for generations have been men and women of brave hearts and undaunted courage, have served in the wars of the country, and have been reliable, industrious and prosperous citizens of the Republic which they aided in founding.

JOHN S STUTSMAN, an honored pioneer of Schuyler county, has been closely identified with its history for many years, and it is fitting that a sketch of his life should appear in these pages. He was born in Dubois county, Indiana, April 10, 1827, a son of Alexander D. and Rhoda (Seybold) Stutsman Alexander D Stutsman was a native of Kentucky, a son of Jacob and Mary (Berkey) Stutsman, natives of Pennsylvania; his father died in Dubois county, Indiana, at the age of eighty years; the mother died in the same place, aged seventy years The Stutsman family is of German origin, the great-grandfather of our subject having emigrated from the fatherland to America. Both Mr and Mrs. John S Stutsman had ancestors that served in the wars of the Revolution and 1812 Rhoda Seybold, the mother of John S Stutsman, was born in Georgia, and was one of a family of seven children; she became the mother of a family of eleven, eight of whom are living. The father died on the old homestead, now occupied by his son, at the age of seventy-eight years He was one of the early pioneers of the State, emigrating to Schuyler county in 1834, and bravely bore the privations of life on the frontier that the way might be paved for the coming of an advanced civilization. He was accompanied by his wife and five children, and made the journey with a four-horse wagon; he purchased a farm of 148 acres, partially improved; for twelve years the family lived in a log cabin that had been built before their coming; this was in time replaced by one of black-walnut logs, which was the home of the parents until death. The mother lived to be eighty years old. John S. remained under the parental roof until he was twenty-three years of age; he attended the district school, and although his opportunities were meager he laid the foundation of a thorough education, and has since come to be recognized as an authority on all historical subjects. Many were the evenings he read to his mother by the light of the flickering candle, as she sewed upon clothing, either for her own or the neighbor's boys.

Mr. Stutsman was united in marriage, March 21, 1850, to Miss Sarah Howell, who was born in Monroe county, Indiana, January 24, 1831. Her parents, Jonathan and Nancy (Gilham) Howell, emigrated to Indiana in 1822, and thence to Brown county, Illinois, in 1838, where they passed the remainder of their lives; the father died at the age of sixty-nine, and the mother at the age of eighty years. They reared a family of ten children, five of whom survive. They had three sons in the Union army in the late war, two of whom died in the service of their country.

Mrs. Howell's parents were natives of North Carolina, as were also Mr. Howells. Mr. and Mrs. Stutsman have had born to them a family of ten children, six of whom are deceased; those living are named as follows: Nancy J. is married and the mother of seven children; Mary E. is at home; Robert W. is married and has two children; John E. is on the old homestead; Mary has taught school very successfully for several years. The family are members of the Methodist Episcopal Church South, and are actively engaged in the good work of this society.

After his marriage Mr. Stutsman lived near his present residence for three years, and then purchased the property he still owns; he first occupied a log cabin, which he replaced in time with a substantial brick structure. His first tract consisted of forty acres of wild land, to which he added as his means would permit, until he now has 195 acres. He does a general farming business, and is more than ordinarily successful and prosperous. It is entirely through his own efforts that he has accumulated his property, as he had no capital excepting that with which nature had endowed him.

Politically, he affiliates with the Democratic party, which he has represented in various positions of trust and honor. He was County Treasurer four years from 1886 to 1890, has been Supervisor seven years, and Township School Treasurer twenty-seven years, holding the latter position at present; he has for many years been a member of the School Board. He is one of the most widely known men in the county, and none is held in higher esteem.

LIBERTY G. PERSINGER, one of the most prominent farmers of Woodstock township, was born in Alleghany county, Virginia, June 6, 1831, a son of Allen and Paulina (Peters) Persinger. Allen Persinger was a native of Virginia, born in Alleghany county, and resided there until he was twenty-three years of age. He then emigrated to Illinois, accompanied by his wife and one child; the journey was made from Virginia in a one-horse wagon, and when he arrived his capital amounted to $25 in cash. He went to work with a will, and began the task of placing a tract of wild land under cultivation. He afterward sold this, and entered eighty acres on another section; to this he added as his means increased, until at one time he owned several hundred acres. He built a log cabin in which he lived four years, and then erected another one of more pretentious size, in which he died at the age of seventy-four years; his wife passed her last days in the same house. Politically, he was closely identified with the early history of the county and State; he held many local offices, and represented his county in the Illinois State Legislature. Liberty G. Persinger, who is named for the old Revolutionary General, Liberty Green, remained with his parents until he was twenty-one years of age. He was then married to Elizabeth Tharpe, a native of Illinois, and a daughter of Jonathan and Anna Tharpe, who were born in North Carolina and were early settlers of Schuyler county. To Mr. and Mrs. Persinger have been born eleven children, ten of whom are living; all are married: William L. has five children; Paulina has five children; Anna C. has three children; Cornelia J. is the mother of three children; Naomi has two children; Louis M. is the father of two children; Allen J. has a family of two children; Elmer E. and Edward have no children; Estella is the mother of one child.

After his marriage, Mr. Persinger rented the land which he now owns; he lived in a little log cabin for a year, and then erected another in which he resided eight years; he then built his present home. He has 300 acres under good cultivation, 111 of which he inherited from his father's estate. He carries on a general farming business, and has met with more than ordinary success. The land was originally heavily timbered, and has required no small amount of energy and labor to reduce it to a state of cultivation.

Mrs. Persinger is a consistent member of the Methodist Episcopal Church. Our subject takes no active interest in politics further than to discharge his duty as a citizen by casting his suffrage, which is with the Republican party. He is a man of superior business qualifications and unquestioned honor and integrity.

NATHAN SUTTON, one of the most prominent citizens of his county was born in Sussex county, New Jersey, January 22, 1819, son of Benjamin and Elizabeth (Robe) Sutton, the former of the same place as his son, where he kept a store for many years, but sold out in 1823 and went to Washtenaw county, Michigan, where he took up land to the amount of 160 acres and improved it. He then sold it to his father, also Nathan, who was born in the same county and State as his son and grandson. This gentleman died Michigan when about seventy-five years of age. His wife, subject's grandmother, was Sarah Sutton and she died on the farm when about seventy-six. The entire family were farmers by occupation. Mr. Nathan Sutton, Sr., was a teamster in the war of 1812. Benjamin Sutton arrived in Illinois July 29, 1833, and settled near the present home of subject, where he entered and bought land to such an extent that he had 2,200 acres at his death, being one of the largest land-owners in central Illinois. He died in October, 1837, aged about forty-five and his wife, who was born in the same place as her husband, died on the old farm, aged about forty-seven.

The Sutton family were of English descent, the Robes of German ancestry. Our subject was one of nine children, five of whom are yet living, and his father was one of six children. His mother's people never came West, but died in New Jersey, when very old: they were farmers. The Sutton family figured largely in the politics of Michigan, several of them serving as Justices of the Peace one was a member of the State Legislature, while another served as Mayor of Ann Arbor, Michigan. The prominence of Benjamin Sutton was not confined to Michigan by any means, as he was one of the most prominent men of his county, in Illinois. He erected the first gristmill in the locality and in order that the children of the section should have the benefit of the subscription schools he paid one half of the teacher's fees for five months. This family did not come West in the moneyless condition that so many were in, as they had nearly $7,000 in cash besides personal effects which had been brought across the country in wagons, the only means of transportation in those days. Mr Sutton, Sr., was a Deacon in the Baptist Church and for a time Clerk, and a member of the order of A F & A. M.

Our subject remained upon the home farm until his marriage, when he rented for a year and then bought seventy-five acres of wild land, on which he built a log house 16 x 18 feet, in which he and his wife lived until he built his present house, in 1856 Mr. Sutton kept adding to his farm until he now has 500 acres of fine land and has given each of his children a fine farm

A son of Nathan Sutton enlisted in the late war, and while in service he was captured and sent to Andersonville, where he remained five months. His health was so impared by confinement that he was obliged to be in the St Louis hospital, but with these exceptions he served throughout the entire war One of his brothers was in the same company for one year, responding to the last call for men.

Mr Sutton was married August 4, 1842, to Miss Elizabeth A. Lemar, born in Mason county, Kentucky, July 9, 1822, daughter of Richard and Elizabeth H. (Merrell) Lemar. The former was a native of New Jersey, who came from Kentucky, which had been his home for some years, to Illinois, in 1840, and after marrying a second time settled in Petersburg, Illinois, where he bought eighty acres of land, five miles from present home of subject His first wife died when her daughter, Mrs Sutton, was thirteen months old. The family was of French descent. The mother of Mrs Sutton was a daughter of Andrew and Elizabeth (Hyde) Merrell and and the Hyde family were the legal heirs to a large estate in England, but which they have never been able to obtain, although they have sufficient proof to establish their claim to it Mrs. Sutton one of five children, two yet living and also two half sisters are still living Mr. and Mrs. Sutton have had eight children, as follows: William Sylvester, born April 21, 1844, married Mary E. Severs three children: Alonzo, born September 9, 1846, married Miss Martha Dick (see sketch of Levi Dick); John H., born August 21, 1848, married Hannah Ogden, deceased; married second time Mary I Garder, two children, David L, born July 28, 1850; Winfield S, born August 19, 1852, married Levina Samuels by whom he had six children, and after her death he married Lucretia Lynn by whom he had four children; Clara J., born October 14, 1854, married Joshua Conyers, and has five living children, one deceased; Benjamin R., born March 24, 1857, married Jennie Morgan, has three children, Stella, Ernest and Ella, the oldest one having died in infancy and another, also an infant, is deceased; and Ella E., born September 8, 1858, married James Odgen, two children.

Mr. Sutton is an ardent Republican, having been an old-line Whig, casting his first vote for General William H. Harrison. Mr. and Mrs. Sutton, with their family are members of the Baptist Church, in which Mr. Sutton has been a Deacon for many years. This is a brief sketch of one of the most prominent families in the county, and we regret that space forbids a more extended notice of such a well known and influential family.

HENRY C. MEYER, a successful brick and tile manufacturer and ice dealer of Beardstown, Illinois, was born in Westphalia, Prussia, September 20, 1835. His parents were Henry C. and E. (Hildabrandt) Meyer. His father was an efficient soldier for fifteen years under the general command of the first Emperor William, when they were both young men. His father participated in many active engagements, and was highly respected by his superior officers. In 1843, the family emigrated to the United States, arriving, after a voyage of fifteen weeks, in New Orleans, from which place they were nearly as long in reaching Evansville, Indiana, by the Mississippi and Ohio rivers. They settled in Knox county, Indiana, where, in 1857, the devoted wife and mother died. Some years later, the father came to Beardstown to visit his son, who had gone to that place some time before. He subsequently died at his son's home in 1878, at the age of seventy years. He was a man of sterling qualities of mind and heart, and enjoyed, with his wife, the heartfelt esteem of all who knew them. Both parents were devout members of the Evangelical church.

The subject of this sketch came to Beardstown in 1857, when a poor, young man, having at that time only $5 in his pocket. He commenced, in a primitive manner, to work at his present business, moulding brick with his hands, which was then the usual way. He was thus employed when the Civil war broke out, and in 1861 he volunteered his services to the Government, but the quota having been filled he was not accepted. He purchased his first land in that year, near Arenzville. By unremitting industry and careful economy, he gradually accumulated means, which he invested in the best improvements obtainable for the manufacture of brick and tile, besides branching out in other directions. He now makes about 1,000,000 brick and many thousand rods of tile annually, being the largest manufacturer in that line in his county. He is also extensively engaged in the ice business, which he has successfuly conducted for the past twenty years, his ice houses now having a capacity of 12,000 tons. He has gradually added to his first purchase of land, until he now owns 1,000 acres of choice realty in Cass county; 900 of which are well improved and cultivated, and 300 being under his own management.

He was married about 1862, to Miss Mollie Boy, who was born and raised near Arenzville, of which vicinity her people were early and respected pioneers. Both of her parents are now dead. Mr. and Mrs. Meyer have had eight children, seven of whom survive: Louis, who married Tilla Piehler;

Elizabeth, wife of A. E Cameron, a successful jeweler of Beardstown; Albert, assisting his father at home; Lydia, wife of Charles Lebkucher, a properous farmer of this county, Mollie, Herold and Adalaide, living at home

Politically, Mr Meyer supports the issues of the Democratic party, and, while being no office seeker, takes an interest in all local and public affairs of importance.

Both he and his worthy wife are useful members of the Fourth Evangelical Lutheran Church

Mr Meyer has not attained his success without earnest and persistent endeavor; wholly unaided, he has, by industry and economy, acquired his present prosperity; while by upright dealings and uniform courtesy he has secured the universal esteem of his fellow men.

HON. ARTHUR A. LEEPER, attorney at law, Virginia, Illinois, was born at Chandlerville, Cass county, this State, August 21, 1855, son of William D Leeper, a native of Edmonson county, Kentucky.

Rev. Robert Leeper, grandfather of Hon. Arthur A. Leeper, is supposed to have been a native of Kentucky He removed from that State to Illinois in 1829, and entered a tract of Government land, a portion of which is now included in the village of Chandlerville, being one of the first settlers there He at once built a log house, and began the improvement of his land He erected the first gristmill ever built in that locality. He operated the mill, superintended the improvement of his land, and resided there until his death

William D. Leeper was twelve years old when his parents moved to Illinois The greater portion of the State was at that time unsettled, and deer, wild turkeys and other game were plentiful in this vicinity. It was long before the railroads entered this section of the country, and for many years Beardstown was the market and depot for supplies for miles around. He entered a tract of Government land that joined his father's farm on the east, located on it at the time of his marriage, and passed his life there, dying in 1866 The maiden name of his first wife, mother of the subject of our sketch, was Mary Runyan She was born in Kentucky, and died in 1857. His second wife, previously Maria Hermeyer, was born in Germany.

In the public schools of Chandlerville, Arthur A received his early education At the age of sixteen he entered Eureka College, and graduated with the class of 1874. He then entered the law department of Iowa University, graduating in 1875. Returning to Chandlerville, he opened an office and practiced his profession there until the fall of 1876, when he came to Virginia, where he has since practiced.

September 18, 1878, he married Eva Howe, a native of Ohio, and a daughter of Rufus and Eva (Miller) Howe. They have two children: Mabel and Alice.

Politically, Mr Leeper is a Democrat. He cast his first vote for Samuel J Tilden In 1876, he was elected State's Attorney for Cass county, and filled that position until 1880. He has served as City Attorney three years, and was School Director three years In 1885 he was the nominee of his party for member of the House of Representatives. This was the time of the memorable contest which finally resulted in the election of John A. Logan to the United States Senate. The Republicans made a still hunt in this campaign, and Mr Leeper was defeated. He was re-nominated, however, in 1888, for State Senator, and was elected, serving through two sessions. He was one of the 101 who voted continually for John M. Palmer. Among the various committees on which he served, we mention the following: Special Drainage, Insurance and Judiciary, Highways and Bridges, Judicial Department, Corporations, Canals and Rivers, Labor and Manufactures, Rules, State Charities, License and Miscellaneous, and County and Township organizations. He faithfully performed the duties of his responsible position, his efficient work being recognized and highly appreciated by his constituents. He was re-nominated for Senator in April, 1892.

Fraternally, he is a member of Virginia Lodge, No. 554, A. F. & A. M., and Saxon Lodge, No. 68, I. O. G. T.

WILLIAM K. SHUPE, one of the most intelligent and enterprising agriculturists of Woodstock township, is a native of the State of Virginia and a son of Peter and Sarah (Wright) Shupe; the date of his birth is October 9, 1824. The father was also born in Virginia and emigrated to this county in 1843; later he went to Iowa, and died there in his fifty-fourth year; his wife was born in Virginia and died in Iowa; they had born to them a family of fifteen children, six of whom are now living. The family is of German lineage, the first ancestors in this country emigrating previous to the war of the Revolution. William K. remained at home until he was twenty years of age, and then worked at the cooper's trade several years. He was united in marriage October 19, 1846, to Miss Mary A. Hoffman, a native of Ohio and a daughter of Joseph and Mary A. (Myers) Hoffman; her parents removed to this county about 1837, and here passed the rest of their lives; they reared a family of eight children, five of whom are living. Mr. and Mrs. Shupe are the parents of six children: Samuel L. is married and has one son; Sarah A. is married and the mother of four children; George H. is married and has eight children; Mary F. is married and the mother of four children; Martha M. is married and has five children; William J. married and his wife died leaving two children.

After his marriage Mr. Shupe settled on the farm he now occupies; he has 120 acres, which he has improved and brought to a high state of cultivation. For many years he lived in a little log cabin, but in 1862 erected his present comfortable dwelling. He carries on a general farming business, manages all branches with much wisdom, and reaps the reward of success.

Peter Shupe, father of William K., was in the war of 1812, and several members of the family participated in the late Civil war. Formerly Mr. Shupe was identified with the Democratic party, but now casts his suffrage for the man rather than the party. He has been Assessor for a number of years, and has held other positions of trust and responsibility. He has given attention to the matter of public education, and has served on the school board. He is now practically retired from active business pursuits, the care and management of the farm being in the hands of the younger son.

The first years our subject spent in this section of country were fraught with trials and hardships, such only as are possible in a new and undeveloped community. The journey from the East was made overland; the funds of the family being exhausted, they stopped and the sons split 1,000 rails to secure money to continue the trip which consumed two months. Mr Shupe is a self-made man in every sense of the word he has never received financial aid, and his present property has been accumulated entirely through his own efforts It was through the influence of Mormon preachers that the father was induced to come to the West, and two of his sons pushed their way to Salt Lake, and pitched their tents on the present site of Salt Lake City. July 24, 1847; one of them still lives there, and celebrates the twenty-fourth day of July Mr Shupe is a man who is fully posted upon current events, is a wide reader, and thoroughly loyal to the interests of his county and State.

JAMES D. MATTHEW was born near the present site of Columbus, Franklin county, Ohio, in 1813, November 24 His father, Simon Matthew, was born in Fauquier county, Virginia, and his father, Nathan Matthew, was, as far as is known, born in the same State. The great-grandfather of subject, Edward Matthew, was born in Wales and came to America, settling in Virginia in colonial times He was a miller by trade, and his son was also a miller, and he erected a mill in Virginia during the Revolutionary war. He resided in Virginia until about 1817, when he went to Washington county, Indiana, and was a resident there until his death. His son was reared in Virginia and went to Ohio when he was twenty-six years of age He settled in Franklin county and was one of the first settlers there. He assisted in cutting the logs to build the penitentiary at Columbus In 1818 he emigrated to Indiana, settling in Washington county, which was a heavily timbered country at that time. He rented a tract of timber land ten miles west of Salem, and erected a log house in the wilderness. There were no railroads in the State at that time, and the nearest market was fifty miles away He lived in Indiana until 1832, and during that time cleared quite a tract of his land In 1832 he sold that and came to Illinois, settling ten miles southeast of Springfield, where he resided until his death The maiden name of his first wife, the mother of our subject, was Ann Dearderff, born near New Castle, of German ancestry She died in Sangamon county, after the arrival of the family

James came with his parents to Sangamon county, Illinois, and was nineteen the day he reached there At that time the capitol of the State was Vandalia, Springfield being but a hamlet, and the nearest market for farmers in Sangamon county was St Louis or Beardstown He resided there until 1838, and then came to Cass county. He had visited this section and entered forty acres of land in 1837, in section 32, township 18, and forty more acres in section 19 of the same township In 1838 he built a hewed-log cabin and commenced at once to clear the land. At that time deer and other kinds of wild game supplied the table with meat Wheat sold from thirty to forty cents a bushel, and corn for ten cents a bushel The wife dressed the children in homespun of her own raising, carding and weaving. He added to his farm until it is now about 365 acres, the greater part improved.

He was married March 27, 1834, to Dorcas Hamilton, born in Virginia, daughter of Pressley and Susana Hamilton. Mr and Mrs. Matthew have had the following children: Simon P, Ann, Charles, Jane Ruth, Rodney, Nettie, Henry L and Lincoln

LIBRARY
OF THE
UNIVERSITY OF ILLINOIS

Edwin Dyson

Mr. Matthew was a member of the Methodist Episcopal Church, as is his wife. He was a Whig and Republican, and was a good and honorable man. He died April 7, 1892, at his home. Thus one of the oldest settlers and a man respected for his sterling integrity has passed away, and the family and large circle of friends and acquaintances are left mourning. He died a firm believer in the Christian religion. His aged wife of fifty-six years, standing, still occupies the old home where they settled in 1838. They celebrated their golden wedding March 27, 1884. They were married in Indiana.

EDWIN DYSON is the editor and proprietor of the Rushville *Times*, a weekly paper devoted to the interests of the Democratic party. It is ably edited and well conducted, and reflects great credit upon the management. Mr. Dyson is an American citizen by adoption, his native land being England; he was born in Lancastershire, July 28, 1838, a son of James Dyson, a native of the same country; there the father was reared and married, his wife's maiden name being Hannah Wilson. He was employed in the cotton-mills until 1841, when accompanied by his wife and four children, he emigrated to America: they sailed from Liverpool and landed at the port of New Orleans after a stormy voyage of nearly three months; they continued their journey to Illinois, and located at Rushville, where Mr. Dyson died a few months later. A few years after her husband's death, Mrs. Dyson married Thomas Hampton, and still lives in Rushville. Edwin Dyson was a child of three years when the family arrived in Schuyler county, Illinois. Here he was reared and educated, and at the age of sixteen years began to learn the printer's trade. He was first in the office of the Schuyler *Democrat*, and served there nearly three years; he then worked in Rushville as a journeyman until 1864, when he went to St. Louis; he was in the office of the *Republican* of that city for four years. At the end of that time he returned to Schuyler county, and purchased the Rushville *Times*, which he has since edited. He has made the *Times* one of the leading papers of the military tract, having a circulation far above the average of county papers. In connection with the publication of the paper he runs a job printing office which turns out work of a very high class.

Mr. Dyson was married in 1861, to Mary F. Irvin, who was born near Danville, Kentucky, and of this union three children have been born: Jennie L., Orean E. and Howard F. Our subject has been prominently identified with the political movements of the Democratic party in this county aside from his editorship of their organ. He has been County Treasurer two terms, and was a member of the Board several years, and has served as a delegate to the various county, district and State conventions. He belongs to Rushville Lodge, No. 9, A. F. & A. M.

JOHN ELLIOTT, a retired farmer, living at the corner of Jackson and Seventh streets in Beardstown, Illinois, was born in county Antrim, Ireland, November, 1820. He came of Scotch ancestry, of a very old family of pure blood, not mixed with Irish by marriage. He is the son of William Elliott of the same place, a farmer and a keeper of a public inn, who lived and died in that county at the age of forty years. His grandfather was

David Elliott, a farmer of Scotland, who died when quite old. William Elliott was married to an Antrim lady of Scotch blood, whose name was Mary Thompson. She was the daughter of Robert and Mattie (Richie) Thompson, who were county Antrim farmers, and there Robert Thompson spent his last years, but his wife came with her son at an early day to Virginia, Cass county, Illinois.

John Elliott came of a large family, grew up in his native county, learned the tailor trade and afterward with his mother and brothers, in 1841, came to America and joined other brothers in Connecticut. In 1845 the mother and son came on to Cass county. Some worked the farm, and others followed their trade. The mother made her hom with her children until her death, which occurred in 1877, aged eighty-four. She was a noble-hearted woman and had done much to help and encourage her children. She was a member of the Presbyterian Church, a great student of Scotch history and literature, a fine reader of the Scotch dialect and a writer of some local repute. She also composed some music, which has been considered very fine. She is remembered as a noble, generous woman.

He lived for some years in Beardstown, working at his trade and with the money he made and saved, with his brother, David, he bought 160 acres of land near Virginia, later sold it and then purchased the 160 acres that became his home until his retirement. His farm, the scene of his labors, lies near the city of Beardstown. The land is highly improved, and has good buildings, and as he now enjoys the comforts of life he can remember that they have been obtained by his own efforts.

He was married the first time in Connecticut, to Margaret Frey of Ireland, who came to the United States in 1841, and after forty-eight years of married life left a bereaved husband, in 1890. The living children are: William W., of San Francisco, California; Thomas F., of Jewell county, Kansas; George W. of Holliday, Kansas; Robert S. of St. Louis, Missouri; Lucy A., wife of John Thompson, of Jewell county, Kansas; and David H., now running his father's farm. Mr. Elliott was married a second time in this county, to Mrs. Ann E. Johnson, formerly, Hiles. She was born in New Jersey, December 12, 1823. She and her first husband came to Macoupin county in 1856, and he died there.

Mr. and Mrs. Elliott are members of the Congregational Church. Mr. Elliott is a Republican in politics and was a Whig.

WILLIAM McKEE, one of the oldest and most prominent citizens of Schuyler county, was born in Crawford county, Indiana, January 22, 1813, a son of William McKee, who was a native of Kentucky. The paternal grandfather, James McKee, emigrated to Kentucky during the war of the Revolution, and thence removed to Indiana, where he passed the remainder of his days. William McKee, Sr., was reared in the Blue-grass State, and there was married; he removed to Indiana when it was yet a Territory, and was a pioneer of Crawford county. He purchased land and made it his home until 1826, when, accompanied by his wife and ten children, he removed to Illinois. The journey was made by teams, which was not devoid of interest. Mr. McKee had visited this section the year previous, making the trip on horseback; he purchased a land warrant which called for 160 acres, paying therefor $100; on his return to Indiana he stopped at Springfield and cleared his title at the

Government office. It was, indeed, a courageous heart that looked at such a future calmly; the country was thinly settled, the poles of the Indian wigwams still stood in the ground, market towns were far distant and provisions were high. Mr. McKee erected a double log cabin, using wooden pegs instead of nails; the door was constructed of puncheons, and was furnished with the historic latch-string.

James Vance built the first horse-mill operated with a rawhide band. This was built when the subject of this sketch came to the county. Calvin Hobart built one in the fall of 1836, then William McKee, father of our subject, built a horse-mill in 1828, it being the third in that section of the country. People came to the mill from as far north as Rock Island.

Mrs. McKee manufactured cloth from the flax and cotton that her husband raised, with which to clothe the family. Mrs. McKee's maiden name was Cassie Frakes; she was a native of Pennsylvania, and a daughter of Henry and Hannah Frakes; her death occurred at the house of her daughter, which is situated close to the old home farm.

The subject of this sketch was thirteen years and four months old when he came to Illinois; on the journey he drove a four-horse team with a jerk line. He has a vivid recollection of many of the experiences which fall only to the lot of the pioneer. He remained in this State until 1839, and then started on a missionary tour among the Indians in the far West; he crossed the plains to Oregon, and spent one year among the savages; at the end of twelve months he returned to Illinois and resumed farming, continuing this occupation until 1847; then he again crossed the plains to Oregon, and during that year the Indians attacked the mission twenty-five miles from Walla Walla and murdered Dr. Whitman and others; he volunteered to assist in subduing the red-skins, and was six months in the service. He was in Oregon until 1849, and then went to California; he was suffering from ill-health, and his funds were limited compared with the extremely high price of provisions, flour selling as high as $2.50 a pound. In 1852 he returned to his home and located on the old homestead which he now occupies.

Mr. McKee was married in 1853, to Sarah C. Wilmot, a native of Steuben county, New York. Mrs. McKee was educated in the pioneer schools and at the age of twenty began to teach. Only one of the directors who examined her could read and write; she received for her services the magnificent sum of $2.50 a week. Mr. and Mrs. McKee are the parents of five daughters: Amanda, wife of Henry Hite, died in February, 1882, leaving an infant son, Archie M., who is being reared by his grandparents; Mary C., died in infancy; Ida S., wife of Samuel D. Wheelhouse, died in April, 1880; Bertha, wife of Cyrus L. DeWitt; and Meta, who died in October, 1889, aged fourteen years.

Politically Mr. McKee affiliates with the Democratic party, although in former times he was a Whig. He is a man of wide experience, having passed through all the phases of life on the frontier. He has always been loyal to the interests of Schuyler county, and has the entire confidence and respect of his fellow-men.

JACOB RITCHEY, an honored pioneer, resides on section 12, Buena Vista township, and was born in Dayton, Montgomery county, Ohio, on December 5, 1821. When but two years of age his mother died, and five years later he had the misfortune to lose his father There were six children, five sons and one daughter. The oldest, John, died in Schuyler county, Illinois; George F died in Rushville, in the same State, Charles is now residing in Rushville, William G. died in Schuyler county; Susan married Jasper Patton, and died in Ohio; our subject was next in birth to the youngest, and on her death-bed his mother gave him to her brother, Jacob Sawyer, with whom he remained five years He then accompanied his brother George to Illinois, living with him until he grew to manhood He attended school but little, as his time was engaged in hard work on the farm When twenty years of age he was hired by a widow to work her farm on shares, which he did for one year. Later, his brother George married the widow, and our subject rented his brother's former farm, which he tilled until 1845, when he rented eighty acres of William McKee, which he cultivated for himself While thus engaged, he met Clara Ann, daughter of the owner of this land, and their acquaintance ripening into mutual affection, they were married in 1849, when his father-in-law presented to him the eighty acres he had been tilling, and on which he and his wife still reside. He has made substantial improvements on his land, in the way of buildings, having a comfortable home and barns for his grain and stock, besides other modern appliances, to facilitate the sowing, harvesting and garnering the products of the farm Besides this eighty acres, which is under a good state of cultivation, he has purchased 167 acres more in Rushville township, which he is also farming.

Mr and Mrs. Ritchey have seven children: William Thomas, residing in Rushville township; Charles R, residing in Camden township; James, residing in Huntsville township, Georgia Ann, living at home, Susan C, wife of F. E. Moore; living in Cowley county, Kansas; Amanda and Mary, living at home

Mr. Ritchey is a member of the Republican party, but takes no active part in politics other than desiring the advancement and welfare of the community. He is not a member of any civic or religious society, but is liberal in his views He is a thoroughly honest and industrious man, a good neighbor, kind husband and indulgent father, and enjoys the esteem of the community and the affection of his family and friends.

CHARLES A. SCHAEFFER, County Superintendent of Schools of Cass county, is thoroughly identified with the educational interests of this county, and is as popular as he is well known. A *résumé* of his life is herewith presented.

Mr. Schaeffer was born in what is now Bluff Spring precinct, Cass county, Illinois, May 24, 1855 His father, Calvin S. Schaeffer, was born in Monroe precinct, same county, son of Phillip Schaeffer, a native of Ohio. Phillip Schaeffer's father, John Schaeffer, was, it is supposed, a native of Pennsylvania, and the family are descended from German ancestry. John Schaeffer removed to Ohio at an early day and was one of the pioneer settlers of that State. He continued his way westward in 1818 and took up his abode in Cass county, Illinois, where he passed his life He and his worthy companion reared six sons and six daughters. Phillip Schaeffer was reared and married in in Ohio, and moved from there to Illinois, becoming one of the first settlers of what is now Monroe precinct, Cass county. Here he entered a tract of Government land and on it erected a cabin which served as the family home for a number of years. Subsequently he built a frame dwelling. At that time Beardstown, Jacksonville and Springfield were the principal markets in this part of the country. There were no gristmills in this vicinity, and on his farm he erected a mill that he operated by horse power. People came for many miles to get their corn ground here. On this place he made his home until the time of his death, in 1854. The maiden name of his wife was Highly Carver. She was born in Ohio, of English descent. Her death occurred at the home place in 1880. The names of their six children are Washington, Valentine W., Calvin S., Cyrus J., Martha A. and Elizabeth. Calvin S. was reared on the farm and remained with his parents until his marriage, soon after which he moved to Petersburg and was engaged in farming there for a time. He then came back to Monroe Precinct and leased a part of his father's estate, built a log house, and lived there about ten years. From there he moved to his present farm, which includes a part of his father-in-law's homestead in Hickory precinct. His wife was before her marriage Miss Mary Schafer, she being a daughter of Christopher and Rachel (Emerick) Shafer. Calvin S. Schaeffer and his wife reared six children, viz.: Charles A.; George W.; Winters L.; William D.; Rachel A.; and Jennie.

Charles A. Schaeffer received his early education in the district schools, afterward attending the Virginia High School and the State Normal School at Normal, Illinois. At the age of twenty-two he commenced teaching, and taught and attended school for nine years. On the thirty-first anniversary of his birth he received the nomination for County Superintendent of Schools, and was elected at the ensuing election. Four years later he was nominated by acclamation, and elected by a largely increased majority. In November, 1890, he bought an interest in the Virginia *Enquirer*, in company with his cousin, William A. S. Schaeffer (since deceased), and soon afterward bought the remaining interest. He was then sole proprietor of this paper until September, 1891, at which time he sold the entire interest in said paper to F. E. Downing.

Mr. Schaeffer was married, in 1882, to Nellie M. Garner, a native of Oregon precinct, Cass county, Illinois, a daughter of William S. and Nancy M. (Crews) Garner. Two children have been born to them: Ledru G. and Edna Belle.

Mr. Schaeffer's political views are in harmony with Democratic principles. He cast his first vote for Samuel J. Tilden. Fraternally, he is associated with Virginia Lodge, No. 544, A. F. & A. M.; Saxon Lodge, No. 68, I. O. O. F.; and Virginia Camp, M. W. A.

HIRAM BENNETT BAXTER, an intelligent and progressive farmer and stock-raiser of township 17-9, near Ashland, Illinois, was born and reared in Jefferson county, Indiana.

His parents were William and Jane (Kerr) Baxter, both natives of Ohio, his father having been born in Dayton. His father's father was a native of Ireland, who came to America and settled in Pittsburg, Pennsylvania, where he married a German lady, named Rebecca Riddle. Mr. Baxter's maternal grandfather was Josiah Kerr, a native of Scotland. Thus he is of Irish, German and Scotch ancestry, three of the most intelligent and progressive nationalities on the face of the earth, and he would be a sad renegade were he not likewise constituted His parents had ten sons and two daughters, of whom the subject of this sketch was the sixth in order of birth James Riddle, the, eldest brother, is an attorney of Bloomfield Greene county, Indiana; Josiah Kerr is a retired physician of Sharpsville, Indiana, Daniel Thomas, a mechanic, died in early manhood, leaving a wife and two children, all now deceased; Oliver H. P. was one of the first white settlers in Pueblo, Colorado, where he engaged in mining and speculating in cattle, in which occupations he has been very successful, having accumulated a fortune of great wealth He is now retired from active business, and spends most of his time in traveling, has been twice to Europe, and last summer was in Alaska William Alexander died in Indianapolis, Indiana, in 1877, the next in order is the subject of this sketch; George W. is a resident of Indianapolis, Indiana; Hayden Hayes is in the cattle business, near Pueblo, Colorado; Edward Arthur is in the livery and undertaking business in Sangamon county, Illinois; Leonidas Napoleon is farming the old Indiana homestead; Havanna Siloam married Robert Williams, a merchant of Madison, Indiana; Irena Hazeltine died in early childhood In 1854 the family were called upon to mourn the loss of the devoted wife and mother, whose life had been one of self-abnegation and subservience to her family's welfare The father afterward married her sister, and to this union one son, Virgil, was born, who died in 1861. The father died in August, 1861, and was interred by the side of his first wife, near the old home in Indiana He was a prominent man in his community and was very popular among his associates, always heading every movement for the moral and material improvement of his locality. The second wife lives on the old homestead She is a lady of much culture and refinement, and is universally beloved

The subject of this sketch was educated in Indiana, and was reared to farm life, and in the peaceful pursuits of rural and home life spent his earlier days. This happy routine was interrupted by civil discord, which rent the country, and on July 14, 1861, he enlisted at Madison, Indiana, in Company K, Twenty-second Indiana Infantry. He participated in the Missouri campaign, the first encounter taking place at Glasgow, that State, where Major Tanner was killed; and also took part in the fight at Blackwater, where the Union forces took 1,300 of the enemy prisoners Thence he accompanied his regiment, under the supervision of General Fremont, to Springfield, Missouri. General Hunter superseding General Fremont, they were returned to their old quarters, under the immediate command of General Curtis, with whom they marched to Springfield and thence to the battle at Pea Ridge, where the right flank suffered severely. Thence they went to Corinth, Mississippi, where they participated in the siege of Corinth, after which they returned to Iuka, that State, going from there to Florence, Alabama, and back again to Louisville, marching 400 miles in August and September, 1862. After this they went to Perryville, Kentucky, where there was an engagement. in which Mr Baxter was shot through the left knee, lying on the battlefield all night after being wounded There were thirty-five men in his company on going into battle, and on emerging there were but eight unharmed, ten having been killed, thirteen wounded and four taken prisoners. Mr Baxter was sent to the hospital at Louisville, where he remained from October 8, 1862, to February of the following year. He rejoined his regiment at Murfreesboro, Tennessee, and there received his commission as First Lieutenant, being promoted from Duty Sergeant to that rank. In the absence of the captain, who had been wounded, Mr. Baxter at once assumed command of the company. His regiment remained in Murfreesboro until June, and then went on the Tullahoma campaign, following the enemy as far as Chattanooga, and participated in the historic battle of Chickamauga. It then fell back to Chattanooga, and engaged for a time in building fortifications. It next took part in the sanguinary battle of Missionary Ridge, at which it was in Sheridan's division, and fought in the center. The following morning it started on a forced march for Knoxville, to relieve Burnside, who was surrounded by Longstreet. During this rapid march, the regiment was short of rations and had no tents. It was encamped on Strawberry Plains for six weeks, while the ground, the greater part of the time, was covered with snow. At this place the regiment re-enlisted for three years, and then returned to Chattanooga, after which the men were given a veteran furlough. At the expiration of their leave of absence, they rejoined their command at Chattanooga, whence they started with General Sherman on his memorable march to the sea, the Twenty-second Indiana being in the advance brigade. The enemy were met in force at Tunnel Hill and Rocky Face Ridge, and next at Resaca, Georgia, whence the Union forces proceeded to Snake Creek Gap, where Mr. Baxter's division was separated from the main army, and sent, under General Jefferson C. Davis, via Rome, Georgia. Here an engagement was fought, at which Mr. Baxter was again wounded in the left leg, the same as before. He remained about a month in Rome, when he secured a leave of absence for forty days, finally reporting to the officer's hospital, in Cincinnati, where the board of examiners ordered his discharge, General Slemmer being the chief of the board. On being discharged, August 29, 1864, he was granted $8.50 a month, that being half of a first lieutenant's pension.

In February, 1865, Mr. Baxter assisted in raising a company for the One Hundred and Forty-eighth Indiana Regiment, of which company he became First Lieutenant and afterward Captain. This regiment was sent to Columbia, Tennessee, where it did patrol duty until September 6, 1865, when it was mustered out of service.

Mr. Baxter then returned to his home in Indiana, and was subsequently employed for a time in the railroad business in Indianapolis. December 15, 1866, he reached Jacksonville, Illinois, near which place he taught school two years; later, he taught school for another two years at Literberry, same State. He was afterward engaged in selling goods in the latter place, where he acted at various times as railroad agent, Postmaster and Justice of the Peace, his residence there extending over a period of nine years.

In 1876 he was married, and included the Centennial Exposition in his wedding tour, visiting in old Virginia and spending a week in Washington city. Miss Lydia Ellen Crum was the lady of his choice, a daughter of Abram A. and Sarah (Buchanan) Crum, old and highly respected residents of the vicinity of Literberry, Illinois, where they still reside. Mr. and Mrs. Baxter have two sons,—Albert, born October 9, 1880, and William Abram, born September 18, 1887.

In 1881, Mr. Baxter sold ohut is mercantile interests in Literberry and removed to his present farm, five miles west of Ashland, where his father-in-law had given him $20,000 worth of land. He owns a farm of 760 acres on the garden spot of Illinois, and, as for that matter, of the world, inasmuch as there is no more fertile country on the globe than that included in the Prairie State. This season (1892), he has 260 acres of corn, 180 of wheat, and eighty of oats, the balance being meadow and pasture land. He has here a substantial farm residence, neatly and comfortably arranged; large barns for his grain and stock; and many other valuable improvements.

Mr. Baxter is a stanch Republican and takes an active interest in political matters. He has been a candidate for various offices, but his party being in the minority he was never elected, yet succeeded in helping to hold the party organization together.

He belongs to the G. A. R. and was the first commander of John L. Douglas Post, No. 591, at Ashland, having served two terms in that capacity.

Seven of Mr. Baxter's brothers were in the army, no two of whom were in the same regiment, and all returned home, and still survive. Dr. Josiah was a Surgeon in the army; and Hayden was taken prisoner, stripped of his clothing and other valuables, paroled and turned loose, walking all the way home from Arkansas Post. Of this family there were one Surgeon, two Captains one Lieutenant, and three privates in the service. The subject of this sketch received three commissions, two as First Lieutenant, and one as Captain, all from the hands of the famous war Governor Oliver P. Morton. Mr. Baxter received two wounds at the hands of the rebels, which compelled him to spend some eight months in the hospital. During the total period of three years and eight months he served two years in command of his company; and, while he was one of the youngest soldiers in it, he thinks he did his part.

Had this family lived in Napoleon's time, they would have been greatly honored, inasmuch as he valued families only in proportion to the number of sons contributed to the insatiable monster of war. It is the disadvantage of republican forms of government, that they bestow no special privileges for services rendered by their inhabitants other than the universal gratitude of millions living and unborn, which is supplemented, in the breasts of those champions of liberty in the late war, by a deep sense of duty done, which soothes the wounded spirit and begets a peace which passeth understanding.

FREDERICK C. LANG, a self-made man and one of the prominent merchants of Virginia, Illinois, belongs to that race of people —the Germans—noted this world over for their energy and thrift. By his own well-directed efforts he has risen to a position of prosperity, and at the same time has won the confidence and respect of all with whom he has had dealings, being now classed with the substantial business men and highly respected citizens of Virginia. It is with pleasure that we present the following facts in regard to his life and ancestry.

Frederick C. Lang was born on the river Tech, village of Omden, in the Kingdom of Württemburg, Germany, September 7, 1848. His father, Christopher Frederick Lang, was born in the same locality. His grandparents, as far as known, spent their entire lives in Württemburg. Christopher F. Lang was reared and educated in his native land and there served an apprenticeship to the trade of a weaver, weaving at that time being chiefly done on the hand loom. He followed that trade in Germany till 1855, in the early part of which year he set sail from Havre de Grace, with his wife and three children, and landed in America in March, after a voyage of nearly three months. He went direct to Indianapolis, where he was employed at various kinds of work. Finally he secured a position as porter in a wholesale drug store, and was thus engaged for a number of years. He resided in Indianapolis until his death, in 1887. The maiden name of his first wife, mother of Frederick C., was Mary Liebrich. She was also a native of Württemburg. She reared three children: Frederick C., George and Mary.

Mr. Lang, being only six years old when he came to America, remembers little of any other save his adopted country. He was educated in the public schools of Indianapolis, was reared to habits of industry, and at the age of fifteen was apprenticed to Jacob Vœgtle, a tinsmith, of Indianapolis, and served four years. He did "jour" work in Indianapolis one year, after which he went to Jacksonville, Illinois, and was employed in the same kind of work six years. He was very industrious, saved his money, and in 1874 came to Virginia and began busines for himself. He first opened a stock of stoves and tinware, and in 1885 added hardware. He now carries a full line of shelf hardware, stoves, tinware, etc. In connection with his store he also conducts a repair shop, having first-class machinery for doing all kinds of job work, tin roofing and the like.

In 1877 Mr. Lang was united in marriage with Mary Tendick, a native of Jacksonville, Illinois, and a daughter of Deidrich and Sibilla Tendick, natives of Germany. They have four children: George, Clara, Flora and Willie.

Mr. and Mrs. Lang are members of the Presbyterian Church. Politically, he is a Republican.

DR. GEORGE A. BYRNS was born in Cincinnati, Ohio, September 30, 1829. His father, John, was born in Pennsylvania, and his father, Michael, was born in Ireland, of Scotch ancestry. He came to America a young man and followed his trade of paper maker, and he met his death in 1825, by an accident in the mill in which he was working. John learned the same trade, followed the trade in Cincinnati for a few years and then began clerking on a steamboat running on the Ohio and Mississippi rivers. In a very early day he came to Illinois as a member of a surveying party and assisted in making surveys in the middle of the State. In 1840 he emigrated thither with his family and settled four miles north of Mt. Sterling, bought a farm and followed farming until 1849. He then started with others for California, and after six months' travel with ox teams, landed there safely. He engaged there in mining for seven years and then returned to Mt. Sterling and lived retired until his death, in 1865. He was a soldier in the war of 1812. His wife was Harriet E. Hobbs, born in Scott county, Kentucky, daughter of Joseph Hobbs. She still lives in Mt. Sterling at the advanced age of eighty-six years.

George was in his eleventh year when he came to Illinois with his parents. He received his early education in the schoools of Cincinnati, advanced by attendance in the schools of Brown county, Illinois. At the age of eighteen he began teaching, and three years later began the study of medicine. In the winter of 1851–'52 he attended lectures at Rush Medical College. He then commenced practice at Cooperstown. In 1854 he returned to Rush Medical College and graduated in the class of 1855, then resumed practice at Cooperstown until 1862. In November of that year he entered the United States service as Assistant Surgeon of the One Hundred and Nineteenth Illinois Infantry, continuing in service until after the close of the war, participating in all the marches and campaigns of his regiment. He was honorably discharged and returned home and was in active practice at Cooperstown, with the exception of two years, 1866 to 1868, when he was in Mt. Sterling, until 1891, when he came to Mt. Sterling and has practiced here since.

He married in 1854, Cynthia A. Henry, born in Cooperstown, Brown county, Illinois. She was the daughter of Orris M. Henry, one of the pioneers of Brown county, and for many years one of the most extensive business men. Dr. and Mrs. Byrns have seven living children: John H., Robert A., Elmer, Susan, Candace, Kate and Hattie. William, the second son, died at the age of thirty-three years. The Doctor is a member of Isaac McNeil Post, No. 289, G. A. R., and of Hardin Lodge, No. 44, A. F. & A. M.

ABNER LEGRAND NOBLE has been for many years prominently identified with the history of Schuyler county, and is entitled to the following space in this volume. He is a native of Madison county, Kentucky, born June 12, 1822, a son of William Noble of Lexington, Kentucky; the father was born, reared and married in the Bluegrass State, and there learned the trade of house painting, which he pursued many years. He resided in Kentucky until 1835, and then with his wife and six children removed to Illinois; they made the journey with teams, camping along the way. Mr. Noble located in what is now Bainbridge township, where he purchased a tract of timber land; a few acres had been cleared and a two-story house had been built of hewn logs; here he lived several years, and finally sold the place and purchased another near by, on which he lived until death. He married Eleanor Ransom of Virginia, and a daughter of Ignatius Ransom, also a Virginian by birth. Abner Legrand Noble was a lad of twelve years when he came with his parents to Illinois, and remembers well many of the privations and hardships endured by the family. He received a limited education, and in early youth began to assist his father on the farm. He has been for years an extensive reader, and has made up for the deficiencies of his early training. He remained with his parents until attaining his majority; he then learned the cooper's trade, and opened a shop in Rushville, manufacturing and selling to the trade for several years; he was compelled to close out the business on account of ill health.

In 1847, Mr. Noble was elected Constable, and for more than thirty-five years attended to the collections of this office; during this time he served three terms as Deputy Sheriff, one term as County Clerk, and one and a half terms as a member of the County Board of Supervisors. He was a very efficient officer, and gave entire satisfaction to the public.

He was married October 28, 1845, to Catherine Serrot, a native of Ohio, and a daughter of Peter and Nancy (Patton) Serrot. Of this union four children were born, two of whom survive: Phœbe Jackson, Dora and Ruth Tetrick; the only son, William H., died at the age of eighteen years; Mary J., the oldest, married William D. Sperry: her death occurred in 1890. Mr. and Mrs. Noble are members of the Methodist Episcopal Church. In early days Mr. Noble was a member of the Whig party, and cast his suffrage for Lincoln; latterly he has voted with the Democratic party. For some time he has held the office of Police Magistrate.

ANDREW CUNNINGHAM, of township 17, range 9, section 6, Virginia post office, Illinois, was born near Edinborough, Scotland, December 17, 1806. His parents were James and Marion (Wright) Cunningham, natives of Scotland, where they lived and died. His father was a baker and miller by occupation and owned and operated a flouring mill in the village of Bonnington, a suburb of Edinborough. They had eight children: Archibald, John, Charles, George, Andrew, Margaret, Jeanette and Mary, now Mrs. Russell, living at Edinborough. The eldest brother died in Scotland. Charles, who was British Consul to Russia and died at Galatz, on the Black sea. John and George died in Cass county, Illinois, leaving families. Margaret was Mrs. Blair and died in Edinborough. Jeanette became Mrs. Shaen and died in England.

Mr. Cunningham was educated in his own country, where he learned the baker trade, and sailed for America March 14, 1834. He was married in Canada, in 1836, to Ellen Allen, who was also born in Scotland, in 1812. She died in 1880. In 1835 he came to Cass county to look up a location and in the beginning of 1837 settled on his present farm. He entered about 700 acres of land, to which he has since added by purchase until he owns about 1,000 acres all, adjoining his present home. On locating here he started a tannery on his farm and followed that business until after the war. He has since superintended his large estate and taken life more easily. He is a literary man, keeps himself surrounded with newspapers and books and has a valuable library where he spends most of his time. Mr. and Mrs. Cunningham have five children: William went into the army in 1862 in the Third Illinois Cavalry, Company C, and died at Helena, Arkansas, Decmber 12, following; Andrew died in infancy; Margaret married Dr. Alfred S. Dodds of Andrew county, Missouri; James A. lives with his father and superintends the farms; Florence married a lawyer, A. G. Jones, at Mt. Pulaski, Illinois. She attends the college at Lincoln, Illinois, but Margaret finished her education in England. The boys all had good school education. Andrew afterward attended a business college at Chicago. Mr. Cunningham is a Unitarian in religious belief, a Republican in politics and was a Whig before the organization of the Republican party. His first presidental vote was cast for Clay. He has been a School Trustee and Director. Both he and his son James are mechanically inclined. He has given a portion of his leisure time to sculpture, having now on exhibition two very fine ideal images of Venus and Hercules, besides other articles of animal sculpture.

James Cunningham settled in Charlestown, South Carolina, previous to the breaking out of the Revolutionary war. He at first served in the militia, under King George, and subsequently joined with the Colonial forces, with which he remained during hostilities.

Mr. Wright, the father of Marion Wright, also served in the war with the mother country.

JOSHUA HEDGCOCK was born in Schuyler county, Illinois, February 2, 1843, onthe place where he now resides, a son of John and Temperance Hedgcock. He received his education at the public schools, remaining at home until August, 1862, when he enlisted, at the age of twenty, as a private in Company G, Seventy-second Regiment Illinois Volunteers, Captain H. D. French commanding the company. His was the first Board of Trade regiment made up in Chicago, commanded by Colonel F. A. Starring. He was in the battles of Champion Hills, Big Black, Benton, Mississippi; siege of Vicksburg; Columbia and Spring Hill, Tennessee; Nashville, December, 1864, and Spanish Fort, Alabama, in April, 1865. He was discharged as Second Sergeant at the close of the war, with the record of which he is justly proud. He returned home in August, 1865, and lived with his father until his death, May 20, 1877, aged seventy-four years, and now occupies the old Spring Hill home of seventy-eight and one-half acres, which his father first bought and settled on in this country. He has now 230 acres.

Joshua was married first January 9, 1870, to Miss Susan E. Glover, born in Hancock county, and died here January 9, 1872, aged twenty-six years. She left one son, who survived her eight months. Joshua was married for the second time, to Miss Anna M. Totten, April 10, 1879, who was born in Adams county, September 26, 1854, and by this marriage there are six children. Mr. and Mrs. Hedgcock attend the Methodist Protestant Church. He is a member of Post No. 302, G. A. R., at Augusta, Illinois; has been Assessor of his township. His first vote was cast while home on furlough, for Lincoln, and every president he has since voted for has been elected, except one.

GEORGE W. McCOY, an extensive farmer of Mt. Sterling, Illinois, was born in Adams county, Ohio, January 1, 1831. His father, Samuel McCoy, was born in Cecil county, Maryland, in 1796. The grandfather of our subject, Alexander McCoy, was born in Ireland, of Scotch ancestry. His parents were poor and he commenced very early to earn his own living, being brought up to work in a factory. He was a lad in his 'teens when he came to America and located in Maryland, where his parents who had preceded him to America were then living. He learned the cooper's trade, which he followed for some time. He was twice married but lost both of his wives before coming to Ohio. After the death of his second wife he removed with his children to Ohio and lived in that State some years, and then spent his last years in Brown county. The father of our subject died in 1882, in the eighty-fifth year of his age. He was about eighteen years old when he went to Ohio. He was very industrious, saved his earnings and finally purchased land in Adams county. He then turned his attention to agricultural pursuits but still followed his trade a portion of each year. He resided in Adams county until 1839, and then sold his farm there and came to Illinois. He was accompanied by his wife and three children, and the entire journey was made overland. After about fifteen days' travel they landed in Brown county. He purchased a tract of land near Versailles, and there devoted his time to farming. He was a resident of Brown county until his death, which occurred as before stated.

The maiden name of the mother of our subject was Sarah Pilston. She was born in in Virginia, a daughter of William and Easter Pilston. She died in Ohio in 1834.

The subject of this writing was in his ninth year when he came to Illinois with his parents. At that time the country was wild and deer, wild turkeys, and other game were quite plentiful. Farming was conducted in the most primitive manner. All the grass was cut with a scythe, and the grain was either cut with a reap hook or a cradle and trampled out with horses or with a flail. There were no fanning-mills, and in order to clean the grain one man would take it in a seive and hold it high and two others would stand by with a sheet with which they fanned the air and in that manner separated the grain from the chaff.

Mr. McCoy remained with his father until nineteen years of age, then commenced farming on rented land. When he attained his majority his father gave him $250, and with that and his earnings he had enough to pay cash on 120 acres of land, which is now included in the farm he now occupies. The whole price of the farm was $680, and he paid six per cent. interest on the balance. He lived in a log cabin and in that humble abode himself and wife commenced housekeeping. They occupied that dwelling about eighteen months and then built a brick house. Since that time he has erected a commodious frame house and other buildings, planted fruit and shade trees and placed the land in a high state of cultivation. He has been very successful as a farmer and has purchased other land at different times and is now the owner of about 500 acres, all in Brown county.

The marriage of Mr. McCoy took place January 27, 1853, to Sarah Harper. She was born in Ohio, August 29, 1835, and was the daughter of Elder James Harper. Mrs. McCoy died November 2, 1868, and Mr. McCoy subsequently married Lucinda, a sister of his former wife, October 28, 1869. She was born in Brown county, Illinois, April 17, 1847, and died May 7, 1890. He was married to Laura J. Putman, October 28, 1891. She was born in Ohio, August 7, 1841. Her father, William Putman, was born in Bourbon county, Kentucky, October 16, 1797, and was the son of Zachariah and Winnifred (Collins) Putman. The parents of Mrs. McCoy moved to Ohio and resided in Champaign county for some years, coming from there to Illinois in 1841, at which time the father purchased a farm in Mt. Sterling township, which he occupied until his death, July 24, 1880. Mr. McCoy has five children by his first marriage: Elvira, Mahala, Mary Jane, Turner and Martha. Of his second marriage there are William and Arthur. Mr. and Mrs. McCoy are members of the Primitive Baptist Church and are good pious people. In politics he affiliates with the Democratic party. He has served long as Supervisor and has been Chairman of the Board.

JOHN DIRREEN, ex-Sheriff of Cass county, was born in Virginia precinct, Cass county, Illinois, July 29, 1840. He is one of the representative men of his county, and as such merits biographical mention in this work. Briefly given, a review of his life is as follows:

While tradition says that the Dirreen family originated in France, their ancestry is traced back only to the grandfather of John Dirreen, who was born in Ireland. Three of his children came from the Emerald Isle to America, and located as follows: John settled in Halifax, Nova Scotia, where he was a customhouse official upwards of forty years, at the end of that time retiring on half-pay. He died there, aged ninety-three years. Michael bought a farm in New York State, and still resides on it. Edward Dirreen was born in county Callan, Ireland, and was there reared. He came to America when a young man and settled in Philadelphia, where he married. He subsequently moved to St. Louis, and from there came to Cass county, Illinois, about 1835, settling in Virginia precinct. Here he entered a tract of Government land, four miles from the site of the present courthouse, and built the log cabin in which the subject of our sketch was born. At that time the country was thinly settled and deer and wild turkey were plenty in this region. The whistle of the locomotive had not sounded here, and Beardstown was the market seat for the surrounding country. In 1855 he sold his farm and bought another in the same locality, where he resided until his death. His widow, whose maiden name was Jane Henphey, still resides on the old homestead. They were the parents of seven children: Catherine, Eliza, Alice, John, Richard, Edward and Michael. Eliza and Richard are deceased.

John Dirreen received his education in the primitive log schoolhouses of his native county. As soon as he was old enough he assisted his father on the farm, remaining under the parental roof until he was twenty-one. He was then employed for three years by others, at the end of which time he engaged in farming on his own account. In the fall of 1877, on account of the ill health of his wife, he went to Texas, remaining there till January, 1878, when he returned to Illinois. That spring he was made a Deputy Sheriff, and has been connected with the office of Sheriff continuously since. In 1886 he was elected Sheriff, and served one term, which is the limit prescribed by law. At the expiration of his term he was again appointed deputy, which position he still holds.

Mr. Dirreen was married in 1871, to Mary Cunningham, a native of Kentucky, and a daughter of George and Maria (Lindsey) Cunningham, natives of Scotland and Kentucky respectively. Mrs. Dirreen died in February, 1878, and in November, 1886, he married Alice Burrows. By his first wife he has one daughter, Josephine, and by the second, a son, Edward.

Mr. Dirreen is a member of Virginia Lodge, A. O. U. W.

WILLIAM JOCKISCH, a retired farmer, of Beardstown, was born in Liepsic, Saxony, Germany, in 1829. His parents, Carl G. and Eliza (Jacob) Jockisch, were born in Saxony. Mr. Jockisch, Sr., was a farmer and distiller for some years before he and his family embarked for the United States in 1834. They went to New Orleans, and then worked their way up the Mississippi river to St. Louis, and there the mother died at the birth of her tenth child. Mr. Jockisch was left with his small children to make the rest of the trip alone. He stopped in Cass county for some time, and then was married a second time to Mrs. Christina Long, of Germany. Mr. Jockisch died in this county, and his wife followed him some ten years later. They were at first Lutherans, and later Methodists.

William Jockisch is the youngest but one of nine children that grew to maturity. Two of his brothers are in the same county. He began farming at an early age, and by his good management has amassed a small fortune, which he now enjoys in retirement in his comfortable and pleasant home on the corner of Sixth and Edwards streets. He owns 300 acres of good, tillable land, besides other lands which lie southwest of Beardstown. The building of the railroad has aided him greatly in making his fortune, as much of the land he owned was increased by the building of the road.

He was married to Elizabeth Rohn, of Beardstown, Illinois. She was born in 1839, in Beardstown, and lived there till 1855. She was the daughter of John and Catharine (Stier) Rohn, of Hesse-Darmstadt. They came to the northwest early in life, and were married in Beardstown. Mrs. Rohn is still living, and is nearly eighty-nine years of age. Mr. Rohn was a plasterer by trade, and was the proprietor of the ferry at Beardstown at the time of his death. He was a Republican in politics, and a Lutheran in religion.

Mrs. Jockisch is the eldest of four children. Mr. and Mrs. Jockisch have had seven children, two of whom are dead, Mary A. and Rosena A. Those living are: Elizabeth, now the wife of J. T. Brines, a farmer in Schuyler county; J. Victor, at home, and clerking for Phil Kuhl; Anna A., now Mrs. Cad Allard (see biography); Rosa, now Mrs. Dr. J. C. Henny, of Beardstown, the leading dentist; Rudolph, deputy clerk in the post office of Beardstown. The children have all been well educated. They are all members of the Methodist Church, of which Mr. Jockisch has been Trustee for four years, and a member of the building committee of the new church that has just been erected.

Mr. Jockisch is one of the promoters and a director of the First National Bank of Beardstown, as well as one of the heaviest stockholders in the same. He was appointed Public Administrator in and for the county of Cass September 13, 1892. He is a worthy citizen of this thriving place, and as he has lived in the county since his fourth year, and in the town for the last twenty years, he is one of the pioneers of the place and is a pioneer of whom Illinois may well be proud.

HENRY VENTRES was born in Smith county, Tennessee, January 25, 1812. His parents, Asa and Nancy (Wakefield) Ventres, were of Welsh and English ancestry respectively. The former was born December 24, 1793, and the latter was born about the same time. Soon after the war of 1812, in which he was a soldier, he located in St. Clair county, Illinois, where he died about 1818.

Henry was the eldest of a family of four children, three of whom are still living. He learned the brick-making trade in early manhood, and worked at that and brick-laying up to the time he came to Illinois, and has engaged in it since coming to this State. Coming to Illinois at such an early date, the family have witnessed a wonderful growth in the country. The Black Hawk band was located on Rock river, and frequently infested the settlers. Mr. Ventres has held the various township offices, and given satisfaction in every one. He settled on his present farm in 1834, and is one of the oldest settlers of the county. There was only an occasional log cabin in the county. The land which he took up was a military tract, which he purchased, consisting of 160 acres of land, to which he has added forty acres since.

He was married in Monroe county, Kentucky, to Miss Elizabeth Jones, January 27, 1833. In 1883 they celebrated their golden wedding, and are looking forward to the celebration of a diamond one. They have had nine children, of whom five are still living, namely: William C., a miller and merchant, located in Kansas; Ophelia, now Mrs. A. R. Marshall, of Gove county, Kansas: her husband is a farmer and stock-raiser; Sarah, now Mrs. T. Shippy, of Plymouth, Illinois: her husband is a teacher by profession; Lucy A., now Mrs. Beck, of Pueblo, Colorado: her husband is a merchant; Walter Maro resides on a farm adjoining his father's: he married Miss Maggie Diamond. Mr. and Mrs. Venters have been consistent members of the Christian Church for sixty years. Mr. Venters has been a life-long Democrat, but is disgusted with both the old parties. He has been a man of exemplary habits, not using any kind of intoxicants or tobacco in any form. Mr. and Mrs. Venters are comfortably situated, and are enjoying the fruits of their early labors.

MRS. SALLIE (BRYANT) LUTTERELL, of section 9, Browning township, was born in Virginia in 1792. She is the oldest person in Schuyler county, and there are very few in the State who can boast of being 100 years old. Should she live until the 25th of June she will be 100 years old. She came to Schuyler county in 1830, and has been a resident of the county ever since. Her husband, Shelton Lutterell, was a soldier in the war of 1812, and fought at the battle of Horse Bud and various other points. They were married November 13, 1813, and their married life lasted for sixty-nine years, four months and seventeen days, when Mr. Lutterell died, in the house where his widow still resides. He was born May 12, 1794. They were among the first settlers of Browning township, where Mr. Lutterell owned a farm. Mrs. Lutterell's parents were natives of Patrick county, Virginia. Mrs. Lutterell raised a family of twelve children, and she has survived all but three of them,—Sarah Skiles, Nancy Wright and Ollie Thornton. Mrs. Lutterell has lived with her daughter, Mrs. Thornton, since the death of her husband. Mr. Thornton, the husband of her daughter, was born in Jackson county, Tennessee, September 10, 1819, and he was the son of Felix and Celetha (Holly) Thornton. They were born and reared to maturity in Raleigh, North Carolina, but came to this county in 1829, and located on a farm near Mr. Lutterell's. They had five sons and the same number of daughters, but only five of them are living. Mr. Thornton was married in Browning township, June 23, 1844, to Miss Ollie Lutterell. They have eight children, but only four are living: William I., deceased; Sarah C., wife of John Flemming, and lives in Browning village; Delilah J., deceased; Patsy Ann, wife of David Steadman, and lives in Browning township; Martha Ellen married William Thornton, and lives in the same place; John A. lives in Browning. Two children died in infancy. A grandson, Chester R., lives with his grandmother.

Mrs. Lutterell's father was a John Bryant, and was the son of another John Bryant.

Her mother was Judy Wentfrey. She is a member of the Christian Church, as are Mr and Mrs Thornton, and she has been one for fifty years Mr. Thornton has been a resident of the township for sixty-three years, and he has seen many wonderful changes take place in the county. He has traveled in the States of Kentucky, Iowa, Missouri, Arkansas, Mississippi, Louisiana and Illinois. He has always been a farmer by occupation. He is a Democrat in politics, and his sons are Democrats in their political views

OVERTON PARKE, a substantial farmer and influential citizen of Woodstock township, Schuyler county, Illinois, was born in Brown county, of the same State, October 8, 1841. His parents were Perry and Mary (Logsdon) Parke. (See sketch of Perry and Joseph Logsdon for history of the Logsdons) They were both natives of Kentucky, and came to Illinois at an early day, and still reside in Woodstock township, near the home of our subject

The subject of our sketch was reared on the home farm and attended the country schools of his district during the winters. He remained at home until he was twenty years of age, assisting his father and going to school, when, on August 11, 1862, he enlisted in Company D, One Hundred and Fifteenth Illinois Infantry, serving in the Civil war until its close, with the exception of a few weeks, during which he was in the hospital at Louisville, Kentucky With the exception of these few weeks he served with his regiment through every skirmish and battle until the great conflict was over After the war he returned to his home in Schuyler county, where he rented a farm for a year, when, in the fall of 1866, he was married to Miss Rosanna C Reddick. She was a native of Woodstock township, Schuyler county, Illinois, where she was born April 25, 1851, her parents being pioneers and prominent people of this county, viz · John J and Mary (Clark) Reddick (See sketch of John Clark for history of Clark family.) John J. Reddick was a son of Jonathan Reddick, and came to this county with his parents when he was only about one or two years of age His parents came from Kentucky about 1830 and located in Schuyler county, being among the earliest settlers of that county, where they resided until their death. They were among the most prominent and successful agriculturists of their vicinity, and highly respected by all who knew them It is on their homestead that our subject now resides, which is one of the finest farms in the country, well improved with substantial house and large barns for grain and stock, while the land is highly cultivated, and supplied with all the modern machinery and appliances for the sowing and harvesting of their products But, immediately after his marriage, Mr. Parke had no such splendid home, living for several years on a part of his father's farm, which he rented. He and his wife resided here until the death of her parents, since when they have lived in the present home, which through the energy and enterprise of our subject has been greatly improved, and which comprises, at the present writing, more than 300 acres of the finest agricultural land in the country

Mr. and Mrs. Parke have had eleven children, five of whom are now living, viz: John E, Maggie A, Elizabeth, Nettie C and Rosanna C.

Politically Mr Parke is a Republican, and ever since his first vote for General U. S. Grant he has voted the straight Republican ticket. He is a member of the G. A. R. Post at Rushville, Illinois. He and his estimable wife are members of the church, for the cause of which they are earnest workers, as, indeed, they are in every worthy cause. Both are ardently interested in the advancement and welfare of their county and the country at large, and both enjoy alike the respect and esteem of the community in which they live.

FRANCIS MARION STOUT, a large land-owner of Mount Sterling, was born near Georgetown, Scott county, Kentucky, January 29, 1823. His ancestors were English, his great-grandfather coming from England, settling in New Jersey at a very early date. His grandfather, Eli Stout, came from New Jersey to Kentucky at the beginning of the present century. He journeyed down the Ohio river, exposed to considerable danger from the Indians, on the banks of the stream. He was a pioneer of Fayette county, Kentucky, and died in Owen county, same State. Isaac Stout, father of subject, was born in Scott county, Kentucky, where he was reared, educated and married. The latter event occurred when he led to the altar Miss Lydia Baxter, native of the same State. He died in Leesburg, Harrison county, Kentucky, of cholera, in 1833, his wife having died a few days previous.

Francis M. Stout was the oldest of four children, and was only ten years old when his parents died. He was reared by his paternal grandfather and grew to manhood in Scott county, Kentucky, and in Owen county where he attended the subscription schools, and high schools, at Owenton, Kentucky. In 1844 he came to Illinois, landing in Brown county in June of that year. He first taught school a few years and then began the pottery business, in Ripley, in which he continued for over thirty years. He also embarked in mercantile pursuits and continued in that busines for about the same length of time. He has now retired from these pursuits and resides on his fine farm in Ripley, where he is a large landowner.

Mr. Stout was married, the first time to Margaret Alexander, native of Tennessee, and this event took place December, 1846. This wife died, September, 1851, and in January, 1853, he married Nancy C. Alexander, a sister of his first wife, who has proven herself a good, faithful wife.

Mr. Stout cast his first vote for Zachary Taylor, and has been a Republican since the formation of the party. He is a devout follower of the teachings of Alexander Campbell.

This gentleman is a representative citizen of this part of the great State of Illinois, and he enjoys the respect and esteem of all his neighbors and friends.

JOSEPH L. COSNER, one of the leading merchants of Virginia, was born on a farm in Philadelphia precinct, Cass county, Illinois, June 26, 1855. Of his life and ancestry we record the following facts:

Thomas Jefferson Cosner, his father, was born in Lincoln county, North Carolina, July 31, 1815, son of Henry Cosner, who is supposed to have been a native of the same State. The latter was a blacksmith by trade, at which he worked in Lincoln county till about 1830, when he went to Indiana, being accompanied by his wife and six children, camping along the way and being six weeks in making the journey He became one of the early settlers of Monroe county, bought a claim and entered a tract of Government land two and one-half miles west of Mt. Tabor There was a log house on the place and a garden spot cleared He worked at his trade, devoted his spare time to the improvement of his land, and lived there until his death The maiden name of his first wife, grandmother of Joseph L, was Elizabeth Isahower She was born in North Carolina, and died in Monroe county, Indiana. She reared seven children, viz: Elizabeth, Sally, Joseph, Thomas J, Andrew, Lewis and Maria Thomas J. was fifteen years old when his parents moved to Indiana, and he remained there with his father till 1836, when, in company with his brother-in-law, Martin Goble, he came to Illinois, making the journey by team Here he was employed at farm work, first receiving $9 per month, and later $13. He continued to work for one man, Jacob Epler, the greater part of the time for a dozen years. He then purchased 120 acres of raw prairie land, built a small frame dwelling, and commenced housekeeping. He was successful as a farmer, bought other lands, and is now the owner of 436 acres, all in township 17 He erected a good set of frame buildings on his farm, and continued his residence there, with the exception of short periods spent in Virginia, until 1887, when he removed to Virginia, and now lives retired. He was married in 1850, to Emily (Stevenson) Beard, who was born one mile from Lexington, Fayette county, Kentucky, December 20, 1827 Her father, Thomas Stevenson, is supposed to have been a native of the same county, his father having been a pioneer of Fayette county, where he spent his last years Thomas Stevenson spent his life on a farm, and died near Lexington in 1831 The maiden name of his wife was Lucy Wyatt, she being a native of Kentucky and a daughter of Walter Wyatt. Her father was a Virginian by birth. He was one of the pioneers of Fayette county, and from there, in 1835, moved to Illinois, settling on Indian creek in Morgan county, where he bought land, improved a farm, and resided there till his death The maiden name of his wife was Julia Bliss She, too, was a native of Virginia, and died in Morgan county, Illinois. After the death of Mr Wyatt she was married to John Creel, and came to Illinois in 1837, settling ten miles northeast of Jacksonville, where she resided till her death. The mother of our subject was ten years old when she came to Illinois with her parents, and remembers well the incidents of the overland journey and of pioneer life here. She assisted her mother in the household duties when quite young, and learned to card, spin and weave. After the death of her mother she went to live with her sister, with whom she made her home until her seventeenth year, when she was married to Maston Beard He was a farmer of Morgan county, and died there The parents of Mrs Cosner are both members of the Methodist Episcopal Church. They reared seven children, viz: John T and Jacob deceased; Henry, Joseph L., Lucy, George and Mollie.

Joseph L. Cosner was reared on a farm He attended the district school a portion of each year, and subsequently advanced his education by a two years' course at Virginia In 1874 he commenced his mercantile career as a clerk in the store of William B Payne, and clerked five years In 1879 he started for the gold fields of Colorado; prospected and mined about a year, had little success in finding gold, and returned home and engaged in farming. A year later he formed a partnership with J. J. Bergen, with whom he was associated in the mercantile business three years, after which the partnership dissolved. He then bought out the firm of Bergslesser & Jones, and has since conducted business alone. He carries an extensive stock of dry goods, clothing, hats, boots and shoes, fancy goods, etc., and does a large business.

Mr. Cosner has an inherent love for fine horses, and, in company with his brother George, is engaged in breeding the same.

He was married June 26, 1888, to Mary Gale Armentrout, who was born in Roodhouse, Illinois, daughter of Adam C. and S. E. Armentrout. She departed this life January 8, 1892, at the age of twenty-five years, six months and twenty-two days. Mrs. Cosner was a member of the Methodist Episcopal Church.

MARTHA J. HARBISON, the estimable lady whose biography it is our pleasure to present to our readers, was born in Greenbriar county, Virginia, November 29, 1844, daughter of John and Emily (Milliner) Mason. The former born in Virginia, came West in 1853, by wagon and boat, landing at Keokuk, Iowa. There he obtained teams and went to Mount Pleasant, where he only remained a short time, and then came to Illinois, by team, settling where his daughter now lives. He bought 120 acres of wild timber land, on which he built a log-house, and there the family lived for many years, then sold and then rented and finally removed to Kansas, where he now resides. The subject's mother died in Missouri, when about seventy years of age, having been a native of Virginia, also. All the family on both sides were farmers, as far as can be discovered, except one member of the family, who operated a woolen mill in Virginia. Mrs. Harbison's grandfather, Milliner, was in the war of 1812.

Our subject remained at home until her marriage, which occurred September 23, 1863. After marriage her husband settled on the farm where she now resides in a fine brick residence that her husband built prior to his death, which occurred August 28, 1890. Mr. Harbison was born September 5, 1837, brother of Moses Harbison (see sketch). Mr. and Mrs. Harbison had four children, one of whom they lost, a daughter, Dolly, at the age of one year and six months. The living ones are: John W., born August 16, 1864, at home renting the old farm, married to Maggie Smith, in 1889. She was born February 26, 1871, daughter of Henry and Elizabeth (Lindsay) Smith. They have one child, James, born October 10, 1890. Mrs. Harbison's second child, Ella M., was born July 9, 1867, and married Frank Wood, February, 1890, have one girl, Lena, born March 8, 1891. The third child, Ida F., was born February 24, 1870, and she married Fred Lippert, and they have one child, Ernest E., born March 16, 1891.

Mr. and Mrs. Harbison were members of the Christian Church and all the family are church people. The son, James, is a strong Democrat. This lady is one of the best known and well liked in the county and well deserves a place in these pages.

REUBEN LANCASTER was born on a farm twelve miles north of Georgetown, Kentucky, June 14, 1842. His father, Lewis Lancaster, was a native of same locality, and his grandfather, Reuben Lancaster, for whom the subject of our sketch was named, was born in the State of Virginia, was reared and married in the Old Dominion and from there removed to Kentucky, locating in Scott county, where he purchased a tract of timber land, and out of the wilderness developed a fine farm. At the time of his settlement on it there were no railroads in Kentucky, and Cincinnati, sixty miles distant, was the nearest market and depot for supplies. Lewis Lancaster was reared to agricultural pursuits. After reaching his majority he bought a tract of partially cleared land near the old home, and at the time of his death, which occurred in September, 1852, had amassed quite a fortune in lands and negroes. His wife, Jane Mallory, was born in Scott county, Kentucky, the daughter of Charles and Mary Mallory, and died in August, 1852, about one month prior to the death of her husband, leaving seven children: Eliza, John, Bettie, Reuben, Thomas, James and Sylvester.

After the death of his parents, the subject of our sketch lived with an uncle, Abram Mallory, one year after that with another uncle, Green Mallory, three years. He then chose as his guardian Aaron Dills, of Harrison county, Kentucky, with whom he lived until September, 1861, when he enlisted as a private in Company B, Sixth Kentucky Cavalry, in the service of the Union. In 1864, he was commissioned Captain of his company, and remained in command until after the close of the war. He participated in the battles of Chickamauga, Mission Ridge, siege of Atlanta and all of the principal engagements of the Army of the Cumberland After the surrender of Lee, he was detached with his company to capture Jefferson Davis, and was only five miles distant when the rebel chieftain was captured, and saw him taken into Macon, Georgia, a prisoner. Captain Lancaster was honorably discharged with his regiment at Louisville, Kentucky, in September, 1865, and returned to his home in Harrison county, Kentucky. In February, 1866, he came to Cass county, Illinois, and engaged in farming near Ashland, continuing there till December, 1874, when he was appointed Deputy by Sheriff William Epler, and continued as such till December, 1876, the expiration of Mr. Epler's term of office. From that time till February, 1890, he was engaged in the livery business. In 1890, he received the appointment of Postmaster, at Virginia, which position he now holds.

In March, 1880, Captain Lancaster married Miss Sue Heaton, a native of Cass county, Illinois, and a daughter of John and Mary J. Heaton. They have two children, Earl and Iva.

Politically, he has always been a stanch Republican. He is a member of Dawning Post, No. 321, G. A. R., Department of Illinois. Mrs. Lancaster is a member of the Christian Church.

THOMAS JONES, a retired farmer of Schuyler county, residing at Rushville, was born in Herefordshire, England, October 7, 1825. His father, John Jones, was a native of Radnorshire, Wales, and when a young man removed thence to Herefordshire, England, where he was married. He remained there until 1850, when he emigrated to America; for a few months he lived in Pennsylvania, and thence came to Illinois and located in Brown county; he purchased forty acres of land near Mount Sterling, and for a number of years was engaged in agricultural pursuits; later he moved to Mount Sterling, and died there, in the ninetieth year of his age His first wife, the mother of the subject of this notice, was Lydia Trull, a native of Herefordshire, England; she died in Brown county, Illinois, having reared a family of four children,—Eliza, Thomas, John and William,— all of whom emigrated to the United States Thomas Jones was reared in Herefordshire, and at the age of sixteen years went to learn the carpenter's trade, serving an apprenticeship of three years In 1850 he crossed the sea to America with his family; they sailed from Liverpool in March, on the vessel William Rathbun, and landed at New York city after a voyage of two months Mr. Jones went directly to Newcastle, Pennsylvania His means were exhausted, in fact were worse than exhausted, as he had borrowed the money for his passage to America He worked at his trade in this place until the following year, and then came to Illinois; he traveled by stage and canal to Pittsburg, and thence via the Ohio, Mississippi and Illinois rivers to Meredosia, and thence by team to Mount Sterling He purchased eighty acres of land in Brown county, the greater portion of which was heavily timbered; there he began his career as a farmer, and has met with more than ordinary success; he rented a a house for a time, but finally built on his own place, and as his means increased made additional investments in land until he is now the proprietor of 430 acres; he also owns a residence in Rushville, built after a modern style of architecture and surrounded by beautiful grounds. Here Mr. Jones lives a retired life, having earned the repose due his years

He has been three times married In Herefordshire, England, at the age of twenty-two years, he was united to Jane Preece, a native of that shire; she died March 27, 1871. The second wife was Minerva Gillenwaters, of Schuyler county, Illinois, a daughter of Joel and Margaret Gillenwaters, pioneers of the county; she died January 3, 1890. In September, 1890, he was united to Ann J, (Nall) Ford, who was born in Rushville township, July 24, 1835, a daughter of Gabriel Nall. Mr Jones has eleven children living: by the first marriage were born; America J., wife of Henry Bartlett; Elmina A., wife of Henry Henhoff, Henry Clay, Walter W , Thomas P., Orvilla A.; Susan W. and Lilly May; the children of the second union are, Robert W., John P and Margaret M Mrs. Jones has one child by her first marriage, George William Tutt. Mr. Jones was reared to the faith of the Methodist Episcopal Church, but in later life he joined the Presbyterian Church. In early days he was a Whig, but for many years past he has affiliated with the Democratic party.

Gabriel Nall, father of Mrs Jones, was born in Scott county, Kentucky, December 23, 1811, a son of Lewis Nall, a native of Virginia, who was a pioneer of Scott county, Kentucky. Her grandfather purchased land nine miles west of Georgetown, and there passed the remainder of his days; his wife's maiden name was Jane Nall, also a Virginian by birth Gabriel Nall emigrated from Scott county, Kentucky, to Illinois, in 1835, and engaged in agricultural pursuits; he owned different tracts of land, and was very successful, in 1887 he retired from active pursuits and came to Rushville to live. He was married in 1834, to Catherine Curtis, who was born in Harrison county, Kentucky, April 25, 1818. Four children were born to them: Ann, Drusilla, Marietta and William F. They have twenty-six grandchildren and six great-grandchildren. Mrs Jones has been married three times; her first husband was George W Tutt, a native of Kentucky; he died in 1852; the second marriage was to Jared P. Ford, a native of Indiana, who came to Illinois in 1857; he died in 1881. Mr. and Mrs. Nall are consistent and worthy members of the Missionary Baptist Church.

HENRY S. SAVAGE was born in Morgan county, Illinois, April 22, 1824. His father, John Savage, was a native of New York State. He emigrated from there to Illinois, making the journey with teams, and becoming one of the first settlers of Morgan county. He located at Diamond Grove, near Jacksonville, and worked at the trade of carpenter for some time. He built the first frame house ever erected in Jacksonville. From Morgan he came to Cass county, and settled six miles southwest of the present site of Virginia. Here he bought a tract of land, built a log house, and subsequently a frame one, and passed the rest of his life on this farm. In politics he was a Whig until the organization of the Republican party, when he identified himself with it. He served as Sheriff of the county. His wife, Elizabeth Smith, daughter of Guy Smith, Esq., was a native of New York. She died on the home farm. The names of their seven children are as follows: Emily, wife of Hon. John W. Pratt; Spencer; George; Henry; Harriet, wife of O. J. Silverthorn; John W.; and Charles W.

Henry S. was reared and educated in Cass county. He remained on the farm till he was sixteen, when he engaged in clerking in Virginia. He clerked here some years and was then employed in the same capacity in Beardstown. He subsequently purchased a farm south of Virginia, and devoted his time to farming, residing there at the time of his death, March 29, 1865, meeting death by accident, having been thrown from a horse. Like his father, he was first a Whig and afterward a Republican.

January 10, 1844, he married Sarah Frances Ward, who was born in Scott county, Kentucky, August 8, 1828. Her father, Jacob Ward, was born in Kentucky in 1800, his parents being natives of Virginia and pioneers of Scott county, Kentucky. Grandmother Ward died in Scott county, and grandfather Ward afterward moved to Missouri, where he spent his last years. Jacob Ward was reared and married in Kentucky, and came to Illinois in 1830, making the journey overland with teams. He located near the present site of Arcadia, where he engaged in farming for a short time, after which he moved into the village of Arcadia and opened a dry-goods and grocery store, at the same time operating a blacksmith and wagon shop and conducting a hotel. Indeed, he was the proprietor of the greater portion of the business there. A number of years later he moved to Cass county, and bought a farm three miles south of the city of Virginia. From this he subsequently moved to a farm on the State road, near Virginia, and was a resident there at the time of his death. He was a prominent and influential man. He served as Associate Judge of the county, having been elected in 1851. The maiden name of his wife was Eliza J. Stevenson. She was born in Kentucky, in 1807, spent her last years in Cass county, Illinois, and died on the farm near Virginia.

Mrs. Savage was small when her parents moved to Illinois. She remembers well the incidents of their pioneer life here, and vividly describes the primitive log school houses with their rude furnishings. She resided with her parents till her marriage, and for some years past has occupied a beautiful home in Virginia. She has five children living, viz.: Charles W., Edward E., Lewis L., Ella Belle and Henry S. Charles W. married Kittie Kelly and has five children; Louise, Bertha May, Harriet, Katie and Chase. Edward E. married Alice Heaton and has four children: Henry H., Walter W., Bessie and Zella. Lewis L. married Emma L. Stribling and has five children: Ada F., Charles J., Fred D., Lewis L. and Tom. Ella Belle is the wife of Henry W. Collins, her children being G. Ward and Elizabeth.

Mr. and Mrs. Savage both joined the Christian Church before their marriage.

REV. FATHER MERSCHER, the popular and efficient pastor of St. Augustine's Catholic Church, Ashland, Illinois, was born in Clinton county, this State, December 4, 1853. His parents were natives of Hanover, Germany, who came to America in 1845, landing in New Orleans, in January of that year. From there they came to Clinton county, Illinois, where they located on a farm which the Rev. Merscher's father continued to conduct until about 1882, when he removed to Nodaway county, Missouri, where he lived until his death, ten years later, January 14, 1892. It may be truly said of him that he inherited all of the good qualities for which the inhabitants of the Fatherland are noted, being thoroughly industrious, honest, intelligent, and extremely kind-hearted, in consequence of which he was universally esteemed by his associates, who greatly lamented his death. Three years previous to his death, the family were called upon to mourn the loss of the devoted wife and mother, who expired February 2, 1889. Her devout spirit, loving heart, and rare Christian virtues, deeply impressed all who knew her, and she enjoyed the esteem of a wide circle of acquaintances and friends. The only brother of the subject of this sketch, B. Henry Merscher, died six months after his mother's death, August 24, 1889, in the same place, Nodaway, county.

Our subject, whose Christian name is John William, obtained his elementary education in the public schools of Clinton county. He then went to St. Joseph's College, at Teutopolis, Illinois, entering in 1866, and attending four years. After this, he attended St. Francis' Seminary, at Milwaukee, Wisconsin, graduating at that noted institution in 1876. While at this latter center of learning, he enjoyed the tutorage of some of the most distinguished men of the Catholic world, among whom were the late lamented Bishop Flasch, of LaCrosse, and Archbishop Katzer, of Milwaukee.

Thus fully equipped, both by instruction and example, he began his ministerial duties in January 12, 1877, at Olney, Illinois, and conducted the services in three churches in that vicinity, at Olney, Stringtown and Bridgeport, continuing in their charge until February, 1884. He was then transferred to Petersburg, of the same State, and conducted services there and at Ashland, with his residence at the former place. In 1885, these churches were placed in separate jurisdictions, and Father Merscher removed to Ashland, where he has since remained, having taken charge of the church in February, 1884. Here he has everything to encourage him in his work, a beautiful church and an attractive parsonage, of modern architectural design, both of which are handsomely finished and neatly furnished. He has charge of a large and intelligent congregation, numbering some eighty-five or ninety families, among whom he has many sincere friends and well wishers.

Thus pleasantly situated, and in the steady pursuance of the path of duty as spread out before him, his time is usefully and happily passed, finding in good works a companionship for his otherwise lonely life.

WILLIAM H. BRACKENRIDGE. The subject of this sketch was born in Washington county, Ohio, November 28, 1835. His father, William, was born in Scotland, in 1805, and came from his native land to Illinois, in 1829, when twenty-four years of age. He was a farmer, and was married to Margaret Harvey, who died, February 11, 1845, leaving our subject, the only child. She was a native of Scotland, and made a good, faithful wife the short time she lived. Her husband was married a second time, to Ellen Reid, of Virginia, by whom he had three children.

W. H. was reared on the farm, and like hundreds of other farmer boys he received a common-school education. At the age of twenty-two he entered a store in Missouri, as a clerk, where he remained four years, and then came to Versailles, May, 1861. Here he volunteered in defense of his country, August, 1862, entering the One Hundred and Nineteenth Illinois Infantry, Company D, as a Second Lieutenant, being honorably discharged after two years and four months of service, on account of failing health. He then returned to Versailles and resumed his clerking, after he had recovered his health.

Mr. Brackenridge was married, October, 1865, to Amanda C. Vandeventer, daughter of Jethro Vandeventer and Jane Olford, natives of Virginia.

Mr. Brackenridge began the mercantile business for himself, in 1866, and has continued doing a thriving business most of the time since. In 1884, he was elected to the Legislature, and was one of the immortal 103 who supported John A. Logan, whom he admired extremely and whose memory he reveres. It is hardly necessary to add that Mr. Brackenridge has been a Republican of the first order, maintaining the principles of that party through thick and thin. He is a member of the Masonic fraternity, being a Blue Lodge Mason. He and his estimable wife are highly respected and esteemed throughout Versailles.

CHRISTIAN DUCHARDT was born in Hesse-Darmstadt, Germany, June 25, 1818. Both his parents and grandparents were natives of that country and passed their lives there. His father, Karl Duchardt, was a butcher by trade and carried on that business. Of his eight children, four came came to America, viz.: John, who settled in Beardstown and died there; Christian; William, a resident of Beardstown; and Mary who was married and died in that place.

Christian Duchardt attended school until he was seventeen years of age, at which time he came to America; sailed from Hamburg in September, 1836, on the Franklin, and six weeks later landed at New York, from whence he came direct to Beardstown, Illinois, landing here a poor boy. The journey from New York to this place was made via the Hudson river, Erie canal, the lakes and canal, and the Ohio, Mississippi and Illinois rivers. At that time Beardstown was a small place and

Cass county was sparsely settled, much of the land being owned by the Government and for sale at $1.25 per acre.

Mr. Duchardt worked at his trade, that of butcher, until his marriage, when he bought eighty acres of land, in section 22, township 18, range 10, covered at the time of purchase with a growth of brush. He bought a log cabin in Virginia, moved it to this place, and commenced at once the work of clearing and improving his farm, and here he has since lived. He has bought other land at different times, prosperity has rewarded his efforts and he is now regarded as one of the substantial men of his vicinity. Nor has his whole time and attention been given to making money. He devotes much time to reading and is well posted on the general topics of the day; is public-spirited and generous, always supporting those measures that tend to advance the best interests of the community where he lives.

In 1846 Mr. Duchardt married Mary A. Nellsch, a native of Wittenberg, Germany. They have two children, John and Lizzie. John was born February 28, 1851. He has the management of the home farm. Lizzie was married March 21, 1882, to William Needham, and has one child, Mary Ann.

Mr. and Mrs. Duchardt and their daughter, Mrs. Needham, are members of the Methodist Episcopal Church.

PAUL P. PHILIPPI, one of the leading and successful young farmers of Cass county, lives on a farm consisting of 200 acres on sections 8 and 5, township 17, range 11, where he was born October 16, 1854. He was reared here by good parents and educated in the public schools and at a German institute in St. Louis. He has always been a farmer and also very industrious, and as he is yet a young man the prospect looks very bright for him. He is the youngest of a family of ten children, five yet living. One, Louisa, wife of John E. Fuhr, a farmer of Christian county, Missouri. The eldest, Mrs. Annie Bohema, is now deceased, and one brother, Victor, fought through the Rebellion for over four years as a private volunteer. He was never wounded or captured, but had a sunstroke in battle and is now dead, leaving a wife and eight children. Herman, a farmer in this county, married Mary Winhold; Bertha is the wife of Ferdinand Winhold, a farmer in this county; Armeda now lives with Paul. Bertha Amelia died when small, and Charles died aged 24.

The father, Pompeius Philippi, was a native of Hamburg, being the eldest of the family of whom the mother and all the children came to the United States, the father having died in Germany. Pompeius Philippi was the inventor of several improvements, which were patented. The last patent issued to him was dated January 24, 1882, for what is now the leading automatic straw-stacker. The family left April 24, 1834, and after a journey of sixty-two days landed in New York. The mother had her three sons, Pompeius, Julius and Victor and her one daughter, Louisa. From New York they came to Cincinnati, Ohio, and later joined the twin brothers, Cæsar and Alexander, at Hamilton, where they had settled when they came over some time before. The family all came West in 1834. Cæsar went to New Orleans, where he was married and where he has since lived, being a book-keeper in the Consumers' Ice Company. He is now eighty years old. The other living children are Dr. Julius, who is a widower with two sons and is eighty-four years old, and is yet smart and active. Another brother, Alexander, is now eighty years old, is married and in St. Louis. The family is remarkable for its health and activity. They all are free-thinkers. One brother, Victor, noted for civil engineering, died in year 1842. The mother died when an old lady at Arenzville.

The father of our subject was a faithful man. He was married in Germany to Caroline Richelman of Hamburg, Germany. She was a very beloved woman in all respects, who came with her husband to the United States in 1834 and afterward lived in Cass county. Here she and her husband improved a large farm of 200 acres, now owned by our subject and named Fair View. Here the father and mother died, the former in 1887 and the latter eleven months later. The father was eighty-one years old at death. They had been married fifty-four years and the wife was seventy-seven years old at her death. They were good people and Freethinkers. Mr. Philippi was a Republican, but not an office seeker. They were recognized as pioneers who helped build up the county.

Our subject and brothers are all Republicans in politics. He has never married and is a reliable good farmer of the county.

ISRAEL HILL, one of the pioneer farmers of Oakland township, was born in Indiana, in 1827, a son of Ishmael Hill, a native of North Carolina, born in October, 1808; when the latter was a child of seven years he was taken to Tennessee, where he lived until a youth of seventeen. The paternal grandfather, Ephraim Hill, was a prosperous farmer and distiller in Tennessee. He removed to Indiana about 1825, and here his son, Ishmael, was married to Miss Elizabeth Wright, a native of Kentucky and a daughter of William and Catherine (Rusher) Wright. This young couple emigrated to Illinois in 1828 with their infant son, Israel; they made the journey overland in the early spring, and came directly to Rushville where they settled on a squatter's claim of 160 acres, eight miles north of the village. Some years later Mr. Hill bought a farm of one hundred and twenty acres in Oakland township. It was wild and heavily timbered, but he went to work with a will, and, assisted by his son, succeeded in making one of the most desirable farms in this section. He resided here until 1878, when he sold the farm to his son, and bought another tract south of Macomb in McDonough county, where he spent the last years of his life. His wife died in 1875, leaving him with a family of eight children; they buried two infant sons; the names of the other children are as follows: Rhoda, Mary, Sarah, Martha, Margaret, Millie A. and Nancy; all are married and have families. Mr. Hill is the only son.

He was married April 4, 1850, to Miss Louisiana Pemberton, a daughter of Thomas Pemberton of Kentucky; the mother's maiden name was Deborah Moore, and she was a daughter of Ephraim Moore, also of Kentucky. Mr. and Mrs. Hill have had a family of ten children, two of whom died in infancy; Minerva J., wife of Thomas Schroder, died at the age of twenty-one years, leaving one daughter; Amanda is now the wife of Thomas Schroder; Eliza married A. J. Heaton; Columbia A. is at home; Deborah, wife of George W. Young; Cora and John are at home; J. N. married a Miss Smith, and they have three children, Wilmar, aged six years, Myrtle, aged four, and Roscoe, aged thirteen months. Mr. Hill bought 120 acres in 1858, to which he added 80 acres in 1871; in 1878 he purchased his father's farm and later added eighty-six acres to the original purchase of 120 acres. In November, 1891, he bought a home in Vermont, where he lives retired from active life.

He has served his town as Supervisor several terms, and has held other minor offices. He was in his early days a Whig, but now affiliates with the Democratic party. He has been very successful in business, and from a small beginning he has accumulated a large estate; he owns 415 acres of good land, well improved, and by a life of honor and integrity has attracted to himself a large number of warm friends, and has won the confidence of the entire community.

FIELDS E. DAVIS, who has been for many years identified with the leading farmers of Schuyler county, is a native of the State of Tennessee, born in Greene county, in 1827, a son of Paul Davis; the paternal grandfather was Fields Davis. Paul Davis was reared in Tennesseee, and there married Sarah Huff, a daughter of Elias Huff. In 1827, accompanied by his wife and child he emigrated to Illinois, and located in what is now Rushville township. He remained here a few months and went to Indiana, and lived near New Albany until 1837, and then returned to Schuyler county, and rented land on which he passed the last days of his life. Elias Huff removed from Tennessee to Illinois in 1827, and settled in Schuyler county; after a few years he removed to McDonough county, Illinois, where he died. Mrs. Sarah H. Davis died in Hancock county, Illinois. Fields E. Davis was an infant when his parents first penetrated the wilds of Schuyler county, and was a lad of ten when they returned to the State. He received his education in the pioneer schools, and has a vivid recollection of the puncheon floors, puncheon seats and puncheon desks, the finishings and furnishings being of almost the same pattern. He remained under the parental roof until he was seventeen years old, when he went to learn the cooper trade; this he followed until 1846, when he enlisted in the Mexican war. He soon fell ill, and was discharged on account of disability; he was in Texas at this time, but returned to his home, and resumed his former occupation. This he pursued until 1851, when he took a trip to the Territory of Minnesota, going via the river to St. Paul which was then a rather straggling village. He returned in the autumn of the same year, worked at his trade, and in the spring of 1855, started for California. This long and weary journey was made across the plains with ox teams, when there were no settlements between the Missouri river and the Pacific coast, excepting the military posts and the Mormons at Salt Lake. He started in March, and reached the Golden State in the following August. He first engaged in mining, the all-absorbing occupation, and afterward followed farming. In 1857 he returned to the East, coming via the Isthmus of Panama. He worked at his trade for two years, and then purchased a farm consisting of 160 acres; this he has by industry and toil brought to high state of cultivation, and he has made many valuable improvements; he has erected good, substantial buildings, all conveniently arranged for farming purposes. He is a thoroughly self-made man, and it is through his own efforts that he has arisen to a position of financial independence.

Mr. Davis was united in marriage April 1, 1860, to Miss Lydia E. Smith, a native of Schuyler county, Illinois, and a daughter of Jonathan and Nancy Smith, whose history appears elsewhere in this work. Eight children have been born of this union: Charles J., Mary, Virginia E., William, Margaret, Samuel, Fanny and John. Mr. Davis is a consistent member of the Missionary Baptist Church, and is highly respected by the citizens of his county.

THOMAS M. REDFIELD was born in Cayuga county, New York, August 27, 1816. His father was Richard Redfield, born in Connecticut in 1768. He was a blacksmith all his life. He had but one brother, Reuben. Richard was married twice and Thomas was a child of the second marriage. His mother's name was Mrs. Lucy Brown, *nee* Main, daughter of Thomas and Lucy (Taylor) Main, of Connecticut, where she was born. Mr. Redfield had one brother, Charles, who died young, and a sister, Mrs. Charles Hulett, the mother of ten children who died in Brown county, aged forty-six: only two of these now survive. The father and mother of Thomas came to Illinois from Indiana with a hired team and wagon in the fall of 1830. They lived about a year at Rushville, where in 1827 he had bought eight lots. He sold these off and moved five miles southwest of Rushville and cleared up a farm on school lands. They moved from these lands to a new place in La Grange, then in Schuyler, but now in Brown. In 1836 they came to Brooklyn and obtained forty acres of Government land.

Thomas lived at home until he was married, in 1839, to Mary Pyle, daughter of Nicholas and Mary Pyle, who came from Kentucky to Illinois about 1832. Mr. Redfield began married life on a farm of forty acres about one mile northeast of the village site, and in 1852 he moved to the village where they lived until 1869, when they sold the home and moved to his present place, September 15. He bought 120 acres of land at $3 an acre. Mr. Redfield lost his wife February 17, 1884. She was in her sixty-sixth year and left five living children. They buried four, Nancy, an infant; Lucy; Mrs. George W. Logan, who died in early married life, and her infant with her; and Melissa, who was Mrs. Daniel Gross; she was first married to George A. Brown, who was Lieutenant of Company A, Seventy-eighth Illinois Volunteer Infantry, and was killed during the war. Her second husband was also a soldier in the army. She died in 1873, aged about thirty-three, leaving five children. Sarah, Mrs. John Krieble, died at the age of twenty-seven, leaving two children. The living children are: Ovandea, at home with her father; George, in McDonough county; Lovisa D. Camp, a widow. Mr. Redfield has been School Director, a life-long Republican and he is a Universalist. Mary, another of his daughters, now Mrs. Logan, lives in Sacramento, California; and Thomas, Jr., lives on part of the farm. Mr. Redfield has twenty-five grandchildren and four great-grandchildren.

WILLIAM H. BURNSIDE, one of the most substantial farmers in Schuyler county, resides on section 29, Buena Vista township. He was born in Bainbridge township, this State, on July 3,

1848, his parents being Thomas and Sarah J. (Henry) Burnside, natives of Ireland and Pittsburg, Pennsylvania, respectively. The father of our subject was born in Ireland in 1816, coming to the United States when seventeen years of age. He was one of a family of six children, three sons and three daughters, named William, James, Thomas, Mary, Lillie and Margaret. On arriving in the United States, he went to Pittsburg, Pennsylvania, where he worked at the trade of cabinet-maker, afterward going into business for himself in that city, but later lost everything, and in 1843 came to Illinois, a poor man. He worked for a time at his trade in Rushville, this State, and afterward engaged in farming, in which he was very successful, eventually becoming the owner of 345 acres of land, highly improved with good house and barns, the land being well cultivated and devoted to mixed farming. He died in 1876, his wife dying a few months previous. They had seven children: Lillie, who married Washington Lawler, of Woodstock township; William H., the subject of our sketch; Sarah, who resides on the homestead; James, also a resident of the homestead; Thomas, living in Buena Vista township; Robert, a resident of Bainbridge township; and Margaret, living on the homestead.

The subject of our sketch was reared on a farm, and attended the country schools. He resided at home until 1883, when he located on the farm on which he now resides. This land he purchased in 1882, which then comprised 320 acres, to which he has since added fifty acres more, making altogether 370 acres of well improved land, which he now owns. He has erected good buildings, a residence and barns for grain and stock and other modern improvements, and has put his land under a high state of cultivation. Besides agriculture, he also raises stock, principally short-horn cattle, in which latter pursuit he is very successful.

He affiliates with the Republican party, but is not an office-seeker, taking only such interest as all good citizens feel in the advancement and welfare of their native county and State.

Beginning life with only such means as his father could spare from the care and support of a large family, he has by economy and thrift become one of the largest land-owners and stock-raisers of the county. Honest in dealings, courteous in manners and cordial to all, he enjoys the respect and esteem of the community and has a host of warm personal friends.

ALFRED M. SMITH, a well-known citizen and an honored veteran of the late war, now residing in Ashland, Illinois, was born in Brown county, Ohio, June 30, 1849. His parents were Wesley and Mary M. (Moore) Smith, both natives of Ohio, the former of Chillicothe and the latter of Feesburgh. They had nine children, five now living: Margaret C., wife of Charles Wiggins, resides in Ashland; James Monroe served four years and three months in the Union army, enlisting in the Twenty-third Kentucky Regiment, and participated in all the principal engagements in which the Twenty-fourth Corps took part; he died, unmarried, of smallpox, in Hamilton county, Ohio, in 1876. John Wesley served in the Fifty-fourth Kentucky (Union) Regiment, is married, and lives in Tallula, Menard county, Illinois; the next in order of birth is the subject of this sketch; William Henry is married, and is a Methodist Episcopal minister in Akron, Ohio; Alice Virginia married John R Hull, and lives in Bracken county, Kentucky, Mary, Joseph and Eliza died in childhood. In 1858, the parents removed to Kentucky, where the father died in 1861, leaving a large family of children to the care of the mother. She afterward married Sovereign Greene, who also died in Kentucky She then removed with her children to Frederick, Illinois, where she married Martin Bridgman, surviving her marriage only about a year, dying in Frederick in 1874

The subject of this sketch was but nine years of age when his parents moved from Ohio to Kentucky, at that time a new and sparsely settled county He was reared on a farm, and followed that vocation until the breaking out of the war. Those happy, peaceful days, spent in rural scenes and homely duties and pastimes, were interrupted by his enlisting, at the age of sixteen years and seven months, in Company K, One Hundred and Ninety-sixth Ohio Infantry, for the period of one year, which he served in full, being under the command of General Hancock, in the Second Army Corps He took the measles while in Camp Chase, Ohio, and was discharged from the hospital to accompany his regiment to the front, when he took cold, and the disease settled in his eyes and lungs, destroying the sight of his right eye, severely injuring the other, and superinducing neuralgia, from which he greatly suffered He now receives a pension for these disabilities.

On September 11, 1865, he was honorably discharged at Baltimore, Maryland, whereupon he returned to his widowed mother in Pendleton county, Kentucky, where he experienced some exciting scenes, caused by the return of the disbanded rebel army of that vicinity. It was while he was at home that his mother became a widow a second time, after which Mr. Smith accompanied her to Frederick, Illinois, where she spent the rest of her life. She is now buried in the Messer cemetery, near Frederick.

Mr Smith was married in Springfield, Illinois, April 1, 1878, to Miss Anna Ratliff, an estimable lady, and a native of Morgan county, Illinois. She is a daughter of Richard and Mary (Bridgman) Ratliff, both of whom had been previously married, the father having one son and three daughters: Lucy J, Mary Ellen, Isaac Wesley, and Lucretia. The mother was formerly married to a Mr Houston, to which union three children were born Hezekiah, Isaac and William Thomas All of these children of both marriages are now living, except Lucy J, and all are married. To the marriage of Mrs. Smith's parents, four children were born, of whom she is the eldest: Anna Nancy J, now Mrs. E. T Welch, resides in Amarillo, Texas; Mary M, married James Allen, of Ashland, Illinois, James Albert, unmarried, is a farmer. The mother still lives, at the age of seventy-one years, and is comfortably situated in Ashland. The father, Hezekiah Bridgman, was a prominent citizen and esteemed pioneer of Morgan county, Illinois, who died in Concord, that county, in 1884. He was was widely known throughout this vicinity and was deeply mourned by a large community

Since the war, Mr Smith has been in rather poor health. Thinking a change might prove beneficial, he traveled through the South for two years, visiting Texas, New Mexico, Mississippi, Arkansas, Louisiana, Tennessee, Georgia and Alabama Some of the time he is able to work, while often he is incapacitated for active pursuits

Mr. and Mrs Smith have five children: Jessie, Clarence, Randolph, Mary Alice,

William Ellsworth and Ada Belle, all at home with their parents. Miss Jessie Smith is particularly intelligent and active. She is now at that age commonly known as "sweet sixteen," and is attending the high school in Ashland, hoping some day to become a teacher. She is an earnest member of the Christian Church, and takes an active part in church and Sunday-school work, never having missed a session of Sunday-school for two years. Mrs. Smith is also a most devoted and useful member of the same church.

Mr. Smith is Democratic in his political affiliations, and takes a deep interest in the affairs of his State and county.

He is a member of Dick Johnson Post, No. 381, of Tallula, Illinois, and of the Brotherhood of United Friends, as well as of the I. O. O. F.

Having followed his career thus far, which has been most honorable, it is reasonable to prognosticate a fitting close, as, surrounded by sympathetic friends, to whom his many sterling qualities have endeared him, and vindicated at the tribunal of his own searching conscience, he peacefully pursues his pathway through life.

GREGORY WAGNER, Jr., farmer and resident of Mt. Sterling township, was born in Owen county, Indiana, March 24, 1853. His father, Gregory, was born at Baden, Germany, February 24, 1820, and his father was also born in Baden, where he learned the trade of a weaver and there followed it. He came to America about 1827, accompanied by his wife and six children. He lived in New York, Philadelphia and Pittsburg, where he worked in the iron works for some years. From there he went to Coshocton county, Ohio and was one of the early settlers there. He continued on the land he then bought until his death in 1837. This was occasioned by the bite of a rattlesnake. His wife's name was Magdaline Riling, also of Baden. After her husband's death she came to Brown county and died here about 1862. Gregory, Sr., was seven years old when he came to America. While the family lived at Pittsburg he worked in the iron works and after their removal to Ohio he assisted his father on the farm. He inherited a part of his father's land and bougth forty acres more from his brother and lived there until 1851. He then moved to Indiana, traded his farm in Ohio for land in Owen township, Indiana, remained there two years, then sold and came to Illinois, and settled in Mt. Sterling township, buying land in sections 1 and 2. There was only a log cabin on the place, but he shortly began improving; later he bought another tract and engaged in farming until 1878, when he moved to Mt. Sterling, where he now resides. He was married November 18, 1840, to Miss Agatha Lash, born in Alsace, Germany, February 5, 1821. Her father was a carpenter of Baden, who came to America in 1827 with his wife and six children. The parents of our subject have ten living children.

Gregory, Jr., was but an infant when he came to Illinois with his parents. He began when very young to help on the farm, was reared to habits of industry, received the benefits of the district schools, and continued to reside with his parents until twenty-one, since when he has been engaged in farming and threshing on his own responsibility. He now owns and occupies a portion of the old homestead, where he has erected a good set of frame buildings and has otherwise improved the place.

He was married January 15, 1878, to Miss Mary Factor of Ohio, daughter of Benjamin Factor, she being one of eleven children. The family are highly regarded members of St. Mary's Roman Catholic Church. He is a Democrat and the whole family is greatly respected. Mr. and Mrs. Wagner have seven children,—four sons and three daughters.

R. H. DUNN, dealer in all kinds of hardware, stoves and gardening implements, in Beardstown, was born in this county. He attended school at home and in Jacksonville College. His father, Luke Dunn, was a native of Cornwall, England. He followed the business of farmer. He married Elizabeth Jasper, of the same place, and soon after, late in the '40s, they reached the United States and settled on the Sangamon bottoms in Cass county, Illinois, upon unbroken land. After making some improvements, he sold the land and took up more land, and still later moved into the city of Beardstown, retiring from active labors. Mr. Dunn still lives, being sixty-eight years of age, but his wife died in 1892, at the age of sixty-six years. She was a good wife, mother and neighbor, of Christian spirit, and a member of the Methodist Episcopal Church. Mr. Dunn is an active politician and has been County Commissioner twice, and has held other local offices. He is a well-known, good citizen.

Our subject is the eldest son and second child of seven children, all yet living. He was for some time engaged in farming, and was also at one time a clerk for Colonel B. G. Wheeler & Co., of Missouri. His present business was established by an old settler, Abner Foster. Except for six months, when Mr. Dunn had associated with M. T. Dunn, Mr. Dunn has been the sole proprietor since 1882. He is a live young man, and is sure of making his business succeed.

He was married in this county, to Miss Lizzie Miller, who was born, reared and educated and taught school in this same county. Her father, E. P. Miller, was born in Kentucky, but married in Beardstown. Mr. Miller was engaged in the livery business when he died in 1884. He was born in 1818; was a sound Republican, but not an office-seeker. His wife, born in Illinois, is yet living and is quite an old lady. Mrs. Dunn is a bright, intelligent lady, and the mother of two children, Edna and E. Miller. She is a member of the Methodist Church.

WILLIAM CAMPBELL was born in county Tyrone, Ireland, April 18, 1818, on the same farm on which his father, Archibald Campbell, and his grandfather, William Campbell, were born. This farm was owned by his grandfather, who passed his entire life on it. William Campbell, Sr., was a member of the Episcopal Church, and in that faith reared his family. Archibald Campbell, like his father, spent his whole life on the farm on which he was born. He lived to the ripe old age of eighty-nine years. The maiden name of his wife was Elizabeth Stewart, she being a native of the same vicinity, and a daughter of James Stewart, who was a native of Ireland and a descendant of Scotch ancestry. Mrs. Campbell died in Ireland, aged seventy-eight years. The names of their six children are: Mary, William, Catherine, James, Archie and Ann. James and Archie are deceased. Mary is the wife of Samuel Shaw, and resides in Dixon, Illinois. Catherine married Hugh Gibney, and lives in Canada. Ann still makes her home in Tyrone, Ireland.

William Campbell, the subject of our sketch, was reared and educated in Ireland, and as soon as he was old enough aided in the farm work. In 1840, bidding farewell to the Emerald Isle, he sailed from Londonderry, May 10, and landed at New York after a voyage of thirty-one days. From New York he came direct to Illinois, making the journey via water, rail and stage, to Pittsburg, and thence by way of the Ohio, Mississippi and Illinois rivers to Beardstown. Then he came by team to the vicinity where he now lives. At that time Cass county was sparsely settled, some of the land still being owned by the Government. He spent a few months with his brother-in-law, Samuel Shaw, and at this time was taken sick with ague. Seeking a change of climate, he went to St. Louis and took charge of a livery stable, remaining there three years. At the end of that time he came back to Cass county and bought a farm three miles and a half west of Virginia. This farm, consisting of 100 acres, he purchased for $5 per acre, a log house and stable and fifty acres under cultivation comprising the improvements on it. Five years later he sold out at an advance, and bought the farm on which he now resides, two miles west of Virginia. The improvements on this place at the time of purchase were a log house with a frame addition, and a frame stable. He has since replaced them with a good set of frame buildings, has purchased other lands at different times, and is now the owner of upwards of 1,000 acres in Cass county.

Mr. Campbell was married in 1845, October 10, to Mary D. Sudbrink, daughter of Frederick and Catherine Sudbrink. She was born in Germany, and came with her parents to America when yonng. Their four children are Henry I., Alfred, Emma Ann and Edwin.

Mr. and Mrs. Campbell are members of the Cumberland Presbyterian Church. Politically he affiliates with the Democratic party. He has served as a member of the Board of County Commissioners.

DR. ARCHIBLE R. ALLEN located in Huntsville in 1882. He was born in Bainbridge township, Schuyler county, Illinois, September 22, 1851, being a son of William J. and Mary G. (Edmondston) Allen, natives of North Carolina and Indiana. The father of our subject was reared in Indiana and in 1844 came to Illinois and settled in Bainbridge where he married; and in 1852. Having some land in Missouri, he left his wife and children with her parents and went to that State. From there he went to Oregon and later to California, where he died. His wife died in Adams county, Illinois. They had two sons, Archible and James E.

Archible is the older, and resided with his grandfather in Schuyler county; but when he was ten years old he removed to Adams county. In 1869. after the death of his mother, he went to Fandon, McDonough county, where he lived with an uncle, Colonel Samuel Wilson, and attended school. In 1874, he commenced the study of medicine with Dr. N. E. Wilson. He subsequently attended college at Keokuk, graduating in 1886. He located in practice at Huntsville.

He was married in May, 1882, to Maggie R., daughter of Marshall and Rebecca Spondenburg) Wells. She was born in Brown county, Illinois, January 8, 1870. They have one child, Bessie May.

The Doctor was in the drug trade from 1874 to 1876, at Birmingham, Illinois. He was quite successful at it.

Dr. Allen is a stanch Republican in politics and a member of the Huntsville Lodge, No. 465, A. F. & A. M., and Cyclone Lodge, I. O. O. F. He and his wife are among the best people of that section, and are highly respected by their large circle of friends.

GEORGE CONOVER, of the firm of Petefish, Skiles & Co., bankers, Virginia, Illinois, was born in Princeton precinct, Cass county, this State, September 11, 1846. Of his life and ancestry we present the following facts:

Dominicus Conover, great-grandfather of George Conover, was born in Holland and came to America in Colonial times, settling in New Jersey, where his son, Levi, was born. The latter served in a cavalry regiment for five years during the Revolutionary war. In In 1790 he moved to Kentucky and settled near Lexington. Five years later he moved to Adair county, where he spent the residue of his life. The maiden name of his second wife, grandmother of our subject, was Jane Galbraith Turnbow. Their son, Levi Conover, Jr., was born in Adair county, Kentucky, and was there reared to manhood. At the age of twenty-two years he came to Cass county, Illinois, arriving here without any means other than the horse he had ridden. He found employment of various kinds, earning his first money by splitting rails at fifty cents per hundred. In 1834 he went to Galena and worked in the mines of that vicinity till fall. He then returned and went to the territory of Iowa, where he took a squatter's claim to Government land. He came back to Illinois and spent the winter, and in the spring returned to Iowa, in company with a friend, making the journey with oxen and wagon. He at once began the work of improving his claim, and soon had his log cabin built. In 1836 he returned to Illinois, married Elizabeth Petefish, and took his bride to their frontier home. In 1837, while they were on a visit to Cass county, this State, Mrs. Conover died, and soon after her death Mr, Conover sold his Iowa claim and settled in Cass county. In 1841 he the Peter Conover homestead, on which he was engaged in farming for some years. From there he moved to the town of Virginia, where he spent the last years of his life. The maiden name of his second wife, mother of George, was Phœbe A. Rosenberger. Her father, John Rosenberger, was born of German parents.

George Conover was reared on his father's farm, attending the district schools a portion of each year. He advanced his education by one term at Beardstown high school and one term at Wesleyan University at Bloomington, after which he entered Bryant and Stratten's Business College at Chicago. After his marriage he located on a farm, owned by his father, two miles and a half southeast of Virginia, which farm his father deeded to him soon afterward. He continued to reside there till 1876, when he came to Virginia to accept the position of book-keeper in the bank of Petefish, Skiles & Co. The same year he became a partner, and so remains, and since 1884 has been cashier. He still owns his farm.

In February, 1870, he married Virginia Lee Bone, a native of Rock Creek, Sangamon county, Illinois, daughter of William and Farinda (Osborn) Bone. To them have been born four children: William B., Ernest B., George B. and Virginia Louise.

Politically Mr. Conover affiliates with the Democratic party. He has served two terms as Mayor and six years as a member of the Board of Education. Though not a third party man, he is a prohibitionist in principle. He was elected Mayor on the temperance issue, and it was during his first term that the saloons were closed in Virginia. They have since remained closed. He is a director in the Virginia Building and Loan Association.

CHARLES M. TINNEY was born in Marion, Grant county, Indiana, November 11, 1852. His father, John M. Tinney, was born in Washington county, Kentucky, son of Nathaniel Tinney, a native of Virginia and a soldier of the Revolutionary war. Grandfather Tinney moved to Kentucky about 1800, and became one of the pioneer farmers of Washington county. He was by trade an architect and builder, but he spent his last years on the farm, and died in his Kentucky home. Grandfather Tinney's maiden name was Caroline Marshall. She was a native of Virginia; spent her last days and died in Tazewell county, Illinois. John M. Tinney was reared in Kentucky and learned the trade of tailor in Cincinnati. He carried on business in that city for a time, and from there went to Dayton, Ohio. In 1859 he moved to Pekin, Illinois, where he engaged in hotel-keeping. He continued his residence at that place until the time of his death. His widow, a native of Dayton, Ohio, was before her marriage Miss Sarah Kaughman. She now makes her home with her children.

Charles M. Tinney was reared and educated in Pekin, Illinois, being a graduate of the high school of that place. He also attended college one year at Oskaloosa, Iowa. After that he studied law in the office of W. D. Maus, of Pekin, being admitted to the bar in 1873. He then commenced the practice of his profession in Virginia, where he has since resided. He conducted a law practice until 1880, when he bought the office and good will of the Virginia *Gazette*, a weekly paper. He has since had charge of this paper, and in connection with it has a job printing office. Politically he is a Republican.

Mr. Tinney was married in November, 1886, to Annie E. Craft, a native of Pennsylvania and a daughter of J. B. and Phebe (Dunanay) Craft.

CHRISTIAN PILGER, a live man and old citizen of Beardstown, was born in Waldeck, Prussia, in 1836, and came of a good old German family. His father, Fred Pilger, was at one time city Mayor, as had been his father and grandfather before him. The same office is now held by one of the sons in the town of Berich, where the family has lived. The father and mother of our subject, were good Lutherans and lived and died in their native country. They had a family of eleven children, five of whom came came to this country, three of whom are yet living. He came to Beardstown in June, 1855, a young man twenty years of age. He was engaged as a bench tailor for some years, when in 1873, he, with Henry Garm started in business as merchant tailors. He enlisted in August, 1862, in Company A, One Hundred and Fourteenth Illinois Volunteer Infantry, Captain John M. Johnson and Colonel James W. Judy, commanding. He was engaged in the battles of

Vicksburg, Jackson, Mississippi, Nashville, thence down to New Orleans, across the Gulf of Mexico to Mobile, and was in all the battles of that section. In all this military duty our subject escaped wounds or capture, but twice suffered sunstroke. He was Corporal of his company when discharged, August 13, 1865. Since his return he has been a live member of the place. In 1882, Mr. Pilger's business was carried on for two years under the name of Pilger & Huge, at which time Mr. Pilger assumed sole charge of the business until 1889. Mr. Pilger is now engaged in the real-estate business, is a Notary Public, and carries a number of lines of insurance. He is agent for the Equitable Building & Loan Society, of Peoria, and is City Clerk of Beardstown. He has been very successful in life, and has amassed a good property in this city. The spot on which his office now stands was formerly the old house site of Mr. Thomas Beard, who first settled here, established the ferry, and later laid out the town. Mr. Pilger was for years the proprietor of the Pilger block on the corner of State and Main streets. He is a worker for the Boys in Blue, and is a charter member of the McLane Post, G. A. R., No. 97, of Beardstown, was its first Quartermaster, and has held the position nearly ever since. The Sons of Veterans of this place also named their camp in his honor. He has been for many years a member of Cass Lodge, No. 25, A. F. & A. M., and has taken an active part in it.

He was married in this city to Miss Margaret Schuman, born in Baden, Germany, and came to this country when eighteen years of age. Her parents also came to Beardstown and died here consistent members of the Lutheran Church. Mr. and Mrs. Pilger are parents of but one daughter, an accomplished young lady, a leader in social circles and now the wife of William F. Stanley, foreman in the paint shop of the Chicago, Burlington & Quincy Railroad Company of this city.

BRYSON M. BLACKBURN was born in Ohio, on the line between Butler and Hamilton counties in 1828. His father was James Blackburn, of the same place, born in 1805, and his father, Bryson Blackburn, came to Ohio from Pennsylvania at an early day, with his wife. Three brothers had preceded him, and the oldest of the family had been killed by the Indians in the same State. The latter left a family. One of the remaining brothers sought to avenge the blood of his brother, named Patterson Blackburn. He was finally lost in the West, after having been in the Lewis and Clark expedition. James Blackburn, the father of our subject, was one of three children. His brother, Hamilton, and his sister, Polly, who married John Mattson, a nephew of William Henry Harrison. The mother of our subject was Neppie Sparks, of Maryland, though born in Kentucky. She was a daughter of Matthew and Prudence (Conway) Sparks. They were farmers who came to Schuyler county in 1830, when Rushville was a very small hamlet. Mr. Blackburn was a tanner and currier, who started a small tannery and soon built up a good business, which he sold out in a few years at a handsome profit. He again embarked in business with a partner who proved a rascal and bankrupted him. He then started anew by taking up eighty acres of land near Plymouth. This was military land, and after making a home and improvements here he found that his title was not good; so lost it. Having studied medicine under the then famous Dr. Thomas, of Cincinnati, he began practicing and soon had a large practice. In 1835-'36 the cholera became epidemic, and he returned to Rushville, against the wishes of his wife and children, to assist the sick.

Mr. Blackburn was one of eleven children: Robert, Bryson, Prudence, Orville, John, Amanda, Amelia, Ann and Thomas: the other two died in infancy. Mr. Blackburn had but a limited district schooling, but he endeavored to improve himself and taught school one winter. He has followed farming and carpentering all his life, for which he had a natural talent.

He was married in Huntsville, Illinois, in 1852, to Susan Brumfield Overstreet, a daughter of Buckley and Nancy Overstreet. Her parents came from Kentucky and Virginia. She was born in Kentucky in 1829, and came to Illinois in 1836. Her parents died in Huntsville, he aged sixty-eight, and she seventy years.

Mr. and Mrs. Blackburn have buried four children in early childhood. They have six still living: Kate, wife of Warren Whitson, of Brooklyn; Frances A., a maiden at home; Fred W. married Sophia Wells and resides near Brooklyn, on a farm of 500 acres; Neppie, wife of Elmer Brown, resides at Brooklyn; Mary M., the wife of George Kruter, lives in McDonough county; and R. H. is a young man at home.

Mr. Blackburn bought his present house and farm in 1854. He has 110 acres of very fertile land. He considers himself a poor financier, although an industrious man. He voted with the Democrats until the Civil war, and did not vote for president until Hayes. He is a stanch Prohibitionist now. He has served the town in some of the minor offices. He and his wife are members of the Methodist Church, and are well known and and influential citizens.

RICHARD J. OSBORN, of Lee township, was born in Adams county, Illinois, November 2, 1838. His father, David N., was born in Connecticut in 1806, and his father died in early life. David learned the shoemaker trade, and worked at it many years in the East. He married Martha Stafford, of Maryland, in Ohio, whither he had come by degrees, working at his trade as he went from town to town, always in a westerly direction. They came with one child to Adams county, Illinois, in 1837. They possessed some means and bought 160 acres of unimproved land, on which they built a small log house, and in which Richard was born. They resided in Adams county fourteen years, and then sold and came to Lee township, Brown county.

When they built their first home the nearest neighbors were five miles, and Mr. Osborn had never seen them, but that did not prevent them from coming to help him. When they reached Lee township, they bought 160 acres of prairie and eighty of timber. They paid $2,400 for these lands, which included a cabin and seventy-two acres broken. This was his life-long home, though he died at Mound Station in 1883, in his seventy-eighth year. He left a widow and six children. She still survives him, making her home with Richard. The latter has been reared to farm life, and obtained only a fair amount of schooling. After Mr. Osborn married he settled here, where he has 198 acres of prairie land and forty of timber. He grows a mixed crop,—

corn, wheat and grass. He keeps about fifteen head of horses and thirty of cattle. He turns off about seventy hogs a year, and has a small dairy in operation. He bought his first eighty acres in 1879, and has added to it from time to time. In 1860 he went to Denver, Colorado, and on to the gold mines forty miles west. He went with an ox team over the plains and followed mining in company with one other. While there he met with a sad accident, by which he lost his left hand and his left eye. It was caused by an accidental discharge of powder, February 11, 1861, hence his trip was not a financial success.

He was married in 1882 to Ella Long, of Brown county, Illinois. She was the daughter of Andrew and Elizabeth (Buxton) Long. They are both natives of Illinois and farmers of this township. Mr. and Mrs. Osborn have two daughters, Edith M. and Alta P. Mrs. Osborn is a member of the Methodist Episcopal Church. Mr. Osborn is a Republican, first, last and all the time. He is School Treasurer of Lee township, and has been Town Clerk. He and his wife are worthy people, and are highly esteemed by all who know them.

DAVID DODDS was born in county Down, Ireland, January 15, 1829, a son of John Dodds, a native of the same county and a descendant of Scotch ancestors; the father was a farmer by occupation, and spent his entire life in his own country; he died in 1863. The mother of our subject was Martha McElroy Dodds, a native of the same county as her husband, and a daughter of John McElroy, of Scotch extraction; she died in 1866, in county Down. They had a family of thirteen children, eleven of whom grew to maturity, and five of whom came to America; Betty, Sallie, Ann, Martha, John, William, James, Samuel, Robert, Thomas and David; John, James, Samuel, Thomas and David came to the United States. Our subject was reared and educated in the county of his birth, and in his youth began to assist on the home farm. He remained with his parents until 1851, when he bade farewell to home and friends and native land, and sailed across the seas to the New World; the voyage consumed five weeks, and after landing at New York he continued his journey to Ohio, and located in Mahoning county. He remained there. working by the month, for more than eight years, and then came to Schuyler county and settled in Bainbridge township.

When the great Civil war arose, Mr. Dodds espoused the cause of his adopted country, and August 5, 1861, enlisted in Company G, Twenty-eighth Illinois Volunteer Infantry. He was with his regiment until April, 1866, and participated in the capture of Forts Hyman and Henry, and in the engagements at Shiloh; Grand Gulf, Champion Hills, the Hatchie, Vicksburg, Forts Beauregard and Blakely and Spanish Fort, and some others of less note. He was honorably discharged, and returned to his home, where he resumed farming. In 1867 he bought the land he now occupies.

Mr. Dodds was married in 1874, to Mrs. Martha Herron Collister, a native of county Down, and a daughter of James and Nancy (Murray) Herron. Mrs. Dodds was first married in Ireland, to Joseph Collister; they emigrated to America in 1856, and the following year came to Schuyler county. Mr. Collister became a member of Company D, One Hundred and Fifteenth Illinois Volunteer Infantry, and after the war settled in Bainbridge township, where he lived until his death, in 1873; they had one daughter, Maggie, who married Thomas Suddith.

Mr. and Mrs. Dodds were both reared to the faith of the Presbyterian Church Mr Dodds is a member of the Republican party, and is an ardent supporter of its principles; he belongs to Colonel Henry Post, No. 131, G A R.

SAMUEL H. PETEFISH was born in Rockingham county, Virginia, April 30, 1824, son of Jacob Petefish, a native of the same State His grandfather, Christian Petefish, was born in Germany.

When a young man, Christian Petefish entered the army. He came to America as a Hessian soldier during the time of the Revolutionary war. His sympathies, however, were not with the British Government, and after the battle of Princeton he joined the Colonial ranks and fought for independence until peace was declared He then settled in Virginia, where he reared his family and spent the remainder of his life.

Jacob Petefish was reared and married in the Old Dominion, and resided there until 1835. That year, with his wife and eight children, he started for Illinois. They made the journey with a four-horse team, brought their cooking utensils along, cooked and camped on the way, and arrived in what is now Cass county in October Mr. Petefish purchased a tract of land in what is now Virginia precinct, engaged in farming, and resided here till the time of his death, in 1849. The maiden name of his wife was Elizabeth Price, she, too, being a native of Virginia. Her death occurred in 1854. They reared a family of eleven children The names of the sons are as follows: William, Jacob, Samuel H., John A , Andrew J and Thomas B Andrew J. was a soldier in the late war, and died in the service Of the daughters we record that Mary wedded Reuben Fultz; Sarah married Robert Maxfield; Elizabeth was the wife of Levi Conover, Ellen married Joseph Crum; and Diana became the wife of Daniel Short.

Samuel H Petefish was eleven years old when he came to Illinois with his parents, and has witnessed almost the entire growth and development of the county. At the time they settled here, much of the land was owned by the Government; it was many years before the whistle of the locomotive sounded in Cass county; the people lived chiefly on wild game and the products of their own land. The pioneer wives and mothers cooked by fireplaces, they dressed their families in homespun manufactured by their own hands, and many were the hardships and privations they endured. In the primitive log schoolhouses, with their rude furnishings, the children of these pioneer families conned their lessons in the three R's.

The subject of our sketch attended school in the winter and worked on the farm in summer. When he was twenty-one his father gave him and his brother, Jacob, a tract of unimproved land, upon which they commenced life as independent farmers. The father furnished them a team and they at once set about the improvement of their land. A year later they made a contract with a neighbor for 350 acres of land near by, the greater portion of it being improved. The contract price was $3,500. They were to take possession one year later, at which time they were to pay $1,000, and then yearly payments of $500, with interest at six per cent. After farming together three years' they divided their land. Samuel H. was very successful, made his payments as they became due, and continued farming till 1857, when he rented his land and went to the Territory of Kansas, going via the Illinois, Mississippi and Missouri rivers. He resided in Leavenworth and Atchison about one year, and in April, 1858, returned to Cass county. In 1859 he located on his farm, and there resided, engaged in agricultural pursuits, until 1867, since which time he has made his home in Virginia. He is still, however, interested in agricultural pursuits, being now one of the largest land-owners in the county, owning upwards of 1,500 acres.

The business career of Mr. Petefish has been a remarkably successful one. He first became interested in banking in 1864, being one of the original stockholders in the Farmers' National Bank. In 1870, the firm of Petefish, Skiles & Co. was formed, which firm has since conducted a banking business in Virginia. He is also a member of the firm of Petefish, Skiles & Mertz, of Chandlerville, this company having been formed in February, 1881; the firm of Skiles, Rearich & Co., bankers of Ashland, established there in August, 1881; the firm of Bloomfield, Skiles & Co., Mount Sterling; and is a stockholder in the Schuyler County Bank, of Rushville. He is the owner of several business blocks in Virginia, and it was he who platted and named the addition to Virginia, known as Grand Villa. Besides his farms in Cass county, he owns 200 acres of fine farming land in Crawford county, Iowa, also 778 acres in Decatur county, Iowa.

Politically, Mr. Petefish was for many years a Democrat. At present he is a Prohibitionist in principle and practice, and votes with that party.

Mr. Petefish is a man of family. March 18, 1848, he wedded Nancy M. Hudson, daughter of Peter and Melinda (Huffman) Hudson. They have two children living, Mary E., wife of E. D. C. Woodward of Virginia, and Louis A. Such is an epitome of the life of one of Virginia's most prominent and popular citizens.

WILLIAM STEVENSON, of township 17, range 10, section 26, Little Indian post office is an honored pioneer of Cass county. He was born in Scott county, Kentucky, December 2, 1813, a son of James and Mary (Elliott) Stevenson, the former a native of Ohio, and the latter of Kentucky. To them were born nine children, of whom three are living at this writing (1892), viz.: Sarah, now Mrs. W. A. Bennett, of Springfield; Louisa, wife of Mr. Anthony Boston, residing near Jacksonville, Illinois; and William of this notice. Those deceased are Wesley, Eliza J., Harriet, James, Robert and Augustus. In 1829, Mrs. Stevenson died, and the same year Mr. Stevenson brought his family of children to Illinois, settling in Morgan county, on the three-mile strip that afterward became a part of Cass county.

Our subject spent his boyhood in his native State, and there received such educational advantages as the common schools of the time afforded, which was supplemented by a few months' schooling after coming to Illinois. While a resident of Kentucky he was well acquainted with that somewhat noted soldier and philanthropist, Colonel Richard Johnson, who claimed the honor of having slain the celebrated Indian chief and warrior, Tecumseh, at the battle of Moraviantown in 1814.

William Stevenson was reared on a farm and farming has been his occupation all through life. On February 11, 1836, he was united in marriage to Miss Frances, daughter of William and Rachel (Roe) Berry, who came from Virginia to Cass county in 1832, and settled on a farm near the Stevenson homestead.

Mr. and Mrs. Stevenson were the parents of seven children, four of whom are still living: Mary Eliza, died in 1838; Thomas, in 1839; Rachel became the wife of William E. Martin, and died in 1879; Robert Roe, married Mary J. Scott, and resides in Jacksonville, Illinois; Sarah Cornelia is the wife of John J. Bergan, a prosperous merchant of Virginia city, Illinois; Joseph B. wedded Dora Vandeventer, and lives in Springfield, Illinois; and Charles married Mary Epler, and resides on the home farm. Mr. and Mrs. Stevenson also reared two orphan children.

In 1884, when in his seventy-first year, Mr. Stevenson contested for the prize of a gold-headed cane offered by the county fair association for horse-back riding, which he won, and shows with a commendable pride. On February 11, 1886, Mr. and Mrs. Stevenson celebrated the fiftieth anniversary of their married life, which joyous event was participated in by all the living relations. Many handsome and valuable testimonials of affection were presented to them on this occasion by their admiring friends.

Mrs. Stevenson died at her home July 13, 1891, after a happy married life of fifty-five years, being in the eighty-eighth year of her age. She was a woman possessing many excellencies of character, a faithful wife, loving mother, kind neighbor, and devout Christian, whose many acts of kindness endeared her to a large circle of friends. By reason of a robust constitution and good habits she attained nearly four-score years, and passed away as peacefully as the coming dawn, in the full consciousness of an immortality beyond the grave.

Mr. Stevenson has been a resident of Cass county for sixty-three years, and has resided on the same section of land since 1829. He has not only witnessed the wonderful change in the country but has actively participated in transforming the wilderness and unbroken prairie into fertile farms. Every enterprise for the material or moral advancement of the community has received his cordial support. He and his family are Presbyterians, and have contributed liberally in support of the church. He was a Whig until the formation of the Republican party, when he joined that organization and has since supported its principles. He has never sought public office, preferring the quiet pursuits of farm life. By honest industry he has been successful in acquiring a handsome competence. He has assisted his children to good starts in life and still owns a fine farm of 375 acres, which which is supplied with good buildings and all modern conveniences. In addition to his duties of superintending his farm, he was until recently agent for the Jacksonville Southeastern Railroad which runs through his farm, on which Little Indian station is located. He was for twenty-four years agent for the Wabash, Peoria, Pekin & Jacksonville and the Jacksonville & Southeastern Railroad Companies, but resigned that position in August, 1892.

JOHN LISTMANN, of the firm of Ruppel & Listmann, extensive dealers in boots and shoes, located at 108 State street, Beardstown, Illinois, was born in Frischborn, Kreis Lauterbach, Hesse-Darmstadt, Germany, October 26, 1853, and grew up in his native place, and passed a full course in the public schools. In 1867 he and a sister with their parents started from Bremen for America, landing in New York city after a safe trip on the steamship Atlanta. The little family came on and made a settlement at Springfield, Illinois, where an elder son and two daughters had preceded them. The family settled at the capital for some time and then the parents located near Burlington, Iowa, where they both died, at the age of about sixty-seven and sixty-eight years respectively. The father who was a native of Hesse-Darmstadt and tiller of the soil died in the fall of 1878; and the mother, whose maiden name was Wienold, lived a few months after her husband's death; then she too died, in the early part of the year 1879.

Our subject is the youngest of a large family of whom but four are living. He continued to perfect his education, principally by self-study, and succeeded in attaining the ability to speak and write both the German and English with fluency. He learned the trade of shoemaker and formed a partnership in February, 1879, with Adam Ruppel, also a practical boot and shoemaker by trade, and these two gentlemen have carried on the business successfully ever since. Mr. Listmann had been in the employ of H. Fayart, Springfield, Illinois, and Ruppel Bros. and Adam Rupple, Beardstown, for some time before entering into the partnership above referred to. He is a stockholder in several building and loan associations, and is identified with the growth of the city. He has a host of friends. He is a Republican in politics and is an active member of the Evangelical Lutheran Church (Fourth Street), and was a delegate to the General Synod of the Lutheran Church, when it held its session at Altoona, Pennsylvania, in 1881. Mr. and Mrs. Listmann take great interest in the social and religious work of their church.

He was married in Beardstown, to Marie Lammers, October 20, 1881. She was born, reared and educated in Beardstown. She was the daughter of Alexander and Henrietta (Christianer) Lammers, natives of Prussia and Hanover, Germany. They were married in Beardstown. They are now both deceased Mr. Lammers died in February, 1879, and was eighty years of age.

Mr. and Mrs. Listmann have three children, Cora, Alice and Phoebe.

OSWELL SKILES, capitalist, Virginia, Illinois, was born in Ross county, Ohio, October 26, 1828. His father, Harmon Skiles, a native of Pennsylvania, went to Ohio when a young man and settled on Pickaway Plains, being one of the early settlers of that section of the country. In those days many of the more extensive farmers had distilleries on their farms, and made their own corn into whiskey, it being much more easily transported to the distant markets in that way. Mr. Skiles had a large distillery on his farm. He removed from Pickaway Plains to Washington Court House, where he died in 1851. He was twice married. His first wife, *nee* Mary Thompson, died in January, 1829, leaving two sons, Ignatius and Oswell. By his second wife he had two daughters, Eleanor and Susan. Oswell Thompson, grandfather of the subject of our sketch, was one of the pioneer settlers of Pickaway Plains. In 1827, he started westward and came to Cass county, Illinois. He located on North

Prairie, where he secured a farm and resided until his death.

Oswell Skiles was an infant when his mother died, and he was reared by a family named Smith. Mr Smith was a poor man, had ten children of his own, and lived on a rented farm. In addition to his farming operations he also had a contract to carry the mails between Washington Court House and Columbus, a distance of thirty-seven miles, and to Chillicothe, twenty-five miles As soon as he was large enough, young Skiles commenced to earn his living by assisting on the farm, and when about fifteen years old he carried the mail, making the journey on horseback. They used to make two trips a week to Columbus Many of the streams were not bridged, and during high water he had either to swim his horse or wait until the water subsided. When he was about twenty years old he began to learn the trade of harnessmaker. He continued work at that trade, in Ohio, until the fall of 1851, when he came to Illinois, making the journey with a horse and buggy, to Springfield. He rode on the cars from there to Jacksonville, that being the first railroad he had ever seen. He landed in Jacksonville with $5 in his pocket, hired a horse and rode to Arcadia, from which place he walked to the home of his uncle, Oswell Thompson, having sent the horse back. On his arrival at his uncle's he received $100 which he had inherited from his grandfather's estate, and with that he bought a horse, saddle and bridle. Thus equipped, he made the journey on horseback the following winter to Iowa, where he joined another uncle residing in Louisa county, for whom he worked about one year. Then he returned to Cass county, and in April, 1853, started for California A man named Welch had fitted out a train of ox teams, and Mr. Skiles paid him $75 to carry his provisions, clothing, etc , and he assisted in driving the oxen and loose stock. They crossed the Illinois river at Beardstown, on the 6th of April, and continued their way westward over rivers, plains and mountains, arriving in the Sacramento valley in October At that time there were no white settlers between the Missouri river and California, except the Mormons at Salt Lake, and the country abounded in game of all kinds Mr Skiles had only about $2 left when he reached California He engaged to work for Mr. Welch on his ranch for $75 per month and board, and the two lived together in a cabin, keeping bach Mr. Skiles was soon taken sick, however, and had to seek quarters where he could receive better attention, and for which he had to pay $9 per week. With the first money he earned after his recovery, he paid his board He remained with Mr. Welch about one year, and then went to Forbestown, Butte county, where he bought an interest in a mining claim, for which he paid $100 He was successful in his mining operations that winter In the spring he sold out and went to Sierra county, prospected for a time, and then for some months was engaged in preparing a tunnel for deep diggings The winter was very severe, the snow falling to the depth of ten feet. In the spring he engaged in mining, being thus occupied there for two years, at the end of which time he sold his interest for $1,000. He then worked by the day about three months, for $5 per day Next we find him in the Sacramento valley, engaged in farming and stock raising, he having purchased an interest in a claim to a tract of Government land near Marysville In 1858 he took passage on the steamer Oregon and went to Victoria, but, instead of being encouraging, the reports from the mines in the British possessions were the opposite, and consequently he returned to his ranch, where he remained till 1862. Then, with four yoke of oxen he started to take a load of flour to Virginia City, Nevada. On his arrival there, he sold his load and engaged in drawing cord wood to the quartz mill, receiving $15 per cord. In the fall he returned to his ranch and spent the winter, and the following spring went back to Virginia City. The next autumn he took a load of shakes to Austin, Reese river, 150 miles distant from Virginia City, selling them for $150 per 1,000. He spent the winter there, and in the spring sold his oxen and wagon, and started on his return East. He journeyed by stage, via Austin and Salt Lake City, to Atchison, Kansas, thence by steamer and rail to Jacksonville, arriving at his uncle Oswell Thompson's on the 4th of July, 1864. His success in California was not unlike that of many others who sought their fortunes in the Golden State—sometimes successful and at other times in hard luck. On his arrival in Cass county, he had about $1,000. He formed a partnership with his brother Ignatius, and engaged in buying and shipping stock, in which he was very successfully engaged for a number of years. For the past few years, however, he has devoted his attention to banking and farming. He is a member of the firm of Petefish, Skiles & Co., of Virginia; of Skiles, Rearick & Co., of Ashland; and of Mertz, Skiles & Co., of Chandlerville; and Bloomfield, Skiles & Co., of Mt. Sterling. He owns farms in different parts of Cass county, some of which he rents and some of which he superintends.

Mr. Skiles has been twice married. In July, 1870, he wedded Miss Ann Conover, a native of Cass county, Illinois, a sister of George Conover (a sketch of whom appears elsewhere in this volume). She died in 1877, and in 1879 he married Eliza J. Epler. He has one child living, by his first marriage, Lee Harmon, who is in the bank at Chandlerville. The children of his present wife are Louis Oswell and Stella.

Politically, Mr. Skiles is a Republican. He and his wife are members of the Presbyterian Church.

PHILIP JOKISCH, a practical young farmer, living on a beautiful farm of 140 acres almost all highly improved, and the same supplied with good farm buildings, was born on the Jokisch homestead belonging to his father, Charles G., in this township January 26, 1854. He was reared and educated in his native county. When arrived at manhood's estate he began farming on his own account. He is the second son and third child of his father, Charles Jokisch (see his biography). Mr. Philip Jokisch had but limited opportunities for acquiring an education, but is a bright, intelligent man, and has been very prosperous. His present farm has been improved by him and lies in the valley of the Illinois river. He has owned this fine farm about ten years and in that time has built the nice residence they occupy. The land has advanced in value since he bought it, and is now very valuable, and he has made his money by hard work.

He was married in this county, near Arenzville, to Miss Sarah Hackman, born in this county on her father's old homestead, near Arenzville, October 28, 1869. She was carefully reared by good parents and received a good education in the schools of the section, and at those of Jacksonville, Illinois. She is the fifth child and fourth daughter of Fred and Minnie M (Meyer) Hackman, natives of Hanover Germany. They grew up in that country, but came to this country when young and single, and were afterward married in Cass county where they began their married life near Arenzville Here they accumulated a fine property of 400 acres of land They are still living there and now enjoy the fruits of their labors Mr. Hackman is not in good health, but Mrs. Hackman is as well as one of her age and after her life of hard work could expect to be. They are members of the Methodist Episcopal Church

Mr and Mrs. Jokisch are members of the German Methodist Episcopal Church. He is a Republican in politics They are the parents of four children· Oswell, Orin P., Viola E and Verna M Mr and Mrs Jokisch are good, reliable farmers, and are highly respected by all who know them

LEWIS T. BARRY, a prominent and esteemed citizen of Mount Sterling, Illinois, was born in Tippecanoe county, Indiana, on a farm four miles northeast of La Fayette, September 29, 1827

His parents were John and Priscilla (Richards) Barry, the former a native of Pennsylvania. His father removed to Ohio in an early day, where he married his first wife, and continued to reside in Scioto valley, that State, until her death. He then removed to Kentucky, where he was again married, his second wife being the widow of Mr. Reynolds and became the mother of the subject of this sketch About 1826, he and his wife removed to Indiana, at that time the frontier of civilization They were pioneers of Tippecanoe county, that State, where the Indians were then more numerous than the whites. The father here secured a large tract of Government land and built a log house, in the construction of which no sawed lumber was used. The floor was of puncheon and the roof was covered with rived boards, held in place by weight poles, while the chimney was made of earth and sticks, called in those days a "cat-and-stick chimney." Both parents resided here until their death, the mother expiring in 1830 and his father in 1836. They both enjoyed the universal esteem of their community and were widely and sincerely lamented.

Thus the subject of this sketch was left an orphan at the tender age of nine years, and early became self-supporting He attended a pioneer subscription school which was taught in a log house, the furniture being of the most primitive kind Rough slabs, supported by wooden pins for legs, formed the seats, which had neither backs nor desks; holes burned in the wall, on which a plank was laid, served as a desk for larger scholars to write on. The country was without railroads or canals for many years, and La Fayette was the nearest market People used to team wheat to Chicago, a distance of about 150 miles He thus continued to live on the home farm and attended school until he attained the age of eighteen years. He then commenced to clerk in Carroll county, Indiana, where he remained for about five years. After this, he engaged in tanning and the manufacture of boots, shoes and harness, at which business he continued four years. At the end of this time, he sold out, and for a couple of years served as Deputy County Auditor, after which he did bookkeeping in Delphi, Carroll county. In 1861, he came to Mount Sterling, where he engaged in the boot and shoe business, besides which, for some years, he made harnesses and saddles. He is still engaged in the boot and shoe trade, and is the only exclusive dealer in that line in the city, being one of the few successful merchants of the place.

He was married in Delphi, Indiana, in 1850, to Ann L. Richardson, an estimable lady, a native of Carroll county, that State, and a daughter of John Richardson, a highly respected citizen. To this union five children were born, all living: A. Priscilla, wife of E. W. Reid, a prosperous resident of Los Angeles, California; Ellen E., wife of Isaiah Price, living in Springfield; Kate L., wife of William Mumford, of Pittsfield, who have one son, named Barry; John H. and Bert.

Mr. Barry is a member of Hardin Lodge, No. 44, A. F. & A. M., and in politics supports the issues of the Democratic party.

Whatever success Mr. Barry has achieved in life has not been acquired without effort, as might be inferred. On the contrary, his prosperity and popularity is directly traceable to his unremitting energy and careful supervision of all the details of his various occupations, and to his uniform integrity and courtesy, thus deservedly attaining success and esteem.

CAPTAIN JOHN HEATON, a retired farmer residing in Virginia, Cass county, Illinois, was born in Wigan, Lancashire county, England, January 1, 1810.

Dennis Heaton, his father, and Bartley Heaton, his grandfather, were also natives of Wigan, the family as far as known being of English ancestry. Grandfather Heaton was a Colonel in the Life Guards. He spent his whole life in England. Dennis Heaton was engaged in the mercantile business in Wigan, where he died about 1816. The maiden name of his wife was Kate Bartley, and she, too, was a native of Wigan. After the death of Mr. Heaton she married James Richardson. Her death occurred in Yorkshire about 1852. By her first husband she had nine children, all of whom reached adult years; by her second husband she reared four children.

The subject of our sketch was reared in Manchester. He was six years old when his father died, and from the time he was seven he earned his own living. From his seventh year till his thirteenth he worked in a cotton factory, after which he began learning the trade of tin and coppersmith with Mr. Moon in Oldham street, Manchester, with whom he worked seven years. He now has a kettle which he made in 1827 and presented to his mother. At the time of his marriage she gave it back to him, and it has been in daily use in his family ever since.

At the age of twenty-one Mr. Heaton enlisted in the Thirty-sixth Begiment of Infantry, and was soon transferred to the Fifty-ninth Regiment, and marched across Ireland to Dublin, joining the regiment at Port Aa Bella Barracks, and served two years and eight months. He was in different parts of Ireland ten months and then made a forced march to Oldham, England, to quell a riot there; thence to Liverpool, where he embarked for Gibraltar, a year later to Malta, then to Carfew, and from there back to Gibraltar, where his discharge and that of nineteen others was purchased, supposed to have been by the Spanish Government. He then became a member of Shaw's brigade for the Spanish army during the war between Don Carlos and the Queen; was commissioned Captain of the Light Company and commanded that company in the different marches, battles, etc, incident to that war. He served a little more than seven years.

When peace was declared Captain Heaton was honorably discharged and returned to Manchester There he began business on his own account as a tin and copper smith, remaining thus occupied until 1850. That year he came to America, sailing from Liverpool on the 27th of May and landing in Quebec after a voyage of seven weeks and three days. His father-in-law was at that time living four miles from Streetsville, Ontario. He joined him, and from there visited the Queen's Bush, a tract of timber land set aside for the soldiers Not caring to have a farm in the wilderness, he came to the United States. After residing in St Louis a few weeks, he sought a home in Cass county, Illinois, taking up his abode seven miles from Virginia, where he entered a tract of Government land. He erected a log house and commenced at once to improve his land. This was before the coming of the railroad and when Beardstown was the principal market for this section of the country. Deer and various kinds of wild game were plenty here. Captain Heaton improved fifty acres of land, and in 1854 sold it to John Fravey. He then moved to Beardstown in order to give his children the benefit of schools He was employed by Horace Billings in his pork house for a time, and later was in the employ of Mr. Crea and Henry Chatsey. While a resident of that place he was sent for from Brooklyn, New York, to superintend a pork-packing establishment there for a Mr. Arris He remained in Brooklyn one season. In 1863 he went to Decatur, Illinois, and established a packing house for Mr Plato He subsequently purchased a farm of Major Arnold, in Monroe precinct, and resided on it till 1870 The following two years he lived in Beardstown His next move was to Virginia He bought property on Gospel Hill, built a house, and resided there till 1884 He then rented that place, and bought and moved to his present home.

Captain Heaton was married at Bolton, Lancashire, England, November 2, 1840, to Mary J. Fullerton She was born in the Tower of London, February 29, 1820, daughter of Major James Fullerton, a native of England. When a young man, her father enlisted in the Seventh Battalion, and was commissioned Major He was in command of the tower at the time of her birth. He served in the army about twenty-two years, after which he was retired on half pay. He then emigrated to Canada, and settled twenty miles from Toronto, Ontario, where he bought a farm and resided till his death. The maiden name of his wife was Martha Glen She was born in England and died in Canada

To Captain Heaton and his wife eleven children have been born, viz: Noble John, who was married by W. R Whitehead to Flavila Yaple, December 24, 1873, and has three children, Charlie, Alford and Noble John, Catharine, who was married by R. C. H Heimerling to Charles Caldwell, December 12, 1860, and has seven children, Patrick, John, Emma, Jennie, who became the wife of James Mead, of Virginia; Lizzie, Katie and Edward, Edward, who lost his life in a railroad accident on the Central Pacific Railroad; James, who was married in November, 1873, to Cora Seaman, has one child, Florence; Mary Jane, who was married by Benjamin Williams to W B. Williams, August 7, 1871, and has two children, Eddie and Henry; William, who was married by John W. Shay to Hannah E. Seaman, November 10, 1875, and has five children, Mary, John, Willard, George and Eva; Charles, who was married January 5, 1885, to Sadie Bohman; Susan, who was married by John W. Allen to Reuben Lancaster, March 11, 1880, and has two children, Earl and Iva; Alice, who was married by John W. Allen to Edward E. Savage, May 10, 1877, and has four children, Henry, Walter, Bessie and Zella; Martha, who was married by J. E. Roach to Richard H. Payne, November 20, 1884, and has four children, Carey, Inis, Hazel and Irine; and Thomas, who is unmarried. They have twenty-nine grandchildren and three great-grandchildren.

The Captain and his worthy companion are devout members of the Catholic Church.

The sword which this veteran carried in Spain he has presented to his son, Noble John, who values it beyond price.

Such is a brief record of one of Virginia's pioneers and highly respected citizens.

WILLIAM L. DEMAREE is a native of Rushville township, having been born there June 7, 1858, and while a young man is a successful farmer, and one who enjoys the confidence and the respect of his friends and neighbors. His father, Ludwell H. Demaree, was born in Mercer county, Kentucky, and his grandfather spent the last years of his life in that State. Ludwell Demaree, after marrying in Kentucky, a lady by the name of Martha J. Yankee, of Washington county, that State, removed to Illinois in 1857, buying a farm in section 16, Rushville township, where he lived until his death, in 1872. He was one of the founders of the Methodist Episcopal Church South, in this county, and spared neither time nor means for its advancement. His wife survived him by sixteen years. Six of her eight children are living, viz.: Belle, married to Leonidas Scott; Laura, married to Alexander Acheson; William L.; John H.; Nora, married to J. C. Harrison; and George L.

William L. Demaree received his education in the schools of his native town. Appreciating the importance and value of a good education, he sought to improve every opportunity. He was but fourteen years of age when his father died, and he continued as before to reside at the home place, only leaving it at the time of his marriage, in 1883. This event took place very happily in that year, to Rebecca Hamilton, daughter of a worthy and esteemed couple, John and Margaret Hamilton, and he then settled upon the farm where he now resides. In 1891, Mr. Demaree added to his possessions by buying another farm in section 22, Rushville township, so that he now owns 460 acres of land, all in the township named. He carries on general farming and stock raising.

Mr. and Mrs. Demaree have two children, Dwight E. and William P. They are earnest members of the Methodist Episcopal Church South, Mr. Demaree being the builder of the McTyeire chapel in 1890. In politics, Mr. Demaree is a Democrat.

CHRISTIAN KUHLMANN, one of the substantial farmers and highly respected citizens of Monroe precinct, Cass county, Illinois, was born in the kingdom of Eilstad, Germany, in April, 1827. His parents were natives of Hanover, and passed their lives there. When Christian was three years old his father died, leaving a wife and three children.

Mr. Kuhlmann attended school until he was fourteen, when he began to earn his own living, working by the year on a farm. The first year he received only $3 and his board. In 1851 he came to America. Setting sail from Bremen in April in the sailing vessel Capanica, he landed at New York after a voyage of forty-two days. He there found employment in a sugar refinery at $26 per month, and thus earned the money to pay his way to the West. In 1852 he came to Illinois, coming via the Hudson river to Albany, Erie canal to Buffalo, the lakes to Cleveland, canal to Portsmouth, and the Ohio and Mississippi rivers to St. Louis. He found employment on a farm in St. Louis county, and remained there till 1854. That year he came to Cass county and was employed at farm work by the month. He was very industrious, saved his earnings, and in the course of time rented land and began farming on his own account. In 1864 he made his first purchase of land, 160 acres, located on section 26, township 18, range 11. There was a log cabin on the place, into which the family moved, and he at once began to make further improvements on the land. Prosperity attended his well-directed efforts, and as the years rolled by he added to his original purchase and erected suitable farm buildings. His home farm now contains 375 acres, and he also owns another farm, 437 acres, in the ame township. Besides these Mrs. Kuhlmann has a farm of 120 acres. Mr. Kuhlmann is indeed a self-made man. His life and achievements serve well to illustrate what a poor young man with ambition, good judgment and plenty of energy can accomplish in this free land of ours.

In 1855 Mr. Kuhlmann was married in Cass county, to Mary Middlebusher, also a native of Hanover. She came to America with her parents. Their union has resulted in the birth of two sons, George H. and John H. The younger resides with his parents. George H. is engaged in farming on his own account. He married Miss Kate A. Hemminghaus, a native of Morgan county, Illinois, daughter of German parents. They have three children: Christian, Adelia and Lydia.

The Kuhlmann family are members of the Lutheran Church at Beardstown.

DEMETRIUS H. ALLEN, a prominent citizen of Versailles, was born in Adams county, this State, in 1855. His father, James, was born in New Jersey in 1819, and he came to this State when a young man, in 1838. His wife was Mary Holten, born May 2, 1825. She died in 1875, having borne her husband nine children, two of whom died in infancy; those who lived to maturity were: Mary C., wife of Jeremiah Stuart; William M., farmer of Missouri, has six children; John, residing with subject; D. H., subject; Amanda, wife of Stephen Smith; Stephen A. D., farm laborer of this township; George resides on the farm with his brother, has but one son.

Our subject's father had but limited schooling, being obliged to work on the farm his father purchased, for many years. He enlisted in the Fiftieth Illinois Infantry, serving two years, when he was discharged on account of sickness, but was home only a few weeks when he re-enlisted in the cavalry service, serving in all some four years and a half, being mustered out at St. Louis at the close of the war. Although not very well educated, he was an able and zealous minister of the Baptist Church.

Our subject was one of the good sons one so seldom sees, remaining at home, assisting with the farm and caring for the little ones, and has never ceased to look after their welfare.

He was married January 3, 1878, to Miss Julia Hall, of the same place, daughter of Elijah and Susan (Cousin) Hall, Virginia farmers, who came to Illinois about 1830, being then very poor, but then they had 240 acres of good land and other valuable property. Five of their children are still living. The father died when seventy years old, and the mother when she was eighty years old, in 1884.

Mr. and Mrs. Allen have buried one son, Charles L., an infant, and one daughter, May Allen, born September, 1880. Mr. Allen is a Democrat, and has served as School Director for something over one term. He is a Deacon in the Baptist Church.

Mr. Allen carries on general farming on his wife's fifty-acre farm, raising wheat and corn, the former yielding about sixteen bushels to the acre, the latter forty to fifty. Mr. and Mrs. Allen are highly respected young people of their township, and enjoy life on their beautiful farm, which is kept in beautiful order by the care of Mr. Allen.

THOMAS S. HOWELL, one of the oldest settlers now residing in Schuyler county, Illinois, was born in Guilford county, North Carolina, February 16, 1825. His grandfather, John Howell, was a native of Wales, and but little of his history is known; he was a farmer by occupation, and emigrated to America, spending his last days in Guilford county, North Carolina. His son, John Howell, Jr., the father of Thomas S., was born and reared in North Carolina, and there learned the cabinet-maker's trade, which he followed until 1829; then, accompanied by his wife and five children, he undertook the overland trip to Illinois, and after eight weeks of travel he arrived in Schuyler county. It had not been long since the first settlers penetrated these wilds, and there were consequently few improvements. Indians still lingered about, and wild game was plentiful. Mr. Howell bought a tract of timber land in Woodstock township, and erected a cabin that was the pride of the community, from the fact that it had a shingle roof; the floor was made of puncheons, and the door of heavy oak boards hung on wooden hinges. There were no railroads, and no steamers plying the Illinois river. Mr. Howell followed his trade in connection with his agricultural pursuits, and lived here until his death, August 10, 1833. His wife's maiden name was Sally Manlove, a native of Guilford county, North Carolina, and a daughter of William Manlove; after her husband's death she was married a second time, to Stephen Frasier; her death occurred May 1, 1843. She was the mother of seven children: Amanda, Oscar C., William M., Thomas S., Jonathan M., John H. and Jacob.

Thomas S. Howell was a child of four years when his parents came to Illinois, but well remembers many of the incidents and experiences peculiar to pioneer life. His father kept sheep and raised flax, and from the wool and flax the mother spun, carded and wove the cloth from which the family wardrobe was supplied. He remained with his mother during her lifetime. The first venture he made in business was threshing 100 bushels of wheat, the agreement being that he was to receive therefor one-tenth of the wheat; he worked three days to pay for three barrels in which to ship the wheat to St. Louis, the whole transaction netting him $3. With this capital he was married, and settled on the home farm; he had inherited twenty-five acres, and he rented the balance of the other heirs, and there began his career as a farmer. In due time he was enabled to purchase this tract.

In March, 1865, he enlisted in Company D, One Hundred and Fifteenth Illinois Volunteer Infantry, and in June, of that year, was transferred to the Twenty-first Illinois, serving until December 16, of the same year; he was honorably discharged at San Antonio, Texas. He resided on the homestead in Woodstock township until 1875, when he sold this place and purchased the Newbury farm, which consists of 220 acres on section 28, Bainbridge township.

Mr. Howell was married May 14, 1843, to Sarah C. Newbury, who was born in Washington county, Ohio, a daughter of Joseph and Margaret Newbury, natives of New York and Virginia respectively, and pioneers of Washington county, Ohio, and Schuyler county, Illinois. Mr. and Mrs. Howell have eight children living: John E., Austin D., Oscar C., Hattie A., William, Lorain C., Dora and T. Edgar. Our subject is a stanch supporter of the principles of the Republican party, and is a man who has the respect and confidence of all who know him.

WILLIAM LUCAS, a farmer of Lee township, was born in Mount Sterling, June 17, 1837. His father, Daniel, was born in Butler county, Ohio, March 21, 1810, and his father was a native of Virginia, of English ancestry. He was a lad of sixteen when the Revolutionary war was declared, and served six years in it. Soon after he emigrated to Kentucky, and was one of the first settlers of that State, and from there went on to Butler county, Ohio, and settled there as a pioneer in 1796 and resided in that county until his death in 1836. His son, Daniel Robins, was the youngest of a large family, was reared to agricultural pursuits, but obtained a good education for those days and by teaching earned enough to educate himself in medicine. He removed from Ohio to Crawfordsville, Indiana, and from there to Brown county, Illinois, in 1836, and was one of the pioneers. He practiced medicine through Brown and Adams counties until his death, January 26, 1884. In 1843 he settled in Lee township, where he bought land and in addition to his practice superintended his farm. He married Sarah Ann Keith, of Kentucky, who died March 22, 1890, aged seventy-two years. They had twelve children: William, Newton, Martha Ann, Mary Elizabeth, Dr. George Washington, John Harding, Ethan Allen, Helen, Daniel Webster, Benjamin Franklin and James Edward. Nine are living and three died young.

William remained on the farm until he was thirty-one years of age. He and his brother went to Texas for a herd of cattle in 1866. They bought 600 head at $20 a head. They drove them through to Illinois, crossed the Red river, April 22, and reached Quincy, September 20. The adventure proved a financial disaster. From 1872 to 1876 he and his brother, Newton, were at Memphis, Missouri, in the grain and hay business. In this he was successful, and now owns 632 acres of land, and is a stock farmer, growing the ordinary crops of this section. He keeps from fifty to a hundred head of cattle, and owns some of the pure-blood registered stock. He often raises as many as 250 hogs.

He was first married January 2, 1866, to Margaret Miller, who died July 7, 1866, of quick consumption in consequence of an exposure while swimming a stream on horseback. He was again married in 1884, to A. E. Lierly, daughter of William R. Lierly, minister of the Dunkard Church. They have one daughter: Sarah Ann, born February 17, 1890.

JOHN H. GOODELL, formerly a prosperous farmer of Cass county, Illinois, now an enterprising lumber merchant of Chandlerville, was born in Windham county, Connecticut, April 15, 1832.

The Goodells were of French ancestry, who settled in Connecticut in an early day. The paternal grandmother of the subject of this sketch was a descendant of the Holbrook family, who were also old and respected residents of the Nutmeg State; while his paternal grandfather was a captain in the Revolutionary war, in which he distinguished himself for bravery and efficiency. The parents of our subject were Horace and Lucy (Rickard) Goodell, both natives of Connecticut, of which State his mother's ancestors were also early settlors. The father of our subject was reared on a farm in Windham county, the same State, where he and his wife continued to reside until 1837. He then sold out, and with his wife and three children removed to Illinois, making the journey by land and water. Arriving on the frontier he rented land for a number of years, which he farmed, finally buying forty acres of wild land, to which he subsequently added, until it now contains eighty acres. On this he erected a substantial farm house, where he continued to reside until his death in May, 1886, at the age of eighty-four years. His wife also died in the year 1868, on the homestead, aged fifty-nine years. This worthy couple were the parents of seven children, all sons, two of whom now survive, the subject of this sketch and a brother, Charles C. Goodell, the latter now residing on the old homestead.

John H. Goodell lived at home until he was twenty years of age, working on the farm until he was eighteen, and attended the district school of that vicinity. When eighteen he learned the carpenter's trade, at which he commenced to work at twenty, continuing in that vocation for ten years.

At this time war was declared and Mr. Goodell enlisted in August, 1862, in Company A, One Hundred and Fourteenth Illinois, under Captain Johnson, and served until the close of the war, being a part of the time on detached duty. He was in the hospital in Memphis for two months in 1864. He was mustered out of the army in Vicksburg, Mississippi, at the close of the war, and received his discharge in Springfield, Illinois.

He then returned to Jacksonville, Illinois, where he worked at his trade for about two years, after which he came to Chandlerville, and bought the farm on which he now lives. He and his wife together now own 235 acres, which is devoted to mixed farming. In 1876, Mr. Goodell started a lumber-yard in Chandlerville, which he has continued to operate successfully ever since, having, by upright dealing and uniform courtesy, built up a large trade in the town and surrounding country.

Mr. Goodell was first married February 27, 1853, to Miss Helen E. Cotton, an intelligent lady, and a native of Franklin county, New York. She was a daughter of Gideon C. and

Miss (Sperry) Cotton, natives of New England, who removed to New York State, where they died. Mr. Goodell's marriage was destined to be of short duration, as ten years later, July 4, 1863, his wife expired at their home in Chandlerville, leaving many sorrowing friends.

On December 28, 1865, Mr. Goodell was married to his present wife, Miss Harriet A. Sewall, an estimable lady who was born April 14, 1838, in the county were she now resides. Her father was born in Augusta, Maine, and was a son of General Henry Sewall, a Major in the Revolutionary war, who was afterward made a Major-General of the Eighth Division of the State militia. He died in his native State, at the advanced age of ninety-four years. His brother, Jotham Sewall, was a prominent home missionary of Maine, and died in that State at the age of ninety-one years. All the family lived to a great age, and many of the name were prominent ministers of the gospel. On account of his father's prominence and services to the country, his son, father of Mrs. Goodell, obtained a lucrative position in Washington, but on his way thither he was shipwrecked on Long Island sound in extreme cold weather, and, on seeing a woman on board suffering for want of more clothes, took off his coat and gave it to her to save her life. Then, to keep from freezing and the ship from sinking, he had to work the ship pump so long that he froze his hands and was rendered unable to write and fill the office. Then after a long illness he went, at the age of twenty-one, to Virginia, where he taught school, having received a liberal education for boys in those days. It was while thus engaged that he met and married his wife in Virginia, which was then a part of Maryland. His wife was a native of Nanjamoy, Maryland, and was a daughter of Samuel and Catharine Tolliver (Hoe) Middleton. The Middletons were of English ancestry, and early settlers of America. Both families were prominent in business and social affairs of the State, and many of their relatives were accomplished literary men, while others were distinguished in the law and other professions. Some of the descendants took an active and prominent part in the Confederate army. Soon after his marriage, about 1829, Mr. Sewall removed to Illinois, then a new and sparsely settled country. They settled in Jacksonville, where Mr. Sewall taught school and entered 640 acres of land in Cass county. He taught school for about two or three years, when he moved on his farm, where he continued to reside until his death. He was a very devout man and did much good in this new country. He was an active worker in Sunday-school and church matters, acting for years as superintendent of the former as long as he lived, and was instrumental in building the first church in the community, of which he was the first Elder. He did more to build up both of these institutions in the early day than any other man in the community. Storms or cold weather never deterred him from his duty. To make sure of prompt attendance he would take his kindling wood with him, and his wife her broom, and ride three miles to the village church, then used as a schoolhouse; and while he made the fire she would sweep and clean up the house before the people of the village had started out.

He and his worthy wife had six children, three of whom are now living. He was universally beloved and respected, and was greatly lamented when he died on his farm, in 1846, aged about forty-nine years. His devoted wife survived him many years, dying at our subject's home at the advanced age of eighty years. What has been said of her husband would apply equally to her, both having led in all good and charitable works, and was always noted for bravery and presence of mind.

Mr. and Mrs. Goodell have six children: Lucy, born May 28, 1868; Lida, born February 2, 1871; William S., born September 16, 1872; John, born March 1, 1875; Andrew J., born March 11, 1877; and Susie, born February 27, 1880.

Mr. Goodell now belongs to the Prohibition party in politics, previous to which he was a Democrat, with the exception of the years 1856 and 1860, when he voted the Republican ticket. He is a member of the Good Templar's Lodge, No. 357. For thirty-five years he has been a Deacon in the church, and he is active in Sunday-school work, having taught the largest Bible class of the older scholars in the Sabbath-school for over thirty years. His worthy wife aids him in all good work. She belongs to the Women's Christian Temperance Union and other ladies' societies, and the whole family are church attendants. They are, in fact, of that class of which it was said they "are the salt of the earth," adding savor to the works of the world.

JOHN C. FLINN, a prominent farmer and successful stock-raiser of township 17, range 9, section 24, near Ashland, Illinois, was born in Morgan county, this State, August 28, 1842. His parents were Royal and Lovicia (Hall) Flinn, his paternal grandfather having come from Ireland. His father was a native of North Carolina, and when twelve years of age went to Kentucky, from which State he came to Morgan county, Illinois, about 1828. Here he purchased land, which he industriously improved, making it a valuable farm, on which he lived a number of years. He was a soldier in the Black Hawk war, and also in the Mexican war, serving efficiently in both. He died at Prentiss, Morgan county, Illinois, January 27, 1892, in his ninetieth year, his having been a remarkably active career, of unusual longevity. The devoted wife and mother still survives at the old homestead, where she is a helpless invalid from rheumatism, being the recipient of the most solicitous care of her children and the deepest regard of a host of friends. This worthy couple were the parents of six sons and four daughters, four of the former now deceased. Those surviving are: Francis M., now living in Prentiss, Morgan county, this State; Thomas, a resident of Waverly, in the same county; and the four sisters, three of whom live in Morgan county, and one in Macoupin county, Illinois, all being married and having families. Two sons by a former marriage of the father still survive, one son having died.

The subject of this sketch attended the subscription schools of Morgan county, and was reared to farm life. At the age of sixteen years he went to southwestern Missouri, where he followed agricultural pursuits, returning to Morgan county in 1862. It was while in Missouri in the early part of the war that he was importuned to unite his fortunes with the Southern cause, but declined to do so, and returned to the North to avoid conscription. Since then he has continued farming pursuits in Morgan and Cass counties, having resided on his present place for nine years. This farm contains 170 acres of choice land, which is principally devoted to grain, besides which some very fine stock is raised. By good management and energy this farm has been very profitable, and he has accumulated a handsome competence.

Mr. Flinn was married in southwestern Missouri, to Miss Hannah Willis, an intelligent lady, and a native of Kentucky, in which State her parents were also born, who emigrated to Missouri when their daughter was a child. To this union have been born ten children, three sons and seven daughters: Ophelia, the oldest, married J. J. Higginson, a prominent merchant of Philadelphia, Illinois; Annie is the wife of L. P. Fisher, a farmer, near Jacksonville, this State; Luella and Alice are teachers in the public schools of this county; Jennie, Oscar, Frank, Lella and Stella (twins), and Earle. The twin daughters, now budding into beautiful womanhood, are so near alike that it puzzles their acquaintances to distinguish them. All except those who are married are under the parental roof, and each and every one of them is intelligent and progressive, being altogether a most interesting family, whom it is a pleasure to meet. All of the young people are interested in educational work. The son, Frank, has in view a course in the Gem City Commercial College for the coming winter, while the young ladies who are not already teachers are fitting themselves to become such. Numerous good books and periodicals are taken and read with avidity, and fully appreciated by their keen intellects. Whatever disappointments may be in store for Mr. Flinn in agricultural pursuits and pecuniary matters, will be amply compensated for by the charming family with which he is surrounded.

Mr. Flinn is Democratic in his political affiliations and takes a deep interest in all public affairs of importance.

Mrs. Flinn and five of the daughters are members of the Christian Church, to which they render much assistance.

Whatever gifts Dame Fortune has bestowed upon Mr. Flinn have not been voluntarily given, but have been wrested from her by perseverance and honest toil, and he richly deserves his present prosperity and happiness.

GEORGE WAGNER, a successful farmer, was born in Hesse-Cassel, in 1825. He had lost his mother when a child, and was brought up by his grandfather. His father came to this country in 1844, but George would not come along, as he did not like his stepmother. In 1848 he was drafted into the army, and after serving two years he came to the United States, but had helped fight five hard battles. He did not like such a dangerous life, and came away, as did many others at that period.

His father, after coming to America, engaged as a piano-maker in New York, in which business he had made much money in Germany. George never joined his father in this country, but came on West to try his fortune in Cass county.

He was married in this county in a short time, to Mary Deer, a German lady, who died in 1862, leaving five children. Mr. Wagner was a second time married, to Catherine Dietrich, born in Hesse-Cassel, who came to America in her youth. She has been a most devoted wife, and the mother of six children, three of whom are married and three of whom are yet at home.

Mr. Wagner has lived in the county since 1850. He first purchased land at 25 cents an acre, and sold it after some improvement, and purchased his present home. He now owns in section 4, township 17, range 11, 100 acres of improved land, and has good farm buildings. He has forty acres of timber land on section 3, township 17, range 11. He purchased the home in 1868, and settled on it in 1870. He was Road Supervisor three terms.

Mr. and Mrs. Wagner are good and well-known people in the county. He is a Republican, and both are upright, honest people.

DOW P. COLT, a leading member of commercial circles in Schuyler county, has resided here since 1843, and is entitled to the following space in this history of the pioneers of the State and county. He was born in Erie county, Pennsylvania, February 2, 1828, a son of Alexander and Lucy (Childs) Colt, natives of Pennsylvania and Massachusetts respectively. The maternal grandfather, Alexander Colt, Sr., emigrated to America from Ireland, accompanied by his wife and children; one brother, Judas Colt, also came to this country and settled in New York State. Alexander Colt, Jr., was the youngest of a large family; he grew to maturity in Erie county, and was married there.

In 1843 he removed to Illinois, and settled on a farm near Rushville, Schuyler county, where he and his wife passed the remainder of their days. They reared a family of fifteen children, thirteen of whom lived to mature years. Dow P. Colt was the second born, and is the oldest of the family now living. When he first came to this State, he was employed in a tannery, and also assisted his father on the farm. At the age of nineteen years he learned the broom-maker's trade, which he followed fourteen years. Having accumulated some means, he embarked in the grocery trade and carried on a thriving business until 1870. During the next five years he sold musical instruments, and from 1875 to 1889 he was engaged in the lumber trade. In the latter year he again took up the grocery business, which he has since continued without interruption.

Mr. Colt was united in marriage, June 2, 1853, to Miss Ellen Kuhn, a daughter of John and Harriet (White) Kuhn; she was born in Westmoreland county, Pennsylvania. To them have been born four children: Alice F., wife of George Bissel, Lucy E., Anna B., wife of James Montieth, and William W. In his political convictions Mr. Colt is allied with the Republican party; he has held the office of member of the village Board, but has not been an office seeker.

He was reared amidst Democratic influences, but after the war his father and brothers became Republicans. During the great civil conflict five of his brothers fought for the nation's flag, the youngest being but fifteen years of age: he enlisted, but was rejected on account of defective vision and hearing. He is not a member of any civic or religious societies at the present time, although for many years he was connected with the I. O. O. F.

JACOB ZIMMERMAN, born in section 26, Pike county, Illinois, son of George Zimmerman (see his sketch in this book), remained at home until he enlisted, August 10, 1862, in Company B, Ninety-ninth Illinois Infantry, Captain Mathews, commanding officer. He remained in service until the close of the war, when he was mustered out at Baton Rouge and discharged at Springfield, Illinois. He was with the company in all their engagements, notwithstanding he was in the hospital for a short time.

He was married in 1864, to Mary L. Winters, born in 1849. After his marriage he resided in Elkhorn, in the first frame house built in that place. He later built his present house, in which the family have lived for ten years. He first owned 157 acres, but has now about 146 acres in this county.

Mr. Zimmerman and wife have been members of the Methodist Episcopal Church for a number of years. He is a member of the People's party, and was a member of the Greenback party some years ago. He is no office seeker, and has had but little time to attend to the local politics.

Mr. and Mrs. Zimmerman have had the following children: Frank O., married, was born in 1868; Edwin, born in 1871; Minnie P., born in 1873; Mark T., born in 1877; and Jessie W., born in 1884. Minnie P. and Frank O. attended Chadock College at Quincy, Illinois, for a term of six months.

Edwin R. is an artist. The children are all temperate, having never tasted any intoxicating drink in their lives, have never used any profane language, and are strictly honest.

Mr. and Mrs. Zimmerman are good, reliable citizens, and are highly respected by their host of friends.

RICHARD MILNER an old settler of Beardstown, was born near Preston, Lancashire, England, thirty miles from Liverpool. He learned the trade of wagonmaker and when young he came to the United States. He was the only one of the family that came to the United States. His parents lived and died in Lancashire, England, the mother when Richard was six years old, the father, Thomas, a life-long farmer, when he was eighty-four years old. He and his wife were ardent Congregationalists. Richard was the eldest of a large family of brothers and half brothers, and left home for Canada in 1842, but he staid there only fifteen months and then came to Jacksonville, Illinois, and followed his trade. At Beardstown he was married to Hannah Wood, of Oldham, Yorkshire, England. She came to the United States in 1844, when young, with her father, John Wood. He died at Beardstown, Cass county, at the house of his daughter, Mrs. Milner, aged eighty-six.

Mr. Milner came to Beardstown in 1849, and began here as a wagonmaker and blacksmith for some years. He formed a partnership with Amasa Hill, and afterward with John Rose, soon after the Chicago, Burlington & Quincy Railroad began to build a line, and he became one of the bridge building force, and he continued building them for seven years, until the bridge for the Q. road was built at Beardstown, when he was made bridge-tender, some twenty years ago. He has retained the position ever since. Later he was made the Government river gauger of of the river at Beardstown, and also was appointed to make observations on the weather and rainfall each day. This position also he has held since its establishment in Beardstown, in 1885.

Mr. and Mrs. Milner had nine children, five of whom still live: Rebecca, wife of Samuel Wroe, of Nodaway county, Missouri, a farmer and cattle dealer; Thomas W., a railroad station master of Denison (now Leavenworth), Kansas; Nannie died one and one-half years after marriage, without issue, at the age of eighteen years ;Mary is at home, although she was a school teacher for some time; Rosa, wife of Henry Baujan (see biography); Maggie is single and at home; Mrs. Milner is a respected member of the Methodist Church and is esteemed by all who know her. Mrs. Milner is the youngest of a large family, nearly all of whom are dead.

ROBERT ATEN was born in West Virginia in 1818, in what was then Brooke county of the old Dominion, a son of William and Jane (Anderson) Aten; his mother died in 1834, leaving a family of seven children. William Aten was a prosperous farmer, and was noted throughout the country for the excellent grade of horses he kept. He was married a second time to Catherine Wycoff, who bore him four children. He died in 1866, leaving an estate of fair value. Five of the children are still living: Robert, the subject of this biographica sketch; William, a resident of Fulton county;I Mary, wife of William K. McClurg; Nancy Lester, a widow residing in McDonough county, Illinois; and Martha Beale, a widow in West Virginia; Aaron H., died in McDonough county, Illinois, at the age of eighty-two years; John C., died in Fulton county; Richard died in the same county; he was a pioneer of Illinois, coming in 1840, accompanied by Richard Aten. The latter returned to Virginia in 1842, and was back and forth until 1854, when he settled here permanently.

He was married in 1850 to Sarah Beale, a daughter of Benjamin Beal and a member of the prominent families of Virginia; she died one year later, to a day, leaving a daughter who died in infancy. Mr. Aten was married again in 1852 to Mary Jane Allison, who belonged to a well-known family. Of this union were born nine children, all of whom are living: Nancy L., now Mrs. Morris; Henry O., W. A. F., Robert Burns, Sarah, wife of Thomas Ashwood; James Grant, Daniel Webster, Flora Ann and John Q.

Mr. Aten's first purchase of land was eighty acres, for which he paid $600, he soon added another tract for which he paid $1,100, and at one time owned 700 acres; he has disposed of all but 400 acres. He carried on a general agricultural business. He makes a specialty of raising live-stock, and ships from two to three car-loads of hogs and as many cattle during the year. He began life with a small capital, but this was strongly supplemented with will and determination to succeed, and has arisen to a position of financial independence. Politically he has affiliated with the Whigs and then the Republicans. He and his wife are members of the Presbyterian Church, and give liberal support to the cause of Christianity. They have lived a useful life, and have borne their share of the burden assumed by the pioneers in their undertaking to redeem the wild prairie and bring it to a high state of cultivation, making of Illinois one of the leading agricultural States of the Union.

SETH C. CRAMPTON, of section 9, Browning township, was born on the farm on which he now lives, January 28, 1864, His father was born in Hartford, Connecticut, in 1797, came to Illinois in 1820, settled on the old homestead about 1835, went to California in 1844, and engaged in mining for two years, being reasonably successful. He returned from California in 1846 and resumed farming in Browning township. He was married the third time in 1858, to Mrs. Elizabeth Mitchell, whose maiden name was Davis. The father died when Seth was but eight years old. He attended the public schools of that district, and at the age of twenty-one entered a telegraph office at Baders, where he learned the business and became a practical operator. He continued at this business at various points on the Chicago, Burlington & Quincy railroad for five years, when failing health compelled him to make a change. He came back to the home farm, put in a crop, continued businsss in the telegraph office, but with the opening of the spring of 1892 he became a full-fledged farmer.

He was married July 7, 1886, in Rushville, to Miss Mary E. Frome, born in this township, October 8, 1863. Her parents were Abram and Nancy Frome; the former died suddenly of heart disease, and the mother married John Ebbert, and lives on an adjoining farm. They have two living children, Meade Horace and Orpha Dot. Mr. Crampton is a Democrat. He belongs to the Brushington Valley Relief Association, a beneficial order.

The Crampton family were among the very early settlers of Browning township, coming here when the country was a wilderness.

WILLIAM H. LEE was born on a farm adjoining his present home, August, 1850. His father, William Lee was born in the State of North Carolina, October 9, 1816. In 1827 the family moved to Tennessee and the next year came to Morgan county, Illinois, where they lived until 1830, when they came to Brown county and entered Govenment land on which William Lee, Sr., lived until he died. He was about fifteen years old when they settled on the farm and died here, January 26, 1884, after a painful and lingering illness. During his fifty years in this county he had been a most useful and influential citizen, filling places of trust and honor with fairness and discretion to all the fellow townsmen. He was a member of the Methodist Episcopal Church and his life was filled with deeds that testified that he practiced as well as preached. He was greatly missed by all who knew him, especially his wife and children. His remains were interred on the farm where he had lived and worked for so long. His wife was Mary A. Thomas of Switzerland county, Indiana. She is the daughter of George and Elizabeth (Jackson) Thomas, the former from Ohio and the latter from Maryland. They were married in Ohio and removed to Indiana, where their daughter was born. In 1830 they removed to Scott county, Illinois. They and their nine children made the journey with teams, and after their arrival in Scott county another child was born to them. Five years later they came to what is now Pea Ridge, in Brown County.

The marriage license was the first issued in Brown county. The mother of Mrs. Lee died at their farm home at the age of forty-nine years and left her husband and ten living children. He was again married, and died at the age of sixty-five years, in Iowa. Mrs. Lee, Sr., began married life on eighty acres, their first purchase, near the present home of their son. To this they added 105 acres, making 185 in all. They had five children, one of whom died.

William Lee, our subject, was reared to farm life and has followed the same life ever since. He was fairly educated for the times.

Mr. William Lee has been carrying on farming and stock-raising, giving special attention to the breeding of some fine road stock of horses. He has some fine young stock and fillies, four good mares and has recently bought a fine young stallion of the Wilkes stock. This is a very promising two-year-old and he hopes to stock his farm with good roadsters. He keeps about 100 sheep of the Shropshire and Merino graded stock and turns off twenty or thirty porkers a year.

Mr. Lee had some experience in his youth in merchandising in his father's employ at Mount Sterling, and later as a clerk at the same place, but his health failing he turned his hand to what he was fitted by nature to do and has made a success of it, although he has the natural ability to fill any commercial position in any city.

He was married in Mt. Sterling, December, 1877, to Miss Jennie Hanna, daughter of F. M. and Sarah (Hobbs) Hanna, residents of Mt. Sterling. They began life on the farm on which they now reside of 150 acres. They have buried one little son, Frank, and have now four children: Mary, in her thirteenth year, a bright child with musical talent which is being cultivated; George A., a bright child of ten; Freddie, five, and William, a Christmas gift of the year 1889. Both Mr. Lee and his wife are highly esteemed by all who know them and they are very influential among their large circle of friends.

WILLIAM W. WARD, a highly esteemed and prosperous retired farmer of township 17 north, range 9 west, near Philadelphia, Illinois, was born in Scott county, Kentucky, June 26, 1822. He was the younger of two children born to William A. and Nancy (Wirt) Ward, the other being his sister Catharine, now Mrs. Hancock, who resides in her native county, in Kentucky. The families on both maternal and paternal sides were Southerners for many generations back. Mr. Ward's father was a native of Kentucky, while his mother was a Virginian by birth, and they were married in Scott county, Kentucky, about 1819. The mother died in Kentucky a number of years ago, while the father expired in Arcadia, Illinois.

The subject of this sketch came to Cass county, Illinois, in 1844, but afterward returned to his home in Kentucky, whence he returned to Illinois permanently in 1848, locating on a farm, where he lived until twenty-five years ago, when he removed to his present location. The last farm comprises 177½ acres, most of which is under a high state of cultivation, and all of it tillable land. He has, besides this, considerable valuable personal property, and owns an attractive residence in Virginia, this State. He has gained all this by honest and toilsome efforts, and is highly deserving of his good fortune.

In 1851, he was married to Miss Sarah M. Turner, an estimable lady, who was born in Cass county, Illinois, in 1834. She is a daughter of Edward W. Turner, a native of Kentucky, and an honored pioneer of Cass county.

To this union eight children have been born, four of whom are now living. America E., the eldest, now Mrs. Long, resides in Virginia, and has had four children, two of whom are deceased; Edward Williams is married; Alice Catharine, born September 22, 1858, married James Whalan, and resides with her father on the old homestead. Mr. Whalan was born in Keokuk, Iowa, November 15, 1855, and was married in Jacksonville, Illinois, in 1874. Mr. and Mrs. Whalan have two children; Mary Margaret, born in Cass county, June 5, 1875, an intelligent and amiable young lady, who holds a diploma of graduation, which she received from the public school in this district; James Edward, born April 22, 1877, is at home, as is also Miss Margaret. Mr. Ward has another daughter, Emma Josephine, who married Joseph Treadway, who was born in Harford county, Maryland, December 29, 1851, and is a prosperous farmer and lives in Sugar Grove, Cass county, Illinois. They have eight children, the eldest of whom is fourteen years old at this writing. Those of Mr. Ward's children now departed this life, are Louisa Jane, who married Henry DeGroot, and who died at Mr. Ward's house February 7, 1891, leaving one child; three of his children died in infancy, unnamed. February 13, 1876, the family were called upon to mourn the loss of the devoted wife and mother, who was beloved by everyone on account of her fervent Christian character. She and the children deceased were at first interred in the private cemetery on the farm, but the remains have since been removed to the cemetery in Ashland, Illinois. Since her mother's death, Mrs. Whalan has kept house for Mr. Ward, both before and since her marriage, thus greatly alleviating the force of this crushing affliction.

Politically, Mr. Ward affiliates with the Democratic party, to which he has belonged for many years. Socially, he is an ardent advocate of the temperance cause, and has been for many years an active member of the I. O. G. T. Mr. Ward is an earnest and useful member of the Baptist Church, as was also his wife. Mrs. Whalan and her daughter, Margaret, belong to the Methodist Episcopal Church.

It is seldom that we have to chronicle a more blameless life than that just written. Intelligent and well informed, yet modest and retiring; energetic and progressive, yet mindful of the rights of others; industrious, persevering and highly moral, we have a combination which insures true success in life, which many others would do well to copy, and verify in their daily life work.

DR. D. W. OWENS was born in Lewis county, Kentucky, August 16, 1845. His father, Lewis, was born in the same county, and his father, Aaron, was born in Fauquier county, Virginia, and removed from there to Kentucky when a young man. He settled in Lewis county, bought land, raised a family and spent the rest of his days there. The maiden name of his wife was Dorotha Hathaway. Lewis was reared on a farm, where he learned the trade of blacksmith which he continued in connection with his farming. He removed from Kentucky to Kansas in 1877, and settled in Labette county, dying there in 1881. His wife, Nancy Owens, was born in Mason county, Kentucky. Her father was born in Fauquier county, Virginia, and moved from there to Mason county, Kentucky. She removed with her husband to Lewis county, where she died in 1869. She reared eight children, of whom Dr. Owens was the seventh. He was raised in his native county, received his early education in the log schoolhouse, assisting his father on the farm until 1864. He enlisted in March of that year in Company K, Sixteenth Kentucky Federal Infantry, and joined the regiment at Louisville. He was with Sherman in the Atlanta campaign and participated in some of the battles en route to the seizure of that city. After that he was with Thomas in pursuit of Hood and fought in the battles of Columbia, Franklin and Nashville. In January, 1865, he took passage on a steamer bound for Cincinnati, and from thence to Washington, District of Columbia, from there to Alexandria, and on to Fort Fisher, North Carolina, and thence to Wilmington. The regiment participated in the capture of Fort Anderson, Town Creek and Wilmington, and then was marched to Goldsboro, where Sherman's men soon joined them. After much marching and counter marching they were placed on garrison duty near Greensboro, and there remained until July, 1865, when they were mustered out of service, and discharged at Louisville, Kentucky, and Mr. Owens returned home in August

He commenced the study of medicine in 1863 After his return he continued it and also resumed farming, and in 1878 he graduated from the College of Physicians and Surgeons at Keokuk, Iowa, and commenced practice at Hersman, Illinois, where he has been in practice ever since He united with the Regular Primitive Baptist Church in 1870, and was licensed to preach and was ordained to the ministry at Rock Creek Church, Hancock county, Illinois, in June, 1873, and that was his first pastorate. He remained there until 1878 when he came to Hersman and was associated with Elder James Harper in the pastorate at Mt Gilead Church, and when the elder died he succeeded him, and in addition to this has supplied the congregation at Camp Creek Church for the past eight years

He married, in 1867, Nanna M. Boggs, daughter of Joseph and Rachel (Means) Boggs, of Lewis county, Kentucky He is a member of the Alumni Association of the College of Physicians and Surgeons, of Keokuk, Iowa, and is at this time its first vice-president. He is also a member of the Board of Examining Surgeons of Mt Sterling, Illinois He is a very successful physician and a useful citizen His influence for good is felt in the community.

LEWIS E. KROHE, an intelligent and enterprising citizen of Bainbridge township, Schuyler county, Illinois, was born in Cass county on May 18, 1837, and removed to Schuyler county March 13, 1859, and has lived here ever since. His father, August Krohe, was a native of Saxony, Germany, and was a son of Frederick Christian Krohe, also a native of Saxony, and a weaver by trade. His father followed the weaver trade in his native country until 1833, when he emigrated to America, making the voyage across the ocean in seven weeks, and landing at New Orleans, Louisiana From there he came direct to Beardstown, Illinois, being a week coming from St. Louis to the former place, a distance made now in two hours. There were at that time but two houses in Beardstown, and the surrounding country was sparsely settled and deer and wild turkey, quail, prairie chicken, and other game abounded in profusion. He bought a tract of land near Virginia, which was mostly covered with timber, the rest being wild prairie land. There was a log cabin on the land when he bought it, and in this he took up his abode, beginning the life of a pioneer He soon met and married Christiana Jockish, daughter of Gotlieb Jockish She was a native of Saxony, where she was born, and came to America with her father After his marriage, August Krohe went to live on his farm, but afterward bought land near Bluff Springs, where he resided many years, until he finally returned to his old home on the farm, where he now lives They had seven children: August, Lewis, Mena, Louisa, Henry, Julia and Amelia. In April, 1889, the faithful wife and fond mother died, leaving many friends to mourn her loss. She was a woman of intelligence and generous impulses, and highly esteemed by all who knew her

Our subject was reared and educated in his native county, that of Cass, and resided with his parents until the time of his marriage, which occurred on March 18, 1859, to Marie Sophia Korte She was a native of Hesse-Cassel, Germany, in which place she was born November 14, 1841, her parents being John Conrad and Christiana (Myer) Korte. Her father was also born in Hesse-Cassel, Germany, where he was reared and afterward married He followed the trade of blacksmithing in his native land until 1857, when with his wife and three children he sailed from Bremen, Germany, for America, landing in Baltimore, Maryland, in August, after a voyage of fifty-eight days. From there he came directly to Illinois, spending a few months in Cass county, and moving thence to Schuyler county, where he worked at his trade, in Bainbridge, until his death, where his wife also died. They reared three children. Henry, Mrs. Krohe and George

After his marriage, the subject of our sketch rented some land in Schuyler county, which he farmed for five years. He then made his first purchase of land, since when he has from time to time made other purchases, until he now owns upward of 700 acres. This is under a good state of cultivation, with a commodious home, besides other modern conveniences to faciliate agricultural pursuits. His home is situated on an attractive site on the bluffs, from which he has an uninterrupted view for miles around, extending across the river to Cass county He has a large orchard He is acknowledged to be one of the most substantial farmers in this locality. All his property he has accumulated by industry and economy

Mr. and Mrs. Krohe have seven children living, viz.: Amelia, wife of Jacob Logsdon; Frank, Louisa, Julia, Edward, Emma and Minnie; William died at the age of thirty-one, and Adolph died in infancy.

Mr Krohe is a Democrat in politics, but takes no active interest in political matters, other than desiring the advancement and welfare of his country He and his wife are members of the Lutheran Church, and have contributed liberally towards its support

Intelligent and able, industrious and frugal, enterprising and progressive, he has bent circumstances to his will, until from nothing he now stands among the first inhabitants of his community, looked up to and esteemed by all who know him.

JOHN H. DEPPE, an old settler and well known and retired carpenter of Beardstown, was born in Hanover, in 1832, August 29 His parents were Casper and Elizabeth (Recor) Deppe, natives of Hanover, and of good German stock After their marriage and the birth of their children, Mr and Mrs Deppe came to the United States, in the fall of 1842, in a sailing vessel of three masts. After a journey of seven weeks and three days they landed in New Orleans After a three weeks' trip on a Mississippi river steamer they landed in St. Louis in January, 1843 After some time in the city they went to Missouri, and they went to Beardstown from there. Casper was a carpenter, having learned his trade in Germany, and he began working at it for $7 a month for some months. Later he received seventy-five cents a day. This seemed big wages to him. After overcoming many hardships and troubles he succeeded in obtaining a foothold in life. He then entered into contracting and building, and as he was a good workman he had many friends in the city. Later in life he purchased land in Indian creek precinct, Cass county, and there lived for a time and then came back to Beardstown. Here he spent the remainder of his days in retirement and quiet. He died in 1889, February 28. He was then eighty-four years of age. His wife died in 1884, at the age of eighty-six. They were well known old settlers of this city and had a host of friends by whom they were missed. They were active members of the Sixth street Lutheran Church, which they helped organize and build up. Mr. Deppe was a Democrat.

Mr. John Deppe was the only son of the family. He had two sisters, but one died, and the other married Charles Kobelenz, and they are both living in Beardstown. Mr. Deppe has always been a hard-working man, and for eighteen years before his retirement from active life was employed in the car shops of the Quincy Railroad at this place doing work as a car builder and woodworker. He learned his trade under his father. Excepting three years, when he engaged in farming, he has always lived in Beardstown and has been successful in whatever he attempted. He bought a farm in Indian Creek precinct of 160 acres, nearly all of which is improved.

He was married in this city to Miss Annie Morman. She was born in Ingra, Prussia, in 1835. She died at her home in this city, May 3, 1883. She was one of the good worthy women of the city, and was the daughter of German parents, who lived and died in Prussia. Mrs. Deppe came to America in early girlhood. She was a worthy member of the Sixth Street Lutheran Church. Mr. and Mrs. Deppe were the parents of eleven children, seven of whom are now living, namely: Louis, tinner by trade, who married Louisa Dieckhous; Gustav, of the dry-goods firm of Deppe Bros.; William, of the same firm; Lydia is at home; Robert H. is a barber of the city; Herman C., a tailor by trade; and Conrad J. at home. The children are young men and women that any one would be proud of, and Mr. Deppe is a father to be envied. He is a Democrat in politics.

JACOB H. SNYDER, an extensive farmer of Brown county, was born about four miles from Duncannon, Perry county, Pennsylvania, June 10, 1831. His father, Jacob Snyder, was born in Germany, and his father, George Snyder, was also a native of Germany, who emigrated with his family to America about 1814, locating in Pennsylvania. Here he spent his last years in Perry county. His son was twelve years old when he came to America, with his parents. He was reared to agricultural pursuits and followed farming in Perry county until 1837, when he removed to Ohio. He and his family made the entire journey overland with teams. He purchased a tract of land in Preble county, which he improved, and on which he resided until his death, in 1858. His wife was named Elizabeth Young, born in Pennsylvania, of German parents. She died on the home farm in Preble county, in 1867.

Jacob was six years old when he moved to Preble county with his parents, and there he was reared and educated. He began when very young to assist on the farm, remaining with his parents until he attained his majority, and then began life for himself on rented land. He continued to rent land in Ohio, until 1865, and then came to Illinois, and bought land in Woodstock township, Schuyler county, and lived there until 1872. He then bought land in Cooperstown township. He also bought other land at different times, and at the present time owns 740 acres in the same township He resided there until 1891, when he bought the farm where he now resides. This is a well improved farm of eighty-six acres, on the Rushville road, two miles east of the Mt Sterling courthouse.

In 1860, he married Margaret Rush, born in Preble county, Ohio. Her father, Cornelius Rush, was born in Virginia, and his father, John Rush, was also a native of Virginia, and he emigrated from there to Ohio, being a pioneer of Preble county. From there he went to Indiana, and spent his last years near Logansport Father of Mrs Snyder was married in Preble county, resided there a few years, then moved to Cass county, Indiana, and was quite an early settler there He purchased a tract of timber land and built a log house and resided there until his death in 1857. His wife was named Barbara Brower She was born in Virginia, daughter of Daniel and Sarah (Flora) Brower. She now lives with her daughter, Mrs Snyder, and has done so since the death of her husband

Mr. and Mrs Snyder have nine children living They are· Joseph F, John B., Ida N, Cora G., Luella B, Angeline A., Charles H., Olive E and Arthur L. Mr and Mrs Snyder are members of the Christian Church Mr. Snyder is a Republican in politics, and both he and his wife have hosts of friends by whom they are admired and respected He was a Union soldier in the late war.

JOHN J. BROWNING was born in Woodstock township, Schuyler county, Illinois, July 4. 1857, a son of James H. and Sarah E. (Hall) Browning. The paternal grandparents, Abner and Nancy Browning, were natives of Virginia, but passed their last days in Hancock county, Illinois, dying at the ages of eighty-two and seventy-eight years James H was born in Virginia, May 8, 1818, and was but four years of age when his parents moved to Kentucky; there he was reared to agricultural pursuits until he was sixteen years of age, when he came to Rushville, Schuyler county, Illinois. In 1834, he purchased a portion of the land on which John J Browning now resides; there he lived until his death, which occurred August 19, 1883. His wife, Sarah E. (Hall) Browning, was born September 28, 1831, in Wayne county, Kentucky, and died February 28, 1883; she was one of a family of ten children, and the father was one of eight Politically he adhered to the principles of the Democratic party; for twenty years he was Justice of the Peace, and he held the office of Supervisor at the time of his death. He was prominently connected with the political history of the county, and for many years was a preacher in the Christian Church. He was married to the mother of our subject, September 7, 1856

Mr. Browning was, himself, united in marriage December 25, 1884, to Miss Mary Sweeney, who was born in Jefferson county, Missouri, March 25, 1858, her parents, Michael and Margaret (Gavin) Sweeney, were natives of county Galway, Ireland, and emigrated to America, first settling in New York State; later they removed to Missouri, and there Mr. Sweeney was engaged in farming until 1861; in that year he came to Schuyler county, where he now resides. Mr. and Mrs. Browning are the parents of three children: Pearl B., born October 23, 1885; Alta M., born July 27, 1888; and Lizzie M., born February 27, 1891. Until 1884 Mr. Browning resided on the home farm; he then purchased a tract of land, which with the inheritance from his father covers 300 acres; the land is under excellent cultivation, and in all branches of husbandry he has been successful. Politically he supports the issues of the Democratic party, but takes no active interest in the movements of that body.

ABRAHAM LINCOLN MARSHALL, of Lee township, was born on his present farm in 1861. His father, James Marshall, was born in Tennessee in 1819, and his father, William Marshall, came to Illinois in 1832. He died in Cass county, at a great age, having reared fifteen children, of whom James was the youngest. All have passed away. James Marshall was a volunteer from Lee township in the One Hundred and Nineteenth Illinois Infantry, Company E. He enlisted in August, 1861, and died in the hospital at Memphis, Tennessee, of a fever, December, 1863. He left a widow and five children. His wife's name was Martha A. Horn, born in Alabama. Her father died when she was about two years old, and she was reared by her mother, her step-father, Elisha Brown, and her uncle, George Criswell, of Morgan county, Illinois. She was married in Missouri, in 1844. They settled here in 1856, on sixty-two acres, to which he added until now the farm is more than 176 acres, of which thirty-five acres is good timber.

The Marshall brothers now own this fine home farm jointly, subject to the mother's life lease. They grow corn, wheat, hay and oats, have from fourteen to twenty horses, ten to twenty head of cattle and turn off from ten to forty hogs, annually. They believe in a rotation of crops and plenty of crops. They have as fine meadow land as there is in the State. An immense barn was built between 1871 and 1888, with ample room for everything. They have a snug farm house, finished and rebuilt in 1889.

Mr. A. L. Marshall was married in January, 1889, to Mary B. Williams, daughter of Thomas and Lucinda (Beam) Williams, he of Ohio and she of Vermont. Mrs. Marshall was born in Clayton, Adams county, and there her mother died, in 1877, in the prime of life. Her father resides in Clayton, Illinois. Mr. and Mrs. Marshall have one little son, named Benjamin Harrison, and Mr. Marshall is a very loyal, ardent Republican.

CONRAD HERZBERGER, now deceased having died at his home in township 19, range 11, March 9, 1882, was born near Frankfort, Germany, November 9, 1831. He came of good and respectable German families, his parents having lived and died in Hesse-Darmstadt, and they had been respected members of the Lutheran Church. Conrad was the only member of his family to come to the United States. He came to America when twenty years old, via New

York city; from there he went to Pittsburg, Pennsylvania, and worked for nine years in a tannery. He afterward made two trips back to his native country. He came to this county in 1860, began as a renter, afterward purchased his farm in section 32, and this remained his home during the rest of his active life. Before he died he owned 281 acres of well improved land. He was a good, hard-working man, a prominent citizen, a successful and practical farmer and one with a host of friends in the county. He was not a politician, but he was a Republican and a worthy member of the Lutheran Church. He had obtained a good education in Germany as a practical surveyor and book-keeper.

He was married in Morgan county, Illinois, to Caroline Dorr. She came to America in 1852, and was the daughter of Lewis and Mary (Retiz) Dorr. These parents settled first at Jacksonville, Illinois, and there the father is still living, being seventy-three years of age. He has been a farmer all his life. His wife died at her home in Morgan county, at the age of fifty-six. They were both highly respected members of the Lutheran Church. Mrs. Herzberger, widow of our subject, is the eldest of six children. Since the death of her husband she has managed the farm with wonderful success, receiving assistance from her children. She is a smart and accomplished lady, interested in everything of importance in the county. She and her children are all members of the Griggs chapel of the Methodist Episcopal Church. The children are as follows: Amelia, wife of Henry Doerr, a farmer of this township; Tillie, wife of William Huppe, a farmer of this county; Lewis, conducting his mother's farm, and has successfully managed her affairs although yet a young man; John William assists his brother; Elva L. remains at home; and Clarence. The children all bid fair to continue a comfort to their widowed mother and a credit to the memory of their honest father.

HERMAN H. KORSMEYER, a practical farmer of section 19, township 17, range 12, has been a resident of this farm since 1851, making some very fine improvements in the buildings and on the land. He first purchased 120 acres, the same being his homestead, and has since added to the original farm until he now owns about 600 acres and nearly one-third of that amount is under the plow. He has also engaged in raising stock of the best grades. He came to this county in 1848 and has since made Cass county his home, beginning here as a poor boy working by the month. He later rented land until he purchased his homestead.

Mr. Korsmeyer was born in the kingdom of Hanover, Germany, September 29, 1831. He is the eldest son and child of the family. His parents were John H. and Anna M. (Lovecamp) Korsmeyer, who were both born and reared in Hanover, coming of good German stock. Our subject, when yet a young man, set out for America alone, taking passage in August, 1848, on the sailing vessel Agnes, which landed him in New Orleans after a sixty days' passage. He then came by steamer to St. Louis, and thence to Beardstown. In 1851 the parents, with their other two children, Fred and Anna, set sail from Germany also, and reached Beardstown that same year. They began farming some miles southwest of Beardstown, the father and his eldest son living together, where the father died in 1860. Our subject's mother died in the same place in 1870. She was born in the early part of the present century. She and her husband had always been members of the Lutheran Church.

Mr. Korsmeyer was married in this county, to Miss Anna M. E. Knipenberg. She was born in Hanover and was the daughter of Frederick and Maria Knipenberg, who came to the United States as a family in 1848, and settled on a farm in Cass county. Mr. Knipenberg was a carpenter by trade. He and his wife continued to reside here until their death, which occurred when they were old people. They were consistent members of the Lutheran Church.

Mrs. Korsmeyer was young when she came to this country, and she lived with her parents until her marriage. She is a good, true woman, and is highly regarded all through her township. She and her husband are members of the German Lutheran Church, and he is a Republican in his political faith

He and his wife are the parents of seven children, all living: John H., remaining at home, assisting his father, married to Minnie Boes; Louisa became the wife of Henry Buscher, a farmer in Morgan county; William, a farmer in the same county, married Mary Rogge; Lena M., wife of Herman Rogge, a farmer of Cass county; Henry is a mechanic now at home with his father, but a graduate of Pearson Institute, of La Porte, Indiana; Anna W., at present with her sister, Mrs. Buscher, of Morgan county; and Sophia, at home.

Mr. Korsmeyer and his wife are highly respected citizens of this county.

HENRY W. HEATON, a well-known farmer of Oakland township, has been prominently identified with the agricultural interests of this section of Illinois for the past thirty-seven years. He was born in Bucks county, Pennsylvania, March 9, 1830. His father, Jeffrey Heaton, was a native of England, born in 1807, but at the age of eight years was brought across the sea to America; he was one of a family of four sons and four daughters. He learned the weaver's trade, of which his father was a master, and followed this vocation several years; he finally abandoned it, however, to take up farming in Ohio, whither he had removed in 1836; he rented land in Jefferson county until 1849, and then went to Fulton county, Illinois, making the trip *via* the Ohio and Illinois rivers. In 1850 he purchased eighty acres, on which he located and there passed the remainder of his days; he died in January, 1858; he left a widow and ten children, of whom our subject is the eldest; the mother still survives, at the age of eighty-four years; she is living in Oakland township with her son, Thomas. One son, Simon, was killed in battle in the war of the Rebellion; he was twenty-nine years of age, and left a wife, one son and a daughter. Henry W. Heaton was was a youth of fifteen years when his father began farming in Ohio; at the age of twenty-one he began the search for his own fortune.

Four years later he was united in marriage to Miss Rebecca B. Patterson, of this county and township, a daughter of Hugh and Ellen Patterson, natives of Ohio and Pennsylvania respectively. Mr. and Mrs. Heaton lived in Astoria township, Fulton county, where they rented land until 1862; in that year they bought a farm on which they lived until 1866, when they sold the place and came to Schuyler county. They bought the old homestead, a tract of 140 acres, on which they have since lived. They buried one daughter, at the age of two years, named Ellen; they now have eight sons and three daughters; the eldest is thirty-three and the youngest is eleven years of age. Their names are as follows: William H.; Franklin H.; Sanford W.; Andrew J.; James; Lewis E.; Cornelius, Albert, Florence R., wife of Sylvester France; Sarah Ann, wife of George Beghtol; and Rosa.

In politics Mr. Heaton votes for the man best suited, in his estimation, for the office in question, but favors the principles of the Democratic party. He carries on a general farming business, raising grain and live-stock. He began life without capital, except that with which nature had endowed him, and by industry and wise management has accumulated a competence for coming age.

The parents of Mrs. Heaton are both deceased, the father at the age of seventy, and the mother at seventy-two years of age.

ADOLPH KALLASCH, a prominent farmer of Elkhorn township in Brown county, is a native of Germany, having been born in that country, February 16, 1840. He is the son of Frederick and Fredrica (Kuntz) Kallasch, natives of the same country, who, in 1852 came to America in a sailing vessel, making the voyage in six weeks and landing in Quebec, where they remained but a short time, coming from there to Chicago, by the lakes and railroad. From that great city they came to this county and settled near where the subject now lives, buying ninety acres of land, partly improved, on which had been erected a little log cabin. This cabin they replaced later by a frame house and here died both the father and the mother, when about seventy-six and fifty-six, respectively. They were the parents of seven children, two yet living. The The father was a carpenter by trade and a stanch Democrat in political faith. Both he and his good wife were earnest Christians, both in life and teachings.

Under the guidance of these good parents our subject remained until 1862, when his country called him from the peaceful occupation of a farmer and he enlisted in Company B, Ninety-ninth Illinois Infantry, Captain Fee in command, in which he remained all through the war, being mustered out at Baton Rouge, Louisiana, and discharged at Springfield. From there he returned home.

After his return home he was married, about Christmas, to Miss Mary Lipkaman, born in Pike county, Illinois, daughter of Frederick and Barbara Lipkaman, who came to this country from Germany at a very early day, renting in Pike county, in the '30s. The father died when about seventy-six, but his wife still lives, on the old farm. The family principally carried on farming, but a few were mechanics. Mr. and Mrs. Kallasch have had seven children, five yet living, namely; Henry, married Minnie Wood, has one boy; Louis, at home running the old farm for his father; Harvey, is also at home; Emma, married Andrew Kelinlein, and they have one child; and Anna, at home.

After his marriage our subject bought seventy acres just across from his father's farm, later adding eighty more acres, 108 acres of which he sold to his son Henry. He first lived in an old log cabin, but now has as fine a house as there is in the county.

This gentleman is a stanch Republican, casting his first vote for General Grant. He and his estimable wife are members of the Lutheran Church, attending at Perry post office, Pike county, where they are regarded as highly respected members of that body. They have always been church members since reaching years of maturity and lead good, earnest lives. Mr. Kallasch has always carried on general farming, at which he has been very successful and can be said to be one of the leading influential men of the township.

MARCELLUS M. CLEEK, resident of Camden, dating from September, 1836, he was born in Boone county, Kentucky, August 27, 1829. His father, Benjamin Cleek, was also born in Kentucky in 1800, and his father John Cleek was a native of Germany, where he married, and came to America, settling at Big Boone Springs, Boone county, Kentucky, where he was one of the pioneers. He engaged in the manufacture of salt and there passed his remaining days, dying at the age of eighty years. He had eight children: John, Benjamin, Jacob, Esau, Sarah, Margaret, Eliza and one other. Benjamin Cleek was the second child and he was raised a farmer, marrying in 1826 Martha Harris of Lexington, Kentucky, daughter of Richard Harris of the same State, who was killed in the Black Hawk war. In 1812 the father with his wife and four children came by boat to Frederick, Illinois, and from there to Rushville, settling on section 7, Camden township, where he purchased 160 acres of land and also entered about as much more. In 1844 the season was very wet and the following year there was so much sickness that he became dissatisfied with the country and so returned to his native State, although he did not sell his land. He remained in Kentucky seven years and then returned to Illinois, settling on his land where he died in 1867. His wife died in 1873. They had eleven children: John, deceased; Marcellus; M. M.; Samuel, deceased; Benjamin, farmer on part of the old home farm; Jacob of Camden; Richard, also on part of the old farm; Mary, deceased, wife of J. J. Yocum; Elizabeth, wife of Henry Price of Huntsville; Lovina, wife of J. J. Yocum of Chariton county, Missouri; Ann, wife of J. H. Hendricks of Camden township; and Martha, wife of Levi Welty, also of Camden township.

Marcellus lived with his parents and on the return from Kentucky pursued the trade of carpenter, which he had learned in Kentucky. He did not return to Illinois until 1854. He continued his trade for four years, when he engaged in farming, purchasing 160 acres, which he farmed until 1861, when he resumed his trade, but also carried on his farm.

In 1884 he removed to Kansas and located in Kiowa county, where he pre-empted 160 acres of land and also purchased 160 more. He worked his farms for two years and then returned to Camden. He owns 185 acres of land in Camden township and 160 acres in Kansas, also valuable property in Camden, all of which he and his wife accumulated.

He was married in 1863, to Lydia A. Welly, daughter of Jacob and Mary Welly, born in Highland county, Ohio, in 1814. Mr. and Mrs. Cleek have eight children, six of whom are still living: Manora, deceased; James, on his father's farm; William, on section 6; Charles, in Camden; Emma, married Presley Price of Huntsville, Schuyler county, Illinois; Alma married G. Alters of Huntsville township: Sadie, deceased; and Clara, at home.

Mr. Cleek is a Democrat in politics. He has been Supervisor and during his term the courthouse was built. He has held nearly all the minor offices in the township. He is a member of the Christian Church and is one of the first members in Camden.

HERMAN H. ROGGE, a successful farmer of section 19, township 17, range 11, was born in Hanover, Germany, September 30, 1843. He is the youngest son of the family, one sister of which yet lives in Germany. The other members are four brothers now living in this country. The father, Fred, was a native of Hanover, Germany, and there died an old man, eighty-five years of age. He was a farmer and a butcher. His wife, whose maiden name was Anna Strube, died after her husband, but at a younger age. She and her husband passed their entire lives in Hanover and were members of the Lutheran Church.

Herman was a butcher by trade, and he engaged in that business until he came to America in the spring of 1867 from Bremen to New York city. He went to Peoria, Illinois, and thence down the Illinois river to Beardstown, where four brothers had preceded him, and he was the last to leave for this country. They are all living and are prosperous citizens. He began here as a day laborer and worked in this way for a year, then started for himself, and in 1877 located on his present farm. He has improved it in a wonderful degree and owns 160 acres. It is now a fine farm.

He was married in Cass county, to Mary Schnelle, born in Beardstown, Illinois, September 26, 1854. She has since lived in this county and is an intelligent wife and mother. She is the daughter of Charles and Mary (Gœstereng) Schnelle, natives of Prussia, where they were reared and married, coming to the United States in the '40s, and their father, who was a carpenter died in 1862, aged forty-one years. He is a good, prosperous German. His wife, who yet lives, resides with her daughter, Mrs. Rogge, and she is now seventy-one years old. She has been a member of the Lutheran Church all her life and the same was true of her husband. Mrs. Rogge is the elder of three daughters born to her parents.

Mr. and Mrs. Rogge are the parents of seven children: John H., Charles G., Henry F., Louis W., Lena M., Aurelia T. and Theo. H; and they are all at home. Mr. Rogge and his wife are Lutherans and Mr. Rogge is a Democrat, has been School Trustee for fifteen years and Road Commissioner for five years. He is a public-spirited man and a good citizen.

CAPTAIN WILLIAM N. MUMFORD of Mound Station, Illinois, was born in Nova Scotia, January 24, 1824. His father, William, was a farmer of that country who lived and died there, having reared nine children. The mother of these was Jane McHattie, of Scotch parentage. The grandfather of the subject was George Mumford of Rhode Island, who died at an advanced age in Nova Scotia.

The Captain grew up a farmer boy with only the common schooling of the period. In his twenty-third year he left home and came to New York city, and from there went on to Alpine depot on the Baltimore & Ohio in Morgan county, West Virginia, where he taught in the public schools. He had experience in his own neighborhood and after that as assistant in a grammar school at Halifax. After closing his three months' term in Morgan county he engaged in a general store as salesman. He brought little money with him, hoping to improve his financial condition. He remained two years in the store, then went to St. Louis and on to Mount Pleasant, Illinois, where he engaged as clerk for S. C. Raymond. While here he was married to Mary Jane Davis, daughter of John and Charlotte (Sears) Davis, both natives of Illinois. In 1861 they moved to Mound Station, then just started, the railroad being just completed. He clerked here until August, 1862, when he enlisted in Company E, One Hundred and Ninteenth Illinois Volunteer Infantry, being unanimously chosen Captain. In September his regiment was organized, Colonel Kinney commanding. The Captain remained on duty for two years, when he was discharged for physical disability at Memphis, Tennessee, and came home to his wife and two little boys at this place. He and his family went on a visit to his Nova Scotia home, but before he reached there his father had died, aged eighty-two years. A striking coincidence in this family is that six of his father's brothers and sisters, including himself, died at the age of eighty-two years. The mother died at the age of eighty-four years. They have three children, Augustus, now practicing physician at Kendall, Minnesota; William, a lawyer at Pittsfield, Illinois, and Charlotte, a wife of J. W. Moore, now residing in Chicago, conducting a stock and commission business. The Captain was Postmaster here under Presidents Arthur and Harrison, but as he is in failing health his step-daughter, Mrs. Deering, acts for him. He buried his first wife June 16, 1868, and was married April 4, 1869, to Mrs. Rebecca Poe, the widow of T. J. Poe and the daughter of the Rev. Granville Bond, a Methodist preacher, well and favorably known in this county. Mrs. Mumford was the widow of T. J. Poe. The Captain is an Episcopalian, but both his wives attended the Methodist Episcopal Church of which the present wife has been an active member for fifty years. Mrs. Mumford has three children of her own and all the family relations are most harmonious and affectionate. A better citizen, neighbor, father or husband could not be found.

WINTSON ANDERSON of section 13, Huntsville township, came here in 1835. He was born in Clermont county, Ohio, in 1833. His father, William Anderson, was born in Mason county, May 14, 1800. He was a son of Andrew Anderson, who was born in Virginia and was of Irish descent. The family has resided in America for several generations. William Anderson was reared a farmer, and married in Kentucky in 1824, a Miss Prudence Wallansford, born in Kentucky, August 15, 1806. They migrated to Ohio in 1832, and resided there at Cincinnati, and in Clermont county, for three years and then came to Illinois and located in Schuyler county. In the spring of 1836 Mr. Anderson purchased a claim on section 13, in which is now Huntsville, and here he passed the remaining years of his life. He entered land and purchased more, until his real estate possessions amounted to 600 acres. He was a cautious man and never went into debt. He was a hard-working man, and in those days when the sickle was used to cut grain, he was an expert in the use of the same, and still continued to use the hook after the cradle came into use. He died

August 16, 1887. His wife is still living and is a member of the Christian Church. The two came with about $200 in capital, and in the time they lived in Illinois became rich and influential people. They had ten children, seven of whom grew up, namely: Jane Cady, Cyrus, Andrew, Vintson, Frank, Sarah McHatten and John.

Subject was two years old when the family settled in Schuyler county, and he resided at home until he attained his majority. His school advantages were limited. At the age of twenty-one he went to Fort Snelling, Minnesota, and broke prairie and engaged as cook to a gang of men who were cutting hay for the Government. At that date Minneapolis consisted of a sawmill and a few houses. He remained in Minnesota about six months and then returned to Illinois and engaged in making brooms at Clayton, Adams county, Illinois. He followed this business four years and then removed to Brown county, but after a few years residence there, removed to Schuyler county and settled where he now resides on land entered by his father. He has a farm of 105 acres. He is a Democrat in politics, and has been Road Commissioner for many years. He has filled that office with great credit to himself.

He was married in 1858 to Jane McDonald of Brown county, born October 15, 1840, daughter of John B. and Sarah C. (Orr) McDonald. The former was born in county Antrim, Ireland, and came to the United States when a young man, and resided in the Southern States for a short time, but finally settled in Brown county in 1833, and soon after married Sarah C. Orr, who was the daughter of Mr. G. Orr, a settler of Brown county in 1831. She was born in Tennessee in 1810. Mr. and Mrs. McDonald had four children, all of whom are now married and well settled.

Mr. and Mrs. Anderson have had seven children: Carrie, wife of William Nelson of Huntsville township; Cora, at home; William J. died in infancy; Frank C. at home; Pearl at home; Myrtle died at the age of four; and Nina E., at home.

Mr. and Mrs. Anderson are members of the Christian Church. Mr. Anderson is a member of Camden Lodge, No. 648, A. F. & A. M., in which he is the Junior Warden.

THOMAS BARTON was born in Brown county, Illinois, October 15, 1839. His father, Thomas, was born in Kentucky, in 1809, and died in Brown county in 1878, aged seventy years. His father was David Barton, who was born in Maryland, and taken to Kentucky when but a lad. He was a teamster when a young man, and later a landholder. His wife was Elizabeth Marsh. They reared five children, Thomas being the second child. The mother of these children died, and the father married again and had five more children. The mother of our subject was named Clarissa Ingles, of Bourbon county, Kentucky, daughter of James Ingles, a large planter and distiller, largely engaged in the manufacture of Bourbon whisky. Thomas came direct to Brown county upon reaching Illinois in 1835. He brought his wife and daughter with him. He bought eighty acres of land at the Government price. They began life in a log cabin. They received their Government deed in 1837, and Mr. Barton was appointed Justice of the Peace. Sixteen children were born to them, many of them dying in infancy, but six of them growing to adult age; three of them are now living. The father and mother now rest in the Huffman graveyard.

Thomas had very limited school advantages, barely learning to read and write. He left his home at twenty-one, and enlisted August 8, 1862, in the Eighty-fourth Illinois Infantry, Company D. He was very soon promoted to be Second Sergeant. He was on duty and at his post every day during his term of nearly three years. He received slight wounds in his left hand and right shoulder, both flesh wounds. He was mustered out at Camp Harker on June 8, and discharged at Camp Butler in Illinois, June 17. He returned to civil life in Brown county in broken health, and paid large doctor bills for six months.

He was married April 30, 1866, to Matilda, daughter of Jacob and Margaret (Briggle) Fry, both of Ohio, coming to Illinois in 1840. He died on the farm in middle age, and left his widow with eight children. His wife survived him and died when about sixty years old. Mrs. Thomas Barton died October 24, 1890, leaving eight children: Charles W., farmer of this county; Nina, prepared at Rushville Normal School for teaching; Edna has had the same advantages; Idalla and Charlotte are prepared to teach; Lawrence Arthur is at home, going to school; James Edgar is a rugged farmer lad, and Jessie H., a bright lass for her years. Mr. Barton is giving his children a good education, and inculcating habits of honesty and industry.

Mr. Barton voted for Lincoln and Grant, but has since been a reformer. Religiously he is free, and does his own thinking for himself, regardless of consequences. He was a candidate for the State Senate in 1888, and for Congress in 1890, on the reform ticket, and is the People's party candidate for the State Senate. He began life barefooted, and owns now 390 acres of good farming land, worth $40 an acre. He built his barns in 1884, and his house which he lives in was built on the ruin of the first. He does a diversified farming, mostly grain. He also raises a number of cattle and sheep, and yearly turns off from forty to fifty hogs.

GEORGE W. LUCAS was born in Lee township, near Mount Sterling, in June, 1845. His father was a native of Butler county, Ohio, named Daniel R. Lucas, born in 1810. His father, John Lucas, was a native of Virginia, a soldier of the Revolutionary war, and emigrated to Ohio, where he died at an advanced age, having reared a large family, of whom our subject's father was the youngest. He was reared on the farm to that kind of life, and was educated in the English branches. After he reached manhood he obtained a medical education by his own efforts. He came to Mount Sterling when quite young, from Crawfordsville, Indiana, and began the practice of medicine. He bought 160 acres of land two and one-half miles southwest of Mounds, and sold it in 1851, three years after he had bought it. From there he went to Texas. Prior to this he and his brother-in-law, Dr. King, practiced medicine together in Clayton, Adams county. He remained in Texas only one summer, and then returned to Lee township and bought a farm of 160 acres one and one-half miles south of this village, on which he settled and where he died in 1884. He bought other lands, amounting in all to over 1,000 acres. He died January 26, 1884. He began life without any money, but the handsome estate he left at his death was worth at least $30,-000. His wife was Sarah Ann Keith, of Kentucky, to whom he was married in 1836. They had twelve children, of whom nine are still living, and all are married except one. Mrs. Lucas died in 1890, six years after her husband.

His son, George W., followed his father in the choice of a profession, and graduated from the College of Physicians and Surgeons at Keokuk in 1878, and began his practice in the fall of the same year. The Doctor takes a great interest in the affairs of his State and county. In 1862, although only a boy of seventeen, he enlisted in the Third Missouri Cavalry, and served three years without receiving any wounds, although his health was impaired by the hardships of camp life. His bravery was rewarded by a medal from Congress. He is a member of the G. A. R., the R. K. McCoy Post, No. 311, of Clayton, Illinois. He has never sought after public office, but is the candidate of the Republicans in this district for the State Senate.

He was married in 1872, to Miss Josephine L. Kilby, daughter of C. G. and Leora E. (Hubbell) Kilby. They were from Cleveland, Ohio, her native State. They came to Illinois in 1870, but after four years returned to Ohio. Mrs. Lucas is one of four children, namely: Mrs. Lucas, Mary G. Kilby, Wilford H. Kilby and Amelia A. The father died in 1889, at the age of sixty-eight, but his wife is still living at her home in Ohio, at the age of sixty-three. The maternal grandmother was Annis Bell, and she lived to the age of ninety-three, not dying until 1881. Mrs. Lucas' maternal grandparents were Solyman and Lucinda Hubbell. Mr. Hubbell was a lineal descendant of one James Hubbell, who came to America in the early days of the settlement of Massachusetts, and came to Ohio in a very early day, locating near Cleveland, where he lived until his death, which occurred in October, 1874. Lucinda Hubbell still lives with her daughter, Mrs. Kilby, aged eighty-three. The paternal grandfather was William Kilby, a farmer of Massachusetts, who died at eighty-six.

Dr. and Mrs. Lucas have the following children: Charles H., Lena L., Mary Ethel and George D., aged nineteen, thirteen, eleven and nine, respectively. The oldest son is at the Normal School at Valparaiso, Indiana, in his second term, and is very proficient in his studies. Dr. Lucas has a good practice and his skill is depended upon by all the best people in the township and surrounding country.

WILLIAM M. WYATT, a prosperous retired farmer and esteemed pioneer of Cass county, Illinois, was born in Fayette county, Kentucky, February 22, 1828.

His parents were James and Sarah (Stevenson) Wyatt, both of whom were natives of Kentucky, and who came to Morgan county, Illinois, in 1830, and located on a farm, on what is known as Golden Prairie. The paternal grandfather of the subject of this sketch, a Virginian by birth, had previously emigrated to Morgan county, in 1828. James Wyatt and wife were the parents of four children, three sons and one daughter, only two of whom are now living. John, the eldest son, died in Cass county about ten years ago; he was married and left three sons and one daughter, one now in Kansas, two in Cass county and one in Braden, Illinois. the sons being farmers by occupation;

our subject was the second child; Elizabeth, the third, married Hugh Sheridan, and died in Lincoln, Logan county, Illinois, leaving a family of one son and two daughters; Walter, the eldest of the children, died in youth

The subject of this sketch was but two years of age when his parents removed from Kentucky to Morgan county, Illinois, and he vividly remembers the experiences of those early pioneer days, which were calculated to test man's endurance and cultivate his powers of invention. The habitation of the family was the primitive log cabin, cooking being done over an open fire-place, while all baking was done in a kettle-shaped oven, on the lid of which coals were placed Wheat bread was unknown for many years, and finally became a treat for Sunday morning When wheat was first raised, it was cut with a reap hook and disengaged from the straw by the treading of horses, afterward being separated from the chaff by being thrown to the wind It was first bolted by machines which were run by hand, the first mill erected, being fifteen miles distant, which was run by wind power, operated by an ox. Corn was plowed with a wooden-moldboard plow, drawn by an ox with an ox harness The whole neighborhood would turn out to assist in raising log buildings, and it never occurred to any one to expect pay for the most valuable services, money being unknown

Surrounded by these peaceful, rural scenes, and in the pursuance of these primitive duties and pastimes, passed the youth and early manhood of the subject of this sketch April 26, 1851, he and an estimable young lady of his neigborhood were united in marriage, commencing life with few earthly possessions but with unbounded faith in each other and the future. The year preceding this momentous event, Mr. Wyatt had raised a small crop of wheat on a portion of his father's land, and hauling a load of this to Beardstown, he procured a marriage license and other necessaries. He was married on Sunday and on Monday they and their friends had dinner at his father's house. Tuesday, having but one horse, he mounted and taking his wife up behind him moved with all their belongings to his brother's house, where they boarded until their cabin was ready for occupancy The two brothers plowed the little farm of forty acres, for which Mr. Wyatt had gone in debt, and, together, erected the cabin. Mr Wyatt's young wife dropped the corn on eighty acres of land, dropping a row every third round of the plow. By 1855, the little home was paid for, while they had a snug little sum of $900 ahead

In 1850, Mr O B. Nance, our subject's father-in-law, had removed to Texas, where he pre-empted a large tract of land, and being desirous of having his daughter near him he offered to bestow a quarter section of land on Mr. Wyatt, if he would remove to that State Accordingly, they went to the Lone Star State, but, not liking the country there, returned to their little Illinois home, where he commenced working his farm with renewed energy. He erected a new fence around it by working up the fallen timber on his father's land, making 100 rails a day and bringing a load home in the evening At night, he would cut corn until ten o'clock, and this experience was repeated day after day for a long time. Heretofore, he had not increased his possessions in land, but as his means accumulated, he bought another forty acres, and in time became the owner of 260 acres of as choice agricultural land as is to be found in the county, which he still retains About eight years ago, he retired from active work on the farm, and located in Ashland.

investing his surplus means in stock in the Ashland Bank, and he and his worthy wife are enjoying in comfort the means which their early industry accumulated.

They have had four children, three now living: John Harding, the eldest, died aged sixteen years; Fannie married Mr. Thompson, a retired farmer of Virginia, Illinois; Alice married Mr. Struble, a prominent farmer and merchant of Newmansville, the same State; James J., who received an excellent education in Jacksonville, Illinois, has been connected with the Ashland Bank, as a stockholder and official, for eleven years, from which he receives a good salary. He married Miss Bertha Lohman, a highly esteemed resident of Ashland, and they have one child.

The entire family are earnest and useful members of the Methodist Episcopal Church

Mr. Wyatt is a man of strong and conscientious convictions, as is evidenced in his political views. He was formerly a Republican, but five years ago joined the Prohibition party, for which he works with his usual energy.

Few men more fully deserves their prosperity and happiness than Mr. Wyatt, who has acquired all by the exercise of intelligent and persistent effort.

KING KERLEY was born in Sumner county, Tennessee, September 25, 1814. His father, William, was born in South Carolina in 1785. When three years of age he was taken to Tennessee by his father, who was also William and who died on his small farm in Tennessee, at the advanced age of ninety-three years. King has heard his grandfather tell how he crawled under the barn in South Carolina to hide their small store of silver coin during the Revolution. His son was a soldier for three months in the war of 1812 and received a land warrant of forty acres for this service. He married Jane Carr of Tennessee, whose father, King Carr, was a native of Virginia. They reared to adult age eleven children and buried two in infancy. The mother died at the age of seventy years and the father lived to be an octogenarian. Both are sleeping side by side on the old farm which is still in the family.

Mr. Kerley went to school only until he was ten years of age, learned to read and write, but had no instruction in numbers. He remained on his father's farm until his majority and was a volunteer in the Seminole war with his brother, John. When he returned home he was married, March 9, 1837, to Elizabeth Brown of Sumner county, Tennessee. They had grown up together. She was the daughter of John and Elizabeth (Ball) Brown. Mr. and Mrs. Kerley began their married life on his brother's farm, but within a year they bought and settled on a farm of their own. Mr. Kerley was in the Seminole war, in which he received a gunshot wound in his thigh. In 1846 Mr. Kerley volunteered in the Mexican war as a private, and was made Second Lieutenant which position he held during his twelve months' service. After his return home he was elected to the Legislature in August, 1847, and next he ran for the State Senate against a prominent man, but was defeated although he ran ahead of his ticket. The first railroad charter was passed during his term of office. In 1851 he left there and by teams he moved his family to Brown county on his present farm in section 17. His wife's family had come to Illinois fourteen years earlier. Mr. Kerley bought eighty acres of land for $1,000, and by a tax title another eighty, which cost him $100 for the patent. He left his family and returned to Tennessee, sold out his farm there and returned to Illinois in February to find his wife dead and buried! She died, as did her father father, stepmother and five others of the family, of ship fever, which had been brought by a returned Californian. Mr. Kerley went on his farm with his three children, but in December, 1853, he married Amanda J. Pell, a daughter of Henry Pell, whose wife was a King. They had eight children. There are four sons of this family still living, one son of the first wife. The stepmother was a real mother to his children, a dearly beloved woman who died January 16, 1891, in her sixty-sixth year. Pleasant Hart Kerley his oldest son, lives at Camp Point, Illinois; Robert is a farmer in Adams county; James N. lives in Oakland, California; Edgar is a farmer near home; and so is the last son, John.

Mr. Kerley was elected to the State Legislature in 1856 and introduced the bill for the railroads running through this county. He was re-elected in 1858 and again in 1864. When he lived in Tennessee he held the office of Sheriff and had to discharge the unpleasant duty of executing a convict. He was Supervisor in 1864 and reelected some fifteen times and several times was chairman of the board. He was the first Assessor for Lee township and held that office for five years. He has been a Democrat and is well named King, as he is a king among jokers. He has retired from active farming and lives with his youngest son on his 200-acre farm. He has been very successful and though nearly seventy-eight years of age is in good health, with the exception of some trouble with his eyesight. Nature has done more for this man than for many of those known to fame. He takes a daily walk to Mound Station and is a very interesting companion as his memory is phenomenal. There is probably no one who can relate in a more interesting manner more incidents of an eventful life than can this well preserved old gentleman. It is the wish of his friends that he may long continue with them.

MRS. MARY F. RAVENSCROFT, is the widow of the late Ashford D. Ravenscroft, and is a native of Versailles, Woodford county, Kentucky. Her father was Henry Casteen of Virginia, and her mother was Lucinda (Peters) Casteen, also of Woodford county. The parents of our subject came to Illinois in May, 1832, when she was but a small child and the long trip was made by water. The first home of the family was on land one mile north of Versailles, on which her father had secured a claim in 1830, when he came through on horseback, and bought the improvements of a squatter settler. They moved into the small, crude, log cabin which this settler had built, and here they lived for a short time until her father could build a good two-story frame house. There were then in the family four daughters and one son, and two daughters and one son were born here in Illinois, making a family of eight children. The mother of Mrs. Ravenscroft died April 16, 1839, and the children she left were: Louisa, who died in the bloom of maidenhood; John A. Casteen, who was for many years a merchant of Versailles and died here September 29, 1887, at the age of sixty-five years; Mary, of this sketch; Martha, residing in Versailles with her sister, Mrs. Julia Bond, widow of the late Dr. John Bond; Catherine, who died at the age of seventeen years; Elizabeth, who died at the age of four years, and William who died in infancy, soon after his mother The father was again married, to Elizabeth Hewett, of Springfield, Illinois, a native of Versailles, Kentucky. By this union there were three children, one son dying in infancy. Thomas Henry died in Versailles, June 27, 1892, aged forty-nine years, and Joseph, a resident of Versailles but now viewing the wonders of Montana He has a wife and four children Henry Casteen died April 14, 1854, aged sixty five years.

The marriage of our subject took place November 21, 1841, to A D. Ravenscroft. He was born near the north branch of the Potomac river in Hampshire county, Virginia, at Romney June 22, 1808, and died in Versailles, Illinois, April 19, 1872, in his sixty-fourth year.

Ashford D Ravenscroft was the son of James and Charlotte (Dowden) Ravenscroft. His paternal ancestry was of English descent and were old settlers of the Old Dominion His maternal ancestors were an old family in Virginia He had one sister and four brothers, and was reared in Virginia, where he had a common-school education, and he had a good business education. Being a bright and brainy man he became a strong, influential business man, developing the characteristics of the statesman and leader among men He left his native place at the age of twenty-four years and went to Hillsboro, Ohio, in 1832, and while here was elected Sheriff During his four year's residence he made a trip to Illinois and soon moved to this State, coming in 1836. This county was a part of Schuyler county and the town of Versailles was only projected, but was attracting attention; so with a limited capital of about $1,000, the savings of his own labor, he decided to embark in the mercantile trade here In the winter of 1836-'37, he built a small frame building of two rooms for a store, which he filled with a stock of goods in the following June. This was the first store in Versailles and still stands, a relic of pioneer times and primitive Versailles. To the first rooms he built an addition and to this home he brought his bride, and they lived here in happiness some time Soon competitors came and with varying success, but Mr Ravenscroft was steadily succeeding, and by his business qualities he built up a prosperous business in his line and became an owner of a part of the town site. Stimulated by the growth of the place, perhaps, or more by his genial manner and upright dealing, he gained the confidence and friendship of the people of this section and built up a trade which made him a wealthy man in the course of many years of merchandising The first entry on his books was made June 25, 1837, and the large piles of his account books corded up in the library of his handsome residence, where he lived until death, show something of the volume of his trade in his thirty-five years in business here. The last few years of his life he was afflicted with rheumatism, but was confined to his couch but a short time and up to the time of his death he was around looking after his business But the summons of that stern Sheriff came suddenly on the 19th of April, 1872 A vast concourse of people at his obsequies testified to the large circle of friends and admirers It is said to have been the largest funeral in this pleasant little hamlet of Illinois. Mr. Ravenscroft was endowed by nature with more than common energy and talent, and would have been successful in almost any calling in life, especially as a statesman or in a judicial line. He was one of the few great men in his own home and domestic relations. To his devoted wife and daughter still at home, this was an overwhelming sorrow, and his memory is most sacredly cherished by them and his other surviving children.

Mr. and Mrs. Ravenscroft had five children, one son and four daughters: Mattie Charlotte died at the age of four years, May 15, 1856. The surviving are: William Henry, a resident of Versailles; Lucinda J. is the wife of Thomas H. Graves of Versailles; Lydia A. is the wife of William Yates of Pike county, Illinois, and Virginia C. Ravenscroft.

JOHN W. DANIEL, an intelligent and progressive farmer of Ashland, Cass county, Illinois, and an honored veteran of the late war, was born in Morgan county, this State, January 12, 1839.

His parents were Joseph and Jemima (Stiltz) Daniel, both of whom were natives of Tennessee, in which State they were married and where their eldest child, Somers T., was born. They had four sons and four daughters, the youngest of whom was a man full grown, when the father died, that being the first death in the family. Somers T. died in mature life, leaving a wife and one son; Mary J. went to California in 1849, and has never been heard from since; she was unmarried; James M., a miller by trade, lives in Kansas, is a widower and has a family; Eliza Ann married Mr. Hodgson, and is now deceased; Ellen is the wife of John Goodall, a prosperous farmer of Kansas; Lavinia, wife of John May, a well-to-do farmer, lives in Arkansas; Joseph is married, and lives in Montana, where he is a miner by occupation.

The subject of this sketch attended the subscription schools of Morgan county, and was reared to farm life. Thus passed his boyhood and early manhood, when the country was shaken to its foundations by the bloody carnage of civil war. Leaving his home, young Mr. Daniel enlisted, August 7, 1862, in Company K, One Hundred and First Illinois Infantry. He was assigned to duty at Cairo, Illinois, for a month, at the end of which time he was transferred to the Sixteenth Corps, accompanying his regiment to Holly Springs, Mississippi, where Mr. Daniel participated in his first engagement. A portion of the regiment was taken prisoners, the remainder being detached to do duty as a guard at General Grant's headquarters. Among the latter was Company K, which accompanied General Grant to Vicksburg. After the capture of that city, the portion of the regiment which had been captured was exchanged, and the regiment went to Union City, Tennessee, thence to Louisville, Kentucky, and from there to Bridgeport, Alabama, whence they went to Chattanooga, Tennessee, where they took part in the battle of Missionary Ridge with the Twentieth Army Corps. This brave company made the memorable winter march to Knoxville, during which they were without sufficient food, and their shoes being worn out they might have been tracked by blood from their bruised and bleeding feet. Mr. Daniel participated with his regiment in all the battles from Chattanooga to Atlanta, Georgia, being 100 days under fire. From Atlanta he accompanied General Sherman in his march to the sea, and thence through the Carolinas, north to Washington City, where he participated in the grand review. In June, 1865, he was mustered out of service at Springfield, Illinois.

Mr. Daniel then returned to his boyhood home in Morgan county, where he was married in September, 1866, to Miss Lutheria

Hubbard, an estimable lady and a native of Illinois. To this union two children were born, Edward Grant and Lorenzo Cass, both living and unmarried, and both employed as telegraph operators. Mr. Daniel's wife died, and he was afterward married to Zilpah Carter, a native of Morgan county. They had three children: Elizabeth E., Charles O. and Daisy, all living at home.

Mr. Daniel owns a small fruit farm in the suburbs of Ashland, and deals quite extensively in poultry, from the proceeds of which, and his pension, he lives very comfortably.

He is a stanch Republican in politics; and belongs to John Douglas Post, No. 592, G. A. R. He and his worthy wife are earnest and useful members of the Missionary Baptist Church.

Thus in brief is given the few most prominent facts of a modest and useful life, which although not blazoned abroad is yet as well lived and important as that of the trumpeted heroes of the war. His duty done, he rests by his fireside in peace and happiness, the recipient of the good wishes of his neighbors, the affection of his family, and the gratitude of his country.

MRS. RACHEL D. MARTIN was born in Redstone county, Pennsylvania, November 20, 1810. Her father was Isaac Turner and her mother, Sarah Minton, and she was born in New Jersey and he in Germany. They were farmers, who moved to Ohio in an early day, in 1815, and located on the little Miami near the junction of the east fork. Mrs. Martin was one of a family of ten children. The family settled on 160 acres of partially improved land and came down the Ohio on a flat-boat from Wheeling and landed at Cincinnati, and brought their teams and household goods. They worked hard and at their death they had the farm all paid for with improvements. The father died at the age of fifty-eight years and his wife some years later. Mrs. Martin and her sister, Sirena, the wife of Abel Light, a farmer in Kansas, are still living. The subject of this sketch is eighty-two years old and her sister is eighty, both active, well preserved women. The most of the family died in youth or early childhood.

Matthias Turner was a farmer in this valley and died at the age of thirty-two years in 1852. His brother, Michael, was a farmer on the old homestead, and had many farms in the county of Hamilton in Ohio. He died at the age of eighty years, in 1890. He had a family of seven children, and the six who survived him have good farms. He never went to school in his childhood with the exception of two years in Ohio, in summer, as they could not provide shoes and clothing in the winter.

When in her seventeenth year Rachel went to school eight weeks and learned to read and write, the reader being the New Testament In her nineteenth year she was married, April 12, 1829, to John Martin, who was born in Ohio, March 2, 1794. His father was Joseph Martin, and his mother was Rebecca (Giebel) Martin. Joseph Martin was a farmer, and was born in Wales and died in Ohio at a ripe old age, nearly eighty. His wife lived but a few months. They had nineteen children, two dying in infancy and one son at the age of nine years. Sixteen of these children came to adult life and became heads of families and the youngest had but one child.

Mrs. Martin and her husband commenced domestic life on a rented farm in Hamilton county, Ohio. They owned a small farm there, which they sold and came to Illinois, in March, 1837, bringing five children. They made the trip to Meredosia by steamboat, and settled on eighty acres in the Illinois bottoms. They sold this place to Mrs. Martin's brother, Matthias, and then bought 160 acres, of which the present home is a part. The beloved father died September 23, 1854, at the age of sixty-one, and then the farm was divided. He left his widow with a comfortable property. He owned at one time 860 acres, and 360 was swamp and bottom land that was overflowed. He came first out here on horseback from Cincinnati with Benjamin Speery, and the choice of land he made was poor, having been deceived by some of the settlers, who had come before him. When they came they brought their wagons and horses, one of the latter outliving his master. Mr. Martin was a stock-raiser and breeder, and was one of the leading ones of his time. He raised cattle, horses, hogs and sheep, and clothed themselves with the wool of the sheep and the flax which they raised. Mrs. Martin has been a heroine in hard work all her life, and is still the most important one on the place. She is bright in mind and strong in body. Of her children: Robert died at the age of ten years, August, 1846; Isaac died in November, 1862; he was a volunteer in Company D, One Hundred and Nineteenth Illinois Volunteers, and died in the hospital at Quincy; he left a widow and two sons; John Edward died October 25, 1883, aged twenty-two, and Sarah, the wife of James P. Craig, died in 1866, at the age of thirty-three, leaving one son and one daughter; Michael E. Martin died June 2, 1878, and left his widow, whose maiden name was Francis E. Hume, and one child, who died in infancy. She is with her aged mother-in-law. The living of the family are; Joseph Martin, a farmer of Ohio, and has four living children: William B. Martin; M. V. Martin, a farmer near by on a part of the old farm. He has six children living and two deceased. John G. Martin, named for his father, is residing on the old farm, and has four children: Rachel F. J., the youngest of the family, is the wife of John E. Taylor, and has eight children. Mrs. Martin is a Baptist. Mr, Martin is a Democrat, while his sons are reformers.

JOHN HENDERSON DAVIS, of section 29, Huntsville, is numbered among the substantial farmers of Schuyler county, where he has resided since 1854. He was born in Rutherford county, Tennessee, September 15, 1819, being a son of John and Mary (Bishop) Davis. John, Jr., was but a small boy when his father died. He was one of three children: John; James M., residing in Carthage, Missouri; and Polly, now Mrs. John Lomax.

When John was eight years old the mother and other children came to Illinois and first settled in Green county, near Whitehall, and later moved to Morgan county, near Jacksonville. From there they went to Winchester, Scott county, and from there to Brown county, settling in Pea Ridge township, where the mother died. John was reared on the farm in Brown county and bought a farm in Brown county, where he resided until 1854, when he settled where he now resides. He purchased at first land that was entirely uncultivated, but now has 300 acres of as good land in as fine condition as any in the county. On this farm are excellent farm buildings. He has farmed and dealt in live stock for many years.

He was married in Brown county to Maria Beckam, born in Ohio, daughter of George and Abigail Beckam. She died in 1867, leaving ten children, namely: William H., and youngest sister, Cornelia, residing in Pratt county, Illinois; John W., married, resides in Huntsville township; James M, married and residing in Huntsville, Minerva, married to Newton Binkley, and resides in Hancock county; Emily, married to Luther Benson, of Harper county, Kansas, Louisa, married to John Swoap, of Adams county; Nancy, wife of William Adams, residing in Adams county; Charles H, at home; next, one that died in infancy; Alexander, married, and is living in Carroll county, Missouri.

Mr. Davis is a Democrat in politics, but has never wanted office He is a man who has made his own way in the world and has done it successfully and gained the respect and esteem of every one who knows him.

JAMES CUNNINGHAM, a prosperous farmer and stockman of township 17 north, range 9 west, living near Philadelphia, Illinois, was born near Edinburgh, Scotland, May 10, 1825. He comes of a family of sturdy, honest yeomanry, whose ancestors have been of that bold, upright class which has infused new energy into the sluggish veins of his country His paternal grandfather was a baker in the British army, during the Revolutionary war The parents of the subject of this sketch were John and Ellen (Taylor) Cunningham, both of them natives of bonny Scotland In 1832, the first great sorrow fell upon the little family, when the devoted mother died, leaving six small children to the care of the bereaved father Soon afterward, the father went alone to the United States, and worked for about three years, at his trade of a miller, in Oswego and Buffalo, New York He then returned to his native country, where he was soon afterward remarried, and in 1836, together with his wife and six children, he again emigrated to the United States. After a voyage of five weeks they arrived in New York city, whence they went up the Hudson river to the Erie canal, via which they arrived at Buffalo, New York. Thence they went by lake to Cleveland, Ohio, whence they staged across the country to the Ohio river, and then, by boat down to St Louis and up the Illinois river, taveling all the time from May 10 until July 4, when they arrived at Beardstown, Cass county, Illinois, after an entire journey of fifty-five days, across an ocean and half-way across the American continent. In Cass county, near Virginia, his father purchased a small farm, on which he erected a log cabin, in which he and his family resided, in pioneer fashion, until his father's death, two years later, in October, 1838. His father was a man of great uprightness of character, generous-hearted and cordial in manner, and left many friends and well wishers to mourn his untimely death.

Two of the six children who accompanied their parents to America have since died. Six children were by the first marriage and two by the second. Of the first family, Margaret was the eldest, who married Martin Hoagland, and died in middle life, near Jacksonville, Illinois, leaving a family; Jeannette married Robert Taylor, a Scotchman by birth and a well-to-do farmer in the Sangamon valley; the third in order of birth is the subject of this sketch; Thomas, married, is a farmer near Virginia, Illinois; Archibald, married, died at Sugar Grove some twenty years ago, leaving one child; John is a farmer in Missouri; Marian, now Mrs. Jacobs, is the sole survivor of the second family, the other child having died in infancy.

The subject of this notice landed in America on his eleventh birthday,, and accompanied his parents to the little farm in Cass county, Illinois. Here he continued his education at the subscription schools of his district, having previously attended school in his native country. His father's death, however, put an end to all further leisure for self-culture, and a year after this sad event our subject was bound out to a neighbor, Stephen Lee, by whom he was reared to manhood. He then worked for a number of years in a steam saw and grist mill in Sugar Grove, in which he, later, bought a half interest, and finally purchased the entire property. This he continued to operate, in connection with his farm, for seven or eight years, when, in 1866, he sold his mill and bought his present farm, where he has since resided. This consists of 280 acres of choice agricultural land, owned by Mr. Cunningham and his son, who also operate eighty acres of leased land. This land is usually devoted to grain, but a great many hogs are also grown for market.

In October, 1856, Mr. Cunningham married Miss Sarah Elizabeth Hopkins, a native of Indiana, who came to Illinois with her parents, Henry and Elizabeth Hopkins, when she was only two years of age. Mr. and Mrs. Cunningham have two children: Henry, born in July, 1857, is unmarried, and manages his father's farm; Dorotha Ellen, born in October, 1858, married F. C. Fox, a prosperous farmer and cattle feeder, who lives near by.

Mr. Cunningham was originally a Whig in politics, but has been a Republican since the organization of that party. His constituents have shown their appreciation of his worth by electing him to the position of Trustee of his township, which office he has held for twenty-four years, serving with integrity and ability.

Mrs. Cunningham is an earnest and useful member of the Methodist Episcopal Church, and although Mr. Cunningham is a non-professor of religion yet he gives liberally of his means to the support of the gospel and other religious and benevolent movements.

Thus, unaided, Mr. Cunningham has attained, by his industry and honesty, not only a competence for himself and family, but has been able to donate to others less fortunate than himself, all of which has endeared him to his community and left his impress on many an honest heart.

HENRY GREVE, a successful manufacturer and dealer in tobacco and cigars, doing business on Main street in Beardstown, Illinois, was born in Hanover, in the town of Wittlage, May 20, 1844. He grew up, obtained his German education and learned his trade before he came to the United States, which he reached in September, 1866. He was the second of the family to come to this country, his brother Anton having preceded him. His parents lived and died in their native country. They were members of the German Lutheran Church all their lives. He worked at his trade in New York city for some time before he came to Beardstown. After his arrival here, April 2, 1867, he at once began as a cigarmaker. He associated his brother Anton with him in 1876 as a partner, and they did business together until 1880, since which time he has been continuing alone. He has a good, substantial trade, doing quite an extensive business and giving employment to several hundred workmen. He has accumulated considerable means, owns a good home and two business houses.

He was married in this city, to Miss Anna M. Reller, from Hanover, Germany, who came over in the same vessel with her husband. She has had two brothers and one sister settle in this city since her arrival. Her parents are both dead. She has been a good wife and mother. She and her husband attend the Lutheran Church, and have nine children: Lizzie, Carrie, Henry A., John F. W., Anna, Fred, William, Emma and Hilda. They have all been educated in the public and parochial schools of Beardstown. Mr. Greve is a member of the A. O. U. W., of the German order, of Beardstown Lodge, of Prussia, No. 21, and is a trustee. He is a Democrat in politics, and is a very reliable man in every way.

ISAAC M. STRIBLING, one of the most extensive and successful farmers of Illinois, a popular and influential citizen of Virginia, was born in Logan county, Kentucky, January 13, 1821.

His parents were Benjamin and Nancy (Washburn) Stribling, both natives of Virginia. His paternal grandparents were Thomas and Elizabeth (Ayres) Stribling, also natives of the Old Dominion, who emigrated to Logan county, Kentucky, in a very early day. There his grandfather purchased a tract of timber land, seven miles from Russellville, which he improved and where he continued to reside until his death. The grandmother survived her husband, and accompanied her son, father of the subject of this sketch, to Illinois, and died at his home. The father of the subject of this notice was married in Kentucky, and resided there until 1827, when he removed, with his wife and two children, to Illinois. The journey was made overland with a team, and they brought provisions and cooking utensils with them, and camped and cooked by the way. He first located in Morgan county, where he bought a tract of land, on which he and his family resided for three years. In 1830 he sold out and came to Cass county, settling a mile and a half northwest of the present site of Virginia, he and his family being among the earliest settlers of the county. He bought eighty acres and entered 720 acres of Government land. On that which he bought there was a small house, the sides and roof of which were covered with split boards, while the floor was made of puncheon. The chimney was made of earth and sticks, known in those days as a "cat-and-stick" chimney. He at once commenced to improve his land, and resided there some years, after which he removed to land which he had purchased on the Sangamon river bottoms. He remained there a few years, eventually moving to Beardstown, and finally to Virginia. In the latter place he bought a comfortable home, and spent his last years retired from active business. His first wife, mother of the subject of this notice, was a daughter of Philip Washburn, and she died on the home farm in 1846. Three of her children attained maturity; Benjamin F. died on the old homestead; and Thomas, the youngest son, now resides in California.

Isaac M., whose name heads this memoir, was six years old when his parents removed to Illinois, and he has a vivid recollection of the overland journey and subsequent pioneer life. Central Illinois was then very sparsely settled, while northern Illinois was uninhabited except by Indians. There were no railroads for many years, and the people lived on the products of their farms and wild game, which abounded in great profusion, such as deer, turkeys, prairie chickens, geese and ducks. His father used to raise flax and cotton, which his mother would card, while he and his brothers would spin it, after which it was woven in a hand-loom. All cooking was done by a fireplace, while the method of farming was quite different from that now employed. Grass was mown by hand and grain was cut with a sickle or cradle. As soon as he was large enough, our subject assisted his father in the improvement of the land, attending school as opportunity afforded. The schools were supported by subscriptions, each family paying according to the number of scholars sent. The schoolhouse was of logs, and the benches were made of rough slabs. Fifty cents a day in trade was the price of labor.

Mr. Stribling remained at home until he attained his majority, after which he earned his first money by mowing ten acres of land, receiving for it $1 an acre. His father gave him a tract of wild land, on which he commenced work for himself. Most of it was raw prairie, and he immediately set about preparing the land for cultivation. He built on it a small house, in which, after marriage, he and his wife commenced life. He resided there for ten years and then moved to his present home. He now owns 2,000 acres of choice farming land, 160 of which is in Menard county, and the remainder in Cass county. His property consists of the best in those localities, for which he paid the highest price demanded for agricultural lands. None of it is rented, but the whole is under his supervision. His principal business is raising and feeding stock, his various farms being well supplied with a high grade of shorthorn cattle, well-bred hogs, and draft and trotting horses.

He was first married in 1843, to Margaret Beggs, an intelligent lady, and a native of Virginia, daughter of Charles Beggs. By this union there are five surviving children: Joan, James, Thomas, Kate, Henry C. and Lou M. The family were called upon to mourn the loss of the devoted wife and mother, whose life had been one of continued exertion in their interest.

Mr. Stribling was married a second time, to Maria Carr, an estimable lady, a native of Cass county, this State, and a daughter of David and Julia Carr. By this marriage there are eight children: Emma, Carrie, Nellia, William B., Hattie, Frank, George and Howard.

Mr. Stribling is pre-eminently a self-made man, and has, by good judgment, steady industry, economy and integrity, attained his present phenomenal prosperity and acquire the universal good will of his fellow men.

LUCINDA J. VANDEVENTER.—This estimable lady is the widow of Barnett B. Vandeventer, is a native of Brown county, this State, and is the daughter of John W. and Margaret (Brown) Reid, both natives of Tennessee, who came to Illinois when single. Here they met each other and after acquaintance were married. John Reid was the son of James C. Reid, of Tennessee, who came to Illinois at a very early date, about 1827 or 1829, settling on a mill site on McKee's creek, about two and one-half miles west of Versailles, where he laid claim to one quarter section. There is no doubt but that James Reid came from Scotland, he having married a Miss Nancy Cameron, of Irish descent, a lady of noble ancestry. Mr. James Reid erected a water-power mill, having preferred a mill site to the more fertile acres of the county, when he took up his claim. This mill was a great success and proved a boon to the settlers who could have their grain ground here, without traveling so far to obtain a little meal or feed. Mr. and Mrs. Reid had eleven children, all of whom lived to maturity. Their son, Mrs. Vandeventer's father, had seven children, of whom Mrs. Vandeventer was the eldest. Four of of this family are still living, namely: Wilson, County Clerk of Mt. Sterling, married Margaret Bell Vandeventer; Martha, wife of Orlando Casteen, residents of Anthony, Kansas, where they live with their two daughters, and where he is County Treasurer of that county; Luzena, wife of Frank Martin, of Kansas; and Mrs. Vandeventer.

The last named lady was married, November 18, 1866, to Barnett Vandeventer, brother of Thomas Vandeventer. He died March 17, 1886, leaving his faithful wife to mourn his loss. She is sustained in her great bereavement by her loving children who are as follows: Fred R., aged twenty-four; O. J., in his twenty-third year; Horace, in his twenty-first year; and Dora, eighteen. They have all been well educated, and incline toward agricultural and domestic pursuits. These young people are all at home and are a great comfort to their widowed mother, who bears her affliction with Christian resignation and patience. She and her lamented husband were members of the Methodist Church, as were most of Mr. Vandeventer's family. This gentleman was only fifty-three years old at the time of his death, yet he left a fine estate, in connection with the estate of the Vandeventer brothers, in which he had a third interest.

Mrs. Vandeventer and her interesting family are among the most respected and highly esteemed in the entire township, and all consider it a pleasure to know them.

CLARKSON DORSETT, of section 21, Huntsville, has had his residence in Illinois since 1835. He was born in Randolph county, North Carolina, April 28, 1823, being a son of Ezra and Mary (Beckerdite) Dorsett. In 1835 the family came to Illinois and first settled in Adams county, and Mr. Dorsett, Sr., entered land in Huntsville township, section 6. There Clarkson grew to manhood, and after marriage settled where he now resides. At first he purchased forty acres of land, which was unimproved, and here he has since resided. He now owns ninety-seven and one-half acres of land, and has a good set of farm buildings.

He was married August 23, 1844, to Sarah Sprigg, born in Meade county, Kentucky, October 11, 1824, being a daughter of Thomas and Elizabeth (Dorsey) Sprigg, natives of Kentucky. The family came to Illinois in 1835 and settled in Huntsville. Mr. Sprigg died in Kentucky while on a visit. His wife survived him and died in Schuyler county.

Mr. and Mrs. Dorsett have had ten children: Eliza Ann, born August 28, 1845, married Thomas B. Graham, of Huntsville township; Linza D, deceased December 25, 1848; Nathan G., born December 12, 1849, resides in Ford county, Kansas; Francis A., born December 10, 1851, resides in Huntsville township; Elizabeth Jane, born July 9, 1861, married Lewis Alexander Prather, resides in Littleton township; William M., born March 11, 1865, at home; Mary M., born May 7,

1867, at home; and Cynthia E., born August 10, 1869.

Mr. and Mrs. Dorsett are earnest members of the Methodist Episcopal Church, of which Mr. Dorsett has been a member since he was fourteen years old. He has been a Class-leader for many years in the church at Shiloh, of which society he was the organizer and liberal supporter. Mr. Dorsett is a Republican and has been School Director. He and his wife are highly esteemed by all who know them.

Mrs. Dorsett had five sisters and three brothers: Mary Pendleton, Eliza Chappell, Nancy Clark, Sarah Jane Dorsett, Matilda (Ezra) Dorsett, Melvina Vetach, Thomas C., and Samuel, deceased.

PETER S. WILLIAMS, of Lee township, was born in Clermont county, Ohio, in 1847. His father, Alexander, now living at the Mounds, was born in Ohio, in 1818, and his father, Thomas Jefferson, was a Maryland farmer who came to Ohio a young man. He died there on his farm of 200 acres. His wife's name was Sarah Jones. Alexander Williams married Lydia Ann, daughter of David and Sarah Smith. Peter is one of nine children. His parents came to Illinois and lived in Adams county five years, where they bought a piece of land. They came by water, bringing two children with them. They came to Brown county in 1856 and bought a farm of 120 acres on section 7 and 8, in Lee township. They moved to Mound Station in 1884, where they have lived ever since. They have lands also in Kansas. They gave their children a good common schooling. Mr. Peter Williams raises as many as 100 hogs. He has from forty to 100 head of stock, keeps from fifty to 300 sheep. He has nearly 500 acres of land all under the plow and also sixty acres of fine timber, from which he has cut the largest and most valuable oaks and walnut trees. They have buried one little son, Charlie, two years old, and have besides five children: Ralph, Elmer, Jennie, James and Blanche. They intend to give them all a good education.

Mr. Williams built his house in 1880. It is a large, two-story frame building. He built his barn in 1884. It is 34 x 44, for stock and hay. He has also built another stock barn, 40 x 44 feet. He has sold about two car loads of cattle per annum for the past fifteen years, but it has not paid of late. Mr. Williams and his wife are worthy citizens of the county in which they live. Mrs. Williams was born at her present home, in September, 1835, and married October 17, 1872. Her parents bought 124 acres in 1832 and also some land in other counties, making in all about 500 acres. She was Cora Campbell, daughter of William and Sarah (McCormick) Campbell. They moved from Tennesssee into Sangamon county in 1829.

Mr. Williams is serving his second term as Supervisor and has served as Road Commissioner for the township. He is a Democrat, a Royal Arch Mason and a Knight Templar. His family belong to the Missionary Baptist society.

JOHN HUESCHEN dates his birth in Prussia, January 20, 1846. A review of his life and ancestry gives the following facts:

His father, Henry Hueschen, was one of a family of four sons: Matthias, George, Henry and Deidrich. His parents were born and passed their lives in Prussia. Matthias and George reared families in their native land, and are still living there, Henry and Deidrich being the only ones to come to America. Deidrich is now a resident of Springfield. Henry Hueschen learned the trade of weaver, and was employed at work at his trade and farming in Prussia until 1852, when, with with his wife and three children, he came to America. They set sail from Bremen and after a voyage of nearly four weeks landed in New Orleans; thence up the Mississippi and Illinois rivers to Beardstown. After his arrival in Illinois, Mr. Hueschen found employment at various kinds of work. He bought a home at Beardstown and resided there for many years. His death occurred at the home of his son John, in 1883. His wife's death occurred some years before his. Of their four children be it recorded that Sophia died in Germany when young; that Sibilla married John Henry Betz, and lives in the State of Washington; the other two are John and William.

John Hueschen was only six years of age when the family emigrated to America; consequently he remembers little of his native land. At the time they settled in Beardstown, although only a small place, it contained a large packing house and was the principal market for this section of the country. He attended a German school, and as soon as he was old enough to work was variously employed. From the time he was twenty-one until he was thirty he worked on a farm by the month, after which for seven years he rented land. At the end of this time he purchased the 120 acres on which he now resides. This place is well improved with good buildings, etc.

March 9, 1876, Mr. Hueschen was united in marriage with Elizabeth Fidler, a native of Hesse-Darmstadt, Germany, and a daughter of Henry and Katherine Fidler. This union has been blessed with three children, namely: Theodore, born January 25, 1877, and died April 5, 1892; Huldah, born June 7, 1887; Alvin, August 6, 1890, and died February 26, 1892.

He and his wife are members of the Lutheran Church.

CASPER STOCK, general farmer on section 34, of the precinct of Beardstown, was born in Hesse-Darmstadt, Germany, 1832. He was the son of Thomas and Margaretta (Shaffer) Stock, who both came of old Hesse famlies of pure German blood. Thomas was reared to the business of distiller and was thus engaged until he came to the United States. He and his wife with their two children came from Bremen and landed in Baltimore after a six weeks' voyage in a three-mast sailing vessel. After the usual trip they arrived in Beardstown, October 26, 1836. The father purchased and settled a year latter on land in the precinct of Arenzville, which he cultivated successfully until his death, March 14, 1846. He was a good hard-working man and was very ambitions, but did not live long enough to realize his hopes. His wife is still living with her son, Thomas, Jr., on the old homestead. She is eighty-one years of age, but is quite active and mentally strong. She and her husband were all their lives members of the German Lutheran Church.

Casper was brought to this county when four years of age and was raised as a farmer. He has always been a resident of this county and one of its most worthy German citizens. He is a quiet, unassuming man, and when he took charge of his farm the land was raw and unbroken, but by quiet, persevering effort he has made it one of the finest places in the county He owns 260 acres, all improved. He has lived on the place for thirty-six years and has owned it for twenty six.

He was married in Cass county to Catherine Seeger of Ohio, and came when very young to Cass county with her parents. Her father, Henry Seeger, is a retired merchant who lives in Beardstown. He is one of the old German settlers and came to the United States in 1830, living in Beardstown since 1849. He was for years a merchant there and his wife died in the same place Mrs. Stock is one of five children, all living. Mr and Mrs. Stock are the parents of three children Henry, a farmer of Beardstown, married to Minnie Hansmeir; Mary Pilger, living in Beardstown; Rosa Hinners married a farmer of Arenzville precinct Mr. and Mrs. Stock attend the Lutheran Church and are good, prosperous people Mr Stock is a member of the Democratic party.

REV. WILLIAM S. GARNER was born in what is now Cass county, Illinois, December 16, 1837. He has passed his whole life in this county, and has witnessed the changes which have transformed the frontier into a well-improved and thickly populated section of country.

His father, Rev James Garner, was born in North Carolina, October 7, 1792; when very young went to Kentucky, and subsequently to Clark county, Indiana, where he was married and resided till 1830. He was converted when a young man, joined the Methodist Episcopal Church, and became identified with the ministry. He was a member of the Indiana Conference, and preached in different places in that State till failing health compelled him to relinquish his labors It was then that he came to Illinois He made the journey to this State with a four-horse team and wagon, being accompanied by his wife and four children. They cooked and camped on the road, and after their arrival here settled in township 17, range 10, where they lived a year or two Mr. Garner then entered a tract of Government land in section 2, township 17, range 9, on which he put up a log house, built after the fashion of those days, with rived boards for roof, stick-and-mud chimney, etc In this humble abode William S. was born It was some years before there were any railroads here. The first railroad built in this vicinity was from Springfield to Jacksonville, the rails being of wood, and the cars drawn by horses After his settlement in Illinois, James R. Garner became a local preacher He was frequently called upon to marry couples and to preach funerals. Often he would ride a number of miles to perform a marriage ceremony, and receive 50 cents or $1 for his pay. In politics he was a Whig, and afterward a Republican. He was a strong anti-slavery man. The subject of our sketch remembers when Beardstown was the chief market and depot of supplies for many miles around The merchants in Springfield used to go to Beardstown with teams for their goods. The price of all farm products was very low. Dressed pork sold for 75 cents to $1 50 per 100 pounds; corn and oats, 10 to 15 cents per bushel; a cow and calf, $8 to $10 Deer and wild turkey were plentiful throughout the State. The people lived on wild game and the products of their own land, dressed in homespun, and withal were as happy, if not more so, than they are to-day. It was not unusual to see the pioneer women walking two or three miles to church and carrying their shoes, putting them on as they neared the church.

In 1855 Mr. Garner divided his land among his children, and moved to section 36, township 18, range 9, where he improved a farm and resided till his death, September 11, 1862. The maiden name of his wife was Elizabeth Robertson. She was born in Clark county, Indiana, October 15, 1795, when that State was a part of the Northwest Territory. These worthy pioneers reared ten children, viz.: Mahulda married George Beggs; Greenbury, Jane Redman; Susan, J. Fox; Amos, Lucy Bingley; Mary J., Robert Robertson; James R., Margaret Wilson; John W., Lucy Carver, and after her death, Melinda Downing; Sarah A., Henry Sherrer; and William S. All their sons joined the Methodist Episcopal Church in youth, and became ministers of the same. Greenbury and Amos united with the Illinois Conference, and the others became local preachers.

The subject of our sketch received his education in the primitive schools of his native county. As soon as he was old enough he began to assist his father on the farm, and remained with his parents till their death. He was converted at the age of nineteen, joined the church, and a few years later was licensed to preach. All his life he has been true to the cause he espoused in his youth, ever showing by example as well as precept that he is a true follower of the Lord. In 1870 he moved from the old homestead to his present farm of 120 acres. Besides this he owns other land, making in all 210 acres.

Mr. Garner was married in 1858, September 30, to Nancy M. Crews, a native of Sangamon county, Illinois, and a daughter of Jesse and Susan (Sneed) Crews, natives of Kentucky and pioneers of that county. Their union has been blessed by the birth of eight children, namely: Hanson A., Nellie May, James H., Lena U., Belle, Jesse, Gertie and Pearl. Nellie May married Charles A. Schaeffer (of whom see sketch in this volume). Lena U. is the wife of La Fayette Shankland.

Politically, Mr. Garner is a Republican. He has served as a member of the School Board, as Justice of the Peace two terms, and as Township Trustee.

Such is a brief outline of the life of one of Cass county's well known and highly esteemed citizens.

FRED R. PRINCE, superintendent of the water service of the St. Louis division of the Chicago, Burlington & Quincy Railroad, having headquarters at Beardstown, was born in Mount Pleasant, Iowa, February 9, 1859. He was the son of Charles Prince, of Coventry, England, born August 30, 1822, of good English stock, who, having grown up in the trade of a machinist, had no difficulty in obtaining work in the shops of Coventry. He here married Emma Taylor, of similar ancestry, and after the birth of three children, in 1855, started for the United States, and landed in New York city. They started on their westward journey with teams, and did not stop until they reached Mount Pleasant, Iowa, which was yet a hamlet. He there worked hard and established a shop, and has since run his business successfully. He is now about seventy years of age, but is still in active business. He and his wife are the only members of their families yet living. They are Universalists in religion, are good, worthy old people. He is a Democrat, and has been Alderman of his city.

Fred is the fifth of a family of eight children. He was reared in his native city, and learned his trade of machinist before he became of age. Soon after this period of his life he associated himself with the Quincy Railroad. He is a thorough machinist, having learned his trade under his father, is a practical and valuable man for the company, and has given good satisfaction to his employers Before accepting his present position, Mr Prince was from April 1, 1881, to September 1, 1883, a machinist at the shops in this place. He has now assumed control of the above mentioned branch of the Quincy business. It covers about 300 miles of road, representing the employment of fifteen men regularly.

While engaged in the mechanical department of the Boys' Reform School at Eldora, Iowa, Mr. Prince was married to Miss Mattie Champion, of Knox county, Illinois, who was born in 1866, reared in Iowa and educated at Oscaloosa, that State Her father, Joseph Champion, was born in Kentucky, January 31, 1810, and died on his farm near Oscaloosa, at an advanced age. Her mother, Rachel Champion, was born in Indiana, September 16, 1816, and is also deceased. The subject of this sketch and his wife are active young people, and much attached to their home. They have no children Mr. Prince is a Democrat, and a member of Ark Lodge, No 16, I. O. O F

ANDREW B. McCORMICK has the honor to be one of the pioneers of Schuyler county, and it is fitting that an outline of his life should be recorded on these pages. He is a native of the Empire State, born April 7, 1828, near Albany, Rensselaer county

His father, Andrew McCormick, was born in Scotland, and is the only member of his family who emigrated to America; his youth was spent in Scotland Emigrating to the United States he settled in New York city, where he was married After that event he located in Rensselaer county, where he was employed in a rolling mill until 1836 In that year he removed to Illinois, coming via the Erie canal to Buffalo, thence by lake to Cleveland, thence by canal to the Ohio river; the journey was continued by the Mississippi and Illinois rivers to Beardstown, and thence by team to Rushville, where he arrived November 15, 1836; where he lived until the spring of 1837, and then settled on land in Woodstock township, where he built a log house, and began the task of developing the wild waste into a fertile farm At the end of two years he disposed of the property and removed to Rushville, where he died, March 17, 1840. His wife's maiden name was Jane Hill; she was one of the girls participating in the reception of La Fayette at Sumbridge, assisting in strewing flowers. She was born in Dutchess county, New York, and was the daughter of David Hill, a native of Ireland, of Scotch ancestry. He emigrated to America a member of the British army, but after coming here his sympathies were transferred to the colonists, and he deserted King George's ranks, and took up the cause of the oppressed When the war was ended he settled in Dutchess county, New York, and engaged in farming; there he spent the remainder of his days The father of our subject was a strict Presbyterian; the mother in earlier life belonged to the same church, but afterward joined the Methodists. She was married a second time, and spent her last years in Rushville, she was the mother of four children, born of her first marriage: Andrew B., David, Jane E. and Samuel.

Andrew B. was a child of eight years when his parents removed to the frontier, as Illinois was then considered. Since that day he has witnessed the wonderful transformation from a wild, almost uninhabited waste into one of the most productive and prosperous States of the Union. He was only twelve years old at the time of his father's death, and was then thrown on his own resources. He found employment on the farm by the month, and worked in this way for three years. At the end of that time he went to learn the cooper's trade, which he followed several years.

When he reached his majority he received an inheritance from Scotland of £100, and with this he purchased the land on which he now resides; he then turned his attention to agriculture, and soon came to be recognized as a leading authority on many questions relating to husbandry.

He was married February 15, 1849, to Miss La Master, who was born in Rushville township, Schuyler county, Illinois, a daughter of James and Nancy (Donahue) La Master; the father was born in Jefferson county, Kentucky, a son of Abraham and Orpha (Erwin) La Master (see sketch of Charles Kennedy), and came to Illinois with his parents in 1826; he resided in Rushville township for a time, and then removed to Bainbridge township. In 1850 he went to California, making the entire journey overland, and after an absence of three years returned to Illinois and to his home in Bainbridge township, Schuyler county; a year later he went to Fulton county and bought a fine farm two miles north of Lewistown, and there lived until death; his wife had died in Bainbridge township, many years previous to his own demise. Mr. and Mrs. McCormick are the parents of ten children, of whom four died in infancy and two boys after twenty-one. One daughter married, and died in 1881, leaving three daughters. David, Robert, Jessie and Della are living now.

Mr. McCormick is one of the representative early settlers. In his youth his opportunities were exceedingly limited; schools were taught on the subscription plan, and were conducted in primitive fashion. He has been a wide and careful reader, and through his own efforts has accomplished, in later years, what was denied him in his youth. Politically, he affiliates with the Republican party, and is an ardent supporter of its principles. He is a man of great integrity of character, and has the confidence and respect of the entire community.

CHARLES KENNEDY, the subject of the following sketch, was born in Hardin county, Kentucky, May 31, 1810. His father, Peter Kennedy, was an old settler of Kentucky, and like many others of that date went through some very thrilling experiences. He was made a prisoner by the Indians when but thirteen years of age, and for nine years was kept captive among them. Finally, making his escape, he managed to reach Louisville, that beautiful city being then but a trading fort. In those days acquaintanceship grew fast, and ere long, Mr. Kennedy married Rachel Colvin, a Kentuckian, and settled on a farm in Hardin county, where they both remained during life. A younger son still occupies the old home which he owned.

Charles Kennedy was married to Sarah Phillips, September 19, 1833, and he and his wife removed Schuyler county, Illinois. In 1835, he purchased a farm and erected neat buildings; here they lived until May 21, 1853, when Mrs. Kennedy died. To them were born four children: Jesse, Francis, John Q., and Charles C., two of whom are still living, Jesse and John Q. The latter served in the One Hundred and Nineteenth Illinois Infantry, under Captain R. L. Greer. Mr. Kennedy's second marriage occurred March 8, 1854, to Miss Nancy La Master, a daughter of Abraham and Orpha La Master. Mr. La Master was born in Maryland, and his wife in Virginia, of French extraction. They were married in Kentucky.

Mrs. Kennedy was but three years old when her parents removed to Illinois. She being an early settler has witnessed the entire development and growth of the country; Mrs. Kennedy is still living. Mr. Kennedy died May 16, 1883; to them were born two children: Leander and Mary, Leander married Ellen Malcomson and has three children: Bessie, Ruby and James; Mary married S. R. Carey.

Mrs. Kennedy has been a member of the Methodist Episcopal Church for more than fifty years, Mr. Kennedy was a Baptist in belief, and was a life member of that denomination.

ROBERT TAYLOR, a pioneer of Illinois, and a prominent citizen of Cass county, dates his birth in Scotland, ten miles south of Campbeltown, Argyleshire, November, 27, 1816. His father, Robert Taylor, a native of same place, was a son of Angus Taylor, who was also born in that locality. Both passed their lives and died there. The father of our subject was a farmer by occupation. He married Miza McCoy, a native of the same shire, and a daughter of Neill McCoy, also a native of that place. Mrs. Taylor survived her husband some years. She came to America in 1837, spent the rest of her life in Cass county, Illinois, and died here in 1845. She reared eight sons and one daughter, namely: Angus, Neill, Alexander, Archibald, Flora, Duncan, John, Robert and William. All came to America.

Robert Taylor was reared and educated in in his native land. When he was three years old his father died, and until he was eight he lived with his mother. He then found a home with his uncle, Archibald Taylor, with whom he remained three years. Returning to his mother, he lived with her till his eighteenth year, when he came to America. He set sail from Greenock May 16, 1835, in the John Hale, accompanied by his brother Angus, and landed in New York on the 4th of July following. His uncle, Alexander Taylor, was a resident of Champaign county, Ohio, and to that place he directed his course. In Urbana he found a home with Douglas Luce, learned the trade of tanner and currier, and remained their four years. In October, 1839, he came to Illinois, accompanied by his four brothers, making the journey with a team. They settled in Cass county and bought a tract of land four miles northwest of Virginia.

At that time this county was sparsely settled. Deer, wild turkeys and other game were plentiful, and for several years there was not a railroad in the country. In 1840 Mr. Taylor made a visit to Chicago, going by the most convenient and expeditious route at that time, namely, by team to Beardstown, steamer to Peru, and stage to Chicago. Chicago's population was then about 5,000. A hotel and a few slab shanties were the only buildings on the north bank of the river. He put up at the Mansion House, which then stood opposite the Tremont, after six weeks spent in the city returned to Cass county. From Chicago to Bureau county he rode with a farmer who had been to the city to market his grain. Then he walked to Peru, where he took a steamer for Beardstown.

For sixteen years he lived on the land he and his brothers purchased. At the expiration of that time he rented it and purchased the farm he now owns and occupies in the Sangamon river bottoms, located in section 18 of township 18, range 10. He has been very successful as a farmer, has purchased other lands at different times, and is now the owner of upward of 1,000 acres.

Mr. Taylor and his wife are members of the Cumberland Presbyterian Church. They were among the original members of the Sangamon Bottom Church. The first meeting of this society was held on the fifth Sunday in July, 1848, and was organized late in the month of August following by Rev. Nathan Downing and by Rev. James White.

Politically, Mr. Taylor was reared a Whig, but joined the Republican party when it was formed. He has always been a Prohibitionist in principle, and of late years has voted with that party in national elections.

ISAAC NEWTON PEVEHOUSE was born on the farm on which he now resides, November 1, 1849. His father, John J. Pevehouse, was born in Kentucky in 1818, and his father, John, also was born in Pennsylvania, while his father was a native of Germany and came to America in colonial times and served in the Revolutionary war. He was a farmer and lived in Washington county, Pennsylvania. John served in the war of 1812 and removed to Kentucky directly after the war, being a pioneer of Wayne county. He has served as County Commissioner several terms. In 1833 he removed to Illinois and settled in Adams county, where he bought land in Honey Creek township, residing there until his death. The maiden name of his wife was Mary Beeson. She survived her husband a few years and died at her home in the house of her son, John, Jr., in Pea Ridge township. The father of our subject, John, Jr., was sixteen years old when he came to Illinois with his parents. He made the entire journey overland with teams. At that time the county was but sparsely settled and Quincy was but a hamlet. He bought eight acres of unimproved land on time, paying $80 for the tract. He bought it at a public sale and did not have the money to pay for it with. He soon found a purchaser for his bargain at a small advance. He married in Brown county and lived there on a farm of 147 acres that he bought at a big bargain, and also bought other tracts of land. He was very successful. Here Isaac was born and when his father died he left 800 acres for his heirs. His death occurred March 17, 1891. The maiden name of his wife was Susanna Pevehouse, born in Wayne county, Kentucky. Her father, Joseph Pevehouse, was well known in Kentucky from which he removed to Illinois, settling in Scott county, where he resided in that part which was Morgan county at that time. He was one of the first teachers of the county. He bought land and followed farming and mercantile business in Clayton and resided there until his death in 1863. The maiden name of his wife was Mary Slagle. She was born in Kentucky and died on the farm. The mother of our subject is still living on the home farm. She reared five children, Thersa A., Elizabeth J., Isaac N., Martha E. and Sarah E.

Isaac was reared and educated in his native township and has always been engaged in agricultural pursuits and still occupies the old homestead where he has always lived.

Politically he has always been identified with the Democratic party. His parents were firm members of the Methodist Episcopal Church. Mr. Pevehouse is an upright gentleman and is greatly respected by all who know him.

FRANK LAWRENCE, a highly respected citizen of Oakland township, was born in Winnebago county, Illinois, in 1851, a son of Thomas Henry Lawrence. His father removed to Illinois about 1848, and settled near Rockford, where he bought a farm on which he passed the remainder of his days; he died in 1853, in the prime of a prosperous life, leaving a widow and eight young children. Soon after his death his wife disposed of the estate, which was valued at $1,300, and returned to Orange county, New York. Her maiden name was Sarah Randle, and she was a daughter of Jesse Randle; she now resides in Warwick, New York, and is still vigorous both in mind and body. Five of the children survive. Thomas H., Jesse R. and A. P. were volunteers in the late war; they all came out alive, but all were wounded; Thomas H. and Jesse R. are both deceased.

Mr. Lawrence came to the West in 1871, his objective point being Council Bluffs, Iowa. In the spring of 1873 he went to Colorado, making part of the journey by rail, and the rest overland by pack train. In 1882 he returned to the East, and then came to Ray, Schuyler county, where he has since resided.

He was united in marriage to Mary E. Baxter Sumner, in 1885; Mrs. Lawrence died July 15, 1889, leaving one son, Thomas H. Lawrence, born in August, 1888. Mr. Lawrence was married a second time, February 8, 1891, when he was united to Josie Glimpse, a daughter of James and Sarah (Shirley) Glimpse, natives of Illinois; the Shirley family is from New Jersey, and the Glimpse family came from Indiana. James Glimpse died in 1891, at the age of forty-five years, leaving a family of five children. Mr. Lawrence occupies a pleasant home in Ray, which he erected in 1891; he owns about sixty acres of land. He has had charge of the Ray tile works as superintendent and foreman; he has filled the position with marked ability. Politically he affiliates with the Democratic party. He is a member of the Masonic order, and belongs to the blue lodge, chapter and commandry.

HENRY STARK, of Mt. Sterling, was born in Prussia, in 1848. His parents were Peter and Elizabeth Stark, both of Prussia. The father spent his entire life there, and after his death the mother and children came to America, and settled in Mt. Sterling, where she spent her last days.

Henry attended school quite steadily, until he was fourteen years old, and then commenced work in the mines for three years, and worked in the rolling mills until 1869, when he concluded to come to America to try and better his condition. He came directly to Rushville, where he landed with empty pockets. He at once found work in the mines, where he continued about three months, went from there to Beardstown, and worked on the railroad for nearly a year, and then went to Peoria and entered the coal mines. A short time after his employer failed and left him with no money. He went from there to Rochelle, and from there to Mt. Sterling, and entered the employ of the Wabash Railroad Company. He then worked two months in a pork-packing establishment, in a brick-yard one summer, then went to St. Louis, in order to learn a trade, and finally back to Mt. Sterling, where with a partner he finally opened a market. He very soon failed again, but a friend lent him money and thus far he has met with remarkable success. In the meantime he has engaged in various lines of business. He was in the junk business, and for two years he ran a skating rink. He was the first ice dealer in the town, and for about twelve years engaged in that business. He continued in the butchering business for eight years, and then entered into his present business. He is one of the largest real-estate owners in the city. In 1890, he erected a handsome business block on Main street, with a forty-foot front, and he owns another block on the same street, 40x100 feet, seven dwelling houses, besides vacant property.

He married in 1877, Sarah Ward, of Mt. Sterling, daughter of Nicholas Ward, of Ireland. He learned the trade of wheelwright, came to America a young man, and carried on his business in Mt. Sterling, where he died as the result of an accident by falling backward from the upper story of his wagon shop, breaking his neck in the fall. He had four daughters. This death left the family in rather straitened circumstances, but by their industry, all learning the dressmakers' trade, they managed to keep the family together. One of Mrs. Stark's sisters, Kate, is married, and lives in Rushville; the other two still continue to carry on the dressmaking trade, in Mt. Sterling. Their mother, *nee* Bridget McCabe, a native of Ireland, is still living.

The only child of Mr. and Mrs. Stark died in infancy. They both are members of St. Mary's Roman Catholic Church. Mr. Stark is a popular and well-thought-of man, he is very liberal to the poor, and is recognized as a good citizen.

JOSEPH ALLISON was born near Dover, Tuscarawas county, Ohio, October 17, 1828. Joseph Allison, his father, was supposed to have been born in Pennsylvania, as he was reared and married in that State, and moved from there to Ohio. He bought a tract of timber land in Tuscarawas county, built a log cabin in the wilderness, settled on his frontier farm and began the work of clearing it. He lived there till 1840, when he came Illinois, being accompanied by his wife and eight children. He made the journey overland with teams, working and camping on the way. After a month's travel in this way, they landed at Jacksonville, Morgan county. At that time Jacksonville was a hamlet and Springfield only a small place, the surrounding country being thinly settled. Renting land in Morgan county, he lived there four years. Then he moved to Cass county, and in 1847, after renting land here three years, bought a farm in section 23, of township 18, range 9, it being unimproved at the time of purchase. He brought a log house from Morgan county and erected it on this place. It was years before there were any railroads here. Settlers were few and wild game was plentiful. Beardstown was the chief market for supplies. Mr. Allison resided on this place till his death, February 11, 1859. He spent years of toil here, improving and beautifying his farm, and at the time of his death had it in a flourishing condition, with good frame buildings, etc. The maiden name of his wife, mother of the subject of our sketch, was Elizabeth Spawn. She was born in Pennsylvania, and died on the home farm, February 18, 1859. They were married in 1812. Following are the names of their eight children: Mary, Margaret, Jane, John, Elizabeth, Martha, Joseph and Catherine.

Joseph was twelve years old when his parents came to Illinois, and he well remembers the incidents connected with their pioneer life here. His mother used to card, spin and weave, and dress her children in homespun. He resided with his parents until their death, and now owns and occupies a part of the old homestead. The farm contains 137 acres and is well improved with good buildings, etc.

Mr. Allison was united in marriage, December 26, 1849, with Cecelia E. Logne, who was born in Warren county, Tennessee, April 26, 1829. Her father, Oliver Logne, was born in the same county, January 17, 1805, son of William Logne, thought to have been a native of Georgia. William Logne was a farmer and teacher, and served as a Justice of the Peace in Warren county, Tennessee, where his death occurred. The maiden name of grandmother Logne was Hannah Sturgis. She, too, died in Warren county. Oliver Logne was reared and married in Warren county, and from there moved to Illinois, in 1829, becoming one of the first settlers of what is now Menard county. About a year later he moved to that part of Morgan county now included in Cass. Here he entered a tract of Government land, improved a farm, and resided till his death. Mrs. Logne, *nee* Rebecca Cole, was born in Warren county, Tennessee, January 12, 1805, daughter of James Cole.

Mr. and Mrs. Allison have three children: John Wesley, who was born March 3, 1851, and married Mary Mellstead, and has two children, Bessie and Cassie; James E., born in 1857, who married Lillie Wyatt, has one child, Etta; and Arthur, born August 11, 1866, who married Sarah Morgan; Elizabeth E., born June 1, 1854, died December 30, 1854.

Politically, Mr. Allison is a Republican. He and his wife are members of the Methodist Episcopal Church.

Mr. Allison has disposed of his farm and intends to retire from active business pursuits.

DANIEL G. SMITH, M. D., who resides on a farm in Hickory precinct, Cass county, Illinois, is well known as a prominent and successful physician of this vicinity. Briefly given, a sketch of his life is as follows:

Daniel G. Smith was born a mile and a half east of Scottsville, Macoupin county, Illinois, October 3, 1847. His father, Samuel Smith, one of the pioneers of Macoupin county, was born in Clinton county, North Carolina. Grandfather Smith removed with his family, from North Carolina to Kentucky, where he spent his last years and died. Samuel Smith was reared in Kentucky, and resided there till 1835, when he moved to Illinois, first locating in Morgan county. At that time much of the land in Morgan county belonged to the Government, and he entered land near Woodson, and resided there a few years. He then sold out and moved to Macoupin county, where he bought a tract of land near Scottville, a part of it being prairie, and a part timber. After improving this land, and residing on it some years, he sold out and moved to Franklin; thence to Waverly, where he lived retired from active business until the time of his wife's death. He then went to Franklin, and spent his last days with his daughter. His wife was before her marriage Miss Dorothy Hull, a native of Tennessee, and a daughter of Jesse Hull. They reared eight of their eleven children.

Dr. Smith first attended the district schools and afterward the Scottville high school. At the age of eighteen he commenced teaching, and taught and worked on the farm for four years. He then began the study of medicine with Dr. G. W. Bradley, of Waverly. He attended one course of lectures at the Cincinnati E. M. Institute, and two courses at the American Medical College at St. Louis, graduating at the latter institution with the class of 1877. He began the practice of his profession in Franklin, and after remaining there four years removed to Virginia. Here he acquired a lucrative practice, and remained a resident till 1889. That year he bought a tract of land in section 1, township 18, range 11, moved upon it, and has since conducted farming operations. He still, however, continues his medical practice, being equally successful in each.

In 1866, Dr. Smith was united in marriage with Melinda J. Thompson, a native of Wayne county, Illinois, and a daughter of William C., and Amelia Thompson. Dr. and Mrs. Smith have five children living: Charles W., Fred M., Dottie E., Lois and Zella F. Myrtie, the first-born, died in her fourth year, and Katie, the fourth, died in her tenth year.

Politically, the Doctor is a Democrat. He and his wife and three oldest children are members of the Christian Church.

LYMAN HAGER, a successful farmer and stock-raiser living near Beardstown, was born in Sullivan county, New Hampshire, August 30, 1828. His father, Reuben Hager, was also a native of New Hampshire, and died in 1871. His parents had died when he was fourteen years of age. He was afterward reared by a Mr. Town until he was of age. While yet in Sullivan county he had become owner of a small farm, which he sold in 1835, and with his wife and children came West, by canals and rivers, until he landed in Beardstown. He made a settlement on a farm consisting of Government land, and later added to it from time to time until he owned a farm of several hundred acres. He spent his last years in quiet comfort in Beardstown. He was a genial, good man, well known for his good judgment. He had been for years a member of the Grand Jury of Beardstown, and was often called upon to arbitrate in difficulties. His wife, who had died in 1846, was named Sarah Reed, and was born in New Hampshire. She had been a good woman, and a consistent member of the Methodist Episcopal Church.

Mr. Lyman Hager could not help being the fine man he is, after having such a good father and mother. He has lived in this county since he was six years of age, and has spent his entire life since then near where he now lives, with the exception of five years spent in California during the '50s. Since early boyhood days he has been a hard worker and he has been fairly successful. He was not able to obtain much early education in the new country.

He was married in this county, to Cordelia Spalding, of Posey county, Indiana. She died at her home, December 23, 1878, at the age of thirty-eight years. She was the mother of seven children. They are: Rose Phelps, living in this county; Douglas, a farmer near this city; Clara Phelps, of this township; Emma Crum, of this county; Christina Redshaw, also of this county; Mary Thompson, of the same; and Joseph at home helping on the farm.

Mr. Hager was a second time married, in Beardstown, to Mrs. Annie Coort. She was born in 1847, in Dublin, Ireland, and came to the United States in 1853, with her parents, who are not living at the present time.

Mr. and Mrs. Hager have three children. One, William was fatally scalded when five years old. The living ones are Charles and Eva.

Mr. and Mrs. Hager are good and intelligent people, and she is of the Catholic faith. Mr. Hager is a Democrat.

HARRISON HINES, foreman in the car shops of the Quincy Railroad, St. Louis division, was born in Montgomery county, New York, February 19, 1841. His father, Henry, and grandfather, John Hines, were natives of New York, but came of Holland ancestry. The latter lived and died in the Empire State a very old man. He had married a kinswoman of Commodore Perry and she also lived and died in New York. Henry Hines grew up in his native State as a carpenter and mechanic. After he came to Illinois he engaged in contracting and building and helped build the Chicago division of what is now the Quincy railroad main line. He lived in Aurora and spent his last years there, dying some fourteen years ago, over eighty years of age. His wife's maiden name was Betsey Howard, who was born and reared in New York, also. The old stock of Hines were Methodists.

Harrison is one of eight children, all living, and was only one year old when his parents came to Aurora, Illinois. He learned his trade as a mechanic under his father and became a skilled artisan. Mr. Hines enlisted in 1861, in the Forty-fifth Regiment, known as Washburn Lead Mine Regiment, Colonel John E. Smith and Captain Holcomb, commanding. He served through three years and six months, being in the First Division of the Third Brigade of the Seventeenth Army Corps, and was in all the terrible battles that that brigade took part in. He received a gunshot wound in his left leg at Shiloh, and at Vicksburg he was wounded in the head by the bursting of a shell. He saw much hard fighting and for meritorious conduct while running the batteries at Vicksburg, he received from General Grant, through General Rawlins, a grant of leave home and a free transportation. He is justly proud of his war record. He was all through the Savannah campaign, march of Sherman to the sea, and finally was honorably discharged at Louisville, Kentucky, July 12, 1865. He has been in his present position at Beardstown for the past twelve years. He came from Ottumwa, Iowa, where he was foreman in a car shop for nine years. In 1866 he began with the Quincy Railroad at Aurora, Illinois. He was there for some years in the building department until 1869, when he was sent to Burlington, Iowa, and was there in the building department from Galva to Keithsburg, Illinois, until 1871, when he became connected with the car-building department and has been a foreman most of the time. He has grown very popular as a citizen.

He was married in Chicago, Illinois, to Miss Nettie Thompson, who was born, reared and educated in Wisconsin. Her parents, now old people, live in Brookings, Dakota. Mr. and Mrs. Hines of this notice are prominent citizens of Beardstown and members of the Congregational Church. They are parents of seven children: Russel, Edgar, Nettie, Augustus, Grace, Mabel and Ralph M.

Mr. Hines is a member of the Board of Education and is a Republican. He is a member of the MacLane Post, No. 91, G. A. R., of Beardstown; of the Masonic chapter, of the Odd Fellows encampment of this place, and of the commandery at Rushville. Mr. Hines' record with the Chicago, Burlington & Quincy Railroad is an excellent one; for his fifteen years of service he has never missed a month's salary. He is a refined gentleman.

WILLIAM MORRELL, a prominent farmer of Elkhorn township, was born September 28, 1825, in Clermont county, Ohio. He was the son of Elmore and Nancy (Wright) Morrell, born in Maine, son of David Morrell, of Portland, that State. The subject's father was reared on a farm and came to Fort Washington, now Cincinnati, in 1812, with his parents and was one of the pioneers who in 1832 came into Illinois. The journey into the wilderness was made by ox team and they suffered all the hardships of that early date. He was married in Campbell county, Kentucky, where his wife was born. He brought his wife and three children to Illinois and settled first in Morgan county, where he bought eighty acres and improved that, and three years later sold this out to buy the farm where our subject now lives and there he spent his life, dying in 1891, aged eighty-six years. He left his original purchase of 100 acres on which he first built a house, the lumber for which was first sawed with an old-fashioned whipsaw. That was the first lumber sawed in this part of Illinois. The father of our subject was one of the first and most active pioneers. He was a Democrat politically. His wfie was a Universalist and her life ended on the old farm when she was about sixty-two. She was born in 1806. The father was born in 1803.

Our subject was one of seven children, three of whom are yet living. He remained at home until his marriage and was employed as are all the sons of farmers. After marriage he picked up the wagonmaking trade and rented the farm where he now lives. He lived there from 1853 to 1876, when he moved into his present home. He first bought forty acres and later bought more until he now has as fine a farm of 154 acres as there is in the country. He also has a fine farm in Buckhorn township, and is one of the most successful farmers in the State. He has carried on a mixed farming.

The marriage of Mr. Morrell took place February 6, 1846, to Miss Abigail Smith, who was born in Ashtabula county, Ohio, July 18, 1826, and was a daughter of Benjamin and Abigail (Hackett) Smith. He was born in New Hampshire and she in Vermont, and after their marriage in Ohio they came as pioneers to Illinois, and in 1889 rented land in Morgan county for two years, and then went over into Brown county and remained there a year, and then finally settled in Cass county, where Mr. Smith, died at the age of forty-six. He has always followed farming. The mother died in Cass county, Illinois, aged about forty-four. George Hackett, an uncle of Mrs. Morrell, came to the county about 1824, and was one of the first settlers in central Illinois, and the owner of the first tanyard west of the Illinois river.

Our subject is a strong Democrat, having given his first vote for Franklin Pierce. He and his wife are both church-going people and are highly esteemed in their neighborhood. They have had seven children: four yet living. Rosalie is a widow and has one grandchild and five children. Delah is married, with four children; William J. is a married man; Henry has two children and rents all the old farm.

The whole family are good, quiet people, and these are the citizens whose names properly appear in a record of this kind.

ROBERT RICH was born in Germany on the Rhine, in Baden, in 1852. He is the son of Matthias Rich of the same place, who came to the United States in 1855, settling in St. Louis with his wife and two children, where he pursued the trade of cooper, which he had learned in Germany. From there he came to Brown county in the fall of 1858, and there continued his trade. He bought 100 acres of timber land that had been cleared, although there was plenty of brush. This farm is Mr. Rich's (Sr.) home at present, and is east of Cooperstown. Although Mr. Rich, Sr., had barely enough to come to this country with, he now owns 300 acres of good land in this county with fine farm buildings on it. He raises a good strain of cattle. Beside this he has 500 acres in the bottoms of Illinois. He is now worth about $35,000. His wife is named Parthina. They buried one infant son, and have ten living children, namely: Robert; Julius, a farmer of this township; Emma, now Mrs. Charles Petei, farmer in this township; Joseph, a farmer in this township; Louisa, wife of Newton Quinn, farmer of Cooperstown; Sophie, wife of John Snyder, farmer; Matthias, farmer; Henry, farmer; Ellora, wife of Charles Barton, farmer of this county; Perfina is at home and brightens up the home circle with her merry presence.

Robert Rich lived on the home farm until he was twenty-one, when he went into a store as a clerk, as he was in falling health and found the farm work too wearing on him. This work did not suit him, either; so a year later he went to California by rail, in the summer of 1873. There he worked out of doors, doing farming, and this proved of great benefit to him. He was there until the winter of 1875, when he returned to Brown county to his old farm. Here he worked on the farm again for two years, and then farmed on his father's bottom lands for three years. He then bought 160 acres of his present place, buying it at a low price, $6,000 in all for the worked land. He moved his wife into a shanty, where they lived until the farm was paid for. In 1888 he built their present comfortable two-story frame house, one of the best in the township, costing nearly $2,000. In 1891 Mr. Rich built a fine new barn, 40 x 60 feet, costing $1,200. This, too, is one of the best in the section. Twenty-four to thirty fine horses or cattle can be housed in the large basement. Mr. Rich devotes himself chiefly to hogs, although he does other farming also. He generally grows an equal amount of corn and wheat, but has eighty acres of wheat this year, which will yield about twenty bushels per acre. On the third year he grows clover about even. Mr. Rich makes money, making about $1,800 clear of expenses. He also has a great deal of fine stock.

Mr. Rich was married to Elizabeth Quinn, in 1877. Mr. and Mrs. Rich have four living children, having buried an infant son. Those living are: Della E., twelve years; Nellie Pearl, ten years; Matthias Benjamin, eight years, and Robert, six years. Their father is giving these children a good education, and he is a School Director. Mr. Rich has been a very successful man of one of his age, forty. He has made all his money himself, making a beginning in California when he saved up $1,000.

JAMES CRUM, of township 17 north, range 11 west, postoffice Arenzville, Illinois, was born in Clark county, Indiana, September 22, 1806. His parents were Matthias and Margaret (Spangler) Crum, the former born in Montgomery county, Virginia, of German ancestry, and the latter in Louisville, Kentucky, in the fort there. Her father was killed there by the Indians. They had twelve children, of whom James was the fourth. Only five of the family are living: Joseph lives at Paxton, Ford county, Illinois, and is a retired farmer; Isaac N. lives in Iowa, a merchant, farmer and preacher; Abraham A. lives in Morgan county, Illinois, farmer and wealthy citizen; John W. owns property in Jacksonville, a widower and well-to-do citizen; William died in Indiana; Christian died at Ashland; David died in Missouri; Samuel died from an accident received in California; Mary married Leander E. Cobb, killed by a horse in Greene county, Illinois; Elizabeth was the widow of Louis O'Neil, and she died in 1892, of the grippe.

James came to Cass county in 1830. The next year his father and mother came and took some land near that of their son, where both parents died. On coming here Mr. Crum and his brother, Christian, entered 160 acres and bought 240, which they divided equally.

He was married to Christine Ream, January 31, 1833. Her parents were Pennsylvanians who moved to Ohio, where she was born. They had a large family. David, deceased, was the eldest; Thomas Jefferson (see biography); James F., a Dakota farmer; Sarah Margaret, wife of Dr. J. F. Wilson, of Tullula, Illinois; Mary Elizabeth, wife of William Howard Thompson, lives in Jacksonville; William Marcellus resides on a farm near Virginia, Illinois; John went to Iowa and Kansas and returning settled in Chapin, Illinois; Amanda C., wife of William Henry Thompson and now lives in Kansas; Marquis L. (see sketch); Charles was killed on the railroad near Keokuk, Iowa, it being a very sad affair; he was a teacher in the high school and left a wife and five children.

Mr. Crum lost his first wife May 1, 1878. He since married Mrs. Eliza Bean, whose husband died in the army. She had two daughters by her first marriage. Mr. Crum has divided his property liberally between his children: most of them have received $10,000 and some a greater amount. Mr. Crum still owns a section of land where he lives, besides having extensive interests in personal property. Few men have been as successful as he in the accumulation of wealth. He has always lived well and endeavored to enjoy life as it came. He is a liberal in religious views and a believer in the Christian religion, to the support of which he has donated liberally out of his means. He has been a life-long Democrat, has voted twice for General Jackson, first in 1828 and again in 1832. Very probably there is not another man in this part of the State that can say as much. He has held various offices of responsibility and trust.

The ancestral history indicates that the Crum family have generally been tillers of the soil, of a hardy, long-lived family, usually successful in anything they undertook.

An event transpired September, 1891, which Mr. Crum will never forget, it being the occasion of their eighty-first birthday. The relatives from far and near came and enjoyed the jubilee. Photographers and newspaper reporters were in demand, as over one hundred relatives were present.

Mr. Crum came here poor and was surrounded by neighbors who were well-to-do at that time. Since then he has outstripped them all in accumulation of wealth. He has given his children more than $100,000 and still owns about $75,000 worth of property. When eighty years of age Mr. Crum competed at the Cass county fair for the old-gentleman's prize for best horseback riding and won it. The prize was a gold-headed cane, inscribed: "Presented to James Crum for the best old-gentleman riding, August 6, 1886."

HIRAM EVANS is a native of the Old Dominion, where he was born, in Washington county, November 4, 1810. His father was Robert Evans, an industrious and upright man, a native of the same State, and was there reared to manhood, and married and there resided until 1811, when he removed to Kentucky, and settled in the famous Rock Castle county, where he continued to reside for several years. He then removed to Woodford county, of the same State, and followed his trade, that of a carpenter, until the year 1853, when he sold out and moved to Missouri, and spent the remainder of his days in Ralls and Monroe counties. His wife, the mother of our subject, was formerly Sarah Peoples, a native of Washington county, Tennessee, who died in Rock Castle county, Kentucky, in 1813, while the family resided there.

After the death of his mother, Hiram Evans went to live with his cousin in Rock Castle county, and resided there until the age of fourteen years. He was then large enough and strong enough to be able to do something for himself, and accordingly joined his father and under his directions commenced to learn the carpenter trade. Thus he continued until the age of twenty years, when he started out on his own responsibility even with the world. He went to Louisville, Kentucky, and secured work at his trade, receiving one dollar and twelve and a half cents per day for his services, working from sunrise to sunset. Thus he continued at hard work for eleven months, when he went to Vicksburg, Mississippi, where he found employment at $60 per month and board. He followed the carpenter trade in Mississippi and Kentucky until 1836, when in June of that year he came to Bushnell, Illinois, and has here since resided. Illinois at that time was very wild, and deer and other wild animals roamed over the prairies. Mr. Evans entered a tract of 200 acres in Henderson and McDonough counties, but did not settle there. He commenced the business of contracting and building, at which he continued successfully for many years; but finally turned his attention to loan and general brokerage. His business life was successful throughout, and was characterized by industry and honesty. He is now well-to-do, and for the past few years has lived a retired life, enjoying the fruits of his labor, and well earned reputation.

In 1845, he was united in marriage to Miss Susanna Carrick, a native of Scott county, Kentucky, and daughter of William and Jennie (Campbell) Carrick. To Mr. and Mrs. Evans were born two children, both of whom died in childhood. Mrs. Evans died in 1849. Mr. Evans has been a useful citizen, and was formerly a Whig, but since the formation of the Republican party has served faithfully in its ranks.

The following interesting incident of early times is related in this vicinity. At that early day little or no attention was paid to the style of dress worn by either women or men. In fact it not uncommonly occurred that when a person attempted to assume a little extra style he was laughed at, if he was not absolutely jeered. On one Sunday a party of civil engineers, unusually well dressed and stylish, attended preaching at one of the Cumberland Presbyterian churches. It so happened on that day that the minister preached on the subject of the sinfulness of dress, and was so severe in his remarks that the party of engineers supposed he intended to be personal, and accordingly became very angry. They thereupon determined to have revenge. The following Saturday, provided with a goodly-sized bag of salt, they went to the church and thoroughly filled the corners and crevices of the same with salt, rubbing it thoroughly upon the steps and around the sides of the building. The next morning about the time services were to begin, all the cattle of the neighborhood seemed to have assembled around the church for a picnic. The people gathered and drove away the cows, but no sooner had they gone inside and begun services than the cattle returned apparently wilder than ever. It is needless to say that very little real devotion was shown in that church on that Sabbath-day. The engineers had their revenge.

CORNELIUS L. ATEN, proprietor of Browning Roller Mills, was born in Astoria, Fulton county, July 28, 1845, his parents being Richard and Ann (Peterson) Aten, both natives of Hancock county, West Virginia. He was raised on a farm and continued there until 1888, when he purchased an interest with Mr. Nagel in the Browning Roller Mills. Recently Mr. Nagel has withdrawn and Mr. Aten has become the sole owner of the mills, which are very valuable, being estimated at several thousand dollars. These mills have a capacity of seventy-five barrels, and Mr. Aten does an exchange business, dealing in grains of all kinds, for which he pays the highest market price. The products of these mills have such an excellent reputation that it keeps Mr. Aten very busy to fill his orders for flour, meal and feed. In addition to the mill property in Browning, Mr. Aten owns a farm of 140 acres in Astoria, and also at Summum, Fulton county, he owns the Home Roller Mills.

Mr. Aten is a Republican in politics, has been a Class-leader and Sunday-school Superintedent for many years, and the whole family take an active interest in the Methodist Episcopal Church and Sunday-school work.

He was married in Fulton county, November 19, 1868, to Susan M. Bryan, of that county. They have nine children, all living: Henry W., Mary Edith, Alta Emeline, Carrie Samilda, Thomas Richard, Sabina Mabel, Jeanette Ann, Chester Arthur and Walter Wayne. Mary E. is a teacher in the public school and all have enjoyed excellent advantages in the public schools.

FRANCIS ASBURY CLARK, a prominent farmer of section 32, Missouri township, has been a resident of Brown county since 1835. He was born in Logan county, Kentucky, September 11, 1820, and is of Scotch-Irish extraction. His father, Abner Clark, was the son of Thomas Clark, who came to this country some time before the Revolutionary war and died at Orangeburg, North Carolina, near the close of that struggle. A copy of his will declares him to have been a yeoman, and the document attests his strength of character and sterling integrity. His widow was left with six children exposed to the ravages of war and the smallpox. She was equal to the emergency. Abner, her youngest son, described her as tall and muscular, with great strength and unflinching courage. To a British officer who rudely demanded to know her political principles she replied: "Sir, I am a helpless widow with six children, but I am an American." She seems to have impressed the stamp of her character upon the family, which is distinguished for simple integrity and resoluteness. The date of her death is unknown, but it must have occurred soon after the death of her husband, for Abner was raised by a Quaker family, and further developed those habits of blunt frankness toward which he had a natural proclivity. In early life he came to Logan county, Kentucky, where he married Nancy Goram, and might have been rich in slaves had he not resolutely chosen free soil and set his face toward the forest and privations of Illinois. In 1835, bringing Francis A., the subject of this sketch, with him, he came to this county; "Dick," as Francis is still familiar known, drove a four horse team across the fire-swept prairies and bridgeless streams of western Kentucky, and central Illinois to Brown county.

The family, composed of the parents and ten children, settled in Missouri township, and soon succeeded in making a home whence the children went out to feather the nests of their own. In 1843 Francis took his new bride, Eliza, *nee* Rankin, into the woods of Pea Ridge township, and they set up in a log-house with a work bench for a table and other things in harmony. Industry and economy, inside and outside, soon transformed the wilderness into a beautiful field, and their empty house to a luxurious home, in which were born nine children, seven of whom are still living. The mother was Irish by birth, having come from Ireland to Philadelphia in her second year.

In that beautiful city she resided until her thirteenth year, and acquired the rudiments of education. At this early age she was taken from school and carried to section 36, Pea Ridge township, where, surrounded with a waste of almost tractless forests on the one side and a sea of prairie grass on the other, she wept in childish grief for the scenes and playmates from whom she was forever separated. She was united in marriage to Mr. Clark July 10, 1843, and the "heart of her husband safely trusted in her, and she did him good and not evil all the days of her life." "Her own works praise her in the gates, and her children rise up and call her blessed."

She died the 15th of February, 1867, leaving her husband with a family of children, some of whom were small, to mourn his bereavement. He soon after married Sarah E. Burk, a widow, with one lovely daughter, Alta Virginia, who, in her nineteenth year when blooming into beautiful womanhood was attacked by fever, to which her frail constitution succumbed.

Mrs. (Burk) Clark is an estimable lady, and has been a kind mother and faithful wife. Soon after his second marriage Mr. Clark came to his present home two miles and a half northwest from Mount Sterling, a farm which he had purchased some ten years before, and which he has finely improved.

His business life, which was "about cattle" rather than farming, though he did and had done much of the latter, has been one of almost uninterrupted success. Beginning while yet a boy by buying a heifer he continued until he became the largest stock dealer of the county and rarely handled either cattle, sheep, hogs, or horses without realizing fair profits. Careful trading with appreciation of values made him a handsome fortune, which he has carefully and equitably distributed by gift or will to his wife and children. In character he is a man affable in manner, sound in judgment, resolute in purpose, sincerely honest and reliable, proud that his paper is always at par. This quality, connected with large descretion and shrewd business instincts, is the key to his success in what he has undertaken. He never tried to succeed by being sharp, though he might have gained temporary advantage by shrewdness, but by being square.

In politics he has been anti-slavery from the first, believes in moderate tariff and today tends to the principle of prohibition as a means of dealing with the liquor-traffic.

In theology he is a Cumberland Presbyterian, but has never been identified with that church or any other. His children are like himself, prosperous, and are gathered round about him: Alexander H., well-known in the county, lives two miles northwest of the county seat; Catherine M. McMurry, his eldest daughter, just outside the corporation; William A. West, of town, one and a half miles; Abner and E. E. are members of the faculty of Chaddock College, Quincy, Illinois; Lydia McDonald, the youngest daughter, with her husband resides in section 36, Pea Ridge township, while Benjamin F. is still on the homestead. Few men sitting in the twilight of life have greater reasons for gratitude than Mr. Clark.

GEORGE W. ZIMMERMAN was born in Pike county, Illinois, August 5, 1837. He was the son of George and Mariah (Lutz) Zimmerman, of German descent. They came to America when young, and to Illinois in 1837, and settled in Pike county and built a frame house on a bit of wild land. He is still living on his farm as is also his wife.

Mr. George Zimmerman remained at home until married, in 1859, and helped his father on the farm. He received a fair business education in a neighboring school. After his marriage he rented a farm in this county, of his mother-in-law. He remained here for two or three years and then bought 100 acres, on which there were no improvements. He built a small frame house and lived in it for fifteen years, and then built a good farm house, in which he still lives. He has added to his farm until now he has 300 acres, while all he had to start with was one pair of horses.

He has held local offices. He voted first for Stephen A. Douglas on the Democratic ticket. When the Greenback movement started he took an active part in it, and still advocates its principles. He was a delegate to the State convention at Danville. He was made a delegate to the People's party Congressional convention at Roodhouse, as for several years he has been giving close and careful attention to their movements. He was elected from Roodhouse in the spring of 1892, to the national convention held at Omaha, July 4, 1892. Mr. Zimmerman is a very important man in politics in this part of the county. He has faith in his convictions and is not afraid to express them upon all occasions. He is president of the Alliance in this township.

He was married in 1859, to Miss Elizabeth Winters, born in Calhoun county, Illinois, a daughter of Peter and Willmina (Shaffer) Winters, who also came from Germany and died on the old farm in Brown county. Mr. and Mrs. Zimmerman have three children, William P., George H. and Nettie, all married. Mr. Zimmerman and his wife are members of the Methodist Church.

DR. CHARLES N. IRWIN, a resident of Mount Sterling, was born in Fayette county, Kentucky, August 30, 1827. His father, John M. C. Irwin, was born in the same county, and his father, William Irwin, was born in Virginia, although his father was born in the north of Ireland, of Scotch ancestry. He came to America in Colonial times and settled in Virginia, where he spent the remainder of his days. His son, William, was reared in Virginia, and after marriage emigrated to Kentucky with his family. The removal was made with pack horses. He located in Fayette county, which was at that time very sparsely settled. When about to trade some horses for some land the horses were stolen from him by the Indians, who were numerous and sometimes hostile. He purchased a tract of land eight miles from Lexington, on the Lexington and Frankfort road. There was a fort in the neighborhood, where the people used to repair for safety. He improved his farm with hard labor, and resided there until his death. The maiden name of his wife was Catharine McClay. She was born in Pennsylvania, of pure Scotch ancestry. She died on the farm in Fayette county. Their son, John, followed agricultural pursuits, and spent his entire life in his native county. He died in 1857. The maiden name of his wife was Martha Nourse, born in Mercer county, Kentucky. Her father, William Nourse, was born in England, where his parents spent their entire lives. He came to America in Colonial times, and was one of the pioneers of Mercer county, Kentucky, where he spent his last years. Mrs. Irwin died on the home farm in Fayette county. She was the second wife of her husband and reared three of her five children, Martha, Charles N. and George.

Charles was reared in his native State, receiving his early education there. In 1846 he came to Illinois, settling in Jacksonville, where he remained a short time and then came on to Mount Sterling, and commenced the study of medicine with Dr. Witty. He attended lectures at Jefferson Medical College in Philadelphia, and in June, 1850, commenced practice in Mount Sterling, which he continued until 1862, when he entered the United States army as Assistant Surgeon of the Third Illinois Cavalry, joining the regiment at Helena, Arkansas. They were with Sherman at the first attack on Vicksburg, and at the battle of Arkansas Post, in Grant's command at the battle of Milliken's Bend. Soon after this the regiment was detailed to do garrison duty on the Memphis & Charleston railroad, guarding different points. During that time the regiment made frequent raids into Mississippi. He continued with the regiment until he was honorably discharged in 1864. He then became Assistant Surgeon in the Provost Marshal's office of the Ninth Illinois District. Upon the resignation of Dr. Worthington as Surgeon, he was appointed his successor, continuing in this office until the close of the war.

In 1865 he bought an interest in the drug and hardware store of Dr. Stone, Dr. Burch being his partner. One year later Dr. Burch sold his interest to George Irwin. In 1877 Martin O'Neil purchased the interest of George Irwin, and the firm became Irwin & O'Neil, and have so continued until the present time. They carry a full line of drugs, agricultural implements, hardware, etc. Since the Doctor engaged in the drug business he has abstained from practice as much as possible. He is frequently called in consultation, besides being called in by former patrons.

He was married in 1851 to Isabella C. Dunlap, born in Fayette county, Kentucky. Her father, Rev. Latin W. Dunlap, was a native of New Jersey, but resided some years in Fayette county, Kentucky, from whence he came to Mount Sterling, and was the pioneer Presbyterian preacher here. He organized the first Presbyterian society here, where he was a resident until his death in 1889.

Dr. and Mrs. Irwin have one child, Nellie R. Their only son, Charles D., died in 1890. They are members of the Presbyterian Church, of which the Doctor is an Elder, and has been for many years. He is an ardent worker and takes a prominent part in the Sunday-school. He formerly was a Whig, and has been a Republican ever since the commencement of the Civil war.

HENRY GARM, of the firm of Garm & Son, was born in Altenburg, Germany, in 1830. He was but a small child when his parents landed in New York city. From there they proceeded to Washington city, but had not been there long when the father, John Garm, was killed by a horse on the roads of the county. He had been a hard-working man and his family felt his loss in a great degree. After some time Mrs. Garm left Washington city and proceeded westward and settled in Beardstown, Illinois, where she resided until the day of her death, at the age of sixty-three. She, like her husband, was a consistent member of the Lutheran Church.

Mr. Garm first engaged in farming when he came to Beardstown. The country was very new and uncultivated. After twelve years spent in farming he went into town, and in company with John H. Harris, now president of the First National Bank of Beardstown, purchased a large stationary saw-mill and for six years manufactured lumber, also engaged in the pine lumber trade with Mr. C. Hagener. He then sold his milling plant and engaged in the ice business with Captain George W. Goodell; after two years Mr. Garm organized a grain and transportation company and carried on an extensive trade in shipping grain to St. Louis, that he purchased in Beardstown and vicinity. This business lasted for four years, and then Mr. Garm entered the merchant tailoring business with his two sons. Robert H. attends to all the financial part of the business as well as being chief salesman, and John T. does the cutting. Mr. Garm is also interested in other local enterprises. He was one of the promoters of the First State Bank, and and is now vice-president and director, as well as an extensive stockholder. This bank was organized in 1889, and was the first bank chartered under the State law providing for the organization of State banks. He is a stockholder as well as a director in the Electric Light Company, is also a director of the Mutual Loan & Saving Association. When the wagon bridge was built across the Illinois river he took an active part in this improvement.

He has been an active politician and the Democratic party has rewarded him in many offices for his zeal and work in the interests of the party. He was twice elected County Commissioner, and is now serving a four-year term as County Treasurer, and he is also the County Assessor of Cass county. It has not been in county offices alone that he has served his party, but he has been extremely useful in the City Council for two terms. As he is one of the leading Democrats in the county, he has been chosen delegate to the State and local conventions a number of times.

Mr. Garm was married in Beardstown, to Mary D. Harris. She had come to the State of Illinois from England, when yet quite young, with the relatives of her parents. They settled in Cass county, and she has been since a resident of Beardstown. Mr. and Mrs. Garm have eight children three of whom are dead. Those still surviving are, Robert H., who married Tillie Dutch; John T., married to Minnie Lamoreux of Mason City, Illinois; Mamie, now the wife of Dr. Norbury, the head of the wards at the insane hospital at Jacksonville, Illinois; Joe E., completing his education at the Depauw University at Greencastle, Indiana; Frank, a graduate of the Beardstown high school, and still at home.

Mr. Garm and the oldest son are members of the blue odge and chapter, A. F. & A. M. The latter is present Master; the former has also served in the same capacity for three terms previously.

Mr. and Mrs. Garm are regular and consistent members of the Methodist Episcopal Church. Mr. Garm is a man of which his town feels proud, as well it may, for he is one of the representative men, not only of his town and county, but of the State to which he came so many years ago.

HARRY J. CRUM, of township 17 north, range 11 west, section 24, post office Virginia, was born in Morgan county, near Prentice, November 24, 1863. He is the son of William A. and Nancy (McHenry) Crum. The McHenry family were among the first settlers of the county. Mr. Crum came here about 1860, and was married. They first lived in Morgan county, and then removed to the eastern part of the State, where he now resides. Harry is the eldest of a family of eleven children, nine of whom are still living. The grandfather was William Crum, brother of James Crum (see biography of James Crum).

Harry was educated in Mattoon, Illinois, in the high school of the place. He lived most of his life in Coles county, but came to this county in 1883, locating on the farm where he now lives.

He was married February 26, 1890, to Mrs. Ida C. Bowers, whose maiden name was Crum, daughter of Robert Crum, and third cousin of Mr. Harry Crum They have one child, Robert A., born December 30, 1890.

Mr Crum is a Democrat in politics, and his wife is a member of the Methodist Episcopal Church. He is a young man of intelligence and progressive ideas. He had a good financial start in the world, which, combined with his industrious habits, will make him one of the foremost men in the county.

A maiden sister of the mother of Mr. Crum resides with him, Miss A. M. McHenry. She is a lady who is a fair representative of the settlers of Cass county. She owns 300 acres of land adjoining the farm of Mr Crum, which is highly cultivated Mr Crum's farm consists of 160 acres in a high state of cultivation

GILDEROY SETTLES, one of the largest landowners in Schuyler county and a man of great force and integrity of character, is the subject of the following biography It is fitting that the history of such men be preserved to the coming generations, that they may have some idea of the vicissitudes and privations and trials which beset the path of those sturdy pioneers which prepared the way for the onward march of progress. To this worthy band belongs Gilderoy Settles, who was born in Fulton county, Illinois, November 14, 1837; one of seven children: Polly Ann, Gilderoy, David J., Serena, Penina, Nancy and Josiah. His father, William Settles, was a native of Tennessee, and emigrated from that State to Illinois, becoming a pioneer of Fulton county; there he was united in marriage to Peggy Carlock, a daughter of Abraham and Mary A Carlock; he spent more than fifty years in Fulton county, but died in Morgan county, Illinois; his wife died in Fulton county; their son Gilderoy was reared to the occupation of a farmer, and remained under the parental roof and guidance until he was twenty years of age; he then began to face the world laying the foundation of the fortune which has since attended his path. He rented land, as he had no capital to invest, and managed in this way until 1859, when he made his first purshase of eighty acres, at $10 per acre; there was a log cabin on the place, and this was the extent of the improvements, but it was truly a home, the first he could call his own.

Mr. Settles was occupying this quiet little place, when in March, 1865, he enlisted in Company I, Third Illinois Cavalry; he joined the regiment at Springfield, and did garrison duty until October of the same year; he was then honorably discharged, returned to his home, and resumed the pursuit of agriculture. The following year he bought another farm in the same township, and afterward sold the farm he had first purchased, he resided in Browning township until 1871, and then removed to land he had bought in Frederick township, this was his home until 1884 when he bought the farm on which he now lives; this tract consists of 204 acres in an advanced state of cultivation and improved with excellent buildings; besides this Mr. Settles owns another farm of 200 acres in the same township, 120 acres in Oakland township, and 160 acres in Clark county, Kansas

In 1857 he was united in marriage to Miss Penina Tracy, who was born in Fulton county, May 24, 1835, one of the eight children of her parents: Perry, Leonard R, Mary A., Thomas C., Penina A., Minerva, Arminda and Cynthia A. Her father, Lyman Tracy, was born in the State of New York, and came to Illinois when a young man, he was one of the early settlers of Fulton county, lived there a few years, and then removed to Missouri; at the end of seven years he came to Schuyler county, and settled in Browning township, where he passed the remainder of his days, his wife, Annie Carlock, died on the farm in Browning township. Mr. and Mrs. Settles are the parents of six children: Leander, Florentine, Logan, Doran, Charles and Orpha. Politically Mr. Settles affiliates with the Republican party

EDWARD GUINN HALL, deceased, was born in Baltimore, Maryland, September 10, 1810 His father, Washington Hall, whose parents were Dutch, was uncertain whether his birthplace was in England or Maryland. He was engaged for a number of years in the wholesale mercantile trade, at the end of which period he removed to Cecil county, same State, where he resided upon a farm for fifteen years, when he returned to Baltimore, where retired from the cares of trade he enjoyed in tranquillity the fruits of a well spent life, dying a good old age, respected by all who knew him. His wife, whose maiden name was Guinn, bore him seven children, namely Edward, Washington, Samuel, Charles, Richard, Ann R. and Achsah.

Edward Guinn Hall was reared and educated in Baltimore He graduated when he was seventeen years old and was admitted to the bar before he attained his twenty-first year. Soon thereafter he settled upon a 600-acre farm owned by his father in Cecil county, living there until the year 1838, in which year he removed to Illinois and took up his residence in what is now known as Rushville township, on land which he inherited from his father He continued to reside there until his death, which occurred July 28, 1857.

He was a man of good, strong sense and excellent judgment. A sound patriot, he took active interest in the affairs of his country. An admirer of old "Tippecanoe" and "Harry" Clay, each of whom received his vote for President, the defeat of the latter sat heavily upon him. He was an ardent Whig and at the organization of the Republican party in 1854 he identified himself with that organization, continuing a faithful member of it to his death Being educated himself, and thoroughly appreciating the advantages of knowledge, he desired his children should have the benefit of a liberal education, which wish his widow carried out

He was married, August 26, 1845, to Priscilla Baker, born in Flemingsburg, Fleming county, Kentucky, April 9, 1825. Her father, Francis Baker, was a native of Maryland, having been born near Baltimore When a young man he removed to Kentucky, engaging in farming in Fleming and Maysville until 1837, when he emigrated with his wife and four children to Illinois, making the entire journey overland. During that winter he visited in Indiana, and in the following spring settled in section 7, Rushville, where he bought a tract of land At that time the country was sparsely settled and frame houses were the exception, the people being well satisfied to own log cabins. Wild turkeys and other game were abundant and the trusty rifles of the neighbors kept their tables well supplied with this kind of food. Mr. Baker died there in 1844, aged eighty-seven years, universally mourned He was a soldier during the war of 1812

The maiden name of Mrs. Hall's mother was Mary Magdalene Brandenburg, who was born in Berlin, Germany, and who died at the home of her son, Dorsey Baker, while on a visit, February 16, 1858. Her home was at Mrs. Hall's. When a girl Mrs. Hall attended the Black Jack school, a house built of logs resting upon underpinning of logs, with slab seats and heated with a fireplace. She resided with her parents until her marriage. Mrs. Hall is the mother of seven children, namely: Achsah A., Washington, Charles, Melinda, Mary, George Edward and Richard. Mrs. Hall is a lady of intelligence and great worth and is held in great esteem by all who know her. Her days pass peacefully and she is happy in the consciousness of having done well the duties and responsibilities of her station.

DAVID CARR was born on a farm in township 18, range 10, Cass county, Illinois, February 21, 1842. As one of the prominent and highly esteemed citizens of this county, and as the son of an early pioneer, biographical mention of him is appropriate on the pages of this volume. We accordingly present the following facts in regard to his life and ancestry:

John Carr, grandfather of David Carr, was born (tradition says) in Ireland, his parents having come from Ireland to America and located in Philadelphia, where they died soon afterward. Thus, left an orphan at an early age, he was reared by strangers. He located in Ohio, and resided there till 1825. In that State his son, David Carr, father of the subject of our sketch was born. In 1825 the Carr family started for the far West. It is said Mr. Carr's destination was the Platte Purchase. He was accompanied not only by his wife and seven children, but also by his son Elisha's wife and two children, and Peter's child, its mother having died in Ohio. They took passage on a keel-boat down the Ohio river to Shawneetown, and from there wended their way northward with teams. They struck the Sangamon river bottom in the locality known as Bluff Springs. Attracted by the natural beauty of the country, they concluded not to go further; selected a site about six miles up the river, and made permanent settlement. At that time there were very few families residing in the present bounds of Cass county, Indians being much more numerous than whites, and all the land was owned by the Government. Mr. Carr at once made claim to a tract of Government land on section 6, township 18, range 10. It is said that the family had but seventy-five cents in cash among them on their arrival here. The first thing he did was to build a log house. No nails whatever or sawed lumber were used in its construction. He rived boards to cover the roof, and they were held in place by poles which were laid lengthwise of the cabin. He made a puncheon floor, and built his chimney of earth and sticks on a rock foundation. For some time there were no flouring mills nearer than St. Louis. Mr. Carr took a section of a log, hollowed out the top, and in that pounded his corn, using the finer part for bread and the coarser for mush. Cornmeal, wild game and fish constituted their chief living. As there was no improved land here and no market for grain even if they had it to sell, the question was how to raise the money to pay for the land, even at $1.25 per acre. The lead mines of the vicinity of Galena were then attracting attention, and in the fall of the year some of the male members of the family walked to Galena, and worked in the mines through the winter. In the spring they returned and continued the improvements they had commenced on the land, afterward working several seasons at Galena. In this way the father and sons earned money with which they acquired large tracts of land in the Sangamon river bottoms. The grandfather resided here until the time of his death. The maiden name of his wife was Sarah Wolliver. She was born in Pennsylvania, of German ancestry, and died on the home farm. She reared seven children: Elisha, Peter, William, James, Benjamin, David and Jemima.

David, the youngest son, came with them to Illinois in 1825, and resided in the parental home until the time of his marriage, when he located on the place where his son David was born and now resides. Here he passed the rest of his life. His wife was before her marriage Julia A. Wells. She was born in Wheeling, Virginia, and died on the home farm.

David Carr, the subject of our sketch, received his education in the pioneer log school houses, the schools being taught on the subscription plan, each family paying according to the number of pupils sent. When a mere lad he commenced to assist in the farm work, and was actively engaged in agricultural pursuits till the breaking out of the war. At the first call for troops he enlisted in the State militia, served one month, and then enlisted in Company A, Fourteenth Illinois Volunteer Infantry, serving until June 24, 1864. During his time of service he was in Missouri, Kentucky, Tennessee, Mississippi, Alabama and Georgia. He took part in nineteen different engagements, the most important of which were the battle of Shiloh and the siege and capture of Vicksburg. He was honorably discharged June 24, 1864, his term of enlistment having expired, and returned home. After his return he located on that part of the homestead which he now owns and occupies. He has bought other land and is now the owner of 305 acres, the home buildings being located on section 8, township 18, range 10.

December 11, 1867, Mr. Carr married Maggie McNeill. She was born in Cass county, Illinois, daughter of Lachlan McNeill; their union resulted in the birth of six children: Florence N., Julia, William D., Lizzie J., Carrie E. and Chalmer M. Mrs. Carr died May 25, 1890.

Mr. Carr is independent in his political views. He is a member of the Cumberland Presbyterian Church, of which he has been Ruling Elder for a number of years.

PETER THOMAS, Supervisor of Cooperstown, was born in Brown county, in 1842. His father, William, was born in Fayette county, Ohio, in 1809, and came to Illinois October 1, 18—, bringing his wife and one daughter. He and his brother-in-law joined teams, and they came emigrant fashion, being four weeks on the way. He took possession of a log cabin in Brown county, in what was then Schuyler. Here he lived four years, making some improvements, which land he sold and then entered 120 acres of Government land. This was wild land, on which he built a rough house, went to work and cleared up a fine farm, where he lived until 1860. He came with but enough means to reach here, and had three bits left when he crossed the Illinois river at Beardstown. Before long he had made enough to obtain a deed for his land, which was in 1837, and he moved on it in February, 1838. His wife was Julia, daughter of Morton and Sarah (Stivers) De Witt, both natives of Kentucky, where this daughter was born. They came to Ohio in 1815. Mr. De Witt died in Texas in 1836 or 1837, and was no doubt killed. His wife died in Brown county in 1857, aged seventy-five. She was the mother of six children.

Mr. Peter Thomas left home for the battle-fields in July, 1862, in Company D, Eighty-fourth Illinois Infantry (Captain Davis), at nineteen years of age. He enlisted as a Corporal, served three years and then was promoted to be Sergeant. His first engagement was at Perryville, where he had the usual experiences of a raw recruit, and the next engagement was Stone River. Here over one-half of the regiment were killed or wounded. The next battle was at Chickamanga, where the loss was heavy. During his three years' service he was confined in the hospital three weeks, and detached some eight months, guarding prisoners at Nashville, Tennessee. They were active in the Cumberland campaign, and the last fight of note of their regiment was in front of Nashville, Tennessee, December, 1864. Mr. Thomas was mustered out at Springfield, June, 1865, and arrived home soon after.

He was married December, 1868, to Irene, daughter of Fielding and Amanda (O'Neil) Glenn. She was born in Brown county, although her parents were Kentuckians, who came to Illinois in 1830.

Mr. and Mrs. Thomas began married life in a log cabin on his father's farm, but at the expiration of three years he bought fifty-five acres, part of his present home, which is now 220 acres. He paid $825 for the fifty-five acres. His next purchase was 152 acres in 1878, costing $1,800; later he bought fifteen acres for $325. He built his present comfortable frame house in 1886, and one barn in 1878, and the second one in 1887. He has under the plow 115 acres, and the balance is in woodland and pasture. He grows wheat, corn and hay, and raises horses, cattle and sheep. He keeps fifteen to forty head of cattle, good stock of dehorned and Shorthorns. He has fifteen head of draft horses which he has bred, and has also a fine Percheron stallion.

They have buried an infant son, and four children are living: Charles S., Oliver O., Daisy E. and James W. They have enjoyed good schooling and are very intelligent. Mr. Thomas has served the township as Road Commissioner and Town Clerk, and was elected Supervisor in 1891, which office he is filling to the satisfaction of his county. He is a member of the Farmers' Alliance and Industrial Union.

LEONARD SERROT, who is well-known throughout Schuyler county as a progressive and intelligent agriculturist was born in Scioto county, Ohio, September 12, 1832, son of Peter F. and Nancy (Patton) Serrot. The paternal grandparents were born in the city of Paris, France, and emigrated to America to take up part of a tract of land that was granted to La Fayette, near Portsmouth, Ohio; there they settled and passed the remainder of their lives. Peter F. Serrot lived in Ohio until 1835, and in the fall of that year removed to Illinois; he made the trip with four horses and a wagon, and was accompanied by his wife and eight children. He first settled in the village of Rushville, and the following spring bought the land on which Leonard Serrot now lives; the tract consisted of 160 acres, and the consideration was $300; there were no improvements, and the land was heavily timbered. He, Peter F., erected a log house which was then regarded as a very superior structure, and which furnished a shelter several years, when it was replaced by a more modern edifice. Mr. Serrot was an old-time Whig, but joined the Republican ranks upon the formation of that party. He died at the home of his son, John, aged seventy-six years; his wife, Nancy Patton Serrot, was born in Ohio, and died at the old homestead, at the age of fifty-six years. Leonard Serrot spent his boyhood and youth at home with his parents. He was married January 4, 1855, to Miss Evelina Thompson, who was born in Cecil county, Maryland, April 6, 1834, a daughter of Ezekiel and Mary (Thompson) Thompson; her father was a native of Pennsylvania, and emigrated to the West at an early day, and was one of the honored pioneers of Schuyler county; he died at the age of eighty-two years, and his wife survived to the age of eighty-four years; they reared a family of seven children. Mr. and Mrs. Serrot each received a fair education in the common schools, and are the parents of two children: Millard F. was born December 24, 1855; he is one of the prominent teachers of the county, and has followed the profession ten years; Mary E. was born May 4, 1860.

After his marriage, Mr. Serrot lived on the home place for thirteen years, and then embarked in the grocery trade in Ripley, Brown county, conducting the business from 1868 to 1871. He is now engaged in general farming. For more than forty years he has been a member of the Methodist Episcopal Church, and has lived a life consistent with its teachings. In politics, he adheres to the principles of the Republican party. He is a member of the Grange, and in all movements for the benefit of the public he takes a deep interest. He has always employed strictly honorable methods in his business relations, and enjoys the highest regard of his fellowmen. Six years ago he erected one of the handsomest houses in the county.

The paternal great-grandfather of Mr. Serrot was Captain of a French man-of-war, and was very prominent among the seamen of his day.

EDWARD S. FRANK, for many years a prominent resident of Brown county, and identified with the busines interests there, was born in Davidson county, North Carolina, May 23, 1848, His father, William Frank, was born in the same county, and his grandfather, Peter, was born in Pennsylvania of German ancestors. He emigrated to North Carolina and was an early settler of Davidson county. He bought a tract of land on the Yadkin river and engaged in farming there, where he spent the rest of his days. William Frank was reared and married in North Carolina, and came from there to Illinois in 1852. The removal was made overland by teams. He located at Buckhorn and there established the post office of which he was the efficient Postmaster. It was kept in his house at that time. His house was in section 33, of what is now Lee township. He followed his trade of gunsmith and resided there eight years, and then removed to the locality known as Mt. Pleasant and still lives there. His wife's name was Sarah, daughter of Godfrey and Martha (Merrill) Winkler.

Edward S. Frank was four years of age when his parents brought him to Illinois.

He was reared and educated in Lee township, and at the early age of fourteen he began to assist his father in the shop, being a natural mechanic, he soon developed into a first-class workman. He finally established himself in the blacksmith business at Mt. Pleasant and continued there nine years, then closed out that branch of the business. In it he lost less than one hundred dollars on account of bad bills, and never sued a customer. He was married in 1878, to Martha J. Morehead of Butler county, Pennsylvania, a daughter of James and Margaret (Monks) Morehead. She is a member of the Baptist Church, and they are the parents of two children, Nona Ruth and Jama E.

He saw the need in that section of a regular undertaking business, and he opened a business of that nature and continued in it successfully for thirteen years. In 1891, failing health compelled him to change his occupation and he sold out this business and bought the farm where he now resides, one mile southeast of Clayton, where he is now engaged in raising sheep, breeding recorded Shropshire sheep. Sheep-raising is not a new business to him. While he was in the blacksmith business he bought a tract of rough land and in clearing it up he stocked it with sheep, so that he has been in the sheep business for upward of twenty years. While in the undertaking business he found it necessary to divert his mind in some way. In this way he began in his leisure hours to make a study of sheep, and he is now thoroughly acquainted with the subject of sheep farming and breeding for vitality. He has raised different breeds, including Merinos, Cotswold, Southdown, Oxforddown and Leicester, and has proven that the Shropshire are by far the superior all-around sheep.

Mr. Frank is a Republican in politics. He has one of the most beautiful homes in the east side of Adams county. It is located on an eminence and is partially surrounded by a beautiful glade. From the natural scenery his home takes the name of the Crescent Glade. Mr. Frank is one of the most prominent men of this section. He is a thorough business man and all his enterprises, which have been many, and has been entirely successful. It would be well if all the men in the county were as well informed, honest and reliable as is Mr. Edward S. Frank.

AMOS HARSHEY, who is well known throughout Schuyler county as a leading farmer of Littleton township, was born in Westmoreland county, Pennsylvania, October 13, 1847, a son of Jacob and Bethiah C. (Barnes) Harshey. His father was a native of the same county, and in 1858 he emigrated to the West, locating near Rushville, Schuyler county, Illinois; after seven years he sold the land he had taken up at that time, and bought the farm now occupied by our subject; here he passed the remainder of his life, his death occurring at the age of forty-nine years; his wife is a native of Westmoreland county, Pennsylvania, and is still living, a resident of Littleton township. Her parents emigrated to Schuyler county in 1859, and were living here at the time of death.

The youth of Mr. Harshey was a quiet, uneventful one, and he was at home until after his marriage. He was united to Miss Marissa R. Prather, September 10, 1872, and they are the parents of one child, Ethel G., born January 24, 1877. Mrs. Harshey was born in Jefferson county, Ohio, April 5, 1848, a daughter of James and Barbara (Young) Prather; the parents removed to this county in 1851, and the father died here at the age of eighty years; the mother is still living.

After his marriage Mr. Harshey engaged in farming on his own account, renting land for a period of five years; at the end of that period he bought his present home, which he has occupied since. He has 130 acres of fertile land in a high state of cultivation. He carries on a general farming business, and by good management and industry makes the business profitable. In politics he affiliates with the Republican party; his father and grandfather were Whigs before the organization of the Republican party, but after its formation they joined its ranks. In 1892 he was elected Supervisor for a term of two years. He and his wife are members of the Presbyterian Church, and are actively interested in the work of this society; he is an Elder, and for many years has been superintendent of the Sabbath-school. He belongs to Friendship Lodge, No. 24, I. O. O. F.

CHARLES HILL, a retired farmer of Mt. Sterling, Illinois, was born in Cooperstown, Brown County, Illinois, November 14, 1834. His father, Robert Hill, was born in North Carolina, and was at the battle of New Orleans in the war of 1812. He was the son of John Hill, who was a General in the Revolutionary war. He was reared and married in his native State and resided there until about 1825, then came to Illinois and was one of the first settlers of Schuyler county. He resided near Rushville for eight years and then moved to that part of Schuyler, now included in Brown county, where he bought a tract of timber land. The log cabin in which our subject was born was the same in which the father resided until his death. The maiden name of his wife was Elizabeth Angel, who lived in North Carolina and was the daughter of John Angel and died at the home of her son-in-law, in Cooperstown.

Our subject was reared in his native State, where he married. He attended the pioneer schools, taught in the log house. In his youthful days there were but few improvements in the county and deer and other kinds of game were plentiful. He resided with his parents until his marriage, and then engaged in farming on his own account and was an active and successful farmer for many years and now lives retired in a beautiful home in this city.

Mr. Charles Hill has been married three times, the first time to Miss Farrington, and she died on the home farm in Cooperstown township. His second marriage was to Mrs. Ella Crooks, and she died at the age of thirty-two years; and his third marriage was with Miss Lizzie Irwin. This lady was born in Mt. Sterling, September 6, 1850. She was the daughter of Willam and Mary A. (White) Irwin. Her grandfather, John Irwin, was a native of Fayette county, where he spent his entire life and died at the age of eighty years. The father of Mrs. Irwin was born in Woodford county, Kentucky, April 15, 1840, and reared and married in his native State. He came from there to Illinois, in 1839, and was one of the pioneers of Brown county. He settled on section 1, of what is now Mt. Sterling township. Here he improved a farm and lived until his death, July 30, 1887. His wife returned to Maysville, Kentucky, in 1830 and died August 12, 1870. The maternal grandparents of Mrs. Hill were James and Elizabeth (Browning) White, natives of Kentucky and pioneers of Pike county: later they moved to Macoupin county and died there.

In politics our subject is a firm supporter of the principles of Democracy and upholds the party measures upon all occasions. In religious matters Mrs. Hill is an active and zealous member of the Presbyterian Church.

DARIUS RUNKLE was born in Champagne county, Ohio, February 10, 1813. He was the son of William and Mary (Pence) Runkle. William was born in Virginia and went to Ohio in an early day, following his trade of tanner until about 1850, when he came to Illinois, rented a farm in Morgan county and lived there until the close of the war. He then came to near where his son now lives, and died, aged eighty-four. His wife, also born in Virginia, died at the same place, aged eighty-six. The Runkles came from Germany, and the grandparents of Darius lost their parents on the trip over to this country.

Darius is one of ten children, four of whom are yet living. He remained at home until twenty-one years of age, working at the tanning business and farming. He had very limited schooling and is entirely a self-made man. After he was twenty-one years old he worked for $10 a month for two years and then clerked for a brother-in-law in a general store in Sidney, Ohio, for two years more. He then started for Illinois, coming to Beardstown, and then walked over to Doddsville, wading two miles in water. This was in the spring of 1837, and he came to take charge of Samuel Dodd's general store. He continued in that for a year and one-half, and during that time entered eighty acres which later he sold and then bought 160 acres of wild land where he now lives. He also bought another eighty acres in the timber. In the fall of 1838, he returned to Ohio and remained with his father working in the tan yard for two years, and then came back here and commenced improving his farm. He broke forty acres, built a story-and-a-half house, and on October 12, 1840, he married Ann Maria Walker, who was born in Adams county, Pennsylvania. She was the daughter of Andrew Walker of Adams county, Pennsylvania, who came here in 1840, and settled on Mr. Dodd's farm. Mrs. Runkle was one of nine children. Mr. and Mrs. Runkle have ten living children. The sons are: James J., William, Charles W., Joseph C. and Stephen A.; and the daughters: Mary A., Laura, Liny and Clara J. Mary A. had two sons and four daughters: Clara J. two daughters and two sons; both the mothers are deceased.

After marriage Mr. and Mrs. Runkle moved into the log house he had built, and remained there until 1866, and then moved into his present fine home, which is one of the best in McDonough, having cost $10,000 and being first-class in every particular. Mr. Runkle has built four or five different times where his sons live, and has bought thee farms with houses upon them. He commenced with $90, and had to borrow $10 to enter his first eighty acres. He now has 3,000 acres of land, 970 in Schuyler county and 1,940 in McDonough county, and he has given each son a fine farm. He makes a specialty of fine stock, and has been engaged in various kinds of business during his life. In 1841 he bought a stock of goods, and was a merchant for two or three years, and was Postmaster in 1843-'44: he also kept a stage. He was Supervisor of School Boards for years, and he with two others built the first schoolhouse in this district, and it also served as a church. He also loaned money to build a pioneer mill and tried to get a railroad through this section. He has helped many a deserving and worthy object. His wife has been a church member ever since their marriage, being one of the first to take an active interest in church and Sunday-school work in the place. She was very active in everything tending toward the building of churches and schools, and was a most worthy companion to as public-spirited a man as Mr. Runkle. Her death occurred in 1889. Mr. Runkle can count his friends by the number of his acquaintances and his enemies are not known. He treats every one well, and the deserving are never turned away without help and words of cheer. Politically he has always affiliated with the Whig and Republican parties. He voted first for Henry Clay, and at the birth of the Republican party voted for Fillmore. He is very well satisfied with Republican principles.

ROBERT NEWMAN, an extensive farmer of Cass county, Illinois, dates his birth in that part of Grayson county now included in Carroll county, Virginia, August 31, 1834. Jesse Newman, his father, was born in Botetourt county, Virginia. He learned and followed the trade of cooper, and in connection with his trade also operated a sawmill. He resided in what is now Carroll county for a number of years. From there he came to Illinois, resided in this State twelve years, and then went back to Virginia, where he is still living. His wife, the mother of Robert, was before her marriage Miss Nancy Bedsall. She was born in Virginia, and spent her whole life in that State. She reared six children.

The subject of our sketch was reared in his native State, and was there married when he was nineteen years old. Accompanied by his bride, he came to Illinois the fall after their marriage, making the western journey via the Ohio, Mississippi and Illinois rivers, at that time the most expeditious route, and landed at Beardstown. He was in very limited circumstances at that time, being unable to go to housekeeping for want of means. He was industrious and persevering, however, and at once found work on the farm, at $15 per month. Little of the land in this section of the country was then improved, most of it being owned by the Government. It was not long after his arrival here till Mr. Newman purchased a squatter's claim to eighty acres of land, in section 9, township 18, range 9, for which he paid $8 per acre. There was a rude log cabin on this place, the cover of which was made of boards rived by hand, there being no floor at all. They at once took possession of the place, and as soon as Mr. Newman could get the money, bought from the Government, under the graduation law, paying twelve and a half cents per acre. As there were no improvements on the land and he had no team, he continued working by the month a portion of the time, putting in his spare hours in grubbing on his own land. This he continued for twelve years. At the time he located on it, his land was covered with a heavy prairie grass, prairie fires having run over it every year and checked the growth of timber. Deer and other wild game abounded here. There were no railroads in the county for some years, and all produce was marketed at Beardstown. The price of grain was low, corn selling as low as ten cents per bushel. Mr. Newman has been very successful as a farmer, has purchased other tracts of land at different times, and is now the owner of 554 acres. Of this amount 245 acres are in Mason county, the rest being in Cass county.

The maiden name of Mrs. Newman was Mary Mangus. She was born in Roanoke county, Virginia. Their union has been blessed by the birth of two children, viz.: Sarah, who married Thomas Wortman, and has seven children; and Alexander, who wedded Ellen Cunningham, and has six children.

JOHN GLANDON was born in Harrison county, Ohio, February, 1834. His father, William, was born in 1780 and moved to Harrison county, Ohio, where he bought a small farm. His wife was Mary Magdalene Peacock, of German descent, probably born in Maryland. Her father was Robert Peacock, a soldier of the Revolution and he laid his land warrant for 160 acres on the historical Mt. Vernon home. She was one of five children, and her parents were stirring farmers of that time and died in Ohio, at an advanced age. Mr. Glandon is one of eleven children, all of whom came to an adult age and became heads of families, but all have passed away except five. The father was an honest, hard working man, but did not accumulate much wealth and died at the age of seventy. His wife was much younger than he and survived him many years. She spent her last years at the home of this son, but while on a visit to McDonough county, in 1866, she died there, aged seventy-two.

Mr. Glandon had but very limited schooling, as he had to work hard in early boyhood. At the age of twelve he carried the mail for one year for his uncle from Cadiz, Ohio, to Cambridge, a distance of forty-two miles. This he continued daily, except Sunday, and this year's experience will never be forgotten. He worked on the home farm from the age of thirteen to sixteen, when he engaged as salesman, on the road in Ohio, Pennsylvania and Virginia, in the fanning-mill business. He was a success at this for two years. He then returned to the home farm, where he remained until the death of his father. He then took the contract to build two miles of railroad in Harrison county on the Pan Handle road. He next went to Kentucky at the mouth of the Big Sandy river, where he built two miles of road on the Lexington & Big Sandy. This, however, was not very profitable. He had married in Harrison county and with his wife and one child he came to Illinois. His wife was Delilah, daughter of Joseph and Catherine (Wood) Banister, both of whom were from Maryland. They first bought 125 acres, at $13 dollars an acre in 1855. Upon this place there were a small log house and a rude stable. Since then from time to time they have added ten to twenty acres at a time, until he now owns 985 acres, all fenced in and 700 acres under culture. Nearly all of this is good, arable land. Much of it is very fertile and is very desirable as it is all in one body. When he built his first large barn, 40 x 70, with basement, it cost him $25,000. It is one of the best barns of the section, with solid stone basement. About six years later he built his second barn in which he can stall 100 head of cattle and ten head of horses. He built his present large farm house in 1885. These buildings are on an eminence, nearly 100 feet above the bottom lands and commands a view of over 500 acres. He grows from 400 to 500 acres of corn, yielding sixty bushels to the acre. He rents much of this land to small farmers, for twenty bushels to the acre. He believes in a rotation of crops and has for twenty-five years fed from fifty to 150 head of cattle. Of late years he feeds less and sells his corn. During the war he kept sheep, as high as 1,700 of the Merinos, and sold his clippings one year for $1 per pound. In 1882 he bought the Brooklyn Water Gristmill of which he had to rebuild the lower portion and put in the roller system. This cost a great deal of money, but proved a great succes for three years. Custom came from far and near, and they had more than they could attend to, as there was no other mill like it nearer than Quincy; but other mills of this kind sprang up and Mr. Glandon moved his machinery to Walker, Ellis county, Kansas, in 1888, but within two years he exchanged it for property in Denver, Colorado. The result of this investment is yet to be seen. Mr. Glandon has all he can do to look after his tenants and business, but he has often followed the plow and swung the ax. He has served as Commissioner and has filled all the minor offices. He always votes the Republican ticket.

In 1865, he, in company with William Hornley, went to Graystone, Texas, by teams for an aged couple who had been stranded there. This journey of about 2,000 miles took from October 4 to December 1. It was an arduous, dangerous journey at this time of civil strife, and strong and resolute as they both were they were glad to land here safely with those dear old people, and the two sons of Mr Hornley who had been left in the South.

Mr. and Mrs. Glandon have four children: Belinda Jane McKelvie, of Clay county, Nebraska; James William, residing in Denver, Colorado; Mary Alice Fowler, on a farm close by; and Edgar Denis, now taking a course at the Eureka College, Illinois. He took one term at Knox College, where his brother John was educated. Mrs. Glandon has always been frail in health, but still superintends and does much of her housework. There are but few finely located homes as this one.

HENRY W. OETGEN, farmer and stock-raiser of Frederick, Illinois, was born near Beardstown, March 10, 1849. His parents, William and Katherine (Middlebusher) Oetgen, were natives of Hanover, Prussia. The father was born May 31, 1817, the mother December 23, 1823. They came to America with their parents when quite young, the paternal grandparents locating in Pennsylvania, and the maternal grandparents came straight to Beardstown.

Our subject was the third child of his parents. He received his education in the public schools of Cass county. He then engaged in farming, which has been his life work. In the fall of 1882 Mr. Oetgen purchased the farm on which he now resides and moved there the following spring. He owns a stock and grain farm of 260 acres, besides some town property in Frederick, all very valuable. His residence is a modern cottage, beautifully located and nicely furnished.

He was married in Cass county, March 13, 1879, to Miss Augusta C. Hansmier, daughter of Henry and Kate (Smidt) Hansmier. Her parents were natives of Germany and both came to America with their parents prior to marriage. The paternal grandmother and two daughters died on the voyage. The grandfather located in Wisconsin, where he remarried, afterward coming to Beardstown, where the father of Mrs. Oetgen married and now resides.

Mr. and Mrs. Oetgen are members of the German Lutheran Church. They have two children: Arthur H. and Inez Hallie. Mr. Oetgen is of straight Republican faith. He has served one term as Tax Collector of Frederick township and is a member of the M. W. of A.

WILLIAM SEWALL, one of the earliest settlers of Cass county, Illinois, was a son of Major-General Henry Sew-all. He was born January 17, 1797, in Augusta, Maine; received a good business education at home, and also took a short academic course. In 1818, at the age of twenty-one, he obtained a clerkship in Washington, but on his way thither was shipwrecked, which event entirely changed his plans, for, in working the ship's pumps his hands were so badly frozen as to render it impossible for him to fill the position. He then spent a year teaching school in Maryland, Virginia and West Virginia, when, in addition to the common branches he taught also bookkeeping and the higher mathematics, including astronomy, navigation and surveying. To illustrate these he used the best brass-mounted terrestrial and celestial globes, with maps, charts and other appliances.

He was married August 9, 1821, to Mrs. Elizabeth W. Adams, who was born in Charles county, Maryland, July 27, 1795, a daughter of Samuel W. Middleton, an extensive planter. Mr. Sewall removed with his family to Jacksonville, Illinois, in the fall of 1829, and while residing there he again taught school. He was present at the organization of the First Presbyterian Church in Jacksonville, and he and his wife were among its first members.

In the spring of 1833 he removed to his farm of 640 acres, entered from the Government and partially opened a short time before. It was in the Sangamon bottom, near the present site of Chandlerville. At that time it was a wilderness which the Indians had not yet wholly abandoned. Here, as was his custom, he zealously engaged in Sabbath-school and other Christian work, and exerted on the new and growing community an influence for good difficult to estimate. Within a radius of eight or ten miles he organized three or four Sunday-schools, one of which was at his own house, where he conducted it for a considerable time, with only the assistance of his wife. They furnished free to each family a large cloth covered Testament for use in this work. Afterward, in the secular schools, these became the only reading books for many of the children for a number of years. By their constant zeal and Christian labor they were instrumental in preparing the way for the first church organization in the vicinity, the First Presbyterian, but afterward a Congregational Church, and located at Woodstock, now Chandlerville. Mr. Sewall was elected its first ruling Elder and Sunday-school Superintendent, and these offices he continued to fill with efficiency as long as he lived. He was a man of extensive reading, and rather in advance of his time—a pioneer in material improvements as well as morals. He had the first washing-machine, the first cook-stove and the first threshing-machine ever used in the county. He also brought the first Durham stock of cattle into his neighborhood, and made the first brick, which were of unsurpassed quality. Shortly after his death his widow bought the first harvesting-machine ever used in Cass county. He also was a good singer and performed on the flute He lived a very useful life in all respects; and although called from his labors in the prime of life, he won the confidence, respect and esteem of all who knew him, and succeeded in laying the foundation for a competency for his family.

Politically, he was a Whig, but never prominent in public affairs He was thoroughly posted, however, on the political questions of the day, and prompt to express his opinion through the ballot-box

He died at his residence near Chandlerville, Illinois, April 7, 1846, at the age of forty-nine years His widow survived him about thirty years, and to her was left the task of educating a large family of children, and of managing the many interests of an extensive farm. She was successful in settling up the estate to advantage, showing great energy and executive ability. She removed an incumbrance on the farm in a very short time, and thus succeeded in saving the place intact for the family Two or three years after the death of her husband she removed to Jacksonville, Illinois, to educate her children, where they received a good training A short time before her death she changed her residence to her daughter's, Mrs J H Goodell, at Chandlerville, where she died October 5, 1874, aged seventy-nine years.

Mr and Mrs. Sewall had two sons and four daughters, as follows:

Henry M., born near Warrenton, Virginia, March 6, 1823, educated at Illinois College, Jacksonville, married Mrs Ann E Clark, formerly Miss Higgins, November 22, 1849, and settled on a part of his father's farm, where he died May 3, 1850, aged twenty-seven years At his father's death, although a Methodist, he was chosen Superintendent of the Congregational Sunday-school, at the age of twenty-three, to fill his father's place. After filling that place for a year or two he was appointed Class-leader in his own church, which position he filled until his death. He had one son

Catharine T. H., born near Warrenton, Virginia, November 6, 1825, educated at Monticello Seminary, married Robert Cole, a farmer of Cass county, and died November 5, 1854, having had three sons and two daughters

Susan E., born in Harrison county, West Virginia, July 29, 1829, graduated at Jacksonville (Illinois) Female Academy in 1851, married in 1867 Abiel Fry, Sheriff of Muscatine county, Iowa, and after his death married, in 1878, Rev. William Barnes of Jacksonville, at one time pastor of the Congregational Church at Chandlerville, she is now a widow, residing at Jacksonville, with no children.

William W , born in Jacksonville, February 11, 1832, graduated at the Illinois College, same city, in 1856, and from that time until 1885 made his home at Virden, this State, where he married Susan E. Cox, in 1858 Enlisting in the Union army during the last war, he served three years, engaging with his regiment in a number of important battles, was severely wounded at the capture of Mobile. After the war he established the North Star Flouring mill, and was for seventeen years a joint proprietor of the same. For many years he was successively Deacon, Trustee and Ruling Elder of his church, the Presbyterian. He now resides at Carthage, Missouri, having two sons and two daughters.

Mary M., born near Chandlerville, July 15, 1834, educated at Jacksonville Female Academy and married Addison L Cole, in 1853. She resided on a part of her father's farm, where she died April 16, 1857. She had five sons.

Harriet A., born near Chandlerville, April 4, 1838, educated at Jacksonville Female Academy, married in 1865 John H. Goodell, a lumber merchant of Chandlerville, where she still resides, having three sons and three daughters.

JOHN HENRY CARLS is a general farmer and stock-raiser, living on sections 24 and 25, township 17, range 12. He was born in Hanover, Germany, December 23, 1831. He grew up in his native province, a farmer boy, but at last decided to come to America. Not wishing to cross the sea alone to the new country, just before he sailed he was married to a neighbor girl whose maiden name was Mary Yoost. She came of a good German family, and proved to him a good wife. Immediately after marriage they took passage at Bremen on the sailing vessel Theodore Connor, and landed in New Orleans after a passage of eleven weeks. From there they went up the Mississippi river to St. Louis and thence to Beardstown. Mr. Carls' ambition was to become a farmer, and he and his wife began in a small way have been very successful.

In 1845 he first purchased forty acres of land, and has since increased his possessions until he has now 240 acres here, and 200 acres in an adjoining township. He has improved the land very much, and has erected excellent buildings.

Mr. and Mrs. Carls are members of the Lutheran Church, and are regarded as very excellent citizens. Mr. Carls is a Republican in politics. He and his wife have ten children, two deceased. Lizzie was the wife of Charles Meyer, but died in the prime of life, and Henry died when two years old. The living children are: William, a farmer in Morgan county, married to Anna Hagener; Mary, wife of William Talkemeyer, of this township; Lena married Gustaff Anoldi, a farmer in this county ;Anna married William Uush, a farmer in Morgan county; Harmon, a farmer in Cass county, married Katie Uush; Tilda married William Jockisch, a farmer in Morgan county; George, farmer in this county, married Dora Linker; and Carrie married William Lovecamp, a farmer in Cass county. They are among the best of our German citizens, and are highly respected by all who know them.

HIRAM M. BACON of Huntsville settled in Schuyler county in 1863. He was born in Hancock county, August 12, 1836. He was a son of Benjamin and Elizabeth (Brevard) Bacon, natives of South and North Carolina. Mr. Bacon, Sr., came West in an early day, and first went to Missouri and then to Illinois and settled in Hancock county in 1835, being one of the pioneers of Augusta. He was a merchant at an early day at Pulaski, later entered land and engaged in farming. He had over 1,000 acres of land. His death occurred in 1860, aged sixty-five years. His wife survived him some twenty years, and was over eighty years old when she died. They had nine children: Alvin G.; Robert; Lamira, deceased; Lois E., deceased; Benjamin F., deceased; Margaret C., Hiram, William H. and Mary E.

He was reared on a farm in Pulaski, and followed farming as his occupation. In 1863 he settled in Birmingham, and has since resided there, and at Huntsville. He followed farming until 1885, then engaged in business at Huntsville, which he continued three years. Since which time he has not been engaged in active business. He owns 180 acres of land.

He was married at Huntsville in 1861, to Miss Emily Louisa Everson, a daughter of Nathan and Cynthia (Cooley) Everson, of New York State. She was born in New York. Mr. and Mrs. Bacon have one daughter, Hila L., married to David E. McCreevy, of Huntsville. They are Methodists in religion, and Mr. Bacon is an ardent Republican in politics. He and his wife are valuable members of society.

WILLIAM TALKEMEYER is a successful farmer of Arenzville, now living on his own fine farm, section 23, township 17, range 12. He was born near Arenzville, this county, in 1849. He grew up and obtained all the education possible in the common school. His father, William Talkemeyer, was a native of Prussia, Germany, and was the first member of his family to come to this country. He came some time in the '30s, landing in New Orleans, and was engaged as a Mississippi boatman. Later he came to Beardstown and engaged in farming, purchasing his first land in Arenzville. About 1855 he purchased a good farm, the same now occupiedby our subject. Here Mr. and Mrs. Talkemeyer, Sr., lived and worked hard, and by honest, economical living, managed to obtain 240 acres. Here they spent their lastyears, Mr. Talkemeyer dying in 1878, aged seventy, and his wife about 1850, when our subject was only a year old. She was a Miss Duvall, who was born and reared in Germany, but came to the United States when a young woman. She and her husband were both members of the Lutheran Church, and he had been a Republican.

William was one of four children: himself and a Mrs. Lizzie Crone, of this county, are all that are now living.

He was married, near Arenzville, to Miss Mary Carles, who was born, reared and educated in Cass county, and was the daughter of J. Henry Carles (see biography). Mrs. Talkemeyer is a fine woman, and has proved herself a good wife and mother, and is very highly respected throughout the community. They have five children; one, George, having died when young; Elizabeth, wife of Henry Bill Smith, a farmer in Morgan county; Lucy, William Henry, H. Robert and Harry are at home.

The political faith of Mr. Talkemeyer is Republican, and he and his wife are highly regarded members of the Lutheran Church.

Mr. Talkemeyer's present farm consists of 600 acres, very well improved and watered by Indian and Bear creeks. He has been very successful, and has everything in first-class order around him.

ISAAC MEATS was born in England, in 1836, December 9, in Herefordshire, son of Isaac and Elizabeth (Lawford) Meats. Isaac, Sr., was born in 1812 and was a farmer. Marrying in 1842, he turned his face for the United States, sailing from Liverpool. Landing in New York he went from there to Chicago, and from there to the Mississippi river, down which he sailed until he came to St. Louis and landed at Griggsville. The trip from Liverpool to New York took five weeks. Mr. Meats brought his wife and four children with him and five more were added to the family after arrival in this country. Mr. Meats first rented in Elkhorn township until 1863 and then bought ninety acres in Hancock county, where he lived until 1868, and then sold out and moved to Woodford county, Kansas, and bought 300 acres of land partly improved. He later sold that and traveled in California for a month or two, then went to Benton county, Oregon, and bought a small farm, where he lived in retirement until his death, at the age of seventy-four years. His wife was born in the same place as he, and she still lives in Benton county, Oregon, with her son, William. Mr. and Mrs. Meats, Sr., were members of the Methodist Episcopal Church for years. Mr. Meats was an old-line Whig and later a Republican. He first voted the Republican ticket for John C. Fremont.

Isaac C. Meats, Jr., lived at home until he was twenty-six years old, working on the farm. He enlisted in 1861, September 5, in Company I, Thirty-third Illinois Infantry. He was mustered out November 24, 1865, at Vicksburg. Mr. Meats receives a pension for injuries received which confined him in a hospital and from which he has never recovered. Part of the time Mr. Meats served in special detached service. After he was discharged at Fort Butler, in 1865, he returned home and spent the winter visiting. In the next spring he went to Hancock and resided there for two years, and in 1869 moved to his present farm and rented for several years. He was so well satisfied with the land that he bought 185 acres, known as the old Winslow farm. Here he has lived ever since. He has been a Commissioner for six years, succeeding Mr. McDonald. He has also held various other offices, among which was Trustee for several years.

He was married, March 4, 1866, to Martha Ingram, born in Pike county, April 17, 1842, a daughter of Henry and Paulina (Kingston) Ingram. The former was born in Smith county, Tennessee, December 1, 1815. He came with his parents to Illinois and settled in Pike county, in 1856; from there he moved to Brown county and bought a farm in Elkhorn township, of 200 acres. Here he died, January 7, 1890. He was a son of John and Rachel Ingram, also of Tennessee, who came here in 1850 and died when very old people. Mrs. Meats was one of six children. The family were all mechanics.

Mr. and Mrs. Meats had eight children, Mary E. residing in Hancock county; George is at home; Fred J. is also at home; Jessie, deceased; Nellie; Francis; Dollie and Ralph.

Mr. Meats is a member of the G. A. R. of Versailles. The family are attendants of the Methodist Episcopal Church. Mr. Meats is a member of the I. O. O. F., Irene Lodge, No. 72, at Versailles, and has held different offices in the order. He is a Democrat in politics and voted for S. A. Douglas. He and his wife are highly respected members of the township in which they live.

THEODORE SCHAAR, dealer in guns and manufacturer of adjustable screens of his own patent, doing business in Beardstown, Illinois, was born in the Province of Posen in Prussia, where he grew up and was educated. From the time he was a small boy, he began to be educated in his native language, and also in that of Latin, French and English in the college of his native town, graduating from it when he was seventeen years of age. He is the son of Carl Schaar, also a native of Posen, who spent his life there and died when an old man He was a skilled musician and a manufacturer of all kinds of musical instruments, being so known in his native country He had taught his children the art of music, and our subject has been a successful and skilled teacher on different instruments. His mother, whose maiden name was Willhelmina Borkenhagen, lived and died in her Prussian home, having been a good wife and mother.

Theodore was the first of the family to come to this country, but he has since been joined by his brother, Charles, now a music dealer on State street, Chicago. He came to this city in 1861 and has since been a resident of the place His adjustable screens are sold extensively to the trade and he employs some eight or ten men all the time. This business was established two years ago and has been built up successfully He is one of the leading public-spirited men of Beardstown, holding the office of Alderman, with which he has before been honored. He is a member of the Board of Equalization of the Twelfth Congressional district, and he has filled that office with credit to himself and acceptably to his constituents. He has taken an active part in local politics, having been a delegate to the Congressional and county conventions. He returned to his native land in 1871, and came back to Beardstown after a pleasant visit.

He was married in 1870, to Miss Johanna Kulhen She was born in Posen and was there reared and educated. She and her brother Fred, a farmer in Colorado, are the only members of the family now living in this country. Mr. and Mrs Schaar have two children· Clara, wife of W T Quirk, now a train dispatcher of Jacksonville, on the Jacksonville Southeastern railroad Mrs Quirk was educated in music in a conservatory in Chicago, and was a teacher until her marriage Martha, a recent graduate of the high school at Beardstown, is the other daughter Mrs. Schaar and the children are members of the Lutheran Church.

Mr. Schaar has stood by the Democratic party, in whose ranks he has been a leader ever since he came to the United States.

HON LEWIS D. ERWIN, formerly of the Illinois State Legislature, now living in retirement in Rushville, was born in Plattsburg, New York, July 1, 1815. His parents were Cornelius M and Lucinda (Fairman) Erwin, both natives of Vermont, the former having been born in Fairhaven, Rutland county, and the latter being a daughter of James Fairman, a man of some prominence in his State.

David Erwin, paternal grandfather of the subject of this sketch, was a native of Newark, New Jersey, and was an able soldier in the Revolutionary war He was with General Washington at the second crossing of the Delaware river and at the retaking of Trenton He afterward went from his native town to Fairhaven, Vermont, where he established a nail factory In 1804, he removed to Franklin county, New York, engaging in the lumber business near Westville, and there spent the rest of his days His wife, formerly Catherine Munson, and a native of New Jersey, also died in Franklin county

Cornelius M. Erwin removed with his parents to New York State, and was engaged with his father in the lumber business in Franklin county He was a resident of Plattsburg until the breaking out of the war of 1812, when he entered the service and was assigned to the Quartermaster's Department. In 1830 he removed to Ohio, then the frontier of civilization, locating in Birmingham, where he operated a sawmill, the country abounding with excellent timber. Four years later he went to Toledo, then a mere village, where he worked at blacksmithing for a short time, later engaging in the grocery business, in which latter occupation he continued until his death in March, 1837. His devoted wife died in Birmingham, Ohio, in August, 1833. They were the parents of six children: Catherine, David, Eliza, Lewis D., George W. and Phoebe.

Lewis D., whose name heads this biograpy, remained with his father, assisting him at the forge until he was twenty-one years of age, when he commenced life on his own account, engaging in clerking. He resided in the Buckeye State until 1839, when he removed to Illinois, making the journey by team, through a wild and sparsely settled country. He secured a position as clerk in Erie, then a small town on the Illinois river, in Schuyler county, which was quite a thriving little center. In 1841 he purchased his land in Schuyler county, near Littleton, on which he engaged in farming. Ten years later, he came to Rushville, which has ever since been his home.

Mr. Erwin was married in 1843, to Elvira Wells, an estimable lady, and a daughter of Charles and Elizabeth Wells. They had eleven children: David D.; Catherine; Matilda; Eliza; Elizabeth L.; Emma; Lewis D., born in 1859 and died in 1887; George L.; Anna C.; Sophie B.; and Edward, who died in infancy. In 1875 the family was called upon to mourn the loss of the devoted wife and mother, who had subordinated her interests to their welfare. She was a woman of rare Christian character, and much esteemed in her community.

The subject of this sketch cast his first vote for Martin Van Buren, ever since which time he has supported the principles of the Democracy. Being a leading man his constituents have conferred upon him various offices of trust and honor, the duties of which have been discharged with ability and fidelity. In 1844 he was appointed Deputy Sheriff, and in 1850 was elected Sheriff. In 1852, he was made Circuit Clerk, to which position he was re-elected in 1854. In 1846 he was elected a member of the Illinois State Legislature, his efforts in that body receiving universal commendation, as shown by his reelection to the same position in the years of 1856, 1858 and 1860, thus serving five sessions, including the extra session at the breaking out of the war.

Such universal endorsement makes further encomiums on his character and qualifications unnecessary, as they are so plainly indicated that "he who runs may read."

MARCUS WHETSTONE was born in Adams county, Illinois, March 6, 1838, son of Abija and Lucinda (Brunton) Whetstone, the former born in 1804, in Ohio, near Cincinnati, following farming when a young man. His father ran a distillery near Cincinnati, where he died. Abija was married in 1832 and then moved to Indiana, where he worked on a farm for twenty-four years. In 1834 he sold out and came to Illinois and rented in Adams county and later bought wild land on which stood a log cabin, where they lived until three years later, when he built a frame house. He lived there until 1853 and then came to this county for three years, returning to Adams at the end of that time. He bought the farm where Marcus now lives, in 1850. He died in Missouri, at the home of a daughter, aged eighty-one years. His father, Nathan, was in the war of 1812. Subject's mother was born in Pennsylvania and came with her parents to Ohio at an early date, and later to Indiana. In 1834 she came to Illinois and settled in McDonough county, later, moved to near Quincy where her mother died, aged eighty years, her father dying at her home, aged ninety years. Mrs. Whetstone is still living with her oldest child in Augusta, Illinois. She and her husband had eleven children, seven yet living. All are farmers as far as known, although one of her brothers is a school teacher, having followed that profession all his life, and one of her daughters follows the same profession. Marcus' people came overland to this State with teams and four yoke of oxen. Mr. Whetstone, Sr., had but very little cash when he came to Illinois, but he was industrious and soon had his farm paid for. He and his wife were church going people and active in any good work, he being instrumental in building several churches and schoolhouses. He started with eighty acres of land, but kept buying more until at his death he had nearly 1,300 acres. He was a good, hard-working man.

Marcus remained at home until twenty years of age, working on the farm, driving oxen and attending the district school in the winter. When he was nine years old he broke prairie and has been one of the hardest-working men in this county. When he had reached the age of twenty he rented the farm on which he now lives, from his father. There were no improvements but the house which was built in 1854. He originally had 160 acres which his father gave him, and he has added to this farm until he has 740 acres of as fine land as there is in central Illinois. He has made numerous improvements on this land.

He was married in 1863, to Clara Tare, who was born in Schuyler county, daughter of Jacob and Nancy (Buck) Tare, natives of Ohio, who came to Illinois in 1834, and died in this county. Mrs. Whetstone was one of eight children, seven yet living. Her family were generally farmers, except a few who were mechanics.

Mr. and Mrs. Whetstone have had eight children, four living, Mary E., married to W. E. Melvin and they have three children: Mattie F., Hattie E. and James G. at home. They are all well educated and graduated from the Augusta and Bushnell schools. Mr. Whetstone cast his first vote for S. A. Douglas and his next one for Abraham Lincoln. He is a Republican and his family were of the Democratic faith, being old-line Andrew Jackson men. He has filled the office of Supervisor for nine years and has also held other offices, among which are Justice of the Peace and Assessor, the former for eight years and the latter for three. He also has been a School Director. Both Mr. and Mrs. Whetstone are attendants at the Methodist Church, of which she is a member. The family are among the most respected and honored in the county, and the entire family are upright in their dealings, commanding the respect of all who know them.

THOMAS W. WATTS, the oldest and leading merchant of Huntsville, is numbered among the pioneers of 1838. He was born in Scott county, Kentucky, November 5, 1834. His father, Simeon Watts, was also a native of Scott county, being born in 1806. He was a farmer, and in 1829 married Harriet D. Scott, and resided in Kentucky until 1838, when he removed to Illinois and settled on a farm near Rushville, where he purchased land, and resided there about five years, and then removed to Brown county and settled on a farm, four miles north of Mt. Sterling, where he pursued farming until 1878, when he removed to Huntsville, where he passed his remaining years and died in 1886. His wife died in Huntsville in 1890. They had nine children, of whom eight grew up. Mary Smith resides in Huntsville township; John F. also resides there; Horace W. resides in Greensburg, Kansas; Simeon was a member of the Christian Church and his wife was a member of the Missionary Baptist Church. He was a poor man when he left Kentucky, but became a successful farmer in Illinois. He had a well improved farm of 240 acres and dealt considerably in real estate.

Thomas was reared and educated in Illinois. He was raised a farmer, but in 1859 he engaged as a clerk in a store in Rushville, where he stayed five years. He then went to Des Moines, Iowa, where he loaned money and also operated a shingle and lath mill, and while thus engaged lost one finger of his right hand. He then went to Mt. Pleasant, Brown county, Illinois, where he became a merchant, but in 1866 he resumed his business in Huntsville, where he has since continued. His brother, Horace, was his partner for some ten years in a large general store. He owns eighty acres of land near Huntsville, also 320 acres in Hall county, Nebraska, 160 in Kiowa county, Kansas, and 160 in Grant county, Kansas. He also is the owner of good property in Huntsville at Wood river, Nevada, at Ford City and Huntington, Indiana, most of which is well improved, and he has made all of this himself.

He was married in 1859 to Nancy A., daughter of Isaiah and Mary (McCarl) Lewton, who were pioneers of Huntsville township. Mr. and Mrs. Watts have five children: William O., Secretary of the Building and Loan Association of Huntington, Indiana; Laura Snyder of Caldwell, Kansas; Fred L., at home; Salena Denny, of Augusta, Illinois, and Frank, still at home. In politics Mr. Watts is a Democrat and has held local office, but only takes enough interest in politics to perform duty as a citizen. His business requires all his time. He is a prominent member of the Methodist Episcopal Church and a very successful man in every way.

PAULIN CAMPBELL, a successful farmer and truck raiser, was born in Gloucester county, New Jersey, October 14, 1849. His father, David, was a native of New Jersey, who was the son of Thomas, who was born, lived and died in the same State. He was a successful farmer and he had built up a large property and had given his children all a farm together, and the place was known as Campbelltown. David grew up in his native State and became a prominent man in a local way. He was successful in life as a farmer, truck grower and lumber man, furnishing lumber to house builders in that community. He gave liberally toward the upbuilding of the Methodist Church and was Steward in it for many years. He died at his home about twelve years ago. His wife had been Ann E. Nelson. Her ancestry was similar to that of her husband's and she lived and died at her home, her death occurring in

1870. She was a good wife and mother and was devoted to the Methodist Church.

Paulin is one of six children and grew up in his father's business. When twenty-one years of age he came to Illinois and has since lived in Cass county. Mr. Campbell makes a specialty of sweet potatoes. He owns a good farm of 120 acres, in section 7, township 18, range 11. He has been in the county since 1872, has lived on his farm since 1880, and has owned it since 1882.

He was married in this county, to Miss Jennie Johnson, born near Brighton, Illinois. She was educated chiefly in New Jersey. Her father was Samuel Johnson, who grew up a farmer in New Jersey, and soon after his marriage to Ann E. Hiles, who came to Illinois and settled on a farm near Brighton. He there engaged in farming, but was accidentally killed while pressing hay. His wife is yet living, the wife of John Elliott.

Mr. and Mrs. Campbell are prominent young people, the parents of one bright boy of eleven, named Roy.

FRANS H. D. KRUSE was born in East Friesland, Germany, in 1821. His father, Dierk Kruse, son of George Kruse, was born in the same place. The father of the present subject learned the trade of millwright and followed it in his native land. He bought several important mills-ites erected mills and set them in successful operation, and sold them. In 1835, he came to America, in the Virginia, a ship sailing from Bremen, bringing with him his sons, Frans H. D. and Sunke M., and landed in New York, July 4.

From there he went to Albany, by way of the Hudson river, thence across to Schenectady, and by Erie canal to Buffalo, thence by lake to Cleveland and from there by land and the Ohio river to Cincinnati. He afterward went West into Illinois to Beardstown, and a few months afterward bought a mill on Sugar creek, ten miles east of Rushville. Six months later he sold the mill and bought a small farm two and one half miles east of Rushville and turned his attention to farming. Here he resided for eight years, when he returned to the old country. Some years afterward he returned to America and settled in Texas, remaining there five years. He afterward came to Illinois and bought a farm in McDonough county. This farm was exchanged for a farm five miles southwest of Rushville in Woodstock township, where he lived until his death in 1860.

The mother of the subject of this sketch was Hiske J. Miller. She was a native of the same country as her husband, and spent her entire life there. She had five children, all of whom grew to manhood, the present subject being the youngest, who was in his fourteenth year when he came to Illinois with his father. The country was but sparsely settled at that time, and some of the land was still owned by the Government. Frans assisted his father at the mill and afterward in cleaning out the farm. As the land was heavily timbered they were able to build a small frame house on it. In 1843 he bought the farm of his father and has had his residence here ever since. Good, substantial buildings have since been erected upon it, and the farm is in a high state of cultivation.

He married, in December, 1843, Elizabeth C. Garrett, who was born in Georgetown, Scott county, Kentucky, in April, 1824. Her father, Thomas Garrett, was born in Delaware and was the son of David Garrett, who lived for many years on the line between that State and

Pennsylvania and spent his last days there. The father of Mrs. Kruse went to Kentucky when a young man, and married in Lexington, Susanah Wigert, who was born in Maryland and went with her parents to Kentucky, while she was an infant. After her marriage she removed to Georgetown with her husband, and some years later again removed with him to Illinois by way of the Cumberland, Ohio and Mississippi rivers. Mr. Garrett made several removals in Illinois and spent the last few years of his life near Browning, Schuyler county. The mother of Mrs. Kruse survived her husband for many years, and died at the residence of a younger daughter, who was a resident of Nebraska, at the advanced age of ninety-one years.

JACOB D. GERRISH, born in Brown county, Illinois, March 12, 1861, is the son of Sewall and Elizabeth (Grove) Gerrish. He owns part of his father's farm, and lives with his mother. In politics he is a Democrat. His father, Sewall Gerrish, was born in Boscawen, New Hampshire, March 18, 1809; came to Brown county September 8, 1836; ran a sawmill on McGee creek, and later was a farmer. He was a Democrat in his political faith, and held several township offices. He was married January 8, 1846, to Elizabeth Grove, who was born in Virginia, February 22, 1825. Sewall Gerrish died May 17, 1879. He was the son of Lieutenant Stephen and Hannah (Ames) Gerrish. His father, born April 16, 1770, died November 11, 1815. He invented the first practical auger for boring logs and pumps, also the attachment of the screw to the pod auger. With his father he used to make the mill saws and cranks on the common forge. He was one of the first in New Hampshire to make cut nails.

February 7, 1796, he married Hannah, daughter of Lieutenant Samuel Ames; she was born January 14, 1776, and died November 18, 1834. Stephen Gerrish was the son of Colonel Henry and Martha (Clough) Gerrish. His father, born May 3, 1742, died May 16, 1806; married Martha, daughter of Jeremiah Clough, November 10, 1763. She was born November 10, 1742, and died October 15, 1826.

Henry Gerrish was the son of Captain Stephen and Joanna (Hale) Gerrish. His father, born January 22, 1711, died in 1788, in Boscawen, New Hampshire. He married Joanna Hale, July 15, 1741, who was born in June, 1715, and died in 1792.

Stephen Gerrish was the son of Colonel Joseph and Mary (Little) Gerrish. Colonel Joseph lived in Newbury, Massachusetts, and was a member of the Colonial Legislature twenty years. He married Mary Little, February 26, 1703. She was born March 20, 1682, and died January 1, 1765.

Joseph Gerrish was the son of Colonel Moses and Jane (Sewall) Gerrish. Colonel Moses Gerrish, born in Newbury, Massachusetts, May 9, 1656, married Jane, daughter of Rev. Henry Sewall, September 24, 1677. She was born in Badesly, England, October 25, 1658, and died in January, 1717; he died in 1694. Colonel Moses Gerrish was a son of Captain William and Joanna (Oliver) Gerrish. Captain William Gerrish was born in Bristol, England, August 20, 1617; came to New England in 1639, and settled that year in Newbury, Massachusetts; was the first captain of the military band in that town, and representative in 1650-'54; married Joanna Oliver, of Newbury, April 17,

1645, who died June 14, 1677, and he moved to Boston in 1678. At the semi-centennial anniversary meeting of Boston, March 14, 1686, Captain Gerrish opened and closed the exercises with prayer. He died in Salem, Massachusetts, August 9, 1687.

Elizabeth (Grove) Gerrish, daughter of Joseph and Catharine (Staley) Grove,—he of Baltimore, Maryland, and she of Lynchburg, Virginia,—came to Illinois in 1826, settling in Sangamon county in 1828; came to Elkhorn township and entered land. She died in 1846, and he was married a second time, to Elizabeth (Hunter) Clamp in 1851, and died in October, 1858. Mrs. Gerrish is one of twelve children. All are prosperous farmers, mostly in Missouri.

Grandfather Jacob Grove was born in Pennsylvania, and died in Virginia. His wife, Margaret (Garinger) Grove, was born in Virginia, and died in Maryland. Grandfather Stephen Staley died in Virginia, and his wife, Barbary (Yeasley) Staley, died in Virginia. She was born in Germany.

Mrs. Gerrish was the mother of ten children; eight are yet living. Hannah married Fred Wenneker, and has four children,—Frank F., Henry G., August C. and Katie M. Harriet married Samuel C. Gerrish, and has three children,—Nettie M., Harry E. and Carlos A. Martha married George E. Richardson, and has five children,—Otis E., Josie L., Sewall H., George E. and Nina L. Samuel S. married Addie Hargus, and they have two children,—Myrtle C. and Loren E. Josephine married Joseph J. Moore, and they have six children,—Joseph G., Edith M., Frank G., Harlan E., Dallas J. and Mabel C. Mary E. married P. C. Sweeny, and has one child,—John. Jacob D. and Cynthia are at home. Her people came to America in 1717, and settled in Pennsylvania. The first was John Grove, who came from Holland,—a Quaker. Some were in the Revolutionary war. The family belong to the Presbyterian Church, and are highly regarded in the county.

CHRISTIAN S. KRUEGER, a farmer of sections 22, 3, and 14, township 17, range 12, was born on the farm he now owns in 1846. He was reared on this farm, and has since lived on it. His father, John, was a native of Hanover, Germany, who grew up and was married there to Mary Hendricker, of the same place. After the birth of two children, in 1839 the family decided to come to America. They came from Bremen, and after many weeks, landed in New Orleans, coming from thence to Beardstown. He purchased the land where he lived and died, the latter event occurring August 11, 1873, in the seventy-fifth year of his age. He was a good, hard-working man, always very quiet and peaceable. He was a Lutheran, and embraced the Republican political faith. His wife, who was also a good Lutheran, died at the age of sixty.

Our subject is the younger of four living sons, a sister having died young. The children are: Henry, a farmer in Morgan county; John and Fred are farmers in Nemaha county, Kansas.

Christian was married in Cass county, to Elizabeth Meyer, who was born May 10, 1853, in this county, and was reared and educated here. She was the daughter of Charles and Minnie (Rusch) Meyer, natives of Prussia, Germany, who came to the United States in the '40s, and made a settlement on a farm in section 17, Cass county, afterward selling that and buying land in range 17, township

12, where they died, both past the age of sixty years. Mrs. Krueger is the youngest of her father's children, and she with the eldest, a brother, Charles H., a farmer in this county, are the only members of the family living.

Mr. Krueger is a Republican, and he and his wife are active members of the Lutheran Church. They have eight children: Christian V., Minnie K., Henry E., Charles F., Lydia N., John F., Amelia M. and Benj. H. Mr. Krueger now owns 160 acres of land, which he purchased from the heirs of his father's estate, having owned it eighteen years. He has improved it, and is considered one of the most success ful farmers of the county.

JAMES M. READ was born in Birmingham township, October 2, 1842. He was the son of Amasa Read, who was born in Massachusetts, and Jane, *nee* Henderson of Ohio. The grandfather, with two brothers, came to America from England when they were young men, and followed farming. Amasa and two brothers came to Ohio at a very early day, and settled at Xenia. In 1837 Amasa sold out his land, and with a wagon came overland to this county. He traded his team to some men to build him a house. In 1837 he went back and brought his family and settled on the farm where our subject now lives. When he came back the house was not finished, and he was obliged to rough it for nine months without doors or windows. The most of the children were born in this old log house.

James was one of six children, three yet living. His father died in the old log house five years after coming here at the age of sixty-six years, and his wife died in 1890, aged eighty years. Amasa Read ran a clock factory in Ohio, and when he first came to Illinois he started a nursery. He was an old-line Whig, and voted for William Henry Harrison.

James remained at home until his marriage, January 3, 1871, to Sophia King, daughter of Louis and Harriet King, who came to Huntsville, Illinois, in 1838 or 1839, and are still living. Up to the time of his marriage, James worked at home, attended the district school, and went one year to Abingdon Seminary. John Brown, of Harper's Ferry fame, was an own cousin of Mr. Read. Mr. and Mrs. Read have five children: Effie M., Ellen J. and Eliza S., now in school at Augusta, and preparing for college; George M. and James M., are both at home.

After his marriage he still lived on the old farm where he had bought out all of the heirs. Later he sold eighty acres, leaving him 240 at present. He has built a fine house and barn, and has as good a farm as is in the county, on which he raises a good deal of stock. He voted first for Lincoln, and has been a Republican ever since. Mr. and Mrs. Read attend the Methodist Episcopal Church. Mr. Read joined the Methodist Episcopal Church at the age of nineteen. His sister, Eliza J., at the age of twenty-six taught kindergarten in Chicago, and is now the wife of Rev. J. T. Sunderland. Mr. Read has a delightful family and a very fine home.

JOHN SCHULTZ, of the firm of Schultz & Baujan, proprietors of the Home Mills and Elevator, located on the south bank of the Illinois river, where they do a large business, was born in Bavaria, in the Rhine province, on the river Rhine, June 1, 1849.

He learned his trade of wagon and carriage maker before he left for America in the summer of 1860. He proceeded to Beardstown, joining his sister, Mrs. Anton Rink, who had come before. The father of our subject was a native of Germany, and died there when sixty. He was a farmer and small land-owner, and married a German lady, Miss Margaret Caalmann, who died when forty-eight. She had six children.

Mr. Schultz began in Beardstown as a carriage and wagon maker. He then became a dealer in wines and liquors for three years. His present business is successfully carried on by himself and the two sons of his old partner, Mr. Baujan, who took their father's place when he died in 1890. Their brands of flour are represented by traveling men and they do business all over the State. The mills have a capacity of 200 barrels per day, and the elevator of 80,000 bushels. They have warehouses also at Spring Bluffs and other places. The mills have nine sets of rollers and are run by steam power. Their main brands are Sunbeam and Sea Foam. It was started in 1875, under the firm name of Baujan & Company.

Mr. Schultz is also connected with other local enterprises, being a stockholder in the First National Bank and the Beardstown Electric Light & Power Company, and a director in both. He has been a leader in many other enterprises that have affected the welfare of the city.

He was married in Beardstown to Miss Rosa A. Baujan, who was born and reared in Cass county. They have four children: Harry, now dead; Olive A., Etta A., Alfred C. Mrs. Schultz is a member of the Roman Catholic Church. Mr. Schultz is a strong Democrat and has been Alderman of the city, and also delegate to the State Congressional Committee. He is a member of the order A. O. U. W., and has filled the chairs. He has been sent to the Grand Lodge.

TAYLOR L. SMITH, Superintendent of the Railroad Round House at Beardstown for the St. Louis & Rock Island division of the Chicago Burlington & Quincy, was born near Zanesville, Ohio. His father, James Smith, was a native of Pennsylvania, of Dutch ancestry. He had grown up in his native county of Washington, at which place his father, William Smith, had followed the occupation of butcher. Later he came to Ohio and there lived and died at Newark, Licking county. It was there that his son James had settled and engaged in the butcher business. He had married Miss Elizabeth Leggett in Pennsylvania. After settling in Newark they became prominent in society, and Mrs. Leggett died there when she was forty-three. Mr. Smith was married a second time to Miss Lotta Frink, in Ohio, and in 1887 moved to Butler, Bates county, Missouri, and are now living there, Mr. Smith still actively engaged in the meat-market business. They are good, hard-working people.

Taylor L. is the third child of six children, all married and prominent persons in life. He grew up an industrious, hard-working boy, and earned his bread by his own personal endeavors. He was reared near the place of his birth, and later became an apprentice to a firm selling portable and stationary engines at Newark, Ohio. Three years afterward, he became connected with the Baltimore & Ohio Railroad. He came to Beardstown a number of years ago, began in the machine shops and being a practical machinist and good workman, soon became overseer of the engine repair shops. He was engaged there for more than three years, when he was promoted to the round house and has since been thus connected, having some twenty-five men under him, besides having to direct about one hundred engineers. He has held this office for two years. He has been very successful, and owns a comfortable home in Beardstown.

He was married in Newark, Ohio, to Miss Mary Dalton of Newark, a very intelligent lady, the daughter of Michael and Mary Dalton, now living in Newark, both in the 60s.

Mr. and Mrs. Smith are the parents of four children: Maybell, Edith, Anna and Warren, all at home. Mr. and Mrs. Smith are prominent in Beardstown society. Mr. Smith is a Master Mason and is a member of Arch Lodge No. 16, I. O. O. F., also of the Knights of Pythias lodge, No. 207. He is a Republican in politics and a genial, pleasant gentleman.

MOSES HARBISON, an intelligent and progressive farmer of Cass county, Illinois, numbered among the substantial men of this section, was born in Barren, now Metcalfe county, Kentucky, September 3, 1831.

His parents were Adam B. and Hannah (Rhea) Harbison, the former a native of Virginia, who, when a young man, operated different mills and also did teaming. In 1831, he came to Illinois with his wife's people, although at the time unmarried, his union taking place in the latter State. Accompanied by his wife, he shortly afterward returned to Kentucky, where they resided for a year or two, after which they removed to Washington county, Missouri, in which place he farmed for about five years. He then sold out and returned to Illinois, settling in Mason county, where he entered 200 acres of good land, and built a log house. Here he died two years later, at the comparatively early age of forty-four years. He was twice married, his first wife being the mother of the subject of this sketch. She died on the farm in Missouri, at the early age of twenty-three years, leaving three small children to the care of her bereaved husband.

The subject of this sketch is the only survivor of these children. He lived at home until his father's death, after which his stepmother bound him out to a farmer. Two years later, however, at the age of thirteen years, he took "French leave," and started out in life for himself. He first worked for $2.50 a month, which was in 1845. At the end of five months, he bought a sow and pig, which was his first speculation in pork. Out of his small income, he provided them with corn, and, like Jacob's kine, they waxed strong and beautiful. This was only the beginning of his schemes for advancement. In 1848 he rented sixteen acres of land, which, with one horse, he started to improve. The following year, he bought another horse, and thus continued to rent land and work it until 1853, when he and a brother came to where our subject now lives, and bought 160 acres of land. An old house was on the place and ninety acres were under cultivation. This land they industriously improved, and, in 1868, Mr. Harbison erected on it his present substantial farm house. He has recently sold some of his land, but still retains 342 acres, most of which is under cultivation.

He was first married, January 7, 1857, to Miss Mary A. Davis, an intelligent and energetic lady, and a native of Cass county.

This union was destined to be of short duration, the devoted wife and mother dying at the age of twenty-three years, leaving a child to the care of her bereaved husband, which afterward died, aged nineteen months. Her people were very old and esteemed settlers of this State.

March 13, 1863, Mr. Harbison was again married, his second wife being Miss Lydia F. Mason, an estimable lady, and a native of Culpeper county, Virginia. She was a daughter of John and Emma (Milliner) Mason, also natives of the Old Dominion. They came to Illinois in 1856, settling first in Cass county, whence they removed to Joplin, Missouri, where the mother died, aged seventy years, the father still surviving. This worthy couple were the parents of eleven children, ten of whom are living.

Mr. and Mrs. Harbison have ten children: Virginia S., married and has one child, a daughter; Charles C., who is at home; Mary C. is married and has one son. The other children are still at home and are as follows: Arthur J., Robert F., Estella, Alice, Martha C., Emma and Nancy A.

Politically, Mr. Harbison is a Democrat, and cast his first presidential vote for General Pierce. His constituents have recognized his ability and integrity of character, and have sought to gain the benefit of these traits by electing him to various local offices, in all of which he has served the best interests of the community. He has been an efficient member of the school board for twenty-two years, which fact of itself speaks volumes in favor of his excellent judgment and moral force of character.

Mr. Harbison's life would furnish an inspiration to many poor, young men, who, alone and unaided, are starting in life, with no compass by which to guide their course. Happy are they, if, like the subject of this sketch, they keep their eyes stedily fixed on the North Star of Truth, while industriously spreading their sails to the breezes of prosperity, which will eventually waft them to the desired haven of comfort and happiness.

NATHANIEL H. BOONE, M. D.—This gentleman was born in Troup county, Georgia, June 6, 1836, and was the son of William and Elizabeth (Bradford) Boone. He was a farmer in South Carolina, and died in Mississippi, aged forty-nine years. The mother of our subject was also born in South Carolina and died at the same place, aged seventy-four.

The subject of the present notice was one of ten children, three of whom are yet living. He remained under the parental roof until he was sixteen years of age, when occurred his father's death. He then was sent to an academy for several years at College Hill, and then to medical college at Nashville. He graduated at this college in 1860, and in 1861 he married Miss Cornelia Blackwell of Georgia, but Dr. Boone had met her at Pine Bluff, where he had gone to practice. Her life was short, as her death occurred at the the age of twenty-three. Her two children died also. She was the daughter of James and Mary Blackwell of Georgia, who later removed to Pine Bluff, Arkansas, and there died, he at the age of fifty-five or sixty, and she about fifty years old. Our subject was married a second time September 25, 1870, to Miss Harriet H. Codington, who was born in Menard county, Illinois, December 21, 1838, and was the daughter of Joseph and Jane (Leeper) Codington. They were natives of Barren county, Kentucky, and he followed blacksmithing until in 1829 or 1830 he came to Illinois. He drove his stock and wagon and a carriage for the family, and first settled in Menard county, and took up Government land and then built a log cabin upon it. Here they lived for quite a time in a tent and in the log house, probably eight years. The father, Mr. Codington, brought three children with them and seven more were born here, and six of this family still live. His life extended to seventy-two years, and that of his wife to sixty-four years. The Codingtons were of German ancestry, and on the mother's side a little Irish. Mrs. Boone says of those early times that the country was sparsely settled and wild game was abundant.

Dr. Boone practiced medicine in Pine Bluff, Arkansas, about three years, and in 1864, he sold out there and came North and settled in Chandlerville, this county. Later, he bought land and kept on adding to it until now he farms over 1,700 acres in this State and in Kansas, and rents the most of it. He works a host of men and presents the unusual spectacle of a successful professional man who is also a successful farmer.

Dr. Boone has taken no active part in politics, but his first vote was for Bell, and since he has been a Democrat and a Prohibitionist. He has served the town for years in the town Council. He and his wife are members of the Christian Church, and the Doctor has been Superintendent of the Sunday-school for many years.

Living with the subject, is his nephew, Howard B. Boone, who was born in Fayette county, Mississippi, May 30, 1870. He was the son of William Sanford and Ophelia (Watson) Boone. William S. Boone was born in the same place as our subject, March 6, 1841, and there died aged about thirty-five or forty years. His wife Ophelia still lives in Mississippi, on the old homestead. Howard B. is a very promising young man and medical student, and will receive every advantage the best medical colleges afford.

C. E. NIEMANN, a successful dealer in wines and liquors at the corner of Washington and Main streets, in Beardstown, was born in West Darling, Prussia, Germany, April 17, 1832. He lost his father, Casper Niemann, who lived and died in his native province in Prussia. His death occurred in his sixty-seventh year. He had been a live-stock dealer and trader. His mother lived to come to this country with her children in 1859, where she spent her last days. She and her husband were consistent members of the Lutheran Church.

Mr. Niemann came to Beardstown in 1859 and began as a poor man and has for twenty years been steamboating on the Mississippi river and for the last few years as mate. He has, however, always lived in Beardstown and been closely connected with the town in its growth. Since he came from Prussia, landing at New Orleans, he has lived to see the great changes come over the steamboating of the great rivers. He has been in his present business fourteen years.

He was married in this city to Miss Elizabeth Howard. She was born in Hanover, Germany, and was twenty years of age when she came to the United States. Her parents and relatives all died in her native country. Mr. and Mrs. Niemann have had eleven children, of whom only four are now living. They were among the first members and organizers of the Lutheran Church at this place, to which they have always subscribed. He has always been a Republican in politics, but in no sense is he an office-seeker. He has many warm friends among his large circle of acquaintances.

THEODORE FRANKENFIELD.—The subject of this sketch was born December 28, 1850, in Prussia, and was the son of Adolph and Johannes (Fielden) Frankenfield, who were natives of the same place. The father was a soldier for thirty years. Our subject came to America when twenty-five years of age and was seventy-five days on the trip, and landed in the city of New York. He was a blacksmith by trade and worked at this business until he came to Illinois. His first change in this new country was from New York to Pennsylvania, and from there he went to various places until in 1861 he settled near where he now lives. He worked by the month and at his trade, and in June, 1863, he was married to Miss Catherine C. Morris, who was born on the farm where our subject now lives. She was born April 28, 1846, and was a daughter of Joshua and Nancy (Hickey) Morris. Her father came from Kentucky and settled here about 1830, locating in this township with his father and mother, Henry and Mary Morris, and lived and died here, aged about seventy years. The father of Mrs. Frankenfield was born in the year 1801 and lived until 1881. He was of Irish ancestry, and was proprietor of a frontier grocery store. He was one of the first of the pioneers of this section and lived in a primitive log house, but at his death he owned 700 acres of land to bequeath to his family. He built the present home about eighteen years ago. He was a kind-hearted man, was very active in politics and was an ardent Republican.

The gentleman of whom we write was one of five children, of whom he is probably the only survivor. He served four years in the German army and soon after his discharge came to America, where he has been a very successful man. He and his good wife have four living children, as follows: Joshua T. was born April 16, 1864, and is now married and the father of one boy; William E. was born September 28, 1866, and a girl is now the comfort of his home; Matilda C. was born May 1, 1869, and now in her home has a boy and girl of her own; Henry P. was born September 27, 1876; and Frank, a lad of eleven years is dead. All the children received an education in the district school.

Mr. Frankenfield believes in the principles of the Democracy and cast his first vote in this country for James Buchannan. He and all of his family are members of the Methodist Episcopal Church and he has been very active in work in the church and Sunday-school. He has carried on a system of mixed farming and has 300 acres of land. He is a man who commands the respect of the whole neighborhood, and the family is one which has been very prominent among the pioneers of this grand old county.

JOHN W. MORRIS, a contractor and builder of Rushville, was born in Rockingham county, Virginia, April 8, 1832. His father, William Morris, was a native of Augusta county, the same State, and the father of the latter was a life-long resident of the Old Dominion. The father of John W. Morris was reared in Virginia, where he learned the trade of a carpenter, a calling he followed there until 1833, when he emigrated to Ohio accompanied by his wife and six children, making the journey with teams. A year was spent at Lancaster, Fairfield county, when another migration was made, this time to Franklin county, where he purchased a tract of timber land near Groveport, where he resided ten years, all the time carrying on the business of contractor and builder, besides superintending the improvement of his farm Selling out again, he again took his family with him, settling in Delaware county, purchasing a farm near Centreville He pursued farming until 1862, when the spirit of change again came over him, and he found a home in Grand View, Edgar county, Illinois, where two daughters and one son continued to reside He lived there, retired from business, until his death, which came peacefully in May, 1879, when he was seventy-seven years old His wife's death preceded his a few months, she having passed away in February of the same year Her maiden name was Eliza Palmer, and she was born in Virginia, and was the daughter of Robert and Martha Palmer She reared eight children: Harriet Stevenson, George, Charles L., James H., William B, John W, Jane F and Caroline Cavendish

John was so young when his parents left Virginia that he has no recollection of his native place He attended the public schools of Franklin and Delavan counties, and when not in school assisted his father at his trade and on the farm. He was a natural mechanic and gave evidence of skill with edged tools at a very early age. He did journeyman's work in Ohio until 1856, when he went to Grand View, Edgar county, where he remained until 1862, when he removed to Fulton county, following his trade at Marietta for two years Mattoon, Coles county was next his home, and then, in 1866, he removed to Rushville, where he engaged in mercantile pursuits for two and a half years, tiring of this he followed farming for two years, when, settling in Rushville, he began the business of contractor and builder, which he has continued ever since The principal business blocks of Rushville were erected by him, and they are so many monuments to his skill and to the fidelity of his work

Mr. Morris was married in 1860, to Elizabeth Cary, who was born in Ohio in 1840. His married life has been a happy one, and three living children bless their union, viz: Mary C., Annie E. and Alice G. Two, Cary and Charles L, are deceased

Mr. Morris united with the Methodist Episcopal Church in 1859, and has continued since that time to be a consistent member of that body. In politics Mr Morris is a Republican, earnestly advocating the measures of that party

REV DANIEL A. BLOSE, pastor of the First Congregational Church of Beardstown, was born in Indiana county, Pennsylvania, May 23, 1854 He was reared on his father's farm, and there remained until seventeen years of age, when he entered Covode academy in the same county, and a year later attended an academy in Armstrong county, and graduated in the class of 1875, and then entered the University of Lewisburg, now known as Bucksnell University, and graduated there with the class of 1878, receiving 100 per cent in all class examinations, also the first honors with the oration in the scientific course. He entered in the fall of 1878, the Auburn Theological Seminary of Auburn, New York, and graduated with the class of 1881. He was then licensed by the Kittanning Presbytery of the synod of Pennsylvania, that being their custom. He was ordained by the Geneva Presbytery of the synod of New York, January 12, 1882, and soon after became pastor of the Presbyterian Church of Dresden, New York. In 1886 he became connected with the Congregational Church, and has since been an earnest worker. It was in De Kalb, Illinois, that he did his first work as a Congregational minister, and the beautiful stone church edifice of that place stands as a silent monument to his labors. Being overworked he was obliged to resign his position against the unanimous protest of the people. He was immediately called to the church at Tonica, Illinois, which he accepted under the promise of being able to rest. During his one year there the membership was doubled. At the close of the year an anti-Masonic faction caused a lack of harmony in the church, and the Rev. Blose resigned against the united request of the congregation. He immediately received a call from four churches, and decided to accept theone from La Harpe, Illinois, where he remained fifteen months, and increased the membership by fifty members. He was then unanimously called to the church at Beardstown, which he accepted much against the wishes of his congregation at La Harpe.

He was married May 1, 1881, at Burns, Allegany county, New York, to Mamie E. Coray, born December 15, 1857, educated in the Union High School of Canaseraga, New York, graduating in 1879. She is an accomplished lady, an enthusiastic worker in the church and in all the avenues where good may be promoted, and is the devoted mother of two very bright children; Minnie Coray and Charles A.

Mr. Blose is a sound Republican, his faith being born of intelligence vitalized by righteousness and patriotism. He feels that he has a right to spread his principles and advocate his political faith from the rostrum as he preaches his religion from the pulpit.

HENRY VETTE, a general farmer, was born in Prussia, May 10, 1864. His father, William Vette, was a brick mason, and died when he was thirty-eight years old. His wife had died the preceding year, and they both were members of the German Lutheran Church.

Henry was left an orphan at the age of ten, and grew up as a maker of cigar boxes in his native province until seventeen years of age, and then he and a friend set out for this country. They set sail from Bremen in 1882, landed in New York city in the same year and then came to Illinois, reaching Beardstown with $1.10 in his pocket. He began work first as a laborer with his uncle, Henry Vette, and after some years of economy he was able to purchase the large farm he is now rapidly paying for. The farm consists of 125 acres, well improved, and other land that is not under plow, amounting to 372 acres. He is a young man of good judgment, and has shown what he can do and is bound to succeed.

He was married in Cass county, to Anna Shave, who was born in Beardstown, March 22, 1867, and was reared and educated in this county. She is the daughter of William and Ingle (Shave) Shave. They are now living in this county, successful farmers, owning fine property. Mr. and Mrs. Vette are members of the Sixth Street Lutheran Church in Beardstown. They are the parents of three children, Hilda L., William H and Edna L Mr Vette is an ardent Republican, and both he and his wife are highly esteemed by all who know them

AARON LOGSDON was born in Madison county, Kentucky, May 7, 1821 His grandfather was Edward Logsdon, a native of Maryland, who moved to Kentucky in early life, where the thirteen children were born These all grew to adult age and reared families of their own. The mother of this family was Polly Brown, also a native of Maryland George Logsdon, the father of the subject of this notice, was the youngest of the family He was reared on a farm and was early accustomed to hard work, only having the meager schooling of the time. He lived at home on the farm, which finally became his own at the death of his father, Edward. The latter was a man of wonderful strength, perfectly fearless, and in his old age was a match for many men who were younger He weighed nearly 200 pounds, and was six feet high. He was one of the pioneers of Kentucky, and in those days strength and courage were the only safeguards of a man He was a very peaceable person, but had some encounters with fighting men, and never was conquered. He married Sally McKinzie, a daughter of John McKinzie The union took place in Kentucky, and there they lived and there their family of eleven children were born. Two of these died in infancy, but all of the others grew up and became heads of families, and seven of them are still living The parents came to Illinois in 1856, bringing three children with them. Our subject had preceded them in 1852, with his wife and five children, coming by water to Lagrange.

The first wife of our subject was Lucinda Dunbar, who died in the prime of life, of consumption, and left him two daughters and an infant which soon died. The daughters were Sally and Minerva. Mr Logsdon was again married, to Martha J. Johnson, the daughter of Thomas Johnson and Rebecca Shearer, the latter from Ireland and the former from Pennsylvania They were early settlers in Kentucky, and the father is still living and hearty at his old home He reared eleven children, ten of whom are still living, the youngest being forty-six years of age

Mr. and Mrs Logsdon came here without means, and rented land for one year, but then bought 160 acres of wild land for $500, paying $200 of it down They occupied the log cabin for several years, were frugal, and as soon as they had paid for their first land they bought forty acres adjoining for $600, and still later bought more until he owned at one time 400 acres. He has sold off and given to his sons until he has only 155 acres left. He has retired from active labor, and his sons, Aaron and Ed, are working the farm. Mr. Logsdon and his present wife have had eleven children The eldest daughter, Mary E, is the wife of John Lear, who died in January, 1883, aged thirty-six, and left two children. Mary is dead, and Grandpa Logsdon has adopted the children The living children are. Minerva, who is the wife of Frank Simmons, who is a farmer in Missouri; Thomas W is a farmer in Nebraska; George lives near by; Rebecca is the wife of Henry Behymer, a farmer near Versailles, Lucinda is the wife of William Betzmer; Aaron married Maria Ballard, of this county; Nancy is the wife of Samuel Wright, a farmer near by; Edward owns a part of the homestead, and lives near with his wife, Minnie Brewer, and two children; Martha A. is the wife of James Harper, a farmer of this county. This fine old couple rejoice in their ten great-grandchildren, and have thirty-two grandchildren, living, and have seen ten buried. There was patriotism in this family, for the brother of Mr. Logsdon went all through the war, and the brother of Mrs. Logsdon carries a bullet wound and had two others; and the son-in-law, Robert Johnson, went three years through the great struggle, and bears three wounds.

Mr. Logsdon has been a Master Mason for thirty years, and has been a Republican for many years. The family are religious people, and belong to the Church of God.

HEZEKIAH LEEK, M. D., has been a resident of Schuyler county, Illinois, since he was a child of seven years. He was born in Peoria county, Illinois, January 25, 1840, a son of Jacob and Adiathia (Leek) Leek. The maternal grandfather, Henry Leek, was a native of Germany, but emigrated to the United States when a young man; he was married in the State of New York, and later resided in Pennsylvania, Ohio and Illinois, being one of the earliest settlers of the last-named commonwealth; he first located in Wabash county, and later removed to Peoria county, and finally came to Schuyler county, where he died at the age of ninety years; his wife lived to the same advanced age. They had a family of eleven children: Benjamin F., William, Allen, Robert, George, Wright, Levi, Adiathia, Abigail, Pernina and Mary. Jacob Leek, the father of our subject, was born in Ohio, and removed from that State to Illinois, settling in Peoria county. In 1847 he came to Schuyler county and entered land in Frederick township, which he occupied until the time of his death in 1842. He left a family of six children; Sarah, wife of Abraham Yuble; Margaret, wife of Annis Davis; Henry, deceased; Hezekiah, the subject of this sketch; Alexander, who died in the old homestead; Jacob F., a minister of the Missionary Baptist Church. The mother died in the autumn of 1891; she was a woman of rare force of character, and for forty years had been a consistent member of the Christian Church

Dr. Leek spent his youth on the farm, and received his literary education in the common schools. Having determined to pursue the science of medicine, he began its study about 1857, in Fulton county, Illinois, under the preceptorship of Dr. Smith of Cuba; he subsequently studied at Olney, Illinois, and in Wabash county. He began the practice of his profession in McDonough county, Illinois, and remained there until 1871, when he returned to Schuyler county. In 1880 he received a certificate from the State Board of Health, having practiced fourteen years. He now resides in Rushville, but ihs patients are scattered over a wide territory. He has been very successful and has won a reputation as a skillful and careful dhysician.

Dr. Leek has been married twice: In 1859 he was united to Drusilla Tungate, who died in 1866, leaving four children: Abel; Margaret, wife of William Shriver; Amos, deceased; and Minerva, deceased. His second marriage was to Angeline M. Johnson, a daughter of Joel Johnson; she died in Aleny, Illinois, leaving four children: Joel C., Harmon J., Asa, deceased, and one child that died in early life. In politics he adheres to the principles of the

Republican party. During the war he was president of the Union League. He was once a minister of the Baptist Church, and later was in the Christian Church in the same capacity; he does no ministerial work at the present time, but devotes himself wholly to his profession He has always been deeply interested in the welfare of his county and town; in his profession he has won the highest respect of his colleagues, and as a citizen he enjoys the respect of all who know him.

REESE H. GRIFFITH, one of the leading merchants of Rushville, is an American by adoption, his native land being Wales; there he was born November 5, 1824. His parents were Humphrey and Mary (Davies) Griffith, the latter a native of Hanover, Wales His father was reared in the Independent faith, and became a minister of that denomination in Wales In 1825 he, with his wife and one child, sailed from Liverpool for America Landing in this country he settled in Somers, Westchester county, New York, where he was pastor of the Presbyterian Church until 1832 He then removed to Michigan Territory, and located in Tecumseh, Lenawee county. Michigan was then a wilderness, and the greater part of the land was owned by the Government. Mr. Griffith purchased a tract near Tecumseh, in which place he was later called to the pastorate of the Presbyterian Church, he being the second minister of the society His family had remained in Detroit while he was preparing a home for them in Tecumseh In the fall he started back for them, but was taken ill at Ypsilanti, where he died Thus his wife was left a widow with four small children, one of whom died soon after the father. Fortunately for her and those dependent on her, she was a woman of superior education and unusual energy. To support herself and children, she opened a select school in Tecumseh and became prominent among the early educators of the State. In addition to providing for her family, she lifted a heavy indebtedness that rested upon the land purchased by her husband Her last days were passed in Rushville, Illinois, where she died in 1877, in her seventy-ninth year. The three children, who attained a mature age, were: Reese H , the subject of this notice; Humphrey, who died in Sacramento, California; and Theophilus D , a resident of Kansas City, Kansas

Reese H was an infant when his parents crossed the sea to this country, and was but eight years old when his father died. He was thus reared and educated by his mother, who, fortunately for him was a woman of unusual intelligence and activity He later attended a branch of the of the Michigan University, and when nineteen years of age commenced to teach, which profession he followed in Michigan for nine years. He then went to northern Alabama, and was engaged for five years in teaching in Florence In the spring of 1852 he came to Rushville, Illinois, where he taught school one year, which terminated his career in that capacity He next embarked in the hardware business, in which he has been very successful He, his son Charles and a nephew, Humphrey Griffith, compose the corporation under the firm name of the Griffith Hardware Company

Mr Griffith was married March 15, 1852, to Susan P Stebbins, an estimable lady, a native of Simsbury, Connecticut, and a daughter of Samuel S. and Laura (Bester) Stebbins, also natives of that State They have six children: Charles, Effie, Harry, Edwin, Laura and William. The nephew, Humphrey Griffith, has been a member of the home circle since early youth, and is esteemed as a son. The parents and children are members of the Presbyterian Church.

Politically, Mr. Griffith was formerly a Whig, and cast his first vote for Zachary Taylor. Since the formation of the Republican party, he has been a supporter of its principles, and has served that party in various positions of trust. He has been a delegate to numerous county, district and State conventions; and in 1892 was alternate delegate from his district to the National Republican Convention at Minneapolis. He also takes a prominent part in all church matters of his denomination. He has always taken a deep interest in Sabbath-school work, has served as president of the Illinois State Sabbath-school Association, and was the first president of the Schuyler county Sunday-School Association, having been a member of the executive committee of the latter society since its organization. In 1861 he acted as delegate to the Presbyterian Conference at Syracuse, New York, and went to New York in the same capacity in 1889.

It is a matter of congratulation that Rushville should have a man of such superior intelligence and morality, for though this combination is very pleasing, it is too often conspicuous for its absence. He who founds his life on these lines builds with success, and is eminently worthy of the esteem of all good men.

GEORGE P. HUFF was born in Schuyler county, Illinois, July 28, 1850. His father was William Huff, born in North Carolina in 1808. and his grandfather was John Huff, also of North Carolina, where he lived and died. The name of his grandmother was Charity Adams, born in North Carolina.

William A. Huff married Betsy Ann Teaney, daughter of John and Nancy Teaney. She was born in Pennsylvania in 1812. When she was fourteen years old, her parents moved to Bartholomew county, Indiana, which they did with their own team. Mrs. Huff was married at the age of twenty-three, fifty-seven years ago. They set out for Illinois with their own horse and buggy and reached Rushville in the fall, where they remained thirteen years, and then moved to their present home. They had enough means to buy ninety-six acres of Government land on which they built a hewn log house containing one room. This land was all wild, the country entirely unsettled, abounding in game, large and small. Mr. Huff afterward bought eighty acres more, making his farm in all 156 acres. In 1860 they built the present frame house, which was nearly completed in the fall of 1861, when he died. They had buried one son, John, who left a widow. Since the death of her husband she has buried, Sarah Huff, aged thirty-four; Melissa Tucker, about forty years old, and Martha Duncan, who died at fifty-two years, leaving ten children. Mrs. Huff has eight children still living: Mary Clampitt of Greeley, Kansas; Amanda Lineburger, of Hancock county, Illinois; Maria Fisher, of Creston, Iowa; Francis, a stock dealer of Hancock; George F. and Homer W., are still at home; Perry P., a farmer on an adjoining farm, and Eliza Wilborn, living on the old homestead.

Mrs. Huff is still well and active in mind and body, and considering that she has been the mother of twelve children, has been a toiler these many years, being now eighty years old, she is a fair sample of the sturdy pioneer women of early days. Mr. Huff died in the faith of the Methodist Church, of which his widow is a member. He and his sons have always been Republicans, and they are highly regarded in the community in which they live.

IRA N. GIBSON, of Browning, Illinois, was born January 1, 1843, near New Castle, Pennsylvania, his parents being John and Mary F. (Fervor) Gibson. They were natives of Pennsylvania. They removed to Morris, Illinois, stayed there seven years; thence they went to the army; at the close of the war, went to Peoria, when the subject was twelve years of age. Both parents are still living.

Ira Gibson grew to manhood in Peoria, but in the fall of 1863, while prospecting in Iowa, he enlisted in the Iowa Cavalry, at Sioux City. He was sent out on the plains, where he remained fighting Indians and guarding the frontier until the close of the war, when he was mustered out, at Davenport, in 1865.

He returned to Peoria and engaged in milling, where he remained seven years. He was head miller in the mill of Frank Fields, for two years.

Quitting the milling, he engaged in the fishery business on the Illinois river, and this has been his occupation since. In it he has acquired a comfortable living and a nice property in Browning, Illinois. He furnishes his stock both winter and summer to J. W. Peters, at St. Louis, where he finds a ready sale for all his products. He puts up his own ice and operates the business in a systematic manner.

Mr. Gibson has been twice married. His first venture into matrimony was when twenty-four years of age, to Miss Frances Smith of Peoria. At her death she left four children: Alice, Frank, Louisa and Viola.

Mr. Gibson was married a second time in Browning, to Miss Mary Williams, who was born in Fulton county, Illinois, in 1858. To this union there are two children: Frances and Ethel, bright little girls, at home.

Mr. Gibson is a Democrat in politics, and is a member of Browning Lodge, No. 309, I. O. O. F. He was formerly a member of the G. A. R., but the post disbanded and he has not yet joined any other.

His first wife was a Roman Catholic in religion, but the present Mrs. Gibson is a member of the Methodist Episcopal Church.

J. THOMAS LAWLER, a widely and favorably known citizen of Woodstock township, Schuyler county, Illinois, is a native of Virginia, having been born in Fauquier county, that State, May 7, 1824. His parents were Alexander and Margaret (White) Lawler, both natives of Virginia. His father served with distinction in the war of 1812. His father was a cooper, and followed his trade in his native State until the spring of 1839, when he with his family drove from Virginia to Ohio, and thence to Schuyler county, bringing all their worldly goods in their wagon. Arrived in Illinois, they purchased 160 acres of wild timber land in Woodstock township, on which they built a log house, and began the life of pioneers. Both father and mother lived here until their death, although it had been much improved during their possession, both with buildings of a substantial kind, as well as the land well cultivated. The father died here at the age of sixty-four years, while the mother survived him for a long time, dying at the advanced age of seventy-three years. The Lawlers were originally from Ireland, where they were well-to-do people.

Our subject was one of a family of fourteen children, seven of whom are now living. He was reared in Woodstock township, and and received his education at the country schools of his day. He lived at home until he was twenty-two years of age, working on the farm and at his trade of coopering. He then enlisted in the army, and served in the Mexican war for thirteen months, and now gets a Mexican pension. After returning from the war, he married, on May 7, 1848, Miss Sarah E. Pinkerton, who was born in Putnam county Indiana, June 14, 1831. She was a daughter of William and Anna (Jackson) Pinkerton. Her father was a native of Kentucky, while her mother was a native of one of the Carolinas, having come with their parents to Indiana in a very early day. Her father died in Indiana, aged about thirty years, after which her mother moved to Illinois, locating in 1855, in Rushville, later moving to Augusta. She is still surviving, and lives with her daughter, the wife of our subject. She had three children, only two of whom are living.

Joseph and Sarah Jackson were Mrs. Lawler's grandparents. They were pioneers of Indiana and later moved to Illinois. Mrs. Jackson died in Indiana aged fifty years, and her husband died in Illinois at the advanced age of ninety-six years. They were related to General Jackson, so famous in the war of 1812.

David and Margaret Pinkerton, the grandparents on her father's side both died in Indiana, at a very advanced age. They were both natives of Kentucky, and of English ancestry.

After marriage, our subject settled where he now lives, residing there continuously ever since. He built at first a little log cabin, in which he and his family lived, until 1865, when he erected his present substantial and comfortable home. His farm was unimproved when he bought it, but it is now one of the best farms in the country, being highly cultivated, and well improved with substantial barns for grain and stock, besides other modern conveniences for the care of grain an other agricultural products.

Mr. and Mrs. Lawler have eleven children, nine of whom are living. Margaret E., married and has seven children; Henry W., married, having three children; Silas E., married, has four children; Albert C., married, has five children; Simon A. and Jane A., twins; Simon, a school teacher; and Jane, married, and has two children; Nancy E., married, with two children; Hattie E., married, and has one child; and Thomas A., at home, and works the farm with his father.

Our subject and wife are consistent members of the Methodist Episcopal Church, and contribute liberally towards its support.

Mr. Lawler and family are highly respected by people of the community on account of their many admirable traits of character.

ALEXANDER MOORE, the prominent citizen of Buck Horn township, whose biography it is our pleasure to present to our readers, was born in Harrison county, Ohio, December 23, 1821, son of Alexander and Sarah (Smith) Moore. Alexander Moore Sr., was born in Maryland, but came to

Ohio with his parents, when very young, settling in Harrison county He was one of eight children, and learned the millwright and carpenter trade, but followed farming principally, and ran a horse-power mill for many years He and his parents took up land in Ohio, that was wild and unimproved, and here he lived in a log cabin all his days, dying on the first farm taken up of Government land, in that section, aged eighty-five years. His wife died on the same place when about eighty-eight, she being a native of Tennessee. The subject's father on the father's side of the family was Alexander Moore, who married, and spent his last days in Ohio, dying when full of years The father of our subject was a Justice of the Peace, and an old Andrew Jackson Democrat, and filled the different township offices, and was active in church and other good work at an early day. He helped to build the first church in that part of Ohio, a Methodist house of worship, and his family were members of it to the close of their lives. There is a record that some of the ancestors of Mr Moore were on the way to join in the war of 1812, but peace was declared before they reached their destination The father of Mr. Moore started out as a fifer, and his uncle as a drummer.

Our subject remained at home until he was seventeen years old, worked summers, and attended school winters, in the old log temples of learning of that day, which were erected within a bit of clearing. At the age of fourteen he went to learn the cabinet-maker trade, and served three years for his board and clothes At the age of twenty he commenced work at the lucrative trade of a carpenter, and continued at this for fifteen years.

Our subject was married November 30, 1841, to Elizabeth P. Johnson, who was born in the same place as was her husband, and was the daughter of Nathan and Jane (Aul) Johnson, who were natives of Maryland, and spent their last days in Ohio; the mother died at the age of thirty-five years. Mr. Moore, of this notice, was one of five children, but one of whom is yet living The first wife of our subject died where he now lives, aged forty-four years, and left five living of her twelve children. They are as follows: Martin L has five children; Margaret J has five children; Amanda has but two little ones, as also has Lizzie; John C is unmarried. Our subject was married a second time in November, 18—, to Mrs. Mary E (Gregory) Ayers, who was born in Pike county, Illinois, November 23, 1842, and was the daughter of John J. and Samantha (Barrett) Gregory. He was born in Tennessee, in 1814, and came to Illinois at a very early day, and died in Pike county, aged forty-seven years. His wife also died in the same county, about forty-four years of age. Mrs Moore's first marriage was November 7, 1858, to Francis M. Ayers, who was born in Ohio, and enlisted in the early part of the war, and died from wounds received at Hartsville, Missouri He was thirty-five years old when he died, and was a member of Company B, Captain Mathews. She drew a pension from the Government until her marriage She had three children, one of whom is William A, who has a family of three children.

After his first marriage our subject first followed the carpenter trade until 1856, when he sold his houses and lots and went to Kansas, but the next year he returned to Ohio, and that fall came back to Illinois, and bought eighty acres of land where he now lives. He first built a log house, and then built a permanent dwelling.

Mr. Moore has been a Republican ever since the formation of the party, and always votes that ticket. He was a Free Soiler until 1856. He and his wife attend the Methodist Episcopal Church, where they hold their membership. This large and prosperous family are much respected in their neighborhood.

JOHN MERZ, general farmer and stock-raiser, was born in Hesse-Darmstadt, Germany, March 21, 1829. He lost his mother when he was fourteen years of age. Her name was Margaretta Darmer, and her husband was John Merz, who lived and died in his native province, at the age of sixty-seven. He was a shoemaker, and followed that trade in connection with his farming. He and his wife were long members of the Lutheran Church. Our subject is the eldest of three children. He grew up as a farmer boy and linen-weaver, and did not come to this country until he was twenty-five years of age. He landed in New York city in 1855, and came right on to Beardstown, and three days later engaged as a farm laborer and has been a tiller of the soil ever since. He has been very economical, like the most of his race, and has acquired a large property by real hard work. He is the only member of his family who has ever come to this country. He now owns 240 acres of very fine land, and has good farm buildings, having owned this since 1858, and strange as it may seem he has made every bit of his fortune by earnest, hard work, receiving help from no one.

He was first married in Beardstown, to Louisa Rohn, who was born and reared at her father's home, not far from Beardstown. She died after five years of married life, being then only twenty-two years of age. She left one daughter, Louisa, who died at fourteen years of age, having been a very intelligent child. Mr. Merz was married in Beardstown a second time, to Miss Louisa Folks, born in Baden, Germany, who came to this country with her parents when very small. Her parents died in Schuyler county. Mr. Folks was a cooper by trade, and followed it all his life.

Mr. and Mrs. Merz have six children: Louisa, Etta and Henry are married; Margaret, Charles and Nora are still at home. They are Lutherans in religion, and Mr. Merz is a Republican. They are among the best of Beardstown's German citizens.

WILLIAM ROHN, a practical farmer and stock-raiser, was born in Cass County, September 27, 1854. His father, Henry, came to the county in 1835, took up Government land near Beardstown, and here lived, labored, and died April 21, 1891. He was then eighty-six years of age. He was a native of Hesse-Darmstadt, of good German blood, came to this country in 1835 with his brother John, and they began life as farmers. Here this brother died when he was seventy years old. (For further family history, see biography of Henry Rohn in this book.) William's mother is yet living, very smart and active, and on her eighty-first birthday, November 21, 1891, enjoyed the kind hospitality of her neighbors in the form of a surprise party.

William Rohn owns 160 acres in Homestead, and eighty acres of bottom land. He has always lived on this farm. He is famous as a local Nimrod, having killed more ducks than any other man in this part of the State.

He has been a hunter all his life, and has made some wonderful scores. In the spring of 1885 he killed 165 ducks in three and one-half hours. His shots are always on the wing, he always giving his game a chance. He has always carried off the prizes in the pigeon and other shooting matches. He takes great interest in these pursuits, and keeps a fine pack of hunting dogs.

He was married in Beardstown, to Gusta Mahan, born and reared in this county, and died, after fourteen years of married life, in 1891. She was thirty-two years of age. She was a good, worthy woman, and the mother of six children, those living being Edwin, Anna and Fred. He was married for the second time, to Anna Mann, who was born, reared and educated in Cass county. Her father, John, died some years ago, but her mother is still living in Beardstown. Both wives, as well as Mr. Rohn, have been worthy members of the Methodist Episcopal Church. Mr. Rohn is a Republican in politics. They are very successful people, hard workers, and much esteemed by the whole neighborhood.

C. M. LANE, a successful wholesale and retail dealer in wines and liquors, located on East Main street, was born in Pennsylvania, and was but four years of age when his people came to Illinois. His father, S. P. Lane, was born in New York, and was married in Pennsylvania, and later came to Winnebago county, Illinois, where he died, in April, 1869. Mrs. Lane still survives him and now lives in Cadillac, Michigan, and is sixty-seven years old. Her maiden name was Mary E. Finn, of Pennsylvania, of German ancestry. She came of a long-lived family, her grandmother being at her death 105 years old, her mother eighty-five and her father ninety-five years of age.

Our subject was never married, but has devoted all his energies to his business. He has been engaged in it for more than ten years and by his own efforts has made his place headquarters for the best people in the city. He has lived in this city since 1871. He was engaged as a miller for some years. He enlisted from Cook county when only fifteen years of age, as a member of the Seventeenth Illinois Cavalry Regiment. He entered the army in 1863 and served until the close of the war, and also spent more than two years serving on the frontier. He escaped unhurt, but saw considerable hard service and received his honorable discharge as a brave soldier. He is known in Beardstown as a great hustler and is a Republican in politics.

JAMES NEELEY, foreman of the store house of the St. Louis division of the Quincy Railroad, was born in Philadelphia, Pennsylvania, March 20, 1857. He was the son of James Neeley, a Pennsylvanian who still lives in Philadelphia, over seventy five years of age. His business has been that of architect. His wife died when James was a few hours old. He was only twelve years of age when he came all alone to Beardstown in 1869, and has lived here ever since. He has gained the knowledge of the business of growing sweet potatoes and that industry was just being developed here. He received $20 dollars a month for his services. He was afterward variously engaged until he became of age and then connected himself with the Quincy Railroad. This took place in 1879, and he was engaged as car inspector for six years and afterward for four years. He was foreman of the lumber yard, which position was similiar to the one which he now holds. He has been the foreman of the store-house for three years and has charge of the receipts and distribution of all store house supplies.

He was married in Beardstown to Mary G. Fulks of Beardstown and a sister of R. B. Fulks (see biography for family history). Mr. and Mrs. Neeley attend the Methodist Episcopal Church, of which Mrs. Neeley is an active member. Mr. Neeley is a member of the subordinate and encampment lodges I. O. O. F., the former Ark Lodge, No. 7, and the latter Mt. Vernon Lodge, No. 7, and has filled the chairs of both lodges. They have no family. Mr. Neeley is a Republican in political, but is no office seeker, having no time to spare from his business.

JOHN GEORGE FREY, who has retired from active business, and living in Beardstown in a pleasant home, was born in Würtemburg, Germany, March 9, 1827. He grew up and worked on his father's farm until twenty-eight years of age. In February, 1854, he took passage on a sailing vessel to New York city, making the trip in thirty days. He then settled at Lancaster, New York, but left that place in six months, and came to Beardstown, which he has since made his home, and has been fairly successful in life. His father, John Frey, died in Germany when eighty years of age. His wife had died many years before, they both being members of the German Lutheran Church.

What Mr. Frey possesses he has made by his own efforts. When he arrived in this city in 1854, he began as a laborer, and was variously engaged for two years. In 1856 he became connected with Mr. Bohlman, and continued with him four years, until he engaged with Mr. Anton Ruck and continued there until he retired from active business.

He was married in Lancaster, New York, to Miss Mary Hoearsch. She was born in Würtemburg, Germany, August 13, 1824. She was a daughter of Mathias and Sarah Hoearsch, who lived and died in Würtemburg. They were birthright members in the Lutheran Church. She was the only member of her family, who came to this country, coming on the same vessel that brought her husband. She died at her home in this city January 26, 1888, having been a member of the Fourth Street Church. Mr. and Mrs. Frey have had four children. Two are living: William, a turner in this city, and is a successful busi ness man; and Mary, who is housekeeper for her father. She is a dutiful girl and an intelligent young woman. Mr. Frey and family are members of the Fourth Street Lutheran Church, and he and his son are Democrats in politics, good quiet citizens and upright, straightforward men.

GEORGE J. SCHMITT, a retired business man living on Sixth street, Beardstown, was born in Bavaria, Germany, May 14, 1828. His parents were Casper and Mary Schmitt, who were born, reared, married and died in their native country. They were members of the Catholic Church and died in middle age.

Our subject was yet a young man when, in 1854, he came to this country and spent one year in New York city, working at his trade of cabinetmaker. After that he journeyed around to many places, seeing the country, before he settled in Beardstown. He reached here in 1861, established a furniture business with his brother, Casper Schmitt, and by good judgment and honest dealing made money and retired from labor in 1882. He was married to Miss Mary Stoner, who was born in Beardstown, November 3, 1837. When she was six weeks old the family moved to Texas, settling in Montgomery county upon a farm and there her father died a few years later. His parents had both come from Germany and settled in Cass county, and were among the oldest settlers of the county. Mrs. Stoner is still living and makes her home with her daughter, Mrs. Schmitt. Although nearly eighty-two years of age she is very bright and active. Her father was Fred Krohe, who came to Illinois very early and died here. Mr. and Mrs. Schmitt have two living children, George J., Jr., now in charge of a drug store, No. 34 Washington street, Chicago; and Victor, who is connected with the same house.

PEYTON R. KEITH, a prominent farmer of section 29, Missouri township, is a native of that same township, having been born here, July 26, 1856. His father, Peyton A. Keith, was born in Kentucky, January 15, 1824, was a son of Peyton R., who reared a family of the following children: Isham, James, John, Alexander, Peyton A., Mary, Eliza A., America, Susan, Caroline and Mary J. The grandfather of our subject lost his wife in Kentucky, and in the fall of 1837, came to Illinois and passed the winter of 1837-'38 in Missouri township. He then rented land in Mt. Sterling township and later purchased land in the same place, becoming the owner of a good farm, where he finally died. His body rests in Mt. Sterling. His son, father of subject, was only a boy of thirteen when he came to Illinois, and continued to live at home during his father's life, settling his estate after his death. He married Mary Moses, a native of Ohio, born in September, 1830, daughter of William and Rhoda Moses, pioneers of 185–. After his marriage, the father settled on section 33, Missouri township, where he became the owner of 320 acres, improving it considerably. He lived here for many years, dealing in live stock, but the last fifteen years of his life he was an invalid and so was unable to carry on the work of his farm. His death occurred January 12, 1887, but his wife is still living, on the old homestead. He was a stanch Republican, but was no office seeker. He lived and died in the faith of the Christian Church. He and his good wife had eleven children, as follows: Peyton; John A., resident of Pea Ridge township; Joseph D. is on part of the old homestead; Francis Marion is on the old homestead with his mother; Charles I. is also with his mother; Mary J. is the wife of John W. Bell, and they are residents of Missouri township; and the other children all died in childhood.

Peyton, the namesake of his grandfather, was reared in his native county, where he attended the district schools and learned the vocation of farming. He remained at home until his marriage, when he settled on his present farm, where he owns 100 acres of fine land and carries on mixed farming.

Mr. Keith was married January 5, 1880, to Mary E. Bell, daughter of Ira and Emeline

Bell. Mr. and Mrs. Keith have three children, Bertie Arthur, William Austin and Ira Anderson.

Mrs. Keith has nine brothers and sisters, namely: Isham died in Columbus, Indiana; James died in Missouri; Alexander, resident of California; Mary married James Kirk and died in Iowa, 1891; Mary J. married Richard Bruce and died in Iowa; Eliza died in Mt. Sterling; America and Susan, married, are both deceased; and Caroline, who married General H. Roberts and died in Missouri township.

Mr. Keith is a strong Republican in politics and always supports the principles of his party. He is a worthy member of the Christian Church, and he and his estimable wife enjoy the respect and esteem of all their fellow citizens.

JOHN W. WEBB representative engineer of the Quincy Railroad, living at Beardstown, was born in Estill county, Kentucky, January 22, 1858. He was reared there until twelve years of age, when his parents moved to Daviess county, Missouri, and settled on a farm. Here he grew up on the farm with only ordinary school advantages. His father is Elijah Webb, son of Richard Webb, of North Carolina. The family came of old Maryland stock, and Richard was brought to Kentucky when eight years old by his parents, who settled on a farm. Here they died after improving the land to a considerable extent. Here Richard grew up and married Miss Clemy Tipton, born in Kentucky, in 1804. After their three children were grown up they removed to Daviess county, Missouri, and joined their son Elijah. They both died in this place, the wife in 1872, her husband ten years later. They both were Baptists. Their son Elijah, born in 1827, was a farmer in Kentucky and followed that profession all his life. He married Sallie A. Brinegar, born in 1841 in Kentucky. They now live in Harrison county, Missouri. Mrs. Webb is a member of the Christian Church, but Mr. Webb is a member of another organization.

John Webb is one of twelve children, of whom nine are yet living. He began his career in the railroad service in 1876 as a brakeman on the Iowa division of the Quincy road. He was then living in Iowa. When he was located at Eldon, Iowa, he was brakesman and extra conductor. Later he was a farmer in DeKalb, Missouri, for two years, and from there returned to the Quincy road, and has been employed by them ever since. He has gained the confidence of the road by his faithful service and good habits. He has been associated with the St. Louis division since June 10, 1886. He was a conductor of local and through freight trains and extra passenger conductor, and only had one wreck. That occurred in the winter of 1884, when engine 194 and eleven cars left the track at Vermont, Illinois. He is a practical man and has made money at his business.

He was married in Wapello county, Iowa, to Miss Hattie Smock, who was born in the same county and was there reared and educated. She is the daughter of Archibald and Hannah (More) Smock, natives of Ohio. They were married near Indianapolis, where Miss More and her parents had settled when she was a small child. Mr. Smock followed his vocation of farming, first in Indiana and then moved to Iowa, and, settling on a farm in Wapello county, remained there the rest of his life with his wife. They were both faithful members of the Baptist Church and were esteemed by all who knew them.

Mr. and Mrs. Webb have had four children, two of whom are dead. Those living are: Maude and Ernest E., two bright little children. Mr. and Mrs. Webb are attendants on the services of the Christian Church, of which Mrs. Webb is a member. Mr. Webb is a K. of P., being a member of the Beardstown Lodge, and he is a Democrat in politics. He and his wife are worthy citizens and are greatly liked for their many good qualities. Mr. Webb is a genial, warm-hearted man, with hosts of friends, and his good natured wife is equally esteemed.

A. S. COIL, editor and publisher of the Beardstown *Enterprise*, was born in Lincoln county, Missouri, October 24, 1860. His father, Jacob Y. Coil, was a native of Kentucky, came of southern parents, who were a stout and long-lived people. Jacob Y. Coil had moved into Missouri after the birth of one child, became a farmer and was thus engaged in Lincoln county until his death in 1873, aged forty-two. He was a kind man to his family, a good neighbor, a prominent Mason and a Democrat in politics. He had offered his services in 1861, but was refused on account of disabilities. Mrs. Jacob Coil's maiden name was Viola Olive Durough of Ohio, and she is yet living, in Mexico, Missouri, the mother of ten children, nine boys and one girl, of whom six are living.

Mr. Coil is the only one of his family in Illinois. His paper is a forty-eight column quarto weekly, published in the interests of the Democratic party. It was started under its present title in Meredosia by F. W. Schierbaum & Company, and in 1879 the plant was moved to Beardstown and continued under the same title. It was run as a daily and weekly. Mr. Schierbaum died in 1886 and C. H. Cummings took the paper as administrator, until Mr. Coil purchased the property in 1888. He is a practical newspaper man and has gone through all the experiences from printer's devil to his present position of editor-in-chief and publisher. He had many discouragements, but by dint of hard work he has been successful in clearing himself from debt and in running the paper successfully. The same perseverance which enabled him to gain a great part of his education by lamplight has served him well in his business. His paper has a good circulation and is ably edited. He is now making it a paying investment and by his own efforts has made it the principal Democratic paper of the county.

He was married in Perry, Pike county, Illinois, to Miss Dora Brandom of Indiana, in June, 1880. She came when young to Quincy, Illinois, with her parents, and her father now resides in Beardstown. Mr. and Mrs. Coil have six bright children: Maybell M., Grace, Arthur L., Harry, Bessie L. and Ruth M.,— all at home with their parents. They attend the Methodist Church. Mr. Coil has been a delegate to local conventions as he is a strong man in his party.

ERNEST H. BOLLE, now running a successful meat market on Second street, was born in Hesse-Darmstadt, near Hesse-Cassel, March 26, 1832. He is the son of John and Keshling Bolle, natives of Hesse, where they were married and their children were born. The family set out for the United States in 1845, landing after five weeks' voyage. They settled in Beardstown in the same year that they came to the country, and here the father died when sixty-eight years of age, and the mother died some time later. They had both been members of the Lutheran Church.

Mr. Bolle has resided in Beardstown ever since he arrived here in 1845. For some years he was a mechanical engineer for the Quincy Railroad. In 1885 Mr. Bolle went into business on his own account and has been quite successful as a dealer in live stock. His present business was established in 1879, under the firm name of Bolle, Ortwine & Co.

He was married in this city to Helena Nice. She was born in Hesse, Germany, and there her parents lived and died. She came with some old friends to this country and lived in this city until her death, December 5, 1887. She was born in 1833 and was a good wife and faithful mother, and bore her husband seven children, five of whom are yet living: Mary, wife of Henry G. Mohlman; Lena, wife of Zenas Sexton, a railroad bridge carpenter now at Galesburg; John is a clerk in the Quincy office in Beardstow n, and married to Ida French; George and Bertha still live at home.

WILLIAM WOOD, a prominent pioneer of 1827, resides on section 17, Huntsville township. He is the son of Mitchell and Nancy (Skiles) Wood, and was born in Wayne county, Missouri, March 8, 1824. His mother was born on the 27th of May, 1802. Her father, William, lived in Maryland and was the son of John and Lizzie Skyles. He was married in North Carolina, and went from there to Jasper county, Tennessee, resided there a few years and then moved to within forty miles of Nashville. There he lived until 1817 and then moved to the Territory of Missouri, remaining there until 1827, when he came to Schuyler county, Illinois, and became one of the first settlers of Rushville township. He resided there until 1844, when he went to Madison, Iowa, and remained there with his sons until his death in 1845. His wife's name was Lydia Chaddick, of North Carolina, and she also died in 1845. Mr. Wood's mother was first married at nineteen years of age, to Mitchell Wood of Kentucky. They were married in Missouri, went from there to Arkansas, but after his death in 1825 she returned to her parents in Missouri. In 1827 she married Jonathan Smith. They lived in a log cabin near Rushville. At that time Rushville consisted of three log houses. She now resides with her daughter, Mrs. Teel. During her married life she dressed her children in homespun, and she raised the flax and spun and wove the cloth out of which they were made.

In 1827 Mr. Wood came with the family to Illinois and grew to manhood in the vicinity of Rushville. He was raised a farmer and embraced all the advantages for learning that was possible in those early days. In the fall of 1848 he married Hulda Ann Teel (see sketch of James A. Teel in this book). After his marriage he continued to live on the home farm.

In 1853 he crossed the plains to California and engaged in mining. After an absence of fourteen months he returned via Isthmus of Panama and New York city. In 1854 he purchased eighty acres of his present farm and settled on same. In August, 1862, he enlisted in Company F, One Hundred and Ninteenth Illinois Volunteer Infantry, and served three years, going through many serious battles, and was mustered out with the rank of Corporal. After the war he resumed business on his farm and now owns 240 acres of land and follows stock-raising.

Mr. and Mrs. Wood have seven children: William H., Ann Elizabeth Wilson, Mitchell C., Dora Josephine, John R., Calvin Mead and Ella Alice. Mr. Wood is a Republican in politics and has been honored with all the local offices and is a member of Cyclone Lodge, I. O. O. F.

ZACHARIAH HASH, a widely known and esteemed pioneer of Cass county, Illinois, now one of the most prosperous farmers of this section, residing in township 19, range 9, was born in Green county, Kentucky, April 6, 1812.

He came of a family of patriots and successful agriculturists, many of whom held responsible positions, in the service of their country, and a few were noted hunters in pioneer days, being unerring marksmen and skillful trappers. His parents were Philip and Sarah (Nance) Hash, both natives of Virginia, who emigrated with their parents to Kentucky in an early day, when they themselves were quite young. The paternal grandparents of the subject of this sketch were Thomas and Ruth (Sturgeon) Hash, also natives of the Old Dominion, who spent their last days in Kentucky. The grandfather was a brave and efficient soldier in the Revolutionary war. The Hash family were of English ancestry, while the Sturgeons were originally from Ireland. The maternal grandfather was Zachariah Nance. Grandfather Nance served all through the Revolutionary war, and was a distinguished soldier. He drew a pension for his services, drawing at one time as high as $700. Others of the family were distinguished soldiers in the old wars of this country, who sought to defend their land in her hour of need. The Nances were mostly mechanics, being skilled in their various callings, and all lived to an advanced age. Our subject's parents and paternal grandparents were pioneers in three different States, and were hardy and energetic men and women, inured to hardship and toil. His father was an extensive traveler in pioneer days throughout the frontier, and visited nearly every settlement in the West during the '30s. He was an old Andrew Jackson Democrat, and took an active interest in pioneer politics. He was for forty years an efficient Justice of the Peace in this section of Illinois, discharging his duties with judgment and impartiality. He was born January 31, 1790, and died August 5, 1849; his wife was born October 24, 1791, and died February 27, 1847. Both expired in southwestern Missouri, whither they had removed from Illinois. They were the parents of fifteen children, six or eight of whom now survive, as far as known. Some of these are prominent men in Indiana.

The subject of this sketch worked on his father's farm in Kentucky and Illinois until he was married. On account of the newness of the country and his busy life, his educational advantages were neglected, and he attended school for the first time when he was twenty-one years of age. He is essentially a self-made man, and having inherited a good intellect and robust constitution, has applied himself with such persistency that he is now a well informed and progressive man, interested in everything that pertains to the welfare of his county, and takes a prominent part in all movements tending to the advancement of the community.

When he first came to this State it was wild and sparsely settled, game and wild fowl abounding in great profusion. He first located on Government land a short distance from where he now lives, on which he erected a log cabin. He lived there only two or three years, when he sold out and bought his present farm. He purchased 220 acres, which is now as fine a farm as can be found in Sangamon valley, or in the State. He paid twenty-five per cent interest on money with which he entered his land, but his industry and careful management soon enabled him to pay all indebtedness, and left him a comfortable income. He raises flourishing crops, has erected a comfortable farm house, and has large barns for his grain and stock, and is numbered among the prosperous farmers of the county.

He was first married, June 26, 1834, to Miss Polly Dick, who was born in Kentucky, February 16, 1817, an intelligent and worthy lady, and a daughter of Peter and Christina (Shutt) Dick, well known and highly respected people. By this marriage there were seven children, two of whom survive: Peter, born May 19, 1853; and Martha, born January 11, 1856, who married John Plunkett, a successful farmer, and they have five children. Two of our subject's children were married before their death: Philip, who had a son and daughter; and Sarah J., married to Benjamin E. Bowman, left two children, one of whom, Orpha, was born November 14, 1872, and has been at the home of the subject of this sketch ever since her birth. Mr. Hash's first wife died where he now lives, June 22, 1857, leaving her family and many friends to mourn her loss.

On April 3, 1862, Mr. Hash was again married, chosing for his second wife Miss Bowman, an estimable lady, who was born in Rutherford county, Tennesssee, March 17, 1825. Her parents were Daniel and Katie (Horn) Bowman, natives of Maryland and Tennessee, respectively. They were the parents of ten children, of whom, as far as known, only four are now living. The Bowmans were originally from Germany. Grandfather, Daniel Bowman, was an old Revolutionary soldier, and drew a liberal pension for his services. Most of Mrs. Hash's people are successful farmers.

Mr. Hash, like all of his people before him, is an Andrew Jackson Democrat, and although not actively engaged in political matters, takes an interest in all public affairs of importance. He is more of a home man, and his private affairs absorb most of his attention.

He and his wife have been earnest and useful members of the Christian Church for many years.

Whatever success in life has been obtained by Mr. Hash, is entirely due to his own exertions; and many a poor young man, just starting in life, would do well to read his history, and adopt the methods pursued by the subject of the sketch. These methods are unfailing, and are persistent industry and careful economy, supplemented by intelligence and uprightness of character.

CHARLES M. DUNLAP, who was for many years engaged in the lumber buusiness in Mt. Sterling, was born in Lexington, Fayette county, Kentucky, in 1836. His father, Rev Latin W. Dunlap was born in New Jersey and went from there to Kentucky when quite young. He was converted in his youthful days and joined the Baptist Church, but later identified himself with the Presbyterian Church He came to Illinois in 1837, landing at La Grange and then located in Mt. Sterling, and here organized the first Presbyterian Church in the county and was its pastor for many years. He was a resident of this place almost continuously from 1837 until he died in 1889, aged eighty-seven years. His wife's name was Rebecca M. Bell, born in Lexington, Kentucky, and died at the age of fifty-four

Charles Dunlap was but one year old when he came to Mt. Sterling with his parents He received his education in the public schools of this city, and when he had reached manhood's estate he engaged in the lumber business and so continued for twenty years. For about fifteen years of this time he was connected with F W Rottger. In 18— he sold out his lumberyard to his partner and moved to the farm which he now occupies This contains 400 acres, located one and one half miles east of the courthouse The buildings which he has erected compare favorably with the best in the county

For his wife he married Helen McCreery, born in Rushville, Schuyler county, daughter of James and Hannah McCreery. Mr. and Mrs Dunlap have four children· Helen, George, Latin and Annie. He is a Democrat and a member of Unity Lodge, I O. O. F.

SINGLETON G. WRIGHT is numbered among the honored pioneers who have passed away He was born in Hardin county, Kentucky, January 12, 1816, and died in Huntsville township, February 24, 1886. He has four brothers, Richard, James, Edmund and William. He came to Illinois on horseback in 1836 and when he arrived in Schuyler county his saddle horse constituted his entire property He worked as a farm hand for William McKee, near Rushville, and while thus engaged made the acquaintance of Sarah E Graham, who afterward became his wife. She was born in Kentucky, a daughter of Fergus and Martha (Tyree) Graham, who settled in Schuyler county in an early day

About two years later Mr. Wright settled on section 17, Huntsville, where he purchased 320 acres of land. He was industrious and observed due economy, and thus soon paid for his land and had money to loan. He carried on stock-raising in addition to his farming He was an active man until 1880, when he was taken sick with softening of the brain, which caused his death six years later

He was a Democrat in politics and a warm friend of public schools, being elected as School Trustee several terms. He donated the land occupied by the schoolhouse in the district

Mrs. Wright still survives her husband and still resides on the old homestead

Mr and Mrs Wright had four children Frances, the wife of William Wood, Jr.; Martha and Columbia, who carry on the home farm; and Alice, the wife of R. Ackley. When Mr Wright's health failed the work of carrying on the farm devolved on his two daughters, Martha and Columbia, as did the other business These two girls have carried on the work of the farm successfully, not only superintending the work but also doing much of the outdoor labor themselves. When their father died the two girls purchased the interest of the others and now own the farm with the exception of their mother's dowry. Martha attended college at Abingdon, Illinois, and taught school for thirteen terms She was a close student, rising at four in the morning in order to study. She is very systematic in all her work. The two are always willing to exert their influence for the Democratic party.

WILLIAM P. GAUT, the subject of this notice, was born in Jefferson county, Tennessee, April 16, 1862. His father was Robert Gaut, born in the same place, in 1800, and his father, the grandfather of our subject, was George Gaut, born in Pennsylvania, who went to Tennessee when a young man. This family is of Huguenot origin. He had by one wife thirteen children, of whom ten grew to adult age. One of these, James Gaut, lived to the age of ninety-seven years, and the average of these ten were over eighty, and the one still living, George Gaut, is on the old home farm. The father of our present subject was reared to farm life and has good common schooling. He married Mary P. Woods in Tennessee, who was born there in 1799. She was of a family of ten children: James, Mary P., Lutetia, John C., Martha J., W. P., E. Flora, Mary E., Sarah P. and Julia Ann M., the last two twins. Some of these children died in infancy. Of the six that came to adult age, five are still living. The mother of this family died in her forty-seventh year and the father lived nineteen years a widower. He died in 1864, in his sixty-fifth year, still mourning his wife.

William P. Gaut is a photographer. At the age of seventeen years he went to work in a blast furnace in Monroe county where he was reared and at this place he worked for six years at low wages. He had the promise of $20 a month, but at that time fifty cents a day was average wages when six cords of wood, pine and chestnut, could be bought for a dollar. He next went to work at the trade of carpenter and millwright and for six years this claimed his attention. From 1861 to 1886 he became a photographer, and he worked at this through Knoxville, Tennessee, and New Orleans.

Our subject was married in Versailles, in 1866, to Miss Elizabeth E. Reily, of Davidson county, North Carolina, who was born there December 21, 1840. She was the daughter of Solomon and Polly (Williams) Reily, both natives of North Carolina. She came to Illinois in 1850 with her mother, in a covered wagon, emigrant style, and were four weeks making the trip. They camped out all but two nights, when the weather was stormy. She was an only child and lived with her mother until her marriage.

After marriage Mr. and Mrs. Gaut lived in Mount Sterling for a few months and then moved to Marietta, Georgia, where they remained about nine years when they returned to Mount Sterling and Mr. Gaut continued the old business which he had started during the war. They bought their present farm of 611 acres, all bottom land except eighty acres, where they reside on the Bluffs, paying $8,000 for it. They have buried two sons and two daughters, all in infancy, but have four of the finest boys left that can be found in the township. R. Eugene is twenty-one, James B. is nineteen, Charles W. is fourteen and George Lea is a bright lad of ten years. All are at home in the sense of not having thought of any separate home; Eugene is attending college at the State University at Champaign; and James B. is following his fancy by learning the carpenter's trade.

Mr. Gaut makes a special crop of his corn, and raises many hogs. He has his hill land for a fruit farm and has it planted mostly in apples and peaches. The native products of uplands are pawpaws and of the bottoms are pecans. He expects his land to yield from fifty to 100 bushels of corn to the acre.

Mr. Gaut is an ancient Odd Fellow and is a Royal Arch Mason and is a Democrat in politics. He was in the Confederate army from 1861 to 1863, and although he was not wounded he lost his health. He was made a prisoner at Knoxville. He has voted for every President since 1861 and has been active in his party.

The aged mother of Mr. Gaut lives with him and is strong and vigorous still.

WILLIAM H. McCREERY is a resident of Huntsville township, residing on section 6, having settled here in 1834. His father, William McCreery, was born in Culpeper county, Virginia, March 1, 1802, being a son of John McCreery, who was also a native of Virginia and a planter. He married Sarah Rousseau, of French ancestry. William McCreery, Sr., was reared on a farm and when seven years of age, the family removed to Kentucky, where he grew to manhood in Pulaski county. Here he entered the ministry of the Methodist Episcopal Church as an itinerant preacher. His work was in Kentucky and Tennessee. In 1827 he preached in Orange county, Indiana. From there, in 1829, he went to Missouri and stayed for a few years, and an account of his work in this State may be found at length in Dr. McNally's History of Methodism in Missouri. In 1832, in Cape Girardeau county, Missouri, he married Harriet E. Long, and two years later they came to Rushville, Schuyler county, Illinois. The next year they settled on section 6, Huntsville township, where Mr. McCreery had purchased a claim August, 1834, and here he resided until his death, November 2, 1884. He was a local preacher and was assigned a circuit in 1848, the Columbus circuit, Adams county. He continued his religious work until within a few weeks of his death. His wife died two days before her husband. He died within two hours after returning from her funeral. Mr. McCreery was a good man and was greatly opposed to slavery, refusing to receive any portion of them from his father's estate. He was an ardent Whig and Republican in politics. They had thirteen children, nine of whom grew up to manhood, namely: James N. and John F., twins: the former was drowned in the Missouri river while working on the bridge at Kansas City; the latter died in Taylor county, Iowa; William H.; Sarah married Robert Ellis and resides at Saline county, Missouri; Eliza married William Kirk and resides in Lincoln county, Washington; Benjamin B. is a merchant and resides in Augusta, Illinois; Henry C. is also a merchant and resides in Illinois; Edward M. resides in Henry county, and Mary married to Quincy Allphin and residing near Andover, Kansas.

Our subject was born in Cape Griardeau county, Missouri, June, 1834, and was only six months old when the family settled in Illinois. He was reared on the farm and attended the country schools two or three miles distant from his home until he was twenty-one. He then attended Rode River seminary one year. He then rented a farm from his father and in 1863 settled where he now resides, and in 1868 became the owner of 160 acres of land. He now owns 333 acres of land and follows stock-raising. He is a good Republican and has always supported the straight ticket. He is interested in all matters tending to improve the welfare of the county or township. He has run for several of the local offices, but, owing to the Republican party being in the minority, he has been defeated. He is a charter member of the Huntsville Lodge, No. 465, A. F. and A. M., and has been Master of the same lodge.

He was married in 1881 to Rachel Baxter, daughter of James and Elizabeth (Cooper) Baxter of Ohio. The Baxter family came to Schuyler county in June, 1857, and settled in Huntsville. Mr. and Mrs. McCreery have had ten children, six grown up, namely: William Morris, for fourteen months in the census office at Washington, is now in Augusta, Illinois; Frank M. and Fred H., twins, the former at home and the latter dealing in implements in Augusta, Illinois; Harry, Ralph and Mary are at home. Mr. and Mrs. McCreery are members of the Methodist Episcopal Church, in which they are earnest workers.

EDWARD HAGENER, one of the firm of Hagener & Schuman, dealers in wines and liquors, located at the corner of State and Main streets, Beardstown, was born here in 1855, and was reared and educated in this same city, and he has always resided here. He is the younger of three sons, all of whom are excellent business men. Their father, William Hagener, now deceased, was for many years prominent in the history of Beardstown. He was a man liked and respected by every one. He was a Republican in politics, and a member of the Lutheran Church. His wife yet living, aged seventy-three years, is one of the best old ladies in the city.

Mr. Hagener established a wood and coal yard in 1877. He also dealt in farm implements, and also managed a farm for some time in Hitchcock county, Nebraska, and spent some time in Colorado and California. His present business was established in February, 1890.

He was married in this city first to Miss Carrie Nieman. She was born in this city, and died at her home in this city, when only twenty-three years of age. She left one child, John, now a clerk for his grandfather, Fred Nieman. Mr. Hagener was married a second time, in St. Louis, Missouri, to Miss Mollie Harmon, January 29, 1889. She was born and reared in Astoria, and she is an excellent housekeeper and the mother of two children, George E. and Pearl. Mr. and Mrs. Hagener attend the Lutheran Church, and Mr. Hagener is a member of the I. O. O. F., Arch Lodge, No. 16. It is an old and very strong lodge. He has been a public-spirited man, and a worker for everything of value for his city and county. He takes no particular part in politics, but votes the Republican ticket.

JOSEPH J. SMITH, of section 8, Pea Ridge township, is a native of North Carolina, having been born in that State, Chatham county, February 25, 1843. His father, Relliff Smith, was also born in the same county, December 4, 1810, being a son of Jonah and Patsy Smith. He married Nancy Dorsett, came to Illinois in 1851, and settling in North East township, Adams county, where he purchased land, becoming the owner of 180 acres of good land. He later removed to a farm near Clayton, and resided there until 1890; then as he had sold his farm to our subject, he began to make his home with his son, and has continued with him ever since. His wife died in 1875. They had three children.

Joseph was reared on a farm, and resided at home until he grew to manhood. He was married in the fall of 1861, to Elizabeth May, daughter of Benjamin May. She was a native of North Carolina. Mr. May and his wife, Mary (Harris) May, were natives of the same State as their daughter, Mrs. Smith. They came to Illinois in the fall of 1846, settling, first in Mt. Sterling, where the father rented land for three years. He then removed to Pea Ridge township, where he first rented land and then purchased ninety acres in section 16, which was partially improved. Here he has since resided, becoming the owner of 280 acres of land. He still owns 150 acres. He dates his birth back to 1818. He had ten children, eight of whom grew up.

Joseph resided at home after his marriage until the death of his mother. In the fall of 1889, he removed to Brown county, and purchased his present farm of 159 acres of land, fifteen acres of this is planted with as fine an orchard as is in this part of the State. This farm is a very good one in every way, as it ought to be, as Mr. Smith has always followed farming, and so ought to know how to develop his land. He deals largely in the culture of small fruits and has been very successful with them.

Mr. Smith's father was a blacksmith by trade, and pursued his trade in his native State. This work had no attraction for Joseph, however, and so he turned his attention to farming, with very satisfactory results, as his nice farm with the two sets of farm buildings testifies.

Mr. and Mrs. Smith have no children. Mr. Smith is a Republican, but like his father before him he has refused any office. He and his wife are members of the Presbyterian Church, of Clayton. They are very estimable people, and enjoy the respect of the whole community.

JOHN BAUJAN, deceased, who died at his home at Beardstown, July 4, 1889, at the age of sixty-nine years, was born in Siegberg, Germany, April 6, 1820. He came of pure German stock and had grown up to the trade of stone and brick mason. He left Antwerp with two of his fellow townsmen, William and Philip Frisbaugh, in the spring of 1849. They landed in New Orleans and came up the river in one of the old river boats to St. Louis. The cholera was raging there at this time and he came on to Arenzville, Cass county, Illinois, and was engaged there for some years at his trade of making brick, building several houses at that place. He then lived one year on a farm three miles from Arenzville, and in 1856 came to Beardstown and made this place his home until his death. He followed his trade and later he with Philip Frisbaugh, put up a sawmill and ran it two years. After that, with John Schultz, he purchased the gristmill at this place under the firm name of Baujan & Schultz. They did a very large and successful business here. At his death the mill interest went to his two sons, Louis and Edward. Mr. Baujan was a good, upright man and one of the city's best and most successful citizens. He was a Democrat in politics and a Roman Catholic in religion. He was an Alderman of Beardstown city and served in that capacity in a faithful manner.

He was married in 1852, to Catharine Yock of Würtemburg, Germany, born September

10, 1828. She was the daughter of Jacob and Christina (Trouth) Yock, who lived and died at Würtemburg. They were members of the Lutheran Church and were worthy, hard-working people. Mrs. Baujan came of a large family, who now reside here. She has been a true, good wife and mother, and is a much respected lady of this county and a most consistent member of the Lutheran Church. Mr. and Mrs. Baujan had eight children, one, Philipena, died young. Those living are: John of the grocery firm of Baujan Brothers, on Fourth street, this city; Rosa, wife of John Schultz, a miller of this city; Henry, who is a liveryman and blacksmith; Kate, wife of Charles Rupple, with his father, Henry Rupple, in the shoe business; Louis and Edward, of the firm of Baujan Brothers, millers; and Otto, of the firm of Baujan Brothers, grocery merchants.

JAMES L. DE WITT, a son of the Rev. James De Witt, whose biography appears on another page of this history, was born in Rushville township, Schuyler county, Illinois, April 30, 1845. He remained at home and led the life which usually falls to the pioneer farmer's son, until twenty-five years of age, when he was united in marriage to Miss Sarah F. Ross, who was born in this township and county, October 6, 1850. Her parents, Talbart and Catharine (Snyder) Ross, were natives of Kentucky and Virginia respectively. The father emigrated to Illinois about the year 1830, and died here at the age of forty-five years; he purchased land and left one of the finest farms in this locality. His wife was a native of the Shenandoah valley, and died in Adams county, Illinois, at the age of fifty-six years. They had born to them a family of nine children, eight of whom are living. In his political opinions Mr. Ross affiliated with the Democratic party until 1844; he then united with the Whigs, to whom he gave his support until 1856; he then cast his suffrage with the Republican party. He and his wife belonged to the Methodist Episcopal Church, and were members of the Rev. James De Witt's congregation, in Littleton township; they were zealous workers in the Sabbath-school, and were among the pioneers in establishing and keeping up organizations.

Mr. De Witt has been a citizen of this community all his life. He has represented the people in the various local offices; has been town Clerk, Justice of the Peace, and Collector, rendering entire satisfaction in his methods of conducting the business of these offices; it should not be omitted that he has filled the position of Supervisor three terms, giving the same faithful service that has characterized his transaction of business, both public and private. Mr. and Mrs. De Witt are the parents of two children: Jessie R. was born February 26, 1875; Clyde L. was born January 1, 1882.

THOMAS J. CHALFANT, a well-known and influential citizen of Beardstown, Illinois, was born in West Virginia in 1823. His parents, William and Helen (Adams) Chalfant, were natives of Pennsylvania. Here they were reared and were married, after which they moved into West Virginia, and Mr. Chalfant followed his trade of ship carpenter until his death, which occurred when he was sixty-five years old. His wife had died previously, in 1832, leaving six children, three of whom are yet living.

Thomas Chalfant is the only one of the family in this State. He came to the State when but twelve years of age, with a family by the name of Clark. He had lived with this family after the death of his mother. He assisted in farming until he was twenty-four, and then learned the trade of machine carpenter and pattern-maker, and after learning was three years in a foundry. At last he went to work on his own account, and started to making wagons. For years he made a greater number of the wagons than were made in the whole surrounding country, but in time he was obliged to give way to the larger manufactories, and he then did repairing until six years ago, when he turned the business over to his son Walter, who now carries on the business with his partner, Mr. Doesser. Mr. Chalfant has lived in the town of Beardstown so long that he has seen it change from a wilderness to the growing, prosperous place it now is. He has lived here ever since coming to the State, with the exception of a trip he took in 1859. He started in that year for Pike's Peak, but became discouraged and returned home. Beardstown was the chief town for conveying goods from St. Louis to inland places, and oxen were used to draw the wagons from one place to the other, and this slow and laborious mode of travel was continued some time after Mr. Chalfant came to the State.

He was married in Beardstown, to Miss Anna E. Norton, of Wheeling, West Virginia, and the daughter of Thomas P. Norton, a worthy pioneer of Illinois. He started the first store and hardware shop of Beardstown. Two of their children are deceased. Their living children are: Helen, now Mrs. David B. Treadway, of Butler county, Nebraska; Matilda, now Mrs. William Danner, of Kansas; Walter S., who carries on his father's old business, married Louisa Looken, and resides in Beardstown; Gertrude, now Mrs. James McClure; Anna, now Mrs. Edwin Stribbs, of Beardstown.

Mr. Chalfant is one of Beardstown's most honored and respected men. He has worked his way up from a poor boy to the position he now enjoys. He has retired from business, and is now reaping the benefits of his years of toil and labor.

JEPTHA PLASTER, an esteemed pioneer of Cass county, Illinois, for four years Associate Justice, and a prominent citizen of Chandlerville, was born in Robinson county, Tennessee, March 19, 1827.

His parents, Thomas and Elizabeth (Batts) Plaster, were also natives of Tennessee, the families on both sides being prominent in the State, many members holding responsible public offices. Thomas and Mary Plaster, the paternal grandparents, were natives of North Carolina, who accompanied their son to Illinois in an early day. The grandfather was a devout and able Baptist minister, who, besides successfully conducting a farm, preached throughout Cass and adjacent counties, doing much good in the dissemination of moral and religious knowledge. No opportunity escaped him of enlightening the people in regard to their obligations, and urging upon them a conscientious fulfillment of their duties. On one occasion, when the subject of this sketch and his grandfather were on their way to the mill, the old gentleman, seeing a group of people, addressed them in an impressive discourse, after which he and his grandson resumed their journey. The grandparents lived to a very old age, and were the recipients of wide-spread and universal esteem The maternal grandparents, Jeremiah Batts and wife, were life-long and respected residents of Tennessee, where they died at an advanced age greatly mourned by a large circle of friends. The father of the subject of this sketch grew to manhood in his native State of Tennessee, and was there married A few years after marriage, in the spring of 1828, leaving his family in Tennessee, he came alone to Illinois, and located Government land In the fall of the same year, he returned after his family, who, with his parents, accompanied him on his removal to the Prairie State. The journey was made overland with an ox team and cart, several weeks being consumed on the way. Once, their cart broke down, and they were obliged to trade a horse for a wagon with which to proceed On their arrival in Illinois, the grandfather settled on Government land in Morgan county, which then embraced what is now Cass county, the latter having been formed out of Morgan county territory in 1835. The father continued to live on rented land for a year or two, when he removed to his own farm. For twelve or fourteen years, he and his family occupied a little log cabin. This was subsequently replaced by a better log and frame house, which, in 1853, gave place to a substantial farm residence His father purchased all his early supplies in Beardstown, which then boasted of but one log store. The country abounded in wild game, such as deer, squirrel, rabbit, turkey, prairie chicken, etc., which, supplemented by the products of the farm, formed the diet of the frontiersman. Thus, industriously and happily, the parents passed their lives on the old homestead, which they had reclaimed from the wilderness. It was in this home, made sacred by many ties, that the beloved mother expired at the age of fifty-five years The father survived her but a short time, dying in 1858, aged fifty-six, as if unable to endure separation from his life long companion This worthy couple had nine children, three of whom survive the subject of this sketch; Mrs Richard M. Johnson, living in Chandlerville precinct, Cass county, Illinois; and Mrs Elizabeth Layman, residing in Lincoln, Logan county, same State

Jeptha Plaster, whose name heads this memoir, spent his early days on the old homestead, and received his education at a subscription school and from private instruction at his teacher's home. In those days, it was customary for the teacher to board around in the various families of the neighborhood, each person subscribing toward the support of the school, according to the number of children sent. Our subject's father agreed to send two pupils, but usually sent and paid for three

When twenty-one years of age, Mr. Plaster rented land from his father, which he farmed until 1852, at which time, induced by the gold excitement in California, he went overland to that State, where he spent a year and a half prospecting and mining. He then returned to his old home, and worked on his father's farm.

On October 14, 1858, he married Miss Elizabeth Johnson, an estimable lady, and a native of Morgan, now Cass, county, where she was born March 15, 1838. She was a daughter of John and Rosanna (Adkins) Johnson, both natives of Tennessee, who were early settlers and esteemed residents of this section of Illinois

Mr. Plaster continued to fellow agricultural pursuits until 1880, when he bought his valuable city property, on which he erected his present comfortable residence, and retired from farm life. His father left at his death about 1,000 acres of land, of which Mr. Plaster now owns about 600 acres, a good share of which he bought.

Coming of a family of lifetime Democrats, Mr. Plaster has followed in their footsteps, casting his first vote in 1848 for Lewis Cass and William O. Butler for president and vice-president. His constituents have emphasized their appreciation of his abilty and worth by electing him Associated Justice of Cass county in 1869. He is also a member of the School Board, his election to the latter position having been non-partisan and unsought, although he appreciates the honor.

Such unanimous endorsement of Judge Plaster's worth renders further remarks on the subject not only unnecessary but impertinent. He has brought to his office a varied and extended experience, unusual acumen, and sustained powers of thought and reason as well as a reputation above reproach, together with a kindly disposition, which can sympathize while condemning, thus winning the hearts of his fellow-men.

CAPTAIN ROBERT E. WILLIAMS, Postmaster and druggist, of Camden, has been one of the most prominent of its residents since 1850. He was born in Montgomery county, Kentucky, April 14, 1829, being a son of Robert P. and Christina A. (Urquhart) Williams, both natives of Kentucky. The family came to Illinois in 1830, and first settled in Hancock county, but soon removed to Quincy. Robert Williams was a lawyer and practiced law the remainder of his life at Quincy. He died in 1840. He was an ardent Whig, and held local offices. He was also a member of the Methodist Episcopal Church, being an earnest worker. When he died he was only thirty-five years old. His wife died in 1833, aged thirty years. They had three children, of whom Robert is the only surviving member. The father of Robert P. was John, and he married Amelia Gill. They came to Illinois, and died in Pike county. They had a large family of twelve children which they raised. They were widely known and respected.

Robert E. received a fair education, and then clerked in several stores until he came to Schuyler county in 1850 and engaged in farming, in Birmingham township, where he purchased 340 acres of land. Three years later he removed to Rushville and engaged in saddlery and harness, continuing in the same nearly twenty years, and was also engaged in the drug trade. In 1879 he came to Camden, and has since represented the drug trade in Camden.

In the time of his country's need he enlisted in Company K, One Hundred and Thirty-seventh Illinois Volunteers, going as Captain. They were stationed at Memphis. Captain Williams raised this company and served 100 days, the time of the enlistment. On his return he assisted in raising Company K, One Hundred and Fifty-first Illinois Volunteer Infantry, of which he was made First Lieutenant. They were ordered to Nashville, and from there to join Sherman in Georgia, at Columbus. Here the company was mustered out of service.

In the cyclone of 1887 Mr. Williams lost his building and a fine stock of goods. He was caught up and lodged in the branches of an apple tree, some distance from where he was.

He was married in 1851, to Mary E. Baker, born in Missouri, a daughter of George Baker. She died in Rushville in 1877, leaving one son, Emory, now with his father. In 1879 Captain Williams was married to Nancy Allen, who was born in Ohio. They have two children, Ellen M. and Myrtle A.

He is a Republican in politics, and has been one since the formation of the party, and has held the position of Postmaster since 1880, with the exception of about ten months during the Cleveland administration. He is a member of Rushville Lodge, No. 9, A. F. & A. M., and Royal Arch and Chapter, at the same place. He was Master of the lodge two terms, and has held many of the minor offices. He is now Secretary of the lodge. He and his wife are worthy members of society, and are highly esteemed by all who know them.

GEORGE EDWARD SNYDER, a prominent farmer and respected citizen of section 15, Buena Vista township, Schuyler county, Illinois, was born in the same section on which he now resides, the date of which event was October 7, 1836. His parents were Jacob and Margaret (Hughes) Snyder, natives of Virginia, who located in Schuyler county, October 5, 1835. His father was born August 9, 1798, and died September 28, 1865, aged sixty-seven years. His mother was born March 23, 1798, and died November 7, 1849, aged fifty-one years. She was a woman of many admirable traits of character, much beloved, and lamented by her family and friends. His parents were married February 10, 1822, and located in Schuyler county, Illinois, October 5, 1835. They had four children: John W., born in Frederick county, Virginia, June 4, 1823; James W., born June 14, 1830, now residing on a farm near Hamilton, Illinois; Joseph W., born July 9, 1833, resides in Littleton township, same State; and the subject of our sketch.

Our subject was reared on a farm, and attended the district schools. He lived at home and assisted on the farm, until he was married, on October 25, 1859, after which he farmed for himself. He married Margaret McCreary, daughter of Robert and Fannie McCreary. After his marriage, he rented land in Buena Vista township, on which he remained for two years, and then purchased 320 acres in Huntsville township, where he lived until the death of his father, in 1865, when he sold his farm and returned to the old homestead, where he has since resided. He owns 162 acres of land and has good improvements. Besides agriculture, he deals largely in live-stock, in which he is very successful.

His wife died March 16, 1877. She was a woman of ability and was much lamented by her family and friends. She left six children: Roland M., who was born September 9, 1862, now a farmer of Buena Vista township; Charles died at the age of seven years, four months and twenty-seven days; Florence was born April 10, 1867, and married P. Bartlow, now residing in Littleton township; Fannie was born August 8, 1870; Dwight C. was born May 27, 1874; and Carl C. was born September 14, 1876.

Our subject married a second time September 26, 1877, his choice being Mrs. Eva Ann Boyles, *nee* Krieole. She was born in Clarion county, Pennsylvania, March 16, 1845. Her parents were David and Mary Krieole, both natives of Pennsylvania, who removed to Ohio about 1846, locating in Benton county. Here their daughter, Eva Ann, married John H. Boyles, October 6, 1861, who in 1869 removed to Illinois, locating in Augusta, Hancock county, later removing to

Schuyler county, where he died September 19, 1873. He was a soldier in the Civil war, a member of Company D, Ninetieth Ohio, and served for three years, dying from the effects of disease contracted during his service. He left five children: Mary E., born November 2, 1862, who died aged sixteen years and three months; Martha Ann, wife of William Krieole, resides in Macomb, Illinois; Nora J. was born April 9, 1868, and died in 1873; Daniel H. was born March 12, 1870, now residing in Littleton township; Viola M. was born December 16, 1872, and died in May, 1874.

Mr. and Mrs. Snyder have two children: Lee Edwin, who was born January 29, 1878, and Eva Lena, born June 22, 1882.

Politically, Mr. Snyder affiliates with the Democratic party, and has been honored by his constituents by an election to a membership of the School Board, in which capacity he has served for twenty-one years, and has also served as Road Commissioner for a period of three years.

Mr. and Mrs. Snyder belong to the Methodist Episcopal Church, of which they are respected members.

Upright in his dealings, of high morality, and great industry, he has accumulated a comfortable supply of this world's goods, and what is best of all, enjoys in addition thereto the hearty good-will of his fellow citizens.

JOHN P. MURPHY, of the firm of Murphy & Co., proprietors of the Camden Roller Mills, at Camden, Illinois, has been a resident of Schuyler county since 1886, born in East Tennessee, August 18, 1833, being a son of William L. and Matilda (Hill) Murphy, natives of Virginia and North Carolina. William's father was a native of Scotland and came to the United States, settling in Virginia. He was a merchant of Richmond, Virginia. William, born in 1805, went to Sullivan county, Tennessee, when a young man, and there married, and still resides there, a farmer. His wife is deceased. They had nine children: Preston W., John, Robert E., William B., David W., James J., Martha Josephine, Mary and Caroline.

John was reared on a farm and received a limited education. When he grew up he learned the trade of a blacksmith. When the war broke out he was exempted from serving, although he was conscripted. He worked for the Confederate Government at his trade at Knoxville. When Burnside captured the city John remained with the Union forces. In March, 1864, he engaged as engineer in a mill. In 1868 he returned to East Tennessee and worked as engineer for four years. In 1872, he returned to Brown county and continued his trade until 1886, when he came to Camden and purchased the Camden Roller Mills. He made many improvements, putting in the newest machinery, and has made it one of the finest mills of its kind in the vicinity. He has a flour, feed and exchange at Mount Sterling.

He was married to Flora Gault, who was born in East Tennessee, a daughter of Robert Gault. She had one child, deceased. She died at Knoxville, Tennessee. Mr. Murphy was married at Mount Sterling, to Mivina M. Black, daughter of Judge Samuel Black. He is a Democrat in politics, but takes very little interest in such matters. Mr. and Mrs. Murphy are members of the Methodist Episcopal Church. Mr. Murphy is a member of the Hardin Lodge, A. F. & A. M., No. 44, and also Chaplain of the R. A. M., at Mount Sterling, of which he was a prominent member for many years. He is also a member of Unity Lodge, No. 310, I. O. O. F., and has passed all the chairs in the same.

REV. WILLIAM WEIGAND in charge of St. Alexis' Catholic Church, Beardstown, was born in Zanesville, Ohio, April 12, 1852. He was reared in Brown county, Illinois, where his parents moved when he was a child. His parents were John and Elizabeth (Leisen) Weigand, natives of Hesse-Darmstadt, Germany. The father was a soldier in the regular German army and he came to the United States after his discharge and married his wife in Baltimore, where she had lived after coming to America with her parents. Mr. and Mrs. Weigand settled in Philadelphia and afterward moved to Zanesville, Ohio, and from there to Brown county, Illinois, in 1864, and settled on a farm. Farming was the vocation of Mr. Weigand. He died soon after coming to Illinois when he was fifty-four years of age. His wife is still living, aged seventy-six years, and is the housekeeper for her son, the subject of this notice. She has eight children, forty-eight grandchildren and twenty-two great-grandchildren. The entire family are good Catholics and are successful in whatever profession they have adopted, making hosts of friends.

Mr. Weigand was thirteen years old when he was sent to St. Francis College, Milwaukee, Wisconsin. Later he was sent to St. Joseph College and finished his course at a college in Ohio. The church at Beardstown is the first charge he has had since he graduated in the spring of 1878. He was ordained by the Right Rev. Father P. J. Balters, now deceased, then of Alton, Illinois. The church has grown under Father Weigand in a wonderful degree. When he came there fourteen years ago he found the church bending under the weight of a heavy debt. He has not only cleared off the debt, but has recently finished a new church edifice that is one of the finest buildings in the county. The corner stone was laid July 7, 1889. It is of brick and all the appointments, both inside and out, are of the most beautiful design. The altar furnishings are in keeping with the general tone of the whole building, and the whole taken together far surpasses any of the buildings used for religious purposes in Beardstown.

The history of the church dates back to the '40s, when a priest from Quincy, Illinois, came to start the church in Beardstown. He built and added to the edifice. There are now about 100 heads of families in the church and it is in a growing condition, although the railroad strike of 1887 caused a decrease of twenty-five families. Father Weigand is a worker and is a man greatly beloved by all his people, having studied their wants. He has charge of the parish at Arenzville. He had a parish school at Beardstown for a time, under his supervision. Father Weigand is a man of true Catholic spirit.

CHRISTIAN BROCKSCHMIDT, a general farmer and stock raiser in Beardstown precinct, was born in Washington county, Illinois, January 30, 1852. His father's name was Henry, who was a native of Hanover, Germany, grew up a blacksmith and came to the United States in 1828. He settled in St. Louis, Missouri, and later his father and stepmother, through his help, also came to America. After Henry came to this country he worked with the Eagle foundry of St. Louis, but losing his health he settled with his family on a farm in Washington county, Illinois. His wife died some years later and he afterward went back to St. Louis and spent his last years there, dying in 1877 at the age of sixty-three years. He was a skilled mechanic, an active citizen and a worthy member of the Lutheran Church. He was a Democrat in politics. His wife was named Katharina Helmick, a native of Prussia, who came to St. Louis when a young girl. She was a mother of nine children and died in 1866, at the age of fifty-seven. She was a good, kind woman and a member of the Lutheran Church.

Christian is the youngest of a family of nine. He came here from St. Louis, where he had lived since he was fourteen years. He had been engaged as a teamster for many years. He came to Cass county, February 1880, first rented his land and then purchased his present farm, August 12, 1890. It consists of 244 acres in what is known as bottom lands, and 120 acres are under the plow. This is considered a fine piece of farming land and is located in township 19, range 11.

He was married in St. Louis, Missouri, to Louisa Shave, who was born in Prussia in 1850 and came to the United States when fourteen years old, located at St. Louis, Missouri, where her father, William died in 1877. He was thrice married. His first wife, the mother of Mrs. B., died in Germany when the latter was very young. Mr. and Mrs. B. have three children: Ida E., Fred W. at home, and Minnie, deceased. They are members of the Sixth Street Lutheran Church. He is a Republican. They are excellent people and highly respected.

WILLIAM L. BRUMBACK, Postmaster and merchant at Huntsville, became a resident of that place October 22, 1864. He was born in Boone county, Kentucky, January 29, 1852, being a son of Peter W. and Ann E. (Estes) Brumback. The former was born in Virginia in 1801, but removed in childhood with his parents to Kentucky, where he passed his early life on a farm, learned the trade of brick mason, also silversmith. He married in Kentucky a lady who was born September 22, 1809, and died March 16, 1884. After his marriage he bought land and engaged in farming. In October 1864, they came to Schuyler county, Illinois, and settled in Huntsville, where he was interested for a short time in merchandise. He died November 27, 1867. He and his wife had twelve children, eight of whom grew to maturity, namely: Oliver, Benjamin, Mildred Harrison, Isabel Barmour, Adelia Smith, Nathan, William L., Jessie Aleshire. Peter Brumback was an old-line Whig and later a Republican, being always prominent in politics. His father, also Peter Brumback, was a German and came to the United States when sixteen years of age. He served seven years in the Revolutionary war, being present at the surrender of Cornwallis. His brother, John, also came to America. The two were sons of a ship-builder in Germany. Mr. Peter Brumback, Jr., was an earnest member of the Methodist Episcopal Church.

William was reared on a farm and tilled the soil until 1881, when he engaged in mercantile business and still continues it. He is a stanch Republican in politics. The appointment of Postmaster was conferred on him during Arthur's administration and he served nearly five years. In 1889 he was again appointed and now holds the office. He is also a Notary Public.

He was married, July 8, 1889, to Mary E., daughter of Budley and Nancy Overstreet. She was born in Huntsville. Mr. Brumback is a member of Huntsville Lodge, No. 465, A. F. & A. M. Mr. and Mrs. Brumback are highly esteemed citizens of Huntsville.

WILLIAM HALE, an honored pioneer of Schuyler county, Illinois, who has contributed materially to the phenomenal advancement and prosperity of this section by his superior executive ability, unremitting energy and progressive disposition, enjoys a well-earned repose in retirement at Rushville. He is a native of New Madrid county, Missouri, where he was born May 18, 1833. His parents were James and Charlotte (Briggs) Hale, the former a native of Georgia and the latter of Vermont. Joshua Hale, paternal grandfather of the subject of this sketch, was also a native of Georgia, while his father was a native of England, who emigrated to this country at a very early day, and located in the South. Joshua Hale moved to Missouri previous to the war of 1812, and was one of the pioneers of that territory, which at that time included a very large area, out of which many States have been formed, but which was then the frontier of civilization. Joshua Hale was a farmer by occupation and secured a large tract of Government land in this new and fertile territory, but spent the last years of his life in New Madrid. James Hale was but a child when his parents removed to Missouri, where he was reared, educated and married, his wife being a lady of superior attainments and culture. She was a daughter of Asa Briggs, a brave and efficient soldier of the Revolutionary war; and widow of John Smith. In 1837, the family, consisting of father, mother and ten children, removed to Illinois. Here, although land could then be purchased for $1.25 an acre, the father, on account of limited means, was obliged to rent a farm for a few years. By industry and economy, he accumulated in time sufficient means to purchase a farm, and bought some choice agricultural land in Buena Vista township, on which he and his family located. This he assiduously cultivated and made on it many valuable improvements, continuing to reside there until his death, his wife also dying on the old homestead. He was a man of sterling qualities of mind and heart, and enjoyed with his worthy wife the highest esteem of all who knew them. Their death was greatly lamented, not only by their immediate family and friends, but by the whole community.

The subject of this sketch was only four years of age when his parents removed to Illinois, but he has a vivid recollection of the privations and vicissitudes of the long and toilsome journey, made in those pioneer days. The country was wild and sparsely settled, while game and wild fowl abounded in great profusion, such as deer, turkey, prairie chickens, etc., while the streams were full of excellent fish. People lived on the products of their land and wild game, while the subject of this biography and the rest of the family were clothed with homespun, manufactured by the unremitting toil of his mother's patient and skillful hands.

Mr. Hale received the limited education afforded by the pioneer schools, and was reared to agricultural pursuits, early becoming accustomed to the hard labor incidental to farm life. Previous to his father's death he had invested in land, to which he subsequently added, until he now owns 480 acres in a body in Buena Vista township, comprising some of the best realty in that vicinity. He continued to reside on this farm, which he brought to a high state of cultivation and greatly improved, until 1892, when he moved to his present home in Rushville. Here he has a substantial home with attractive and tasteful surroundings, all the appointments of which suggest comfort and refinement, where he and his worthy wife are enjoying in ease the fruits of their early industrious efforts.

Mr. Hale was married in 1855, to Miss Margaret Priscilla Sponamore, an estimable lády, a native of Schuyler county, Illinois, and a daughter of William and Mary (Green) Sponamore, pioneers and prominent residents of this county. They have had nine children, seven of whom now survive: Mary F.; Sarah Malinda;. James F., Hester A., William C., Lydia Belle, and John Martin, — all of whom fill positions of honor in business and society. The parents are earnest and useful members of the Methodist Episcopal Church South, to the support of which they contribute liberally of their means and influence.

Politically, Mr. Hale affiliates with the Democratic party, and although not a politician in the modern acceptance of the word, takes an active interest in all public affairs of importance. He is public-spirited and is always ready to assist any worthy enterprise, tending to the moral, educational or material advancement of his vicinity.

Whatever prosperity Mr. Hale has attained is entirely due to his own unaided efforts. By persistent industry, careful economy and intelligent management he has accumulated a competency, while his unimpeachable integrity, unwavering fidelity and uniform courtesy have gained for him the universal esteem of his fellowmen.

WILLIAM PILGER was born in the Rhine province, Prussia, Germany, in 1832. He remained with his father in farming until 1853, when he took passage for the United States on the ship Yaeger which was making its first voyage. He landed in New Orleans after a six weeks' voyage, and then came up to St. Louis by way of the Mississippi, and from there came on to Beardstown. He spent the first five or six years here as a laborer. He was the first son of the family to come to this country, one sister having preceded him, another brother and two other sisters came over and settled in St. Louis. Here one died. Mr. Pilger came here a poor young man just twenty-one years of age. He began to farm here in 1858, and was actively engaged in farming and stock-raising from 1858 to 1891, when he retired to Beardstown. He owns 240 acres of very good land, forty being in timber, the rest improved and supplied with good buildings. He has made money by his own efforts and is now enjoying the result of those efforts. He has been a hard-working citizen and is well known in the county, and now resides on the corner of Eleventh and Adams streets.

Mr. Pilger was married to Elizabeth Schmidt, who was born in Hesse-Darmstadt, Germany, October 20, 1830, and she died at her home on the farm, March 4, 1881. She was young, when, with her mother and other children, she came to the United States and settled in Cass county, where her father had preceded them two years.

Mr. and Mrs. Pilger had six children, four of whom are living, viz.: Louis, a teamster in Beardstown, married Mary Stock; Lena, is the wife of Marshall J. Ratineau, a painter by trade; Henry C., is a farmer; William is also a farmer on his father's homestead, and married Mary Holbrook. Mr. and Mrs. Pilger and family are members of the Lutheran Church. Mr. Pilger is a Republican in politics, and is a man of influence in the city in which he has made his present wealth. He is great respected by all who know him.

FRANCIS EUGENE CADY is one of the prominent pioneers and substantial farmers of Schuyler county, born in Stafford county, Connecticut, December 4, 1825, being a son of Isaac and Sarah (Chapman) Cady. Francis was ten years old when the family came to Illinois, landing June 12, 1835. The family soon settled in Camden township, entering the northwest one quarter, section 18. Here he grew to manhood. He was reared on the farm, but learned the trade of bricklaying and plastering. After he was married he settled on section 18, on eighty acres of land, entered by his half brother, Alonzo Jones. Mr. Cady gave his attention to his trade for awhile, and then went to California in April, 1853, crossing the plains with an ox team most of the way. He was accompanied by his brother, M. E. Cady, and they took 150 head of cattle and thirteen head of horses. He remained two years and pursued mining, being successful at that occupation. He returned via the Isthmus and New York city. He now owns 160 acres of land, which he has well improved and on which he has erected a nice set of farm buildings.

He was married in 1855 to Percilla Norvall, of Claiborne county, Tennessee, a daughter of William and Mary (Jenkins) Norvall, of Scotch parentage, the former born in Virginia, the latter in North Carolina. Mr. Norvall received a good education and was a lawyer by profession, and was married twice, his second wife being Mrs. Cady's mother. He died at the age of sixty-five years, in 1825. Mrs. Cady was one of eleven children. A part of the family came to Illinois and settled in Huntsville in 1835, and Mrs. Cady was among the number. Here the mother died in 1858, aged seventy-two years. Her brothers and sisters are: William, Timothy, Ralph, John, Sarah, Henry, Nancy, Rufus Andren and Mrs. Cady.

Mr. and Mrs. Cady have had four children: Mary, wife of Henry King, of Huntsville township; Isaac N., a ranchman in California; William E., farmer of Huntsville township; Francis E., at home. He is a Democrat, but has never sought public office. He is a member of Camden Lodge, No. 668, A. F. & A. M.

JAMES M. EDWARDS, of the firm of Edwards & Cavens, Camden, Illinois, general merchants, was born in the northern part of Greene county, Illinois, September 12, 1839. He was the son of Isham B. and Sarah (Day) Edwards, natives of Virginia and Kentucky. The father of our subject went to Kentucky when a young man, where he married and in the winter of 1830 came to Illinois and settled in Greene county, entering land and engaging in farming, and he there passed his remaining years. He died in February, 1882, aged seventy-nine years. His wife died at the age of sixty-two years.

Father of subject owned over 1,000 acres of land, and at one time he was a large stock-raiser. They had thirteen sons and three daughters; twelve of whom grew up. The subject was the thirteenth child. He was raised on the farm, and in August, 1857, was married to Miss Melinda E. Hoots, daughter of David Hoots, of Scott county. Our subject, after his marriage, purchased land and pursued farming in Greene county until 1862, in August, of which year he enlisted and was mustered into service with Company H, Ninety-first Illinois Volunteer Infantry, and served for two years and nine months as a private soldier.

He was in the battles of Elizabethtown, Mabeto, Richmond, Red River expedition and many other battles. After the war he resumed farming in Greene county for one year, and then sold out his farm and went to the Cherokee lands in Indian Nation, and one year later he returned to Greene county, and two years later came to Schuyler county, and purchased 160 acres of land, which he improved further and sold. He has since improved ten farms in Schuyler county, numbering at least 2,000 acres. He has been a hard worker and has improved more farms than any other man in Schuyler county.

He owned a sawmill for eight years, and for thirty-two years has run the mill for threshing machines. He has at all times been ready to engage in any business which would promise to make any money. He has been at all times very successful in all of his enterprises. He now owns 160 acres of land, and property in Camden.

In 1891, he engaged in his present business. He dealt in live stock for twenty years. Mr. and Mrs. Edwards have had eight children, six are living: Sarah J. married Harvey Bleckledge of Henderson county, Illinois; Etta married George Watt and resides in Camden township; Trissie married Nicholas Notson of Schuyler county; Ollie Belle married Amos Cavens, her father's partner; Mary Emeline and Daisie D.

In politics, Mr. Edwards is a Republican. He has been Justice of the Peace and other local offices. He is a member of the Camden Lodge, No. 648, A. F. & A. M. He is also a member of the G. A. R. Post in Brooklyn.

HENRY J. BAUJAN, a successful liveryman, blacksmith, dealer in implements and buggies and owner of the Palace Hotel, was born December 20, 1859, in this city, and was here reared and educated. He is the second son of John Baujan, who was born in Germany and who, when he was twenty-nine years old, came to the United States. He followed his trade of brick mason in St. Louis for one year and then came to Cass county, and was married at Arenzville, and later came to Beardstown. Here he established a brick-yard, did a manufacturing business for some time and later became connected with the gristmilling business under the firm name of J. Baujan & Co., until his death, in July, 1889. He was over sixty-nine years of age when he died and was a well-known and popular German of this city.

Our subject is one of seven children. He has always lived in this city and here learned his trade of blacksmith, before which he worked in his father's mill. He has been in the livery business for one year and carries a fine class of outfits and good horses. He has been a blacksmith and farm implement dealer for nine years, and has always made money. No doubt a great deal of it is owing to his good habits and his energy as a business man.

He was married to Rosa Milner, born in this city August 23, 1861. She was here educated, although she completed it at St. Louis, and she is an intelligent, agreeable lady. Her parents, Hannah and Richard Milner, of English descent, are well known settlers of this city. Mr. Milner has for sixteen years been the Chicago, Burlington & Quincy bridge tender and Government water gauger of the Illinois river. These old people are connected with the better elements of the city. They are Methodists and consistent Christians.

Mr. and Mrs. Baujan attend the Methodist Episcopal Church. He is a Democrat in politics, has been Alderman of the city, and is a public-spirited young man. They have three children, Nellie, Verna and Glenna.

JAMES PERRY, a prominent citizen of Versailles, is a native of the Blue Grass country, being born there in 1817. His father was Edmond Perry, a farmer of South Carolina, and his father was Nathan Perry, a farmer of the same State, who came to Illinois in the fall of 1830. Edmond Perry had made the journey the year before, in the company of his two brothers and a brother-in-law. They spent the winter of 1829-'30 in Illinois and were here during the big snowstorm, which is a historical one. In June of 1830, he returned to his family and brought them and his parents to the new country. The trip was made in the regulation style, covered wagons and ox teams, and, although they were a month on the journey, they enjoyed it to a remarkable degree. There was a fascination in the free life they led, camping by the roadside when they made their stops. One night the party had the luxury of sleeping in a vacant house in Springfield. The party consisted of seven families of the Perrys, including two brothers-in-law. They came with limited means, but before long by industry they all were in comfortable circumstances. The old grandmother Perry had been a Miss Rebecca Yarbrey, and she was the mother of eight children, all of whom eventually came to Illinois. She and her husband lived to be aged people, he dying at the age of eighty-two years and she some three years before him. Their children were: Edmond Perry, father of subject, eighty-two; Luke Perry, eighty; Melvina, seventy; William died in the prime of life; Edward, about seventy; Sarah, over seventy; Irving, about sixty; Benjamin, baptized in the Baptist Church, is about sixty; John, baptized in the same faith when seventy-five years of age; Edmond Perry, married Rachel Bridges of North Carolina, and they had eleven children, all of whom grew up and had families, namely: Martha, died when she was about fifty, leaving nine children; Phoebe, died when a young woman, leaving four children; Rebecca, wife of Samuel Briggs, of Versailles; Ichabod, a retired farmer in Mt. Sterling is a widower; James, of this sketch; Nathan, a farmer of this township; Sarah died in this township, leaving six children, being about fifty at her death; Melvina died in the prime of life, leaving one child; Louisa married and in middle life; Francis, farmer of Mt. Sterling, has six sons; and Luke, a farmer of Stone county, Missouri, who has six children. The mother died when about seventy-six years of age and the father four years later, when he was eighty-two years of age. They left a good estate and are remembered as being among the best of the pioneer families of the State.

Mr. Perry was married, in his twenty-third year to Eliza Hills of Indiana, daughter of Robert and Betsy (Angel) Hills, who came to Schuyler county before the big snowstorm. They died on their farm at an advanced age, he when he was seventy-five, and she when she was a year younger.

Mr. and Mrs. Perry settled on their present home of eighty acres in the fall of 1841, October 15. He now pays taxes on about 560 acres of land, although he started with very little money. All of their eleven children are living, the eldest fifty-three and the youngest twenty-six. There is not a death in the family and all of the children are married and settled in life. These children are: Charles, now a banker in Knoxville, Iowa, with two sons; William Perry (see sketch); Olive, wife of J. B. Masters, a retired farmer of Denver, with three children; Francis, a farmer of this township, with four children; Robin, a farmer of Mt. Sterling township, with one daughter; Almira, wife of Richard Underwood, a farmer living near by, has four sons; Elizabeth, wife of James Butler, a farmer of this township, six children; Edmond, a farmer of this township with two children; Eliza, wife of E. W. Lanier, a a farmer living near by, four children; and James K., a farmer on the old homestead, two children.

Mr. Perry supports the principles of the Democratic party and he and his wife are members of the Baptist Church. Mr. Perry is now an old man, being about seventy-five, while his faithful wife is about two years younger. He is practically retired, but takes a strong interest in all that is taking place, and is as much interested in the welfare of his children and grandchildren as if he were yet a young man. These children are persons to be proud of, as none of them ever contract any debts that they are not perfectly able to pay, all have been well educated, and are worthy sons and daughters of their respected and honored parents. The old people's hearts are gladdened by the merry prattle of the thirty-three grandchildren who have been added to this large and prosperous family.

T. J. ROWLAND was born in Frederick county, Virginia, near Winchester, January 15, 1864. His father, Matthew M. Rowland, was born in the same county. His father was a native of Wales and came to Virginia where he lived until his death at an advanced old age. Mr. Matthew Rowland was a farmer all his life; he married Miss Margaret Campbell, also of Virginia, who died in Jacksonville, Illinois. Mr. Rowland died in Virginia, in 1834, when his son was still very small.

Our subject began to support himself when he was eleven years old. He learned the saddle and harness business at Zanesville, Ohio. Here he remained after learning his trade. He then removed to Newark, Ohio, and began business for himself and remained there six years. From there he went to Coshocton county, Spring Mountain, and from there to Coshocton, the county seat. The war then broke out and he enlisted in the One Hundred and Third Ohio Infantry and served about two years when he was discharged by the close of the war. He made a fine record in the army and was a brave soldier. He settled in Keokuk, Iowa, and remained there three years and then removed to Brown county, and has resided here ever since.

He was married in Newark, Ohio, to Miss Lenora Barring, of Slatestown, New York, born September 18, 1850. They have had eleven children, seven of whom are living, namely: Blendon L., Louise, Lucinda C., Abner C., Lovey Augusta, Bessie I. and Homer M. Mr. Rowland worked at his trade at this place until he retired. He is connected with the Methodist Episcopal Church and has been for forty years. He has been a member of the Masonic fraternity for about the same number of years. He and his wife are good, highly esteemed citizens of the place and have earned their right to their present life of ease by years of toil in their younger days.

JACKSON C. HOFFMAN was born in Lexington, Virginia, February 14, 1826. His father, Joseph Hoffman, was born in 1801 at the same place, but his grandfather, David, was born in Germany and came to America at the close of the Revolutionary war and settled one mile west of Lexington, Virginia. His occupation was that of a farmer and tanner, which he continued as long as he lived, dying at the age of eighty-nine years. His father, Joseph, was also a tanner, continuing the business of his father until his death, which occurred at the age of fifty-two years. He was a great temperance man and advocated his doctrines upon any and all occasions. His mother's name was Elizabeth Windel, born in Lexington, Virginia, and dying in Huntsville, Alabama, at the age of fifty-six. She left five children, three of whom are still living.

Mr. Hoffman started out to carve his own fortune one year after the death of his father in Lexington, Virginia, and worked there until nineteen years of age. He then volunteered for the Mexican war and served twelve months. The regiment was detailed for guarding train provisions from Camargo to Monterey. It was discharged at the former place and Mr. Hoffman returned to Frankfort, Kentucky, where he remained for two years. He then built a mill on Camp creek, in Estill county, Kentucky, and carried it on as a saw and gristmill for a time and then moved to Irvine and worked at his trade for about two years and then moved to Madison county, Kentucky, near Clay county. Here he remained for four or five years. He then moved from there to Clark county, Kentucky, near Winchester, and there run a sawmill for two years. From there he moved to Armistead, Blackwood's place, the same county. After that he went to Mt. Sterling and followed his usual occupation of carpentering. He remained there six years and then removed to Cooperstown township, and there remained six years, then went to Missouri and farmed for one year, and then returned to Versailles, where he has since remained.

He was married in Kentucky, to Margaret Eads, born in Estill county, Kentucky, about 1825, and is still living. Mr. and Mrs. Hoffman have five children: Elizabeth, Charlton, Matilda, Joseph and Mary Ann. Mr. Hoffman has held the offices of Magistrate and School Trustee and has belonged to the Methodist Episcopal Church for seventeen years. Politically he is a Democrat, and a member of the I. O. O. F., and for eighteen years has held all the offices of a subordinate lodge. He has twenty-eight grandchildren and two great grandchildren. He is the owner of a well improved farm of forty acres.

FRED W. HUGE, one of Beardstown's most influential contractors and builders, was born in Hanover in 1832, January 27. He learned his trade of carpenter with his father and worked with him until twenty years of age. He was the first to leave the home roof when he set forth for America. He came from Bremen to New Orleans and landed after a voyage of six weeks and three days. Fifteen more days were consumed in going to St. Louis, and from there he came to Beardstown. Here he has had his home ever since. Four of his brothers and sisters have joined him, and one brother, William, was a soldier in the Rebellion for two years. The other brother is a furniture dealer in Beardstown. The parents of Mr. Huge, Casper H. and Anna M. (Peters) Huge, both lived and died in their native country. One daughter still lives in Germany.

Mr. Huge had made a success of his business, and has built nearly all of the business houses in Beardstown and a good many of the residences. He is a member of the Central Building and Loan Association, and is influential in many other ways. He is a Democrat in politics and a Lutheran in religion.

Mr. Huge was married in Beardstown, to Miss Anna Slater of the same town in Germany as Mr. Huge. She grew up there, and was educated there, also. Her parents lived and died there, but she and a sister, Eliza, came to the United States. They were the only ones, however, of the family that ventured across the deep sea. Mrs. Huge was only seventeen years of age when she landed in this country. She has resided, ever since her arrival, in Beardstown. Mr. and Mrs. Huge are members of the Sixth Street Lutheran Church, of which Mr. Huge is Trustee, and has been for sixteen years. They have six children: Dina, now Mrs. John Leger, a shoe dealer of the city; William, a tailoring cutter in Chicago; Lizzie, who died in her fifth year; Fred, a hotel clerk in St. Nicholas Hotel, Springfield; and Julius, who died when six months old.

Such men as Mr. Huge are wonderful aids in the building up and growth of the town. He is honored and respected by all who know him.

RICHARD B. FULKS is a retired merchant, living at his pleasant home at Beardstown. He was born at Rushville, Schuyler county, New York, February 6, 1840. This boy grew up under the name of Dick, and has borne that title ever since, being scarcely known by any other title. He is a man who has made his own fortune and carved his own history. His early life was a struggle to acquire book knowledge. During his boyhood days he studied hard and served as clerk as early as fourteen. He was with the firm of Shaw & Merriman of Beardstown for some time, and in 1857 he became a clerk for Charse, Rich & Parker, of this city, and was thus engaged until the breaking out of the war. He enlisted August 21, 1861, as a private in Company K, Thirty-third Illinois Volunteer Infantry, Captain Lippincott and Colonel Charlės Hovey, of Normal, Illinois, in command. In 1862, while encamped at Ironton, Missouri, Mr. Fulks issued for three months a camp journal called the *Camp Cricket.* This knowledge of newspaper work he had acquired when but yet a boy; and later, in 1860, by working at night and at odd times in the office of Thompson & Irwin as assistant in publishing *The Central Illinoian* of Beardstown. After a service of two and a half years as a private Mr. Fulks was commissioned as Quartermaster Sergeant and in that capacity served till the close of the war on the staff of General Lippincott. After serving as a brave soldier he was mustered out and discharged properly and honorably at Springfield, in December, 1865. During the war he was in many engagements, including the burning of the big bridge on the Iron mountain railroad in 1861, later at Fredrickstown, Missouri, and afterward did guard work on the Mississippi river, and he saw much active service, but escaped without a scratch. He went through the battles of Vicksburg, Jackson, Mobile and Spanish Point and at Placco, Texas. While at Meridian, Mississippi, he received a severe sunstroke, from which he has never recovered. The Government remembers him with a pension. When the war closed he laid aside the soldier's habiliments and resumed citizen's dress and returned to Beardstown. He then resumed his mercantile pursuits. The qualities for which Mr. Fulks is noted are grit and push, and as he put them in his business he has made a success of it. He has added to the general welfare of the city, which gives him credit for making it the thriving place it has become. No misfortune ever shocked or worried Dick. He has had three disastrous fires, which in each case represented heavy losses to his stock and his business, but he has pulled through and managed to have a surplus at the bankers, to supply all demands. Hard work and years finally told upon him, he lost his health, and had to retire from active labors in 1887. He has owned and dealt, sometimes quite extensively, in city property.

He was married first, in this city, to Lydia M. McClure, who was born and reared in Cass county and died at Denver, Colorado, April 10, 1878. Her body was brought to this city and interred in Oakwood cemetery. She was then in the prime of life, being born about 1843, and was a well educated woman, having been second principal of the school in this city. She was a member of the Congregational Church, and left one daughter, now a well educated young lady, named Inas. He was a second time married, in this city, to Miss Mattie, of Louisville, Kentucky, a bright young woman, who died two years after, and was buried at her old home. He was married a third and last time to Miss Etta Brown, who was born and reared here, but died at the birth of her first child, in 1885. The child is a bright little girl of seven years, named Anna D. He has been a member of I. O. O. F. for some twenty-five years, a member of the Knights of Honor, and one of the promoters and charter members of the G. A. R. order. He has served the city as an Alderman for some time, and has been a member of the Board of Education. He has always been a strong Republican.

THOMAS EDWARD CUNNINGHAM, a highly respected citizen of section 30, Buena Vista township, Schuyler county, Illinois, was born in Rushville, of this State, on May 2, 1860.

His paternal grandfather, William Cunningham, was a native of Kentucky, in which State he was married, and in 1837, came to

Rushville, near which place he was for some years engaged in farming. Later, he has kept a hotel, and still later, removed to Mt Sterling, where he continued in the hotel business until the time of his death, which occurred in February, 1871 He was twice married His first wife, the grandmother of our subject, died, leaving nine children He had no children by his second marriage. The nine children were as follows· William, born on October 31, 1816, died in Schuyler county, Nancy J was born on October 31, 1818, and married William Cooney, who died in Canton, Illinois; Woodson was born on September 23, 1820, and died in Brown county; Caleb was born on August 22, 1822, and died in California; Joseph was born on October 17, 1824, and died in Brown county, Ellen was born on November 17, 1826, and married William Bowling, who died in Schuyler county, John was born on November 30, 1828, and died also in Schuyler county; Thomas was the father of our subject; Lucinda, the only surviving member of the family, was born on October 16, 1834; she married Isaac Warrington, and resides in Camden township, Schuyler county

The father of our subject was born on December 23, 1830, and removed with his parents to Illinois. He was reared in Rushville, where he was married on March 16, 1859, to Nancy Ann, seventh daughter of Edmund and Lucy Ann Smith She was born in Kentucky, on February 23, 1833, and came to Illinois when sixteen years of age. The father of our subject resided in Rushville, until the close of the Civil war, and owned and operated the stage route between Rushville and Mt. Sterling, for many years. In 1866, he settled on a farm in Buena Vista township, where he purchased 160 acres of land, where he passed his declining years On this property he built a large, handsome brick residence, and made other substantial improvements He died at his home on September 22, 1882, leaving a wife and family to mourn his loss. His faithful wife survived him seven years, passing away on March 30, 1889, lamented by all who knew her They were consistent members of the Christian Church, contributing liberally toward its support

Politically, he was a Democrat, and was elected by his constituents to the office of Supervisor of Buena Vista township, serving in that capacity for several years.

They had eight children: William, born on February 17, 1885, married Margaret Green; Charles D., born on August 5, 1857, married Mary C. Unger; Thomas E, born on May 2, 1860, married Clara A Wilmott; Lucy A, born on July 30, 1863; Amanda E, born on May 19, 1866; Nancy J. was born on April 2, 1869, married Charles Hester; Woodson J, born on July 19, 1873, John M, born on July 9, 1876, died on July 10, 1876 Of these, seven are still living, all being residents of Schuyler county.

Thomas Edward, the subject of our sketch, was reared on the home farm, and attended the district schools In 1881, he was married to Miss Clara A Wilmott, a native of Schuyler county, where she was born on June 3, 1859 She was a daughter of Morris and Dorotha Wilmott, highly respected citizens of that county She died on September 30, 1890, leaving a husband and three children to mourn her loss, besides a large circle of friends They had three children: Reverda, who was born on March 13, 1884; Bertha, born on November 9, 1885; Raymond, born on November 13, 1887

Mr. Cunningham carries on the homestead, besides which he owns forty acres of his own, all of which is under a high state of cultivation, and which is applied with all modern improvements, of machinery and buildings, to facilitate the planting and gathering of his crops.

In politics, he follows in the footsteps of his fathers, affiliating with the Democratic party.

Of high integrity and morality, courteous and cordial in manner, and interesting in conversation, he enjoys the esteem of his fellow citizens and the affectionate regard of his family and friends.

ISAAC MISENHIMER, farmer and stock-raiser of Frederick township, was born in Clay county, Illinois, September 28, 1839. His parents were Jacob and Elizabeth (McGrew) Harris. Mr. Harris was a native of Pennsylvania and his wife of Indiana. They were married in Clay county, Illinois, where their parents had moved, being among the first pioneers of that county. Mr. Harris died in 1843, and his widow survived him some ten years. The family moved to Schuyler county when Isaac was about nine years old. He was educated in Schuyler county and was reared on the farm, and he has followed that business ever since. He enlisted in Company I, First Illinois Infantry, and served three years in the Western army. He participated in the battles of Shiloh, Britain Lane, siege of Vicksburg, and was present at the capture of Little Rock, Arkansas. When he returned from a furlough the regiment was back in Tennessee and he there re-enlisted and was in Tennessee until he was mustered out in March, 1865. Returning home after this, he settled down to farming. He owns 223 acres of land in excellent farming condition, and two years ago he built one of the most commodious and comfortable houses in the county. He has large barns, and altogether his farm is among the best in the county. His grade of stock, too, is very fine and he is among the most prosperous of the citizens of this section.

He was married, September 27, 1867, to Miss Penelope Gillet, of Schuyler county. Her parents were Elijah and Eliza Gillet, who were among the very first settlers of the county. She was the youngest of seven children. Mr. Misenhimer was one of five children, only two of whom are living. They have one child, Jennie, born December 28, 1874, and is still at home. She is a young lady of fine attainments and holds a teacher's certificate. She is a fine musician, also. Mr. Misenhimer is a Democrat in politics.

LEWIS SCHISLER, Jr., son of Lewis Schesler and Anna Schisler, was born in York county, Pennsylvania, April 14, 1851. His parents were natives of the same State, but came to Illinois among the first settlers and located near Astoria. Here Mr. Schisler died when only twenty-seven. His widow married again, but her second husband died in Iowa when out there visiting. Mrs. Schisler bore her husband fifteen children and all are living. Of this large family, Louis was next to the youngest. He was educated in the country schools and worked on the farm. His father was a miller, and worked at his trade until the time of his death, but afterward his widow bought a farm and removed there with her family. Mr.

Schisler still resides on this farm with his mother and attends to all the management of it for her.

He was married to Miss Julia Coldrider, of York county, Pennsylvania. Mr. and Mrs. Schisler have eight children, all of whom are living: Ananias, John, Josephine, Sarah, Anna, Daniel, Noah and Harry.

The family of Schislers is of German origin, although remote, as the family has been established in America for several generations. Mr. Schisler is a Republican in politics and he belongs to the United Brotherhood Church, known as Dunkards. The 160 acres that he farms for his mother are in splendid condition, and speak well for his management and thrift, for which the well cultivated fields and comfortable farm buildings the place is one of the finest in the county.

WESLEY M. GRIMWOOD, merchant of Frederick, Illinois, was born at Akron, Ohio, February 7, 1855. He is the only surviving member of a family of four children. The father was a mechanic by profession and a native of England, where he was born February 18, 1816. His father was also born in England and married Maria Clapper, daughter of Daniel Clapper. He started for America with his family in 1830, but was wrecked off the coast of Prince Edward's Island, and he and his family resided there for two years and then removed to Providence, Rhode Island. In 1858 he moved to Akron, Ohio, where he died in 1864. His wife died at Akron, Ohio, in 1876. The father of our subject was born, reared and educated in England and came to America with his parents in 1833. He was aboard the steamship Royal William on her first trip across the Atlantic, thus demonstrating the feasibility of steam navigation. In the fall of 1837 he removed from Rhode Island to Pekin, Illinois, where he married Miss Anna Eliza Brewingam. In 1859 he removed to Schuyler county, where his wife died, in 1868. He was a stanch Abolitionist and later a Republican. During a political riot at Alton, Illinois, he was struck on the head with a club, and almost killed by a member of the mob, who afterward killed that honored patriot Elisha P. Lovejoy. He served his county as Supervisor, Justice of the Peace and various other offices of responsibility. He was an honored and respected citizen. He married Miss Alice A. Bartholow, of Astoria. She was a daughter of Jasper and Olive Bartholow, natives of Ohio. Both are now dead. They were pioneers of Fulton county. They had four children.

Mr. Grimwood was educated in the common schools of Schuyler county, and at Wabash College, at Crawfordsville, Indiana. He learned the wagonmaker's trade with his father, and followed it for about twenty years, when he engaged at merchandising at Frederick, here he carries on a general store. Mrs. Grimwood is a member of the Christian Church, and Mr. Grimwood is a member of Browning Lodge. No. 389, I. O. O. F., and of the M. W. of A., a beneficial order. Mr. and Mrs. Grimwood have three living children: Charles L., Ferol Fern and Don Wesley. Mr. Grimwood is a stanch Republican, and has been Clerk of Frederick township for the last twelve years. He is the candidate of his party from the Thirty-fourth District, for Senator. He did not seek this honor, but when notified of his selection, consented to allow his name to appear on the ticket.

This is a genuine case of the office seeking the man. He stands very high in the estimation of the people.

JOHN T. HILLS was born in Oakland township, Schuyler county, Illinois, in 1841, a son of Jackson Hills, who was born in 1812; his father died in June, 1842, so that in infancy he was deprived of his guidance and care. The paternal grandfather, Ephraim Hills, was a native of Pennsylvania; he was a farmer by occupation, and came to Oakland township from Indiana when Jackson Hills was a lad of twelve years; he settled on a farm of 160 acres, on which he lived until death during the war; he had attained near four-score years of age. His first wife died, leaving a family of five children, but his second wife survived him; one son, James, died at the age of twenty-four years, leaving a wife and one son; Ephraim is a farmer, residing in Missouri; Jackson, the father of our subject, died at the age of twenty-five years, leaving a widow and two sons, William Henry and John T.; his wife's maiden name was Delilah Fowler, a daughter of Thomas Fowler, of New York, who came to Illinois as early as 1825. John T. Hills was reared from his twelfth year by his uncle, Henry Hills: his mother was married a second time to William Schroder.

He had just attained his majority when the great war of the Rebellion arose, and he offered his service in defense of the old flag. He went to the front a member of Company C, Seventh Missouri Cavalry, and served three years and three months as a private. He was mustered out at St. Louis, after which he returned to Oakland township; he was held a prisoner at Fort Smith, Arkansas, for three months, at the end of which time he was exchanged; he experienced many of the horrors of prison life, but was fortunate in being released before the confinement had sapped his life away.

Mr. Hills was united in marriage the first day of the year 1866, to Miss Mary E. Chockley, of McDonough county, Illinois, a daughter of Benjamin and Sally (Du Wese) Chockley, natives of Kentucky, who settled in Illinois at an early day. He then settled in Littleton township, on 160 acres of land, which he sold at the end of the first year; he rented one year of his wife's father, and then purchased a tract of forty acres; here he resided three years, returning to his wife's home where they passed six years. In 1880 he bought eighty acres of his present farm, paying therefor $700; he has sixty acres under excellent cultivation, and he has made many valuable improvements. He carries on a general farming business, raising corn, wheat and clover, and some live-stock; twenty acres have been set to timber, which is in a flourishing condition.

Mr. and Mrs. Hills have buried three infant children, two sons and a daughter, and four children survive; the mother died in 1882. Mr. Hills was married a second time to Mrs. Martha Fowler, *nee* Chockley, sister to his first wife. The children of the first marriage are: Delilah I., wife of Hiram Fowler; Genevra; Lilladocia, wife of William O'Donnell; and Tennessee; the children of the present wife are: Eldow C., aged eight years; Inez L., five years old; and Perry E., an infant of two years. Mr. Hill has a foster son, a nephew, named Alvin E. Toland, aged twenty-three years, now a resident of McDonough county. He is a member of Fremont Post, No. 33, G. A. R. He is a man of good business ability, has been fortunate in all his undertakings, and enjoys the respect and esteem of his fellow men.

REV. HARVEY A SKILES, pastor of the Union Baptist Churches at Browning and Denver, in Hancock county and Spring Creek in Sangamon county, is one of the very early settlers of Schuyler county, born here August 29, 1829. His parents were William and Sarah (Perkins) Skiles, who located in Schuyler county after their marriage sixty-eight years ago. The grandfather was a farmer in Rushville township, where he settled in his early manhood and died. The mother died during the cholera epidemic in 1852.

Harvey A. Skiles says that he received his education in the backwoods seminary, to which he walked two and one-half miles night and morning. Later in life he applied himself to study in the line of theology. Thirty-nine years ago he was ordained a minister in the Union Baptist Church, and has been constantly in the ministry to the present time. He has on ten or more occasions walked forty miles in a day and preached at night. His labors in those days were not pathways lined with roses, by any means. The pay consisted largely in provisions and necessaries, and they were not always in very liberal quantities. He preached two years in Fulton county for a wagon load of frost-bitten corn. It is certain Mr. Skiles did not preach for the emoluments derived from it. In late years his pay has been satisfactory and work not arduous. He worked on a farm in his early manhood, and continued until the last twenty years, thus securing a livehihood for his family, giving his services in the ministry for the good of humanity. Little was expected in return for his labors except the satisfaction of duty well done; certainly, little was realized in a temporal sense. Mr. Skiles spent fourteen years preaching in Iowa, and has preached two years at Keokuk since locating at Browning, going from here to his appointments.

He married, September 15, 1854, Mary A. Wright, daughter of William and Rebecca Wright, who came to Schuyler county in 1835. Mrs. Skiles was born October 31, 1836. She was the eldest of a family of nine children, eight of whom are still living. Her father died August 15, 1884, and the mother died March 13, 1891. Mr. and Mrs. Skiles were born within one and one-half miles of each other, attended the same school, grew to maturity as young acquaintances and friends, which resulted in matrimony. They have had six children, but only one is living, Bele, now Mrs. Billingsley, and resides near Camden, Illinois, her husband a farmer. Mr. Skiles is a stanch Republican, and takes a lively interest in political matters. The family owns a pleasant home, located in Browning.

GEORGE W. CAMPBELL was born in Richland county, Ohio, October 30, 1827. He was the son of Peter L. Campbell, a native of Virginia. He was of Scotch ancestry, and his father and he removed from Virginia to the Northwest Territory about 1797. As the Indians at that time were hostile, he returned to Virginia and resided there for a short time, but in 1800 he concluded that he was much more likely to gain a fortune in the new West than in the old East, so he returned to his western home and settled on the west bank of the Ohio river, and remained there a few years. He then wandered to Richland, and from there to Crawford county. Mr. Peter Campbell learned the trade of tanner, and followed it till 1843, and then came to Illinois in the fall of 1844. He was accompanied by his wife and eight of his twelve children. They made the entire journey overland with teams. He settled in what is now Bainbridge township, where he had previously bought a tract of land in section 4, the northwest quarter. Like all the land of that date, there were no improvements, and they resided with another family for a short time after their arrival. The following year he built a cabin on his own land, where he lived to the day of his death. He made many improvements on the farm and erected tasteful buildings. His death occurred August 19, 1881. His wife's name before her marriage was Agnes Jones, and she was born in Virginia, July 6, 1801. She was the daughter of Oliver Jones. Mr. Campbell was a Democrat in politics, and served as County Assessor for two years, and several terms as Justice of the Peace of the township, and County Treasurer. He was a strict Predestinarian Baptist, of which denomination he was an Elder.

The subject of this sketch was seventeen years old when he came to Illinois. He did not come until the following year after his parents came. He came with a team. Coming here as he did when there were so few settlers, and about the only inhabitants were the wild game, he had a good opportunity to watch the growth of the country, as he has been a resident of this township ever since. He has occupied the farm he now resides upon since 1870. He married, January 20, 1853, Laura A. Neill, the daughter of James Neill. She was born in Weatherfield township, Trumbull county, Ohio. Her father was a native of Tyrone, Ireland. His first wife was a native of the same county, and he and she died there. After her death he came to America, bringing his only child with him, and settled in Trumbull county, and bought timber land and erected the log house in which Mrs. Campbell was born. Here he lived until 1846, and then moved to Illinois, accompanied by his five children, and settled in Rushville. Here he bought land and pursued the occupation of farming until his death in 1864. The maiden name of his second wife was Mary Stewart, daughter of Archibald Stewart, a native of Ireland, and of Scotch ancestry. She was a native of Ohio, and died in Trumbull county about 1843.

Mr. and Mrs. Campbell have ten children living, namely: James N., Agnes M., C. Stewart, Edward L., Mary W., Lewis E., Jonathan, Milton, Amy L., Della K.; L. Jennie and Lucy M. died in infancy.

Mr. Campbell is a Democrat and cast his first vote for Lewis Cass. He has served twelve years as Justice of the Peace, and seven years as Assessor. He also served several terms as Supervisor, and one term as Sheriff.

JAMES GROVER, farmer of Mt. Sterling township, was born in 1841. He is the son of Henry P. Grover (see this book). James attended the pioneer school, and afterward taught in a log house where the furniture was of the most primitive kind, —seats made of rough slabs, with wooden pegs for legs. He worked for his father until twenty-one, and then rented some land from him for two years. He then bought some land in Mt. Sterling township, and there built a log house, 16 x 18 feet. The log house gave place in time to neat buildings of all kinds, and he resided here until 1882, when he traded with his father for the old homestead. His present farm contains 160 acres, highly improved, with farm buildings that compare favorably with any in the township.

He married, August 13, 1863, Miss Margaret C. Putnam, of Brown county, Illinois. She is the daughter of William and Martha Putnam. Mr. and Mrs. Grover have three bright, intelligent children,—Minnie, Arthur and Oscar H. Mr. Grover and wife are members of the Primitive Baptist Church. Mr. Grover is a stanch Democrat in politics.

EDWARD BERTHOLF has been so closely identified with the early political history of Schuyler county that this volume would not be complete without an extended review of his career, which began here May 1, 1836. He is a native of Orange county, New York, born April 9, 1816, a son of John and Elizabeth (Perry) Bertholf, natives of New York and New Jersey respectively. The family is descended from the Hollanders, who emigrated in colonial days to New York. The father was a farmer by occupation, and resided all his life in the Empire State. They had a family of thirteen children, twelve of whom grew to maturity; ten married and reared families. Edward grew to manhood amid the scenes of farm life, and attended the common schools; at the age of sixteen he began to teach school; and followed this profession until he was twenty. At that age he removed to Illinois and located at Rushville, Schuyler county, his older brother, Henry B., having settled here previously; here he taught a school and assisted his brother, who was Judge of the probate court, deputy Clerk and county Recorder; he was thus introduced into court-house work, and has since passed one-half of his time in various offices. In 1848 he was appointed Treasurer of the school fund, and held the office until 1869; he continued teaching, served as deputy for other offices, clerked and kept books for the merchants of Rushville. In 1848 he was also elected Justice of the Peace, and retained the office for more than twenty years; he finally resigned both this and the office of school trustee. In 1847–'48 he was deputy Sheriff and Collector of Taxes; he was elected deputy Clerk in 1855, and six month later, on the death of the Clerk, Nathan Moon, he was appointed to the office of county Clerk. In 1860 he was elected Sheriff and served one term; two years later Thomas J. Kinney, went into the war, and he took charge of the office of Circuit Clerk, which Mr. Kinney had previously filled, and continued to transact the business during the remainder of the term; he was then deputy County Clerk, and is still in the office of Circuit Clerk during court.

Mr. Bertholf was married in November, 1838, to Mary E. Jackson, a daughter of Levi and Lydia (Wilcoxen) Jackson; nine children have been born to them; one died in infancy and the eldest, William H., died at the age of twenty-one years; Horace is a resident of Cherokee county, Kansas; Frank E. is a citizen of Rushville; Fred L. is a farmer of this county; John Jesse is also a farmer; Emily Ann married Thomas W. Moon; Harriet E.; Mary E. is the wife of E. W. Bickford of Plymouth, Illinois.

In his political convictions Mr. Bertholf adhered to the principles of the Whig party until 1856, and since that time has been a

Democrat. He is a member of the Methodist Episcopal Church, and has been a liberal supporter of the society. In 1862 he purchased the farm on which his father settled, and owned this land until March, 1891. He has never been connected with any civic society except the Sons of Temperance. Levi Jackson, father of Mrs. Bertholf, was a native of Connecticut, and was there reared and married; he removed from that State to Ohio, and thence in 1836, to Schuyler county, Illinois; he died in July, 1868; his wife died in 1839; they reared a family of four daughters and three sons. Mr. Jackson was a shoemaker by trade, but followed farming from the time he settled in Ohio until his death. He was married a second time, bnt had no children by this union. Politically he afflliated with the Republican party.

STEPHEN BRANNAN, deceased, having died at his home in Beardstown, Illinois, September 16, 1875, was born in Queen's connty, Ireland, about seventy-two years ago. He came of pure Irish ancestry. His mother had died in her native country, when in middle life. Her name was Anorah Brannan. His father later came to this country, joined his son in Cass connty, and after having lived here twelve years, died at his home, aged eighty-four. He and his wife were all their lives Roman Catholics.

Mr. Brannan came to Cass connty a poor man in 1849. He had given up a farmer's life in Ireland and when twenty-three years of age went to England, spent three years in Liverpool and in 1849 reached the United States. He had been nine weeks in the city of New York before he came on to Beardstown and here the scenes of his active life began. He was a hard-working farmer and stock-raiser and became prominent as such in the county. He was successful in accumulating land, having worked around for seven years; he then purchased and began to farm for himself. He first bought eighty acres, which before his death he had increased to 380, and 340 of it is still in the family. This land is in Indian precinct.

He was married, in Beardstown, to Elizabeth A. Riley, who was born in Londonderry, Ireland, August 7, 1835. She was the daughter of John and Margaret (Kenan) Riley, natives of Dublin, Ireland. Mr. Riley and his wife had both come to England when young people, were married in Ashton, England, and there Mr. Riley followed for a time the trade of a baker and was so engaged throughout England until 1836, when he came to the United States and located in Beardstown. Four years later his wife and children came over on the same ship with Mr. Brannan of this notice. Mr. Riley obtained land in Indian precinct, about 650 acres, and it was upon this place that John Riley and wife labored, successfully, and died abont the age of fifty-five years, having been all their lives good Roman Catholics. Mrs. Brannan was her parent's only child. She has kept the property together and is a good manager. They had thirteen children, four of whom are dead. Nicholas is now a farmer on the old homestead; John Jr., is also a farmer at the same place; R. Edward is a partner with his brother in farming; Mary A., at present housekeeper for her brothers on the farm; Nora is at home with her mother; Thomas is a clerk for Werner & Stoneagle; Lizzie is at home, while William and Stephen work for their brothers on the farm.

Mr. Brannan was a good neighbor, a kind father and husband and a consistent member of the Roman Catholic Church.

ELIAS CLARK, a prosperous retired farmer and an esteemed pioneer citizen of Cooperstown, Illinois, was born in Virginia in 1808.

His parents were Josiah and Jane (Adams) Clark, both natives of the Old Dominion. The latter was a daughter of John Adams, a native of Maryland, who removed to Virginia in an early day, but who later returned to his native State. By this marriage there were ten children, six sons and four daughters. The devoted wife and mother died in middle life, and was buried on the old farm in Virginia. The father afterward married again, his second wife being Lucy Menifee, a native of Pennsylvania, who belonged to a large and prominent family of that State. By this marriage there were also ten children, eight sons and two daughters, most of whom are still living and reside in Ohio.

The subject of this sketch spent his boyhood on the home farm in Virginia, and had but few educational advantages, having attended the subscription schools but for a short time. He was trained to drive four and five horses by one line, riding one of the wheel horses, and in this manner made many long trips to Washington, District of Columbia, Fredericksburgh and Falmouth, on the Potomac. He made one trip to Baltimore, a distance of 100 miles, with ten barrels of flour, and returned with merchandise. He counts these as among his happiest days, when, in company with other teamsters, he would camp out in his wagon at night.

In 1835, he and his father and family moved from Virginia to Ohio with a covered wagon and a team of horses, the party numbering thirteen persons. His father and family settled on eighty acres of timbered land, the timber being mostly chestnut and dogwood. Here they resided until the venerable man died. He was well into the nineties at the time of his death, about 1850.

In the fall of 1851, Mr. Clark sold his Ohio farm and removed to Illinois, which was then the frontier of civilization. He was accompanied by his wife and eight children, six sons and two daughters. The long journey was made overland with two lumber wagons and two double teams of horses, and was rendered exceedingly tedious on account of bad weather and miserable roads, in addition to which his children were taken sick with the ague. He inquired on the way for a healthy location, and was directed ta Adams county, Illinois. Before reaching there he rented a house east of Mt. Sterling, where he and his family remained until the following spring. He then rented the farms of two brothers, Henry and Mike Huffman, who were going to California. He was to reap the wheat, which was then half grown, and this helped him to a good start, as he realized therefrom 250 bushels as his share. This was a windfall to him, as he had little or no means, and it secured for him bread and seed for the following year. One of his sons worked in a tanyard and earned the the price of two cows, which then cost $10. His other son took a job of clearing timber from some land, and drew the wood to market. Thus all put their shoulder to the wheel until brighter days dawned upon them.

Mr. Clark afterward rented an old farm of 160 acres, which was a part of his present place. He lived there two years, when he built a good brick house on his own farm, his house having an excellent cellar under the whole of it. He paid $1,000 for 160 acres, and most of it was wild and covered with brush. He now has 140 acres of this under good cultivation, while twenty acres are of timber, which is planted with blue grass, which makes good pasture. He has fertilized his land with clover, and grows about forty acres each of corn and wheat, realizing as high as forty bushels of wheat to an acre, and sixty and seventy bushels of corn. He has ceased, for some years, from active labors on his place, although still enjoying fair health.

His first wife died, aged nearly seventy years, and is buried on the farm. They had seven children, three of whom are living: Joseph W. died May 31, 1859, leaving a wife and three children; Elias died in Ohio, when an infant, in January, 1842; Jonah was stabbed at Cooperstown, Virginia, when twenty-one years of age, and died November 29, 1859; Moses was a volunteer in the Civil war, and died March 7, 1871, aged twenty-eight years; Martin, also a volunteer in the late war, passed through the conflict in safety to return home and meet with an accident by which he lost a leg in a threshing machine. He is now farming on his father's land. This son and two daughters are the only living children. One daughter, Tabitha, now Mrs. George Kendrick, lives on a farm near Mt. Sterling, and has four children; Massy J., the other daughter, is the wife of George Hollis, a prosperous farmer, who lives in Gibson City, this State; they have eight sons.

Mr. Clark's present wife, with whom he has lived ten years, was the widow of William Lozden. Her maiden name was Eliza Curlew, and she was born in Kentucky, in 1835, and was reared on the frontier in Missouri, when the aborigines were plentiful. She had seven children by her former marriage, four sons and three daughters.

Politically, Mr. Clark has been a Democrat until recently, and now votes independently, regardless of politics. Religiously, his faith for twenty-five years has been that of the Methodist Church, to which he renders much valuable assistance.

These are a few of the most prominent events of an eminently busy and useful life, which is deservedly crowned with prosperity and the esteem of his fellow-men.

JAMES W. BLEYER was born near Franklin, Franklin township, Pennsylvania, June 17, 1860. His father, Samuel Bleyer, was born in Connecticut, and his father, Alex. Bleyer, was a native of the New England States. The ancestry of the family is Scotch. Mr. Alex. Bleyer removed from Connecticut to Pennsylvania, and died in that State, and his son was reared in the State of his birth. Here he followed farming until he removed to Williamsport and remained a few years, and then returned to Franklin county, and still resides on a farm. The maiden name of his first wife was Barbara Kane, and she was the mother of James. She was a native of Connecticut, and she died in Franklin county, Pennsylvania, in 1875. James was reared and educated in his native State. He was fifteen years old when his mother died, and from that time he cared for himself. He had learned the printer's trade in the office of the *Press* at Chambersburg, at the age of fourteen, worked there one year, and with the exception of a few months has followed the trade ever since, and has set type in the principal offices east of the Mississippi river. In May, 1891, he bought the office and good will of the *Brown County Republican*, a weekly paper devoted to the interests of the Republican party.

He was married in 1890, to Hattie May. She was born in St. Louis, Missouri, the daughter of David and Alice May. Mr. Bleyer is a member of Cincinnatus Lodge, No. 287, K. of P., and of the National Telegraph Union. He has always been a sound Republican.

JACOB HOWELL is one of the oldest settlers of the county now living in Bainbridge, he having been born in what is now Woodstock township, Schuyler county, Illinois, April 23, 1833. His father, John Howell, was a native of Guilford county, North Carolina, where he was reared and where he married. He emigrated to Illinois across country with teams, accompanied by his wife and five children, locating in what is now Woodstock township. It was a wild and cheerless country, that in which the pioneer North Carolinian and his family settled. The cry of the wolves startled the children by night. Deer and turkeys haunted the big woods. Most of the land was owned by the Government. Neighbors lived far apart. Yet he went to work with a stout heart upon a tract of land, sixteen acres of which had been cleared. A log cabin stood upon the tract and there the subject of this sketch was born. The father resided there until his death, in August, 1833.

The maiden name of the mother of Jacob Howell was Sarah Manlove, daughter of William Manlove, born in North Carolina. After the death of her husband she married a second time, a man named Stephen Frazer. She died on the home farm in 1842.

But an infant when his father died he was doubly an orphan when but nine years old. From that time onward the brave and persevering lad was made to care for himself. He was able to attend the primitive school of his youth—the conventional log cabin with its splintered seats and puncheon floors, where, somehow, boys did manage to pick up knowledge nearly, if not altogether, as good as that of the present date, when the pupils are given the advantages of culture, aesthetic furnishings and scientific appliances. He began work upon the farm at $5 per month, continuing to work out until 1853. In February of that year he started out with others to make the overland journey with ox teams to California. It was a perilous undertaking for this inexperienced lad of less than twenty. The only white settlement between the Missouri river and California was the Mormon one in Utah, which report declared was to be nearly as much to be dreaded as the hostile Indians who scoured the plains in search of victims. Reaching California he first engaged as cook for a threshing party, receiving $3 per day. A few weeks of this life sufficed and he undertook mining, which disagreed with him and he went to southern California, where he engaged in the raising of hogs. In 1859 he returned to Schuyler county, and bought the farm he now owns and occupies. Since that time he has devoted himself to agricultural pursuits.

In the following year, 1860, he was united in marriage to Rachel Parker, who has borne him four children: Emma, Addie, John and Fred. Mrs. Howell was born in Bainbridge township, and is a daughter of John and Emily Parker, who are natives of North Carolina and pioneer settlers of Schuyler county.

Mr. and Mrs. Howell are members of the Methodist Episcopal Church. Mr. Howell is a Republican in politics.

DAVID THRON, an old resident and well-to-do farmer, now living at his old home on section 27, township 17, range 12, was born in Baden, near Heidelberg, Germany, June 3, 1823. He was only twelve years old when his father, Michael, died, at the age of forty-four. For eleven years he had been a soldier in the Spanish provinces, and had seen much hardship and had many unpleasant experiences. He is remembered as a brave German soldier. His wife, who survived him, came to the United States shortly after the death of her husband, bringing with her five children, two having come before. She sailed from Bremen and came via New Orleans, being fifty-six days on the water. The family, including the mother and seven children, settled in Cass county, except one who died in New Orleans. The mother died at the home of our subject in 1880, aged eighty-four. She had spent her last years with him. She had been a good woman all her life, and she and her husband were consistent members of the German Lutheran Church.

David came to this county in 1844, and began life as a laborer in Beardstown. He then decided to become a farmer, after having worked and saved his money for nine years. He rented one year and then bought the farm where he now lives. His first purchase was of eighty acres, and he afterward entered forty acres of Congress land, adjoining his first purchase. He afterward improved this and added to it until he owned 200 acres. He disposed of part of his land to August Hausmeyer, and expects to retire and move into Arenzville after the spring of 1893. He added buildings to his farm and made it comfortable in every way.

He was married in Beardstown to Maria A. Eradt, who was born in the same town and province as himself, coming to America on the same vessel with him, and they were married soon after landing. Her parents came to this country a few years later and settled in Bellville, where they continued until the end of their lives. They are members of the Lutheran Church.

Mr. and Mrs. Thron are honored and respected members of the Lutheran Church, and he is a Democrat in politics, and they are the parents of seven children. They experienced a great grief in the loss of four of them in a few weeks, in the fall of 1863, of diptheria. Their names were: Valentine, fifteen years old; Henry, thirteen years old; David, Jr., nine years old; and Anna M., seven years old. The living are: Michael, a workman on the Quincy Railroad, who married Elizabeth Garrick; Elizabeth, wife of Henry Kneke, a farmer in this county; and Louis, a farmer in Cass county, who married Dora Fellow. Mr. and Mrs. Thron are among the best of our German citizens, and are highly respected by all who know them.

GEORGE W. FRISBY, a prosperous farmer of Schuyler county, was one of the pioneers of this section, and is justly entitled to the following space in this history. He was born near Watertown, Jefferson county, New York, June 21, 1821, a son of Sparrow Frisby, a native of the same State; the maternal grandfather emigrated to the United States from Wales; he resided in New York for some years, and then removed to Connecticut, where he passed the last years of his life The father of George W. was but an infant when his mother died, and he was then taken into the family of Dr Wesley Willoughby, of Herkimer county, New York, and there grew to mature years. In the spring of 1837 he made a trip to Illinois in search of a permanent location; he came to Schuyler county, and selected a tract of land in what is now Woodstock township; he built a log house in the midst of the wilderness, and in the fall was joined by his family, after a few years he sold this place and removed to Rushville, where he worked at the trade of painting and paper-hanging; he was a resident of that place at the time of his death. The maiden name of the mother of our subject was Lydia Willoughby, a native of Herkimer county, New York, and a daughter of James and Lydia (Cook) Willoughby, natives of Connecticut and pioneers of Herkimer county; the last years of her life were spent in Rushville George W was sixteen years old when he came to Illinois in the fall of 1837; the journey was made by the most convenient route at the time; via team to Utica, thence via the Erie canal to Buffalo, thence by steamer to Cleveland, thence by canal to Zanesville, thence by team to Portsmouth, thence via the Ohio, Mississippi and Illinois rivers to Schuyler county, landing at a point then known as Erie Mr. Frisby had attended the schools in New York State quite regularly, and after coming to Schuyler county was a pupil one term in the primitive school of the frontier He lived at home with his parents until he was twenty-one years of age, and then he worked at the shoemaker's trade for two years He next took up the cooper's trade, which he followed five years, and then engaged in farming In 1860 he settled on the place he now owns and occupies, section 8, Bainbridge township

Mr. Frisby was married in 1845, to Elizabeth Thompson, who was born in Greene county, Pennsylvania. They have five children living: Ann Elizabeth, William V., Mary C., James and Serilla H. The parents are members of the Free Methodist Church

Politically our subject is identified with the Republican party, and has represented the people of his township in many offices of trust and honor; he has been School Trustee and Director, Collector, Town Clerk, Constable, Magistrate, and at the present time is School Treasurer, an office he has held more than twenty five years. He has discharged all the duties devolving upon him with rare fidelity, and has the utmost confidence of his fellow-men.

ANDREW LOGSDON, a prominent farmer of Bainbridge township, has been a resident of Schuyler county, Illinois, since he was a child of seven years He was born in Cooperstown township, Brown county, Illinois, March 13, 1858. His father, Joseph Logsdon, was a native of Kentucky, born in Madison county, September 6, 1809, and the grandfather, William Logsdon, was also born in Madison county, Kentucky, he was a planter by occupation, and spent all his life in the county of his birth He married Elizabeth Beheimer, a Virginian by birth; after the death of her husband she emigrated from Kentucky to Illinois, and died in Brown county, at the age of eighty-four years. Joseph Logsdon was reared in Kentucky, and was there married. In 1844 he came to Illinois and located in Brown county, where he purchased sixty acres of unimproved land in Cooperstown township; there he resided until 1865, when he removed to Woodstock township, Schuyler county; here he bought a tract of land that had been improved, and on it he has since lived. He was married to Lucy Parker, who was born in Madison county, Kentucky, May 1, 1815, a daughter of Jonathan and Patsey (Everson) Parker. Of this union were born eight children, seven of whom lived to mature years.

Andrew Logsdon, the subject of this notice, was reared from his seventh year in Woodstock township, and received his education in the common schools of that neighborhood. At the age of twenty years he assumed the responsibilities of life, and began his career as a farmer on rented land. In 1882 he purchased the land which he now occupies, located on section 6, Bainbridge township. He is engaged in general farming, and has been quite successful in his operations.

He was united in marriage in 1879, to Rohamah Terrill, a native of Bainbridge township, and a daughter of Jackson and Elizabeth Terrill. To them have been born four children: Maude, Hugh, Lucy and Elizabeth. Politically Mr. Logsdon has always been independent, and is now identified with the People's party.

GEORGE H. KIRKHAM, a prominent farmer and progressive citizen of Littleton township, Schuyler county, was born in Brooklyn township, this county, April 22, 1846. His parents were Henry and Elizabeth Kirkham, his father still living in Buena Vista township, this county.

Our subject received his education from a private teacher, who boarded about at the different homes, teaching in the various families, his facilities were thus necessarily limited, all of which have been supplemented by subsequent endeavor and self instruction. At the age of twenty, he enlisted in the war on August 15, 1861, serving in Company G and D, Twenty-eighth Illinois Infantry for four years, under the command of Captain B. C. Gillam. He was with his regiment all through the war, with the exception of about four months, when he was sick and in the hospital at Monterey, and went through the international struggle without receiving so much as a scratch. He was mustered out of the service in Brownsville, Texas, and honorably discharged in March, 1866. He had a brother and two step-brothers also in the late war, his brother in the same regiment as himself, while his step-brothers served in the Fiftieth Illinois Infantry. His brother served for three years, at the end of which time he went as a substitute, serving until the close of the war. Both of his step-brothers were re-enlisted.

After the war he returned to Schuyler county, and on November 6, 1870, was married to Anna E. Garrison, who was born in this township and county, July 31, 1846. She was a daughter of George and Sarah Garrison, prominent pioneers of this county, who both died here, her father at the age of seventy-seven years. She was one of eleven children, ten still living. Our subject is one of six children, five living, all of them farmers.

After marriage, he located where he now resides, on a part of the old Garrison farm, he having made all the improvements at present noticeable on the place. He built, in 1882. his present large and comfortable home, and now has good barns for his grain and stock, besides various other modern conveniences, facilitating the handling of the various products of his farm, which is devoted to mixed agriculture He has recently added to his original farm by purchasing 160 acres, and now has one of the largest and best farms in the county, having more than 800 rods of tiling on his place.

Mr. and Mrs. Kirkham have ten children Charles L, at Normal school, born January 6, 1872; Elizabeth, born March 27, 1873, wife of William Blodgett; Ida F, born November 16, 1874, now attending the Normal school; William R, born December 14, 1876; Margaret G, born August 4, 1878; George H., born May 16, 1882; Anna B. M., born September 4, 1884; James O, born January 4, 1888.

Politically, Mr. Kirkham is a Republican, and cast his first vote for General Grant's first term He served as Collector of his township during 1890, doing in that capacity creditable and satisfactory work. He is a member of Colonel Horney Post, G A R, No. 131.

He and wife are consistent members of the Christian Church, of which Mr Kirkham is Deacon, and for the support of which he and wife are ardent workers and liberal contributors

Intelligent, honest and public-spirited, he commands the respect of all, while his more amiable virtues have won the affectionate regard of his fellow citizens.

HENRY KIRKHAM, one of the oldest living pioneers and most highly esteemed citizens of Schuyler county, dates his first appearrnce on the stirring scene of this locality on January 4, 1835. He is a native of Ohio His father, Henry Kirkham, was born in Virginia, September 2, 1769, while his grandfather, Michael Kirkham, came from Ireland, where he was married, to the United States, locating first in Virginia, and later moved to Kentucky, residing in Lexington, that State, for seven years, during the Indian troubles He died in Kentucky in 1835, aged ninety-six years His wife died on the same day, aged ninety-four years, both dying of cholera

The father of our subject removed from Virginia when a boy, accompanying the family to Kentucky, where he was married to Mary Gay. She was a native of Kentucky, having been born in that State in 1773 She died September 9, 1820. The parents of our subject removed from Kentucky to Ohio, coming in 1834 to Illinois, locating in Rushville township. Here his father died April 12, 1840

His parents had ten children: Agnes, born February 3, 1794, married John Patterson, and died in Ohio; Sarah, born February 15, 1796, married John Kaze, and died in Missouri, Margaret, born January 6, 1798, was married, and died in Bloomfield Illinois; James, born January 11, 1800, died in Ohio, John, born September 6, 1802, died in Schuyler county, Illinois; Michael, born February 20, 1805, died in Schuyler county, Illinois; Mary, born August 7, 1808, married Martin Huffstetter, and died in Iowa, Rebecca, born February 20, 1810, married Peter Wempler, and died in Schuyler county, Illinois; the subject of our sketch, was born in Ohio; William, born August 1, 1815, died in California

At the age of five or six years, our subject removed with his parents to Monroe county, Indiana. Here he was reared on a farm, attending the district school, but receiving but little instruction On January 4, 1835, he married Elizabeth Hinkle, and at once came to Illinois, locating in Schuyler county. He was poor, consequently rented land for some years, finally purchasing land in Woodstock township, Schuyler county, where he remained until the close of the war, when he removed to Buena Vista township, where he now resides. Here he owns eighty-two acres, which he has vastly improved, having erected a substantial residence and barns for grain and stock, besides numerous other modern conveniences for the pursuit of farming. His land is under a good state of cultivation, being devoted to mixed agriculture. It was here that his wife died, September 26, 1847, leaving six children to his care. She was a lady of much intelligence and many admirable traits of character, and was greatly regretted by her family and friends. The children were: James, born February 13, 1836, still residing with his father; William, born September 26, 1837, was a soldier in Company G, Twenty-eighth Illinois, serving three years in the army, then re-enlisted and did duty until the close of the war, and now resides in Portland, Oregon; Mary, born September 4, 1839, married Jabez Vatters, residing in Macomb, Illinois; George H., born April 22, 1841, was a soldier in the Twenty-eighth Illinois, serving until the close of the war, now residing in Littleton township, Illinois; Sarah E., born March 20, 1843, married, and now resides in Springfield, Illinois; Margaret, born December 7, 1844, married Amos Burgee, and resides in Portland Oregon.

Our subject was married a second time, March 26, 1846, his second wife being Frances Swan, born in 1803. They had one son: Robert John, born December 28, 1849. By a former marriage to Morris Swan, she had had six children: Martha, Matilda, Mary Ann, James, Jason W. and one that died in infancy. His second wife died in 1875, much lamented by all who knew her, as a worthy woman, a faithful wife and devoted mother'

Politically, our subject first voted the Whig ticket, and is now a Republican. His constituents have honored him by electing him to one of the most responsible positions in their power to bestow, he having served as School Treasurer for forty years, which is the only office he would accept.

The Kirkhams are Presbyterians, although our subject is not a member of any church. He is, however, a believer in the Christian religion, and has never used a profane word, or tasted intoxicating liquor in his life. A kind of rara avis, sometimes heard of but seldom seen.

His endorsement by the community, and his conduct of life, make further remarks unnecessary. His integrity and fidelity are noticeable in this day of uncertainty in such matters, and are as refreshing as they are rare, and appear to be fully appreciated by his community. Would that the world might have more of such men, that the millennium might be hastened!

JOHN H. CLARK was born in Westmoreland county, Pennsylvania, September 8, 1815, a son of William and Rosana (Hurst) Clark. The father was a native of Ohio, and in 1838 penetrated the frontier to Illinois, and located in Schuyler county. He erected a sawmill, which he operated for eight years, and then disposed of the property, retiring from active labor; he died at the home of John J. Redick, aged seventy four years; his wife was born in Westmoreland county, Pennsylvania, and died at the old homestead in Schuyler county, aged sixty-four years. John H. is one of a family of eight children, and the only surviving member. He remained under the parental roof until his marriage, which occurred March 1, 1852, when he was united to Miss Rena Black; she was born in Schuyler county, Illinois, and died here in early womanhood; she was the mother of four children, two of whom are living: Mary E. is married and has four children; Lorena is married and the mother of one child. Mr. Clark was married again in 1858, to Miss Mary Carter, a native of Ohio, who died in Schuyler county, Illinois, at the age of forty years. The third union was in 1870, when Mr. Clark was married to Miss Sarah E. Lawler; she was born in Fauquier county, Virginia, October 22, 1821, a daughter of James and Nancy (Harris) Lawler.

In 1870, Mr. Clark settled on a farm near his father's home, and began the task of clearing a heavily timbered tract; there he labored industriously for eight years, and then sold the place; he bought the farm he now owns soon afterward, but only eleven acres were cleared, and a log cabin was the only place of habitation. Since then he has witnessed the many changes that have been wrought by the hand of progress, and has done his share in making the path clear for the advance of civilization. His dealings with his fellow-men have been characterized by a strict integrity and keen sense of honor that have won the highest respect of all who know him.

The parents of Mrs. Clark, James and Diana (Thomas) Lawler, reared a family of five children, four of whom survive; the maternal ancestors came from Ireland, and the father participated in the war of the Revolution; he died at the age of seventy-five years, and she survived to the age of sixty.

Politically the subject of this sketch affiliates with the Democratic party, and has always supported its issues. He and his wife are consistent members of the Christian Church.

HENRY P. GROVER, Mount Sterling, Illinois, one of the oldest settlers of the county, was born in Mason county, Kentucky. His father, Joseph, came from Virginia, and the grandfather, Jonathan, spent his last years in Lewis county, Kentucky. Joseph was a farmer in Mason county, where he spent the last years of his life. His wife was named Sarah Putnam. She was the daughter of Elizabeth and Henry Putnam, who came from Kentucky to Illinois in 1836, and she spent her last years in Brown county.

Henry was ten years old when his father died, and when he was sixteen years old his mother and her family moved to Ohio, and settled in Champaign county, where they were pioneers. They lived there until 1836, when Henry concluded to go West and try to better his fortune in a new country; consequently he came by teams as did other emigrants, and after eighteen days of travel landed in that part of Schuyler now included in Brown county. His means were very limited, and therefore, although there was plenty of Government land to be had for $1.25 an acre, he was not able to secure any for a time. He rented for two years, and then entered a Government tract, near Mount Sterling township. It was timber land, and he built the usual log hut, and existed for a long time upon the game that at that time was very plentiful. It was many years before there was any railroad through that section. He made frequent trips to Quincy, forty miles distant with wheat. Those were days of privations, but are now looked back upon as being very happy ones.

His first wife was very industrious, was able to card, spin and weave and dressed her entire family in homespun, made entirely by her own hands. Mr. Grover cleared the land and built a brick house and lived there until 1882, and traded with his son James for the farm he now owns and occupies.

He married first in 1833, Lucinda Putnam of Champaign county, Ohio, a daughter of William and Mary Putnam. She died about 1860. His second wife was named Martha Putnam. He has seven children, who were all born by his first marriage, and are named: Erwin, Caroline, John G., Marion, James, Joseph and Angeline. Mr. Grover is a member of the Regular Primitive Baptist Church, and is a Democrat in politics. He has served two terms as a member of the County Board of Supervisors.

JOSEPH LOGSDON, a venerable pioneer of Schuyler county, has been a resident of the State of Illinois since 1844. He was born in Madison county, Kentucky, September 6, 1809, a son of William and Elizabeth (Behcimer) Logsdon; his father was a native of the same county, and died there, at the age of fifty-five years; the mother survived until her eighty-fifth year, and died in Brown county, Illinois. The paternal grandparents, Edward and Polly Logsdon, also lived to a good old age. Joseph Logsdon is one of a family of eleven children, four of whom are yet living. He spent his youth at home, and in 1837 was united in marriage to Miss Lucy Parker, a native of his own county, born May 1, 1815. Her parents, Jonathan and Patsey (Everson) Parker, were born in Madison county, Kentucky, and were pioneers of Ohio. After his marriage Mr. Logsdon settled in Kentucky and followed agricultural pursuits there until 1844, when he came to Brown county, Illinois; he purchased sixty acres of wild land, and made it his home until coming to Schuyler county, when he bought a tract of 184 acres, which was well improved. He has done a general farming business, and has met with merited success.

Mr. and Mrs. Logsdon have had born to them nine children, seven of whom survive; they are all married and the heads of families, excepting one: Elizabeth R. has seven children; Perry is the subject of a sketch which will be found elsewhere in this volume; Sarah is the mother of seven children; Ellen has a family of six children; George is married, but has no children; Jacob has two children; Andrew is the father of a family of four; the two who are deceased were twins. The ancestors have been people of long lives, noted for their honor and uprightness, respected by all who knew them.

CHARLES H. PHELPS was born in Dutchess county, New York, January 25, 1836. He is the son of E. B. and Jane (Wright) Phelps, the former born in New Medford, Connecticut, taught school for twenty-six years, and also ran a tile factory, working at different trades. He died at the age of fifty-five, in Dutchess county, New York. His wife was born in Fishkill, New York, and died in Hancock county, aged fifty-five years. Her family were from the New England States, where they followed the occupation of farmers.

Charles remained at home until he was twenty-three years of age, when he came to Illinois in 1857 and settled near Huntsville on a rented farm. He then rented in Birmingham township for five years, and two years in Hancock county. He then bought a farm in Hancock county, and lived there for ten years, then sold and bought in this county, in Huntsville, 240 acres of improved land, where he lived for four years, and then sold and rented a farm in Adams county, and in 1887 bought his present farm of 200 acres, partly improved, near the geographical center of the township. He has also been engaged in threshing.

Until Lincoln's second term he was a Democrat, but since that has been a stanch Republican. He has been Supervisor for four years, being first elected in 1888. He succeeded Marcus Helston.

He was married February 3, 1859, to Nancy Scott, of Carroll county, Ohio, who came here with her parents when two years old. She was the daughter of William and Elizabeth (Hunter) Scott, the former a son of John Scott, of Ireland, who came with his wife and son to the United States when William was only eight years old. He rented in Carroll county, Ohio, in 1817, and came from there to Illinois in 1842, settling in Huntsville, Schuyler county. John Scott was seventy years old at his death, and his wife, Isabel, died on the old farm. Elizabeth Hunter was born in Maryland, but her father was a native of Ireland. She died on the old farm, aged sixty-five years. She and her husband had five children, four yet living.

Mr. Phelps was one of fourteen children, but he himself has only nine, as follows: Sarah Alice, wife of B. Craft, and they have three children; William E., married to Nana Tyree, four children; Charles F., married to Josephine Farewell, two children; Eliza May, married to George Burnett, one child; Ervin is at home, as are also George B., John R., Bert R. and Clara Belle.

Mr. and Mrs. Phelps are members of the Methodist Episcopal Church. Mr. Phelps has been the Master of the Masonic lodge, No. 465, of Huntsville, for eighteen years. He was once a member of the I. O. O. F. He is a Granger, and was Master and State Deputy in same, and no one has been more popular, both in the offices he has held and in the various business dealings he has had with his fellow-men. He was one of the men who put John A. Logan in the United States Senate. He worked for him personally, and as long as the history of the Thirty-fourth Illinois Congressional District contest, which put J. A. Logan in the Senate, is preserved, just so long will the biography of Charles H. Phelps be on record as one of the workers, if not the hardest worker, in that cause. He knew no such word as fail, and much of the enthusiasm of that time was due to his efforts. He is a man of honor and uprightness, and is loved by every one, regardless of party affiliations.

ABRAHAM LINCOLN STOUT, was born in Ripley township, Brown county, Illinois, November 9, 1860. He is the fifth son of Francis M. and Catherine Stout (see biography of same). He was reared and educated at Ripley. In his youthful days he attended school and helped his father on the farm. He lived with his parents until his marriage and then settled on the farm he now owns and occupies. This contains 180 acres, pleasantly located on the Rushville road one mile east of the courthouse. He has erected a good set of farm buildings, planted fruit and shade trees and otherwise improved the farm.

He was married in November, 1884, to Miss Louisa Lanning. She was born in Cooperstown township and was the daughter of Isaiah and Ellen Lanning. They have three children: Ethel, Eleanor Lottie and Helen.

Mrs. Stout is a member of the Christian Church. Mr. Stout is a Republican in politics. Both he and his wife are good, hard-working farmers and are greatly esteemed by all who know them.

RICHARD BUSH, of Mt. Sterling, a successful manufacturer of tile and brick, was born in Zanesville, Ohio, December 20, 1827. His father, Thomas, was born near Easton, Pennsylvania, in 1802, and his father, Richard, was born in the same State. He removed from there to Ohio and was one of the pioneers of Muskingum county. The removal was made on pack horses in 1801. He secured Government land on Meig's creek. At that time the Indians were more numerous than whites, but all of them were friendly. For many years there were no railroads, no canals, no markets, and the people lived on the products of their lands. His wife's name was Dorothy Ryman, born in Pennsylvania of German ancestry. Thomas was eight years old when his parents made this move to Ohio, and there he was reared and married. He learned the trade of carpenter, and in his early life would hew all the timber and then saw all the lumber with a whipsaw to build a barn. He remained in Ohio until 1834, and then with his wife and nine children came to this State. This removal was made by team, cooking and camping by the way. Mr. Bush entered Government land, one and one-half miles east of Exeter. There was a small cabin on the land. As soon as he could well do so he erected a frame house with two rooms, and that was one of the five houses of that section. At the time he settled there the county was but sparsely inhabited and much of the land was still owned by the Government. He remained there until 1849, when he sold and came to Brown county and settled in Lee township, and bought land and lived there until his death. The name of his wife was Elizabeth Morrison, born in Virginia, daughter of Alexander Morrison, who had come from Ireland. He had settled in Virginia and from there had moved to Muskingum county, Ohio, and died near Zanesville, his wife being also from Ireland. She reared seven children and finally died on the home farm.

Richard was six years of age when he came to Illinois with his parents and attended the log schoolhouse. He remained with his parents until 1848 and the same fall he moved to Brown county, and settled in Lee township. There he bought eighty acres of land, all wild, part timber and part prairie. He improved the farm and resided there until 1856, and then sold out and moved to Texas, making the journey with teams. He bought 400 acres of land in Lamar county, at $5 an acre, and engaged in farming and stock-raising, and lived there until 1860, and then sold out, for $10 an acre. He had in the meantime accumulated quite a stock of cattle, so that his investment there had proved very profitable. On selling out he returned to Lee township and bought 200 acres of land, three miles west of Mt. Sterling, and continued farming there until 1889, when he sold the farm and moved into Mt. Sterling. He then engaged in the manufacture of tile and brick. The most solid and enduring brick in existence is made by Mr. Bush at his yards. It is exclusively used for the paving of Jacksonville and Quincy. He introduced the first portable steam sawmill into Brown county, and owned and operated the first mower and reaper combined, the first twine binder and the first thresher in that part of the State. Mr. Bush is an intelligent man, he has progressive ideas and he is not afraid to put them into practice.

He was married in 1848, to Lucinda Stayle, born in that part of Morgan now included in Scott county, a daughter of Peter and Parthena Stayle, natives of Kentucky and pioneers of Morgan county. Mr. and Mrs. Bush have eight children: Elizabeth A., Peter T., Emma J., Alexander J., Parthena S., Asenath, Minnie and R. Arthur. He is a Republican in politics.

WILLIAM J. LAMBERT, a prominent citizen of Schuyler county, has been a resident of the State of Illinois since his childhood, and has aided in developing the wild, uncultivated land into one of the most fertile farming sections in the United States. He is a native of Washington county, Kentucky, born January 21, 1832, a son of William and Catharine (Dennis) Lambert. William Lambert, Sr., was born in Washington county, Kentucky, and was reared to the occupation of a farmer, which he followed all his life. He emigrated to Illinois in 1836, and settled at Rushville, where he operated a pioneer hotel until 1844; he died in that year, at the age of forty-five years. The trip to Illinois was made with a covered wagon and four horses, and the trials and hardships endured by the family were many, and such as are incident to life on the frontier. The mother of our subject was born in Mercer county, Kentucky, and died at Rushville, Illinois, at an advanced age; she was married a second time, this union being to Charles Wells; she reared a family of three children, two of whom survive, Mrs. M. O. Snyder and William J., the subject of this notice.

He was a youth of fourteen years when he left the home of his childhood, and went out to meet some of the responsibilities of life; he first worked for his brother by the month, and in 1847 he came to Littleton township, and bought a tract of wild prairie land, which he undertook to improve and place under cultivation. Here he was married April 18, 1852, to Miss Josephine Rose, who was born on the farm which is now her home, June 29, 1833. Her parents, Randolph and Sarah Rose, were natives of Kentucky, but emigrated to Illinois and settled in Schuyler county in 1826; they had to undergo all the hardships of pioneer life, and did their share in the development and improvement of the country; they had a family of three children. Mr. and Mrs. Lambert are the parents of eight children, six of whom are living: Mabel is the wife of George Little, and has two children; William L. is married and has two children; Ellen, a talented artist, is a pupil in the Art Institute, Chicago; Edward is on the home farm; Josephine is a teacher in the Littleton schools; Fannie is at home. The family have had excellent educational advantages, and are among the most prominent citizens of the county.

Mr. Lambert in his youth enjoyed only such educational facilities as were afforded in the district schools, but he improved his time and secured a fund of information that fitted him for the ordinary duties of life. After his marriage he settled on a farm which he occupied for some time and then sold; he now owns nearly 500 acres of as choice land as lies within the borders of the county. He is engaged in general farming, but gives especial attention to the raising of high-grade cattle.

Politically he affiliates with the Democratic party. For more than twenty years he has been School Director, and has always given a liberal support to those movements which tend to advance the interests of the county and State. In his religious faith he is a Baptist, and has been a member of that church for many years. The children being reared to this faith, are also members of the church.

CHARLES H. JUETT, a well-known farmer of Woodstock township is the subject of the following biographical sketch. He is a native of the State of Kentucky, born in Fayette county, June 7, 1831, a son of John and Catharine (Hoffman) Juett; the parents were natives ef the Bluegrass State, and there passed all their days; they had born to them a family of nine children, two of whom died in infancy, and four of whom are yet living. Charles H. was married February 22, 1859, to Miss Mary Jane Hoffman, a native of Fayette county Kentucky, and a daughter of Michael and Syba Hoffman. Nine children have been born of this union, two of whom died in infancy: John M.; William, who is married and has one child; Anna M., married and the mother of two children; Catharine A., married and the mother of three children; Eliza E.; Charles H.; Benjamin D.; Effie S. and Francis M.

After his marriage Mr. Juett removed to Illinois, and settled in Brown county; later he came to Schuyler county, and here he purchased 160 acres of timber land; he then undertook the task of clearing this and placing it under cultivation; he erected a log cabin, 16 x 18 feet, which was afterward destroyed by fire. As his means increased he made additional investments in land, and now owns 320 acres, all under cultivation. He is engaged in general farming, and has been very successful. He has filled various local offices, and in both public and private life he has made a record for honorable and correct methods of dealing that command the confidence of the entire community.

In politics he was allied with the Whig party until its dissolution, and since that time he has voted the Democratic ticket.

HENRY MEYER, an old and retired German farmer of section 19, township 17, range 11, was born in Prussia, Germany, in 1814. His parents lived and died in Prussia, when quite old. The father, Conrad, was a small farmer, and he and his wife were members of the Lutheran Church. Henry is the youngest but one of the family. He and a brother Fred are the only surviving members of the family. Henry has earned his own living since he was eight years old and has made his present large fortune entirely by his own efforts. He was yet a young man when in the spring of 1833 he sailed from Bremen, on a sailing vessel, arriving at New Orleans after a voyage of nine weeks. He came up the Mississippi river and spent some few months in Missouri, but not liking it he came on to Beardstown, Illinois, and settled here, being among the first settlers of the locality. They were all strangers to him. He is now the oldest settler now living in the county, which was all unbroken when he came to it in the spring of 1833. Arenzville was a small town indeed when he settled there, consisting of two log houses. Beardstown and Virginia were hamlets, and no roads marked out the sectional and township lines. In fact there were no improvements in the county to amount to anything. As there were no railroads the pioneers had but few advantages to sell their produce when they had raised it. Mr. Meyer has lived to see all this changed, doing his full share to effect this change. He has worked hard to increase his original 186 acres to his present number of 380 acres, of which 250 are highly improved. The 380 acres are divided into two separate farms, each supplied with a complete set of farm buildings. Until about five years ago Mr. Meyer worked hard, but then, as advancing age told upon him, he retired, and has been living quietly ever since, enjoying the fruits of his labors. He is now seventy-eight years old, and can point to a life of usefulness that would put to shame many an idle man.

He was married in this county to Elizabeth Talkemeyer, born near the old home of her husband in Prussia, Germany. She came to America with a brother, Frederick, in the '40s, their parents having died in Germany. After they landed in New Orleans, they came north to Beardstown, and here they both lived and died. Mrs. Meyer died at her home where her husband yet lives, September, 1884, aged sixty-seven. She was a good wife, a devoted mother, and a kind neighbor. Mr. and Mrs. Meyer were the parents of four children: Caroline Keane, of Arenzville; Mary, wife of William Duvelmeier, of Beardstown; Henry manages the farm, and married Caroline Baujan, of Arenzville; Louisa, wife of Fred Wienkenc̈man, a farmer on one of Mr. Meyer's farms.

Mr. Meyer has been a leading man for many years in his section, and one of the most prominent members of the Lutheran Church in Beardstown, and one near Arenzville. He is an ardent Republican in politics.

ANGUS McPHAIL was born in Glasgow, Scotland, April 25, 1810. His father, Angus, was born on the island of Mull, and served an apprenticeship in Glasgow, to the trade of haberdasher. He then went into business for himself, but was not successful, losing all he had. He then decided to come to America, and try his fortune in the new world. His son, Angus, sent money to defray the expenses of his parents to America in 1844. He spent his last days in Lee township, and died aged eighty-four years. His wife's name was Jane, daughter of James and Flora (McVicker) Crawford. She was born in Argyleshire, Scotland, and died at the home of our subject. Her father was born in Renfrewshire, Scotland, and descended from the early settlers of that place who fled from France during the time of the persecution by the Roman Catholics. He was a sailor, and followed the sea many years. He fell from the mast, finally, and was killed. His wife passed her entire life in Scotland. The mother of our subject reared seven children: Archibald, Jane, and our subject, were the only ones that came to America.

Angus was reared in Glasgow, and served six years' apprenticeship to the tailor's trade, and then did journey work in different parts of Great Britain He came to America in 1835, and stopped in New York a few weeks, and then made his way to Toronto, there bought property and opened a shop, continuing at his trade until 1837. Early in the spring of 1838, he left for the States by a roundabout route, and at last reached St. Louis, which then contained but 2,000 people. He stopped there a short time, and then came on to Beardstown, and from there to Rushville, and here opened a shop where he conducted his business until 1840, and then went to Mt. Sterling, and there opened a shop and continued until 1850. He then moved to the farm he now owns, and has since been engaged in farming

He was married in Glasgow, in 1833, to Mary Crawford, born in Scotland, who died in 1852 He was married a second time in 1855, to Jane McCaskill, born in Sangamon county, Illinois, February 26, 1828. Her father, Daniel, was born in North Carolina, and his father, John, was born in Scotland, and coming to America settled in North Carolina, and then went to South Carolina, where he died The father of Mrs McPhail went to Indiana when a young man, and studied medicine, and continued practicing there He then became one of the pioneers of Sangamon county, Illinois He practiced medicine in that county until 1835, and then took eighty acres of Government land in Pea Ridge township, and bought 240 acres more in the same township. He remained there until his death, at the age of fifty nine The maiden name of the mother was Esther Turner, the daughter of Archibald Turner, a native of Ireland, who died at the home of the family in Pea Ridge township

Mr. and Mrs McPhail have four living children: Daniel, William, Archibald John and Flora Ellen He has also four living children by his first wife: Mary, Catherine, James and Scotland They are members of the Presbyterian and Methodist Churches, and he is a Republican

HENRY A. HIERMAN, a young and energetic farmer, living on section 12, township 17, range 12, was born on this farm on June 6, 1865 He was educated in the public schools, and lived at home until the death of his father, since which time he has farmed on his own account He is the fourth son of nine children born to his parents, Bernhardt and Mary (Legermeier) Hierman, natives of Germany, whose parents both lived and died in the fatherland. The father was yet a young man, about twenty years of age, when he came to the United States in the '50s and made a settlement at Beardstown He there followed his trade of painter, which he had learned in Germany. He afterward decided to go to farming, and purchased land six miles from Beardstown, in township 17, range 11 He here improved a large and beautiful tract of land embracing more than 300 acres There are eighty acres of timber. He put up good farm buildings and made everything pleasant around him. Here he died, November 16, 1887, in the fifty sixth year of his life He was a good man, well known throughout the community He was a Republican, and a member of the Methodist Episcopal Church His wife, who survives him, had come to the United States when a young woman. She married Mr. Hierman in Beardstown, and after his death married a second time, Fred Housmier, a retired farmer His first wife had died here. Mr and Mrs Housmier are members of the

Methodist Episcopal Church, and Mr. Housmier is a Republican in politics.

Mr. Hierman now conducts a large farm of 320 acres, belonging to his mother. He has been operating it for the past three years very successfully. It is in a high state of cultivation and is one of the substantial farms of the township. The brothers of our subject are: William A., a farmer of Schuyler county, married to Mary Winklehack; Edward, a dealer in agricultural implements in Arenzville, married Josie Beard; Thedora married Cinda Hackman, and they are farmers in Morgan county; our subject married Lizzie Nordsick, who was born and reared in Cass county, and is the mother of one child, Inas; Frank lives with his brother Edward, in Arenzville; George lives with his brother Theo, in Morgan county; Louis and Albert, twins; and Charles is with his brother Henry.

Mr. Hierman is a Lutheran, but his wife is a Methodist. Mr. Hierman is a Republican, and both he and his wife are highly respected throughout the community where they live.

CONRAD BECKER, now a retired farmer living in section 32, township 17, range 11, near Arenzville, was born in Hesse-Darmstadt, Germany, August 18, 1826. He grew up and was educated in his native province, being twenty-one years old when he came to the United States, sailing from Bremen on a sailing vessel that landed him in New Orleans after an eight weeks' voyage. He came from there up the Mississippi river to St. Louis, and from there to Beardstown, taking five weeks to make the trip. He settled in the last named city, February, 1847. He was a poor man at that time and among strangers, but by hard work and economy he has accumulated a fortune. He is the only member of his family who came to the United States. The parents of Mr. Becker died in Germany, and were farmers, as were their parents before them, and they were Lutherans in religion.

Mr. Becker has lived in Cass county for forty years, and has been a successful farmer and stock-raiser. His property embraces some very fine land, besides his fine residence and a large number of Government bonds.

Mr. Becker was married in Arenzville in 1851, to Miss Sarah Hakes, born in Nottinghamshire, March 7, 1828, daughter of William and Elizabeth (Freeman) Hakes, natives of Nottinghamshire, England, where they lived and died. Mrs. Becker lost her mother when quite young, and so was obliged to take care of herself. She is the only member of her family who came to the United States, and she made the trip in 1848, sailing from Liverpool, England. She landed in New York city after a voyage of some weeks, and came thence to Morgan county, Illinois, where she remained a few weeks, and then came on to Arenzville, which has since been her home. She has proved herself a true wife and mother, always willing to do any amount of hard work. Mr. and Mrs. Becker have three children: Henry married Mattie Boyer, and resides in Arenzville; Mary died in 1882, at the age of twenty-four, being the wife of Herman Weber; Lizzie, wife of Ed. Petefish, farmers of Virginia, this county.

JOHN H. WALKER was born in Grayson county, Kentucky, October 5, 1831. His father was Felix, born in Breckenridge county, Kentucky, November 14, 1804.

He was a farmer whose father, William Walker, was a farmer who lived and died in the same county. He owned a good home and raised a large family. Felix Walker came to Rushville and settled four miles north of Buena Vista township, in 1837. He rented lands for some years, but in 1844 he bought forty acres in Brooklyn township. This was wild land, on which he lived for only a short time He had but a few hundred dollars and soon moved to the hamlet of Brooklyn, where he died November 14, 1845. He left a wife, five daughters and his only son, John Soon after his death, his daughter Harriet died, in her sixteenth year. The mother of these children was Rachel Watts, of Hardin county, Kentucky. She died January 22, 1884, aged eighty years She was lame many years from a dislocated hip caused by a fall, but other than that she was well and bright to the last There are four of her children still living: Mr Walker; Sarah Blackburn, living in Brooklyn township; Catherine Hine, also of Brooklyn; Callie Shaler, living in Adams county, Iowa

Mr. Walker grew up on the farm and remained at home until thirty-one years of age, when he enlisted, August 11, 1862, in Company A, Seventy-eighth Illinois Infantry. He served nearly three years, and was in but one general engagement, and that against Hood at Nashville, Tennessee He was in seven skirmishes, but was confined to the hospital most of the time He returned to Brooklyn and resumed farming the forty acres his father had left In 1866, with his brother-in-law, Orville Blackburn, he bought eighty acres on section 29 for $1,700 They farmed this in company for three years.

In 1869 he was married to Lydia McAllister, born in Shelby county, Kentucky, daughter of Enoch and Elizabeth (Smiley) McAllister, who came to Illinois in 1854 The father died in the Confederate army, at Corinth, Mississippi, in 1862, aged fifty-one His wife is living near Huntsville, eighty-one years of age, and is still well and active. Mr. and Mrs Walker have buried one child, but they have five living: Felix, Adolphus, George A., Maude A. and an unnamed baby. Mr. Walker has eighty acres in his home farm and 120 elsewhere He raises horses, cattle and hogs, buying and selling them. He has been Road Commissioner many years, Supervisor five years and is also Assessor He is a Republican, member of G. A. R, George A Brown Post, and is a Master Mason.

JOHN W. McCLINTOCK was born in Ireland, August 12, 1812. His father was also John, a farmer in Ireland, who died there in middle life, when his son was a youth His wife was Jane Thompson, the mother of fifteen children She lived to be quite aged. Of this family, Isabella came to this country first, when a young lady and her sister, Margaret, joined her Our subject came next, when twenty-eight years of age, bringing his wife and two children His wife was Eliza Hebron They came in 1840 on the sail ship, Sardiana, and were six weeks and three days between Liverpool and New York. They encountered a great storm, and for two nights they were nailed below the decks Mr. McClintock had $100 after paying his way. They lived first with a farmer of Chester county, named William Webb, a grand, good man, a Quaker. Mr. McClintock lived with him for five years, in which he had house rent, cow and feed, free. In 1846 they to Ohio, and two years later he bought two acres of land, for $200, at

Youngstown, Ohio. He lived here five years, farming, and within five years he bought eight acres in the suburbs of that village, for $166 an acre, and brush at that! At this time there were eight railroads there. This eight acres brought him $500 in money and 120 acres of land here in Brooklyn township. His two acres brought him $500, and he came to his present farm home in the fall of 1871.

They have buried one son, John, who died in 1882, aged thirty-three years. The living ones are: William, a farmer on the old homestead; Andrew, at home; Sarah, now Mrs. James Henderson, farmers in this township; Hugh, on an adjoining farm.

Mr. McClintock has voted the Republican ticket since Horace Greeley ran for President. They are members of the Baptist Church, and have given their children a good education. Although Mr. McClintock had only $100 when he landed in this country, he and his family now have 300 acres of land, worth $30 an acre, with no mortgage upon it. They are worthy people and are justly proud of their success.

RICHARD BOYD, a farmer on section 34, Oakland township, Schuyler county, is a native of county Donegal, Ireland, born in 1858, the son of James and Catherine Boyd; the parents of both died on the Emerald Isle, the father at the age of sixty years, and the mother at the age of ninety-nine. At the age of sixteen years Richard Boyd bade farewell to his home and friends and native land, and crossed the sea to America; he landed at the port of New York, and continued his journey to Pittsburgh, Pennsylvania, to which point his ticket carried him. He soon secured employment at $2 a day, and worked until he had paid back his passage money which he was obliged to borrow; he remained in Pittsburgh three years, and at the end of that time came West with his brother James, who had preceded him to America. He was in the employ of John Young for three years, at $16 a month; he then spent a year in prospecting, and ended his observations by purchasing a tract of eighty acres, a part of his present farm, the consideration being $600; he has since added forty-three acres, and has made many improvements, developing one of the most desirable farms in the township.

Mr. Boyd was married in March, 1891, to Miss Jessie Ackman, a daughter of Isaac and Nancy (Harmon) Ackman. Mrs. Ackman died when Jessie was a child of six years, and Mr. Ackman married a second time to Miss Maria Hay, of Ohio; he died May 26, 1886. He was a farmer by occupation, and was one of the pioneers of this county, settling here in 1842. There were nine children of the first marriage, and to these the second wife was a good and kind mother; she was as deeply and truly mourned as was the father: David Ackman lives in northern Kentucky; Georgiana is the wife of Edward Garrett, and lives in Kansas; Mary married Blair Simpson, a farmer of northern Wisconsin; the rest of the family live in Schuyler county. Mr. Boyd does a general farming business, raising grains and livestock; his preference in the latter is Shorthorn cattle and Poland-China hogs.

Mr. and Mrs. Boyd are both members of church, and are liberal supporters of the religious denominations. Politically, he affiliates with the Republican party. Two of his brothers and two of his sisters are living in the United States, but the remainder of the family are in Ireland. Mr. Boyd is a man of many sterling traits of character, and has the respect of his adopted countrymen.

SAMUEL W. COOK, a highly respected member of the farming community of Oakland township, was born in Marion county, Ohio, in 1833, a son of Peter L. Cook. The father was born in 1808, and died May 2, 1892, aged eighty-four years; he enjoyed excellent health until about three weeks previous to his death. The paternal grandfather of our subject, John Cook, was a blacksmith by trade, and also carried on farming in Marion county, Ohio; he was sixty-two years of age at the time of his death, and left his second wife a widow. His first wife was Susan Londerback, a native of Pennsylvania, and in that State they were married; thence they removed to Ohio, when Peter L. was a small lad; he is one of a family of nine children, seven of whom grew to adult age. He married Hannah Hankle, a native of Bucks county, Pennsylvania, and a daughter of Henry Hankle, who died at the advanced age of ninety-six years. Eleven children were born of this union; the mother died in the fall of 1887, in her seventy-sixth year; one son died in the summer of 1859, aged twenty-eight years; he left a wife and five children; the other members of the family are living, all are married and have families, the first, second and third generations numbering about 125 souls.

Samuel W. Cook, our worthy subject, was married in 1857, to Elizabeth Lovell, of Schuyler county, a daughter of William and Elizabeth (Seaver) Lovell; Mrs. Cook's father

was a native of Kentucky, and her mother was of German extraction; the maternal grandmother lived to the extreme old age of 104 years; Mrs. Cook was born in 1840. They began their married life here in Schuyler county, and with the exception of a legacy of $3,000, which was recently received by Mrs. Cook, have accumulated their property through their own efforts. They own a fine, fertile farm of 110 acres, and Mrs. Cook has a tract near by which consists of fifty-six acres.

They are the parents of eleven children: one son and two daughters died in infancy; Charles E. died at the age of nineteen years, in 1885; Mary E. is the wife of Thomas Chalkley; William T. married Laura Strausbaugh, and has two children; Lizzie is the wife of Harry Smith; Hannah married James Lybarger, and is the mother of one child; Inez L., Samuel W. and Wilmar F. are at home.

In his political opinions Mr. Cook adheres to the principles of the Democratic party; he has represented his township in some of the local offices, and has discharged his duties with great credit to himself. Mrs. Cook is a consistent member of the Church of the Disciples.

NOAH W. BAKER was born in Summit county, Ohio, June 25, 1835. He was the son of James M. and Eliza (Taylor) Baker. James M. Baker was of New York, and came from there to Ohio, and rented in Summit county, and soon after bought and began farming. In 1840, he sold his Ohio property and drove of oxen and one wagon, and settled in Pike county, near Griggsville, and lived there eight months. He then came to this county and bought forty acres and built a log house in which they lived He then bought sixty acres more, and he lived there till his death, which occurred when he was eighty-six years of age

Our subject's father was one of five children Our subject's mother was born in Connecticut and came West to Ohio with her people, and she died here about seventy-one years of age. Noah W. was one of eight children, four yet living, and all in this neighborhood but one The subject of this sketch is a Democrat, and was from his twenty-first year. His people all belong to the Methodist Episcopal Church He was at home till he was of age, and then worked out by the month

He was married February 21, 1867, to Miss Margaret Greenleaf, who was born in Elkhorn township, July 10, 1843 She was the daughter of Peter and Mary (Furguson) Greenleaf, she being of Ohio, and he came from Canada to Illinois Their daughter Margaret, was one of four children, and all are living Margaret's father and mother died in Elkhorn township and had about 160 acres of land at his death. He went to California overland and part of the way he walked and rode. He staid there four years, and while there he practiced the trade of a tanner. He returned by land.

Our subject's wife had nine children, seven of whom are living: Hattie M was born December, 1869, Perry was born February 4, 1870; Susie was born October 22, 1873; Nellie was born September 6, 1875, Fred was born November 16, 1878; Carson was born October 13, 1883, and Mart was born April 13, 1885. After his marriage our subject settled on the forty acres he had bought and built a log house and then a frame one. He lived there till 1888. He has now in the neighborhood, over 480 acres and eighty under cultivation

Subject's children are all cultivated and intellectual. One of them is teaching, two are musical, and the others are more or less gifted He himself is a Democrat and voted for Stephen A Douglas He is a member of the Methodist Episcopal Church, and he is also a member of the I. O. O. F. He is a fine man, and very much respected by all of his fellow citizens.

ALLEN WEBB was born in Madison county, Kentucky. July 25, 1820. He was the son of Joshua and Letta (Haward) Webb. The former was born in Virginia and came with his parents at an early day to Kentucky, where he lived and died at the age of eighty years. He was in the war of 1812 and drew a pension, having been a brave soldier He was the son of John and Millie Webb, who were both natives of Virginia and died in Kentucky, the former at eighty five, the latter at 103 All the family were farmers Mrs. Letta Webb was born in Virginia and died in the same State as her husband when she was fifty-five She was a daughter of John and Nancy Haward. A brother of Joshua Webb was in the Revolutionary war and was at the Cornwallis surrender.

Allen Webb was one of five children and remained at home until nineteen years of age, working on the farm. He then hired himself out to a man as blacksmith's apprentice and stayed with him two years, and then started a business for himself in Clark county, Kentucky. He continued working at his trade until 1851, and then started by wagon for Illinois He first located at Mt. Sterling

His original farm was 160 acres, worth but little at that time, and he lived in a log house for some time. He then sold that farm for 100 per cent. profit and bought another farm of 225 acres. He built a good farm house and soon had one of the best farms in the county. This farm he sold also, and moved to another place for a year. He then settled on the old Dennis farm and lived there for three years, when he again sold out and moved back to Mt. Sterling and retired from active business, having been an extensive stock-grower. He now has a fine town house and the old General Signtetan farm of twenty acres. He was an old Whig and voted first for Henry Clay and in 1856 for John Fremont. He has voted the Republican ticket ever since. Mr. Webb had only six month's schooling in his entire life, but he has educated himself and is a well-read man. Mr. Webb now enjoys life in an easy way looking after his property and real estate interests.

He was married for the first time to Emily Oliver, of Madison county. She died in Lee township aged forty-eight years. She bore her husband ten children, four now living, namely: Jennie, John A., Emeline and Isaac.

Mr. Webb was married for the second time to Miss Martha Harper of Ohio, daughter of Stephen and Martha Harper, who came here at an early day. Mrs. Webb died in this county, aged forty-eight years. She bore him one child, that died at the age of four years. Mr. Webb was married for the third time, to Miss Sarah Dennis of Bourbon county, Kentucky, near Georgetown. She was the daughter of Clark and Elizabeth Dennis. They were also natives of Kentucky and came to this State at an early date, and Mr. Dennis was made the first Sheriff of the county. Mrs. Webb was one of nine children, five yet living. Her whole family were members of the Christian Church of which her father was an Elder.

Mr. and Mrs. Webb have educated the four living children of Mr. Webb very finely, and the oldest son was in the late war, being one of the first 100-day men. Mr. and Mrs. Webb are influential people who are greatly respected by their large circle of friends.

MRS. ALMIRA YOUNG, widow of John Young, is the daughter of William and Elizabeth (Seaver) Lovell, natives of Ohio. Her parents emigrated to Illinois in the fall of 1836, when she was an infant of two years; they made the journey overland with horses and a prairie schooner, being five weeks on the way; the family consisted of the parents and three children. They first settled on the Illinois river, but shortly afterward removed to the present home of Mrs. Young. The mother died in 1841, leaving a family of six children, four sons and two daughters; she was forty-two years of age; the father survived her forty-nine years, and died at the age of eighty-six years.

Mrs. Young was married in 1849 to Ladon Beghtol, a native of Kentucky, a son of Peter Beghtol, who emigrated to Illinois about 1840; they lived here until the death of Mr. Beghtol, which occurred in 1857; he left a family of three children: Mary Elizabeth, Sarah Melvina and William Levi. Mrs. Beghtol was then married a second time, this union being with John Young; he was a native of Pennsylvania, was reared in the State of Ohio, and removed to Illinois with his first wife and four children in 1855; the wife died soon after their arrival in this State. Mr. and Mrs. Young were married in 1859, and seven years later they moved to Hamilton county, Iowa, where they settled on a small farm; there they resided until the death of Mr. Young, which occurred March 20, 1876, at the age of fifty-seven years. Nine children were born of this union: John died in infancy; Oscar was accidentally killed in childhood; Justine is the wife of Marion Stockton; William, Eli, George, Nola, Marion, Joseph; Nola is married to Webster Aten of Schuyler county.

JOSEPH PARKE was born in Chester county, Pennsylvania, in 1818. His father, Jonathan, was born in the same place and died at an advanced age, when his son was so small that he has no recollection of him. There were ten sons and the same number of daughters in this family, all coming to adult years, but all have now died. The mother of this remarkable family was Marjory Woodward of the same county. She lived some fourteen years after her husband's death and they both now rest in the Marshalltown cemetery, a large Quaker cemetery. These parents were well-to-do and gave the family a good education.

Joseph was sent to a Quaker school at Western Academy. He was reared to farm life, but at twenty-one he began school-teaching, taught two years in Pennsylvania and four years in Ohio. At his mother's death he was put under a guardian, who gave him additional educational advantages.

He was married in Logan county, Ohio, in his twenty-sixth year, to Mary Ann Wilson. She was a daugther of Robert and Elizabeth (Holt) Wilson. They, Mr. and Mrs. Parke lived for five years in this county and taught school. In October, 1840, they came West, overland, and settled in Brooklyn township, entering 160 acres. This was wild and they made the first improvements, building a log cabin with a sod chimney. Mr. Parke still has the cabin as a part of his present dwelling but the sod chimney is now a brick one and the cabin is weather-boarded externally and lathed and plastered inside. He has 300 acres, a part of which he has deeded to his daughter. About 1865 they buried one son, Jonathan, aged twenty. They next buried Elizabeth, Mrs. Taylor Gray, at the age of twenty-six; in 1885 their daughter, Ada Sario, aged about eighteen years old, died at Dr. Prince's establishment at Jacksonville. His wife had fits for some twenty years and in March, 1891, fell into the fire and died the same day. He has only one living daughter, Eliza, second wife of Taylor Gray. She has four children: George W., Mary Florence, Estelle and Nellie Jane. She has buried one infant son. She and her husband are operating the farm for her father, who lives with them. Mr. Parke has been a constant toiler since 1840, when he came to this home. He has served in some of the township offices and taught school one year. He has been a general farmer, although he has made the most out of wheat, growing from fifteen to thirty bushels per acre. Hogs have been the best-paying stock and horses have paid well in a small way.

He has voted the Democratic and Republican tickets, but is now a Farmers' Alliance man. He and his family have been Universalists, although he has been reared a Quaker.

JAMES E. NEELEY, a prominent farmer and dealer in live-stock, Littleton township, was born at Fort Larned, Kansas, March 3, 1864, a son of John and Lucinda

(Snyder) Neeley. The father was a native of Pennsylvania, but emigrated to Kansas, where he engaged in farming. James E. is the only child of the first marriage; the mother died April 8, 1864, at Larned, Kansas. Mr. Neeley married a second time, and had one child by this union. After the death of his mother our subject was taken to the home of Major Wheeler, where he was reared with all the affectionate care that could be bestowed upon him. The farm he now occupies was inherited from the Major, and he is engaged in general agriculture.

Mr. Neeley made a specialty of breeding and raising fine, thoroughbred horses, and fine stock of excellent pedigree; Roan Dick is an animal of good record, and a colt that he is now raising promises to be one of the fastest horses in the State. He has managed all branches of farming with keen intelligence, and has met with merited success.

In 1886, November 25, he was united in marriage to Miss Rachel A. Greer. Mr. and Mrs. Neeley are the parents of one child: John F., born March 13, 1891. Politically, our subject adheres zealously to the principles of the Republican party, having cast his first presidental vote for James G. Blaine. He is a young man of superior business qualifications, and his judgment carries due weight throughout the agricultural district of this section of Illinois.

HENRY FISCHER, a successful and practical farmer, living on section 24, township 17, range 11, was born November 1, 1854, and is the son of Henry Fischer, a native of Hesse-Darmstadt, where he learned the trade of shoemaker. There he was married to Miss Margaret Kraft, a native of the same province. After the birth of two daughters and a son, the family emigrated, in the '40s, to the United States, settling in Beardstown, Illinois, where Mr. Fischer established a shoemaking business, and ran it for some years with the assistance of his son, our subject; but when the latter began to farm the father withdrew from his trade and is now retired. Although now quite an old man he is still very active and energetic, and is a Lutheran in religion and a Democrat in politics. His mother is still living, in Beardstown, with her daughter, Mrs. Elizabeth Bohrnman, and is over ninety years old. The excellent wife of Henry Fischer is yet living, about seventy years old. She has been a valued member of the Lutheran Church for many years. Our subject and two sisters are yet living: the latter are Margaret, widow of Martin Bolle, deceased, having died from the effects of an accident on the Quincy railroad; and Sophia, wife of George Speaker, who is now foreman of the wrecking department of the Quincy railroad.

Our subject has been a farmer for eleven years. He enjoys it more than his former trade of shoemaker. He is now located on section 24, and the land of which he owns one-half interest is known under the firm name of Keil & Co. They purchased together the old John Weiss homestead, embracing 500 acres of land, mostly well improved with good farm buildings. On this land is Hagener station, and besides this they own 200 acres in this township, known as pasture land, and forty acres of timber in township 17, range 11, which is very valuable. He has, for the last eleven years, had the management of this land and is a practical man and an excellent farmer.

Mr. Fischer was married to Miss Mamie Weiss, who was born on the farm where she now lives, April 26, 1856. She is the youngest child of John and Katherine (Hahn) Weiss, natives of Germany. They married immediately before sailing to the United States, in 1842, and on reaching here made a settlement on a farm in township 17, range 11, which is now the home of Mr. Fischer. They began to make improvements and bought more land, and in time Mr. Weiss' possessions increased until he owned 900 acres of valuable land. Here they remained the rest of their lives. Mr. Weiss died in 1876, aged seventy-two years. He had been an active, hard-working man all his life and was regarded by his neighbors as an upright citizen, worthy of their respect and regard. He was a member of the Lutheran Church and was a Republican. His wife died some years later, at her old home, in 1887, aged sixty-two years. She had been a member of the Lutheran Church all her life. Of the family of four children left by Mr. and Mrs. Weiss, all were daughters: Lizzie, wife of Christian Meyer, died at the age of forty, leaving a family of eight children; Katie is the wife of William Hackman, grocer of Jacksonville; Sophia is the wife of Henry C. Keil (see sketch of same).

Mr. and Mrs. Fischer are the parents of five children: Adelaide, Ervin L., Ray H., Rena K. and Albert H., who died when an infant. This is one of the wealthy and greatly respected families of the township with whom it is a pleasure to become acquainted.

CHARLES D. RITCHEY, a substantial farmer and influential citizen of Littleton township, Schuyler county, was born in this county on June 11, 1862. His father, Addison B. Ritchey, is a prominent pioneer of Schuyler county, and a sketch of his life is subjoined. Our subject was reared on a farm and was educated at a college in Vaparaiso, Indiana, from which institution he graduated with honor.

He was married June 13, 1889, to Miss Dena Saunders, a native of Atlanta, Macon county, Missouri, in which place she was born June 15, 1864. She was a daughter of James W. and Martha A. (Stone) Saunders. Her father was born in Kentucky, and accompanied his parents to Missouri when he was but nine months old. His father, Woodward G. Saunders, is also a native of Kentucky, and is still living, at an advanced age, in Missouri. George W. Saunders, father of Woodward G., was a school teacher, and died in Missouri a number of years ago. Woodward G. Saunders located on a farm in Missouri, where he and family began the life of pioneers, experiencing all the inconveniences and hardships incident to those similarly circumstanced. Here, James W. Saunders was reared, and was educated at the William Jewell College, located at Liberty, Missouri, and was for twenty years a Baptist minister. It was in Missouri that he met and married Martha A. Stone, a very attractive lady, and daughter of Hiram and Laura J. (De Freire) Stone, both natives of Tennessee, the father still surviving in Macon county, Missouri, a graduate from the high school in Ellettsville, Monroe county, Indiana. Our subject's wife was a school teacher for more than sixteen years, and is a highly educated and interesting lady, of superior ability and culture.

After his marriage, Mr. Ritchey went into business with Mr. De Witt, in a general store, where he remained for some time. He was later elected Clerk of Littleton township, in which capacity he served for one year. He was afterward elected Collector of that township, serving for two years in a highly creditable manner.

Mr. and Mrs. Ritchey have one child. Edna M., who was born December 25, 1890.

Mrs. Ritchey is a member of the Baptist Church, to which she contributes liberal aid

He is a Republican, and cast his first vote for James G. Blaine His constituents have demonstrated their esteeem by electing him to two of the most responsible positions in their power to bestow.

Of unswerving fidelity and integrity, and high morality, together with generous impulses and cordial manners, he enjoys the respect and esteem of his fellow citizens.

ADDISON B RITCHEY, one of the oldest pioneers of Schuyler county, is a native of Ohio, and was born in Green county, of that State, September 17, 1817 His parents were John and Elizabeth (Reed) Ritchey His father, a native of Pennsylvania, was born in Alleghany, that State, and was a farmer all his life He went to Ohio in 1816, and in 1824 came all the way to near Rushville with a four-horse wagon All the worldly possessions of the family were in the wagon and they had very little money besides, as they paid their last fifty cents for being ferried across the river at Beardstown, then known as Beard's Ferry. He had come out for the purpose of taking land, for which he had a patent, but after camping on the land, for one night, he would not remain, and moved to near Rushville, where he located on a quarter section, building there a small log cabin about 16 x 18, in which they lived for several years His was the thirteenth family in the county. In 1826, he traded his claim for 160 acres of land in Littleton township, in section 35, on which he built another log house, where they lived for one season, then rented land and removed to his former farm, where on account of some trouble about trade, he moved to Rushville, buying there 160 acres adjoining the town, on which he built another log house, in which he and family lived for about eight years. He then sold and came back to Littleton township During all this time our subject was employed in various pioneer work, splitting rails, plowing and doing whatever other work he found to do. His father died in 1842, aged fifty-three years. His father's father was a native of Ireland, from which country he emigrated in the early days of this country, and died many years ago, in Pennsylvania His mother, Elizabeth Reed, was born in Pennsylvania, and died in Ohio when our subject was but three years of age. Our subject remained at home until his father's death, after which he spent one year with a brother, in the meantime farming the old homestead on his own account

On June 4, 1845, Mr. Ritchey was married to Miss Mary Ann Hayes, a native of Vermilion county, Illinois, where she was born October 3, 1829 Her parents were John and Debora (Hankins) Hayes Her father was a native of Virginia, from which State he emigrated, first to Kentucky, afterward to Illinois, at a very early day, where in Vermilion county he rented a farm, which he worked for some time, when he later came to Carroll county, and still later to Putnam county, finally going to Henry county, all in Illinois, in which latter place he died, aged seventy years. His wife, Debora Hankins, was a native of Tennessee, in which State she was born and is at present living with a daughter in Kansas Grandfather Hankins also came to Illinois at an early day, where he died, at the advanced age of ninety-three years. Grandmother Hankins also died in Illinois, aged sixty-five years Grandfather and grandmother Hayes were also pioneers of Illinois, where they died, in Whiteside county, both very old people. The Hayes were of Irish descent. Our subject's wife was one of seven children, four of whom are yet living. Our subject is one of three children, of whom he ist he only survivor; he has, however, a half-sister and half-brother, both of whom are living.

After marriage, our subject lived in section 34, in his old home, where he remained for two years, at the end of which time he bought 160 acres of wild land, on which there was a log house. Here he and his wife lived until he built his present home. He has improved the farm in numerous ways, until now it is the finest in the county. He has erected a large and comfortable residence, and commodious barns for the accommodation of grain, stock and machinery, besides adding other modern improvements and conveniences to facilitate agricultural pursuits. He has planted ornamental trees and shrubs around his house, which now only renders his place attractive from a distance, but is a welcome retreat from the sun's too ardent rays on a mid-summer day.

He has reared fifteen children, eleven of whom are living. His oldest son, John Q. Ritchey, served for four months in the war in Company K, One Hundred and Thirty seventh Illinois Infantry, and also was in the hundred days' service.

Our subject's father was an old-line Whig, as was also his son, who was later a Free-soiler, and now a Republican. Our subject cast his first vote for General William H. Harrison. His father voted for John Quincy Adams. Neither he nor his father were politicians in the modern acceptation of the term, never desiring office but wishing only the advancement and welfare of their country.

Mr. Ritchey and wife are members of the Baptist Church, to which they have liberally contributed.

Commencing life in a new country, without means and without friends, he now has both money and friends, which have accumulated and increased with the progress of the country. He is the oldest living pioneer of his county, and as such enjoys a pre-eminence among his neighbors, which superior age always bestows. Of superior ability and unswerving integrity, he has retained the regard of all through his checkered career, and now holds an eminent position in the community.

PEYTON HARDING, farmer of township 17, range 9, section 19, Philadelphia postoffice, was born in Barren county, Kentucky, December 17, 1817. His parents were Martin and Isabella (Beard) Harding. The father came from Virginia, born in 1792, and the mother from Tennessee, born in 1794. They were married in Barren county, Kentucky, where their eldest children were born: Peyton, Paschal, William, Sarah and Andrew; and after coming to Illinois, Winnie, Isabella and Martin were born. Paschal lives with Peyton; Andrew is a farmer in this precinct; Martin lives in Virginia, Illinois; and Isabella, now Mrs. Foster, resides in Lucas county, Iowa. The parents removed from Kentucky to Illinois in 1826, and located on the farm where Andrew now lives. The father entered a large tract of land here on which he died in 1854, and the mother died in 1867. At the time the Harding family located here the country was entirely new. There was no improved land, except two small improved tracts in this neighborhood. The forest was overrun with wild game and Indians. Mr. Harding has lived to witness the development of this wilderness into one of the most fertile and valuable sections in the United States. He has also witnessed the growth of inventions, the extent of which is wonderful, railroads, plows, reapers, mowers, binders, separating threshers, telephones, electric lights and thousands of other inventions, more than in the past 200 years previously. Mr. Harding taught school here in 1840, but preferred the less confining occupation of farming. He has been a farmer and stock-raiser all his life He is comfortably situated and will spend his old age in ease He owns 280 acres of good land. He has never married, but his brother, Paschal, resides with him with his four children. He is a Democrat in politics and cast his first vote for Martin Van Buren His father was a soldier in the war of 1812 and the Black Hawk war, also in the Mormon troubles, but none of the family took part in the late Civil war.

ISAAC BLACK, a retired farmer, is probably the oldest settler of Schuyler county now living in Rushville; he has endured the trials and toil in a pioneer country, and is entitled to more than passing mention in this history He is a native of Indiana, born in Dubois county, February 24, 1824, a son of Richard Black, the father was born in Mecklenburgh county, North Carolina, and was reared in that State; he removed thence to Hancock county, Kentucky, and lived there a few years; he then went to the Territory of Indiana, and was one of the pioneers of Dubois county. In 1826 he again started to the West, keeping close upon the frontier border Accompanied by his wife and four children, he made a journey to Illinois, and located in Schuyler county, where he purchased a claim to land entered by Willis O'Neil; this land is the present site of the city of Rushville. When the county was organized the claim was selected as the county seat, and so was taken from Mr. Black; he was afterward reimbursed in part He then went five miles to the southwest, near the present site of Bethel Church, and there bought a tract of patent land, on which he erected a log cabin, sixteen feet square, there were a puncheon floor and a stick-and-clay chimney. Later he made an addition to this domicile, and resided there until his death in 1853 The maiden name of his second wife was Elizabeth Fowler, a native of Jefferson county, Kentucky; she spent her last years with her son Isaac, the subject of this notice The family reared by her consisted of eight children, two of whom were born of her husband's former marriage. Elizabeth, William, Isaac, Cecelia, John L., Richard S, Austin F and Monroe.

Isaac Black was an infant when his parents removed to this county, the country was thinly settled, and Indians still tarried in the vicinity of Rushville, game was abundant and the pioneers lived on wild turkeys, deer, and the product of their land; the children were clothed in homespun, woven by the mother's hands Young Isaac attended the primitive pioneer schools during the winter season, and in the summer he lent valuable assistance in subduing the wild land and preparing the way for the coming generation, it is to such men that a deep debt of gratitude is owing from those who have reaped the benefits of those years of privation and labor. Until he was twenty years of age he remained with his parents, and then with his brother rented a farm near Littleton, they cultivated this land four years, and then Isaac Black purchased ninety acres in Woodstock township; there he lived two years, and in 1850 sold it, purchasing a tract in Bainbridge township. He was very successful in all his undertakings, made profitable investments, and secured 450 acres of as choice land as lies within the borders of the county. He lived on his farm until 1889, when he retired to Rushville, where he leads a quiet, contented life.

In 1848 he was united in marriage to Cynthia A. Edmonston, a daughter of Enoch Edmonston, who located in Schuyler county in 1831; he became prominently identified with public affairs, and served two terms as Sheriff of the county; he was also County Treasurer and Assessor; his wife's maiden name was Susan Allen. Mr. and Mrs. Black are the parents of eight children: Susan, Emily, Sarah E., George M., James P., Enoch, Flora A., Elvira and E. Louisa. George M. Black has represented the people of his county in the State Legislature. Mr. Black affiliates with the Democratic party, and at one time represented Bainbridge township on the County Board of Supervisors. He has been a loyal citizen, always giving a liberal support to worthy movements and to those enterprises tending to benefit the general public.

HENRY ZAHN, a practical farmer and stock-raiser, living on the old Zahn homestead, which he has owned since 1882, was born in Pike county, near Waverly, in 1857. He came with his father to Illinois when only fourteen years of age, and has since lived in this county. His father, Frederick Zahn, was a native of Hesse-Darmstadt, and was a boy of sixteen years when his parents came to America and settled in Pike county, Ohio, where they were pioneers. There the parents of Frederick Zahn died when he was quite young. There he grew up as a farmer, and was there married to Tinna Creek, who had settled there, with her parents. The latter had come with a colony at the same time the Zahn family had come from Hesse-Darmstadt. Frederick and his wife began life in the usual pioneer fashion, both working very hard, raising a family of eight children. There Frederick's wife died, being then thirty-two years of age. He was married for the second time, in Pike county, Ohio, to Miss Margaret Halensteine, who was born in Germany, but reared in the United States. In 1864 they decided to remove to Illinois and settled on a large farm of 507 acres, where they remained two years, and then purchased 200 acres on the line of Morgan and Cass counties. There they lived until 1876. They then removed to Missouri, where they now live. Mr. Kahn was seventy-three years of age, December 29, 1891, his wife being not quite so old. They are members of the Methodist Episcopal Church, and are good, respectable people. Mr. Zahn has been a lifelong Democrat.

Our subject was reared a farmer lad and lived at home until he took a farm to run on his own account. He has lived on this farm, which is one and one-half miles from Arenzville, section 36, township 17, range 12, and consists of 250 acres, well improved and well stocked. He has excellent farm buildings and everything convenient about him.

He was married, in this county, to Miss Mary Hinners, who was born, reared and educated in Cass county, her birth occurring October 7, 1852. She was the daughter of John and Caroline (Miller) Hinners, who were born in Hesse-Darmstadt, Germany. They came to the United States, and were married in Morgan county, and here lived to amass a fine property. In 1891 Mr. and Mrs. Hinners retired to Meredosia, Illinois, where they live, respected members of the Methodist Episcopal Church. Mr. and Mrs. Zahn are members of the same denomination, and Mr. Zahn has been an official member of the church.

Mr. and Mrs. Zahn are the parents of three bright, well educated children: Mamie Ella, Lusetta and Henry A. This is a fine family, well thought of in and around Arenzville.

GEORGE H. HOFFMAN, a successful farmer of section 2, township 17, range 11, was born in Hesse-Darmstadt, May 20, 1840, and when young came alone to the United States. In 1856 he sailed from Bremen and after forty-nine days of the ocean he landed in New York city. He came on to Chicago, and thence to Springfield, from there to Jacksonville, and across the country to Arenzville. When he landed in Arenzville he was $5 in debt. He is the only member of the family who came to this country. His father, George, is still living in Germany, and is hale and hearty, at the age of eighty-six, but his mother, Mary, died when he was eight years old. They always were members of the Lutheran Church. Two of our subject's brothers are still living in Germany, and are married, pursuing the occupation of farmers.

After our subject first came to this county he began work, near Hagener Station. After some years he began his agricultural life as a renter, and later purchased his present farm.

Mr. Hoffman was first married to Elizabeth Schuman, who was born and reared in this county at what is known as Hagener Station, March 9, 1849. She is the eldest child of John Schuman (see biography of Adam Schuman for family history). Mr. and Mrs. Hoffman are members of the Lutheran Church, in which Mr. Hoffman has been a Deacon for six years. He is a Democrat in politics, and he and his wife are the parents of eleven children: Mary, wife of Adolph Kruse, a farmer in this county; John A., at home, helping his father; Attia, Henry, Emma, Edward, William, Eva, Ralph, Martha, and the two-year-old baby, are all healthy, intelligent children. The older children have been well educated in both German and English, and are able to speak and write in both languages. Mr. Hoffman is a very progressive farmer, and owns a fine place, containing 170 acres, 135 of which is under the plow. He came into possession of this in 1865, and has since this made all of his excellent improvements.

FRED MEYER, a retired farmer of Arenzville, was born in Prussia, Germany, in 1805. He came of Prussian parents, who lived and died when quite old. His father, Gotlieb H. Meyer, was a German farmer, and his wife was a Prussian lady, formerly Anna Roche. They were members of the Lutheran Church.

Fred was one of five sons and one daughter. The latter lived and died in Germany. The five sons all came to the United States at different times. Fred and a brother, Henry, are the only surviving members of the family. The former grew up and was married in his native province, to Catherine M. Burkesikus. She came of an old Prussian family. After the birth of all their children but one, they came to the United States, in December, 1848, leaving Bremen on a sailing vessel and landing at New Orleans after a trip of nine weeks and three days. They proceeded up the Mississippi river to St. Louis, and from there to Beardstown, and began farming the next year. Here Mrs. Meyer died, in 1865, at the age of forty-three. She and her husband were members of the Lutheran Church. They had five children: William, a farmer in this precinct, married Carrie Talkemeier; Mary, wife of William Dougal, farmer near Taylorsville, Illinois; Minnie, formerly wife of Fred Nordsiek, and the mother of seven children; Mary A., at home; Lizzie, wife of Henry Hierman, farmer of this county; Emma, wife of Ed. Kloker, farmer in this county; Henry, Lena, Ann and John are all at home. Another son of Mr. Meyer, now deceased, named Henry A., married Minnie Yost.

Mr. Meyer began in this county in 1848, and in the time since then has by hard work accumulated a large property. He had only 100 acres at first, but now has 474 acres, most of which is well improved, with good farm buildings. He has always been a hard-working man, and although now eighty-eight years of age, is as active as ever and in perfect health. He has been a good citizen, a Republican in politics, and now lives in retirement with his daughter Minnie (Mrs. Nordsiek), on section 7, township 17, range 11. He is a good old man, greatly respected by all who know him.

SAMUEL HINDMAN was born in Richland county, Ohio, January 24, 1834; his father, Elijah Hindman, was born in Allegheny county, Pennsylvania, November 4, 1798, a son of Samuel Hindman, whose nativity is not positively known; the year of his birth was 1763, and after his marriage he emigrated to Allegheny county, Pennsylvania, where he was one of the pioneers; he was a cooper by trade and followed that vocation until his death; he was married to Letitia M. Clinithan, a native of Allegheny county, Pennsylvania. Elijah Hindman was married in Alleghany county and resided there until 1833: in that year he emigrated with his wife and four children to Ohio, making the journey overland with a four-horse wagon; he located in Richland county, on a tract of timber land which he occupied until 1838, he again started westward, coming to Illinois and settling where Rushville township, Schuyler county, now is; here he improved a tract of land and passed the remainder of his life. He married Anna Mace, a daughter of John Mace, a native of London, England, who emigrated to America and fought in the war of the Revolution. Mrs. Hindman, the mother of our subject, resides with a daughter in Rushville township, at the advanced age of ninety-one years. Samuel Hindman, Jr., was four years old when his parents removed to Illinois. Here he grew to manhood, among the vicissitudes and privations of frontier life; the mother carded and spun the cloth with which the children were dressed, and they lived from the products of their land; Mr. Hindman relates that on one occasion his father sold a load of wheat at twenty-five cents a bushel, and at the same time paid thirty-seven and one-half cents a yard for calico. He received his education in the pioneer schools, the furniture and house being constructed in the most primitive style; in early youth he began to assist in the cultivation of the land, and has since followed farming.

In 1859 he determined to make a trip to Pike's Peak, but at Fort Kearney the party met many returning with discouraging reports; Mr. Hindman then changed his course, going to Coffey county, Kansas, whence he returned home after an absence of three months. He had once before started to the West, in 1855, accompanied by his brother John, their destination was Kansas, and they traveled via the Illinois, Mississippi and Missouri rivers to Richfield, Missouri, at which point his brother died of cholera, Mr. Hindman pushed on to western Missouri, but on account of his brother's death he came back.

He was married November 8, 1876, to Julia (Ward) Mathews, a native of Washington county, Pennsylvania, and a daughter of James Ward, and a granddaughter of Thomas Ward, a native of England, who passed his life in the British kingdom. James Ward married Nancy Hamilton, a native of New Jersey and a daughter of Richard Hamilton. Mrs. Hindman was first married in 1853 to Thomas H Mathews, a son of James and Sarah (McIntire) Mathews, he died in 1873, one child was born of this union, Lemonia H. Mr and Mrs Hindman have one child, Juniata. Mr Hindman inherited a part of the old homestead, and has devoted his life to agricultural pursuits.

HENRY C NIESTRADT, a general farmer living on section 12, township 17, range 12, is a young, progressive man. He has always lived in this county where he was born September 29, 1861. He was reared and educated in the public schools, remaining home with his father until his majority. He is the third son of Henry B Niestradt, who was born in Prussia, Germany, where he grew up and remained until he was twenty five years of age. He then came to the United States and settled where he now lives and now owns a large property. He is the only member of his father's family that came to the United States. He is very active for his eighty years, and is proud of his good, healthy German blood. He was married, in Cass county to Charlotta Miller, who was born in Prussia, Germany and who came alone, the first of her father's family who ventured to this country. Her parents have died, but the most of her brothers and sisters have joined her here. Henry B and wife are both active members of the Lutheran Church and he has been an officer in the same for some years. Henry C. is one of seven children, two having died in infancy.

Mr. Niestradt has been a farmer for some years, having carried on farming for three years before he took the present farm. This he purchased September 30, 1890. He is a very practical man and has so improved his eighty acres that one would predict great success for him in the future.

He was married, in this county, to Miss Minnie Lawner, who was born in this township, August, 1868. Her early life was spent at home with her parents, Frederick and Carrie (Meyer) Lawner, both natives of Illinois. They were married in Cass county and began life as farmers in township 17, range 11, and there Mr. Lawner died, in 1878, being under forty years of age. He was a good citizen, a fine farmer, a member of the Lutheran Church and a Republican in politics. His wife was married for a second time, to John Kern, who lives in Arenzville, Illinois.

Mrs Niestradt is the only child born to her father. She is an intelligent women and makes a good wife and mother. She and her husband have one child, Anna B. Mr. and Mrs. Niedstradt are Lutherans in religion and Mr. Niedstradt belongs to a Republican family. They are highly respected people of their neighborhood.

HERMAN H. LOVECAMP, one of the most successful farmers and stock-raisers of township 17, range 11, near Arenzville, Illinois, was born in this county in 1840. He has passed his life in this section and is the son of Katherine and Fred Lovecamp, both natives of Germany, born and reared in Hanover, and married after they came to St. Louis. They were early settlers of Cass county, coming to Cass county about 1835. They were both industrious and economical, and bravely contended against all the trials that beset the early settlers. They spent their last days on the large farm which their united efforts had earned. Mr. Lovecamp only lived to be forty-five years old, but his wife survived him until she was seventy-eight. They had both been Lutherans, and Mr. Lovecamp was a Republican, a worthy, good citizen and his wife was one of the best and kindest women in the world.

Herman grew up under his mother's care and became a farmer also. He was married in this county to Mary Peters, born in Hanover, Germany, December 19, 1843. She came to the United States and to Beardstown with her parents, Mary and Fred Peters, in 1845. Mr. Peters was a blacksmith by trade, a good mechanic and had always been a hard-working man until the time of his death. He was a Democrat and belonged to the Lutheran Church. He died in 1877, aged sixty-five. His wife is still living in Beardstown, and upon her last birthday, August 13, 1892, was seventy-three years old. She is still active and has been a member of the Lutheran Church all her life. Mrs. Lovecamp is one of nine children, three yet living. She is one of the good, German women where she resides and she has the respect of the whole neighborhood. She is the mother of twelve children: Emma and Cora died young; John is a harnessmaker in Arenzville; William, a farmer in Cass county, married Miss Caroline Carls; Henry assists in running the home farm; Mary, Christina, Lucinda, Louisa, Alma Albert and Julius all are at home. They are Lutherans and they have had the pleasure of seeing their children confirmed in the same faith. Mr. Lovecamp and his grown sons agree in their political faith, being members of the Democratic party.

Mr. Lovecamp owns over 240 of well improved land, and has been the possessor of it for the past fifteen years. He has made a great many improvements on the place and now resides very comfortably in his nice home with his family around him.

EDWARD T. MILBY was born in Sussex county, Delaware, August 4, 1835. His father, Nathaniel J. Milby, emigrated with his wife and four children to Illinois in 1840, settling in Rushville township. The journey was made by canals and rivers and proved a tiresome one. The father bought a tract of land and hastened to make it ready for settlement. Two acres of the land had been cleared and a plain log cabin had been built. This was all. But deft and willing fingers soon made things assume a fairly comfortable shape, and western life was fairly under way. This log cabin, by the way, was the first permanent house of its kind in Illinois. Mr. Milby, Sr., occupied the farm to the day of his death. The maiden name of the mother of the subject of this sketch was Mary Wilson, born in Sussex county, Delaware. She died on the Schuyler county home farm.

In those days nearly every one lived in log cabins of one room. The housewife spun and wove the cloth used for the clothes for both sexes. She also had many other duties to which the wives of farmers now are strangers.

Edward attended school attired in homespun that his mother had made for him with her own hands. Notwithstanding his school duties he assisted on the farm and continued to do so until his marriage, when he began for himself on rented land in Huntsville. He continued to pay rent for land for about ten years, when he bought two and a half acres in Buena Vista township. He lived in the latter place but two months as he went to his father's farm, where he stayed for seven years and then bought eighty acres in section 23. After ten years' residence there he sold out and bought the place where he now resides. On his farm of 223 acres he does general farming and stock-raising.

Mr. Milby has been married thrice. The first time he was twenty-three years of age when he married, and the lady who honored him with her hand was Lydia Hillis, of Rushville, the daughter of John and Jane Ferres Hillis. She died in 1865 and Mr. Milby remained single until 1872, when he again entered the married state. The second lady was Lizzie J. Davidson, of Kentucky, and she died in 1879. Mary A. Bauer, of Highland county, Ohio, the daughter of Valentine Bauer, was the lady to whom he was married January, 21, 1886.

Mr. Milby has had six children, all of which save one, are living. Three of the children are the issue of the first marriage: Frank, Clement and Lizzie, and the other three are the issue of the second marriage. The second child of the second marriage, Herne, died when three years old, but the other two, Walter and Ida, are living.

Mr. Milby is an earnest member of the Methodist Episcopal Church South, while the present Mrs. Milby is a member of the same church in the North.

In politics Mr. Milby is a disciple of "Old Hickory," he being a Democrat.

CATHERINE SAUNDERS, who has kept a little store for years at La Grange, Brown county, Illinois, is the widow of John Saunders, and was born in Huntingdon county, Pennsylvania, in 1826. Her father, John Whited, and her mother, Mary Sheckler, were of the same place in Pennsylvania. Her husband was from Maryland. Mrs. Saunders is the fourth child of a family of eleven. As her parents were poor, Mrs. Saunders has had no educational advantages, but has worked hard from early childhood.

She was married at the age of twenty-three to William Thomas, with whom she lived ten years, bearing him four children, all of whom have died. In 1855, she came West to this part of Brown county, where she has lived the most of the time. She was married a second time when she was thirty-four years old, to George Welbourn, of England. By this marriage, there were two children, one of whom died in infancy, the other at eighteen years of age. Mr. Welbourn died in 1862, aged thirty-two years, of congestive chills. She was married to her last husband, John Saunders, of Virginia. By this husband, she had one daughter: Lizzie, now Mrs. John Cisco. Her husband is a native of Ohio, and a farmer by occupation, working by the day. They live at home with her mother. She received a good education at the public schools, and now conducts the store for her aged mother.

Mrs. Saunders has seen some hard times in her life, but she has bravely met her troubles and conquered them. She owns her little home and store, which are nestled under the hill on the banks of the Illinois river, where she has done a snug little business, paying as she went. Mrs. Saunders is not wealthy, but she owes no one, and expects to finish her days here happily. She is a good and worthy woman, and deserves much praise for the way in which she has supported herself, keeping out of debt as she has.

MRS. MINERVA HINMAN was born near her present farm home, January 2, 1832. Her father was Ralph Alexander, and her mother, Elizabeth Fields. She was born in Indiana, and he in Hillsboro, Ohio, in 1808. Elizabeth Fields was left an orphan at eight years, was reared by a Mr. Scott, of Indiana, who gave her a good schooling for that period. She was married in Indiana, at sixteen years of age, to Ralph Alexander, when he was twenty-six. He was a tanner and currier by trade, and followed that business until they came West to Brown county, in 1829. They came as other emigrants did, and made their first stop in this neighborhood, at the home of Ezekiel Rosses, who had come here about six months earlier. The two families dwelt in this one log house during that memorable winter of deep snow, and it was not a large cabin, either. With his good span of horses, Mr. Alexander helped Mr. Rosses harvest his first crop of grain and hay. He took a half section of land close by, to which they moved in the spring of 1830, and lived in the rough log cabin on the place. It was in this mansion that our subject first saw the light. Eight years later they moved into the two-story hewn-log house, and in this very good dwelling the father died, in 1846. He died a comparatively young man, leaving his wife, who survived him some thirty years, and died in Kansas, aged seventy. She was the mother of twelve children, many of whom have also passed away. The living ones are: Thomas M., a ranchman in Arizona, now seventy-one years old, who killed two mountain lions at this age; Milton H., living at Versailles, Illinois; Mrs. Hinman; James, now in Arizona, and the youngest of the family; John P., pastor of the Baptist Church at Auburn, Illinois.

Mrs. Hinman was married in this county, in 1851, to Gideon Hinman, who was a widower with three sons. They have had eight children: Clara, Otis, Ralph and Hester have died. The living are: Minerva J. Withrow, of Cooperstown; Nellie Swenson, wife of a farmer at Mound Station; Abraham Lincoln, the unfortunate son, crippled and nervous from infancy from whooping-cough. He is very bright in some things, especially in figures. He cannot express himself. Elizabeth is the next child, and is known as Dolly, a young lady at home, who graduated at the Rushville Normal College, being the valedictorian. Two of the sons of Mr. Hinman's first marriage are still living, large farmers and stock dealers.

Mr. Hinman left his wife this fine estate of 160 acres of rich farm land with good buildings, well stocked. She has made a success of conducting it, pays taxes like her male neighbors, even if she cannot vote. She believes in a rotation of crops and clover. She grows from forty to sixty acres of corn, yielding from fifty to sixty bushels per acre, and feeds the most of it to hogs, of which she sells from fifty to sixty-five per year. She has colts, and about thirty head of cattle raised on the farm. The farm is in a finer condition than ever before.

Mr. Hinman came here about 1840. He was a school teacher, and he soon settled on eighty acres south of Cooperstown, and two years later he entered 160 acres. He started with no means at all, but by his industry he accumulated a large property. He was in ill health some time before his death, and Mrs. Hinman had the experience that has proved so valuable to her in the management of the farm.

MARO HARRIS was born in Schuyler county, Illinois, November 10, 1864. His parents were F. Marion and Arthusia (Hollingsworth) Harris. Mr. Harris, Sr., was born on the farm, on which his son now lives, in 1844, and he died March 27, 1892.

Maro Harris is the only surviving child, and he was educated in Schuyler county. When about fourteen he decided to see something of the world outside of Illinois; so visited Pikes Peak, Denver, etc. He is a fine musician, and there is a great demand for his talents. He enjoyed himself to such a degree during his trip that he did not return until three years ago. He tried farming when in the West, and was successful in his undertakings. He has inherited a fine farm of 320 acres in Schuyler county from his father, and owns valuable property in the vicinity of Beardstown, besides the fine farm in Colorado.

He was married about three years ago to Miss Melinda Betville, of Arkansas. They have one child. Mr. Harris is a Republican in politics, and is a good business man, and is respected by all who know him.

WILLIAM PERRY.—The gentleman whose sketch it is our pleasure to present to our readers, was born in Cooperstown township, at the present home of his father, March, 1844. His father, James Perry, was born on Powel's river, in Tennessee, in 1808, coming to Illinois in 1830.

William Perry was reared to farm life, and was well educated in the common schools, teaching several terms after finishing his education.

His marriage occurred, in 1866, when he was only twenty-two to Miss Mary E. Grover, daughter of W. P. Grover, and his wife, a Miss Patterson, both natives of Ohio, but residents of Brown county.

Mr. and Mrs. Perry first rented the old home farm, and in 1876 bought eight acres for $3,200, which he sold two years later, buying his present farm of eighty acres on section 32, paying the same price for it.

By this marriage Mr. Perry had six children, one of whom died when an infant. Mrs. Perry died in 1878, leaving three sons and one daughter, namely: Oscar, twenty-four; Elmer, twenty-two; Scott, eighteen, and Hattie, fourteen. He was again married in

1882, to Miss Anna Whitehead, of this county, daughter of Dr. John and Mary (Gilford) Whitehead. Mr. and Mrs. Perry have one living child, Orpha, aged six.

Mr. Perry was Town Collector, at twenty-two years, and served as Assessor for two years, from the time he was twenty-three until he was twenty-five. He next served as Township Treasurer for twelve years. Until 1876 he was a Democrat, but since that time he has been an advocate of reforms, being now a member of the Farmers' Alliance, or People's Party.

Mr. Perry carries on general farming on his beautiful farm, where he resides, surrounded by his children and his loving wife; and if ever a man had cause to be proud of his past life, it is the subject of this sketch, William Perry.

WILLIAM H. GRIFFITH is a native son of the State of Illinois, born in Woodstock township, Schuyler county, April 5, 1847. His father, Joshua Griffith, was born in Tuscarawas county, Ohio, and was there reared to the occupation of a farmer. In 1837 he accompanied his father to Iowa, and three years later he came to Schuyler county, Illinois, and purchased forty acres of wild, timber land. He built a log-house, which was his dwelling for fifteen or twenty years. In connection with his agricultural pursuits he had mastered the cooper's trade, which he followed after coming to this county. His father was Nathan Griffith, and he died in this county at the residence of his son, Joshua, aged ninety-three years; he was a soldier in the war of 1812, and drew a pension from the Government in recognition of his service. Joshua Griffith married Margaret Hoffman, who died at the age of fifty-seven years; they reared a family of eleven children, all of whom are living. Mr. Griffith is living a retired life at Lewistown, Fulton county, Illinois. He has a few acres of land, and is devoting his energies to fruit culture. Politically he is identified with the Republican party, and while a resident of Schuyler county was Justice of the Peace for many years. He is a self-made man, and has accumulated his entire property since coming to the State; he has been very successful in his farming operations, but has relinquished the care and management of his land to his son, William H. He has bravely done his share in the development of the resources of Schuyler county, and the present prosperity of the commonwealth is due to the men of his type.

William H. Griffith was married October 9, 1870, to Miss Susanna Custer, a native of Washington county, Iowa, born August 12, 1852. Her parents, Abraham and Susanna (Antrim) Custer, were natives of the State of Ohio; the father died in Iowa, but the mother survives, and is a resident of this county. Mr. and Mrs. Griffith are the parents of four children: Elmer E. was born September 17, 1871; Wilmer E. was born January 26, 1877; Edith L. was born February 26, 1880; Myrtle was born March 22, 1888. After his marriage Mr. Griffith settled on a farm with his grandfather, renting for a year; he then purchased forty acres, to which he removed, and later bought an additional forty; he has the management of the entire farm, which consists of 200 acres.

In politics he affiliates with the Republican party, having cast his first vote for General Grant's second term.

The paternal grandfather of our subject was one of the pioneers of the county; he made the journey to the frontier when the distance was wearily covered by driving or walking, and met the privations and hardships unflinchingly, as became the sturdy soul who undertook to rescue this wilderness and convert it into one of the most fertile States of the Union Let the coming generations never forget the debt of gratitude they owe their worthy forefathers

JAMES M. PATTERSON, one of the successful farmers of Cooperstown, residing on section 21, was born in this county, June, 1849 His father was Joseph Patterson, a native of Highland county, Ohio, who lost his father when very young and was reared by an uncle, learning the wool-carding business He came to Brown county, when young, in company with the family of James B. Russell, making the journey by team, in 1830. The gentleman with whom he came brought his family of seven Mr Patterson married one of the daughters of Mr. Russell, Phœbe, whose mother had been a Miss Sarah Lincoln, a native of Pennsylvania Her husband, however, hailed from the State of Vermont. They were married in Fulton county, between 1843 and 1845, and Mr Patterson pursued his trade at the Cardic mills, near Versailles, and then in Versailles. Their next place of settlement was in Elkhorn township, and later they moved to this county, where he worked in a flouring mill. He also cleared a fine farm of heavy timber

The gentleman whose name appears at the heading of this sketch was reared to farm life, and was offered plenty of opportunity for improvement, but like many boys of that age he did not appreciate nor take advantage of his opportunities When twenty-one he began working by the day and month.

Mr Patterson was married, January 16, 1879, to Miss Sarah Howell, born May, 1856, daughter of Thomas and Rebecca (Bearel) Howell, natives of Indiana and North Carolina, respectively. Mr. Howell came to Illinois when he was eleven or twelve years old, in 1832, and was there married, twelve years later. They bought eighty acres of land, built a log house, where they spent the first year of their married life, and then moved to a much better piece of land on which they built a permanent house, and lived there for twenty-one years, when they moved one half a mile away. Mrs. Howell died November, 1878, aged fifty-three years and fourteen weeks; on February 14, the husband followed the partner of his joys and sorrows, dying at the age of fifty-seven They had ten children, but lost all but three, they all dying at the farm, some in infancy and others later. These good people had been extremely poor when they were married, but when they died they had 100 acres of fine land and a property worth about $30,000. They were good, worthy people who richly deserved their good fortune.

Mr and Mrs. Patterson began their married life on the old homestead, where they remained for one and one half years, then, in 1881 bought their present farm of 160 acres, paying $8,000 for it. On this farm was the present fine frame farm house, built by the former owner, J Stiles. They built their large, ornamental barn in 1885 It is a fine structure, 40 x 60 feet, with eighteen-foot posts and a shed 12 x 60, and they can house sixteen horses

These good people have buried one infant son and still have two living: Otho T and Lee R., the former twelve years old, the latter nine. They are intelligent little lads, who are fond of their books.

Mr. Patterson is pursuing general farming, growing corn, wheat and hay, of which he has just cut a fine crop, filling both barns. He engages in stock-raising, having some forty to sixty head of cattle, hogs, and now feeds sixteen head of horses, three of whom he has raised.

Mr. Patterson is a member of the Masonic fraternity, and adheres strictly to the principles of the Democratic party. Mrs. Patterson is a devout member of the Christian Church, and she and her husband are worthy members of the society of Cooperstown.

ARTHUR A. McCABE, M. D., one of the most prominent physicians of Versailles, was born in Macomb, McDonough county, Illinois, December 17, 1856. His father, John McCabe, was a native of Ohio, and his father, also John McCabe, was a native of the same State. The latter gentleman was a blacksmith who came to Fulton county, Illinois, about 1849, where he followed his trade until he went into the army, in 1862. He had a family of seven sons and one son-in-law when he went to the defense of the old flag. Four of his sons, he, himself and the son-in-law, all perished in the army. Mr. McCabe dying from the effects of poison in a mince pie, which was bought of a Confederate and contained poison. The names of his sons who fought in the late struggle, were: John, father of subject; Miles, James, Marion, Westley and the son-in-law, James W. Jefferson, who married the daughter, Mary McCabe. There were four other brothers, also. Miles survived the war, but died of consumption, contracted in the service. John was a volunteer in the Eighty-fourth Illinois Infantry, entering as a private and coming out as an Orderly of Company A, after a service of three years. He was wounded at the battle of Lookout Mountain, a ball passing through his ankle. He received a furlough, but on his way back to Washington he was hurt by jumping from the cars; so badly was he injured that he was obliged to delay joining his command for some weeks. While waiting he joined the Masonic fraternity, and while sick in a strange city proved the worth of the order. When he returned, he was given a commissary position, and served his time out. His brother James was in the service three years and came out of the war sound and hearty, and is now a resident of Texas, in the employ of the railroad. He had quite a romantic accident some time since. He was injured by an explosion in Ohio, and he was nursed back to life in a Catholic hospital by the Catholic Sisters. So impressed was he by their sweet faces and kind, skillful treatment that he declares that if he ever marries, one of those sisters will be his wife!

John McCabe was married, at Indianapolis, Indiana, to Mary Ann Clark of that city, when twenty-two years of age. They came to Illinois soon after marriage, and made their home on a farm in Littleton township, Schuyler county, moving from there to Macomb, and from there to Rushville, where they have lived ever since. Here Mr. McCabe has carried on a successful business in the manufactory of brick and tile, in connection with his son, James. Mr. McCabe has three sons and one daughter, namely: James; Arthur, subject; Howard C.; Cora May, wife of Allen Walker, of Rushville. Two sons and one daughter died in infancy.

Dr. McCabe was educated at the Rushville high school, and in the College of Physicians and Surgeons of Keokuk, Iowa, graduating in the class of 1878. He began his practice in Bath, Mason county, where he remained for two years, then removing to Littleton, Schuyler county, where he remained for two years, when he finally removed to Versailles. Here he practiced for four years and then removed to Mt. Sterling and remained for one year, returning to Versailles, where he has remained ever since, enjoying a good practice.

The Doctor was married, January 1, 1879, to Carrie E. Seely, of Rushville, daughter of James Seely and Mary Sanford, born in New York. They have one daughter, Myrtle Isabelle, a promising, beautiful child of ten years of age, whose musical attainments on the piano are wonderful for one of her tender years.

The Doctor is a Master Mason, and a member of the fraternity of Modern Woodmen. He has been a Republican since the start of the party, and has always voted according to the principles of that party. He has served on the central committee for some time.

The Doctor has gained the confidence and respect of all who know him, and his large practice testifies to the appreciation in which his services are held. He and his estimable wife hold an enviable position in Versailles society.

W. S. GLOVER, of Beardstown, was born about thirty years ago at Winnemac, Indiana, and was there reared and partly educated, but desiring to to improve his knowledge of books he attended a college at Valparaiso, Indiana. Upon completing his course there he became a telegraph operator there, working in the city of his birth for some time and later at Logansport, Indiana, for the Pittsburg, Chicago & St. Louis Railroad. He remained here three years and then went to Nickerson, Kansas, in a similar position on the Santa Fe road. He was in active service there as a train dispatcher until he came to Beardstown and the Quincy system, February, 1882. Like most railroad men, he has since that time seen very active service. Mr. Glover's personal appearance and jovial manner are sufficient to make friends for him everywhere. He comes of a respectable line of ancestry, who date their first settlement in this country prior to the Revolutionary war. His grandparents lived and died in Ohio, where his father, Samuel Glover, was born, at Portsmouth, Ohio. He came to Winnemac when young and there became a successful mechanic, and was thus engaged when the Rebellion broke out. He enlisted in the Eighty-First Indiana Infantry, but was transferred later to the Ninth Indiana Cavalry, and continued in the service for three years, seeing much hard fighting. He was neither captured nor wounded, but he contracted a terrible camp malady, from the effects of which he died in 1866. He married in Winnemac, Indiana, Hannah Hawes, of Kentucky, who had been brought to Indiana by her parents in the '40s, where they lived and died, respected by all. Mrs. Hannah Glover is still living, and is very active in spite of her fifty-seven years, and makes her home with her son, W. S. Glover. She is a Christian lady and has been a member of the Methodist Episcopal Church for years.

September 5, 1886, Mr. Glover received the promotion of chief train dispatcher for the St. Louis & Rock Island Division of the Chicago, Burlington & Quincy, affecting 285 miles of line and railroad and places him over several men. His energy and fidelity to business is what brought him this promotion.

While in Nickerson, Kansas, Mr. Glover met and married Sarah Van Arnsdale, a leading lady of that place. She received a practical education in Ohio, that being her place of nativity. She has no children, but is known as a worthy wife and kind neighbor, and she and her husband take an interest in bettering humanity. They affiliate with no particular church creed. They are interested in everything that benefits Beardstown, and have recently built a fine residence with all modern improvements in the best part of the city. Mr. Glover is a sound Republican, and is interested in local politics. He is a prominent member of Beardstown Lodge, No. 107, Knights of Pythias, and has filled all the chairs.

AUGUST KROHE, an old settler and well-to-do farmer, was born on Saxony, Germany, on August 19, 1812. He came of good German blood and good family. He is the son of Christian and Rosina (Reicker) Krohe, natives of Saxony, where they grew up and lived until the family of children were all born and part of them grown up. They then took passage on a sailing vessel in August, 1835, and after a seven weeks' voyage landed in New Orleans, coming thence up the Mississippi and Illinois rivers to Beardstown. From there they soon went to Spring Bluff, and here they bought and improved new lands, part of which was Government land. It was on this farm that the father and mother spent their last days, the former dying at the age of seventy-nine years; the latter was eighty-eight when she died. They were a healthy and prosperous family, and the same quality is in their son, August, who is as bright and healthy at eighty years as he ever was. The father and mother of our subject were members of the Lutheran Church.

Mr. Krohe has a fine farm with good buildings on it, on which he has lived since 1840. It is in section 8, township 17, range 11. He has always been identified with the best interests of the county, and has lived to see wonderful improvements here.

He was married in this county to Miss Christianna Jockisch, born near the farm of her husband in Saxony, Germany, in 1810. She was yet a young woman when her parents and grandparents came to the United States, in 1835, on the same vessel that the Krohes came on, and they, like the latter, found good homes in Cass county. Soon after coming here, Mr. Krohe and Miss Jockisch were married, and lived together until 1889, when Mrs. Krohe died. She was a good mother and wife and was a faithful member of the Lutheran Church. She was the only daughter of Gottlieb and Christianna (Jacob) Jockisch. Grandfather Jockisch died here in 1836, after he had been here about a year. He was then about sixty-four and was a good, reliable old man. His name was Gottlieb Jockisch, and he was the founder of the family in this country.

Mr. and Mrs. Krohe had six living children: Louis, a farmer in Schuyler county, married to Sophia Korte; Minnie, wife of Henry Korte (see biography); Louisa, wife of a farmer of Morgan county; Henry (see biography); Amelia, wife of Henry Rupel, a farmer on Mr. Krohe's homestead.

Mr. Krohe, wife and all the family have been members of the Lutheran Church, and Mr. Krohe and his sons are Democrats. They are all worthy people.

NATHANIEL P. MESERVE, a resident farmer of section 30, Lee township, was born in Caledonia county, Vermont, March 25, 1825. His father, Nathaniel, was a native of Barnstable, New Hampshire, born about 1794, and died at the age of ninety-two, in Vermont.

The subject of this sketch was educated in the best New England schools for a teacher, which profession he followed for over twenty years, in the East and West. He taught several years in Illinois, both before and after his marriage. He married Mary J. Meserve, a cousin who was born in 1839. She was a daughter of Joseph and Elizabeth Meserve, who were English people. The peculiar incident that led to this marriage was romantic. After Mr. Meserve had been in Illinois some time, he was shown a letter from this young miss, and he said to his friend who showed it to him, "That girl shall be my wife;" and sure enough, when she came West she became his wife. They were married in Brown county, in 1856, and settled on their present farm two years later, first buying eighty acres and later 100 more. In 1870 they went to Colorado Springs, where they remained six years. This move was made partly on account of Mr. Meserve's failing health. While there he invested in silver mines, and now owns one mine and has an interest in another. They returned to their Illinoian home. They have two children, Ai Meserve, born in 1857, and Rosabelle, born in 1871. The son is a farmer, and both are at home where they have enjoyed every advantage and have improved every opportunity. Mr. Meserve is not strongly partisan, but votes the Republican ticket. His wife is a Presbyterian, and is an interesting lady. He is in failing health and strength, and has retired from all business. They are both admirable people, and are greatly esteemed by all who know them.

HON. WILLIAM C. RENO, of Browning, Illinois, dealer in grain and stock, is a native of this township, born in 1838. He is the son of Jonathan and Louisa (Thornton) Reno, both natives of east Tennessee, father born in 1811, the mother in 1813. The paternal grandfather, also named Jonathan, came to Schuyler county in 1825, and was accompanied by his son, Jonathan. The latter was married in 1834.

William Reno grew to manhood in Browning township, spent a year traveling through Kansas, Nebraska and Colorado, and on his return was married to Rebecca A. Wallace of Browning township, in 1860. She was born in 1841, grew up in the same neighborhood, as her parents were very early settlers in this county. Mr. Reno was raised on a farm and followed that occupation until nine years ago, when he went into his present business. He has been an active man all his life.

In 1880, he was elected Representative to the State Legislature, and served one term of two years, having been elected on the Democratic ticket. For many years he has been an active worker in political affairs, and on the national and State issues has always affiliated with the Democrats, but in county and township affairs he has voted for men rather than measures. Mr. Reno is a man of sterling integrity, having the esteem of all with whom he has been associated, either socially or in business capacity. He has been Justice of the Peace for Browning township for the last sixteen years, and has represented his township on the Board of Supervisors for five or six years, and has held the various offices of the county.

Mr. and Mrs. Reno have seven living children, having lost one, namely: Samuel F. is cashier of the bank at Rushville, Illinois; Salina and Jennie are at home, the former a teacher in the public schools; Mark M. is a telegraph operator at Creston, Iowa; Minnie M. is a teacher in the public schools; Jay and Fred are still at home. Mrs. Reno belongs to the Methodist Episcopal Church. The Reno family are of French ancestry on the father's side and of Welsh and Dutch on the mother's. The family was established in America five generations ago and all were given to agricultural pursuits. His father was a soldier in the Black Hawk war.

BLENDON L. ROWLAND, one of the most prominent citizens of Versailles, Illinois, was born in Newark, Ohio, December 5, 1856. His father, Thomas Jackson Rowland, was born near Winchester, Virginia, about 1826, and his father, grandfather of subject, was named Martin Rowland, who was a farmer of Virginia, who died there in 1830, in early manhood, of consumption. He was married and had four children, namely: Julia Ann, wife of Mr. McCapp; Abner died near Jacksonville, Illinois, leaving four children; Thomas, father of subject; Lucinda, wife of Henry Lybarger, died in middle life, leaving two children. Thomas Rowland married Leonora Barney of Sackett's Harbor, New York, daughter of Thomas J. and Louisa (Wells) Barney, of Wellsville, New York. The latter died in Watertown, New York, and the mother of subject was reared by an uncle, James Barney, who moved to Newark, Ohio, when she was a small child. Here she was married to the father of subject, who was a harnessmaker and worked at his trade at Newark, Millwood and Spring Mountain, Ohio. He and Senator Joseph Wilson were shopmates and warm friends. They came West in 1864, to Keokuk, Iowa, but three years later landed in Versailles. They were in humble circumstances and had only $200 when they arrived in Versailles. Mrs. Rowland bore her husband eleven children, three of whom died in infancy, and another, Emma, died when seven years old. The adults, seven in number, are as follows: Blendon L., of this notice; Anna, wife of Charles W. Wainnon, of Rushville, Illinois; Lucinda C., wife of Oscar Van Deventer; Abner C., of the mercantile firm of Rowland Brothers, hardware and farm implements; Love Augusta, of Versailles; Bessie, wife of J. C. Cleveland of Versailles; and Homer M., bookkeeper and salesman for the firm of Rowland Brothers, a promising young man of twenty. These children all received a good common-school education and are all well informed, intelligent people. The parents, while not wealthy, were able to give them a good start in life. The mother died in 1884, but the father is still living a retired life in Versailles, making his home with Abner C. The maternal grandfather, Thomas J. Barney, died in St. Paul, in his seventy-eighth year, leaving an estate of $100,000, which he willed to his nephews and nieces, making no mention of this daughter. This injustice was too great, so Blendon broke the will and recovered $40,000 to the family, showing great ability in the contest, although he had received no education in this direction. He persistently worked at the case in the face of much discouragement from a prominent lawyer, who told him that there was nothing in the case. His efforts were richly rewarded and much credit is due him.

Mr. Blondon Rowland left the harness trade, in 1884, having worked at it for twenty years, and embarked in his present business, with his brothers. They do nearly all of the business in this line, and he is the leader in this line, as he always was in the harness business

Mr Rowland is chairman of the Democratic Central Committee of Brown county, and has filled all the township offices, being School Director for ten years and the Supervisor from this township He is a Master Mason, and is a very influential man in his township.

He and his charming wife have four children, Dollie Rowland, a young lady of twenty; Nellie, wife of A R. Groves of Versailles; Nettie, fourteen; and Ethel, eight

Mrs Rowland is a Methodist and her husband is favorably inclined toward that church.

NATHANIEL G. SLACK, M. D., deceased, stood at the head of his profession in Schuyler county, and it is fitting that his name should be recorded in this history as one of the most skillful and benevolent practitioners He was a native of England, born April 9, 1830, a son of John and Ann Slack; the father spent all his life in England, but after his death the mother emigrated to America and settled in Fulton Illinois; she had married a second time, a Mr Potts, who died a few years after they came to this country. Nathaniel G. was a mere lad when his father died, and still in his youth when he came to the United States with an older brother; he first settled in Rhode Island, and thence removed to Fulton county, Illinois He attended Farmington Academy, and afterward went to Cedar Rapids; but the funds to defray his expenses were raised through his own efforts; possessing a natural talent for painting, he secured pupils in this art, and taught until he had saved sufficient means to carry him through his literary course; he then taught school for a time, and choosing the profession of dentistry he was in due time engaged in practice All his leisure time, however, was given to study, and he attended medical lectures at Keokuk later on; he finally abandoned the profession of dentistry, and began practicing medicine in Fulton county, Illinois In 1859 he removed to Rushville, Schuyler county, and in November of that year entered upon a career, every action of which reflected honor upon his name. He was very successful in the practice of medicine and was a skillful surgeon The poor found in him the truest and kindest of friends, and the best knowledge was as freely given to them in their distress as was expended in the care of the wealthiest patient.

In addition to his professional duties, Dr. Slack found time to engage in mercantile pursuits, and was also interested in the woolen mills here.

He was united in marriage November 12, 1858, to Eliza C. Berry, a native of Fulton county, Illinois, and a daughter of Henry C. Berry, who was a native of Berkshire, England; the grandfather, Joseph Berry, also a native of England, emigrated to America, accompanied by his family, and settled in Canada; he removed from the Dominion to

Fulton county, Illinois, about 1839; he purchased a tract of land there on which he resided until his death; his wife's maiden name was Elizabeth Blanche; her death occurred in Fulton county. Henry C. Berry was a miller by trade, having mastered this vocation in England; he followsd this pursuit after coming to America, and also engaged in farming. Later he disposed of his land and embarked in mercantile business in Fulton county, Illinois. Thence he removed to California, and lived in Santa Ana for a number of years; his death occurred there. He married Elizabeth Temple, a native of England, who emigrated to this country with an uncle. Dr. and Mrs. Slack had born to them six children: Clement L., Sheridan Grant, Flora M., Bessie, Clara and Henry.

Politically, the Doctor affiliated with the Republican party. During the war he was United States Marshal, and passed through many dangers and perils in the discharge of his duty. He was a member of the Rushville Lodge, I. O. O. F., and also belonged to the Encampment. He continued in the active practice of his profession until overtaken by death, August 9, 1887. The country lost a loyal, noble-hearted citizen, the medical profession a skilled practitioner, and the family a beloved husband and indulgent father.

SAMUEL A. MOORE, of Lee township, was born in the State of North Carolina, in 1820. His father was William Moore, a farmer and blacksmith, who emigrated from North Carolina to Indiana when about sixty years of age. He settled on a farm in Monroe county, where he resided some fifteen years, when he again sold and moved to Illinois, in the fall of 1852. He died on his farm near Kingston, when about eighty-five years old. His wife was Margaret Summers, born near Baltimore, and died when nearly eighty years old. They left what was considered a good estate at that time.

Samuel had but little schooling, as there were no public schools where he was reared. His parents had but a small farm, but did the best they could for their children. He worked by the day and month for some years, and was married at twenty-six years of age, in Indiana, to Sarah, daughter of John and Agnes (Jones) Goodnight. They were farmers and moved to McDonough county, Illinois, about two years after Mr. and Mrs. Moore came to Illinois. Mr. and Mrs. Moore started with no means when they were married and they worked rented lands three years near Bloomington, the county seat of Monroe county. They then started with a pair of horses, a covered lumber wagon, bedding, furniture and clothing, all that they could draw for a new home. They camped nights in their tent, which they brought along. They drove two milch cows, and had a pleasant journey of some three weeks. They settled in Adams county, where they now have a good farm of 240 acres and other lands there, making 720 acres in this part of Illinois. They have seven living children: A. W., of Chicago, a stock-dealer in the Exchange building; Elizabeth, at home with her parents; Esther Ann, wife of J. H. Amran, a farmer of Lee township; Sarah M., wife of I. M. Sout, of Ripley, Illinois; Paris D. is on the old homestead; S. D. remains on the old farm, and Mary E. is still at home. Mr. and Mrs. Moore, with most of the children, are professors of the Christian faith.

Mr. Moore is a Democrat. He never sought office, but was made Supervisor of the township, and for sixteen years a director of the County Agricultural Society.

HENRY R. SUTHERLAND was born in Knox county, Ohio. His father, Joseph B., was born in Trumbull county, Ohio, and his father, Benjamin, married Jane Beard, of Pennsylvania. They were farmers and spent the most of their lives in that county. Joseph Sutherland married, in Ohio, in 1834, Jane, daughter of Joseph and Sarah (Crider) Eaton both of Pennsylvania. They were married in Ohio, where the father died, in middle age, and the mother died in Littleton, Illinois, aged fifty. Mr. Joseph Sutherland died in Ohio, aged twenty-four, leaving his widow and this one son. She was married again, to Henry Schoonover, of Ohio, by whom she had two children, both dying young. They came to Illinois in 1858, and settled near the present home soon after coming. They bought 140 acres first, paying $800, and they have lived here since, where Mr. Schoonover died, aged forty-four years. Mrs. Schoonover and her son, Henry R. Sutherland, have added to the original purchase of eighty acres, making 220. All of this, except twenty acres, is under good cultivation, and these twenty are in pasture and timber. They were left in good circumstances, and by good management have prospered since.

Henry married Ella R. Pratt, of Licking county, Ohio, daughter of Hector and Susan E. (Reed) Pratt. They have two children: Twilie D., born July 3, 1887, and Glen C., born August 30, 1889.

Mr. Sutherland has been a School Director for many years. He has a good education, and is an intelligent, reading man. He is a Democrat. They have one a general farmer, raising the usual crops, but he sells no grain but wheat. He has six cows and the same number of horses, and fattens forty to sixty hogs, also feeding some cattle. They raise a great plenty of orchard and small fruits.

Mrs. Sutherland is a Baptist, and the whole family are greatly esteemed by their large circle of admiring friends.

ADAM L. HAGEMAN was born February 26, 1857, on the farm which he now owns. Here he grew to manhood, and was educated. His father, Isaac Hageman, was born in Schuyler county, Pennsylvania, in 1809, of English and Scotch ancestry. His wife was Susanna Lischy, born in York county, Pennsylvania, in 1813, of German and Scotch ancestry. They were married in 1837, in Ohio, and removed to Illinois in 1839. They settled on the farm where their son now lives in Monroe precinct, Cass county, Illinois, where both died, the father in 1873 and the mother in 1883. They had eight children: Jesse, William, Emanuel, Noah, Miller, Adam, Amanda and Sarah. All the children except Jesse were born on the old homestead in Monroe precinct. He was born in Ohio. Mrs. Hageman was raised in the Lutheran faith, but after marriage she joined the Methodist Episcopal Church with her husband. Both were consistent members of that church at their death and were respected by all.

Adam bought out the other heirs and now owns the old homestead. The farm comprises 422½ acres of farming land well adapted to stock-raising. There are sixty acres of timber on the land. He has rented the farm for five years. Next year he purposes moving his family to Virginia to live in comfort and ease. He is a Republican in politics.

He was married to Miss Lizzie Jockisch of Bluff Springs, Cass county, Illinois, born May 20, 1865, he being thirty years of age. Her parents were Charles T. and Eleanora (Carls) Jockisch, who were very early settlers of Bluff Springs. To Mr. and Mrs. Hageman have been born four children, three of whom are living: Mary Eleanora, Emma Madora, Effie Cornelia and a son who is yet unnamed. Effie C. is the one not living.

Mrs. Hageman is a member of the Methodist Episcopal Church and both she and her husband are worthy people.

JOHN J. BEATTY, Sheriff of Cass county and a member of the firm of Beatty & Hammer, formerly Rearick & Beatty, was born in Franklin county, Pennsylvania. He lost his father when very young. The latter was of Irish descent and died in the prime of life. He was a miller by trade. His mother died soon after and he was reared by Jacob Rearick and wife, who brought him to Cass county, when he was six years old. They were early settlers of Cass county and here they lived and died, leaving three sons. The latter were very prominent in politics for many years. Mr. Beatty, after he had grown up, started out to seek his own fortune, always with the love and respect of his foster parents. He came to Beardstown in 1856, and afterward spent some five years in Missouri, engaged in the hardware business. His present business is dealing in farm implements and hardware. He is located on Main street and the present firm has been in business seven years. The store is an old one and was first started in the '40s and has been considered one of the leading stores of the city since it was started. Some years ago he was elected Mayor and held that office five terms. In 1980 he was elected Sheriff of the county, and has held this office with great credit to himself and satisfaction to the people. Being an ardent Democrat, he has taken an active part in local politics and has been a delegate to the Congressional conventions.

He was married in Canton, Missouri, to Miss Mary Francis Pickering, of Boston, Massachusetts. Her father, John, was born in New England, and came from there to Chicago, and at one time was well-known as a railroad contractor and builder and now lives retired in Portland. His wife is yet living and is also quite old. They are both quite intelligent and are highly respected by all who know them.

Mrs. Beatty was carefully educated and is the devoted mother of two bright young sons, William P. and Edward L. Mr. and Mrs. Beatty are prominent people of Beardstown and leaders in society. Mr. Beatty is a leading Mason, member of the blue and chapter lodges in Beardstown.

THOMAS ARMSTRONG, a retired farmer now residing in Bainbridge township, was born in county Monaghan, Ireland, in March, 1837. His father, Robert Armstrong, was a native of the same county, but unquestionably of Scotch extraction; he was a farmer by occupation, and passed his life in his own country. He married Jane Crozier, a native of county

Tyrone, Ireland, and a daughter of William Crozier; she emigrated to America in 1852, resided in the State of New York four years, and then came to Illinois, where she spent the remainder of her days; she was the mother of sixteen children. Thomas Armstrong was a youth of sixteen years when he came to America; he sailed from Dundalk to Liverpool, and there embarked upon an American vessel; he landed at the port of New York after a voyage of five weeks and three days. He now found himself a stranger in a strange land, without money. After a time he found work at the cabinetmaker's trade which he followed about a year and a half, and then turned his attention to marble-cutting. Times were hard, business dull, and he could earn but little more than a living. He therefore determined to emigrate to the West, and try his fortunes on the frontier. He located at Rushville, Illinois, and worked by the day, month or job for three years. He then rented land for a time, and a little later, purchased forty acres in Bainbridge township; there was a small house on the place, and seven acres had been cleared; this constituted the improvements. Mr. Armstrong lived here four years, and at the end of that time sold at an advance; he then bought seventy-five acres in the same township, made many valuable improvements, occupying the place two years; he disposed of this farm and purchased 106 acres, which are included in his present farm. He has erected a nice set of frame buildings, has invested in other lands as his means increased, and now owns 285 acres. He was actively engaged in agricultural pursuits until 1892, when he removed to the home he now occupies; he erected this dwelling in 1891, and is surrounded with all the comforts which his years of industry have secured.

Mr. Armstrong was married, in 1859, to Catherine Ryan, who was born in Buena Vista township, February 1, 1840, a daughter of Charles and Margaret Ryan (see sketch of Thomas Ryan). They have six children living: John, Mary, Charles, Robert, Samuel and Frank. The parents are consistent members of the Protestant Methodist Church. Mr. Armstrong is a supporter of the principles of the Democratic party. He is a man of strict integrity, and has the respect of the entire community.

WILLIAM SCHEWE, a large farmer and stock-raiser living in section 5, range 18, has a large farm of 160 acres. He owns in other parts of the county large amounts of land. He has altogether 680 acres, mostly in the Sangamon bottoms, and is unusually well improved. He has lived in this county ever since 1866. He has always been a farmer on his own account since 1869, having spent the first two years in Beardstown.

He was born in Westphalia, Prussia, Germany, in 1839, and was reared and educated in his native country. When he was of age he set out for the United States, being the first of the family to come. He left Bremen in 1859, crossing on a sailing vessel to New Orleans, and thence up the Mississippi river to St. Louis. After spending some years in the southern part of Illinois and around St. Louis, he came on to Beardstown, and has since been a tiller of the soil in Cass county.

He was joined, some years after his coming to this country, by his father, William Schewe, who died in Cass county when forty-four years of age. He had lost his wife in Germany, when she was in middle life. Her maiden name was Louisa Meyer. She and her husband were members of the Lutheran Church all their lives. Our subject and a sister, Mrs. Charles Brokemeier, are all that are living of the children born to their parents.

Our subject was married in St. Louis county, Missouri, to Miss Ingra Otschwe. She was born and reared in Prussia, Germany, and came to the United States when twenty years of age, and since her marriage has been a hard-working woman, and has borne her husband eight children: Anna, wife of Henry Wette; Louisa, wife of Henry Merz, a farmer in this county; William, Charles, Herman, Minnie, Henry and Emiel are at home.

Mr. and Mrs. Schewe are members of the German Lutheran Church. Mr. Schewe is a Republican.

DAVID C. LINN, who ably represents Frederick township on the County Board of Supervisors, was born in Franklin county, Indiana, March 29, 1834, a son of John Linn, a native of Sidney, Ohio. The father was a carpenter and wheelwright by trade, and was engaged in the manufacture of large spinning and small flax wheels. He removed to Indiana when a young man, and followed his trade in Franklin county until 1839, when he started westward with his family, his objective point being Illinois; the entire journey was made overland, and after about five weeks of travel he landed in Adams county. At first he rented land near Camp Point, and two years later he bought a tract of land; here he erected a log house and a shop, and worked at his trade, at the same time superintending the cultivation of his farm. He made many valuable improvements, and resided on the place until his death in 1881. His wife's maiden name was Nancy Gant; she now resides at Camp Point, at the advanced age of eighty-three years. David C. is one of a family of eleven children, and was but six years of age when he came to Illinois with his parents. At that time Adams county was sparsely settled; deer, wild turkeys and other game abounded, and the iron horse had not yet penetrated the frontier. Quincy was the nearest market town, and was the depot of supplies for many miles around.

Dr. Linn received his early education in the primitive schools which were taught in the log schoolhouse. At the age of eighteen he began the study of medicine under the preceptorship of Dr. Ashton, of Cincinnati; he also attended lectures at the Eclectic Medical College, and in 1857 began the practice of his profession at Birmingham; he had been there but a short time when he went to Plymouth, where he practiced until 1859. In the spring of that year he was graduated from the Eclectic Medical College of Cincinnati, and then located in Frederick township, where he has practiced continuously since. He has been a close student of his profession, and has availed himself of every opportunity of improvement. In 1883 he attended a course of medical lectures at Bellevue Hospital Medical College, and in 1888 he was graduated from the Ohio Medical College at Cincinnati.

In the month of March, 1865, Dr. Linn entered the service of the United States, as Assistant Surgeon of the One Hundred and Forty-eighth Volunteer Infantry, and was on duty until the following September, when he was honorably discharged, the war being ended.

He was married in March, 1861, to Ada Folsom, a native of Illinois; she died in August, 1862. The Doctor was married again in 1863, to Della Truett, of Baltimore. Politically he is a Republican, and a stanch supporter of the principles of that party. He was first elected Supervisor in 1886, and has served continuously since that time. He has been a capable and efficient officer, working always for the best interests of the county. He has been successful in his profession, and has a large and appreciative practice.

WILLIAM THOMAS was born in Fayette county, Ohio, January 9, 1809. His father was John, a Virginian, who came to Ohio while the Indians were still plentiful on Paint creek. His first wife was Nancy Putnam of Pennsylvania, who died in early life, leaving six young children. Four years later he was married again, but she was drowned about one year later, while trying to save the life of his child. Some years later he was married again, and by this marriage he had six children, making in all thirteen. He died at eighty years, on his farm. These children have all passed away but our subject and Benjamin Thomas, a farmer in his eighty-fifth year, living in Iowa.

William has been a farmer all his life and had very little schooling. He was married in Ohio, to Julia DeWitt, and came West in the fall of 1831, with wife and one child. They came in a four-horse wagon and with three loose horses, which they rode part of the time. In good weather his wife rode his little pacing mare and carried the baby. He had very little money left when he crossed the river at Beardstown. He took up a homestead, and, not being able to deed it, sold out his improvements and then had enough to enter 120 acres, for which he obtained a Government deed, and then had eighty acres under the plow and an orchard and two good hewed-log houses. There he lived from 1837 to 1860. He traded it for 160 acres of his present farm and moved upon it. There was an old log house into which he moved until he could build a good log house, and in 1866 or 1867 he built a part of his present frame house. In 1882 he built his good barn, and in 1884 he built the frame addition to his house. There is not a man living in this section that was living here when Mr. Thomas first came.

Mr. Thomas lost his first wife in March, 1855, by whom he had seven children, Drusilla Shield, deceased; John M., deceased; James, deceased; Sarah C., a maiden lady at home with her parents; William A., a merchant in Cooperstown; Peter A., farmer close by; Parmelia Ann Gibson, living on the homestead; Eliza Jane Garnett, in Arkansas. Mr. Thomas was married again, to Mrs. Nancy Brown, *nee* Clayton. She died, aged seventy-eight years, in 1884, after having been his faithful wife for twenty-four years. He is a Master Mason and organized the Versailles Lodge, of which he is the last living member. He believes in moral reform in politics.

EMANUEL LEIB, deceased, was one of the most highly respected farmers of Schuyler county, and it is fitting that his name should be preserved to the coming generations as an honored citizen of the great commonwealth of Illinois. He was born in York county, Pennsylvania, August 26, 1808, a son of Abraham Leib, a native of the same county; the paternal grandfather spent his entire life in York county, and there Abraham Leib was reared to agricultural pursuits; he, too, remained in York county until the day of his death He married Matilda Ziegler of the same county, and she died on the homestead. Emanuel Leib grew to maturity, surrounded by rural scenes and occupations; he remained in the place where he was born until 1865, when he emigrated to Illinois and settled in Rushville township, Schuyler county, he purchased a farm and spent the remainder of his life He was an intelligent, successful farmer, and developed one of the most desirable tracts of land in Schuyler county

He was united in marriage to Miss Mary Ann Kimmel, a native of York county, Pennsylvania, and a daughter of Philip and Elizabeth (King) Kimmel. Three children were born to them. Henry E, who married Addie Wells, is a resident of Chicago, Alice Leota, a stenographer. is also in Chicago; and John Robert resides with his mother.

After the death of her husband, Mrs Leib remained on the farm for three years, managing it with marked success; in 1890, however, she rented the land, and is now making her home in Rushville.

J W ORWIG, of the firm of Orwig Brothers, successful house painters of Beardstown, is one of the prominent men of the city The firm employs from two to ten men and are noted for the excellence of their work They make a speciality of fine graining The firm includes J. W. and a brother, George. They have been doing business under the present firm name for the past twenty-two years formerly the firm was known as William D Orwig & Sons Mr Orwig started the business as early as 1857 He was engaged in business with them as journeymen workmen for two years, coming to Beardstown in 1867 Here he died in 1875, aged sixty-three. He was born in Pennsylvania of Pennsylvania Dutch parents He grew up in his native State, following in his trade of distiller, and was yet a young man when he came to Illinois, settling in Morgan county Here he was married to Jane Whipp born in Yorkshire, England She emigrated to this country with her parents, settling in Morgan county in the '30s. Mrs Orwig remained with her parents until her marriage, and she made her husband a most faithful wife until his death.

For some time after his marriage Mr. Orwig engaged in the mercantile business in Morgan county, but later went to Rushville, Schuyler county, where he was engaged in the same business for a time. In 1857 he entered the painter's trade, having learned his trade in Sandusky, Ohio He was a good citizen and his loss was felt by all who knew him He was a Republican in politics from the formation of the party. He was a sound friend and acquaintance of Mr Lincoln's, having formed his acquaintance while he, Mr. Orwig, was a clerk in the treasury department at Springfield His wife is still living with her son, George L, at Beardstown and, although she is in her seventy-first year she is very active for her years and is a devoted Methodist and a good Christian woman Her husband was of the same religious faith

Our subject is the eldest of two sons and three daughters, namely. Lizzie, wife of John Shaw, retired farmer of Beardstown, Mary, wife of Charles Fulks, wholesale grocer of Peoria, Illinois, Rosa I , wife of Milton McClure of Beardstown; J W , born in Rushville, Illinois, November 12, 1845, and George.

Our subject was reared and educated in this city and was married here to Ann Summers of Rochester, New York, born in 1869 She came to Beardstown when young with her parents They are still living in this place and are past middle life They are well known and highly respected people.

Mr. and Mrs Orwig are parents of one child: Charles William. The are prominent young married people and are greatly liked by their large circle of friends

LEWIS ZIMMER is now retired from active labor as a farmer and is living at the corner of Jefferson and Twelfth streets in Beardstown. He was born in Frankfort-on-the-Main in Hesse-Darmstadt, July 28, 1819 He came of Hesse-Darmstadt parents, his father, John Zimmer being a German farmer in a small way and died when ninety-two years of age He was an active old man to the last, and when seventy-five thought nothing of walking twelve miles He was a tried and loyal soldier and served his country for six years as one His wife, whose maiden name was Margaret Snyder, died at the age of eighty, at the same place as her husband She came of a long lived-family. They were both members of the State Church of Hesse-Darmstadt

Lewis is the youngest, but one of nine children born to his parents Several of the family are still living and married, but Lewis is the only one who came to the United States. He grew up on the farm in his native country

and after he became of age he enlisted as a soldier in the regular Germany army, serving six years; when he received his honorable discharge he came to the United States, leaving in August, 1846 He sailed from France on a three-mast sailing vessel, landing in New York city after thirty-one days' passage He came thence to Milwaukee, Wisconsin, locating fourteen miles west of that city and began life in the new country as a day laborer. After about three years he came to Cass county, Illinois, through the influence of a German friend who lived there. Here he has lived ever since He has a nice farm of 200 acres, a good portion of which is well improved and the soil is as fine as any in the county. The farm lies against Bluff Springs, in the valley of the same name. He came to the county a poor man, renting his farm, but in 1859 he purchased sixty-eight acres and on this began to farm on his own account. He added to this original farm until he had accumulated a fine property and fortune, and this without assistance from anybody but his faithful wife

He was married in Beardstown to Mrs Catharine Price, *nee* Keil She was born in Hesse-Darmstadt and after growing up was married to Conrad Price, a gentleman of the same province. After marriage Mr Price with his parents and young wife came, in 1845, from Bremen to Baltimore and thence to Beardstown, Illinois, and here a few years later he died very suddenly from paralysis, leaving his widow with quite a family, two sons who are now grown up and prosperous, Henry and John The parents of Mrs Price died in Beardstown when old people, their names were Conrad and Catherine (Shelman) Price They were both natives of Hesse-Darmstadt and were all Lutherans.

Mr. and Mrs. Zimmer are the parents of two children: Lewis, Jr. (see biography), and Margaret, wife of Theo. Krohe, an implement dealer in the city.

Mr. Zimmer moved into the city in 1888 and is now enjoying the fruits of his early labors. He is a Democrat in politics and he and his wife are members of the Lutheran Church.

ROBERT LITTLE was born in county Tyrone, Ireland, August 8, 1808. He was the son of William and Jane (Crozier) Little, who were both born in Ireland, where he died, at the age of sixty years, but she, surviving, came to Pittsburg, where she died, at the age of sixty-five years. William L. came to this country in 1831, in a sailing vessel, Captain Haines, commanding. They were nearly six weeks on the trip and first landed at Quebec, Canada, and remained there that summer. He worked in Queen Victoria's works for about three months at dry masonry, and he was injured there by a large stone falling upon him which laid him up for about two months. He seems to have had a good deal of sickness and misfortune, and it was not until that fall that he was able to go to Eastern Canada, where he worked for two years. The next spring he came to Pennsylvania, and went into a boot and shoe store with his uncle. He left Canada against the wishes of the English company by whom he was employed, who offered to make him an officer and deed him a large tract of land. He remained in Pennsylvania twelve to fifteen years, engaged for the most part in superintending the construction of railroads.

He was married the day before he left Ireland, and his wife came with him. He, his wife and eight children left Pittsburg for Illinois via St. Louis and Fredericktown, and from there came to Rushville. In 1844 he rented a farm for three years, and then bought a farm of partly improved land in Littleton township. The next spring he moved to this farm, into a little log house about ready to tumble down. The next year he built a substantial log house, and then built a frame addition and otherwise improved the entire house. He has now over 600 acres of fine land and two houses, and several lots in Littleton. About eleven years ago he retired from farm work, and rented his land to his boys. His wife was named Eliza Cunningham, was born in 1814, on the estate of Lord Mt. Joy, in Tyrone county, Ireland, Easter Monday. She was the daughter of Henry Cunningham, who came to Quebec, and the father, who was pensioner of the British army, died at the age of sixty, and his wife at the age of sixty-five.

Mr. Little's wife died in 1890, at home where he now lives. Mr. and Mrs. Little had ten children, seven of whom are yet living.

GEORGE E. RICHARDSON of Elkhorn township was born in St. Louis, Missouri, in 1846. He was the son of Robert H. and Sophia (Armbrewster) Richardson. He came with his parents to Illinois when a boy, and before he was of age went on the river and learned to be an engineer and followed that business until 1864, when he died. His father's family were farmers and mechanics.

George remained at home until he was nineteen years old, having remained at school until fourteen. He entered an office in St. Louis as shipping clerk, and afterward came to this county and settled in Mt. Pleasant, and worked for an uncle one year on a farm. He then took to running a portable sawmill. Since then he has farmed and continued his business in the sawmill. He has been Assessor and Collector, and is now a Democrat, although he first voted the Republican ticket.

He was married April 22, 1875, to Miss Martha J. Gerrish, who was born in this county April 9, 1854. She is the daughter of Sewall and Elizabeth (Grove) Gerrish. Mr. and Mrs. Richardson have five children, namely: Otis E., Josie L., Sewall H., George Everett and Nina L. Mr. Richardson and family are prominent people in the township and they are steady church-going people.

HENRY Y. NEWBOLD, now deceased, was born in Lippe-Detmold, Prussia, Germany, September 22, 1828. He came of a respectable family and his mother died in her native province when he was eight years old. His father, Henry, who was a small German farmer, came with his four children, in 1850, to New York city, and from thence to Stephenson county, Illinois, where they all settled for a time, and where a part remained. The father continued there with one of his sons until his death. He and his wife were Lutherans all their lives.

Henry Y. came to Beardstown in 1854, and two years later was married, and after a few years purchased a good farm, five miles east of Beardstown, where he lived and died. He was a practical farmer, improved his land nicely, put up a fine residence and good outbuildings. At the time of his death he owned 152 acres of good, improved land in the bottoms. He was a much respected citizen and a working member of the Lutheran Church. His wife, who still survives him, and is managing the farm with remarkable success, is a very capable woman. Her maiden name was Mary Mohlman, and she was born in Westphalia, Prussia, September 25, 1838. She was twelve years of age when her parents came to the United States and to Beardstown. There the father, Henry Mohlman, died, being nearly sixty years old. He was a good mechanic and operated a large planing-mill, and also did business as a merchant. He was a well-known and worthy citizen, a Republican, and an active member of the Lutheran Church. His wife is yet living, and bears her eighty years as well as can be expected. She has always been a consistent Lutheran.

Mrs. Newbold lived with her parents until her marriage. She is the mother of six intelligent children, all living: Henry A., a farmer of Christian county, Illinois, married to Phoebe Livergood; Ellen, wife of Herman Drawer, a farmer of Christian county; Charles, also a farmer, married Amelia Tribswater; William runs his father's old farm; Emma is the wife of Parker Hammer and Lily M., a charming young lady, is at home with her mother. The children are all well educated, and are highly respected throughout this county.

AMASA HILL was born two and a half miles from Friendship, Allegany county, New York, July 1, 1830. His grandfather Hill, a pioneer of Allegany county, and a farmer by occupation, died in 1832. His father, Nathaniel Hill, was born in Delaware county, New York; removed from there to Allegany county, bought a tract of timber land, and from the wilderness developed a farm. He spent his life there, and died in 1838. The maiden name of the wife of Nathaniel Hill and the mother of Amasa was Rhoda Tiffney. She was born in Delaware county, New York, daughter of Horace Tiffney. She came to Illinois, and died at the home of her son, Amasa, in 1875. Mr. and Mrs. Hill reared four children: Chancey, Horace, Mary and Amasa. Chancey now lives at Fredericktown, Knox county, Ohio. Horace and Mary are deceased.

The subject of our sketch attended the primitive schools of Allegany county, which were held in log schoolhouses, with greased paper for windows and the seats made of slabs with wooden pins for legs. When he was nine years old his mother sold the farm, his father having died the previous year, and emigrated to Ohio, the western journey being made in a two-horse wagon. They settled in Knox county. There were no railroads in Ohio then, and the people lived off the products of their farms and wild game. The mother bought fifty acres of land, eight miles from Mount Vernon, and there Amasa Hill was reared to manhood. At the age of fourteen he began to make his own way in the world, starting out from home with all his possessions tied up in a handkerchief. He went to Fredericktown, and there served a three years' apprenticeship to the trade of wagon and carriage maker. After learning his trade he did journeyman work there one year. In 1846 he came to Illinois, landing in Cass county, September 20. He found employment in a carriage shop at Beardstown, where he worked four years. He then started in business in company with Richard Miller, and together they conducted a carriage shop four years. At the end of that time he and his brother, Horace, bought a farm and engaged in agricultural pursuits. They farmed together till the latter's death, April 13, 1877. Since then Mr. Hill has operated it alone.

He was married, in 1850, to Mary A. Streeter, who was born in Pennsylvania, August 11, 1832, daughter of Andrew J. and Diana Streeter. Mr. and Mrs. Hill had three children: Chancey, Amanda and William. Chancey married Lucy Schaeffer, and Amanda is the wife of J. Theirget, and has one child, Nettie. Mrs. Hill died December 3, 1885. She was a consistent member of the Presbyterian Church, of which her children are also members.

ENGLEBERT CRAMER, farmer on section 33, township 18, range 11, was born in Beardstown, November 7, 1856. He was reared and educated in his native city. He is the son of Jacob H. Cramer, a native of Hanover, Germany, who came to America when a young, single man. He set sail from Bremen, on a sailing vessel, and after a long and stormy passage he landed in this country, and coming up the Mississippi river he located at Beardstown, Illinois. This was in the spring of 1848. He was a cabinetmaker, and had no difficulty in obtaining work, as he was a skilled workman. He later engaged as mechanic, and housebuilder, and carpenter. He was thus engaged the remainder of his life, dying at his home in Beardstown, in 1874, when he was fifty-four years of age, having been born in 1820. He was a Republican in politics, and a member of the German Methodist Episcopal Church, and a good substantial citizen. He was married in Beardstown, to Charlotte Frankle, born in Prussia, Germany, coming to this country with a sister. They settled in St. Louis, where they remained for a time.

She was a true wife and good mother, and a worthy woman, dying in 1888, being about sixty years of age. She was a member of the German Methodist Episcopal Church. She was the mother of ten children, seven yet living, three of them being married.

Englebert grew to manhood in this county. He has a fine farm of 160 acres, which lies in the Illinois valley, and is well improved. He has good buildings on it, and also very good stock. He is a practical farmer, and a good manager.

He was married to Paulina M. Hackman, born in this county, in 1858, where she was reared and educated. She is a very intelligent woman and good housekeeper. She has proved herself a kind and devoted wife and mother. She is the daughter of John H. and Louisa (Jockisch) Hackman. Mr. Hackman was born in Hanover, Germany, and came to the United States when thirteen years old with his parents, John E. and Mary E. (Stuben) Hackman. The family located in Cass county, in the early '40s. They bought a farm on which the father died soon afterward, and the mother some years later. John Hackman was reared to manhood on a farm in this county, and was married here. After marriage he purchased land in township 17, range 11 (which is the home of our subject) and here Mr. Hackman and wife worked and built up a fine home and large farm of 320 acres in one body, and here they both died, the former April 18, 1874, aged fifty. He was a prominent man, a Republican in politics, and was one of the builders and leading members of the Zion Methodist Episcopal Church. His wife died July 26, 1877. She was born in this county, in 1837. (For full biography of her family see history of William Jockisch). She was a kind and good neighbor, a worthy wife and mother, and a member of the Methodist Episcopal Church. She was the mother of four children, yet living.

Mrs. Cramer is the eldest; Frank J. R., a farmer in this county, married Rosa Wagoner; Lydia C., wife of Henry Sitter, now a farmer in Petersburg, Illinois; Julius H. is single and lives with his brother, Frank.

Mr. and Mrs. Cramer have four children: Louisa B., Jacob H., Julius W. and Englebert C. Mr. Cramer is a stanch Republican, and takes a very prominent part in politics, having held all of the precinct offices. He and his wife are leading people in the county.

W. H. DRUSE, passenger and freight agent at Beardstown for the Chicago, Burlington & Quincy Railroad since 1886, was born in Henry county, Illinois and was reared, educated and has always lived in this State. His father lived on a farm when he was born and reared in that calling; later he learned the trade of a carrriage painter, but after pursuing the trade for a short time he found it was not congenial and so did not continue it. He then entered into the employ of the railroad. Since then he has been successful and has saved part of his income, with which he has purchased various pieces of real estate: in this is the valuable farm in Clay county of 160 acres. It was uncultivated when he purchased it, but he has improved it until it is one of the best farms in the county. He has put a good farm house and farm building on it and has planted a large number of fine trees.

Mr. Druse comes of Eastern people, his parents being from Kentucky. His father, Stephen Druse, was a farmer in Illinois and finally ended his days with his son in Leland,

Illinois. His wife, whose maiden name was Driggs, is still living and makes her home with Mr. Druse. She is now an old lady and holds to the doctrines of the Presbyterian Church. She has only five living children, all of whom, excepting Mr. Druse, are residents of Nebraska.

Mr. Druse came to Beardstown in 1882 and has not lost at single day since from the pursuit of his duty. He has exclusive charge of the passenger and freight depots and has always proved himself worthy of the trust imposed in him. There are from twelve to twenty-five men under him all the time. He is a popular young man in his city and has the confidence of his employers. He has a thorough knowledge of his business and is a man of good habits. When he first came to the city he was clerk and night agent for the Quincy Railroad until 1886. He was also connected with the main line, with headquarters at Leland for some time. When he was first employed he was the youngest man in the employ of the road.

He was married in Beardstown, to Miss Bertha Boehme of Williamsville, Illinois. She was yet young when her parents came to Beardstown and here she was reared and educated. Her father, Julius Boehme, was a naive of Germany who settled in Illinois and was engaged as a mechanic until his death. His wife followed her husband some years afterward and was about the same age when she died. Her maiden name was Anna Phillipi and she also was a native of Germany. She came to this country with her husband and they became pioneers of Beardstown. Here they spent the remainder of their days. They were people quite well known to the people of this city and county and can be properly associated with the history of this place.

Mr. and Mrs. Druse have a close social relation with the better class of Beardstown society, and are prosperous, progressive young people who will make life a success. They adhere to the moral principles of life, but hold to no church creed. Mr. Druse is a stanch Democrat, but is no office seeker. He is an active worker for the principles of his party in a local way. He is a working member of the Masonic order, Cass Lodge, No. 23, and takes a live interest in public matters tending to benefit the city and county.

JAMES L. GREER, who was for more than twenty years the popular landlord of one of the best hotels in Rushville, was born near Five Mile Town, county Tyrone, Ireland, January 14, 1820, the son of Robert and Catherine (Lendrum) Greer. (See sketch of George Greer.) He was a lad of nine years when his parents left the beautiful Emerald Isle and crossed the sea to America. When thirteen years of age he was sent to sea as a cabin boy on a cruising vessel, making the principal ports of bóth the Atlantic and Pacific coasts. A portion of the time he was drillmaster, and after seven years he was discharged as an able-bodied seaman.

In 1841 he removed to Rushville and there engaged in the manufacture of brooms for a few years. During the war he was engaged in buying horses under contract from the Government. Previous to the war he had bought a farm in Littleton township, on which he resided until 1869, when he sold out and came to Rushville. He purchased the property which has been used as a hotel, and became the proprietor of a hotel which he managed with rare ability; he had a large and enthusiastic patronage, and a reputation that reached as far as his guests traveled.

Mr. Greer was married in 1841, to Nancy Wilson, who was born in Nelson county, Kentucky, a daughter of Elijah M. and Jane (Hawley) Wilson. Six children have been born to this union, who are still living: Emily, now Mrs. McCreery, Robert, George, Charles and Milton. Robert and Charles are engaged in the mercantile business at Kearney, Nebraska; George is a carpenter, and Milton is in the livery business at Rushville. Mr. Greer and wife are members of the Methodist Episcopal Church. He assisted in organizing the first Methodist Episcopal class in Littleton, and aided very materially in the building of the church. For a number of years he was superintendent of the Sabbath-school, and has always been a devoted worker in the cause of the Master. He is a man of excellent traits, and has the respect of all who know him.

REV. JOHN W. HAYES, general farmer on section 7, township 17, range 11, was born in Clark county, Missouri, but was reared in Schuyler county, Illinois. He is the son of George W. Hayes, a native of Kentucky, and own cousin of ex-President Hayes. His mother was a relation of J. Q. Adams. Mr. George Hayes came to Indiana when a young man, and followed his trade of general mechanic and cooper carpenter. Here he was married to Martha Fifier, of Jennings county. Here he lived for a few years, and then moved to Missouri, coming to Schuyler county, Illinois, in 1862, and began life as a farmer. Later he settled in Rushville, and there the wife and mother died, in 1886, when in middle life. Mr. Hayes still lives in Rushville, and is sixty-six years of age. He is a Methodist, as is his wife. He was a Democrat. He has three living children: Nancy, wife of Mr. Lee of Rushville; L. Jennie, wife of M. B. Woods, living at Havana, Illinois, and John W.

John W. Hayes has been in this place only a short time, formerly living in Schuyler county, Illinois, where he had lived the most of his life after he was five years old.

He was married in Schuyler county, to Annie Horton, who bore him no children. He was married a second time, in Cass county, to Mrs. Martha E. Buck, *nee* Wegle, born in Cass county, where she has since lived. She is the daughter of Jeptha and Phebe (Tood) Wegle, natives of Kentucky, where they were reared and married. They came to Illinois in the '30s and settled in Brown county. Later they came to Cass county, and settled on a farm, where Mr. Wegle died, in 1861, in middle life, being born in 1812. He was a farmer, a Republican, and a member of the Union Baptist Church. His wife makes her home with her daughter, Mrs. John Hayes. She is quite old, being born in 1812. She is a Baptist, and was the mother of twelve children. Mrs. Hayes is the youngest of the nine now living, all married with families.

Mrs. Hayes was married for the first time in Cass county, to Stephen D. Buck, who was born on the farm he lived to own and improve. Here he died, September 16, 1890. He was then fifty-seven years old, being born of a family of pioneers, who came here at an early date from North Carolina. Mr. Buck was a kind husband and a good citizen, a Democrat in politics, but not an office seeker. He was the father of ten children, two deceased. Those living are: Flora, wife of Elza Merrot, of Cass county, a farmer; Julius H. works for a farmer in this county; Stephen D. and Ella, at home. Edith M., Lillian

M., and Walter A. are triplets, and are bright healthy children. Mr. Hayes is a minister of the Church of God, and has been the pastor of the church for several years. He is a forcible speaker, and prominent minister. His wife is a member of the Baptist Church. Both are worthy people.

GEORGE W. BARNEYCASTLE, Alderman of the First Ward, Beardstown, and blacksmith for the Quincy railroad, was born in Bertie county, North Carolina, October 1, 1844. His father, George W. Barneycastle was born and spent all his life in Bertie county. He spent his life in farming, and died at the age of seventy years. His wife died when little George was twelve years old. At the death of his mother, little George was taken by an uncle and aunt, James and Sarah Wilson, and taken by them to Cass county, Illinois. They settled on a farm in Arenzville precinct. Here George was raised and his uncle and aunt lived and died. He learned his trade in Beardstown under the oldest firm in the city, John Webb & Co., and completed his trade a little before he was twenty-one. He then tried his hand at farming for three years, but finally entered the Quincy shops, and has since been engaged there. He has been on their pay rolls ever since 1878.

When George was eighteen, he enlisted in Company I, Third Illinois Cavalry, Captain Samuel Shelenberger in command. They went as a regiment to the front in 1864, and engaged in many small battles in the Cumberland mountains and Mississippi, under General Hatch. After serving for about one year he was mustered out at Snelling, Minnesota, October 20, 1865. He escaped unhurt and was never captured. He was always on duty and never was sick. Since the war he has lived in Beardstown most of the time and has been an enterprising citizen. He is a member of the G. A. R., McLane Post, 97, also a member of the subordinate lodge I. O. O. F., and is Past Grand Commander, having filled all the chairs. He takes an active part in local politics and serves his party, Democratic, in a very proficient manner. He has been closely associated with the best interests of the city.

He was married in this city, to Miss Elizabeth Dengler of Schuylkill county, Pennsylvania, born in 1845. She came West with her parents when very young, the family settling in Bath, Mason county. Her father and mother died when quite old, Mr. Dengler being an engineer.

Mr. and Mrs. Barneycastle attend the Methodist Episcopal Church, of which Mrs. Barneycastle is a member. They have three children besides the one child, William, who died when young. The living children are: Lillie M., a type-writer in the office of the "Star of the West;" Clyde, at home.

ROBERT ANDERSON, the capable and enterprising manager of the lumber business of J. S. & G. S. Russell, and a popular citizen of Ashland, Illinois, was born in county Tyrone, Ireland, December 22, 1842. His parents were William and Martha (Kimpston) Anderson, both of whom were natives of county Tyrone, where they were married and where all of their children were born. In 1847, they came to America, and located in Philadelphia, Pennsylvania, where both parents afterward died. This worthy couple were the parents of five children, of whom the subject of this sketch was the first son. Jane, the first in order of birth, died in young womanhood, in Philadelphia; next in order was our subject; Kate, the third child, resides in Bucks county, Pennsylvania; Sarah, now Mrs. Finley, lives in Philadelphia where her husband is a carpet manufacturer; Willie was born in Philadelphia, but died in infancy.

Mr. Anderson lived with his maternal grandfather in Ireland, until he was twenty-two years of age, when, in June, 1865, he came to Philadelphia. He remained in the city of Brotherly Love until the fall of 1872, and was, in the meantime, on May 2, 1868, married there, to Miss Mary A. Lucas, who was born in his native county, in Ireland, and who had been a schoolmate of his in the beautiful Emerald Isle, in which country her parents spent their entire lives.

In 1872, Mr. Anderson came to Jacksonville, Illinois, where he entered the employ of Russell Brothers, with whom he has been connected ever since. In 1876, he started the business in Ashland, which he now operates, which is the only lumber-yard in that city, and they enjoy a large and lucrative trade. The entire management of this large enterprise is vested in Mr. Anderson's hands. It is he who pays the men, does all the collecting, and handles all the money, and is, in fact, a trusted employee, whose integrity is unimpeachable and his faithfulness unsurpassed.

Mr. and Mrs. Anderson have four children: Robert L., twenty-four years of age and unmarried, is the manager of a lumber business in Virginia, Illinois; Henrietta, is the wife of Ferdinand L. Strawn, a prominent and successful young farmer near Jacksonville, Illinois, to whom she was married January 6, 1892; Sarah E. and Willie Johnson are still under the parental roof: the former, now past eighteen years of age, is an efficient teacher in the public schools of Sangamon county; the latter is employed, during vacation, about the lumber-yard or on the farm belonging to the Russell Brothers. All of the children have had excellent educational opportunities in the common and high schools of Ashland. Robert L., the oldest son, is a graduate of the Jacksonville Business College, and Henrietta graduated in music at the Jacksonville Conservatory of Music, and taught that beautiful art in Ashland for several years, being very successful.

In his political affiliations, Mr. Anderson is a stanch Republican, advocating most thoroughly the principles of that party. He abhors free-trade England, and deeply sympathizes with his oppressed countrymen across the water. Socially, he affiliates with the I. O. O. F., Knights of Pythias and with the A. O. U. W. The entire family are earnest and useful members of Pleasant Plains Presbyterian Church, contributing liberally to its support and advancement.

Ireland and America being such friends, it is natural that their respective countrymen should entertain the kindest regard for each other, especially if, as in Mr. Anderson's case, they are irreproachable in business and social life, inspiring all worthy men with the deepest respect and esteem.

ISAAC R. GARNER, a prominent and esteemed citizen of Ashland, Illinois, and an honored veteran of the late war, was born in Cass county, Illinois, February 21, 1846. His parents were Greenberry and Mary J. (Redman) Garner, his father being a native of Indiana, while his mother was born in

Morgan county, Illinois, in which latter county their marriage took place in 1837. The father was a prominent and useful minister of the Methodist Episcopal Church, and was an active member of the Illinois conference for more than forty years. The paternal grandfather of the subject of this sketch, Rev James Garner, was also an able minister of the same denomination, while four brothers of our subject's father were also ministers of the same church. The family was originally from Hollaad, but have been established in America since an early day. The subject of this notice was one of ten children, seven of whom are now living Hannah E., the oldest, is the wife of Rev G. B. Wolfe, an itinerant minister in the Methodist Episcopal Church in the Illinois Conference; Charles W, married, is a farmer in Pike county, Illinois; Isaac R, the subject of this biography; Mary A., widow of J. Bagby, resides in Ashland, Hattie E, wife of Ross Ister, lives on a farm in Pike county, Illinois; George, unmarried, is a horse trainer in Virginia, Illinois; Minnie Lee, wife of Jerry Ritter, lives in Ashland; James died in childhood; William N died aged eight years; and Elina Bell aged thirteen.

The early life of our subject was spent in school and in working in a store, up to the time of his enlistment in the army. He offered his services to the Twenty-first Illinois Regiment, under General Grant, but was rejected on account of his youth; a year later, however, he was accepted in Company I of the Sixty-second Illinois Infantry, and was assigned to duty in the Army of the West. For a time he served in the Sixteenth Army Corps, and was afterward under General Steele in the Seventeenth Corps. Mr. Garner was appointed Drum-major of his regiment, serving in that capacity most of his army life. His duties were to drill his own band, and he was afterward detached and placed in charge of the bands of new regiments as drillmaster. He participated with his regiment in several skirmishes, and took part in the battle of Little Rock. It was while on board a boat, in the spring of 1864, that he met with a distressing accident, which destroyed his sight, and he has been totally blind since the spring of 1866. The anguish occasioned by the deprivation of sight has been intense, and for twenty-six years he has never looked upon the face of his wife and children On May 2, 1865, he was honorably discharged, and at once returned to his parental home in Cass county, Illinois He afterward entered the Blind Institution at Jacksonville, where he remained four years, taking the entire five years' course. He then engaged in selling musical instruments, in which business he continued for seven years. After this, he was for two years in the livery business at Plymouth, Hancock county. Later, he followed trading for a time, but, since coming to Ashland, about twelve years ago, he has retired from active business. He receives a liberal pension on account of his misfortunes

Mr. Garner was married November 10, 1885, to Miss Grace E Douglass,'a highly esteemed lady and a daughter of W. S. and Virginia (Job) Douglass, honored pioneers of Cass county, Illinois, who now own and operate the Central Hotel, in Ashland. Mrs. Garner is the second of five children, of whom Charles, the eldest, is unmarried, and is in the insurance business in Ashland, Edward, died in infancy; Ellen is the wife of Dr. William Bane, a practicing physician of Springfield, Illinois; William is employed in a drug store in Ashland, and is unmarried.

Mr and Mrs. Garner have two children,

Harold D., born in Ashland, September 10, 1886; and Helen Lee, born September 2, 1888.

Politically, Mr. Garner is a straight Republican, and takes a deep interest in the affairs of his country. Socially, he is a prominent member of Douglass Post, No. 592, G. A. R., in Ashland.

He is a devout and useful member of the Methodist Episcopal Church, and is active in forwarding the interests of the church, Sunday-school and other religions and charitable enterprises.

Thus, notwithstanding his deep affliction, he does more for his fellow-men than many others who have nothing of that kind with which to contend. In the midst of all his sorrow, he is buoyed up with the sense of a duty done by which he is assisted in liberating thousands of suffering humanity, who might yet be groaning in bondage. This and the universal esteem of his associates and friends tend to brighten his otherwise dark pathway through life.

WILLIAM HARVEY McCASKILL is one of the oldest of the native-born citizens of Illinois now residing in Brown county. He was born in Sangamon county, Illinois, July 23, 1826. His father, Daniel McCaskill, was born in North Carolina, and his father, John McCaskill, was born in Scotland, coming to America when a young man, locating in North Carolina, where he married a lady of Scotch birth, and spent the remainder of his days there. His son was reared and educated in his native State, but came North when a young man and engaged in teaching. He married in Indiana, at the age of thirty-four, and either in the fall of 1825 or the spring of 1826 came to Illinois, making the journey overland with teams. He located in Sangamon county. At that time the State capital was at Vandalia; Springfield was but a hamlet, and the surrounding country was sparsely settled. He engaged in teaching, and resided there until 1834, when he emigrated to Schuyler county, settling in that part now included in Pea Ridge township, Brown county. He entered a tract of Government land, and at once built on the place. He was one of the first teachers in the county, and followed his profession for many years. He superintended the improvement of his farm, which he occupied until his death in 1851. His wife was Esther Turner, daughter of Archibald Turner, of Ireland, of Scottish descent.

William has been a resident of this county since his eighth year, and has witnessed the improvement and development of this section of country. Deer, wild turkeys and other game were plentiful. There were no railroads for years, and the people were obliged to convey their grain by team to a distant market. The people lived principally off of the products of their own farms. His father used to raise flax and sheep, and his mother manufactured all the cloth used in the family, dressing the children in homespun made by her own hands.

William received an ordinary education, but began when very young to assist his father on the farm. After his marriage he settled on a farm on section 1, where he resided until 1864, when he settled on the old homestead, which he had bought from the other heirs. The farm, which is well improved, contains 240 acres; besides this he has a farm of ninety acres in Bates county, Missouri.

He was married in October, 1851, to Jane

Crooks. She was born in England, and came to America with her parents when an infant. Mr. and Mrs. McCaskill have eight children living: Daniel Morgan, Mary, William H., Thomas L., Ella, Esther, Cora and Kate.

Mr. McCaskill is a Republican in politics, and he and his wife are highly respected members of society.

FINIS E. DOWNING, the present Clerk of the Circuit Court, and a resident of Virginia, was born in Virginia, Cass county, Illinois, August 24, 1846. Of his life and ancestry we record the following facts:

Rev. Nathan H. Downing, his father, was the son of John Downing, son of William Downing. The father of William was a native of Scotland or Ireland, of Scotch ancestry, and was one of three brothers who came to America in early Colonial times. He settled in Virginia and there spent his last years. William Downing was born, reared and married in Virginia, and about 1784 moved to Kentucky, becoming one of the first settlers of Garrard county. For some years after his settlement there the Indians were numerous and troublesome, and the whites lived in block-houses. He cleared and developed a farm, and resided there till his death. John Downing was about eight years old when the family moved to Kentucky. He resided there till 1828, when, with his wife and ten children, he moved to Missouri and settled in Marion county. He entered a tract of Government land, twenty miles from Hannibal, erected a log cabin, and there spent the remainder of his days, dying in his frontier home on the 7th of June, in 1832. The maiden name of his wife, grandmother of the subject of our sketch, was Susanna Hall. She was born in Virginia, daughter of Randolph and Sally (Woodson) Hall. Her death occurred at Newark, Knox county, Missouri, March 4, 1861. She reared nine of her twelve children.

While John was a resident of Garrard county, Kentucky, his son Nathan H. was born there, November 11, 1811. The latter was seventeen years old when the family moved to Missouri. His youthful days were spent in assisting his father on the farm, and when he was twenty-one he entered Marion College, Marion county, Missouri, and worked his way through college. Before leaving Kentucky he was converted, and while a college student joined the Presbyterian Church. After completing his studies he was employed at various kinds of work. He subsequently bought an interest in a sawmill at Hannibal, which he operated six or seven years. In 1842 he came to Virginia. During this time he had severed his connection with the Presbyterian Church and had joined the Cumberland Presbyterian Church, and was ordained as preacher of the Salt River Presbytery. He came to Virginia to accept the pastorate over a small society here and other charges in this vicinity. He was instrumental in building a church and having a college located here. His death occurred in Virginia, November 30, 1853. On March 16, 1836, he was united in marriage with Eliza J. Head, who was born in Boone county, Missouri, July 16, 1821, a daughter of Alfred R. Head, a native of Virginia. Her grandfather, William Head, was born in England; came to America and served in the Revolutionary war. After residing in Virginia some years, he moved to Missouri long before it was a State. He erected a block-house on his place, four miles from Rocheport, which is now known as Head's Fort. He resided there till death. His son Alfred, grandfather of Mr. Downing, went to Missouri with his parents, and on their frontier farm he was reared. All his life he was engaged in agricultural pursuits. He bought a tract of land near the old home in Boone county, and lived on it till his death. His wife, *nee* Margaret Heard, a native of Garrard county, Kentucky, was a daughter of John and Jane (Stevenson) Heard, pioneers of Howard county, Missouri. Her second husband was John Arnold, and her death occurred at the home of her son, Jesse Arnold, near Los Angeles, California. The mother of Mr. Downing is now a resident of Virginia. She reared three children, viz: John C., who served in the One Hundred and Fourteenth Regiment of Illinois Volunteer Infantry, and died in the service at Memphis, in 1863; Finis E.; and Lucy J., who married Russel G. Middleton.

The subject of our sketch was seven years old when his father died. He continued to reside with his mother, attending the public schools and working on the farm. When he was twenty years old he was employed as clerk in a dry-goods store in Virginia, remaining as such five years. Then he engaged in the mercantile business on his own account in Virginia, and conducted the same until 1869. Next we find him at Butler, Missouri, where he clerked till 1874, after which he returned to Virginia, and continued clerking here till 1880. That year he was elected to his present position; has since been re-elected twice, and is now serving his third term. He has been quite an extensive dealer in real estate, both in city property and farm lands.

In 1868 Mr. Downing was united in marriage with Sue H. Payne, who was born in Fayette county, Kentucky, daughter of William B. and H. E. Payne. They have one son, Harry F., who graduated from Knox College in the class of '90, and from the law department of the University of Michigan in 1891.

Soon after Mr. Downing was elected to his present office he commenced the study of law, and in January, 1887, was admitted to the bar.

Politically, he has always affiliated with the Democratic party. He has served as a member of the City Council, and has been a member of the Senatorial and Congressional committees.

Fraternally, Mr. Downing is associated with the Virginia Lodge, No. 544, A. F. & A. M; Clark Chapter, No. 29, R. A. M.; Hospitaller Commandery, No. 31, K. T.; Saxon Lodge, No. 68, I. O. O. F., and Virginia Camp, M. W. A.

FRANCIS MUHLERT, now deceased, was born in the kingdom of Hanover, Germany, April 4, 1820. He grew up there and obtained a good German education. His father was a professor of mathematics in Hildesheim University, and as a linguist he could speak five different languages. He had three brothers and two sisters. Frederick, the eldest brother, and Ferdinand, the youngest, are professors in the University of Göthingen. Herman went to the East Indies, where he became head physician of the East India hospitals. The two sisters, Bertha and Amelia, are still in their native country, married. All are members of the Lutheran Church. His parents lived and died in their native province and he was the only one of the family to come to the United States. When twenty-eight years of age he embarked on a sailing vessel from Hamburg to New

Orleans, and after the usual tedious trip arrived in Beardstown, February, 1848 In Germany Mr. Muhlert had been overseer of a large farm, but after his arrival here he became for two years a merchant in Arenzville. About this time he was married to Paulina Winhold, born in Kurhessen, Germany, January 4, 1831. She was the daughter of William and Barbara (Weber) Winhold, who were born in the same place in Germany and came to the United States after the birth of their two children This was in 1834 They landed in Baltimore, Maryland, after a seven weeks' voyage and afterward settled near Pittsburg, Pennsylvania Seven years later they came to Illinois, and settled on a farm in Cass county, township 17, range 11, and here they lived and died, the father aged seventy-seven, and the mother eighty-two They were good, hard-working people, members of the Catholic Church

Mrs Muhlert is the eldest of a family of which seven are still living.

Mr and Mrs Muhlert purchased a good farm after their marriage in section 4, township 17, range 11, and there Mr. Muhlert spent the remainder of his life He was a well respected and favorably known citizen. His widow now lives on and owns a fine property of sixty acres of land, all highly improved. She is a noble, good, kind woman and has many friends here She attends the German Lutheran Church, as did her husband She is the mother of eleven children, one having died young The living children are: Sophia, wife of Jacob Heinen, now farmers in Kansas; William, living with his mother on the home place; Amelia, wife of William Meyer, farmer in this county; Edward is a farmer in Kansas and he married Matilda Heinen; Henry is a carpenter and lives with his mother; Herman is a farmer in Kansas and lives with his sister; Lena is the wife of John Parish, a railroad engineer at Jacksonville, Illinois; Charles, Frank and Ernest are at home

JOHN WEBB, who was for many years prominently identified with the manufacturing interests of Beardstown, Illinois, is now a resident of Bainbridge township, Schuyler county. He was born in Lancashire, England, December 9, 1813, a son of Samuel Webb, who was a native of the same shire; the paternal grandfather, John Webb, was a manufacturer of cotton goods, and operated in Lancashire, where he spent his entire life. Samuel Webb learned the trade in his father's factory, and became a skilled workman In 1817 he determined to come to America, and, as it was at that time time against the law for expert mechanics to leave Great Britain, he sailed under an assumed name. He located in Baltimore, and there secured a situation as foreman in a cotton factory three miles from the city, after a few years he took the same position in another mill, where he continued until 1827 He then went to Mercer county, Pennsylvania, and leased a mill, engaging in the manufacture of cloth He afterward returned to Baltimore, and in 1842 he came to Illinois; he was foreman of a woolen factory at Petersburg, Menard county, several years, and then purchased a farm near Mason City, on which he resided until death. He married Ellen Fletcher, a native of Manchester, England and a daughter of James Fletcher, a soldier in the British army and a participant in the battle of Waterloo: she died at Petersburg about 1848 The family consisted of ten children: Mary, Ellen, Olive, Sarah, John, James, Samuel, Nathaniel, Thomas and William. John Webb was a child of five years when he was brought to America; he attended school in Baltimore, and when he had finished his studies began to learn the machinist's trade; he served an apprenticeship of three years, and at the end of that time took charge of a shop for his employer; he held this position three years, and then entered the service of the Baltimore & Ohio Railroad at Mt. Clare; after a year he went to work in a marine foundry in Baltimore; twelve months later he entered the employ of the Savage Manufacturing Company, and remained with this firm until 1817. In that year he came to Illinois, via stage to Pittsburg, and thence by the Ohio, Mississippi and Illinois rivers. He was in poor health, and did not at once engage in business. September 12, of the same year, he started back to Baltimore with a horse and carriage making the entire journey overland, and arriving at his destination October 22. December 2, he started on the return trip, accompanied by his family; this journey was also made with a horse and carriage.

Mr. Webb remained in Springfield until 1839, and in the fall of that year went to Petersburg, where he had purchased a flour mill; in 1844 he went to Cass county, and there built the first circular-saw mill west of the Alleghany mountains; this he operated until 1848, and then went to Beardstown where he opened a machine shop and foundry. December 5, 1856, the buildings and entire plant were destroyed by fire, and the following year he rebuilt, and continued there until 1866, when he sold out. Later he built a carriage-shop which he operated a number of years. For the past nineteen years he has been interested in agriculture; he owns 500 acres of land, and is one of the directors of the First State Bank of Beardstown.

He was married in the city of Baltimore in 1834 to Miss Eliza Callaley, a native of Virginia; she died November 20, 1888. His second marriage was in November, 1890, when he was united to Maria Serrat, a native of Scioto county, Ohio, and a daughter of Peter and Mary Serrat. Five children were born of this union: John, Joseph, Samuel, William and Mary; the children are all married, and there are twenty-eight grand-children in the family.

THOMAS GAPEN, a retired farmer of Rushville township, Schuyler county, is the subject of the following biographical sketch. He was born in Clearfield county, Pennsylvania, May 3, 1833, a son of Zachariah T. Gapen, also a native of the Keystone State. The paternal grandfather, John Gapen, was descended from English ancestors; he was a farmer by occupation, and owned land in Greene county, Pennsylvania, on which he lived the last years of his life. His son, Zachariah T., was reared and married in Pennsylvania; there he resided until 1841, when he removed to Illinois; the journey was begun March 19; he floated down the Monongahela to Pittsburg, and there took a boat, going via the Ohio, Mississippi and Illinois rivers to a point in Schuyler county then known as Erie; by team he came to Rushville township. His means were very small, and he was obliged to rent the lands he cultivated; later he purchased the tract on which he had expended so much labor, and lived there until his death in 1846. His wife's maiden name was Margaret McGee; she was born in Pennsylvania and died in Rushville township, Schuyler county, Illinois, in 1851; they reared a family of eleven chil dren. Thomas Gapen was a child of eight years when his parents came to Illinois. He has since witnessed many changes in the country, wrought by the march of progress He remained under the parental roof until bereft of both father and mother. He then purchased the old homestead, and now has 320 acres, 130 acres being in an advanced state of cultivation. He now rents the land and lives a quiet life at Rushville.

Mr. Gapen was married, in 1872, to Isabelle Williamson, a daughter of L. S. and Margaret Williamson; she was born in Peoria county, Illinois. Three children have been born to them, two of whom died in infancy: Maggie is the name of the surviving child. Mr. Gapen is a man of high and honorable principles, and has the respect of the entire community.

WILLIAM T. EMMERSON of Beardstown was born in Morgan county, November 27, 1840. His father was Richard Emmerson of Yorkshire, England, who was the son of Thomas Emmerson. The latter came to the United States and settled on a large tract of Government land in Morgan county, Illinois, amounting to over a thousand acres, near St. Clair station, and went back to England, and returned four years later with his wife and children, and finally they became the most prominent people in Morgan county. Of their four children, Richard was the eldest, and was married, as was also one of his sisters, before leaving England. A nephew of his now lives on the old homestead in Morgan county. Richard Emmerson, after he came to the United States, became a farmer of Morgan county. He came to Beardstown in 1850, and died here the following December, at the age of forty. His wife survived him many years and died at the home of her son, in 1869. She and her husband were Methodists, and she was born, reared and married at Scarborough, England. Her maiden name was Elizabeth Musham. She was a mother of a family, of whom five are still living.

William Emmerson was reared in this county and has never married. He was only nine years old when his parents came to Cass county, and has always lived here, except from 1862 to 1864, when he served as a soldier in the quartermaster's department, at Rolla, Missouri, and at Helena, Arkansas. After two years' service he was honorably discharged, and returned to Cass county, where he has since lived, and made most of his fortune by his own efforts. He lives near the city precinct. He owns a well improved farm adjoining the city limits. Here he has lived since 1867. He also owns and has a controlling interest in 600 acres in other parts of the county, all well improved. He is a Democrat in politics and a public-spirited citizen. His brothers and sisters are as follows: Mary Thornley, lives in Morgan county; Ann Harris is the wife of the president of the First National Bank of Beardstown; Edward lives with his brother, and Emma Harris lives in this county.

DAVID W. ORR was born in Sumner county, Tennessee, March 17, 1826. His father was Greenberry Orr, widely known as "Berry Orr", who came to Illinois in the fall of 1828. He stopped two years in Morgan county, and then moved to Mount Sterling township, near the village, which was then in Schuyler county. He made some improvements on 160 acres of Government land, which he sold, and one year later moved to what is now section 34, Pea Ridge township. They had twelve children, born in Tennessee, and left two behind and buried one on the way. Their journey was made in one of the old-style prairie schooners, drawn by three horses, and were six weeks on the way. They arrived in Morgan county, November, 1830, and at Pea Ridge the night of the great snow storm. Their new log house had not been well chinked, and he was obliged to take up the puncheon floor to get dirt to make mud for the walls, in order to keep out the fearful storm. They reached here with very little means, but he was fortunate in getting work in wood hauling, and when his farm came into the market he was able to obtain his deed for 160 acres. It was part prairie and part timber. He built a house here, where he died, February, 1850, aged sixty-five. He left his widow with eleven children. She had been Mary Brown of Tennessee. His children all had to work hard in life, and had but very little schooling. One of their employments was to beat the hominy mortar, which Mr. Orr obtained by trading a shot gun. The nearest doctor was at Jacksonville, and they were obliged to go there over the paths that the Indians had trod.

David remained at home until after his father's death, and August 1, 1850, he was married to his first wife, Mary Jane Pells, who died a year and a half later. April 6, 1854, he was married to his present wife, Patience H. Osborn, daughter of Lewis and Amelia (Corwin) Osborn, of Ohio, where she was born, reared and educated. She was a teacher there and in Illinois before her marriage. Her father was a Baptist minister, and he died in Hancock county, while on a visit, in his eighty-fifth year. His wife died in 1875, aged seventy-one, leaving four children, Mrs. Orr being the only one now living. She is a niece of Tom Corwin, of Ohio, and is a relative of the family of General Halleck. Mr. Osborn owned the farm on which his daughter, Mrs. Orr, lives, for fifty years. He had no regular charge for some ten years prior to his death, but preached occasionally. Mr. Orr left the old homestead of his parents in 1858, and moved to Hancock county. He has lived in Kansas and Missouri, and came back to Illinois and settled on his present farm of 112 acres, in 1874. This has forty acres of timber. He has been doing general farming. Mr. and Mrs. Orr have four children: John M., now a resident of Anthony, Kansas; Mary Halleck, at home, and Lewis H., residing in Mount Sterling. Mr. and Mrs. Orr had reared this son to farm life, and hoped to have him with them on the farm during their declining years, but he preferred the life of a mechanic; hence of late years they rent out their land. He has made much money out of corn and hogs, and also breeds some horses. He has a stallion of Leviathan stock, which is turning out well.

He has served the town as Road Commissioner, and both he and and his wife are Missionary Baptists.

IRA BELL, a prominent citizen of section 28, Missouri township, Brown county, was born in this township, October 27, 1830. His grandfather, Robert Bell, was a native of Virginia, and married Jane Anderhan. These two reared a family of nine children, namely: James, Richard, Emily, Ira, John, Patsey, Sarah, Catherine, Rebecca, and they all came to Illinois, settling in Brown county, after a residence of a short period in Morgan county. The aged grandfather of our subject died in Brown county, surrounded by his children. The father of our subject was born in the State of Virginia, February 5, 1800, and was married in Morgan county, Illinois, to Elizabeth Mullen, coming to Brown county after marriage where he settled, and entering land in Missouri township. This he improved and finally became the owner of a farm of 200 acres of very fine land. He died February 13, 1882. His wife died in 1836, having been the mother of six children, namely: Mary Jane, wife of Moses Coffman, of Quincy, Illinois; Robert, of Missouri township; Ira, our subject; James died at Nashville, Tennessee, was a member of the Eighty-fourth Illinois Volunteer Infantry; Lizzie, wife of John Carter, of Kansas; John W., died in childhood.

Ira was reared in Missouri township, where he helped on the home farm until he was married, when he settled on forty acres given him by his father and erected a dwelling on it. Soon he added another forty and then removed to his present residence, where he has eighty acres of land. The land was but little improved when he took charge of it and it owes its present state of cultivation to his efforts.

Mr. Bell was married to Emiline Bates, daughter of William and Elizabeth Bates. Mrs. Bell is a native of Winchester, Scott county, Illinois, born January 1, 1837. Her father was born in Kentucky, near Lexington, and was a son of Thomas Bates. He was reared to farm life in his native State, but migrated to Indiana, where he married Elizabeth Carr, a native of that State, born in 1818. They came to Illinois in 1835, residing in Scott county until 1839, when they came to Brown county, where the father died. His wife still survives him, however, and is a very interesting lady. She and her husband had five children: Emiline, Mathew T., Francis M., Mary A. and Sarah Jane.

Mr. and Mrs. Bell have five children: Mary E., wife of Peyton R. Keith; John W., of Missouri township; George D., of same township; James A., at home: and Charles Bertie, also at home.

In politics Mr. Bell supports the principles of the Democratic party, but his time is so fully occupied that he has not been willing to accept any of the public offices, except that of School Director, which office was thrust upon him. He is a consistent member of the Christian Church and he and his intelligent wife are influential members of society in Missouri township.

MRS. MARY (PETERS) JACKSON was born in Alleghany county, Virginia, February 18, 1820, a daughter of John Peters. The father was also a Virginian, and was reared and married in his native State; he purchased land, owned slaves, and was in very good circumstances at one time; he endorsed notes for other parties, which he had to pay, and as the sums were heavy his property was swept away. He resided in Virginia until 1825, and then emigrated to Missouri, where he spent the remainder of his days. His wife's maiden name was Catherine Lane, a native of Virginia; she came from Missouri to Illinois, and here passed the last years of her life with her children in Schuyler county. Mrs. Jackson was a young child when her parents removed to Missouri, and at the age of eight years she came to Illinois with her sister and brother-in-law, Allen Persinger. The country was then sparsely settled, deer and wild turkeys were plentiful, and the privations of the pioneer were many. Mrs. Jackson lived with her sister until her marriage, September 3, 1835, when she was united to Jeremiah Jackson.

Mr. Jackson was born in North Carolina, November 27, 1807, a son of James and Mary Jackson. He emigrated to Illinois about the year 1826, and was one of the pioneers of Schuyler county. Two years after his marriage he purchased the farm now occupied by his widow, and engaged in agricultural pursuits, which he followed until his death in June, 1883.

Mrs. Jackson has reared a family of nine children: Martha J. Chitwood, died in Nebraska; Harriet Riley is a resident of Missouri; Andrew J. served in the late war in the One Hundred and Fifteenth Illinois Volunteer Infantry, and died before the war was ended; John was a member of the same regiment, and now resides in Kansas; Jesse, enlisted twice in the late war, and is now a citizen of the State of Washington; Calvin and Garrett live in Nebraska; Emrita Kokenours and Mary McCormick are residents of Schuyler county. Mrs. Jackson belongs to the Methodist Episcopal Church, of which her husband was also a consistent member. Politically he affiliated with the Democratic party.

DR. W. G. UNLAND, one of the successful physicians and surgeons of Beardstown, was born and chiefly reared in Cass county, Illinois. His people are pioneers of the county. He came of good, respectable German stock, his parents being born in Hanover. His father, Rev. Casper H. Unland, had grown up there and for some time associated in ministerial way with the old German Reformed Church. After coming to this country and settling in Cass county, Mr. Unland connected himself with the Methodist Episcopal Church and was associated with the local work as a Methodist minister. He was so engaged at the time of his death, March 8, 1889, when nearly eighty-two years of age. With the money he had brought with him he bought and improved land, erecting houses and a gristmill, which was one of the first in the county for making flour. He was a good and worthy citizen, a prominent man. At first a Whig, but in later years a stanch Republican. His wife who survived him died September 25, 1891, and was eighty years of age on the day of her burial. Her maiden name was Maria Carlas. She was a worthy woman and a good neighbor.

The parents of Dr. Unland, recognizing in their son a bright mind and a liking for books, afforded him opportunities for improvement by sending him to the best schools in Quincy, Illinois. After this he completed his classical education at the Wesleyan college at Warrenton, Missouri. The Doctor practices upon a broad and liberal scale, following no particular school. He is a graduate of two different schools: Hahnemann Medical College of Chicago, in the class of 1871 (later he spent one year at Quincy, Illinois); after that he went to Berlin, Germany, and graduated there again in medicine, and returned, remained in Quincy for a time, going thence to Lincoln, Nebraska, later to Fremont, and afterward to Pekin, Illinois, spending some time in each place. Since 1881 he has practiced in Beardstown. His genial nature and cheerful manner have made him very popular in his chosen profession. His experience and thorough education in all branches of medicine have made him very popular and his practice is a very large and paying one.

The Doctor was married here to Miss Emily Minton, of Ohio, who lived in Schuyler county for six years after coming to Illinois. Her parents died in Caldwell, Kansas, some years ago. They have a bright little daughter of eight years of age, named Ethel. They are members of the Methodist Episcopal Church.

SAMUEL MILLER, an intelligent farmer and prominent veteran of the late war, residing in Ashland, Illinois, is a native of Tazewell county, this State, where he was born July 6, 1837.

His parents were Joseph and Sarah (Kemper) Miller, the former a native of Philadelphia, Pennsylvania, while the latter was born in Kentucky, in which latter State they were married, and whence they removed in an early day to Tazewell county, Illinois. Eight children were born to this union, four sons and four daughters, only three children now surviving. The deceased are, Christiana, Eliza, Harriet, Diana, Thomas and William, of whom Harriet and Diana died in childhood and the other two daughters in mature life, being married and leaving families; William also died in mature age, leaving a wife and child. Thomas, Joseph and the subject of this sketch comprise the surviving members of this once large family. Thomas, who served two years in the army, is now married, and is a farmer in Harper county, Kansas; Joseph is a prosperous farmer, and resides in Delavan, Tazewell county; he is also married, and both have families. The father of this family died in 1843, widely mourned by the pioneers of his county. He left a large family to the care of his faithful wife, who ably performed her duty by them, finally going to her reward in 1863, while the subject of this notice was absent in the war.

Mr. Miller received a common-school education in Tazewell county, and was reared to farm life. November 8, 1858, he married Miss Nancy Nash, an intelligent lady, who was also a native of Tazewell county. She was a daughter of Andrew and Lucinda Vancil, prominent pioneers of that county, and was one of seven children, three of whom are now living. Andrew J., the oldest, died in childhood; Mrs. Miller is the second; Catharine died aged two years; George served in the Twenty-sixth Illinois Infantry, is married, and is a farmer in Harper county, Kansas; William Graham, a half-brother, was also a soldier in the late war, and resides in Tazewell county,; Sarah and John A. died in youth.

Mr. Miller enlisted in Company C, Eleventh Illinois Cavalry, at Peoria, this State, in November, 1861, serving in the regiment commanded by the noted Colonel R. G. Ingersoll. He was sworn into the United States service December 20, 1861, remaining at Camp Lyon until February 22, 1862, when he accompanied his regiment to Benton Barracks, St. Louis, Missouri, where they were armed and mounted. Thence they proceeded to Shiloh, to take part in that sanguinary engagement, under the command of General Lew Wallace. After two days at that point, they moved forward to Corinth, participating at the siege of that city. They remained there until the fall of 1862, when they were attacked by Van Dorn and Price, who sought to recapture Corinth, but the enemy were repulsed with heavy loss of killed, wounded and prisoners. The regiment next went to

Rienzi, Mississippi, where they had a severe battle, capturing the place and returning to Corinth. They afterward went to Lagrange, Tennessee, under the command of General Grant, and were cut off at Holly Springs, being obliged to return; whereupon they took boats and went to Vicksburg, participating in the siege of that city. They captured Yazoo City and went in camp between Jackson and Vicksburg, on the Black river. While lying there, the regiment and two sections of artillery were ordered on a forced march to Lexington, Tennessee, where a portion of the regiment, including Colonel Ingersoll, were taken prisoners by General Forrest's men, and were paroled on the field. At Parker's cross-roads they had a fight, in which the Union forces defeated the enemy, and pursued them into Tennesseee. Mr. Miller's regiment was with General Sherman in his march to Meridian, Mississippi, in February, 1864. Their time having expired, nearly all re-enlisted, and were mustered in at Vicksburg, December 20, 1863. They then returned to Illinois on a veteran furlough, at the expiration of which they went back to Vicksburg, where they spent the spring and summer in scouting and watching guerillas and bushwhackers. It was while here that Mr. Miller received a severe injury, by his horse falling on him, for which he now receives a pension. He was mustered out of the service, September 30, 1865, and was paid off and discharged at Springfield, October 20, 1865.

He then hastened to return to his family in Tazewell county, Illinois, where he missed one kindly face and heart-felt welcome, his mother having died during his absence. He gradually assumed his former daily routine of duties, and notwithstanding loss of dear ones, many hardships endured and misfortunes sustained, the sense of having fulfilled his duty, as he realized it, gave him renewed energy for the prosecution of life's tasks.

He and his worthy wife are the parents of six children, all of whom are now married and at the head of families. Thomas is a farmer near Delavan, Illinois; Alpheus lives in Ashland; Clara, now Mrs. Thompson, lives in Virginia, this State; Ida, married Ralph Nixon, a superintendent of coal mines, and resides in Wesley City,, near Peoria, this State; Martha, now Mrs. Smith, lives at her parents' home; Della married Mr. Perrin, and resides in Virginia, Illinois;

Mr. Miller is a stanch Republican in politics, and is a prominent member of Downing Post, No. 321, Virginia, Illinois. His worthy wife is an earnest and useful member of the Baptist Church, to the support of which they both contribute.

An honest and industrious citizen, a brave and efficient soldier, and devoted husband and father, he deserves the high esteem in which he is universally held.

DANIEL LYONS, M. D., an eminent physician and surgeon, of Ashland, Illinois, was born in La Salle, of the same State, June 16, 1848. His parents were Daniel and Mary (Morris) Lyons, both natives of Ireland, who came to America in 1832, soon after their marriage. His father was a railroad contractor, which business he followed during his life in this country. The first death which the family was called upon to mourn was that of the devoted wife and mother, who expired in Arkansas, in 1861, greatly lamented by her associates and friends. The father survived his faithful companion fifteen years, dying in Brierfield, Alabama, in 1876.

He was a man of the highest integrity, extremely kind-hearted and benevolent, and was very popular among his acquaintances. This worthy couple had six children: Lawrence, Michael, Daniel, David, Mary and Katie. All but two of these are now deceased, the subject of this sketch and a brother David, who is engaged in mining at Crystal, Colorado.

Dr. Lyons received his elementary education in the public schools of La Salle county, where his boyhood and early manhood were spent. After attaining his majority, he was engaged for about seven years in civil engineering. During the Rebellion, he was for three years in the Quartermaster's Department, in St. Louis. In 1878, he commenced the study of Eclectic medicine, in the American Medical College, St. Louis, taking four courses, and continuing his studies until 1883. While pursuing his studies, he spent most of his time in the city hospitals of St. Louis, gaining practical experience in his chosen work. In 1883, on graduating in St. Louis, he came to Ashland, where he commenced the practice of his profession. He has steadily grown in favor until he now does a large and lucrative business, being universally regarded as thoroughly skilled in his profession, conscientious and careful.

He was married in St. Louis, in 1869, to Miss Johanna Connelly, an estimable lady, and a native of Canada. Her parents were James and Catharine Connelly, and she was one of seven children, three sons and four daughters. Dr. and Mrs. Lyons have two children: Deloraine J., now twenty-two years of age, is unmarried, and is a telegraph operator in Colorado; Gertrude, now thirteen years old, is at home and in school.

The Doctor is Democratic in his political affiliations, on which ticket he was elected to the position of Coroner of Cass county, serving in that capacity with acknowledged ability.

Socially, he is a member of the M. W. of A., and is prominently associated with the Masonic order, which latter society he joined in St. Louis.

These are a few of the most important facts of a busy and useful life, which has been spent in the amelioration of human suffering, and in promoting the happiness and welfare of his fellow beings.

WILLIAM FREESEN, now deceased, having died near Oxville, Scott county, Illinois, in 1884. He was fifty-four years of age, being born in the Rhine province, Prussia, Germany, near the river Rhine, in November 1829. He came of German parents, who lived and died in Germany. He was the only member of his family to come to this country, which he did when he was twenty-three years of age, setting out from Antwerp, in 1852, for the United States in a sailing vessel. He landed in New Orleans after a seven weeks' voyage. He came to Beardstown, and after the first year became a farmer, purchasing land in Cass county, where he became a successful farmer. He owned 200 acres of good land in Cass county, and 240 acres in Scott, at the time of his death. His widow still owns the Cass county farm. Mr. Freesen was a good, worthy citizen, a member of the Lutheran Church, and a stanch Democrat.

He was married after the first year in this county, in Beardstown township, to Elizabeth Stauttler, who proved herself a most devoted wife, and a woman in every way worthy of the good husband she had. She now enjoys the property she helped her husband accumulate. She was born in the same place as her husband March 9, 1838, and was reared and educated by her German parents, William and Margaret (Speaker) Stanttler. The former died in Germany, when a young man, and his daughter, Mrs. Freesen, was only eighteen years old. Her mother is yet living in Beardstown, and is eighty years old, and is now the wife of F. W. Friday, and both old people have been prominent members all their lives, of the Lutheran Church.

Mrs. Freesen came to America with her mother and stepfather, on the same vessel as Mr. Freesen. She is the mother of twelve children, four of whom are deceased: Margaret, Bell, Anna and Hannah, all died young. The living ones are: William, now a farmer in Scott county, married to Matilda Baully; George Garrett, a farmer in Scott county; Fred, a resident of St. Louis; Katie, at home, and she and her sister Maggie, also at home, dressmakers; Henry is at home, as are also Lewis and Edward. Mrs. Freesen and all the children are members of the Lutheran Church.

THEOPHILUS C. LAUNER, a large and prosperous farmer, lives on sections 6 and 7, township 17, range 11, where he owns 270 acres of well-improved land, with good farm buildings. He also owns 320 acres, almost all well improved. Besides this he owns a fine lot of timber land amounting to 182 acres, and eighty acres draining land in section 20. He came to the county a poor young man, but has since accumulated much valuable property. He has always lived in Cass county, except a year in Morgan county. He began here as a farmer on his own account, first purchasing forty acres, which he sold and with the proceeds bought 120 acres, and later sold that and increased his sales until he now owns a fine property, all earned by his own efforts.

He was born in Buffalo, New York, January 30, 1838, and was yet a very young child when his parents removed to Philadelphia, Pennsylvania. Two years later they came to Cass county, which he has since made his home, and where he has been a prominent farmer. His father, Rev. Frederic G. Launer, was a native of Berne, Switzerland, born February 18, 1793. He was very highly educated, receiving instruction in his native country and other places, including London. He was educated as a Lutheran minister, and became master of five languages, being a man of quick perception and powerful intellect. He came to America in 1832, and first held a professorship in a college in Buffalo, New York, and later at Philadelphia, also preaching in both places. He afterward came to Beardstown and built up the first Lutheran Church of the place, and was also at Havana and Pekin, Illinois. He was widely and well known throughout the State as a preacher, and had a great deal of influence in that capacity. He was the pioneer minister in this part of the State, and did a great deal of good. He died in Beardstown, September 28, 1867. He was then seventy-four years, six months and ten days old. He worked hard all his life for his church, and made a host of friends. He was a missionary in this State, after filling that position in Africa for three years. His wife, Lydia, was born November 23, 1811, and died several years after him, in Beardstown, January 1, 1873. She was then over sixty years of age, being born in Canton Peal, Switzerland, where she lived until her marriage. She was a devoted wife and mother, and a good Christian woman. She was a daughter of General Marthe, and a grandchild of General David Marthe, Commander-in-Chief of the army of Napoleon the Great, during the time that general was frozen out of Russia, near Moscow. Of seven children three are now deceased. Charles served five years in the Union army; Peter was a brave and efficient soldier in the Mexican war; Theodore is now living in Morgan county, this State; and Mary resides in Beardstown.

Our subject was married in this county, March 10, 1863, to Josephine Winhold, born near Pittsburg, Pennsylvania, September 12, 1838, coming to Cass county with her parents. Mr. and Mrs. Launer are members of the Lutheran Church, and are prominent, good people. Mr. Launer has held almost all the local offices. He is a Republican in politics, as are his sons. They are the parents of six children: Bertha, wife of Prof. John Hagener, a teacher of the county; Ida, wife of John Kloker, farmer of this county; Rose, Cora, Richard and Robert are all at home, and all the children are intelligent, well educated, a credit to the family, society and the State.

FERDINAND WINHOLD, a very prosperous German farmer, living on section 8 of township 18, range 11, was born in Pennsylvania, near Pittsburg, in 1839. He is the son of William Winhold, born in Hesse-Darmstadt, of Hessian parents, who, after all their children were born and a good part of them married, including the son, William, came to the United States in 1833. They set sail from Bremen, Hanover, and after a voyage of fifty-seven days landed in Baltimore, Maryland, later settling in Pennsylvania, near Pittsburg, where the father of William died, an old man. Later, William, who was the only child who came with his parents to America, came with his mother and own family to Illinois, settling in 1840 on a new farm in township 18, range 11. Here the mother of William spent her last years and died when an old woman. William began to make a home for his wife and children. He first bought forty acres, and added to it from time to time, improving it all the while until it was one of the finest farms in the county. He died in 1886, when nearly seventy-eight years old. He was a good citizen, a successful farmer and a stanch Republican. He held to no church, although his parents were Catholics. His wife is now deceased, dying on the old farm in 1887, when quite an old woman. She was born, reared and married in Hesse-Darmstadt, Germany, coming of good old stock. She was the good mother of seven children, five of whom are married and all are living in Cass county.

Ferdinand is the fifth child of the family and was reared in this county, being but eighteen months old when brought to Illinois by his parents in 1840. He now owns 230 acres of land, all well improved, which he has owned for some years, having begun farming for himself when twenty-three. He had but few opportunities for education, but made the most of what he had, and has made up for lack of education in common sense and intelligence.

He was married in this county to Bertha Philippi, born near where she now lives in 1847. She was reared and educated in this county, and is one of a large family. (For history of same see biography of parents.) Mr. and Mrs. Winhold are prominent people of their county. Mr. Winhold is a Republican, and has held local offices. He and his wife are the parents of nine children, all yet at home: Rudolph F., Julius P., William P., Lena B., Charles H., Eugene S., Paul P., Bodo H. and Hugo V. Mr. and Mrs Winhold deserve their present prosperity, as they have been hard workers all their lives.

LEWIS ZIMMER, Jr., a practical general farmer, of section 21, township 18, range 11, was born on his present farm March 19, 1861. He has since lived on the farm and was educated in Bluff Springs precinct. He lived with his parents until after he became of age, and since that time he has had control of the home farm, which he has run successfully. He is the son of Lewis Zimmer, a native of Prussia, Germany, and came of German ancestry. He was reared a farmer and while yet a young man he came all alone to America and settled in Cass county. This was in the '40s. He later began to buy land and finally accumulated the large and substantial farm he now owns. Here Mr. Zimmer, Sr., and his wife lived until some six years ago, when they retired to Beardstown, and are spending their last days quietly, leaving the farm in the charge of Lewis. Mr. Zimmer, Sr., married his wife in this county, her name being Catharine Keil, a native of Germany, who came to America when young. She has proven herself a good wife and mother. Mr. and Mrs. Zimmer are members of the German Lutheran Church of Beardstown. Mr. Zimmer is a Democrat.

Our subject is the second child and only son, his only sister being Maggie, wife of Theo. Krohe, an agricultural dealer in Beardstown. The farm consists of 200 acres, 100 of which he owns himself. It is in fine condition.

Lewis was married in this county, to Matilda Krohe, born in this county, February 1, 1862, and was reared and educated in her native county. She is the daughter of August and Mary Krohe, who now live in Beardstown and are retired farmers, owning a large improved farm in township 18, range 11. Mr. and Mrs. Krohe are both natives of Germany, but have lived in Cass county since their marriage. They are Lutherans. Mr. and Mrs. Zimmer are members of the Lutheran Church, and Mr. Zimmer is a Democrat. They have three children: Calvin L. P., Clara M. C. and Theodore E. Both Mr. Zimmer and his wife are highly respected, and have hosts of friends in the county, where they are well known as honest, hard-working people.

HON. JESSE DARNELL, deceased, a resident of Rushville township, and one of the oldest settlers of the county, is worthy of representation in this history. He was born eight miles from Wooster, Wayne county, Ohio, October 4, 1811, a son of Henry Darnell, a native of West Virginia. The father was a volunteer in the Colonial army, participated in the battle of Yorktown, and was present at the surrender of Lord Cornwallis. About the year 1800, with his own and nine other families, he emigrated to the Northwest Territory, being among the earliest settlers of Ohio. He first located in the Scioto valley, but as it was sickly there, he went to Wayne county; here he secured a tract of land which was part timber and part prairie. For several years there were no other settlers in that section. Indians were numerous and often hostile. The colony built a block-house with a stockade around it, and it was within these walls that our subject was born. The father improved a fine farm there, on which he resided until his death in 1847. His wife's maiden name was Elizabeth Lee, also a native of Virginia; she died in 1818.

Jesse Darnell, whose name heads this notice, was reared in his native State, where his educational opportunities were limited to the subscription schools, which were taught in private houses. There were no railroads or canals: consequently no market towns. The people lived upon the products of their own land and wild game, which was plentiful. The mother carded, spun and wove all the cloth used by the family.

At the age of fifteen years our subject went from the home which had sheltered his childhood, out into the world to begin life for himself. He remained in Ohio until 1833, and then came to Illinois via the Ohio and Mississippi rivers, landing at Oquawka, where he remained about a year, after which he came to Schuyler county. There were few settlers in the county, and agriculture was carried on in a most primitive fashion. He settled at Frederick and engaged quite extensively in the manufacture of fanning-mills, which he continued for seven or eight years, and then turned his attention to farming. He lived in Frederick township until 1886, at which time he removed to a farm he had purchased several years before; this is a tract of 160 acres, the greater portion of which is well improved; he also owned another farm of 200 acres in Frederick township.

Mr. Darnell was married in April, 1841, to Louisa Utter, a native of Illinois and a daughter of Lyman and Martha Utter, natives of the State of New York and pioneers of Schuyler county, and located on a farm east of Pleasant View. His wife died in 1847, but he never married again. Two sons and one daughter survive him: John Monroe, James K. Polk and Mrs. H. A. Nelson, the latter living in Santa Barbara county, California. His son James is a resident of Breckinridge, Colorado, having located in that State twenty-two years ago.

Mr. Darnell was a sincere Democrat, and had been from early youth. The principles laid down by Jefferson were thoroughly instilled into his very being, and he was always found allied with the cause he believed to be right. In 1848 he represented this county in the Legislature, and for eight years he was Supervisor from Frederick township, filling the position of chairman of the board for several years. He was a prominent member of Rushville Lodge, No. 9, A. F. & A. M., to which he had belonged for nearly half a century. He was a man of sterling integrity, esteemed and respected by all who knew him.

GEORGE H. WIER of Birmingham township, was born here September 16, 1841. He is the son of Samuel and Sarah (Clampet) Wier. Mr. Samuel Wier is a native of North Carolina, a farmer, and came to Illinois in the fall of 1835 and settled where the subject now lives, and bought eighty acres and later purchased more, leaving 160 acres at his death. He made the trip with his wife and child, with one horse and wagon. He first built a log house 16 x 18 feet and remained in it until his present house was built in 1869. In politics he was an old-line Whig and was a minister of the

Methodist Episcopal Church. He continued preaching occasionally until his death in 1865. His wife was born in North Carolina and died where our subject now lives, in middle life.

George Wier remained home until his marriage, when he rented part of his father's farm and after the latter's death he bought the land and now owns 365 acres. He is a thoroughly self-made man, politically a Republican and a highly valued church member for eighteen years.

He was married for the first time in 1863, to Martha Wells, who died a year later, leaving one child which also died. In 1870 he was again married, to Mary McPherson. She was a native of Morgan county, Illinois, born in 1847, daughter of Benjamin F. and Harriet (Thompson) McPherson. Her father is still living, but her mother died here, aged forty-five. They were pioneers of Illinois.

Mr. Wier has five children, namely; Harriet L., William A., Edwin R., Samuel B., and Harrison R.

GEORGE W. ERWIN, one of the most prominent farmers of Littleton township, Schuyler county, Illinois, was born in Constable, Franklin county, Ohio, December 1, 1818. His parents were Cornelius M. and Lucinda (Furman) Erwin. His father was born in Rutland county, Vermont, and died in Ohio, aged fifty years. (See sketch of L. D. Erwin.)

Our subject was reared and educated in Ohio, living at home until his father's death, when in June, 1838, he came to Illinois, where he walked all through the lead mines, looking for work, and finally located in Rushville, working by the month on a farm. He continued in this capacity until the year 1847, when he enlisted in Captain Dunlap's company and served for a year and a half in the Mexican war. At the end of this time, he returned to Rushville, and soon after married Agnes Corrie, on New Year's Day, 1851. She was born in Orange county, Illinois, and was a daughter of John Corrie, a substantial farmer of the State. After his marriage, our subject bought a farm of 160 acres of partly improved land, on which he built in 1855, the home in which he still resides, which is a substantial pile, suggestive of comfort and convenience. He has added large barns and other buildings for his grain and stock, and has his land under a high state of cultivation, being devoted to mixed farming. His former farm is worked by his son-in-law, Mr. Bosworth, a highly esteemed young man and intelligent farmer.

Mr. and Mrs. Erwin have had ten children, four of whom are now living, viz.: Ellen A., wife of Richard R. Bosworth, has five children, three boys and two girls; Cornelius M., married Sara B. Taylor, and they have four children; Frank C. married Mary Cordell; William S. lives in Montana. He has had his children carefully educated in the schools of the vicinity, and all are intelligent members of the communities in which they live.

Mr. Erwin had the misfortune to lose his wife, after thirty-four years of happy wedded life. She died May 10, 1885, aged fifty-five years, mourned by her family and a large circle of friends. She was a lady of intelligence and many charms of person and character, a faithful wife and fond mother, and sympathetic friend.

Our subject is a member of the Democratic party, having cast his first vote for Martin Van Buren, since when he has voted the straight Democratic ticket. His constituents have honored him by an election to the office of collector of the township, in which capacity he was the first to serve after its organization He has also been a school trustee and director for many years, which position he has filled with ability and to the general satisfaction of the community.

He is a consistent member of the Methodist Episcopal Church, to the support of which he has always liberally contributed

Of superior ability, energetic and progressive, and of high morality and integrity, Mr. Erwin enjoys the esteem of his fellow-citizens to an unusual degree.

DE WITT CLINTON JOHNSTON, deceased, was born in Clermont county, Ohio, April 2, 1824 His father, James T. Johnston, was born at Washington, Pennsylvania and his father and grandfather lived in Scotland, and on coming to America settled in New Jersey They removed to Pennsylvania and there engaged in farming until they died

The father of the subject was a graduate of Jefferson College and became a practicing physician in Clermont county, Ohio, but he spent his last days at New Richmond. His wife was a Mary Whetstone, of Hamilton county, Ohio. She died in the same town as her husband.

The subject of this sketch received his education at the public schools of New Richmond, and from private tutors, and graduated from the same college as his father, in the year 1843. He commenced the study of law at Batavia, Ohio, and was admitted to the bar at Hillsborough, Ohio, and practiced there till 1850, when he removed to New Richmond, Ohio, an opened an office and continued there until 1853, when he came to Rushville and practiced there until January 28, 1866.

He married, in 1845, a lady whose maiden name was Margaret Bauer, a native of Bavaria, Germany. Her grandfather had lived in the same country all his life, and so had her father until 1832, when he resolved to try his fortune in the new world, so with his family he set sail from Havre de Grace in the fall of the same year His father, Conrad Bauer, also came over to America in the same ship The trip was made in thirty-three days From New York, where they landed, the older man went to Ohio by the way of Pennsylvania, making the journey by the canal and stage to Pittsburg, and then down the Ohio river. He located in Brown county, and bought a farm and engaged in tilling the soil until his death

Mrs. Johnston's father was accompanied by his wife and two children, and he located in the same county as his father, bought a farm, and resided there until 1856, when he sold out and came to Illinois, and located in Rushville township. Here he also bought a farm, on section 25, and engaged in agricultural pursuits until his death.

The maiden name of the mother of Mrs. Johnston was Margaret Heigh. She was born in the same locality as her husband, and spent the last years of her life on the home farm

Mrs Johnston continued to reside in Rushville for some time after her husband's death, but she now occupies her father's old homestead in Rushville township. She has two sons living, James B and Harold W The former is a graduate of the Chicago University and is a practicing attorney. The second son is a graduate of the Illinois College, Jacksonville, where he is professor of Latin. He is also an author, his first work is entitled "Select Orations and Letters of Cicero."

Mr. and Mrs. Johnston were earnest members of the Episcopal Church. Mr. Johnson was a stanch supporter of the principles of the Democratic party, of which he was a member. He was an able lawyer and a fine citizen. His record is one of which his family and friends may justly be proud, not only in his capacity as County Judge, but in the occupations of daily life. Having many advantages which other early settlers did not have, he became well-known throughout the State as a legal authority, as well as a man of literary attainments.

FRANK T. RITCHEY, a farmer and resident of Rushville township, was born in what is now Buena Vista township, Schuyler county, Illinois, September 19, 1844, being the only son of George S. and Lucinda Ritchey. His father was born in Dayton, Ohio, and lived there until 1831, when he emigrated to Schuyler county, having nothing but a large stock of health and youthful spirits upon which to draw for a livelihood. Energy and industry spurred him on and he continued a hard-working man, living to see himself possessed of a good competence.

In 1831 neighbors were far apart in old Schuyler, deer being far more numerous than human beings. When he married Lucinda Walker, of Kentucky, he took her home to a log cabin, where the subject of this sketch was born. The year following this latter event Mr. Ritchey removed with his family to section 6, Rushville township, upon land he had previously purchased, and, except two years spent in California, he resided there until his death. His wife also died on the old home farm. Mr. Ritchey, Sr., was mourned as a good farmer, a kind neighbor and a good friend.

Frank Ritchey received his early education at the district school, the first one being held in a log house with furniture of the most primitive kind, the benches being mere slabs. Later he took advanced steps in the public schools of Rushville, where he was fitted as a teacher. He engaged in teaching and farming until 1872, when he went to Crawford county, Kansas, and there taught school for two terms, after which he returned to Illinois, and has resided ever since, in Rushville, where he now owns a nice farm of 255 acres and is engaged in general farming and stock-raising.

He was married in 1876, to Catharine F. Sands, of Rushville township, daughter of Robert and Frances Nall Sands (see sketch of R. E Sands). Four children have blessed this union, namely: Lora E., Lucinda F., George F. and Robert.

Mr. and Mrs. Ritchey are consistent members of the Christian Church. He is an active member of the Republican party, and, as all good citizens should do, takes a deep interest in all that concerns the well being of his county, State and the Union.

HON. J. M. HAMBAUGH.—The subject of this brief sketch is one of the men of whom the State of Illinois is proud. His career in the last Legislature, as a Representative from the Thirty-sixth Senatorial District, has made a national reputation for him as a champion of the rights and privileges of apiarists.

This gentleman was born in Versailles township, Brown county, Illinois, July 16, 1846, hence he is over forty-five years of age His father, Stephen D Hambaugh, emigrated from Kentucky, and pre-empted the farm now occupied as a homestead by his son, in the year 1828, being one of the very first settlers of this section of the country Stephen was the son of Henry, a native of Louisiana, born in 1771, who married Rebecca Morris. Henry was the son of John, a native of Germany, married to a lady of Detroit, Michigan, having come to this country when quite a young man. He and his wife died in Louisiana, leaving quite a family. Stephen was one of ten children, of whom he was the third He was reared to farm life, receiving a fair schooling, and married Elmina Stone, daughter of John and Abigail (Crook) Stone, natives of New Hampshire and Vermont, respectively The mother of our subject was born in 1814, and was taken to Kentucky by her parents when only five years old, and is the last surviving member of her father's large family of ten children, who were reared to maturity and became the heads of families The grandfather of our subject came to Illinois in 1824, with his wife and three children, leaving one son behind He had no property, but settled first at Edwardsville, Illinois, in the fall of 1824, and in the spring of 1828 he came to the present home of our subject Here he moved his family into a small log cabin, which his brother had built. The brother had preceded him and built this cabin on eighty acres of land. They made the journey to their new home in a "prairie schooner," drawn by four horses The company that made the trip was composed of Mr. and Mrs. Henry Hambaugh and their children,—John P, Stephen D, Philip G, and Francis, the only living daughter, who became the wife of Governor Ford, of this State S. D. Hambaugh, father of J M Hambaugh, died November 4, 1877 J P Hambaugh, brother of S. D. Hambaugh, a bachelor who had always made his home in the family of S. D, died September 3, 1886, leaving his nephew, J M Hambaugh, executor of his estate, and in his will bequeathed $1,000 to be expended on a monument to the Hambaugh family, and an iron fence around the cemetery; and Mr. Hambaugh had a most unique model of the old pioneer log cabin erected on the bluff in Hambaugh cemetery near the old home, which has been visited by thousands of people and admired by all who have seen it.

At the time the Hambaugh family made their advent into Illinois there was not a railroad in the State, and but few in the United States. The father of our subject was united in marriage to Miss Elmina Stone on the eve of the great snow-storm, December 28, 1830, so historical and memorable in the minds of old settlers, the snow falling to a depth of four feet on a level, and remaining on the ground until the 1st of April.

Nestling among the trees of the forest, where scarcely a ray of sunshine could penetrate, Mr. Hambaugh had built his hut, which was in keeping with its rude surroundings, and it was to this rude structure that Mr. Hambaugh introduced his bride, to share his lot in the miseries and pleasures coincident with a truly pioneer life They were the advance guards of the on-coming tide of civilization With nerves of steel they endured privations and sufferings and made possible the deeds of to-day

It was during the first winter of his pioneer experience that Mr. Hambaugh obtained a few colonies of bees from hollow trees, by felling them, and sawing above and below the colony, covering one end with boards and mounting them upon platforms prepared for that purpose, then transporting them to his cabin on a sled In this way the first bees were obtained, from which he increased their numbers year by year, until they reached as many as fifty or sixty colonies. The hive used was very primitive, and the method of taking the honey was with the brimstone match; but, strange as this may seem, wax and honey was quite a financial factor with the early pioneers, and many a hearthstone has been made happy by the timely exchange of this product for linsey, jeans and other necessities for home comforts; and one settler states that he paid for eighty acres of land with the money obtained from honey and wax

Mr. and Mrs. Hambaugh had seven children born to them, four of whom are still living, Joseph M. being the youngest; and it has fallen to his lot to remain on the old homestead to look after the fences and the bees Having inherited a passionate fondness for this wonderful little insect, like his father, he declares that the old homestead will never be deprived of their merry hum; but it was not until 1881 that he began to study modern methods, and prepare for a new era in bee culture. Up to that time he had never seen the inside of a bee-book. He had been taught to produce honey in small boxes, and believed it to be the *ne plus ultra* of all other methods, when a little circumstance led him to an investigation, which was a ray of light cast upon a new field of labor, grand and beautiful beyond discription. It was in the fall of 1881 that, chancing to step into the grocery house of J A Givens, in Mount Sterling, he discovered a huge pyramid of beautiful white clover honey put up in two and three pound packages, and upon inquiry he found that they had been produced by a citizen of his own county, by the name of Dunbar. He sought out Mr. Dunbar and found out that to be a successful honey-producer one must study the art About this time he read A I. Root's advertisement in an agricultural paper and sent for a catalogue of his bee supplies, and he was soon in possession of Cook's Manual of the Apiary, Dzierzon's Rational Beekeeping and many other works of note, and it was after a careful persual of these works that he ventured on modern improved methods. Did not space forbid we might follow Mr. Hambaugh through all his evolutions, but suffice to say that he prefers the Dadant hive for extracting purposes; and, as his success as a honey-producer is well known throughout the county, his opinion is valuable

He was married October 26, 1869, to Miss Josephine Shamp, of Edina, Knox county, Missouri, daughter of H S. Shamp, who gladdened his home but the short space of two and a half years, when she crossed the dark valley, leaving to him an infant but six hours old This sorrowful experience in Mr Hambaugh's life came near turning his brain, and he says that only those who pass through a similar experience can ever understand the intensity of the heartache and laceration of the soul such a disaster occasions Mr Hambaugh was married for the second time, February 29, 1879, to Miss Frances Cullinan, of Mount Sterling, daughter of William and Ann (Brown) Cullinan She is the mother of five children, all living. but one infant The living ones are. Elmina, aged twelve; Anna M, aged nine years; William James, aged six years, Stephen D., aged two years

Mr. Hambaugh has borne his share of the minor township offices, and was elected to the Legislature, November, 1890. He has pursued mixed farming and stock-raising, in addition to honey production, and has always been prominent in bee societies all over the State, and is a member of the North American Beekeepers' Association, the Beekeepers' Union, and is President of the Illinois State Beekeepers' Association.

Our subject is a devout Catholic in religion. In politics he has maintained the principles of the Democratic party, is strictly temperate, and an ardent advocate of the abolishment of the American saloon.

ROBERT E. SANDS, a highly respected citizen of Rushville, Illinois, was born in Rushville township, Schuyler county, Illinois, April 15, 1849, a son of Robert R. Sands, who was born in Washington, District of Columbia. The paternal grandfather of our subject, Robert Sands, was a native of Ireland, of Scotch ancestry; upon coming to to the United States he located in the capital city, where he resided several years. In 1831 he removed to Schuyler county, Illinois, and was one of the pioneers of Rushville township; he entered a tract of Government land on section 8, improved the place, and occupied it until his death. Robert R. Sands was a child of eight years when his parents come to Illinois; at that time there were few settlers, and Rushville was but a hamlet; deer, wild turkeys and other game were plentiful; there were no railroads and for many years the river towns were the market places. The following incident related by Mr. Sands is worthy of record: One season his father raised about 1,000 bushels of corn; he shelled it in a machine operated by hand, teamed it to Frederick, and sold it for fifteen cents a bushel! Robert R. Sands inherited land from his father which he occupied until his death. His wife, whose maiden name was Frances Nall, was a native of Kentucky, and a daughter of Gabriel Nall, also a Kentuckian by birth, and a pioneer of Schuyler county; she died on the home farm in April, 1870.

Robert E. Sands was reared and educated in his native town, and was never separated from his parents until the hand of death was laid upon them. He then purchased the interest of the other heirs in the homestead, and was actively engaged in agricultural pursuits until March 14, 1892, when he sold the farm, and removed to Rushville.

Mr. Sands was united in marriage, in 1873, to Sarah Montooth, a native of Pittsburg, Pennsylvania. They are the parents of three children: Walter E., Kate Alice and Mary Stella. Mr. and Mrs. Sands are worthy and consistent members of the Methodist Episcopal Church. Politically he supports the issues of the Republican party.

JOHN F. SNYDER, a progressive and enterprising agriculturist of Littleton township, is a native son of Illinois, born at Rushville, Schuyler county, November 20, 1849, a son of William and Jane (Little) Snyder; the father was born in Lancaster county, Pennsylvania, April 23, 1803, and was a cabinetmaker by trade; he penetrated the frontier in 1835, and settled at Rushville, where he followed his trade until removing to Littleton township in 1854; here he engaged in farming in connection with his other vocation. His father, Henry Snyder, was also a native of the Keystone State, but emigrated to the West and died in Rushville township at the age of sixty-seven, October 23, 1835 William Snyder died on the farm now occupied by his son John F., September 22, 1875, at the age of seventy-three years, his wife was a Pennsylvanian by by birth, and now deceased. They reared a family of seven children, five of whom are now living, viz . John F . who lived upon his father's farm until the death of the latter; Mrs M. A Davidson, Mrs Ellen De Witt Mrs. Susan Dooley, and William. James Little, the maternal grandfather of John F Snyder, departed this life October 19, 1855, aged seventy-one years, and his wife September 10, 1864, in the sixty-fourth year of her age

The subject of this sketch was first married October 2, 1873, to Miss Frances Park, who was born, reared, and died in this county, she was a daughter of Washington and Maria Park, natives of Ohio, who were among the early settlers of this county; the parents are deceased. Mr. Snyder's second marriage was May 12, 1880, when he was united to Miss Brunette Spragg; she was born in Lewis county, Kentucky, August 25, 1858. Five children have been born of this union, three of whom are now living: Mary J. dates her birth March 12, 1881; Martha E. was born September 10, 1883, and died April 16, 1889; William H., born December 23, 1885, died September 16, 1887; John L. was born December 8, 1889, and Charles Beam, July 26, 1892 Mrs Snyder's parents are William P. and Mary B. (Scott) Spragg, natives of Ohio and Kentucky, respectively; they are now residents of Nashville, Tennessee William P Spragg was born November 22, 1837, in Fairfield county, Ohio His father, N. B. Spragg, was born in the State of Pennsylvania, October 1, 1797. His wife, Rhoda Green, was born in Fairfield county, Ohio, July, 1795, the second white child born in that county. Mary B. Spragg, Mrs. Snyder's mother, was born in Greenup county, Kentucky, November 4, 1835, and married William P Spragg, December 2, 1855. Her father, Jacob Scott, was born in the State of North Carolina, January 15, 1798, and his wife, *nee* Catherine Thompson, was born in Lewis county, Kentucky, June 24, 1802.

Mr Snyder settled on his father's farm after his marriage, purchasing fifty-four acres of land; as his means increased, he made additional investments, and now owns 210 acres, all in a high state of cultivation He carried on his agricultural pursuits with great intelligence and energy, and has met with merited success; he gives especial attention to the raising of live-stock, and has some very fine specimens on his place

Politically our worthy subject adheres to the principles of the Republican party, as did his father before him He has filled some of the local offices, and has discharged the duties intrusted to him with a zeal and ability that have won the confidence of the community. He and his wife are members of the Methodist Episcopal Church, and are both active workers in the cause of the Master. His father was also a zealous churchman, and for many years, was a Class-leader on the frontier. Mr Snyder belongs to Littleton Lodge, No. 766, A. F & A M. He was not a soldier in the late war, but his brother William was in the service two years, in Company A, Tenth Missouri Volunteer Infantry, and was wounded in the battle of Corinth.

Concerning Mrs. Jane Snyder, deceased, the mother of the subject of the foregoing sketch, we are furnished with the following additional items: She was a daughter of Mr. James and Mrs. Rebecca Little, and was born in Columbia, Lancaster county, Pennsylvania, on the 26th day of July, 1810. On April 2, 1833, she was united in marriage with Mr. George Carson, who survived this marriage but fifty-seven days, leaving a young bride to mourn his untimely death. After a widowhood of nearly two years, she married Mr. William Snyder, on May 20, 1835, and soon after they removed to Illinois, first to Jacksonville, and then to Rushville, where they resided till 1854, when they removed to Littleton. Mr. Snyder died in September, 1875, and Mrs. Snyder remained on the farm with her son, John F., till, within the last few years, she has been making her home with her daughter, first at Augusta, and then at Plymouth, spending some time every year with her son at the old home.

She had returned but a short time to her home, from an extended visit with her son, when she was stricken down with a violent attack of flux, and notwithstanding all that physicians could do, with the loving care and nursing of children and friends, she calmly departed out of this life on Friday, September 23, 1892, after only five days' illness, in the eighty-third year of her age.

Mrs. Snyder was converted and united with the Methodist Episcopal Church, when she was but fifteen years old, and she held fast the beginning of her confidence firm unto the end.

MRS. MARGARET FRANCIS BOWE, widow of Thomas Bowe, was born July 27, 1857. Her parents were Lawrence and Mary (Adams) Costello, both natives of the Emerald Isle, the father having been born in Westmeath Athlone, Ireland, in 1822. In 1844, at the age of twenty-two years, he emigrated to America, landing in New York, where he remained for a short time, going thence to Pennsylvania. He afterward came West to Mt. Sterling, Illinois, where he was married, October 11, 1856. The worthy parents still reside on their farm, two and one-half miles west of Mt. Sterling. They first bought eighty acres and lived for several years in a small log house: later they built the pleasant home they now occupy. It is a seven-room, two-story house. Soon afterward, they added a large barn to their frame buildings. They began life with but little means, but are now well-to-do farmers. They buried an infant son and daughter, also a son, James, born July 23, 1864, died January 22, 1880, in his sixteenth year; and Thomas, born April 6, 1860, died April 3, 1880; both thus dying within three months of each other. Another son, Walter, was injured by a runaway, and died at the age of thirty-two, in Woodland Park, Colorado, where he had gone in search of health. The living members of the family are, Mrs. Bowe; John, First Sergeant, Second Artillery, in the regular army, stationed at Fort Riley. He began as a teamster when eighteen, but volunteered at twenty-one, and was made Post Librarian, and has been regularly promoted until he is now First Sergeant. This young man is quite an adventurer, having started out on his life of adventures at the age of twelve, without the knowledge of his parents, who thought for a long while that he was dead, and were rejoiced to hear from him, some four years later, that he was safe and well. The next child was Catherine H., who was married to Elmer Byrns, July 6, 1829, and now resides in Mt. Sterling, where she and her husband intend to make their future home William and Chris are young men at home on the farm Their parents came to Illinois when young, Mr. Costello from Pennsylvania, and Mrs. Costello direct from Ireland. Both came without means, and worked by the week and month, and they have been very successful, and by hard work and economy have accumulated a large fortune of $20,000, besides their other property, which is very valuable.

August 7, 1892, Mr. Costello started for the land of his birth, to benefit his health and visit his three sisters and two brothers, who still reside there He reached his home in safety, and has every prospect of a pleasant visit

Mrs Bowe had only a common-school education, but has improved her mind by reading. She has one daughter, Eva May, born January 23,1886, twenty-nine days after the death of her husband Mr. Bowe left 500 acres of land, but Mrs Bowe only received fifty-five acres of it. She now has 150 acres, having bought the remainder herself, and this large farm with its nice buildings she superintends herself. She is a very remarkable lady in that she can manage the estate in so able a manner

JOHN KIRCHER, a practical farmer and stock-raiser, living on section 29, township 17, range 11, was born not many miles from Frankfort on the Main, Germany, October 4, 1835. His father, Henry, was a native of Hesse-Darmstadt. He grew up a farmer, and was there married to Elizabeth Folp, who was born and reared in the same province. After they had six children, they decided to try their fortunes in a new country In 1847, they took passage on board a sailing vessel at Havre de Grace, France, and after forty-seven days landed in New Orleans, and came from there up the rivers to Beardstown. Here they lived a short time, and a few months after landing the mother died, at the birth of another child, when she was in her fortieth year. The infant died also. The children have been taught to revere her name Her husband is yet living, aged eighty-seven, making his home with his son, our subject. He has been a cripple for forty years, having lost his leg by the accidental discharge of a gun in the hands of a friend, when they were out hunting The Lutheran Church has always been his choice, as it was that of his wife, and he has always been a Democrat Our subject and a sister, Elizabeth, wife of Michael Fortune, of Rich Hill, Missouri, are the only remaining children

John Kircher landed in Beardstown in 1847 His mother died before he was twelve years old, and he had to go out among strangers to work for a living. In 1856, he bought his first forty acres of land; he was married the same year; he hired to a man to work on a farm at $20 per month, and boarded himself The next year he rented a small farm and commenced farming for himself, and improving his forty acres His first corn was shelled by a hand sheller, and he hauled it fifteen miles to market, and got fourteen cents per bushel for it. From then on, he bought one piece of land after another, adjoining his, when he could get it, until he now has a farm of 280 acres.

He was married in Cass county, Illinois, to Elizabeth Rahn, born in Hesse-Darmstadt, near the birthplace of her husband, coming in 1854 with her parents, John and Mary Rahn, to Cass county. Mr. Rahn was a farmer near Arenzville. He died February 1, 1892, aged eighty-two years He had come to this country in 1854, with his wife and family. The wife, who is yet living, is eighty years old and lives with her daughter, Mrs. Kircher. They were always members of the Lutheran Church. Mrs. Kircher is the only daughter, although she has three brothers, George, living in Christian county, and John and Henry, living in Cass county.

Mr. and Mrs. Kircher have had eleven children: Louisa and an infant died young; Edward married Laura Buck, and is a farmer in this county; William married Josephine Buck, and is also a farmer in this county; Henry, Frank, Mary E., Lena, Anna, Lucy and Rosa are all at home.

Mr. and Mrs. Kircher are members of the Lutheran Church, and Mr. Kircher and his grown sons are sound Democrats. They are excellent representatives of the thrifty German element in this township.

EBENEZER SPINK, the able editor of the *Sangamon Valley Times*, of Chandlerville, Illinois, was born in Mason county, this State, January 8, 1857, his parents being Ebenezer and Fannie (Baylor) Spink.

The originator of the paternal branch of the family in this country was Daniel Spink a native of England, who emigrated to America in middle life, settling in Rhode Island where he spent the rest of his life. Samuel his son, was born in Rhode Island, about 1784, and married Ruth Slocumb, also a native of that State. Her parents were Pelick Slocumb and Ruth (Cappes), her mother also being a native of England, and both parents residing in Rhode Island until their death. Both Samuel Spink and his wife resided in the State in which they were born until their death, which occurred in 1814, at the age of thirty years. They were the parents of four children: Washington, William, Louise Ann and Ebenezer, the father of the subject of this sketch. Ebenezer Spink, Sr., was born in Prudence Island, in Narragansett Bay, Rhode Island, April 12, 1812. After the death of his father, Ebenezer went with his mother to Wickford, on Narragansett bay, and thence to Providence, in 1822, where he received instruction in the rudimentary branches of education. In 1825, he left home and worked in various localities, doing whatever he could to turn an honest penny. He finally went to Boston, Massachusetts, where he met and married his first wife, Juliet Nichols, their marriage taking place in 1832. Two years later, he removed with his family to Indiana, whence they moved, in 1836, to Kentucky. Two children, Alonzo and Melissa, were born to this marriage.

Mr. Spink, Sr., was, sometime later, separated from his wife, and in 1843 married Fannie Baylor, an estimable lady and the mother of the subject of this sketch. Her parents were George P. and Louise E. (Moy) Baylor, who were married in Pennsylvania in 1823. Her father was a native of Germany, and served twelve years in the Revolutionary war, for which he received a large tract of land in Fulton county, this State; her mother was a native of Pennsylvania, where she was born in 1803. They were the parents of eleven children, seven now living, their daughter, Fannie, the mother of our subject, having been born in Pennsylvania, July 18, 1826. The parents eventually removed from the Keystone State to Fulton county, Illinois, where they both died, the mother at the age of fifty-one years and the father aged seventy-two.

In 1853, Mr Spink, Sr, removed with his wife and children to Illinois, by boat, landing at Havana, and continued to reside in and near that city until his death, August 14, 1892, aged eighty years, three months and twenty-seven days.

There were twelve children born to bless this union. Two daughters died in infancy. The eldest, Charles H, was born in Kentucky, February 11, 1844 He enlisted in Company B, Eighty-fifth Regiment of Illinois Volunteers, in 1862, and was killed in the battle at Peach Tree creek, Georgia, July 20, 1864. The remaining children are as follows. Mary E. Haynes, of Blue Mound, Kansas; Isabelle Chambers, of Mason City, Illinois; Joseph E., of Guthrie, Oklahoma; George W., of Petersburg. Illinois; Clara Yates, of Havana, Illinois; Ebenezer, of Chandlerville, Illinois; Walter W. and James W of Havana, Illinois; and Lilly M Morgenstein, of Topeka, Illinois.

Ebenezer Spink, Sr., being one of the pioneer settlers of Mason county, was well known by all the older residents, and was held in high esteem as a neighbor and friend In 1856 he joined the New Lebanon Baptist Church, on Crane creek, and lived a consistent Christian life ever afterward. Having a large family he never accumulated much property, but was ever a most kind and indulgent father and husband.

Ebenezer Spink, Jr., whose name heads this notice, attended the schools in his vicinity and learned the printer's trade in Havana, Illinois He resided in Havana until 1879, when he came to Chandlerville and engaged in the publication of *The Independent*, returning in 1881 to Havana The following year, however, he again removed to Chandlerville, and bought out the *Independent* and changed the name to *The Sangamon Valley Times*, which he has ever since continued to edit and publish.

When eighteen years of age, he was married, in Havana, Illinois, August 8, 1875, to Miss Anna R Morrison, an estimable lady, a native of Havana, where she was born January 19, 1859. She was a daughter of John and Virginia (Derry) Morrison, prominent and early settlers of Illinois Her paternal grandmother's people came directly from the Emerald Isle to America, where her grandmother married Thomas Morrison They had four children, one of whom was John Morrison, the father of Mrs. Spink. He was born in Pennsylvania, December 27, 1821, and came to Illinois in an early day He was a blacksmith, which occupation he followed through life He was twice married: first to Aurilla E. Jones, July 1, 1848, and they had two children: Amelia A and Marcus J. The latter child was born December 27, 1852, and became a prominent man; he died October 16, 1883. On February 16, 1853, the devoted wife and mother died, leaving the son to the care of her husband, the daughter having died in infancy. On December 31, 1854, the father married again, the only child by this marriage being Mrs. Spink The father died in Havana, Illinois, November 25, 1859. Mrs. Spink's mother, Virginia Derry, was born February 14, 1832, in Virginia, and was a daughter of Jacob and Mary A S Baggett, both natives of the Old Dominion, the latter having been born near Alexandria, Virginia, on September 20, 1808, and died September 21, 1890. The couple were married March 14, 1834, and reared eleven children, eight of whom are now living, there being also thirty-four grandchildren and twenty-nine great-grandchildren Virginia Derry's grand parents were Townsend and —— (Howard) Baggett, both natives of Virginia, who, as far as known, lived and died there, surviving to an advanced age.

Mr. and Mrs. Spink have seven children: Marcus L., born in Havana, July 21, 1877; John C., born in the same place, January 7, 1879; Ernest O., born January 23, 1881; Fay R., born February 21, 1884; Earl M., born March 16, 1888; Flossie M., born January 8, 1890; and Wallace, born January 31, 1892.

Mr. Spink belongs to the Republican party, casting his first vote for General James A. Garfield, for President. The citizens of Chandlerville have honored him with official positions several times. He served two terms as Treasurer of the village and is a member of the School Board. He is a prominent member of the Woodmen, and attends the Congregational Church. Mrs. Spink is an earnest member of the Woman's Christian Temperance Union.

It is eminently fitting that a person who wields the influence of an editor should be of high moral character and possess the courage to express his honest convictions, both of which are characteristics of the subject of this sketch, and as such he deserves the commendation which he so widely receives.

EDWIN M. ANDERSON, member of the County Board of Supervisors and president of the Rushville Village Board, first saw the light of day in Louisburg, Greenbrier county, Virginia, April 1, 1837. His father, James L. Anderson, was a native of Scotland, "the land of cakes," and the home of Robert Burns, the greatest amatory poet the world has ever known. The grandfather of our subject was also a native of Scotland, in which historic land he passed his entire life. His widow, however, came to America, and spent her last years with her son, James L., in Rushville. She reared four children, of whom our subject's father was the only one to cross the Atlantic to America. When a young man he learned the trade of a silversmith, and upon his arrival here lived for a short time in North Carolina, thence going to Louisburgh, Virginia, where he married. In 1848 he moved with his wife and infant child to Illinois, coming via the Ohio, Missouri and Illinois rivers to Erie, Schuyler county, thence by team to Rushville. He followed his trade for a short time and then founded a weekly newspaper, which he conducted successfully for eight or ten years. During this time he studied law and was admitted to the bar, and for a time was associated in practice with Judge Bagby. He resided here until his death in 1865. His wife, and the mother of our subject, was Maria W. Moore. Her parents were Samuel and Jane (Matthews) Moore, natives of Virginia, as was also their daughter Maria. The latter passed away February 21, 1872. James L. Anderson was formerly a Whig, but later became a Democrat. He was a man of more than usual ability and strength of character, and served several years as Police Magistrate and Probate Judge. He is a thirty-second degree Mason, and served as Grand Secretary and Grand Master of the Grand Lodge of the State, a distinction conferred upon him by reason of his intelligence and high character. His four children were named Edwin M., Bessie, Edgar and Porter, the two latter being deceased.

Edwin M. Anderson was reared and educated in Rushville, and resided here continuously until 1862, when in July of that year he enlisted in Company C, One Hundred and Nineteenth Illinois Volunteer Infantry, and served until the close of the war. He participated in the Red River campaign under General Banks, and with the movements at Nashville under General Thomas. He was engaged in all the arduous duties, campaigns and battles participated in by his regiment, passing through it all with gallantry and patriotism until he was discharged in August, 1865. Upon his return home he secured employment as bookkeeper for the firm of Little & Ray, and remained in their employ continuously for fourteen years, since which time he has not been engaged in active business. Socially he is a member of the Rushville Lodge, No. 9, A. F. & A. M., and of Rushville Chapter, No. 184, F. A. M. Politically he has always affiliated with the Democratic party. He was elected one term as County Treasurer, and handled the finances of the county in an able and creditable manner. He had served several terms as a member of the County Board and as a member of the building committee appointed to supervise the construction of the county courthouse. He has shown himself eminently qualified for any office within the gift of his fellow-citizens.

CHRIST. J. HUSS is a retired farmer, living in Beardstown, and was born near Westphalia, Prussia, March 11, 1827. He came of respectable German parents and was the second of the family to come to the United States, coming from Bremer-Haven on a sailing vessel, which was forty-two days on the water. He landed in New Orleans and came thence up the Illinois and Mississippi rivers to Beardstown, making the trip in nine days. He had a brother, August, now deceased who had come to Beardstown in 1845, being the first to come to the country. Our subject was fifteen years old when his father, Henry, a farmer, died, having been engaged on a farm in Prussia, Germany; for forty-nine years. He was seventy-two years old when he died, and was a Lutheran in religion. The maiden name of his wife was Caroline Andres, and she survived her husband some years, dying in Prussia at the age of seventy-two. She was a life-long and faithful member of the German Lutheran Church. Christ. is the only member of the family now living in this county. A sister, Charlotta, wife of Henry Backman, lives on the old farm in Germany.

Our subject came here in 1849 when a young man twenty-three years of age. He worked one year on a farm as a laborer. In 1850 he began teaming in Beardstown and in 1861 he sold out this business and bought a good farm, where he afterward did a large stock business in connection with grain farming. In 1890 he retired to the city of Arenzville, where he lives in comfort, enjoying a well-earned fortune, which he obtained by his own efforts, as sisted by his good wife.

He was married in Beardstown to Miss Mary Bronkar, who was born August 29, 1833, in Hanover, Germany, and came to the United States in 1848 with her parents, who settled in Cass county, where they lived and died. Her father, Ernest Bronkar, was a successful farmer and lived to be eighty years of age. His wife lived to be sixty-five. Her maiden name was Mary Kelver. They were members of the Lutheran Church.

Mr. and Mrs. Huss are parents of eleven children, four died young, an infant, Edward, William, Sr., and William, Jr. The living are, August, married Mary Kuhlman and is a farmer in his county; Henry is a shoemaker and dealer in the firm of Fish & Huss, married to Minnie Coblones; Christian, dealer in agricultural implements and groceries, married Mary Hurbert; John operates his father's farm in this county, and married Amelia Buck; Minnie is the wife of Peter Hems, a farmer in this county; George is a farmer of this county, and Lizzie is at home.

This is one of the large and most respectable families in the county.

HENRY C. FUNK, a well-to-do farmer and stock-raiser of township 17 north, range 11 west, section 14, near Virginia, Illinois, was born in this precinct February 13, 1860. His parents were Conrad and Frederica (Steiner) Funk. The father was born in Hesse-Darmstadt, Germany, December 26, 1832, and his mother in Texas, December 5, 1839. They were married in Beardstown, Illinois, July 28, 1857. Conrad came to Cass county in 1842 with his mother, his father having died on the ocean. They came directly from Europe to Arenzville, where they rented for a short time, afterward removing to this precinct, where Conrad purchased a farm, having at the time of his death 1,150 acres of land, all except 304 acres being in Monroe precinct. He died upon the farm where our subject now resides, March 8, 1888. His wife still resides at the old homestead where her unmarried children live.

They had eight children, who are as follows: Willis Conrad died in childhood; Henry C., our subject; Louis A. resides upon a farm near; Rosa, Mary, George, Emma, and Frank, living at home. This whole family has enjoyed good educational advantages and have an excellent home.

Henry grew to manhood upon the farm and received his education in the common schools. He now owns 360 acres of good land, which he rents. He furnishes all the seed and gets one half the grain. The girls have good farms and the brothers are equally well off. The voters of the family are Democrats. The parents were members of the Lutheran Church and the whole family is prominent, and possesses the confidence and esteem of all who are fortunate enough to know them. George Edward is not married, and is of a roving spirit, having visited many of the cities of the West. Early in life he developed a fondness for fire-arms, and is now one of the best rifle-shots in the country. He has given numerous exhibitions of his skill at target practice, shooting glass balls, etc., and has always come out best in competition with local authorities. He was born November 13, 1868, on the farm where his mother and family live and which is his home.

JOHN G. KENDRICK, of Elkhorn township, was born in Lebanon, New Hampshire, February 18, 1828. He is a son of Stephen and Martha (Gerrish) Kendrick. Stephen came to Illinois in 1841 with his wife and two children, his possessions being an ox team and $50 in cash. He first rented in this county and bought forty acres of land, where he died when eighty-four years of age. Stephen's father was a merchant of Lebanon, New Hampshire, and died there a very old man. Stephen's wife was named Thankful Howe, and she died when an old woman. The father of our subject was one of eight children, and his mother one of seven children. She was born in New Hampshire, and died at the home of her son, aged sixty-one years.

John remained at home until married, and went to the district school with James A. Garfield. He learned the trade of a blacksmith and wagon maker. After he married he rented a farm near his father, and there lived until 1872, when he moved into his own house, and now owns 300 acres. He carries on mixed farming and has been very successful. He is a Republican in politics.

He was married in 1850 to Mary Jaques, born in Allegany county, New York, April 14, 1843, daughter of Samuel and Effie (Fagort) Jaques. They were New Yorkers, who came to Illinois in 1841. Mrs. Kendrick is one of twelve children. Mr. and Mrs. Kendrick have three living children: Edward R., Fred W. and Emma. The boys are on the land their father owned. They are members of the Methodist Episcopal Church, and Mr. Kendrick is a Class-leader, and the whole family are very active in Sunday-school work; in fact Mr. Kendrick is active in every good work, especially temperance work, and has organized several temperance societies. No man in the county has been more active than Mr. Kendrick in placing it in the position it now enjoys. He has a grand record for local temperance and church work, and is highly steemed throughout the county.

JAMES M., BENJAMIN R., AND WILLIAM B. WILSON are farmers of Elkhorn township, where they have been residents for a long time. Their father, John S. Wilson, was born in New Jersey, May 15, 1817. He was the son of Reuben Wilson, who was of English parents and a successful farmer of New Jersey. (See sketch of George W. and F. M. Wilson.) Reuben Wilson removed to Ohio and resided there a few years, and in 1829 he visited Illinois on horseback, and was so pleased with the country that he emigrated to Illinois in 1833, and settled in Adams county. He entered sixteen sections of Government land, 10,240 acres, part of which was included in the township of Quincy. Soon after his arrival in this State he was taken quite sick, and was rendered helpless until his death some three years later. He married Susan Carver, of New Jersey, and of Holland parents. She died about two years after her husband. John Wilson was about sixteen years old when he came to Illinois with his parents. At that time Adams was but little settled, and Quincy was only a village, although it served as the market place for the farmers for many miles around. He was the pioneer teacher for Adams county and also Brown county, and as there were no districts all were taught in the subscription school in a little log house. The teacher was obliged to board around among the people. He was married November 30, 1843, to Miss Elizabeth J. Adams, born in 1827, daughter of Mr. Benjamin Adams, Sr. They had six children, namely: Benjamin B., born November 3, 1844; Perlina, born December, 1846; Pernita, born March 25, 1849; James M., born May 26, 1851; Dora E. was born February 5, 1854; William B., born November 4, 1859. Mr. Wilson bought land in section 5, and built a log-cabin, in which all of his children were born, and where he lived until the day of his death, on April 22, 1875. His wife died in 1892.

The brothers have always resided on the old homestead, and have been engaged in farming. They have received a good education, and they are extensive readers, putting into practice the ideas they receive from their papers. Their farm is one of the best and most improved in the county.

JOHN H. TUREMAN.—Mr. Tureman' father, in the year 1827, emigrated to what is now Cass county, with his family, which then comprised a wife and seven children. He purchased from a man named Myers a claim to a tract of Government land, and some time later, as soon as he could obtain the money, entered the same direct from the Government. It is the same that is now owned by the subject of this sketch. There was then a log cabin on the place, having in it neither sawed lumber nor nails; the boards on the roof were rived by hand and held in place by weight-poles; those of the floor were split and one side hewed smooth,—called "puncheons," about six feet in length. The chimney was built of earth and sticks on the end and outside of the building. And it was in this humble abode that John H. Tureman was born. The family occupied this dwelling about four years, when Mr. Tureman erected a story-and-a-half frame house,—one of the first frame dwellings in the county. The lumber for this structure was all sawed by hand, as there was no sawmill in the country. A platform was constructed, on which the logs were rolled, and two men operated the saw, what was called a "whip saw," one man standing above, the other below. The father was a resident of this place until his death, in June, 1835, when he was aged about fifty-two years. His wife survived him many years, dying in 1868, aged seventy-nine years. Her maiden name was Elizabeth Harbold, and she was born in Pennsylvania, of Germany ancestry. Until seven years of age she spoke no other language than the German, and after moving from Pennsylvania there was a period of twenty-one years during which time she did not even see a German-speaking person.

Following are the names of the twelve children in the above family: Eliza, the wife of William Carr; Ann, who married James Cook; David, George, Leonard, Catherine, who married William Patterson; Arsenoin, who married Cabel Patterson; John H.; Elizabeth, the wife of James Allison; William A.; Tracy; and Virginia, who married George Davis. Of the foregoing, Catherine, John H., William and Virginia are living.

Mr. Tureman, our subject, was born and has passed his entire life on the place he now owns and occupies and has therefore lived longer on one place than any other person now residing in the county. He has a very retentive memory and relates many interesting incidents of pioneer days, illustrating the contrast between the peculiarities of those days and the present. He was in his sixth year when his father died, and he remembers how he seemed to be his father's favorite, for his father often took him along on his travels, thus widening our subject's experience and the scope of his pleasures. Their grain and other products were all marketed at Beardstown, much of it being drawn there with ox teams.

On one occasion they camped over night a short distance from that place, which was then the principal market for this part of Illinois. There were then many campers there, some having come from Jacksonville, Springfield, and Decatur for merchandise. It was on one of these return trips that the elder Tureman drew the second load of merchandise that was ever taken to Virginia, the goods being for Dr. Hall, who, at the time, kept the only store in the place On another occasion he took a carding-machine to Jacksonville, and on this trip they stopped on the way at a distillery to quench their thirst, distilleries being then very numerous and their products pure and cheap. The people subsisted principally upon wild game and produce of their own raising Deer, wild turkey, prairie chickens, etc, were abundant Bread was considered a great luxury, Corn meal was the principal breadstuff in use, sometimes exclusively so for long periods.

For several years there were no gristmills other than horse-mills in this part of the country, and often the inhabitants had to grate their corn on a perforated tin grater, or pound it in a mortar The first gristmills started were operated by horse-power When but a boy our subject used to take a sack of shelled corn on the back of a horse to mill, where he often had to wait all day for his grist When he was about fourteen there was a water-power mill at Arenzville, to which he took grists

His father was a true friend of popular education. He hired a teacher, giving him a room in his own house. But in those days "licking" and learning went together, and John came in for his share of the "lickings" His sister, Mrs. Cook, took pity on him, and on one occasion lined his jacket with card-board made of brown paper, which was placed under his clothes, as a protection against the customary rough usage of the "schoolmaster."

His other brothers having left home, young Tureman found himself at the age of fifteen with the management of the farm devolving upon him. Being industrious and possessing good judgment, he was successful from the start In the course of time he bought the interest of the other heirs in the homestead, and he has also purchased other tracts of land The home farm contains 400 acres; another farm, in Logan county, also contains 400 acres. Mr Tureman's life has not only been characterized by industry and enterprise, but also by generosity and public spirit. In 1884 he erected the opera-house in Virginia,—a handsome, well built structure, 64 x 120 feet in dimensions, two stories high besides basement, and was, at the time it was erected, the finest building in any town of its size in the State of Illinois. He is also a stockholder and a director in the First National Bank in Virginia.

Politically Mr Tureman was originally a Democrat. In 1876 he voted for Peter Cooper, but, previous to this, a revolution in his political creed had occurred, which had its incipiency in the first issue of greenbacks by the Government He accepted these as safe money, because it had the stamp of the land, was a creation of the law, and consequently was good, and would remain so as long as the Government by which it had been issued was solvent In this he was an original greenbacker At this time, or perhaps a little later, Mr. Tureman began to realize the drift of the old party he had left; saw that the famous Kansas and Nebraska bills were shallow pretenses of democracy, championed by Douglas and other pro-slavery leaders to ultimately carry slavery into all the unorganized domains of the Government This after-light caused him many doubts about clinging to the fortunes of a party bent upon fostering slavery in the free Territories from 1856 to 1864 From the latter date on, he has not been in harmony with either of the old parties, the financial policy of the Republican party being particularly distasteful to him in all its collateral branches. He wants no dollar redeemable in another dollar, no specie base to hoodwink and give the appearance of security to a currency, which is as good without a promise to redeem in specie as it is with a promise to redeem and without the specie with which to do it.

Socially he is a member of the Morgan and Cass County Pioneer Society, of which he has served both as president and vice-president.

He was married December 5, 1851, to Mary J. Davis, a native of Cass county. Their two children are Parthena and John F. The former is the wife of Hugh W. Harrison, of Belleville, this State, and has one child, named Zoe. John F. married Mary Caldwell, and he is engaged in the grocery business in Virginia.

RICHARD S. BLACK, an intelligent, progressive and highly esteemed citizen of Mound Station, Illinois, and representing one of the best families of Schuyler county, was born in Woodstock township, this county, May 28, 1832.

His father, Richard Black, was a native of Mecklenburg county, North Carolina, where he attained to manhood. Of an adventurous and progressive disposition, he removed from his native county to Hancock county, Kentucky, in an early day. The spirit of emigration, however, was too strong for him to resist, and after a few years' sojourn in Kentucky, we again see him moving Westward. His second settlement was made in Dubois county, in what was then Indiana Territory. In 1826, he again moved toward the setting sun, moving by team overland to Schuyler county, Illinois, accompanied by his wife and four children. Arrived at his destination, he purchased of Willis O'Neil a claim to the land which is now the site of the city of Rushville. On the organization of Schuyler county, this claim was selected as the county seat, and it was consequently taken from Mr. Black, the county afterward reimbursing him in part. Thus deprived of his home, he removed five miles southward, near the present site of Bethel Church, where he bought a tract of patent land. He erected on this a log cabin sixteen feet square, for the roof of which he rived clapboards, and split puncheon for the floor, while he made his chimney of sticks and clay, called in those days a "cat-and-stick chimney." He, later, built an addition, making a double log cabin with an entry between, at that time a very pretentious residence, where he dwelt until his death, in 1853. The maiden name of his second wife was Elizabeth Fowler, a native of Jefferson county, Kentucky. She reared eight children, two of whom were her husband's by his former marriage. These children were: Elizabeth, William, Isaac, Cecelia, John L., Richard S., the subject of this sketch; Austin S., and Monroe. The devoted wife and mother survived her husband and spent her declining years in comfort with her son Isaac.

Richard S., whose name heads this biography, was reared and educated in Schuyler county, where he was born. He attended the pioneer schools, which were held in log houses without any floors. The seats were made of small logs, split and hewed smooth on one side, with wooden pegs for legs. A piece of puncheon, supported by wooden pins inserted in the sides of the building, served as a writing desk for the larger scholars. The country was sparsely settled, all land that was not patent or soldier's land being owned by the Government. The country was mostly inhabited by wild Indians, while game abounded in great profusion, such as deer, bear, rabbit, turkey, prairie chicken, grouse, etc., and the streams were alive with the choicest fish. No mills were in the country at that time, and all grain was ground by hand. The pioneers subsisted on wild game, fish, and such products as they raised on their land. All clothing was of homespun, which was manufactured by the women of the family, who carded and spun the materials and afterward cut and made the garments, and that at a time when sewing machines were unknown.

The subject of this sketch resided with his parents until he attained his majority, when he commenced farming for himself on rented land in Bainbridge township. After a few years of industry and careful management, he had sufficiently prospered to be able to buy land, which he accordingly did, purchasing a tract in the same township. He continued to farm this land until 1869, when he sold out and bought another tract in Brown county, on which he remained for three years. This, he also sold, and removed to Adams county, purchasing a farm in Concord township, where he resided until 1884. He then again disposed of his interests and removed to Lawrence, Kansas, where he engaged in the manufacture of cider and vinegar for eight months. The climate there not agreeing with him, he returned to Mound Station, and entered the mercantile business, which he successfully continued for five years. For the the last two years he has been prosperously conducting the principal hotel of Mound Station.

Mr. Black was first married, in 1857, to Harriet Terrill, an estimable lady, daughter of Andrew and Elizabeth Terrill, who were early and prominent settlers of Bainbridge township, where their daughter, Harriet, was born. This marriage was dissolved by death in 1883, the devoted wife and mother going to her reward. Matilda, the only surviving child, is now the wife of John M. Anderson, a well-to-do farmer of Huntsville township, Schuyler county. They have three children: Hattie, Ora and John Richard.

In 1887, Mr. Black was again married, his second wife being Mary M. McBrackney, a native of Clayton, Adams county, Illinois. Her parents were Robert and Elizabeth (Marshall) McBrackney, both born in Ireland, of Scotch ancestry. Her parents resided in their native country until 1834, when they removed to Clayton, Adams county, this State, where the father purchased and improved land, on which he resided until his death. Both parents were devout members of the Presbyterian Church, in which faith they reared three children.

Mr. Black is, politically, a Democrat, and has been elected by his constituents to various offices of trust. He was for seven years an efficient member of the Adams county Board of Supervisors, and for the past two years has represented Lee township on the Brown County Board. He and his worthy wife are esteemed members of society, being as widely respected as they are known.

JOHN SMITH WALKER was born in Adams county, Pennsylvania, in November, 1826, the son of Andrew Walker, a native of the same State and county; there the father was reared and married; he was a farmer by occupation, and followed agricultural pursuits in Adams county until 1839, when he emigrated to Illinois, accompanied by his wife and eight children. They made the entire trip overland, and on their arrival to Schuyler county they settled on what is now Littleton township. Mr. Walker rented land, and later purchased a tract uncultivated and without improvements; he built a small frame house and log stable, and here passed the remainder of his days; he died in 1843. His wife's maiden name was Ann Wilson, a native of Adams county, Pennsylvania. After her husband's death Mrs. Walker lived with her children at their various homes until her decease, which occurred in October, 1870, at the residence of her daughter, Mrs. John McGaughey, near Industry, McDonough county, Illinois. She was buried beside her husband in the Camp Creek cemetery south of Macomb, Illinois.

John Smith Walker is one of a family of ten children; he was thirteen years of age when the family left their Pennsylvania home and penetrated the wilds of the frontier, as Illinois was then called. The country was thinly settled; there were no railroads, game was abundant; they were pioneers, and had to undergo all the privations incident to the settling of a new country. Our subject attended the common schools taught in the primitive log house, conned his lesson while sitting on a puncheon seat, and learned to write on a puncheon desk. He assisted in the farm work and resided with his parents during their lifetime. He has been successfnf in his farming operations, and owns at this time 200 acres of choice farming land. He resided on his farm until 1887, when he removed to Rushville, where he now makes his home.

Mr. Walker was united in marriage, in 1868, to Elizabeth Huckeby, a native of Breckenridge county, Kentucky, and a daughter of Thomas Huckeby, her parents emigrated to Illinois in 1836, making the journey by the river on steamboat; they were pioneers of Schuyler county.

The mother died within three years after coming to this State and was buried in the Thompson cemetery a short distance southwest of the village of Littleton. The father married again and removed to Fulton county, where he resided until the time of his death in March, 1847.

Mrs. Walker was but sixteen months old when she was brought to Illinois, and has therefore witnessed the transformation of the country from a wild prairie to a rich farming community. Mr. and Mrs. Walker are the parents of two children, Anna and John.

JOHN FOOTE, the senior member of the firm of John Foote & Son, proprietors of the Rushville Hosiery Factory, was born in Leeds, Yorkshire, England, January 17, 1827. His father, John Foote, was a native of England, and a weaver by trade; he operated a hand loom for many years, and spent his last days in Leeds. He married Margaret Hines, who spent her entire life in England. Three of their children came to America, Frank, Mary and John. The last named, the subject of this biography, began when quite young to learn the trade of cloth dresser, and followed this vocation in Leeds until 1844. In July of that year he sailed from Liverpool on board the Greenock, and landed in New York city after a voyage of six weeks. He went directly to Boston, and thence to Millbury, Massachusetts, where he followed his trade for two years; he was afterward in Cherry Valley and Foxboro; and later went to Oxford, Massachussetts, where he was employed in a satinette factory for a few months. Next he went to Winchester, where he was in a flannel factory, and after that to a place now called Bridgewater, Massachusets, where he worked at the boot and shoe trade until the beginning of the Civil war. At this time he went to Newport, New Hampshire, and secured employment in a flannel factory. After the close of the war he removed to Charleston, but in 1866 went to Michigan; he resided in that State for two years, and then removed to Rock Island, Illinois, where he was foreman in the carding and spinning department of the Rock Island Woolen Mills, a position he filled until 1874. In that year he came to Rushville, and two years later established the Rushville Hosiery Factory, which has been in successful operation since that time; both cotton and woolen hose are manufactured, and are sold directly to the trade in Illinois, Indiana, Iowa and Nebraska.

Mr. Foote was united in marriage in Foxboro, Massachusetts, in May, 1846, to Martha A. Childs. a native of Maine and a daughter of Amos Childs; there are five surviving children born of this union: Charles F., Alfred A., Ada, John W. and George H. The last named is in partnership with his father. Mr. and Mrs. Foot are zealous members of the Methodist Episcopal Church, and are active in all movements tending to elevate humanity. Politically, Mr. Foote affiliates with the Republican party.

GEORGE W. AND F. M. WILSON are among the few men in Brown county who own and occupy the same farm on which they were born and on which they have resided continuously since childhood. Their grandfather, Savile Wilson, was born in Egg Harbor city, New Jersey, in 1770, of English parents. He was a farmer by occupation, owning several hundred acres of choice agricultural land. He made a specialty of dairying, having several hundred milk cows, and made cheese and butter, which he marketed in New York city and Philadelphia. He also engaged extensively in truck farming and poultry raising. In 1790, he married Susan Carver, and they had seven children, four sons and three daughters. On the outbreak of the war of 1812, he enlisted in a New York regiment, and participated in most of the great battles. He was in the battle of Bladensburg and saw Washington city burned. In 1817, he emigrated to Ohio, settling near Cincinnati, where he engaged in farming. His entire family, some of whom were married and had children of their own, emigrated with him. In 1825, he removed farther westward, settling near Indianapolis, Indiana. Here he bought 640 acres of wild land, from which he and his sons proceeded to clear the timber, preparatory to its cultivation. One would have thought that a man who had passed the meridian of life, and who had borne the hardships and privations of two settlements in the wilderness, would be content to remain where he was, but such was not the case. Indeed, a desire for change increased with the gratification of a naturally adventurous and roving disposition. Consequently, we again find him, in 1836, turning his steps toward the setting sun. This time he removed to Illinois, settling in Adams county, where he bought twelve sections of land, some of which now lies within the limits of the city of Quincy. In this same year, shortly after their arrival in the Prairie State, the devoted wife and mother was called to her reward, leaving a break in in the family which time could never repair. As if the severance of those tender ties was too severe a blow to be endured, the husband

and father also expired, two years afterward, in 1838. They were aptly mated, both being persons of intelligence, activity and great perseverance, which contributed to their marked success in life Mr. Wilson's influence and strong sense of justice retained his family around him until his death, many of his children having families of their own. The interests of these were consolidated, their land and agricultural interests being held in partnership, and all accomplished with the utmost satisfaction and good will. His forethought and perseverance were remarkable, and seldom failed to carry him forward to success. As witness of this, we append an incident, showing with what care the last removal of the family to Illinois was contemplated and brought to a happy consummation· Previous to disposing of his farm in Indiana, which in itself was contrary to the time-honored custom, of leaping first and looking afterward, he and his eldest son, John S Wilson, went all over the proposed route to the "West," as Illinois and Missouri were then called, traveling through the Prairie State to St Louis, thence to Fort Scott and Fort Leavenworth, at that time the extreme western part of Missouri At the latter place they rested a few days, after covering this long stretch of territory on horseback, and then resumed their journey homeward, returning by way of Iowa and central Illinois. This was, indeed, an undertaking in those days, the magnitude of which cannot be correctly estimated in these times of rapid and comfortable transit. Their way led over lonely distances, the silence of which was, at times, oppressive, many days sometimes elapsing without disclosing to view a single habitation or the face of a white man All glory be to those who went before and blazed the path for others to follow!

Reuben Wilson, father of the subjects of this sketch, was born in New Jersey in 1790. The schools in that State were then but primitive affairs, but his quick perception and inherited judgment stood him in good stead, and he imbibed a fair amount of knowledge of books. He married Sarah Spencer, a bright, active girl, whose parents were German. His father, some time later, becoming inspired with his customary desire for travel, Reuben accompanied him to Ohio, afterward to Indiana, and finally to Illinois. He at first settled in Adams county, the latter State, whence he removed, two years later, to Brown county, locating on the west half of section 32, township 1 south, 3 west Reuben Wilson was thus a pioneer in three different States, and was well acquainted with the hardships and privations incidental to settling a wild, new country. He was always a champion of education, and especially favored free public schools He was one of three or four men, who built the first school-house in district No. 1 township 1 south 3, west, which served for school purposes for twenty years It was christened White Oak College, from the white oak logs used in its construction, and that name still clings to the large frame house, which took its place years afterward. He was a devoted member of the Methodist Episcopal Church, to which he had belonged from his twentieth year; and he helped organize the first Methodist Episcopal Church in Brown county, his residence often serving for the public meeting-house This good and greatly esteemed man was called from this life in 1855, leaving a stricken family and many friends to mourn his loss His worthy wife, Sarah, the companion of his youth and sharer of his hardships, survived him many years, expiring in 1873. They had ten children, seven sons and three daughters, all but the two, whose names head this biography, having passed away Following are their names·

John S., born in New Jersey, May 15, 1817, came to Brown county, where he died April 22, 1885; he married Elizabeth Adams, in 1845, who was born March 14, 1827, and died June 13, 1892; they had six children, three sons and three daughters, all now living in Brown county.

Savile Wilson, born in New Jersey, came to Brown county, married Mary McDaniel, in 1845; he emigrated to Texas in 1853, and his wife died in Shreveport, Louisiana, with the cholera, on the way to their destination, he settled near Gainesville, Cooke county, where he died in 1880; his children consisted of four sons and two daughters, all but two now dead.

Reuben J, born in Ohio, came with his parents to Brown county, where he died in 1860; he married Lucinda Marden in 1846, who died in 1889; they had three daughters and one son

Jesse J, born in Ohio, died in Brown county, in 1877, unmarried.

Susan, born in Indiana, married Silas Campbell in 1868, and died in 1878; they had three daughters, two of whom survive

Hester, born in Indiana, married Dr. T. J. Norvell, and died in 1885.

James M., born in Indiana, died in 1847, in boyhood

Sarah Ann, born in Adams county, Illinois, married Arthur Newenhan, in 1872; she died in Missouri, in 1879; they had two sons, one of whom is now living.

George W Wilson, senior partner of Wilson & Brother, was born January 19, 1837, on the west half of section 32, township 1 south, 3 west, Brown county, Illinois, where he has resided continuously ever since. He was educated in the country schools, which were crude at that time, attending usually for three months during the winter He soon learned that it was a virtue to be industrious. The chief occupations were: cultivating and harvesting the various crops; attending and feeding stock; clearing off new land; splitting rails and building fence There was ample recreation in the hunting of wild game, with which the prairies and woods on the streams abounded, especially wild turkey and smaller game, such as squirrels, quails, etc., affording great sport in shooting and trapping.

When twelve years of age, he and his younger brother, F. M. Wilson, built a small pen out of fence rails, covering it with the same, and made a trap door, which they set for turkey. They caught ten at one time, besides one or two on various other occasions.

He was never married. He was never identified with any church, although a strictly moral and upright man. He experienced a great affliction in 1855, when his father died, leaving him and F M Wilson, the youngest of the family, and their mother, alone, the older members being married and having homes of their own. Such had been their training, however, that they successfully carried on the farm as usual. It was this trying ordeal, sharing a common sorrow through the long and lonesome days, as they went about their daily tasks, that laid the foundation for the partnership which has survived for more than a generation. In 1880, they, in company with William Eckler and Manville Larkin, took a trip out West, to look for a more favorable location. After visiting Missouri, Kansas and other portions of the West, they concluded Illinois was the best place, and accordingly commenced life in earnest.

In 1865, they formed a partnership in sawmilling, of which the members were, Jesse J , George W. and F. M. Wilson, the firm name being Wilson & Brother They continued successfully in the lumber business for eight years, sawing large quantities, which they shipped to Turner, Jacksonville and other places, besides supplying a large home trade, and in the meantime they were also farming. In the spring of 1866 and 1867, they set out a large orchard of apple trees, covering 120 acres, which, after a great expense, proved a failure, the winter of 1875 killing the trees, so they had to be cut down

In 1873, they were called upon to mourn the loss of their devoted mother, who went to her reward after a life of the purest unselfishness and entire subservience to the happiness of her children She was widely known in her community, and was sincerely mourned by a large circle of friends

In 1877, Jesse J. Wilson died, and the business was continued by the two brothers, who, for several years past, have carried on general farming and stock-raising At the present time they have a feed mill, where they grind all the grain for their stock; and they have also a small sawmill, which they operate principally for their own use.

F M Wilson was born March 3, 1839, in Brown county, on the west half of section 32, township 1 south, 3 west; and has resided continuously on the same farm ever since. He was known as a quiet, unassuming boy, ever ready to stand for the right and condemn the wrong, which characteristic is equally marked in him as a man. He never belonged to any church, but is an upright man, accepting for his guide the greatest of rules, that "Whatsoever ye would that men should do unto you, do ye also even unto them" He was a member of the Grange until that lodge was discontinued He belongs to the Farmers' Alliance, is president of the Board, and has been School Director for twenty years, which position he still holds.

He has been twice married first, in 1862, to Martha Carpenter, who died the following year. In 1866, he married Minerva J. Richey, who died in 1874, leaving two children to his care, a son and daughter, who are living at home with him.

Mr Wilson was educated in the common schools of his vicinity, then called subscription schools, which he attended for three months each winter The term "subscription" arose in consequence of each parent signing a paper, which assured a teacher a certain number of scholars, the tuition being usually $2 for each child for a term of sixty days, including the teacher's board, who lived around for equal lengths of time among the various families The school houses were crude, being built of logs, usually sixteen feet square, with a stove in the center. The furniture corresponded with the appearance of the house, the seats being made of slabs, a slab being the first piece sawed from a log These were supported by wooden pins, inserted in auger holes bored in the bark side. These seats were placed around the stove, usually about two feet apart For writing-desks a plank was fastened to the walls, all around the room. Thus in this room would be crowded probably forty pupils, of ages ranging from five to twenty years. The studies were necessarily crude, nothing being attempted but the rudiments of reading, writing and ciphering, often denominated the "three R's" However, on the foundation thus attained many built well, and afterward took their place in the world as useful members of society.

The Messrs. Wilson have witnessed the improvements extending over a period of half a century, many of which are interesting for a later generation to note. The first plowing was done with a wooden plow, furnished with an iron share. A complete revolution has been made in agricultural implements and methods within their lifetime. One of them still bears the scars on his hands, which were made by a reaping hook, in his first efforts at harvesting wheat. After this came the cradle, which superseded the reaping hook; later the horse-power machines, the grain being cut by horse-power, after which it was raked from the platform and made into bundles by hand. Subsequently to this came the self-raking reaper, which was a great saving of labor entailed in hand raking. After this, the self-binder; first with wire, then with twine, and bunching the sheaves together ready for shocking. But, there have been more improvements, if possible, in threshing and cleaning the grain. First, the flail and tramping floor were used, the *modus operandi* being as follows: A circle of sheaves, five or six feet wide and ten or twelve paces in diameter, over which four or six horses would tramp, until the grain was out. Then the straw was separated from the chaff and wheat, after which the wheat was run through a fanning-mill, to clean the grain. Fanning-mills were at first few in number; men often hauled their wheat and chaff five or six miles in order to get it cleaned; often paying as much to get their wheat fanned as it now costs to have it threshed. The first threshing machines were composed of a cylinder, operated by a belt, which threshed the grain, but did not separate it from the straw, which was afterward accomplished by hand. The next improvement made, was a separator which, as the name implied, separated the straw from the wheat and chaff, after which the wheat had to be fanned free from the chaff. The cleaners were then used, which cleaned the grain as it was threshed.

One would naturally suppose that labor-saving devices would have been readily adopted, but such was not the case. There were men who opposed every advance that was made. They clung tenaciously to the reap-hook, after they could have a cradle; others would still use the cradle when they could have a horse-power machine; and, incredible as it may seem, there were binders destroyed in Brown county during the first year of their use, by the professional harvest hands, who said they could get no work to do.

ERNEST JOCKISCH, a practical farmer and stock-raiser of section 5 and 6, of township 17, range 11, owns a fine and well improved property where he lives. Altogether he owns about 500 acres of first-class land, 400 acres of which is highly improved and supplied with first-class buildings. He has lived in the county since he was ten years of age and has owned land farming it for himself since he was twenty seven. He has been very successful and is very proud of his efforts.

He was born in Saxony, Germany, February 6, 1825, and came with his parents and grandparents to the United States. The family began life here as poor people did in those days, but they did not remain poor very long and are all rich at the present writing. They have done much to build up Cass county, where many of them yet live, and they are all progressive people. (See biography of William Jockisch.)

Ernest was married in this county to Margaret Deiglemeier, born in Hanover, Germany, coming with her mother and brother to the United States when she was young. The family settled in Cass county. The head of the family had died in Germany before they started on their trip across the ocean. The widowed mother died soon after her arrival in this county.

Mr. and Mrs. Jockisch are the parents of seven children: Wilhelmina, deceased after marriage and birth of three children, yet living. The living children are: Caroline, wife of Oscar Lane, farmer of Concord, Morgan county, Illinois; William A., a farmer, married to Tilda Carls; Frank, a farmer in Cass county, married Emma Hesler; Louisa, at home; Charles and Henry are at home and farm with their father. All are good hard-working people. Mr. Jockisch, wife and children are members of Zion German Methodist Episcopal Church, of which they are generous supporters. Mr. Jockisch and sons are all Republicans and Mr. Jockisch has held local offices. He is a genial man and kind-hearted neighbor, and is highly respected by all.

CPSIA information can be obtained
at www.ICGtesting.com
Printed in the USA
BVHW082114120620
581252BV00002B/25

9 781376 113396